AF539105

VIF PERSPECTIVE

ISSUES AND TRENDS | 2017

SECURING INDIA

STRENGTHENING INDIA'S NUCLEAR DETERRENCE

NEIGHBOURHOOD–IMMEDIATE & EXTENDED • CIVILISATIONAL VISION

COUNTER-RADICALISATION • ECONOMY • CLIMATE CHANGE

Vivekananda International Foundation
3 San Martin Marg, Chanakyapuri
New Delhi-110021, India
info@vifindia.org
Follow us @VIFINDIA
www.vifindia.org

First published 2017
Photographs: pp 2, 46, 74, 93, 94, 122, 144, 157, 158: commons.wikimedia.org; p 1: narendramodi.in; p 20: vsmandal.org; p 36: mygov.in; p 57: 4gwar.wordpress.com, Sergeant Tyler C Gregory; pp 58, 73: pmindia.gov.in; p 84: pbs.twimg.com; p 109: pbs.org; p 110: theindependentbd.com; p 134: moi.gov.mm; p 173: independent.co.uk; p 174: pulitzercenter.org; p 183: manoa.hawaii.edu; p 184: rocketstem.org, Bigelow Aerospace

ISBN 978-81-8328-495-0

Published by
Wisdom Tree
4779/23, Ansari Road
Darya Ganj, New Delhi-110 002
Ph.: 011-23247966/67/68
wisdomtreebooks@gmail.com

Printed in India

Contents

Preface v

Strengthening India's Nuclear Deterrence 2
General NC Vij,
PVSM, UYSM, AVSM, and VIF Expert Group

Swami Vivekananda's Message and Vision:
Some Keynotes and their Contemporary Relevance 20
Dr Anirban Ganguly

Case for India-specific Economic Model 36
S Gurumurthy

Evolving US Foreign Policy under
Trump and its Implications for India 46
Kanwal Sibal

Engaging China in an Uncertain World 58
Ashok K Kantha

The China–Pakistan Nexus 74
Prabhat P Shukla

Evolving Dynamics in Pakistan 84
Tilak Devasher

Prospects and Problems of Transition and Stability in Afghanistan 94
Lt Gen Ravi Sawhney, PVSM, AVSM & Sushant Sareen

Daring to Dream: Restoring Connectivity in South Asia for Regional Development 110
Tariq Karim

India and the Indian Ocean—the Dynamics of Multiple Centralities 122
Vice Admiral Anil Chopra, PVSM, AVSM

Emerging Contours of BIMSTEC 134
Rajeet Mitter

The Arab World—A Region in Transition 144
Dinkar Srivastava

Radicalisation: Developing a Counter-narrative 158
Alvite Ningthoujam & CD Sahay

The New Climate Change Regime and Its Implications for India 174
Chandrashekhar Dasgupta

Weaponisation of Outer Space—A Major Security Challenge 184
Lt Gen Davinder Kumar, PVSM, VSM BAR, ADC

Index *195*

Preface

As a sovereign, democratic nation, we are just seventy years in the making. Our expressions of various aspects of freedoms, rights and aspirations, therefore, have—of necessity—to be conceived, nurtured and articulated with great degree of deliberations. Obviously, such discussions have to be rooted in innate national wisdom covering political, strategic, administrative and economic experiences. The commitment to national consolidation is rendered more challenging when tested against the diversities of our nationhood and adversities imposed by geopolitical avarice in our neighbourhood.

The Vivekananda International Foundation (VIF) was founded nearly a decade ago to sustain, promote and catalyse a noble commitment to our nationalist consolidation. In this pursuit, the Foundation has found its cause from the powerful and patriotic teachings of Swami Vivekananda while the ever-venerated Vivekananda Kendra gave our Foundation a platform for its institutional functions. That made it possible for a group of highly regarded professionals from the fields of security, military, diplomacy, economics to generate ideas in the VIF and stimulate actions for greater national security and prosperity.

The analyses, prognoses and options articulated by scholars of the Foundation have thus made a mark in shaping opinion amongst our higher State, public and private functionaries. Similarly, our factual, prejudice-free and candid confabulations with highly regarded think tanks and top intellectuals of the larger world has made it possible for the Foundation to gain deeper insight into the various challenges facing India, and so helped us in our search for appropriate policy options for the country.

VIF has been disseminating its analytical papers and reports through its website www.vifindia.org. In this endeavour, occasional papers, monographs and books having long-term applicability are being published both in the printed form and in the e-version. This year, we decided to take another stride by requesting some of the most renowned experts in the strategic circles to pen down their observations on subjects of their expertise. These have been largely related to the aspect of 'Securing India' which has been carried as the central theme for this year's publication. These enlightening and thought-provoking essays have been compiled in the form of a set of incisive papers for dissemination as our inaugural publication: *VIF Perspective: Issues and Trends*.

There are in all fifteen papers of various lengths, each devoted to dissection of one of the salient aspects of our nation building. Papers of such nature, wherein deep knowledge and understandings have been packaged with experience and insight, are generally tedious to access for the thinking community at large. It has, therefore, been our effort to ease that avenue to analyses, enquiry and wisdom through the medium of this publication.

I am sanguine that the publication, *VIF Perspective: Issues and Trends*, would serve its purpose in its cognitive reach-out to the State, academic, public and private institutions and both at national and international levels.

Jai Hind!

—General NC Vij
Director
Vivekananda International Foundation

April 2017
New Delhi

Strengthening India's Nuclear Deterrence

General NC Vij, PVSM, UYSM, AVSM,

and

VIF Expert Group

Abstract

This paper looks at India's nuclear deterrence as it exists today and recommends ways to strengthen it by identifying current gaps and suggesting remedies to address these. This exercise is driven by a two-fold requirement: First, to generate options to counter the ongoing nuclear brinkmanship by Pakistan; and secondly, to examine the larger issues of India's nuclear doctrine in context of both Pakistan and China.

The paper also covers the genesis of Pakistan's tactical nuclear weapons (TNWs) and examines the impact of these on India's nuclear deterrence. Measures to restore the credibility of India's nuclear deterrence in a responsible and credible manner, through a wider spectrum of counter measures, have also been analysed in this paper.

INDIA'S NUCLEAR DETERRENCE: GAPS AND REMEDIES

Salient Points of India's Nuclear Doctrine

In essence, the salient points of India's nuclear doctrine as per the Cabinet Committee on Security (CCS) notification of 4 January 2003 are that India will build up and maintain a 'credible minimum deterrence' while following a 'No First Use' (NFU) policy. It proceeds to elaborate that India will use nuclear weapons only in retaliation against nuclear attack on Indian territory or on Indian forces anywhere and that retaliation will be 'massive and designed to inflict unacceptable damage'. Further, nuclear weapons would not be used against non-nuclear weapon States; however, the option of retaliating with nuclear weapons in the event of a major attack against it with biological or chemical weapons will be open. Finally, retaliatory nuclear attacks will be authorised only by the civilian political leadership through the Nuclear Command Authority (NCA).

It is against the backdrop of the above-mentioned features of India's nuclear doctrine and the contemporary nuclear developments in the region that various contextual issues are examined in this paper.

The Dilemma of Nuclear Response

In its promulgation of 'massive retaliation' to cause 'unacceptable damage', India's nuclear deterrence is but a 'one massive leap' response against one and every situation which India wants its potential adversaries to register. In that stance—essentially a mind game—as conceived by the architects of India's nuclear doctrine, lies the punch of India's deterrence. Another cardinal feature of the Indian doctrine is related to its apex command and control. In that, it is stated unambiguously that retaliatory nuclear response could only be authorised by the civilian political leadership through the NCA.

In contrast, Pakistan follows a nuclear 'first-use' policy. This policy more or less propagates Pakistan's policy of resorting to thwart any possible Indian aggression with its superior conventional forces. In late 2001, the Pakistan NCA defined their nuclear 'red lines' in the form of four potential thresholds. These were later published by the International Institute for Strategic Studies (IIIS). It is relevant to note that these formulations are mere pronouncements by Pakistan's NCA; there *per se* is no formally promulgated nuclear doctrine or nuclear strategy by the State. Arguably therefore, these thresholds are merely stated positions at a point in time and may well be subject to change at any time based on the ever-changing dynamics of India–Pakistan relations. Presently, the said thresholds stand stated as under:

- **Spatial Threshold**. This threshold is crossed if and when the Indian military forces penetrate on a large scale into Pakistan's territory which Pakistan is unable to thwart. The actual limits of this penetration have been left to the imagination of the analysts; the general belief is that it could be the line of Indus River—the lifeline of Pakistan. Penetration of Indian forces up to the Indus Valley and capture of key objectives along its most sensitive eastern territorial belt is therefore considered to be a situation serious enough for Pakistan to trigger nuclear first use.
- **Military Threshold**. Comprehensive destruction of a large part of its conventional forces by Indian offensive, particularly the armoured and air forces, could lead to Pakistan resorting to nuclear response. Attack on nuclear installations, or use of chemical or biological weapons against Pakistan could also trigger nuclear response.

- **Economic Threshold.** This threshold refers to a possible Indian naval blockade of the Sindh province or the Makran Coast of Baluchistan province, significant reduction of Pakistan's share of Indus, Jhelum and Chenab rivers, or the capture of vital centres and arteries of Pakistan's core economic activities.
- **Political Threshold.** Political or serious internal destabilisation that could lead to a stage when Pakistan's national integrity is threatened.

A read through of the above-mentioned thresholds suggests that these have been kept deliberately vague and sweeping to the extent that Pakistan's use of nuclear weapons might not necessarily be linked just to conventional military thrusts but it could also be triggered by economic blockade and political destabilisation. But the moot question is that why should India create such a situation that Pakistan must reach for its nuclear button? The answer lies in Pakistan's core purpose: all the nuclear posturing is to keep itself unrestrained from bleeding India with sub-conventional aggression in various forms, without having to suffer military consequences from a conventionally stronger India. With Pakistan's compulsively revisionist ideology, that is the crux of the whole issue—continuation of sub-conventional aggression with immunity, that is, restraining the victim from retaliating with its conventionally superior forces.

On the conventional front, India followed what was called as the Sunderji Doctrine. As per this doctrine, while the seven 'Holding Corps' of the Indian Army deployed along the Indo-Pakistan Border had only limited offensive capability that was just adequate to check any possible cross-border aggression from Pakistan, the main punch of offensive power rested with the three 'Strike Corps', based well away from the border, in the hinterland. Thus while the Holding Corps contained Pakistan's aggression, Strike Corps were to mobilise from their peacetime locations and launch punitive counter-offensives. Post Pakistan's formal nuclearisation, and in anticipation of its possible 'first-use' of nuclear weapons in such scenarios, the Indian Army prepared itself to conduct what it termed as 'conventional operations under a nuclear overhang', wherein the offensive operations were slated to culminate short of what could be construed as Pakistan's nuclear threshold.

Limitations of the Indian doctrine became evident during the 'Operation Parakram', which was launched after the Pakistani terrorists' attack on the Indian parliament on 13 December 2001. Herein, it took nearly three weeks for the strike forces to mobilise, thus giving not only adequate time for Pakistan to be operationally prepared, but also for the international community to intervene by urging India to exercise restraint. The Doctrine thus revealed three main weaknesses. Firstly, it was realised that the Strike Corps were far too large and located far away to make it possible for them to mobilise for offensive in quick time. Secondly, given the levels of battle transparency that existed even during that time over a decade ago, movement of such large forces across the length and breadth of the country just could not be shrouded, whereas the long mobilisation period negated the achievement of strategic surprise. And lastly, lack of offensive power with the Holding Corps prevented them from undertaking significant offensive operations to seize fleeting opportunities.

In order to address the above weaknesses, a new doctrinal development took place in the aftermath of Operation Parakram. Colloquially referred to as the 'Cold Start Doctrine'—conceived in General Vij's time—and meant to address the three weaknesses as stated above, this development made a modification to the existing defence posture. It aimed to establish a proactive strategic stance with the capability to launch conventional offensives against Pakistan, and involved rapid multiple thrusts by Indian mechanised forces, supported by air, over a wide front across the Punjab and Rajasthan sectors. Needless to state that India meant to keep the objectives limited to relatively shallow depths and so deny Pakistan any provocation to use its nuclear weapons. The new doctrine thus addressed the lacunae experienced during Operation Parakram.

Introduction of TNWs in the Equation

At this stage, Pakistan, having realised that its nuclear posturing, as defined by its nuclear thresholds, had been unhinged by the Indian strategy of opting for shallow multiple offensive thrusts astride a wide front, sought to recalibrate its response strategy. Starting with a series of joint military exercises by the name of 'Azm-e-Nau III', it focused on an offensive-defence type of response to counter the Cold Start Doctrine. One significant fallout of this focus was the testing of 'Nasr' (Hatf IX), a short-range ballistic missile (SRBM) with a range of 60 km. Nasr is a multiple launch rocket system capable of carrying four ready-to-fire nuclear-capable missiles with a weapon yield in the region of 0.5 to 15 kilo tonne. Starting from its first flight test on 19 Apr 2011, the missile was claimed to be operational on 5 October 2013. In the aftermath of induction of Nasr SRBM, Lt Gen Khalid Ahmed Kidwai, the then director general of Pakistan's Strategic Plans Division (SPD) stated that in Nasr, Pakistan had consolidated its nuclear deterrence at all levels of the threat spectrum—that is, at the strategic, operational and tactical levels. It is relevant to note here that in the 'Hatf' series of surface-to-surface missiles (SSM), Pakistan possesses the nuclear-capable Shaheen I (Hatf IV–750 km), Shaheen IA (1100 km), Shaheen II (Hatf VI–2000 km), Shaheen III (2750 km), Babur (Hatf VII Cruise–700 Km) and Nasr (Hatf IX SRBM–60 Km). This inventory roughly spans the complete range of strategic, operational and tactical levels of warfare.

Consequent to the 'Azm-e-Nau III' military exercises, Pakistan stated that the development of 'Nasr' SSM was in response to India's Cold Start Doctrine. This impression is sustained by Pakistan's possession of its newly operationalised arsenal of Nasr 'low yield' or 'tactical nuclear weapons' (TNW)—essentially counter-force weapons—which are considered to be useable within a localised battlefield space, with limited and localised fallout-effects, to close India's option of undertaking even shallow-objective offensives. Thus through hints, insinuations and posturing, Pakistan implies to convey the message that its nuclear red line, aimed at defeating even limited conventional Indian offensive, stands substantially lowered, and that the strategic 'space' left for India to prosecute conventional offensive has shrunk further. Pakistani strategists proclaim that TNWs are war-fighting weapons; but that stated, it has been clarified that the competence to authorise the use of such weapons will remain to be with the Political Council of the NCA. This clarification is aimed at allaying the universal concern regarding the option of employing TNWs being left to local or theatre commanders.

With the above posture of nuclear brinkmanship in place, Pakistan continues to engage in acts of bloody cross-border aggression—terror attacks in Mumbai, Pathankot, Uri, Nagrota etc. to cite just a few. In so doing, Pakistani strategists draw assurance from their conviction that their Indian counterparts, understanding that Pakistan's thresholds of nuclear weapons-use has indeed been further lowered, are restrained from retaliating with punitive conventional strikes upon even shallow objectives. On their part, every time a hostile cross-border attack is perpetrated from Pakistan, Indian leaders have to contend with a decision dilemma regarding putting boots across the border in order to make the intransigent pay for its mischief. One of the factors of this hesitation is the matter of inviting Pakistan's use of low-yield weapons, or what it calls as 'battlefield nuclear weapon', in retaliation to India's punitive operations.

As stated, Pakistani strategists consider that even if India opted to retaliate by conventional offensive action through whatever limited strategic 'space' to do so was still left open for it under the aforementioned 'nuclear overhang', Pakistan could use low destructivity of TNWs to recoil such offensives. In their opinion, Pakistan could do so with minimal chances of India responding with 'massive' nuclear retaliation because such a situation could make it hard for Indian leaders to find justification for infliction of disproportionate damage to avenge against what limited damage the TNWs could inflict. There is indeed a serious decision dilemma amongst many of the Indian strategic community who find it hard to justify that in response to Pakistan's use of low-yield tactical battlefield nuclear weapons, the Indian leadership would react by wiping out a few cities in Pakistan—besides opening up the escalatory ladder of nuclear exchange culminating into mutual destruction. In sum, it is in the incredulity of India's policy of 'one massive leap' of massive response in their perception that emboldens Pakistan in playing the game of nuclear brinkmanship. Thus, while Pakistan's nuclear brinkmanship succeeds, continuous acts of cross-border aggression are perpetrated under its umbrella. The question therefore arises as to who is actually getting deterred—India or Pakistan?

In the overall context, the concern is that even a limited conventional operation to punish Pakistan's proxy war could provoke Pakistan's use of TNWs against Indian forces. In that eventuality, the Indian decision-makers might find that any nuclear retaliation could eventually snowball into an uncontrollable nuclear war, something that was neither desirable nor in India's national interest. Conversely, by its passive inaction against Pakistan's relentless aggression, India would deter itself, thus allowing Pakistan's nuclear brinkmanship to succeed. More worryingly, that kind of policy passivity could lead to the Indian decision-makers inferring that the 'space' left for prosecution of conventional offensive had purportedly shrunk to inconsequential levels, and therefore there could be no option left but to sequester India's conventional power and continue to stoically suffer the consequences of Pakistan's proxy war.

Pakistan's possession of the Nasr SSM has cropped up another significant asymmetry against Indian forces, wherein the adversary has battlefield nuclear weapons which are clearly intended to be used while the own side does not possess a matching capability. The human angle to such grave asymmetry manifests by the unwelcome morale effect upon the field force commanders and the troops they command. Adversary's use of nuclear weapons, even if low-yield and localised-effect, would oblige the troops to fight through the nuclear attack with only the conventional weapons that they possess. Such feeling of inequality does not auger well for fighting morale and thus may fault the outcome of war.

Relevance of Low-yield Weapons in Own Context

To be clear of the above discussed adverse asymmetry—mental, morale and physical—the sensible option for India may be to have its own low-yield nuclear weapons.

But converse opinions contend that by reacting to Pakistan's game of fielding low-yield nuclear weapons in a tit-for-tat mode, India will actually debilitate the sanctity of its nuclear deterrence, anchored as it is upon the declaration of inflicting 'massive retaliation with unacceptable damage' against any use of nuclear weapon, of any yield, by the adversary. India would thus signal to Pakistan that a compromise of proportional or graduated response would be acceptable in the gamut of India's nuclear deterrence. That understanding would in turn encourage Pakistan to brandish its TNWs—or battlefield nuclear weapons—even against India's small and shallow conventional offensive actions, and limit India's retaliation to nothing more than similar low-yield weapon counter-attack. In such a case, the keys to 'conventional stalemate' as well as 'escalation control' would be in Pakistan's hands, for it to continue with its mission of bleeding India with impunity while India's nuclear as well as conventional deterrence remains stalled. This opinion therefore contends that India's policy of 'massive retaliation' should remain to be in force in order to deter Pakistan from using its TNWs in the battlefield for the fear of inviting 'unacceptable damage'. The inference drawn in this argument therefore is that India does not require low-yield nuclear weaponry in its nuclear arsenal.

The case for maintenance of status quo is, however, countered by the hard reality that in spite of the expression of India's resolve to wreck retribution by 'massive retaliation to inflict unacceptable damage', Pakistan remains comfortable in its belief that in the contingency of its using low-yield, limited-effect weapons in a localised battlefield, the 'one massive leap' response of 'massive retaliation'—being maximalist and disproportionate over-reaction besides being escalatory—is unlikely to prevail over India's conscious political decision dilemma. Such comfort of immunity emboldens Pakistan to indulge in its unending misadventures like the proxy war and cross-border terrorism activities all over India. Indeed, that perception of immunity is the centre pillar of Pakistan's nuclear brinkmanship. On the other hand, accommodating TNWs within India's existing nuclear doctrine would only add to its options of weapon selection without compromising its provisions of 'massive retaliation' and 'unacceptable damage'. It would thus curb Pakistan's nuclear brinkmanship.

Case for India's Possession of Low-yield Weapons

The bottom line in the Indo-Pak context is that while it is universally accepted that nuclear weapons are political weapons of deterrence, Pakistan subscribes to the notion that its battlefield nuclear weapons are an extension of the country's conventional deterrent capability—'full spectrum capability' so to state. This 'make-believe stance' however does not change the reality—and each side knows it too well—that nuclear weapons, irrespective of the yield, remain very much the political weapons of deterrence, and that once started, a nuclear exchange just cannot be controlled from spiralling out of control into an all-out nuclear war. That indeed is abhorrent because no nation wants to destroy its civilisation and progress made over time.

As to Pakistan's TNWs, there are basically three schools of thought. According to the first school, TNWs merely serve to extend Pakistan's deterrence posture further down the conflict-intensity spectrum. The second school believes that it indicates a shift in strategy from deterrence to nuclear war-fighting; while the third school has questioned the utility of TNWs in stopping India's offensives—it is estimated that hundreds of TNWs would be needed to really attrite the multiple-thrust line-mechanised attacks across a wide front.

Whatever be the case, the arguments in favour of India opting to possess TMWs are hinged at the following considerations:

- If Pakistan intends to put TNWs to military use, then it would be necessary for India to have the flexibility of possessing a matching capability in addition to its maximalist response of massive retaliation. In any case, use or otherwise of nuclear weapons of various ranges, yields and destructive effects would be decided by India according to its own plans, and in such cases it is always preferable to have more options.
- If Pakistan's possession of TNWs is to bolster its posture in deterring India across the full spectrum of strategic, operational and tactical levels of warfare, then it would make sense for India to repudiate that kind of imposition, particularly at the tactical level wherein lies the promise of India's retaliation.
- With the comfort of believing in incredulity of India's 'one massive leap' response, if Pakistan, by flouting its TNWs, seeks immunity from the consequences of its hostilities against India, then India has no option but to keep its own options secure—that of tactical retribution through offensive strikes. Such retribution would require India to possess TNWs, and display it to derail Pakistan's new-found notion of 'full spectrum' immunity.
- A most significant advantage of possessing TNWs, irrespective of its intended use, would be in allaying misgivings in the minds of our commanders and troops, that of our forces being less capable in any way as compared to the adversary. It would also allow the Indian leadership to be instilled with more conviction and confidence and freedom to make the desired decision at the time of reckoning. With low-yield weapons in our arsenal too, the feeling of a perceived inequality among the Indian forces would be obliterated, and India's deterrence-deficit against Pakistan would be overcome to good extent.

It is relevant to note that during India's nuclear tests in 1998, out of the five nuclear weapons, the first group consisted of a thermonuclear device (Shakti I), the second was the fission device (Shakti II) and the third was a sub-kiloton device (Shakti III). Nearly two decades later, and with 'Prithvi' series of SSMs well operationalised, it may be fairly simple for India to possess low-yield weapons, with no obligation to revise its nuclear doctrine. To reiterate, by implication, the possession of low-yield weapons to maintain a complete range of nuclear arsenal would expand the perceived 'space' for India to prosecute offensive conventional operations to disarm the habitual troublemaker—Pakistan.

Nuclear deterrence, as a subset of comprehensive national power (CNP), rests on three pillars. In that, while warheads of tactical, operational and strategic yields form the first pillar, the triad of delivery capability on land, sea and air make up for the second one. Finally, the third pillar is the decision, command, control and execution structure that is dedicated to the management of nuclear posture as defined in the nuclear doctrine.

The credibility of nuclear deterrence being derived from the combined strength of all the three pillars and as it is registered by the adversary, it is needless to state that strengthening of nuclear deterrence requires reinforcing all the above three pillars. The added option of India's possession of low-yield weapons would bolster the effectiveness of all the above listed pillars with the least of effort and maximum effect.

ON DETERRENCE OTHER THAN NUCLEAR

While salience of the above-mentioned three pillars is true of nuclear deterrence, there is another very strong and expanding domain of developing nuclear deterrence capability in the non-nuclear domain. This domain of deterrence has lately assumed tremendous significance given the netcentricity of the future battlefield and its near-total dependence on the electromagnetic spectrum.

The tools of such a deterrence arsenal make use of enablers like electronic warfare, cyberwarfare and other soft kill means. The aim is to interfere, hack and debilitate adversary's surveillance networks, target acquisition capability, missile guidance capability and more, as also, to strike at its command and control networks controlling nuclear launch. The soft kill arsenal is actually huge in range and depth and is only limited by the imagination of the attacker and the technologies at hand.

The above arsenal, cumulatively referred to as electronic combat capability (ECC), spans both the offensive, as well as the defensive domains. Hierarchically, it covers the continuum starting at the national level, where it manifests as the policy and decision-making functions, and comes down to the armed forces level where execution of the said policies and decisions is to take place in a manner and sequence to be stated in our national war fighting doctrine. Needless to mention that the above 'teeth' capability needs to be meshed with the 'flesh' consisting of requisite organisations, infrastructure and the 'skin ware' with required skills and training.

In specifics, the ECC stated above would comprise electronic warfare including non-nuclear e-bombs, cyberwarfare, electromagnetic (EM) space management, EM spectrum warfare, electronic deception, optical warfare, counter-space operations and appropriate platforms for operations on land, sea, air and space. Exercise of this capability would seriously degrade the adversary's command, control, communications, computer, intelligence, surveillance, target acquisition and reconnaissance (C4ISTAR) systems, weapon systems, navigation, guidance and logistics, and impede his overall battlefield transparency while providing to own forces real-time intelligence and assist them in counter-intelligence.

In fact, so exponentially galloping is the pace of technology and information flow in the current era that these two verticals are going to be the new 'normals' in the future battlefield. With that as the stark reality whose time has come, it is imperative that we must develop the capability of unimpeded use of these while negating that option to our adversary. This requirement, in the context of this paper, relates to the vertical of generating such ECC that adds strength to our nuclear deterrence by denying the use of such technologies and information flow to the adversary that may be employed in delivery of his nuclear punch—in other words, first strike. The areas to be targeted by own ECC must encompass soft-crippling adversary's those battle function areas end-to-end which unfold in the delivery of the nuclear strike. These may include the adversary's surveillance of battle space, target acquisition, command and control structures to include hierarchical chain of authorisations and successive levels of control, and finally, to cripple, dissuade and waylay the electronics and electromagnetic systems that are involved in his guidance and control of the delivery means in flight—a very tall order, no doubt.

To address the above requirement in the manner stated above is such a huge vertical and has so many complex requirements that it will call for a corresponding organisational transformation at successive levels of command. Such a transformation will aim to develop capabilities of electronic interference and soft kill means in our arsenal that will aim to cripple adversary's nuclear punch as a whole (surveillance, target acquisition, command and control et al) thereby providing strength to our nuclear deterrence by 'means other than nuclear'. Such a capability, if well disseminated will add considerable credibility to our deterrence. That such a capability needs to be developed as a part of strengthening our nuclear deterrence is a strategic imperative.

REVISITING THE POLICY OF 'NO FIRST USE' AND 'MASSIVE RETALIATION'

'No First Use' (NFU) of nuclear weapons and the resolve to inflict 'massive retaliation' against the initiator of nuclear attack are the central pillars of India's nuclear response policy. Since there is much discussion on the issue, it would be in order to examine if there is any need to modify that policy.

One of the primary reasons of opting for the NFU policy post the nuclear weapon tests in 1998 was to assure the world of India's responsible intent. Indeed, that stance has reinforced the world view of India as a responsible nuclear power, which in turn has yielded several positives at various international confabulations, like the Indo-US Civil Nuclear Agreement and acceptability from the Nuclear Suppliers Group (NSG). Besides, the policy of NFU, read with the stipulations of 'credible minimum deterrence' (CMD), and 'massive retaliation to inflict unacceptable damage' also offer certain implied advantages. Briefly put, these expressions absolve India from engaging in nuclear arms race and yet impose adequate level of deterrence for the adversaries to desist against the pain of having to suffer the unwanted consequences of India's debilitating nuclear retaliation. Indeed, this is a policy that has held well on a couple of occasions during the last two decades.

By similar considerations, there is no requirement to redefine the expression 'massive retaliation' either with the description of 'punitive retaliation' that had been used in the draft doctrine, or by adding new qualifications to it. In fact, retracing to the draft stage expression is likely to signal an ambivalent intent on India's part and that is a very dangerous situation in the context of nuclear posturing. Indeed, that might be viewed as India's stance shifting to accommodate proportional or graduated response to the adversary's first strike, which in any case is not repudiated in India's nuclear doctrine. Such a signal would compromise the basic feature of India's nuclear doctrine without the accrual of any corresponding advantage. Conversely, India will get embroiled into warhead-matching, numbers game and readiness stress—all this just to promote a weapon which the world considers to be unusable in war.

Truly, a doctrine cannot be so rigid and fixated that it leaves no scope for periodic review or modification if found necessary. Indeed, it will remain India's sovereign right not only to revisit its nuclear doctrine but also to interpret its policy articulations in the manner as considered congruent to national interests. However, our current nuclear doctrine allows the advantages of flexible interpretation of its expressions and articulations without necessitating any change. There is nothing to debar India from resorting to nuclear warfare at tactical or strategic levels if and when it cannot avoid doing so, nor does it tie India's commitment to any preconceived scale of its own 'massive retaliation' and the adversary's 'unacceptable damage'. In the overall analysis therefore, it should be very clear to all parties that 'India will retain the right to defend itself in whatever manner it deems fit'.

At this stage of discussion on India's nuclear deterrence, it would be necessary to delve into our other nuclear neighbour and Pakistan's strong ally China's nuclear policy and its implications.

ASSESSMENT OF CHINA'S NUCLEAR STRATEGY

The Chinese Government published its nuclear strategy in 2005. However, in its most articulated Defence White Paper of 2013, there was no specific reference to its nuclear NFU policy, leading to speculation on whether China was moving away from its previous stance. That speculation was rested in China's white paper on 'China's Military Strategy' of May 2015, wherein the Chinese Government reiterated that 'China has always pursued the Policy of NFU of nuclear weapons and has adhered to a self-defensive nuclear strategy that is defensive in nature'. Some other salient points stated in this white paper are:

- China's nuclear force is a strategic cornerstone for safeguarding its national sovereignty and security.
- China will not use or threaten to use nuclear weapons against non-nuclear weapon

States, or in nuclear-weapon free zones, and will never enter into a nuclear arms race with any other country.

- China would continue to maintain its nuclear capabilities at the minimum level required to maintain national security.
- China will optimise its nuclear force structure, improve strategic warning, command and control, missile penetration, rapid reaction, survivability and protection, and deter other countries from using or threatening to use nuclear weapons against China.

Notwithstanding all that has been stated, the paper also states that China upholds the principal of 'counter-attack in self-defence' and limited development of nuclear weapons to maintain a 'credible nuclear deterrent force'. At the same time, there is reiteration of the stance that China does not consider nuclear weapons as offensive weapons for first use.

Strategy analysts tend to argue that China's nuclear deterrence is basically focused on the United States (US); the India factor does not materially affect the concerns of Chinese strategists. Being aware of the military and technological gap between the two, they do not consider that India could have the capability to pose military threat to China. China's pronouncements too refute the general perception that India chose to develop nuclear weapons to save itself from China's nuclear arm-twisting, and instead ascribes the cause to India's purported great power ambitions. According to Chinese experts, the mention of China during the 1998 tests was made to address domestic opposition and to help legitimise the tests to the international community. To that extent, India's nuclear capability may not seriously impact on China's policy articulations on nuclear deterrence, strategic stability or security threats.

Besides India's adverse capability gap, experts further opine that China does not consider that India would seriously intend to go to war against it either on nuclear or on conventional front, even if escalation of tension on account of the border dispute remains plausible. This assessment is based on India's strategic culture wherein China feels that India will be more cautious and would not take any provocative action that might lead to a war with China. In the context of China–Pakistan alliance, experts like Toby Dalton and George Perkovich opine that in any Indo-Pakistan confrontation, while creation of heightened tension is likely, China is unlikely to intervene with its own nuclear forces, especially if India does not initiate the use of nuclear weapons in the conflict.

While the above perceptions of the nuclear experts might stand considered at one pole of strategic thinking, it will also be a grave mistake to stand fixated in the belief that China does not consider India as a security threat and therefore, by reciprocity, it poses no threat to India. In fact, not just the history, but also the Chinese behaviour and dynamics of its policies over the decades of co-existence has taught us never ever to dilute—or worse, not even acknowledge—the China threat factor, be it nuclear or conventional. It will be safer to assume that while China may not pose an immediate threat, it would always remain a 'threat-in-being' and India should always remain prepared accordingly.

China, however, considers India, for not having formally endorsed the Nuclear Proliferation Treaty (NPT), Comprehensive Test Ban Treaty (CTBT) and Fissile Material Cut-off Treaty (FMCT), as an illegal nuclear power. It is very critical of the India–US Civil Nuclear Deal and has been blocking India's entry into the NSG. While China may not show concern with India's civil and peaceful use of nuclear energy, it remains very serious about the grey area between civil and military nuclear use, especially in the matter of fissile material production which, on date, is not regulated by the International Atomic Energy Agency (IAEA) safeguards or the NSG technical control procedures. In the above context, China sees two main security challenges created by India's nuclear programme. First, enhanced civil nuclear capabilities and practical difficulties in verifying dual-use nuclear materials would permit India to modernise its nuclear weapons. Secondly, it perceives that should India compromise on its NFU stand, it might dilute the nuclear taboo by signalling to the other non-NPT nuclear weapon States that use of nuclear weapons might be an option during a war, and this would in turn dilute the basis for stability of nuclear deterrence.

Without prejudice to the aforementioned considerations, China could still perceive a threat from India in the medium term. This perception is apparently based on three factors, namely: Foreign support to India's great power aspirations; enhancement of India's conventional military capability; and, China's distrust of India with regard to the territorial dispute and stability in Tibet. China views the growing strategic cooperation between the US and India and the emerging US-driven bilateral and trilateral arrangements in the Asia–Pacific, including its idea of 'power rebalance', with India co-opted as a key partner, with great concern.

In the overall context of strategic factors prevailing, it would be wise to be cautious in concluding that since China does not consider India as a foreseeable security threat, and therefore, by implication it poses no threat to India. In fact, China's behavioural trend warns us not to ever discount the possibility of China posing threat to India, be it conventional or nuclear—China's military build-up is a clear indication to that end. Even if the threat is not considered to be imminent, China remains a threat-in-being and India would be wise to be prepared accordingly. Indeed, it is a strategic imperative for India to keep close watch over political, military, scientific and technological developments in China and to ensure that adequate measures are in place, effectively, to protect India's national interests, without ever committing the error of diluting or negating the Chinese threat or failing to recognise it as a threat-in-being.

CONCLUDING OBSERVATIONS

In view of the realities of Pakistan–China–India strategic matrix as discussed above, and relating these to the issues of introduction of low-yield weapons and revisit of India's nuclear doctrine, it is fair to conclude that there is no reason for India to amend its nuclear doctrine and modify its NFU policy, neither is there any need to be restrained in possessing low-yield weapons capability. That said, we should continue our efforts in seeking cooperation and collaboration from like-minded global powers—US, Australia, Japan, Russia…—in furtherance of our strategic capabilities, and forge partnerships that serve our overall national security interests.

RECOMMENDATIONS OF THE STUDY

In sum, the above discussion may be crystallised into the following recommendations:

- India should develop low-yield weapons to address the gaps in its nuclear arsenal and to further strengthen our nuclear deterrent in the face of the never-ending nuclear brinkmanship by Pakistan.
- Efforts should be made to strengthen our deterrence in fields other than nuclear by building the requisite electronic combat capability and putting in place a transformed organisational structure that is necessary to sustain that capability.
- No change is recommended in our existing nuclear doctrine and its articulation of 'No First Use' as well as 'massive retaliation to inflict unacceptable damage'.

***

THE EXPERT GROUP

General NC Vij, PVSM, UYSM, AVSM (Retd), was India's twenty-first Chief of the Army Staff and is a former founder Vice Chairman of the National Disaster Management Authority in the rank of Cabinet Minister. Presently he is the Director of the Vivekananda International Foundation (VIF), New Delhi.

Lieutenant General Ravi Sawhney, PVSM, AVSM (Retd), is a former Director General of Military Intelligence and a former Deputy Chief of the Army Staff. He is a Dean, Centre for Defence Studies, at the VIF.

Ambassador PP Shukla, Distinguished Fellow, VIF, has served in diplomatic assignments at Moscow, Brussels, London and Kathmandu, and finally as India's Ambassador to Russia. He has also served as the Diplomatic Adviser to the Prime Minister in the late 1990s.

Ambassador TCA Rangachari, Distinguished Fellow, VIF, is a former Ambassador to France and Germany.

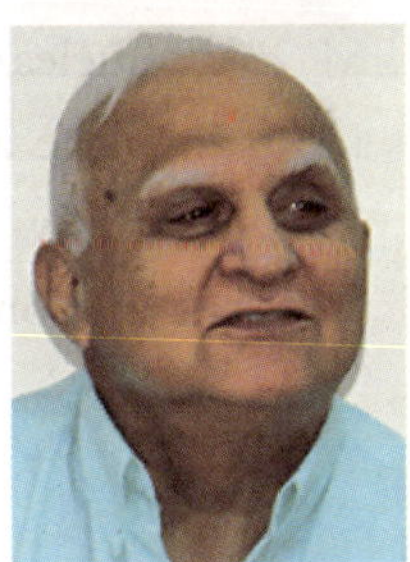

Vice Admiral Raman Puri, PVSM, AVSM, VSM (Retd) is a former Commander-in-Chief, Eastern Naval Command, and a former Chief of Integrated Defence Staff, Ministry of Defence, Government of India.

Lieutenant General Gautam Banerjee, PVSM, AVSM, YSM (Retd) is a former Chief of Staff, Central Command and Commandant of the Officers' Training Academy, Chennai. He is a Member of the Executive Council and a Distinguished Fellow at the VIF, New Delhi.

Ambassador Ashok Kantha, Distinguished Fellow, VIF, is a former Indian Ambassador to China.

Ambassador DP Srivastava, Distinguished Fellow, VIF is a former Indian Ambassador to Iran.

Lieutenant General JP Singh, PVSM, AVSM (Retd), Visiting Fellow, VIF, is a former Deputy Chief of Army Staff, and later, an Adviser to the DRDO.

Lieutenant General Davinder Kumar, PVSM, VSM BAR, ADC retired as the Signal Officer-in-Chief of Indian Army after a distinguished service of forty-one years.

Lieutenant General VK Saxena, PVSM, AVSM, VSM (Retd) is a former Director General of the Corps of Army Air Defence, and presently an adviser to a leading DPSU.

Vice Admiral Anil Chopra, PVSM, AVSM (Retd), Visiting Fellow, VIF, is a former Director General, Indian Coast Guard, former Commander-in-Chief, Eastern and then Western Naval Command. Presently, he is a Member of the National Security Advisory Board.

Lieutenant General Anil Ahuja, PVSM, UYSM, AVSM, SM, VSM & Bar (Retd) is a former Deputy Chief of the Integrated Defence Staff, Ministry of Defence, Government of India.

Commodore Gopal Suri is a Senior Fellow at the VIF.

Col AR Sirsikar is a Senior Fellow at the VIF.

Swami Vivekananda's Message and Vision: Some Keynotes and their Contemporary Relevance

DR ANIRBAN GANGULY

Abstract

Swami Vivekananda was unarguably one of the principal progenitors and drivers of modern India. Steeped in tradition, immersed in Indian civilisational wisdom and experience—of which he became one of the most articulate and forceful proponents—and yet remarkably up to date with the currents of world thought, Vivekananda spoke for and symbolised an aspiring India, which yearned to take her rightful place in the comity of nations.

Vivekananda's articulations came at a time when the burden of subjection in India was acutely felt and had its repercussions in almost all spheres of our national life. His words, first spoken and heard in the World Parliament at Chicago, generated a wave of enthusiasm back home, which gradually worked to crystallise the aspiration for freedom. I have argued that Vivekananda, while being acutely conscious of the deficiencies in our national life, was also supremely affirmative of India's potentials and future. He called for basing this movement for the 'recovery of India' on her civilisational wisdom; it is this wisdom which, he asserted, would free her from her many debilitations, direct her march towards the future and successfully enable her to recover her pre-eminence as a civilisational State. In these articulations of his, one discerns a remarkable level of contemporariness and relevance. I have put together certain pointers—keynotes as I have termed them—from his thoughts for India that continue to remain vital for the present efforts for national regeneration.

THE MESSAGE AT CHICAGO AND ITS IMPACT IN INDIA

The significance and contribution of Swami Vivekananda's message in articulating the aspirations of modern India, in shaping the Indian narrative of nationalism and in defining the need for an overarching national unity has often been discussed, especially by those who have interpreted his work in some detail or have put aspects of his message into contemporary practices. India, her plight, as he saw it around himself at that point in time, her state of subjection, her aspirations, her eventual liberation and her future was what dominated Vivekananda's articulation, especially over a period of nine years that began from his appearance at the World Parliament of Religions at Chicago in 1893 and ended with his passing away in 1902, at the age of thirty-nine at Belur in Bengal.

The appearance of Vivekananda at Chicago as a representative of Hinduism and of India, showed, as Sri Aurobindo, one of India's leading modern philosopher-sage, has argued, that 'the spiritual ideas' for which India stood was no longer a defensive one, but an 'aggressive and invading' one, which challenged the 'materialised mentality of the Occident'[1]. The Swami's appearance at the World Parliament of Religions had succeeded in creating an unmistakable wave back home in India, despite many a later-day callow critics trying to play it down. As news of that grand event and Vivekananda's peroration on behalf of a colonised and unsure people, percolated back in India, a wave of enthusiasm began gathering steam. This effect of his visit to the West has been well documented and recorded.

One of Vivekananda's pre-eminent biographers and chronicler, Sankari Prasad Basu (1928-2014) noted that the Monk's words spoken in the West, instilled a national self-faith (*ātma-viśwās*) and a national self-dignity (*ātma-sammān*), among his compatriots back home[2], leading to a wide and wave-generating awakening. Sister Nivedita (Margaret Noble, 1867-1911), one of Vivekananda's foremost Hinduised Western disciples, perhaps best summed up the effect of Vivekananda's words on India when she wrote that as the Swami spoke in the West, 'a nation sleeping in the shadows of the darkened half of the earth, on the far side of the Pacific, waited in spirit for the words that would be borne on the dawn that was travelling towards them, to reveal to them the secret of their own greatness and strength[3].'

What set Vivekananda apart from many others of his age was the fact that 'it never occurred to him that his own people were in any respect less than the equals of any other nation whatsoever...'[4] It was this firm conviction that enabled him to move minds and infuse a deeper collective confidence in his people, especially the youth of that epoch. Vivekananda's success at Chicago and his inspiring speeches, delivered literally across the length and breadth of India upon return, were also 'a source of inspiration to young nationalists'. Though he played no part in active politics, 'his contribution to the

Indian national movement was invaluable'. Vivekananda's messages put the image of the motherland on a high pedestal. He gave expression to India's growing 'nationalism and spirit of self-help and independence' and was seen 'as the very embodiment of courage, self-confidence and strength'[5].

THE PREOCCUPATION WITH INDIA AND HER FUTURE

In a sense, 'very little that Swami Vivekananda spoke or wrote [can] be sharply separated from his thoughts on India and fellow Indians'[6]. As one of Vivekananda's foremost Western biographers, the French social and political philosopher Romain Rolland (1866-1944) lyrically, yet movingly wrote, 'It was the misery under his eyes, the misery of India, which filled his mind to the exclusion of every other thought. It pursued him, like a tiger following its prey, from the north to the south in his flight across India. It consumed him during sleepless nights'[7]. Rolland saw in Vivekananda's indefatigable peregrinations for India's awakening a firm seeking for a 'public salvation...the regeneration of the mother-country, the resurrection of spiritual powers of India and their diffusion throughout the universe...'[8]

For Sister Nivedita, also among his principal chroniclers, the Master's pre-occupation with the condition and fate of India was ceaseless and this concern of his found expression in his utterances on India, which breathed a conviction of India's rise and of her capacity to unshackle herself. Nivedita argued in her masterly assessment of Vivekananda's life, that the Swami's concern and worship of his 'own land' was focused on the 'conviction that India was not old and effete, as her critics had supposed, but young, ripe with potentiality, and standing, at the beginning of the twentieth century, on the threshold of even greater developments than she had known in the past'[9]. Throughout the years that she worked with him, Nivedita saw how 'the thought of India was to him [Vivekananda] like the air he breathed'[10]. It was this unceasing preoccupation with India that led Vivekananda to lay 'the foundation for the crystallisation of Indian nationalism', when he gave a call in Madras on 14 February 1897, asking all his listeners to worship the motherland alone and exclusively for the next fifty years. 'Give up,' he said, 'being a slave [and] for the next fifty years this alone shall be our keynote—this, our great Mother India. Let all other vain gods disappear for the time from our minds[11].'

It is this ceaseless concern and preoccupation of his with the condition and the destiny of India that has made thinkers and leaders of a later age look upon him as the crystalliser and shaper of India's modern narrative, as one who articulated and imparted direction and energy to the then amorphous quest for a national self-expression. For CP Ramaswami Aiyar (1879-1966), the scholar–administrator, Vivekananda's work and action 'revived for us the idea of nationhood'. He saw Vivekananda as the 'first of those, who made it possible to think of India as [a] whole irrespective of the existing differences of class, creed, colour and custom', as one who 'pleaded for driving away of everything that would prevent the union of India' and knew that 'unless India was one spiritually and intellectually, India could not step into the outer world'[12].

As an intense patriot, the Swami felt remorse for the decline of his country and perhaps therefore, 'he wanted at times to act as the iconoclast coming like a bombshell on the evils of society'. Vivekananda may not have been a political philosopher in the strict sense of the term; he did not, for example, 'enter into the analytical study of the concepts of political philosophy, nor [did] he probe into the dynamics of political processes and behaviour', but his teachings and personality had a great influence on the nationalist movement in India. 'He was a great patriot with a burning love for the motherland' and had a vision of the unity of the country, and 'although primarily, he taught the concept of spiritual freedom, this gospel was bound to result in the popularisation of the other aspects of freedom which included the political as well'[13].

TALKING OF A MULTIDIMENSIONAL NATIONAL REGENERATION

Vivekananda's approach, his case for India's regeneration was multidimensional and centred on the need to first reawaken a sense of wide national unity, then a reclaiming of our civilisational knowledge systems, an opening up of the national mind to the currents of world thought—scientific and technological, a wide educational sweep right down to the masses—a democratisation of education as it were, a strengthening of indigenous industries, imparting fillip to the Indian entrepreneurial spirit, a comprehensive effort for the empowerment of women as the neglect of Indian women 'distressed him'[14], along with a systematic effort at religious reform in an affirmative spirit, a dynamic effort at inclusion and ending discriminations of all types and bringing about an end to sectarian strife, and all of these were to have as their basis a wide spiritual awakening. The essence of the intellectual awakening that Vivekananda spoke of was the need to effectuate foremost a 'decolonising of the Indian mind'[15], the more material side of his vision for the regeneration of India, a panacea for 'India's several ills was mass education: training in useful sciences and crafts, manual skills and manufactures'[16].

It can be argued that throughout his tours across India, Vivekananda's speeches focused essentially on three aspects: first, 'his sense of a supreme mission, which almost appeared as a historical imperative', second, 'his conviction of the indestructibility of the "Indian soul" and the invincibility of Indian "spirituality"', and third was 'his belief in "nationalism", which alone could become an effective and adequate instrument for the fulfillment of India's destiny'. These, in fact, formed the bedrock of his philosophy of Indian nationalism[17]. While he spoke and articulated lofty philosophical positions and took on some of the leading thinkers of the world and quite easily mingled with the elites of the West, Vivekananda never lost connect with the aspirations of India and of her people. As one of his assessors has pointed out, during these travels, 'everywhere he mixed with the people—one day living with a pariah in his hut and the next day conversing on equal terms with the maharajas and dewans (prime ministers) at their palaces, or another day with the orthodox pandits and liberal college professors in their houses and clubs. He was as conversant with the knowledge of the pandits as with the problems of industrial and rural economy, whereby the life of the people is controlled. He came face to face with the joys and sorrows, hopes and frustrations, ideals and aspirations of all classes of people'[18].

In these years of his wandering across India, Vivekananda was like 'a diver plunged into the Ocean of India, and the Ocean of India covered his tracks'[19]; he started his *Bhārat parikramā* 'as a holy man, but became a patriot-prophet at the end'. Identifying himself with the happiness and miseries, hopes and frustrations, ideals and aspirations of India, he became, as he declared later to a Western disciple, 'a condensed India'[20].

In fact, one of the reasons that propelled Vivekananda to go to the West was to raise resources with which he could return to work out his plan of India's regeneration; as he wrote once, 'I have now travelled all over India...but alas it was agony to me, my brothers, to see with my own eyes the terrible poverty and misery of the masses, and I could not restrain my tears! It is now my firm conviction that it is futile to preach religion amongst them without trying to remove their poverty and sufferings. It is for this reason—to find more means—for the salvation of the poor of India that I am now going to America'[21].

The Swami's sojourn in the West, his visits and travels across America and continental Europe, gave him as it were an experience of the freedom that the West lived in, while also exposing him to the many deficiencies of these systems and frameworks, for he was an astute and discerning observer of civilisations, of societies and of nations. This gave him perspectives, which he examined in the light of the past—the past of his people and his country—and wove through these examinations a road map for their salvation.

RECOVERY FROM THE CIVILISATIONAL ROOT

The upholding base, the basis, the foundation of Vivekananda's national regeneration was India's spiritual and civilisational strengths. To him it was a rekindling of these inseparable and intrinsic dimensions of India's civilisational march that distinguished her from other civilisations of the world. These needed to be restated, rejuvenated and disseminated. This emphasis of his on rediscovering India's civilisational watersheds came at a time when deracinating tendencies abounded due to a system of education and discourse, which primarily divorced young minds from their civilisational roots. As KM Pannikar

(1894-1963) argued, when colonial education had made the Hindus more royal than the king by denationalising them and by making them abjure or secretly despise the beliefs and customs of their forefathers, Sri Ramakrishna, Swami Vivekananda and Swami Dayananda Saraswati's emergence substantially contributed in arresting that trend by evolving a counter narrative:

> The first leaders of the National Movement were Indian by birth, but they had abjured most of the things which their fathers had prized—all that complex tradition which had been aforetime the very soul of their people...those leaders no longer had root in their native soil; they were parasitic upon the West. Their religion was that of Spenser and Comte, their philosophy that of Bentham and the Mills, their tradition that of Macaulay...they were déracinés.

There was a hidden life in India which felt this like a challenge, and, in the works of two remarkable men, it became an answer and a corrective energy. The religious revival, brought about by Dayananda Saraswati and Swami Vivekananda, was India's first modern effort at self-protection, her first reply to the challenges of Western culture. From that time onwards, an indivisible nationalism had two aspects—one political and the other religious[22]. But Vivekananda's emphasis on deriving essential and propelling national strength from the roots of India's civilisational past, from her traditions and their life-infusing spirit, from the entire corpus of the high watermarks of her past was not a backpedaling revivalism, but rather an energy that would push forth India, then in a state of subjugation, towards a greater and liberated future.

That India's aspiration for freedom, for selfhood and for a coequal partnership in the comity of nations had to be inspired and driven by this rediscovery and restating of her rich and multi-hued civilisational experience was clear to the Swami, and he in turn made it clear in his hundreds of public talks, writings, letters and personal communications. He was never apologetic about such an approach; through it he perceived a clear path and direction towards national salvation. Vivekananda's life and action turned young India nationalist and that nationalism, in turn, 'realised its true nature' and was 'informed, illumined and inspired by a strong consciousness of the past achievements of India, of the glorious part which, in spite of the vicissitudes...she had played in history, and of the high and noble mission which, in the inscrutable dispensation of providence, she was called upon to play in the modern world'[23].

Vivekananda's conviction that any forward national direction must be imbued with a sense of past achievements, essentially stemmed from his deep and meditative study of India's past. He was not 'only a great philosopher but also a close student of history'. 'Long before the publication of KP Jayaswal's (1881-1937) *Hindu Polity*'[24], for example,

Vivekananda spoke 'of ancient Indian republics' and argued 'that the government by the people was not totally unknown in ancient India'. He spoke of how 'the doctrine of self-government was fully developed in the Buddhist monasteries' and 'refused to parrot the findings of the Orientalists' while diving 'deep into the ancient Sanskrit literature to find out the sequence of social development in the country'[25]. His extensive and prolific studies and his travels across India convinced Vivekananda, thus, that the source, the inspiring fountain of India's regeneration was to be initially found in her civilisational past. In this approach he was unequivocal and unambiguous:

> ...Many times have I been told that looking into the past only degenerates and leads to nothing, and that we should look to the future. That is true. But out of the past is built the future. Look back, therefore, as far as you can, drink deep of the eternal fountains that are behind, and after that, look forward, march forward and make India brighter, greater and much higher than she ever was. Our ancestors were great. We must recall that. We must learn the elements of our being, the blood that courses in our veins; we must have faith in that blood and what it did in the past; and out of that faith and consciousness of past greatness, we must build an India yet greater than what she has been...[26]

It was this approach of the Swami that inspired legions of young Indians across the decades, long after his passing, lending continuous fuel to India's quest for freedom. In this, Vivekananda is indeed the originator of spiritual nationalism, one, who before many others, articulated and shaped India's collective quest for emancipation. Vivekananda's task 'was to provide a solid spiritual foundation to the national movement. None before him had taken such a view of the social and political problems of India'[27]. For him, 'spirituality and patriotism were evidently continuous in his awareness. Only rarely was he impatient with the duties imposed by his concern for his countrymen and longed to break away into an uninterrupted mystical quest'[28].

It is this seamless continuity of spirituality and of patriotism in Vivekananda's nature and work which, I argue, was an aspect that was unique and inspiring and over the years, long after he had ceased to physically exist, continued to inspire legions of young minds and thinkers. Because he was seen as having imparted a vision of spiritual and material freedom, Vivekananda came to be looked upon by a large section of Indians as a prophet, who indicated a distinct path of liberty and freedom to his subject people.

THE PLAN

Vivekananda proposed a distinct plan for India's regeneration, the fundamental elements of which, some of its key signposts, continue to remain relevant to our contemporary collective aspirations and challenges. Through his vast corpus of intellectual and spiritual output, certain distinct keynotes emerge—keynotes that essentially define India's national life and form and in a sense, offer a distinct programme for a continuous national regeneration. It is through these keynotes that the contemporary relevance of Vivekananda's message continues to shine forth and it is in that sense that these keynotes need to be reexamined and worked out.

Vivekananda emphasised on 'unity in variety'—in other words on diversity in oneness or unity in diversity. 'Unity in variety', he noted 'is the plan of nature' and that varieties of expressions and manifestations must remain. In God, he argued, we are 'all one' but, 'in manifestation, these differences must always remain'[29]. 'Differentiation, infinitely contradictory, must remain, but it is not necessary that we should hate each other; it is not necessary therefore that we should fight each other'[30], he argued. He did not accept uniformity as an expression of unity, but rather talked of the Indian way of preserving diversities within an essential and all encompassing unity.

Vivekananda spoke of 'assimilation and not destruction', he did not believe in mere tolerance—tolerance for him still had a certain amount of coercion, he advocated instead, acceptance, which he saw as a more complete step towards a harmonious collective coexistence, especially in societies and nations that pulsated with diversities of many types. 'Holiness, purity and charity,' he told his Western audience and through them sent a message to those evangelists among them who insisted on the sole right of their concept of divinity, 'are not the exclusive possession of any church in the world, every system has produced men and women of the most exalted character. In the face of this evidence, if anybody dreams of the exclusive survival of his own religion and the destruction of others, I pity him from the bottom of my heart[31].'

In almost all the regions and countries that he visited, Vivekananda perceived this deficiency in acceptance, 'Take my experience for that...there is tremendous religious persecution yet in every country in which I have been, and the same old objections are raised against learning anything new'. The little toleration that he saw in the world was in India: 'The little toleration that is in the world, the little sympathy that is yet in the world for religious thought, is practically here in the land of the Aryas, and nowhere else[32].' It was this uniqueness that India had to preserve and to perpetuate in order to emerge as a great power that successfully harmonised her diversities and unity.

The Swami also argued that both individuals as well as nations had missions. For him, the essential task was the discovery of that mission and the nurturing of aims that would lead to its accomplishment. Such an action, he argued, could enable an uninterrupted existence and progression, both for the individual as well as the collective. It was clear that the nation for Vivekananda was a living entity with a soul and had a distinct mission of its own. Like the individual, he saw the nation too as having a mission, a destiny to fulfil and a message to deliver. In his characteristic style, speaking on the theme, the Swami argued that as every human being is the embodiment of an ideal, a mission and so long as the ideal was not lost, the mission was not lost, nothing could destroy the individual, similarly, the nation too is 'multiplied individuals' and 'each nation has a mission of its own to perform in this harmony of races; and so long as that nation keeps to that ideal, that nation nothing can kill...'[33] It was essential for him that India rediscovers and restates this civilisational mission of hers. Such a mission for India was primarily the dissemination of her unique civilisational, cultural and spiritual wisdom.

Vivekananda almost always referred to a spiritual conquest—that of India conquering or going forth into the world with the power of her spiritual message and genius. He spoke of how India could perennially renew the world's hope through her spiritual and civilisational message and vision of life. India's mission, he argued in his first public lecture after returning from the West in 1897 is 'to conserve, to preserve, to accumulate, as it were, into a dynamo, all the spiritual energy of the race, and that concentrated energy is to pour forth in a deluge on the world whenever circumstances are propitious...India's gift to the world is the light spiritual'[34]. This was her unique mission as a civilisation, she had to be made conscious of it, and her people had to actively participate in its fruition.

At the time of articulating this position, Vivekananda also pointed out that India's civilisational thoughts, her wisdom were already permeating the West. His interaction with the German Indologist Max Mueller (1823-1900), with the other German Indologist and philosopher Paul Deussen (1845-1919), who had studied and written extensively on the Upanishads and Vedanta, must have also convinced him of the progress of that process. 'Those who keep their eyes open, those who understand the workings in the minds of different nations of the West, those who are thinkers and study different nations,' he told his Indian adherents, 'will find the immense change that has been produced in tone, the procedure, in the methods, and in the literature of the world by this slow, never-ceasing permeation of Indian thought[35].'

SOME KEYNOTES AND THEIR CONTEMPORARY RELEVANCE

The contemporary relevance of this position that India's civilisational wisdom can indeed be a salvaging power for a world where a variety of conflicts continue, can never be over-emphasised, especially now, when one is increasingly faced with challenges of dissolving human ties, accelerated competition—both individual and collective—unbridled consumerism and friction with increased predatory tendencies evident between nations and collectivities. In India, as in the world, the relevance of this position continues to grow, Indian spiritual and civilisational thought is in fact permeating global thinking and working at altering mindsets and narratives. The power of Indian yoga, of her scriptural wisdom, of the storehouse of higher knowledge and truth of her various philosophies have begun to increasingly attract people across the world. Vivekananda's vision of India's spiritual conquest of the world is indeed proceeding apace.

India remained central to Swami Vivekananda's entire philosophical formulation. Scattered throughout his vast corpus of work, are interesting and thought-provoking signposts that continue to retain a perpetual degree of relevance in the present times. Vivekananda's talk on 'The Future of India'[36], for example, remains as relevant today as when it was delivered more than a century ago. The 'Future of India' address is a comprehensive exposition of the fundamentals of his thoughts and vision for India. He discussed in it certain problems and proffered certain proposals for a national action. The address thus articulates and expresses, some of the key dimensions for national regeneration and national unity.

Some of the fundamental pointers that emerge from this seminal address of his are reiterations of the cardinal points that we have discussed above: It was essential to develop an understanding, faith and consciousness of past greatness in order to build an India greater than what she was. Looking back into the past does not necessarily degenerate or lead to atrophy. India's problems are varied and complicated, but unity can be based on traditions and on religion, religion in India's case can actually unite; common grounds of religions and sects therefore, must be discovered and explored. Vivekananda saw 'our sacred traditions, our religion' as providing a common ground. 'In Europe', he argued, it was 'political ideas' that formed 'national unity', whereas in Asia, 'religious ideals form the national unity', and therefore, 'unity in religion' was an 'absolute necessity as the first condition of the future of India'[37].

Vivekananda's first plank towards the making of a future India was that Hindus had to unite and not be diverted and divided by sectional and sectarian strife and differences. 'All of us have to be taught,' he reminded his audience, 'that we Hindus—dualists, qualified monists, or monists, Shaivas, Vaishnavas or Pashupatas—to whatever denomination we may belong, have certain common ideas behind us, and that the time has come when for the well-being of ourselves, for the well-being of our race, we must give up all our little quarrels and differences[38].'

He saw spirituality (*ādhyatma*) as India's lifeblood, which strengthens the national body, prevents diseases and decay (in this address Vivekananda uses the word religion and spirituality interchangeably), and therefore, it cannot be negated or ignored. 'Our lifeblood is spirituality', he exhorted his people. 'If it flows clear, if it flows strong and pure and vigorous, everything is right; political, social, any other material defects, even the poverty of the land, will all be cured if that blood is pure'[39]. Therefore, it was essential, imperative for India, to preserve, perpetuate and disseminate this vast corpus of spiritual knowledge and experience; it is this that has always been India's civilisational distinctness.

As an obituary, making an assessment of Vivekananda's brief meteor-like life noted: 'He bitterly felt that India had completely degenerated; and his idea of curing her was to make her recognise that in spiritualism lay her strength and what was wanted was only faith in herself'[40].

One of Vivekananda's formula, the secret, which he perceived could push India to greatness lay in organisation, accumulation of power, coordination of wills, and for that to effectively happen, the trivial caste-, religion- and sect-enjoined quarrels had to end. These only served to dissipate the accumulated energies and wills. He was electric when he placed his point on this aspect, 'Why is it,' he asked, 'to take a case in point, that forty million of Englishmen rule three hundred million of people here? What is the psychological explanation? These forty million put their wills together and that means infinite power, and you three hundred million have a will each separate from the other. Therefore, to make a great future India, the whole secret lies in organisation, accumulation of power, coordination of will...for mark you, the future India depends entirely upon that. That is the secret—accumulation of willpower, coordination, bringing them all... into one focus[41]'. These words galvanised young India then, like never before; it was an unheard of assertion on the way forward towards achieving national greatness.

The other unambiguous line of action that Vivekananda propounded, a line that he was convinced was essential for an overall and comprehensive national growth was, as he said, attacking customs and practices that perpetuated oppression and subjugation of the marginalised, 'The solution is not by bringing down the higher, but by raising the lower up to the level of the higher'.[42] It was clear to him that 'so long as Indians do not raise the standard of life of the masses and enlist their wholehearted cooperation'[43], salvation and national emancipation would be 'fruitless'. That proposition continues to remain as relevant in this age, as it was when Vivekananda had pointed it out.

For Vivekananda, the empowerment and upliftment of India's women was a sine qua non for our integral national growth and he argued that it would alone, in a sense guarantee, the 'recovery of India'. He was unequivocal in this stance of his, in fact he had already drawn up plans for erecting another unit, which would also train women workers for disseminating his master's message[44]. It exasperated him to see how women were discriminated against. 'It is very difficult to understand why in this country,' he once exclaimed, 'so much difference is made between men and women, whereas the Vedanta declares that one and the same conscious self is present in all beings. You always criticise the women, but say what have you done for their uplift? Writing down *Smritis,* etc., and binding them by hard rules, the men have turned the women into mere manufacturing machines! If you do not raise the women, who are the living embodiment of the Divine Mother, don't think that you have any other way to rise[45].' In his characteristic style, he threw a constant challenge to the extreme orthodox thinking, which propagated a secondary or tertiary role and status for women in our national life. In what scriptures, he asked:

> ...Do you find statements that women are not competent for knowledge and devotion? In the period of degradation, when the priests made other castes incompetent for the study of the Vedas, they deprived the women also of all their rights. Otherwise you will find that in the Vedic or Upanishad age, Maitreyi, Gargi and other ladies of revered memory have taken the places of rishis through their skill in discussing about Brahman. In an assembly of a thousand Brahmans, who were all erudite in the Vedas, Gargi boldly challenged Yajnavalkya in a discussion about Brahman. Since such ideal women were entitled to spiritual knowledge, why shall not the women have the same privilege now? What has happened once can certainly happen again. History repeats itself. All nations have attained greatness by paying proper respect to women. That country and that nation which do not respect women have never become great, nor will ever be in future. The principal reason why your race has so much degenerated is that you have no respect for these living images of Shakti. Manu says, "Where women are respected, there the gods delight; and where they are not, there all works and efforts come to naught."(Manu.III.56) There is no hope of rise for that family or country where there is no estimation of women, where they live in sadness. For this reason, they have to be raised first...[46]

Finally, in Vivekananda's scheme of things, like in those of most of the epochal leaders and thinkers who followed him in India, education played a defining role. At a time when the colonial system of education dominated, when the movement for taking control of Indian education, for evolving a national system of education had not yet been conceived of, Vivekananda spoke of the need to take control of our education and to evolve and to alter its focus and objective towards a different goal altogether. He called for taking hold of both 'spiritual and secular' (material) education. Vivekananda was clear on why the education system as he witnessed it was detrimental to our national awakening and growth. 'The education that you are getting now has some good points, but it has a tremendous disadvantage which is so great that the good things are all weighed down. In the first place, it is not man-making education, it is merely and entirely a negative education. A negative education or any training that is based on negation is worse than death'[47].

Such a negative education works to eradicate the young learners' civilisational beliefs, traditions and rootedness and, as he observed, they eventually become 'a mass of negation'. Vivekananda famously delineated his fundamental philosophy of education when he said that, 'Education is not the amount of information that is put into your brain and runs riot there, undigested, all your life. We must have life-building, man-making, character-making assimilation of ideas.' The ideal was therefore, to have the 'whole education of our country, spiritual and secular, in our own hands, and it must be on national lines, through national methods as far as practical'[48]. The national dimension of education, a national system of education that would be rooted in India's civilisational ethos and was responsive to and respectful of her vast cultural and philosophical wisdom and outpouring remains an ongoing quest.

'A CERTAIN HOPE'

The relevance and vibrancy of Vivekananda's message, the keynotes of his vision continue to retain their original dynamism. In the task of India's national regeneration, the dream of which has been seen by leaders of the intellectual, political and spiritual realm across the decades, Vivekananda's example and words continue to remain key ignition points for further rumination and action. Every problem or challenge that is faced by a nation and a civilisationally evolved people striving to evolve a modern polity out of an ancient civilisational experience shall continue to find signposts and keynotes in Vivekananda's thoughts and message.

Vivekananda's own life embodied that possibility, in him the intrinsic mingling of action and thought with the aspirations of this vast and varied land was genuine and established, it was at least evident to those who saw him at close quarters and in the early years had toiled to set his mission on track. One of the foremost among such ones was Sister Nivedita, and in a succinct yet profound assessment of the Swami's life and work she recalled how, 'seated in his retreat at Belur, Vivekananda received visits and communications from all quarters' of the land, '...no hope but was spoken into his ear, no woe but he knew it, and strove to comfort or rouse...he held in his hands the thread of all that was fundamental, organic, vital; he knew the secret springs of life; he knew with what word to touch the hearts of millions. And he had gathered from all this knowledge a clear and certain hope'[49].

The dimensions of that vision, of that 'certain hope', continue to exercise our collective mind. It is in Vivekananda's articulations on India, in his utterances of her civilisational mission and potential that one continues to discover the vital milestones of India's national march. I have argued that in reigniting and crystallising the sense of selfhood, in providing an early direction to an all-encompassing national overhaul, in rekindling faith in India's civilisational strength and in her perennial message, Vivekananda played a decisive role. Coming as it did in the throes of subjection, his vision and conviction galvanised the national mind and psyche and placed these on an irreversible forward trajectory.

In his reading of Vivekananda, Romain Rolland had written thus: 'Sixteen years passed between Ramakrishna's death [1886] and that of his great disciple [1902]...years of conflagration...he was less than forty years of age when the athlete lay stretched upon the pyre...but the flame of that pyre is still alight today. From his ashes, like those of the Phoenix of old, has sprung—the magic bird—[of] faith in her [India's] unity and in the Great Message..."[50]

Who can disagree on the still radiating power of that lighted pyre!

***

Dr Anirban Ganguly is the Director of Dr Syama Prasad Mookerjee Research Foundation (SPMRF), New Delhi. He is a Member of the Central Advisory Board of Education (CABE) and a Visiting Faculty at Banaras Hindu University (BHU), Varanasi. Dr Ganguly holds a PhD in Education from Jadavpur University, Kolkata. Dr Ganguly has authored and edited a number of books, among them being: *The Modi Doctrine: New Paradigms in India's Foreign Policy* (2016), *Redefining Governance: Essays on One Year of Narendra Modi Government* (2015), *Swami Vivekananda, Buddha & Buddhism* (2014), *Debating Culture* (2013), *Education: Philosophy & Practice* (2011). He is also a columnist with *The Daily Pioneer*, *The Millennium Post* and the *New Indian Express*.

END NOTES

1. Aurobindo, Sri. *The Renaissance in India & Other Essays on Indian Culture*, Sri Aurobindo Ashram Publication Department, Puducherry, 2nd imp., 2002, p 64.
2. Basu, Sankari Prasad. *Vivekananda O Samakalin Bharatvarsha*, (Bengali), Vol. 1, Mandal Book House, Kolkata, 11th rpt. 2011, p 123.
3. Nivedita, Sister. 'Introduction-Our Master and His Message', in *The Complete Works of Swami Vivekananda*, Vol. 1, Mayavati Memorial Edition, Advaita Ashrama, Kolkata, 27th imp. 2009, p xii.
4. Nivedita, Sister. 'The National Significance of the Swami Vivekananda's Life and Work' in *The Complete Works of Sister Nivedita*, Vol. 1 (Birth Centenary Publication), Sister Nivedita Girl's School, Kolkata, 1967, p 379.
5. Bose, Nemai Sadhan. *Indian Awakening and Bengal*, Firma KLM Pvt. Ltd, Kolkata, (1960), revised edition 1976, p 240.
6. Sen, Amiya P (ed.). *The Indispensable Vivekananda: An Anthology for Our Times*, Permanent Black, New Delhi, 2006, p 27.
7. Rolland, Romain. *Prophets of New India*, (trans. Smith, EF Malcom), Cassell & Company, Ltd, London, 1928, p 250.
8. Ibid., p 252.
9. Nivedita, Sister. *The Master as I Saw Him: Being Pages from the Life of the Swami Vivekananda*, Longmans, Green & Co, New York, 1910, p 70.
10. Ibid., p 64.
11. *The Complete Works of Swami Vivekananda* (CWSV), Vol. 3, (Mayavati Memorial Edition), Advaita Ashrama, Kolkata, p 300.
12. Aiyar, CP Ramaswami. 'The Message of Swami Vivekananda', in *Vedanta Kesari*, April 1929 cited in Basu, Sankari Prasad. *Vivekananda O Samakalin Bharatvarsha* (Bengali) Vol. 7, Mandal Book House, Kolkata, 4th rpt. p 223.

13. Varma, VP. *Modern Indian Political Thought*, Lakshmi Narain Agarwal Publisher, 3rd, revised edition, Agra, 1967, p 101.
14. Lokeshwarananda, Swami. 'Introduction' in *Swami Vivekananda – A Hundred Years Since Chicago: A Commemorative Volume*, Ramakrishna Math & Ramakrishna Mission, Kolkata, p xxix.
15. Sen, Amiya P. op.cit. p 30.
16. Ibid., p 34.
17. Gokhale, BG. 'Swami Vivekananda and Indian Nationalism' in *Journal of Bible and Religion, Vol. 32, No. 1* (January 1964), p 37.'
18. Mumukshananda, Swami. 'Swami Vivekananda's Bharat Parikrama' in *Swami Vivekananda-A Hundred Years Since Chicago*, op.cit., pp 49-50.
19. Rolland, Romain. op.cit., p 245.
20. Mumukshananda, Swami. op.cit., p 58.
21. Rolland, Romain. op.cit. p 253.
22. Pannikar, KM. *Indian Nationalism: its Origin, History and Ideals*, 1920, pp 16-17.
23. Pradhan, RG. *India's Struggle for Swaraj*, GA Natesan & Co., Madras, 1930, p 60.
24. Jayaswal, Kashi Prasad (1881-1937, historian and scholar of Indian civilisation). His classic *Hindu Polity* (*A Constitutional History of India in Hindu Times*) (1918) was considered a path-breaking work that generated wide discussion and provided a major push to the nationalist quest for evolving a new narrative of India's history.
25. Majumdar, Biman Behari. *Militant Nationalism in India and its Socio-religious Background (1897-1917)*, General Printers & Publishers, Kolkata, 1966, p 19.
26. *The Complete Works of Swami Vivekananda* (CWSV), Vol. 3, (Mayavati Memorial Edition), Advaita Ashrama, Kolkata, 21st imp. 2008, pp 285-286.
27. Biman Behari Majumdar, op.cit. p 17.
28. Tapan Raychaudhuri, *Europe Reconsidered: Perceptions of the West in Nineteenth Century Bengal*, OUP, New Delhi, 1988, p 248.
29. Vivekananda, Swami. 'Paper on Hinduism' 19 September 1893 in *Complete Works of Swami Vivekananda* (CWSV) Vol. 1 op.cit. p 17. *CWSV* Vol. 2, (Mayavati Memorial Edition), Advaita Ashrama, Kolkata, 23rd imp. 2009, pp 381-382.
30. *CWSV*, Vol. 3, p 115.
31. *CWSV*, Vol. 1, op.cit. p 24.
32. *CWSV*, Vol. 3, op.cit. p 114.
33. *CWSV*, Vol. 2, op.cit. pp 370-371.
34. *CWSV*, Vol. 3, op.cit. pp 108-109
35. *CWSV*, Vol. 3, op.cit. p 109.
36. 'The Future of India' in Lectures from Colombo to Almora, *CWSV*, Vol. 3, op.cit. pp 285-304.
37. Ibid., pp 286-287.
38. Ibid., pp 287-288.
39. Ibid., p 288.
40. 'In Memoriam: Swami Vivekananda', *The Mahratta*, Poona, 13 July 1902 in *Prabuddha Bharat*, August 1902, pp 140-145.
41. 'The Future of India', *CWSV*, Vol. 3, op.cit. p 299.
42. Ibid., p 295.
43. Majumdar, Biman Behari. op.cit. p 36.
44. *CWSV*, Vol. 7, p 214.
45. Ibid.
46. Ibid., pp 214-215.
47. 'The Future of India', *CWSV*, Vol. 3, p 301.
48. Ibid., p 302.
49. Nivedita, Sister. *The National Significance of the Swami Vivekananda's Life and Work*, op.cit., pp 379-380.
50. Rolland, Romain. op.cit. p 234.

Financial Inclusion Plan
An initiative of Ministry of Finance

Case for India-specific Economic Model

S Gurumurthy

Abstract

In the year 1951, the world economic establishment mandated One-Size-Fit-All [OSFA] economic model to remove poverty and bring prosperity for all underdeveloped nations. Since the early and mid-1990s, the belief turned into an ideological conviction and the guild of world economists put total trust in globalisation and free trade as the new OSFA vehicle. The world nations—the West and the rest together—institutionalised it through World Trade Organization (WTO) and other multilateral setups. While the global market players still swear by the OSFA model, the world leaders have, of late, begun doubting its viability. The critical question that has been raised is whether the economic model is to be tweaked and tuned for each nation and society to suit its distinct characteristics including its culture. This question is being debated among world leaders since least 2005. Yet, surprisingly, it is not debated—in fact it is not even noticed—in the Indian economic discourse.

OSFA DEVELOPMENT MODEL

The philosophy and premise of One-Size-Fit-All (OSFA) as a modern development economic model that dominated the global economic discourse for over half a century post World War II, was no theory or body of expert opinion. It was virtually mandated by the West for the rest through the United Nations itself as early as in 1951. The UN had said: 'There is a sense in which rapid economic progress is impossible without painful adjustments. Ancient philosophies have to be scrapped; old social institutions have to disintegrate; bonds of caste, creed and racc have to burst; and large numbers of persons who cannot keep up with progress have to have their expectations of a comfortable life frustrated. Very few communities are willing to pay the full price of economic progress[1].'

This mandate was based on US President Harry Truman's inaugural address as the US president on 20 January 1949 announcing his concept of 'fair deal' for the entire world[2]. The Truman-influenced UN mandate suggested no less than total restructuring of underdeveloped societies—on the model of the West—in an amazingly ethno-centric and arrogant, at best naive, manner. Yet, by the early 1950s, the UN mandate had become hegemonic at the levels of circles of power[3].

WESTERN ANTHROPOLOGICAL MODERNITY AND MODERN ECONOMICS

The OSFA was sourced in the evolution of Western anthropological modernity—or simply Western modernity, which extended as, and into, modern economics. Modern economics is founded on the Western anthropological assumption that humans are rational economic beings (homo economicus). Being from the West, the theory had its origins in Christianity. Max Weber, the German sociologist, theorised that Protestant Christianity led to the rise of individualism, which encouraged entrepreneurship and enterprise, and consequently, Protestant ethic became the foundation of modern capitalism[4]. Weber, arguably the foremost social theorist of the twentieth century, is known as a principal architect of modern social science along with Karl Marx and Emile Durkheim[5]. In Weber's theory originated methodological individualism that led to the advent of rational economic man[6] on which development of efficient market hypothesis rested[7]. Efficient market hypothesis became the foundation of neo-classical economics[8].

Consequently, the modern Western anthropology extended as modern economics. Western modernity, which was theorised and structured to contract people out of traditions, in effect meant negation of social and filial relations with contracts substituting for relations including, as it turned out later, not just social relations like community or caste, but also for family relations[9]. Modernity meant contracting people out of their traditions. Even Karl Marx accepted the concept of modernity[10] except that he would rely on the communist doctrine instead of capitalism to achieve it[11]. Both capitalism and Marxism advocated break with all traditions and traditional relations—namely a total break from the past as conditional precedent for economic development[12]. This was actualised increasingly in the post-World War II Anglo-Saxon West and commended to the rest of world by no less than the UN in 1951 as mentioned earlier.

Deepening this view, sociologist Karl Popper first declared that there was no such thing as society, and later an influential political economist, Margaret Thatcher, accepted him with a rider, 'except family'[13]. At present, even the family has collapsed in the West with most children born being born to unwed mothers in the UK[14], as many as four out of ten in the US[15] and less than half the US households now consist of traditional families[16]. To make it worse, 55 per cent of first marriages end in divorce, while 67 per cent of the second and 73 per cent of the third too meet a similar fate[17]. When this trend was visible in the 1970s, the State began to step in to provide universal social security for the unemployed, the infirm and the aged. This further broke up families and relations, as was feared in 1980s by well-known economists, including Milton Friedman[18]. Finally, the publicly-funded universal social security and increasing health security costs, the present value of which in US is estimated at a minimum of USD 87 trillion and a maximum of USD 222 trillion[19], meant nationalisation of families and making people State dependent! As the nationalisation of families accelerated in late 1970s and 1980s, the concept of privatisation of government functions commenced in the US with the appointment of US President's Commission on Privatisation, 1987-88[20].

G-20, WORLD BANK, UN REJECT OSFA, TURN TO NATION-SPECIFIC, CULTURE-CENTRIC ECONOMIC MODEL

Global trust in the OSFA model peaked in early 1990s after the fall of the Soviet Union through the escalation of globalisation. Globalisation was founded on the conviction that the Western model had emerged as the final victor[21] over the rest and therefore, the rest of the world wanting to develop should integrate into the West-led global economy soonest. Therefore, the West-centric OSFA economic philosophy became the accepted way forward and consequently global rule-making institutions like the WTO emerged in 1995. But, in little more than a decade, globalisation seems to have fatigued. It is now not seriously disputed that globalisation, which was held out as the OSFA escalator for all nations to develop is fading into history[22].

How did the idea of OSFA-driven globalisation, which was considered as the vehicle for growth and prosperity, nearly collapse so soon? Globalisation as the escalator for development was seen as manifesting in the global trade growing at double the global GDP from 1970s[23], which lifted hundreds of millions in the developing world, including in Southeast Asia and China, out of poverty in 1980s and 1990s[24]. But global trade as related to global GDP began to decline from 2001[25]. The global meltdown in 2008 intervened as never before and questioned the viability of the global financial order[26]. The global trade is now struggling to grow at less than the global GDP[27]. Even earlier, particularly when this trend was getting visible in 2005, the global leaders began rethinking on the OSFA model.

The central bank governors and finance ministers of G-20 nations declared in October 2005, 'We note development approaches are evolving over time, and thus need to be updated as economic challenges unfold.... We recognised there is no uniform development approach that fits all countries. Each country should be able to choose the development approaches and policies that best suit its specific characteristics', while benefiting from accumulated experiences of the past[28]. Later, in May 2008, just ahead of the global meltdown, the World Bank said in its newsletter: 'In our work across the world, the World Bank has learned the hard way that there is no one model that fits all. Development...means taking the best ideas, testing them in new situations, and throwing away what doesn't work. It means, above all, having the ability to recognise when we have failed. This is never an easy thing to do. It is even more difficult for an organisation to do so, be it the government or the World Bank, which constantly need to adapt to the changing nature of the development challenge[29].'

The UN, which had officially endorsed the modern Western anthropological model of development for all and called for the destruction of the indigenous philosophies and values in 1951, formally joined the band-wagon of 'no one size fits all' paradigm in 2010—a bit late though. 'Development must be nationally driven', the then Deputy Secretary-General UN Asha-Rose Migiro stressed, rejecting the OSFA approach to eradicate poverty and foster economic growth[30]. It took over half a century for the West and the world to realise that the Western model would not work everywhere and every nation and society would have to work out its own model.

IMPACT OF WESTERN INTELLECTUALISM ON INDIA

But long before, thanks to colonisation, the elite Indian mind was overawed by modern Western intellectualism, and in default of de-colonisation after independence, it continued to remain under its dominance. With the Indian mind still impacted by the West, while India became a free nation, it did not really become an independent one in the real sense. The story of dominance of the West over Indian thinking has a long history. In mid-nineteenth century, Karl Marx described the cow- and monkey-worshipping Hindu society as semi-barbaric. He endorsed the British destruction of the Hindu society which, he said, had not changed for two thousand years, as painful, yet pleasurable one to prepare Indians for revolution and modernity[31]. Max Weber considered Hinduism and Buddhism, which believed in karma and rebirth, as militating against entrepreneurship and enterprise[32] thus virtually disqualifying India and China from development under modern capitalism[33]. Studies have established that Karl Marx and Max Weber, despite the fact that neither of them came to India nor met any Indian scholar or leader to know about India, exerted the greatest influence on the Indian mindset in the twentieth century[34].

That was why when socialist India was growing slowly, Prof Raj Krishna made his famous observation linking it to Hinduism—and called it as Hindu rate of growth[35], which is being repeated even today by many Indian intellectuals and leaders[36]. But all these theories which regarded Hinduism and Indian civilisation as other-worldly and therefore, not suited for development, predated the works of Paul Bairoch in 1983[37] and

Angus Madison in 2001[38], which established that Hindu India was the leader of the world economy for almost 1800 years and lost its lead position only in the last two hundred years, when it had remained colonised. However, by the time these studies showed that India was a high performer in world economy, the Western view that unless Indians gave up their philosophy and social structure they are unfit to develop, had become a matter of almost a conviction for many educated Indians. The advent of globalisation further deepened the belief that India could not develop unless it distanced itself from its past and embraced the West. Ironically, it is at this stage that the Western world has begun to say that there is no OSFA based on the West and each nation has to work out its own model consistent with its conditions including its culture!

NITI AAYOG RECOGNISES THE NEED FOR INDIA-SPECIFIC DEVELOPMENT MODEL

While the Indian economic discourse is still rooted in the idea of OSFA approach, after the present government led by Narendra Modi took over, it has begun recognising the need for an India-specific development model. The cabinet resolution constituting the National Institution for Transforming India (NITI) Aayog passed by the Modi government on 1 January 2015 stated: 'Perhaps most importantly, the institution must adhere to the tenet that while incorporating positive influences from the world, no single model can be transplanted from outside into the Indian scenario. We need to find our own strategy for growth. The new institution has to zero in on what will work in and for India. It will be a Bharatiya approach to development[39].' This means a huge U-turn on what India has been believing and doing for the last six decades under the socialist regime till 1990, and later under the liberalisation and globalisation period since then.

The NITI Aayog mandate implies not just policy tweaking for India but recognises the need for deeper re-education and reorientation of India. The NITI Aayog talks about 'social capital'[40]—a term which Marxism believing in social engineering would detest and capitalism founded on methodological individualism would abhor. Social capital is the relation of a collective of people inter se, like a family, caste, community and mutual associations, which unburdens the State. The NITI Aayog document says: 'In fact, the "social capital" that is present in our people has been a major contributor to the development of the country thus far and, therefore, it needs to be leveraged through appropriate policy initiatives[41].' The recognition of social capital is a total repudiation of the mandate of the 1951 United Nations that the old social institutions have to disintegrate and bonds of caste and creed have to burst. This also completely negates the assumptions of both Marx and the market. Marx believed that socialism would make the society irrelevant. Capitalism trusted the market to do what Marx felt the State would do. The NITI Aayog's emphasis on social capital, which is founded on relations, also implicitly rejects the contract-based and methodological individualism-shaped OSFA model commended by the West for the rest, post World War II. But now the new theories evolving in the West believe that social capital is society's commons, like environment and ecology, which operates outside the State and the market. The NITI Aayog also refers to millions of non-corporate businesses, two-thirds of which are owned by backward castes, scheduled castes and scheduled tribes as the area of focus for job creation and knowledge, technology and skill upgradation[42].

INDIANISED EDUCATION, INDIGENISED PUBLIC DISCOURSE MUST FOR EVOLVING INDIA-SPECIFIC ECONOMIC MODEL

Yet, even after more than a decade, the Indian economic and public discourse has still not responded to the global view that each nation has to evolve its own development model. It does not seem to have taken notice of the NITI Aayog mandate to work out an India-specific economic model for India. This shows that the Indian economic thinking and academics has been merely a carbon copy of the Western model without any Indian content or context. Indian content in economy or polity cannot emerge unless the education system is revamped to make it culturally Indian and to give indigenous orientation to the public discourse. While in 1950s national culture was seen by the United Nations as the disabler of economic development[43], now the same United Nations has turned around and said that without culture, development is difficult, even impossible. In the General Assembly debates in June 2013[44], the Secretary-General Ban Ki-moon said: 'Too many well-intended development programmes have failed, because they did not take cultural settings into account. This must be an overarching principle for all development efforts[45].' Saying that, 'Development has not always focused enough on people,' he added, 'To mobilise people, we need to understand and embrace their culture. This means encouraging dialogue, listening to individual voices, and ensuring that culture and human rights inform the new course for sustainable development. The fundamental role of culture was not fully acknowledged within the MDGs (millennium development goals) as a goal, an overarching principle, or as an enabler[46].'

Given the UN view that without a reference to culture there is no development possible and unless Indian culture studies become fully integral to the Indian education system, there is no way that a developmental economic model specific to India can be created in the Indian academia and in the public discourse. Unless national cultural and social impulses are fully grasped and understood in our educational system, reorienting the national discourse to prepare the people and the establishment for the task of building a national economic model suited to India and Indian culture and values will be difficult, if not impossible. In short, what is needed is an Indianised educational system and indigenised public discourse.

NEED LATERAL THINKING AND LATERAL AND STRATEGIC INTERVENTIONS IN EDUCATION AND PUBLIC DISCOURSE

It is unfortunate that the political ecosystem of India virtually prevents the emergence of an Indianised education system. It is least conducive to any substantial intervention in the present education model which is largely influenced by the Marx and Weber view of Indians, and their philosophy, culture and worldview[47]. Therefore, there is urgent need to eliminate the Marx–Weber domination in the Indian educational system. Without eliminating the Marx–Weber web over the Indian education system, the influence of the Western duo in Indian public discourse cannot be eliminated. And unless the public discourse is rid of the Marx–Weber influence, the education system cannot be revamped and Indianised. It is thus a Catch-22 situation which can only be resolved by political will. But till the Catch-22 situation is resolved and the education is Indianised and the public discourse is indigenised, it is necessary to think laterally and intervene laterally in both through the holistic efforts of the society. Lateral intervention goes hand in hand with lateral thinking. Lateral thinking 'solves problems by an indirect and creative approach, typically through viewing the problem in a new and unusual light'[48]. This is in contrast to vertical thinking[49], which is hierarchic and top-down in approach and effect.

The vertical and hierarchic thinking in India is frozen in Marx–Weber formulations imposing the OSFA model which has proven to be no more valid or appropriate. What is needed is lateral thinking and lateral interventions in the currently operative vertical and hierarchic thought structures. This can be done by independent think tanks and private educational and research institutions outside the formal control of the establishment, which is a prisoner of the Marx–Weber ideologies, which need to be challenged. As the former US President Bill Clinton said, 'Ideologies do not allow debates which philosophies do'[50]. OSFA is based on ideology, while recognising that diversity is founded on philosophy. Ideological approach, which is essentially Western, needs to be converted into philosophic approach, which is inherently Indian. Philosophy tends to unite humans but ideology aims to divide them[51].

The Indian society has huge private educational, academic and media infrastructure which can be leveraged to influence the academics and the public discourse. Concerned citizens who have influence over educational institutions, research institutions, think tanks and media should be approached with the need for developing an India-specific economic model for which they need to be convinced that education needs to be Indianised and the public discourse has to be indigenised. They need to be co-opted in the task. It is necessary and even inevitable to strategise lateral interventions in Indian education and public discourse through individuals and institutions committed to national interest, in order to break the intransigence of national education and public discourse.

Swaminathan Gurumurthy is a professional, writer, academic and activist, who regularly contributes columns in leading newspapers like the *Hindu Business Line*, the *New Indian Express* and others on issues of critical importance to the society and the country. A Visiting Faculty of the Indian Institute of Technology, Bombay, and a Distinguished Professor of Legal Anthropology at the Palkhiwala Centre for Legal Anthropology, Sastra University, Thanjavur, he started as a chartered accountant and corporate adviser and became the adviser to the *Indian Express* newspaper. He was an investigative journalist of high repute in 1980s exposing the corrupt nexus between corporates and government. Noted for his high sense of probity and his investigative writing, and rated as 'outstanding' in his knowledge of economics, finance and accounts, the media repeatedly rated Gurumurthy among the 50 most powerful persons in India.

ENDNOTES

1. United Nations, Department of Social and Economic Affairs 1951.
2. *Introduction: Development and Anthropology of Modernity*, press.princeton.edu/chapters/s9564.pdf
3. Ibid.
4. *The Protestant Ethic and the Spirit of Capitalism*, Max Weber, Review Essay by Engerman, Stanley. Departments of Economics and History, University of Rochester http://eh.net/book_reviews/the-protestant-ethic-and-the-spirit-of-capitalism/
5. Max Weber (Stanford Encyclopedia of Philosophy) plato.stanford.edu/entries/weber/
6. *Methodological Individualism* Stanford Encyclopaedia of Philosophy First published 3 February 2005; substantive revision 16 November 2010 plato.stanford.edu/entries/methodological-individualism/
7. *Economic Development and Financial Instability: Selected Essays* Anthem Other Canon Economics Author: Kregel, Jan A. Editor: Kattel, Rainer, Contributor: Harcourt, GC. Publisher: Anthem Press, 2014, p 99.
8. *Principles of Economics,* Gans, Joshua; King, Stephen; Libich, Jan; Byford, Martin; Mankiw, Gregory and Stonecash, Robin. Publisher Cengage Learning Australia, 2014, p 854.
9. *Family and Intimate Relationships: A Review of the Sociological Research,* Val Gillies Families & Social Capital ESRC Research Group South Bank University http://www1.lsbu.ac.uk/ahs/downloads/families/familieswp2.pdf
10. *The Political Humanism of Hannah Arendt G-Reference, Information and Interdisciplinary Subjects* Series Author McCarthy, Michael H. Rowman & Littlefield, 2012, p 181.
11. *Key Writers on Art: From Antiquity to the Nineteenth Century*, Murray, Chris. Psychology Press, 2003 Routledge Taylor and Francis Group London and New York.
12. *On the Anthropology of Modernity, or, Some Triumphs of Culture over Despondency Theory*, Sahlins, Marshall E. press. anu.edu.au/wp-content/uploads/2011/06/ch0316.pdf
13. *Thatcher was Right – There is No 'Society'*, Brittan, Samuel. *The Financial Times* 23 April 2013 https://www.ft.com/content/d1387b70-a5d5-11e2-9b77-00144feabdc0
14. *Most Children will be Born out of Wedlock by 2016 Telegraph* UK 10 July 2013 http://www.telegraph.co.uk/news/politics/10172627/Most-children-will-be-born-out-of-wedlock-by-2016.html
15. *CDC: Forty per cent+ of US Babies Born to Unmarried Women for Eighth Straight Year* cnsnews.com http://www.cnsnews.com/news/article/terence-p-jeffrey/cdc-babies-born-unmarried-women-exceeded-40-8th-straight-year
16. *Fewer than Half of US Kids Today Live in a 'Traditional' Family*, Livingston, Gretchen. PEW Research http://www.pewresearch.org/fact-tank/2014/12/22/less-than-half-of-u-s-kids-today-live-in-a-traditional-family/
17. *The High Failure Rate of Second and Third Marriages: Why are Second and Third Marriages More Likely to Fail?*

Psychology Today, 6 February 2012. https://www.psychologytoday.com/blog/the-intelligent-divorce/201202/the-high-failure-rate-second-and-third-marriages

18. *The American Economy in Transition, National Bureau of Economic Research Conference Report* Author: National Bureau of Economic Research, Feldstein. Martin (ed.). University of Chicago Press, 2009.
19. Mercatus Centre George Mason University https://www.mercatus.org/system/files/debt-in-perspective-analysis.pdf
20. *Privatisation Toward More Effective* Government. Report of the President's Commission on Privatisation, March 1988 http://pdf.usaid.gov/pdf_docs/PNABB472.pdf
21. *The End of History and The Last Man* by Fukuyama, Francis. The Free Press: A Division of Macmillan New York.
22. Vaidyanathan, R. *The Rise and Fall of Globalisation,* https://rvaidya2000.com/2017/02/20/the-rise-and-fall-of-globalisation/
23. *Prospects for Global Trade* Prepared by the IMF and World Bank, May 2015 http://www.oecd.org/tad/events/-WBG-IMF-G20-paper-Prospects-%20Global-Trade-29-May-2015.pdf
24. *With Little Notice, Globalisation Reduced Poverty* Yale Global Online http://yaleglobal.yale.edu/content/little-notice-globalization-reduced-poverty
25. Ibid 21.
26. The New International Financial Crisis: Causes, Consequences and Perspectives by Vieira, Flavio Vilela. Universidade Federal de Uberlândia. http://www.scielo.br/scielo.php?script=sci_arttext&pid=S0101-31572011000200003
27. Ibid 21.
28. G-20 COMMUNIQUÉ Meeting of Finance Ministers and Central Bank Governors Xianghe, Hebei, China, 15-16 October 2005 www.g20.utoronto.ca/2005/2005communique.pdf
29. *In Development There is Mo one Model that Fits All*, Isabel Guerrero: Newsletter—May-June 2008 This article was originally published in the *Outlook* magazine on 31 March 2008. Permanent URL for this page: http://go.worldbank.org/K1OSH3Y7X0
30. UN News Centre www.un.org/apps/news/story.asp?NewsID=35048
31. Karl Marx in the *New York Herald Tribune* 1853, *The British Rule in India*, First published: 25 June 1853 https://www.marxists.org/archive/marx/works/1853/06/25.htm
32. Bendix, Reinhard. Max Weber: *An Intellectual Portrait*, University of California Press, 1977, p 196.
33. Ibid.
34. Weber in Asian Studies by Buss, Andreas E. Publishers Brill Archive [1985] cited in *India's Culture, Society and Economy-Past, Present and Future* by Gurumurthy, S.
35. Ahluwalia, Montek Singh. First Raj Krishna Memorial Lecture, 1995: *Economic Reforms for the Nineties*, Planning Commission, Government of India.
36. Ibid.
37. *Economics and World History: Myths and Paradoxes* by Bairoch, Paul. University of Chicago Press, Chicago, 1993.
38. *The World Economy: A Millennial Perspective* by Maddison, Angus. Development Studies Centre OECD. http://www.oecd.org/dev developmentcentrestudiestheworldeconomyamillennialperspective.htm.
39. Press Information Bureau Government of India Cabinet 1 January 2015 17:9 IST *Government Constitutes National Institution for Transforming India* (NITI) Aayog. Press Note http://pib.nic.in/newsite/PrintRelease.aspx?relid=114268.
40. Ibid.
41. Ibid.
43. Supra [1].
44. UN News Centre http://www.un.org/apps/news/story.asp?NewsID=45156#.Vd3X0XjWX-Y
45. Ibid.
46. Ibid.
47. Supra 34.
48. https://en.oxforddictionaries.com/definition/lateral_thinking
49. https://en.oxforddictionaries.com/definition/vertical_thinking
50. http://snerdgronk.blogspot.in/2006/11/philosophy-vs-ideology-excerpts-from.html
51. *Ideology, Philosophy, and Politics* by Copleston, Frederick Charles. Calgary Institute for the Humanities, Conference for the Study of Political Thought. Parel, Anthony (ed.). Calgary Institute for the Humanities Publisher: Wilfrid Laurier Univ. Press, 1983, p 29.

Evolving US Foreign Policy under Trump and its Implications for India

Kanwal Sibal

Abstract

The global scenario has become uncertain and unpredictable with President Trump in the White House. He had promised during his election campaign that his political, security and economic policies would be materially different from the misguided policies of previous administrations that damaged US national interest. His slogans of 'Make America Great Again', 'America First' foreshadowed a more inward-looking America, more transactional, repudiating globalisation and non-interventionist abroad. His advocacy during the election campaign of more 'Brexits' from the European Union (EU), tougher postures towards China, willingness to work with Russia, caused consternation amongst the neocons, the ultra-liberals, those linked to the Democratic establishment, even prominent Republicans, the mainstream media, the think tanks and the intelligence agencies.

Faced with enormous political pressures at home by diverse lobbies, Trump has had to change tack on many issues. On Russia, many members of his own cabinet have made discordant noises. Early hopes that US–Russia relations that had sharply deteriorated under Obama might improve under Trump have been laid to rest by Trump's decision to launch cruise missile attacks against Syria. It is the first time that the US has intervened militarily directly against the Assad regime, opening new uncertainties in the region and the US–Russia relations.

On Japan, Trump has moved from jolting the relationship to reassuring Prime Minister Shinzo Abe of US commitment to Japanese security, specifically including the Senkakus within the ambit of the US–Japan defence treaty. On China, Trump has reiterated US adherence to the 'One China' policy after questioning it. The decision to step back from a confrontational posture towards China and move towards engagement, but failing to issue a joint statement during President Xi's visit to the US suggests uncertainty ahead. On the EU, Trump has softened his rhetoric though German Chancellor Merkel's visit to Washington was not too successful. He now does not find NATO obsolete as he did earlier.

If Trump's election raised a great deal of uncertainty abroad because of his unorthodox positions, his move towards more traditional ones only increases this uncertainty, as the President is exposing himself as an opportunist, with no firm convictions and capable of disavowing his postures without embarrassment. Even the reversal of his positions on Russia, China or Japan cannot give the assurance that yet more reversals will not take place as the situation develops. The way that the Trump administration is functioning, with family members engaged in foreign policymaking, the State Department sidelined, Trump's team adopting positions that contradict his stances, the President distracted by persistent efforts domestically to undo his presidency and so on, this concern is real.

India is not a priority country for Trump, if only because we are not the source of his concerns about issues on which he has wanted to reverse earlier US policies. We are not part of trade blocs which he feels were badly negotiated by the US and which he wants to revise or has repudiated. We are not the source of his concerns about Islamic radicalism and terrorism. We are not part of the refugee influx into the US that he has wanted to stem. India not being a military ally, we cannot be accused of not paying for our protection. But there are issues on which bilaterally and more widely Trump's policies could affect us for better or for worse. If US–Russia relations were to improve we could be beneficiaries. The sentiment in Russia is growing that India is moving into the US camp, diluting in the process the geopolitical importance of formats such as the Russia–India–China dialogue, Brazil, Russia, India, China and South Africa (BRICS) and the Shanghai Cooperation Organisation (SCO). This perception is strengthened by the expanding India–US defence trade, seen in Russia as being at its expense. If Russia–US relations were to move into a positive phase, these Russian concerns would diminish.

US and EU pressure on Russia has pushed it increasingly into the arms of China. Better US–Russia ties would prevent a still tighter Russia–China strategic embrace. Treating Russia as the principal geopolitical enemy is too trans-Atlantic a view, rooted in Cold War politics. If the US loses its global hegemony, the process will start in the Asia–Pacific. China is already challenging US power in the Western Pacific.

It has begun to dominate Central Asia economically; it has strongly positioned itself in Iran taking advantage of US sanctions. Its geopolitical commitment to Pakistan has increased manifold with the announcement of the China–Pakistan Economic Corridor (CPEC). With its One Belt One Road (OBOR) project, China is expanding geopolitically across Asia, taking advantage of the vacuum created by the weakening of Russia and US failure to establish itself in the area because of differences with Russia, the decision to withdraw from Afghanistan, tensions with Iran and inability to shape developments in Central Asia.

For India, US encouragement to China to play a role in Afghanistan is a problem as China's role there would be inevitably aligned with Pakistani interests, given China's decision to invest massively in Pakistan for gaining access through it to the Arabian Sea and eventually building Gwadar into a naval base for its fleet. India fails to see the logic of the US treating China as an adversary in the Western Pacific and a partner in our region. It is unclear how much we can rely on Trump to deal with Pakistan forcefully on the issue of terrorism. His Ambassador to the UN, Nikki Haley, has in early April raised the possibility of US intervening to defuse a developing India–Pakistan conflict proactively at an early state and push for a dialogue in order to prevent escalation. The blinkered US view of Pakistan and India–Pakistan relations was evident again in the testimony of the US Central Command (CENTCOM) chief before the Senate Armed Services Committee on 9 March in which he implicitly criticised India's public policy to diplomatically isolate Pakistan as it hinders any prospects of improved relations, which he found troubling because of the danger of an India–Pakistan conflict escalating into a nuclear exchange.

The uncertainty that is hovering over US–EU ties can become more problematic with the internal turmoil in Europe with the refugee crisis, the rise of nationalist parties, election results in France and Germany this year and the instabilities in the Euro-zone. This has implications for India, as the EU is India's biggest trade and investment partner. It is important that as we develop our global strategy we send a clear message that we reserve a prominent place for Europe in it. Europe and India have a shared interest in opposing protectionism, safeguarding the World Trade Organization (WTO) system and preserving the Paris Agreement on climate change, all points on which Trump's thinking presents a challenge.

The global scenario has become uncertain and unpredictable with President Donald Trump in the White House. He had promised during his election campaign that his political, security and economic policies would be materially different from the misguided policies of previous administrations that damaged US national interest. They had weakened the United States (US), especially economically, with loss of manufacturing jobs and imposition of an excessive burden on it to defend others. His slogans of 'Make America Great Again', 'America First' foreshadowed a more inward-looking America, more transactional, repudiating globalisation and non-interventionist abroad.

Even during Barack Obama's presidency, concerns in the US and European circles were widespread that the international order was breaking down and serious instability lay ahead as no single power was now capable of upholding it. The American public was seen as being tired of foreign interventions and the economic costs they entailed for an America whose infrastructure was breaking down and needed heavy investment to rebuild, where inequalities had widened, the condition of the middle class had deteriorated and the working class had suffered massive job losses because of globalisation. Obama's perceived unwillingness to lead from the front and resist further military entanglements abroad, as in the case of Syria, fuelled this geopolitical angst about impending global disarray.

With the positions Trump took during the run up to the presidency, consternation about the US ceasing to exercise hegemony over global affairs was widespread amongst the neocons, the ultra-liberals, those linked to the Democratic establishment, even prominent Republicans, the mainstream media, the think tanks and the intelligence agencies. After assuming power, Trump issued several presidential directives to implement some of his campaign promises on repudiating the Trans-Pacific Partnership (TPP), renegotiating North American Free Trade Agreement (NAFTA), temporarily suspending the entry of nationals of seven Islamic countries into the US, erecting a wall on the Mexican border and devising a time-bound strategy to destroy the Islamic State (IS) and so on. His position on climate change and clearing the way for controversial pipelines within the US scoffed at environmental lobbies at home and abroad.

His advocacy of more 'Brexits' from the European Union (EU), accusing Germany of hurting US economic interests and attacking the Euro-riled major European countries raised murmurs of a possible trade war between the US and EU. He berated the Europeans for not spending 2 per cent of their GDP on defence and went to the extent of demanding Germany to reimburse the US for the contributions it failed to make within the ambit of North Atlantic Treaty Organization (NATO) for the defence it provided to German security. Indeed, he questioned the continuing relevance of NATO, causing flutters in Europe and the US security establishment. He took hard positions on China, upsetting many assumptions of the relationship. He spoke on the telephone to the independence-minded Taiwanese president, questioned US continuing adherence to a One China policy and threatened to impose 40 per cent tariff on Chinese exports to the US. He called on Japan to assume more responsibility for its own defence, to the point of suggesting, during his campaign, that Japan could go nuclear to defend itself against China.

On Russia, he maintained an open posture during his election campaign and even after, angering the American 'deep state' who continues to see Russia as the biggest geopolitical enemy of the US. The allegations of Russian interference in the presidential elections in favour of Trump and against the candidature of Hillary Clinton bugged the Trump campaign and continue to bug his presidency. This has become a huge political issue domestically, with legal ramifications. The US intelligence agencies appear to have engaged in leaks to the press to keep the issue politically alive, embarrass Trump and countering his declared intention to find some *modus vivendi* with Russia, at least in West Asia for combating the IS.

Faced with enormous political pressures at home by diverse lobbies that want to erode his capacity to pursue his disruptive policies, and who believe he is unfit to be president and are not reconciled to the electoral verdict in his favour, Trump has had to change tack on many issues and his own team has suffered blows. His National Security Adviser (NSA), General Michael Flynn, for instance, had to resign because of his contacts with Russia during the election campaign. The head of the Senate Intelligence Committee, Senator Devin Nunes had to recuse himself under pressure from chairing the Senate investigation into the Russian role in the presidential election. It is widely believed that no US president can succeed in a confrontation with the intelligence agencies and their nexus with the mainstream media. Trump's resistance has suffered erosion as can be seen from the reversal of his position on several issues.

On Russia, many members of his own cabinet have made discordant noises. The new NSA Lt General Herbert McMaster views Russia as a hostile country and so do Defence Secretary James Mattis and Vice President Mike Pence. Secretary of State Rex Tillerson has used strong language against Russia on the Ukraine issue and Crimea. The US Ambassador to the United Nations (UN) Nikki Haley has been notably aggressive towards Russia. Early hopes that US–Russia relations that had sharply deteriorated under Obama might improve under Trump have been laid to rest by Trump's decision to launch cruise missile attacks against Syria. It is the first time that the US has intervened militarily directly against the Assad regime, opening new uncertainties in the region and US–Russia relations. Trump's action contradicts his administration's statements just before the bombing of Syria that removing Assad was not a priority and that he was reality on the ground that the US had to deal with, besides gainsaying his oft-repeated desire to work with Russia to destroy the IS as well as opposition to US military interventions abroad. Russia has condemned the US action as a violation of international law and President Putin has called it a significant blow to Russia–US relations. From an expectation that US–Russia relations might move towards a semblance of normalcy, the opposite is happening.

On Japan, Trump has moved from jolting the relationship to reassuring Prime Minister Abe of US commitment to Japanese security, specifically including the Senkaku Islands within the ambit of the US–Japan defence treaty. On China, Trump showed an anxiety to have a telephonic contact with President Xi that became possible only when the US side accepted the condition that Trump would reiterate support to the One China policy during the conversation, which he did. Trump even characterised his talk with Xi as 'excellent', standing alongside Abe in Florida. This has been followed up with an early visit by Xi to the US, though its political focus was lost in view of the US attack on Syria while the visit was on. The decision to step back from the early confrontational posture towards China—reflected also in Tillerson's statements to the Senate during his confirmation hearings that the US will deny access to China to the newly militarised islands in the South China Sea and engage China early—raised speculation that the US and China may move towards a G-2 in Asia with which Obama had flirted at the start of his first presidency. Tillerson's statement during his visit to Beijing using the vocabulary used by China to describe the kind of 'equal' relationship it, as a big power, sought with the US strengthened this impression. Eventually, Xi's visit had low visibility, with no joint statement issued. The two countries have given themselves 100 days to address the economic issues troubling their relationship. The future contours of the US–China relationship remain unclear.

On the EU and NATO, Trump has softened his rhetoric though German Chancellor Angela Merkel's visit to Washington seems to have had limited success. Merkel has, in fact, been positioning herself as a defender of Western values that Trump is perceived as abandoning, but whether she can sustain this posture that would pit Germany against the US is questionable. Germany can hardly afford to confront both the US and Russia on 'Western values' and have tensions with both countries. One could argue that its attention should be primarily focused on reviving the EU politically and economically after Brexit and the rise of nationalist parties within the Union who question it.

If Trump's election raised a great deal of uncertainty abroad because of his unorthodox positions, his move towards more traditional ones only increases this uncertainty, as the President is exposing himself as an opportunist, with no firm convictions, and capable of disavowing his postures without embarrassment, which was an accusation against him by his detractors during the election campaign and continues to be made. Even the reversal of his positions on Russia, China or Japan cannot give the assurance that yet more reversals will not take place as the situation develops. The way that the Trump administration is functioning, with family members engaged in foreign policymaking, the State Department sidelined, Tillerson losing ground, Trump's team adopting positions that contradict his stances, the infighting within his team, the President distracted by persistent efforts domestically to undo his presidency and so on—this concern is real. Because the US remains the foremost global power and its policies and actions have repercussions worldwide, a changeable leader at helm in Washington can be destabilising for both allies and adversaries and those in between.

India is not a priority country for Trump, if only because we are not the source of his concerns about issues on which he has wanted to reverse earlier US policies. We are not part of trade blocs which he feels were badly negotiated by the US and which he wants to revise or has repudiated. We are not the source of his concerns about Islamic radicalism and terrorism. We are not part of the refugee influx into the US that he has wanted to stem. India not being a military ally, we cannot be accused of not paying for our protection. But there are issues on which bilaterally and more widely Trump's policies could affect us for better or for worse. If US–Russia relations were to improve we could be beneficiaries. In Russia a sentiment is growing that India is moving into the US camp, diluting in the process the geopolitical importance of formats such as the Russia–India–China dialogue, Brazil, Russia, India, China and South Africa (BRICS) and the Shanghai Cooperation Organisation (SCO). This perception is strengthened by the expanding India–US defence trade, seen in Russia as being at its expense. If Russia–US relations were to move into a positive phase, these Russian concerns would diminish. Russia's overtures to Pakistan seem to be motivated by a desire to develop a new leverage against India, besides signifying some alignment of its Pakistan policy with China. A worsening of US–Russia ties will make Russia increasingly suspicious of US intentions in the Afghanistan–Central Asian region aimed at exploiting radical Islamist ideology, including the IS, to destabilise Russia's periphery in the east. Such scenarios can only damage India's security by exposing us even more to radical Islam and terrorism.

US and EU pressure on Russia has pushed it increasingly into the arms of China. Better US–Russia ties would prevent a still tighter Russia–China strategic embrace. Treating Russia as the principal geopolitical enemy is too trans-Atlantic a view, rooted in Cold War politics. The post-Cold War world has been marked by the decline of Russia and the spectacular rise of China. It is China, with its economic and financial muscle and increasing military strength that is threatening US power in Asia and even beyond. If the US loses its global hegemony, the process will start in the Asia–Pacific. China is already challenging US power in the Western Pacific. It has reclaimed rocks and militarised artificial islands in the South China Sea under the nose of a formidable US military presence in this area represented by the Seventh Fleet, several military bases and thousands of US forces stationed in the region. China is threatening US allies like Japan, knowing America's treaty obligations to defend that country. It has succeeded in dividing Association of Southeast Asian Nations (ASEAN), even weaning the Philippines president away from the US despite Philippines obtaining satisfaction on all points against China's claims in the South China Sea from the United Nations Convention on the Law of the Sea (UNCLOS) Tribunal (the Permanent Court of Arbitration, or PCA). China has begun to dominate Central Asia economically; it has strongly positioned itself in Iran taking advantage of US sanctions. Its geopolitical commitment to Pakistan has increased manifold with the announcement of the China–Pakistan Economic Corridor (CPEC). With its One Belt One Road (OBOR) project, China is expanding geopolitically across Asia, taking advantage of the vacuum created by the weakening of Russia and US failure to establish itself in the area because of differences with Russia, the decision to withdraw from Afghanistan, tensions with Iran and inability to shape developments in Central Asia.

For India, US encouragement to China to play a role in Afghanistan is a problem as China's role there would be inevitably aligned with Pakistani interests, given China's decision to invest massively in Pakistan for gaining access through it to the Arabian Sea and eventually building Gwadar into a naval base for its fleet. India fails to see the logic of the US treating China as an adversary in the Western Pacific and a partner in our region. It is by no means certain that US–China tensions in the Western Pacific will make the US more willing to counter China's expanding influence around us in the west. Many Americans, otherwise negative towards China, believe that the CPEC can be helpful in stabilising Pakistan and thus be to India's benefit eventually. Beyond that, the US has interests in Pakistan that it wants to conserve, with a strategic balance in South Asia in its mind too. Pakistan is viewed as a major Islamic country equipped with nuclear weapons and therefore, too important not to be engaged.

It is unclear how much we can rely on Trump to deal with Pakistan forcefully on the issue of terrorism. His Ambassador to the UN, Nikki Haley, has in early April raised the possibility of US intervening to defuse a developing India–Pakistan conflict proactively at an early state and push for a dialogue in order to prevent escalation, without waiting for something to happen. She added that Trump himself may participate in this exercise that the National Security Council would initiate. The US seems to have a blind spot when it comes to dealing forcefully with Pakistan's involvement with terrorism from which it too has suffered. The root cause of tensions and a potential conflict between India and Pakistan is terrorism, but the US establishment refuses to acknowledge this reality while expressing concern about the situation between India and Pakistan. The blinkered US view of Pakistan and India–Pakistan relations was evident again in the testimony of the US Central Command (CENTCOM) chief before the Senate Armed Services Committee on 9 March in which he spoke of Pakistan remaining a critical partner in the counterterrorism fight.

He spoke with moderation about Pakistani support for the terrorist Haqqani network, noted positively some promising coordination between the Pakistan and Afghanistan militaries aimed at addressing instability in the Afghanistan–Pakistan border region, and acknowledged Pakistani support for the operation of the coalition forces in Afghanistan. He expressed concern about India's military response to terrorist attacks in 'India-held' territory leading to miscalculation on both sides. He implicitly criticised India's public policy to diplomatically isolate Pakistan as it hinders any prospects of improved relations, which he found troubling because of the danger of an India–Pakistan conflict escalating into a nuclear exchange, besides Pakistan's increased focus on its eastern border detracting from its efforts to secure the western border. He noted that the Pakistani military also continues to support US efforts elsewhere in the region. Viewed in the context of this testimony, the US would welcome Pakistani military involvement in support of Saudi Arabia against the Houthis in Yemen. This kind of diehard US military thinking about Pakistan's usefulness will remain a problem for us. While the US Commander-in-Chief Pacific Command (CINCPAC) will continue to woo us to counter China geopolitically, the Pentagon will continue its dual policy of shielding Pakistan against India.

The uncertainty that is hovering over US–EU ties can become more problematic with the internal turmoil in Europe with the refugee crisis, the rise of nationalist parties, election results in France and Germany this year and the instabilities in the Eurozone. This has implications for India, as the EU is India's biggest trade and investment partner. It is important that as we develop our global strategy we send a clear message that we reserve a prominent place for Europe in it. Economic growth is India's priority. Collectively, EU is India's biggest trading and investment partner. Within Europe, three or four of the world's largest economies are located. With each of them India's trade and investment relationship is on the ascendant. In developing our inadequate infrastructure, Europe can provide the material, technical and financial resources. In Information Technology (IT) and Information Technology Enabled Services (ITES) sectors, our overdependence on the US market requires a shift towards Europe. The tapping of vast reservoirs of frontline technologies in European small and medium enterprises will be required for deepening the base of our industrial economy. Potentially, our young and plentiful human resource base can meet the needs of Europe's ageing societies within the logic of globalisation, economic interdependence and all round prosperity. Europe and India have a shared interest in opposing protectionism, safeguarding the World Trade Organization (WTO) system and preserving the Paris Agreement on climate change, all points on which Trump's thinking presents a challenge.

***

Kanwal Sibal is a former Foreign Secretary to the Government of India, earlier having served as India's Ambassador to Turkey, Egypt, France and Russia, besides as the Deputy Chief of Mission in the United States. A former member of India's National Security Advisory Board, he is on the Board of the New York East–West Institute, Advisory Board of the Vivekananda International Foundation, Editorial Consultant to *The Indian Defence Review*, Foreign Affairs Editor of *The Force*—and is the Chairman of the Forum of Strategic and Security Studies. Ambassador Sibal has written more than 400 op-eds and other articles for major national journals and periodicals on international affairs, and is the author of a book of poems, *Snowflakes of Time*. He is decorated with the 'Grand Officer of the French Ordre National du Merite', the second highest in this prestigious category, and was conferred with Padma Shree award in 2017.

Engaging China in an Uncertain World

Ashok K Kantha

Abstract

Acknowledging that India–China relations are currently suffering from an overhang of differences and suspicions, the paper suggests that this important but difficult relationship has entered a phase which is even more challenging, involving an uncertain mix of cooperation and competition. The future directions of this relationship will increasingly be shaped by the course taken by the rise of China, the parallel rise of India and others, and the related issue of the changing and unpredictable dynamics of the international landscape around them. The paper analyses the present challenges in India–China relations and offers some suggestions for devising a new modus vivendi and an updated framework for managing this relationship and for taking it along a pragmatic path, complex and demanding and yet, constructive and forward-looking.

India–China relations are today passing through a period of marked stress. We are faced with an accumulation of issues and concerns in bilateral engagement, ranging from the boundary question to trans-border rivers to stapled visas for residents of Arunachal Pradesh to disquiet about China's stand on India's membership of the UN Security Council (UNSC) and the Nuclear Suppliers Group (NSG) and listing of well-known terrorists like Masood Azhar in the 1267 Committee of the UNSC. China has its own set of concerns, including non-acceptance by India of its 'Belt and Road Initiative' (BRI) and concerns over India's stance on Tibet, Dalai Lama and South China Sea. Since early last year in particular, the two sides have, unfortunately, got into a negative cycle of public airing of differences in an action-reaction mode. This has affected the narrative of the relationship.

Bilateral differences have acquired greater prominence as the convergence between the two countries on geopolitical issues is seen to be weakening. In India, China is increasingly being viewed as not being supportive of India's rise or responsive to its concerns, interests and aspirations. There are discernible anxieties about China's growing footprint in South Asia and in the Indian Ocean Region (IOR). In China, India is seen in some quarters as getting co-opted in the US-led strategy to counter its rise. Moreover, we need to manage our relations with China in an international context which is increasingly volatile and unpredictable.

The election of Donald Trump, the vote for 'Brexit' and the fact that populist parties are now part of the government in about a dozen Western democracies, represent powerful forces which are bringing about fundamental shifts in the US and Western societies in general. Over the past year, we have witnessed emergence of populist movements in the West that oppose key elements of the liberal-democratic status quo, question pluralism and liberalism, and rail against perceived threats ranging from immigration to globalisation, international institutions and multilateralism. Linked to the rise of populist and protectionist sentiments is the Donald Trump phenomenon. With his 'America First' slogan, his aggressive agenda on trade and immigration issues, and his ambivalence over the USA's global leadership role and the continued relevance of its alliance system, as also his cynicism about the merits of globalisation and multilateral institutions, Trump has caused disquiet and enhanced unpredictability in the international environment. Notwithstanding his unorthodox methods, however, Trump represents the most prominent manifestation of an important trend in the West. Ironically, China has quickly moved to position itself as an anchor of stability in an uncertain international climate and as a defender of globalisation, multilateralism and rule-based open trade.

Notwithstanding Trump's harsh rhetoric on China, Sino-US relations appear to have stabilised after the initial Chinese jostling with the new administration. Trump reaffirmed the 'One China' policy during his telephonic conversation with President Xi Jinping; US Secretary of State Rex Tillerson unexpectedly repeated the Chinese mantra of 'no-conflict, non-confrontation, mutual respect and win-win cooperation' during his visit to Beijing; the US has unilaterally ceded space to China by withdrawing from the Trans-Pacific Partnership (TPP); Trump has abandoned his oft-repeated campaign pledge to declare China a currency manipulator; and the outcome of the Trump–Xi summit at Florida is being projected by both sides in positive light, even though it did not result in anything spectacular and was upstaged, to an extent, by the US missile attack on Syria. However, Trump enjoys being unpredictable and we may yet have disruptions in store.

The current international uncertainty is in part stemming from, and is compounded by, the protracted geopolitical shift triggered by the rise of China, India and other countries. With China progressively asserting itself, the flux and contestation in the geopolitical landscape, particularly in Asia–Pacific, has increased significantly. The brief period of unipolar dominance enjoyed by the US is over, but a new equilibrium is yet to emerge. We are in the midst of a period of transition with uncertain outcomes. It is important to take note of these broader international trends because they will increasingly shape the engagement between India and China. For instance, the task of dealing with China will become more challenging for us if the rise of China and its assertive behaviour is juxtaposed with a gradual retreat by the USA from the Asia–Pacific region. However, one can argue that with his 'Make America Great Again' goal and 350-ship US Navy target, Trump may not lead the US into a period of retrenchment from its leadership role in the Asia–Pacific region, as many fear at present. Likewise, the US, with its considerable edge in technology, innovation and the corporate domain and given its tremendous capacity for self-renewal, is far from a declining power, even though the gap between the economic and military capabilities of the USA and China is narrowing.

Coming to our relations with China, the relationship is at present under some strain, as noted above. However, if one steps back and takes an objective and longer-term view, the overall report card for India–China relations will come across as reasonably substantial. It has been rightly assessed that today India and China are more engaged with each other than ever before[1]. India–China ties are complex with outstanding issues but have also advanced well in multiple fields. The leaders of both India and China have invested in fostering engagement between the two countries, as reflected in the remarkable frequency of summit-level exchanges. There is a major economic component in the relationship, though trade remains lopsided in China's favour. Sub-national cooperation between provinces and cities has emerged as a potent instrument for scaling up bilateral ties, particularly in developing economic and commercial links. Contacts at the level of ordinary people, though still limited, are expanding. There are over 16,000 Indian students in China[2]. Indian movies are once again finding a large and welcoming market in China. During the Chinese Lunar New Year holidays this year, two of the top four grossing movies, *Kungfu Yoga* and *Buddies in India*, were India–China joint ventures which became possible due to the film co-production agreement signed during President Xi's visit to India in September 2014[3]. Border areas are essentially peaceful.

Beyond bilateral engagement, the two countries have built upon their shared interests to develop a cooperative though limited agenda on multilateral and global issues. India–China relations have acquired attributes of normal State-to-State and people-to-people relations. While the gains in India–China relations are substantial, so are the challenges.

One can argue that India–China relations have entered a phase which is more complex and challenging. It involves an uncertain mix of cooperation and competition between the two countries which are simultaneously rising in a highly unpredictable international environment. Hence, it is evident that the future directions of our relations with China will increasingly be shaped by the course taken by the rise of China, the parallel rise of India and others, and the related issue of the changing dynamics of the geopolitical landscape around us, described above. At the same time, there are aspects of the emergence of China that are becoming reasonably clear.

First, there is little doubt now that China is prepared to aggressively deploy its considerable political, economic, military and diplomatic clout in pursuit of its strategic objectives. Deng Xiaoping's dictum of 'hiding one's capabilities and biding time' is rapidly receding in the rear-view mirror. China seeks supremacy in Asia–Pacific at the expense of the US, even though the element of interdependence in their relationship remains strong.

Secondly, China is also a country at an inflection point, adjusting to a 'new normal' not only in its economy but also in its polity and diplomacy. The new normal in politics and diplomacy involves emergence of the 'core' leader in Xi Jinping who is systematically pursuing the 'Chinese dream' of great rejuvenation of the Chinese nation. Under his leadership, China is seeking to shape its neighbourhood, through the BRI and other initiatives, deploying huge resources. At the same time, the Chinese economy is slowing down with a host of structural challenges, even while the country deals with an aging population, internal security risks and other domestic issues.

At a path-breaking Work Conference on Peripheral Diplomacy convened in October 2013, Xi Jinping noted that neighbours had 'extremely significant strategic value' and remarked:

> Maintaining stability in China's neighbourhood is the key objective of peripheral diplomacy. We must encourage and participate in the process of regional economic integration and speed up the process of building up infrastructure and connectivity. We must build the Silk Road Economic Belt and Twenty-first Century Maritime Silk Road, creating a new regional economic order[4].

The BRI has several pragmatic considerations linked to China's connectivity agenda, the quest for new growth engines for its slowing economy and the desire to stabilise its western periphery. However, it is also a geostrategic play aimed at carving out a continental-cum-maritime realm with China as the anchor and central player. It helps China achieve its geopolitical objectives by binding its neighbouring countries more closely to its own growth story. China is systematically putting in place a universe of institutions led by it, without challenging existing international institutions, where it seeks to play a larger role.

China is a revisionist power which seeks to incrementally alter the status quo to its advantage, but it is not a revolutionary power determined to upturn the global order.

Thirdly, given Trump's 'America First' policy and his ambivalence over the US's global leadership role, China discerns a strategic opening today to further expand its regional and global profile. This could be the third wave of assertion by China of its leadership role, the first two being in the aftermath of the global economic crisis of 2008 and following Xi Jinping coming to power in late-2012. However, it is still reluctant to expand its international responsibility too rapidly.

Fourthly, the rapid accumulation of power by China has led to balancing and hedging by countries of the region but this has not deterred it. China's assessment has been that long-term benefits of its assertive stance outweigh attendant risks. For instance, it is prepared to pay the price of some diplomatic damage as it entrenches its physical and military presence in the South China Sea. It is counting on its economic pull and the reluctance of the Association of Southeast Asian Nations (ASEAN) to take sides between the US and China. The US does not seem to have any effective strategy so far to prevent China from incrementally changing facts on the ground to its advantage in the South China Sea. There is, however, an element of hubris in the Chinese behaviour as can be seen in the punishment currently being meted out to South Korea to coerce it to change its policy on hosting the anti-missile system, 'Terminal High Altitude Area Defence' or THAAD, on its territory. China's assertive attitude is opening up opportunities which countries like the US and Japan are seeking to utilise.

Finally, it is important to note that China now considers protection of overseas interests and its emergence as a maritime power as strategic priorities. In the Chinese white paper on military strategy released in May 2015, there was a major shift in the focus of the Peoples Liberation Army (PLA) Navy, or PLAN, with addition of 'open seas protection' to its existing role of 'offshore waters defence'. The white paper stated that the 'traditional mentality that land outweighs the sea must be abandoned'. This doctrinal shift, the rolling out of the Maritime Silk Road initiative and other actions taken by China on the ground will progressively result in a much bigger footprint of the Chinese Navy in the IOR, in consonance with China's stated policy of becoming a maritime power.

Indeed, we are witnessing a new phase in the PLA's expanding footprint abroad. Overseas military bases were until recently considered anathema by the Chinese, but now Djibouti is likely to be only the first of many such facilities for China. Instead of constructing large US-style overseas military bases in the Indian Ocean, China may prefer a mixture of preferred access to overseas commercial ports and a limited number of exclusive PLA Navy logistic facilities, possibly co-located with commercial ports[5]. China is likely to establish logistics hubs at Gwadar and possibly even Karachi or Ormara in Pakistan. There is even talk of deploying Chinese Marines at Djibouti and Gwadar. In our immediate neighbourhood, there are concerns about China's plans for ports like Hambantota and Colombo where it has secured long-term presence and operational control. We may expect that the operations of the Indian Navy and the PLA Navy will increasingly coincide, both in the IOR and the Western Pacific. We are going to face enlarged Chinese military presence closer to us in the maritime domain, apart from along the land borders.

Looking ahead, a primary challenge for us is going to be managing the simultaneous rise of China and India. The areas of influence of the two countries overlap and there will be growing competition in their shared periphery. As China's global footprint is expanding so is its political, economic and strategic presence in India's immediate and extended neighbourhood. China's actions will increasingly impact India's pursuit of its national interests in its vicinity.

Growing strategic linkages between China and Pakistan have become a major concern in India. China appears to be doubling down on its commitment to Pakistan, as manifested recently in its actions in the Nuclear Suppliers Group (NSG) and the 1267 Committee. With the China–Pakistan Economic Corridor (CPEC), the relationship is acquiring a major economic component, in addition to its traditional politico-security preoccupation. China is, for the first time, getting involved in the business of delivering stability and economic development in Pakistan. Pakistan today has increased utility in China's foreign policy priorities. It is taking advantage of its strategic economic geography, bilateral trust developed over the last six decades, and Chinese concerns about growing strategic ties between India and the USA, to position itself as a major partner in advancing China's regional and global aspirations. Pakistan is at the intersection of the land and maritime dimensions of the BRI, and the CPEC is its flagship project and most advanced component. CPEC has limited economic rationale for China but its geostrategic drivers are compelling. Pakistani ports are likely to play an important role in China's emergence as a leading maritime power with major presence in the IOR, as noted above. The upgraded Karakoram Highway is finally emerging as a relatively viable transit route. However, given its terrain and high cost of transit, it is unlikely to become a major trade and energy corridor as billed; its value will be more strategic and military, than commercial. China has decided to disregard India's concerns, including on the CPEC passing through POK, and has continued to assist in building up Pakistan's strategic capabilities, which will be used against India.

India has its own aspirations of emerging as a leading power, though the Indian dream is less clearly articulated so far. It has disavowed any interest in being part of any containment strategy directed towards China. However, like many others in the region,

India too, is hedging to deal with the uncertainties associated with the rise of China and a geopolitical landscape in flux. India prefers a multipolar world and a multipolar Asia. India does not want to see an Asia–Pacific region dominated by China. The challenge of dealing with China is compounded by the fact that a yawning gap has opened between India and China in terms of their economic, technological and military capabilities. China's GDP at around USD 11.5 trillion is five times larger than India's USD 2.2 trillion. China spends over four times as much on defence than India does[6], and has much larger resources at its command to advance its regional and global agenda, including in our neighbourhood. Thus, we do not have the option of outbidding China for projects in our periphery. Instead, we will have to build on our strengths in terms of natural synergies and connectivity, which are considerable. We should also not lose sight of the fact that, given its size, civilisational heritage, economic achievements and potential, manpower resources, basic stability and demographic advantage, India is best placed among the emerging countries to eventually catch up with China, if it puts its act together. However, the gap between India and China will continue to widen in the near term, which could make China more assertive in its behaviour.

How do we navigate India–China relations in these unpredictable waters? Some recalibrating and reimagining of the paradigm of the relationship is called for. Let us consider some suggestions.

One, we must build on and update the basic template of the relationship adopted by the two countries since the late 1980s. This pragmatic approach involves compartmentalising and managing differences, not letting them come in the way of development of positive engagement to the extent feasible and of exploring areas of convergence, cooperation and collaboration in bilateral, regional and multilateral domains. It has served us well till now.

At the same time, we must acknowledge that outstanding issues are affecting expansion of India–China relations and fuelling mutual distrust. There is a clear case for addressing these issues with a sense of urgency rather than merely seeking to compartmentalise them. Even incremental but steady progress on unresolved matters will generate positive sentiments about India–China relations.

Let us take up the issue of terrorism. At the bilateral level, there are shared concerns and indeed a good beginning has been made in terms of cooperation. This was quite evident during the talks Home Minister Rajnath Singh had in China during his official visit in November 2015. The subsequent visit of the Secretary of the Central Political and Legal Affairs Commission of the Communist Party of China, Meng Jianzhu, to India in November 2016 also reflected a degree of convergence of interests on terrorism between the two countries. Yet, the Chinese stance opposing the listing of Masood Azhar under the

1267 Committee has become a major irritant in bilateral relations, souring perceptions in India about China. The Chinese position is linked to their readiness to be Pakistan's diplomatic protector. Is it possible to make progress on this question through quiet, patient discussions without making it a make-or-break issue in relations? In parallel, the two sides can develop bilateral and even multilateral cooperation on terrorism, utilising the ministerial-level dialogue and other mechanisms agreed upon in November 2015.

There are other complex issues like the boundary question which have defied solution. Both sides have averred on multiple occasions that an early boundary settlement will advance the basic interests of the two countries and should, therefore, be pursued as a strategic objective. There was an important breakthrough in April 2005 when the Agreement on the Political Parameters and Guiding Principles for the Settlement of the Boundary Question (APPGP)[7] was concluded. Under the Agreement, both sides decided to seek a 'political settlement of the boundary question in the context of their overall and long-term interests', abandoning the dreary and unproductive path of trying to reconcile their highly divergent and entrenched historical narratives on the issue. This was to be done on the basis of a number of eminently sensible and pragmatic propositions (such as, 'due consideration to each other's strategic and reasonable interests, and the principle of mutual and equal security'; taking into account 'historical evidence, national sentiments, practical difficulties and reasonable concerns and sensitivities of both sides, and the actual state of border areas'; identifying boundary 'along well-defined and easily identifiable natural geographical features'; both sides to 'safeguard due interests of their settled populations in the border areas'; and so on).

However, when negotiations moved to the next stage of exploring an 'agreed framework for a boundary settlement', the Chinese side started reinterpreting the agreed parameters and principles, showing little keenness to move towards an early settlement. The Agreement of 2005 requires the two sides to 'make meaningful and mutually acceptable adjustments to their respective positions on the boundary question, so as to arrive at a package settlement' to the boundary question. In the negotiations leading up to the APPGP and subsequently, it was conveyed without any ambiguity that India could not make any major adjustments in the Eastern Sector, let alone ceding Tawang or any of the areas with settled populations. Indeed, any pragmatic solution would involve 'meaningful adjustments' in the positions of India and China in the west and east respectively, as the Chinese side had also proposed earlier as part of Deng Xiaoping's 'package' solution[8]. Unfortunately, any major advance in the negotiations on the 'agreed framework' has eluded the special representatives in their talks since 2005.

The Chinese side is also not ready to proceed with the line of actual control (LAC) clarification exercise, disregarding the agreement to arrive at common understanding of the alignment of the LAC which is a prerequisite for implementation of several agreed confidence building measures (CBMs). It is relevant to recall Article X(1) of the Agreement of November 1996 on CBMs in the military field along the LAC in the India–China border areas, which stipulated:

> Recognising that the full implementation of some of the provisions of the present Agreement will depend on the two sides arriving at a *common understanding of the alignment* of the line of actual control in the India–China border areas, the two sides agree to speed up the process of clarification and confirmation of the line of actual control. As an initial step in this process, they are clarifying the alignment of the line of actual control in those segments where they have different perceptions. They also agree to exchange maps indicating their respective perceptions of the *entire alignment* of the line of actual control as soon as possible[9].

Unfortunately, the Chinese side stalled LAC clarification after differences emerged in 2002 when maps depicting respective perceptions of the LAC were shown to each other but not exchanged. The LAC clarification process has not been resumed by the Chinese side even though this commitment was reiterated subsequently, including in the APPGP of 2005[10]. Different perceptions of the LAC have contributed to border incidents, including stand-offs involving military forces of the two sides, and also prevented implementation of several agreed CBMs.

China has shown a measure of reluctance to accept the LAC as the basis for trans-border interactions, including for border trade and pilgrimage, even though both sides had pragmatically accepted such an approach in the past, beginning with the Border Peace and Tranquillity Agreement of September 1993. It is worth recalling that the understanding reached in 1993 accepting the legal validity of the LAC involved a major shift in India's stand which created obligation on the part of the two countries to respect the status quo, pending an ultimate boundary settlement[11]. The Chinese protestations regarding the activities on our side of the LAC (in Arunachal Pradesh, for instance) are, therefore, puzzling for the Indian side. There is need to revisit these issues, respecting the understandings earlier reached between the two countries. At the same time, we must not underestimate positive gains of ensuring that border areas are peaceful despite major differences on the boundary question and significant divergence with regard to the alignment of the LAC. This has been achieved as a result of clear political commitment on both sides, mechanisms and CBMs assiduously put in place through as many as six agreements, and close contacts and cooperation between the border-guarding forces of the two countries. Both sides recognise that the maintenance of peace and tranquillity in the border areas is an essential prerequisite for the continued development of relations between the two countries.

It is also important that we anticipate contentious issues and prevent them from becoming troublesome irritants in the relationship. For example, we have the sensitive question of trans-border rivers where we can build on the existing mechanisms and move towards greater transparency and comprehensive arrangements for cooperation among co-riparians. This will help allay worries in India about the possible downstream impact of Chinese projects. Even while we must not duck contentious issues, we cannot afford to let them overwhelm the overall agenda of relations and thereby put this important relationship on a downward slope. While we seek to address our differences meaningfully, we must also learn to manage them, keeping in mind that India–China relations are vital, complex and sensitive.

This brings us to the second suggestion, the imperative of constantly investing in the positive contents of the relationship; otherwise, we run the risk of negatives dominating the bilateral discourse.

Today, India and China are the two fastest growing large economies. Present indications are that by 2030, the US, China and India will be the three largest economies in the world. While we cannot make linear extrapolation of present trends to anticipate future growth, both India and China are reasonably confident of maintaining their respective domestic transformations. How the two countries respond to and utilise each other's growth stories will be of great significance for both of them and for the global economy. This assessment was the basis of the understanding on 'closer developmental partnership' reached during President Xi's visit to India in September 2014[12], which was reinforced during Prime Minister Modi's visit to China in May 2015[13].

On our side, the objective was to leverage China's capabilities to advance India's domestic development agenda through participation of Chinese companies and other entities in infrastructure, manufacturing, skill development and other sectors. On the Chinese side, the decision perhaps reflects that India is now a major account for Chinese companies (seventh-largest export destination with exports of USD 62 billion last year; projects in excess of USD 60 billion; emerging destination for foreign direct investment (FDI); major market for e-commerce giants like Alibaba; and so on). One key element of rebalancing of Chinese economy is greater investment abroad; China's outward FDI of USD 148 billion exceeded inward FDI last year. It makes business sense for Chinese companies to have India as an essential part of their global portfolio.

We have made progress, as the Prime Minister noted during his visit to China in September last year. However, there are concerns in India about the lopsided and imbalanced nature of trade relations between India and China. In the last fiscal year, India had a trade deficit of USD 53 billion with China, which was 44 per cent of its global trade deficit which is clearly unsustainable. We need some visible progress on getting enhanced access to the Chinese market for Indian goods and services. Our economic engagement is also undergoing transition as we have reached the limits of the earlier model that relied on increasingly asymmetric trade expansion. Investment, e-commerce and services have emerged as new drivers of growth, as trade in goods, especially our exports, has stagnated. Much more needs to be done to identify and utilise complementarities in the two economies and forge production and supply chain linkages.

The two sides can be more ambitious in setting and implementing the agenda of bilateral cooperation. This is particularly true of the developmental partnership. There are a whole lot of other possibilities, including in newer areas. For instance, during Prime Minister Modi's visit to China in May 2015, we agreed to cooperate on peaceful applications of nuclear energy and outer space. Can India and China look at an agreement on civil nuclear cooperation? China is, after all, one of the most competitive suppliers of nuclear power plants. Can we consider a joint project in space which will project a positive narrative of India–China cooperation?

Thirdly, while exploring opportunities for collaboration, it is important to remain pragmatic in our approach. Let me illustrate with China's Belt and Road Initiative. India has its valid reservations regarding this important Chinese initiative and it is unrealistic for the latter to expect an endorsement from India. At the same time, the two sides can explore synergies between their respective connectivity and developmental agendas and agree on specific projects. Such a practical orientation resulted in India joining the Asian Infrastructure Investment Bank (AIIB). The AIIB was initially mooted as part of the Belt and Road Initiative, but launched in June 2015 as a multilateral financial institution with the participation of fifty-seven countries, with India being the second-largest stakeholder, next only to China.

Fourthly, as noted above, a primary challenge for us in the future is going to be managing the simultaneous rise of China and India. During Prime Minister Modi's visit to China in May 2015, we sought to develop a basic political consensus on the issue of simultaneous rise of India and China. It was agreed that the re-emergence of India and China as two major powers in the region and the world must unfold in a mutually supportive manner, and that mutual sensitivity for each other's concerns, interests and aspirations will be the key to managing this process[14]. However, this template is aspirational and much work needs to be done to substantiate it.

The geopolitics of the simultaneous re-emergence of China and India can best be addressed through better strategic communication and mutual accommodation in respect of specific theatres, situations and issues to the extent feasible. This will involve substantive and continuous discussions and understanding each other's vital interests while avoiding any expansive definition of those interests. It will be useful for China to recognise that a measure of hedging by India is a legitimate response in an uncertain geopolitical landscape and that India will work with third countries to offset its disadvantage arising from large asymmetries in its strengths and capabilities vis-à-vis China. On its part, India must recognise that Chinese activities in its neighbourhood are not necessarily directed against it. In the maritime domain, our navies will have to develop the habit of working together. This strategic dialogue, which should also address and manage major issues and differences in the bilateral domain and identify areas of convergence and cooperation, will essentially seek to develop a new modus vivendi and an updated template for India–China relations.

A beginning has been made with strategic consultations between National Security Adviser Ajit Doval and State Councillor Yang Jiechi in Hyderabad in November 2016 and the launching of restructured strategic talks between Foreign Secretary S Jaishankar and Executive Vice Foreign Minister Zhang Yesui in Beijing in February this year. Announcing the latter talks, the spokesperson of Ministry of External Affairs acknowledged that there are 'friction points' in the relationship and that the dialogue will 'take a holistic view of India–China relations, and see to what extent the two sides can accommodate each other's concerns and interests'[15]. This process of reconciling the interests, concerns and aspirations of the two countries must be carried forward in a structured, sustained and constructive manner.

Fifthly, we need to forge a fresh agenda for our collaboration on regional, multilateral and global issues, proceeding from common interests. For example, India and China are two of the major beneficiaries of economic globalisation. Equally, they have the most to lose if it breaks down or even declines. Looking at what is happening around us—the populist and protectionist backlash in the US and Europe, for instance—we realise that India and China, as the two largest developing economies and sovereignty-conscious States, have greater convergence in their interests and concerns than often recognised.

Finally, as noted earlier, the challenge of management of India's relations with an assertive China is compounded by the large gap in economic and military capabilities of the two countries. In fashioning our response to China, we should take a leaf out of China's playbook for dealing with the US, at least until recently. While China is a potential adversary, it is not in our interest to cast it as an enemy. It will be prudent for us to assiduously narrow the still-widening capability gap. It will obviously not be possible to match the Chinese armed forces in numbers or overall strength. While stepping up our military modernisation programme, we will have to focus on developing asymmetric capabilities to offset the Chinese advantage. This will involve a mix of defensive and offensive capabilities as a deterrent along the India–China borders, and building on the naval edge in our periphery, exploiting our strategic geography and our 'home-field advantage' in our proximity. A major part of our response will have to be to utilise our natural synergies and potential connectivities with our neighbours.

While seeking constructive engagement with the Chinese and utilising trade, investment and other economic linkages with China to advance our developmental agenda, we will have to, in parallel, develop leverage that China respects. Here again, our response may be asymmetric in terms of the choice of issues and theatres where we can act in a cost-effective manner, without being unduly provocative. The present geopolitical scenario where the rise of India is largely perceived as benign while there are growing anxieties regarding the rise of China, has its possibilities. At the same time, it is in our interest to ensure that our critical relationship with China remains on an even keel and moves in a positive direction to the extent feasible. This will require strategic maturity on both sides. We must keep in mind the big picture of our relations and avoid knee-jerk reactions to individual events and issues in this media-driven age.

As noted earlier, India–China relations have entered an even more challenging phase involving a changing mix of cooperation and competition in a complex and shifting geopolitical environment. Managing this relationship and ensuring that it remains on a constructive track while we hold our own ground and bide our time will possibly be the most important challenge of our foreign policy. Significantly, India and China still consider this to be a period of opportunity in their relations, despite their differences. Both have a shared desire to project bilateral relations in a positive light, even though they harbour doubts about each other's strategic intentions. Both recognise the aspect of competition but neither wishes to cast the other as an adversary. Both are today concentrating on their internal adjustments and development and do not desire confrontation with each other. Today India–China relations are suffering from an overhang of differences and suspicions, but it is eminently feasible and desirable to develop it along a pragmatic trajectory, complex and challenging and yet, forward-looking.

***

A career diplomat, **Ashok K Kantha** was Ambassador of India to China until January 2016. Prior to this, he was Secretary (East) at Ministry of External Affairs. His past assignments include High Commissioner of India to Sri Lanka and Malaysia, Consul General in Hong Kong, Deputy Chief of Mission in Kathmandu and Joint Secretary (East Asia) in Ministry of External Affairs. Presently, he is Director of the Institute of Chinese Studies, Delhi, and a Distinguished Fellow at the Vivekananda International Foundation, New Delhi.

END NOTES

1. Menon, Shivshankar. *Choices: Inside the Making of India's Foreign Policy*, Allen Lane, 2016, p 29.
2. According to Project Atlas, managed by the Institute for International Education, the total number of Indian students in China in 2015 was reported at 16,694 as compared to 765 just a decade ago. http://chinaindiadialogue.com/indian-students-in-china-the-case-of-medical-education#/home.
3. http://www.latimes.com/business/hollywood/la-fi-ct-20170207-china-box-office-20170207-story.html.
4. Lowy Institute, Understanding China's Belt and Road Initiative https://www.lowyinstitute.org/publications/understanding-belt-and-road-initiative.
5. US Department of Defence Annual Report to the Congress: Military and Security Developments Involving the People's Republic of China 2016 https://www.defense.gov/Portals/1/Documents/pubs/2016%20China%20Military%20Power%20Report.pdf.
6. SIPRI estimates China's military expenditure in 2015 at USD 215 billion and puts India's defence spending at USD 51.3 billion in the same year. http://books.sipri.org/files/FS/SIPRIFS1604.pdf.
7. The text of the Agreement at http://www.mea.gov.in/bilateral-documents.htm?dtl/6534/Agreement+between+the+Government+of+the+Republic+of+India+and+the+Government+of+the+Peoples+Republic+of+China+on+the+Political+Parameters+and+Guiding+Principles+for+the+Settlement+of+the+IndiaChina+Boundary+Question.
8. In an interview to the India journal *Vikrant* in 1982, Deng Xiaoping had said, "...for instance in the Eastern Sector, can we recognize the existing status quo, I mean the so-called McMahon Line? This was left over from history but in the Western Sector, the Indian government should also recognize the existing status quo." At https://thewire.in/1457/not-quite-out-of-the-box-right-yet/. Saran, Shyam. 'An Out of the Box Solution to the India-China Boundary Dispute?', *The Wire*, 12 May 2015.
9. The text of the Agreement at http://peacemaker.un.org/sites/peacemaker.un.org/files/CN%20IN_961129_Agreement%20between%20China%20and%20India.pdf.
10. Article IX of the APPGP of 2005.
11. Menon, Shivshankar. *Choices: Inside the Making of India's Foreign Policy*, Allen Lane, 2016, p 24.
12. Joint Statement issued in New Delhi on 19 September 2014; text at http://www.mea.gov.in/incoming-visit-detail.htm?24022/Joint+Statement+between+the+Republic+of+India+and+the+Peoples+Republic+of+China+on+Building+a+Closer+Developmental+Partnership.
13. Joint Statement issued on 15 May 2015; text at http://www.mea.gov.in/bilateral-documents.htm?dtl/25240/Joint_Statement_between_the_India_and_China_during_Prime_Ministers_visit_to_China.
14. Paragraph 3 of the Joint Statement issued on 15 May 2015 during PM's visit to China http://mea.gov.in/outoging-visit-detail.htm?25240/Joint+Statement+between+the+India+and+China+during+Prime+Ministers+visit+to+China.
15. http://www.ptinews.com/news/8413719_India--China-to-discuss--friction-points--like-NSG--Azhar-.html.

The China–Pakistan Nexus

PRABHAT P SHUKLA

Abstract

The Chinese–Pakistani nexus has been building up over the decades since the 1960s. While some in India have downplayed the strength of the Chinese commitment to Pakistan, the history of these relations reveals a different picture. The Chinese have been deterred in the past by a conjuncture of external forces, but today, those constraints no longer operate. The 2005 Sino-Pakistan Treaty of Friendship, Cooperation and Neighbourly Relations symbolises the strategic and economic commitment of China to Pakistan's security. It has emboldened the latter to confront both India and the US-led forces in Afghanistan, and has been indulged by both India and the US. It is time for India to understand the hard realities of the situation and take measures to address the growing threat to its own interests.

The China–Pakistan relationship goes back to the early 1960s. In fact, 1963 saw the boundary agreement, and served notice of a new axis emerging in the Indian subcontinent. Under this agreement, Pakistan ceded the Shaksgam Valley of the state of Jammu & Kashmir (J&K) to China at a time when India and Pakistan were engaged in serious negotiations over J&K, following the 1962 India–China War. Not surprisingly, it effectively destroyed any prospect of a settlement between India and Pakistan.

But it was the 1965 Indo-Pakistan War that brought out the strength and closeness of China and Pakistan, and the danger this posed to India in a military sense. It is worthwhile going into some detail on this, as there is a general belief that China has never intervened in any of the India–Pakistan wars. In fact, China issued two ultimatums to India during the course of the war. The first was on 8 September 1965 and in its note, the Chinese warned that an Indian attempt to take over Pakistani territory would entail 'grave consequences'. This was in response to the Indian decision to cross the international boundary on 6 September in response to the Pakistani attack in J&K. An Indian combined arms attack was then heading inside Pakistani territory towards Sindh and Lahore.

This was a sufficiently serious matter for a discussion between the Indian and American leaders, and within the US itself. President Lyndon Johnson and Defense Secretary Robert McNamara agreed that the US needed to prepare for a contingency where China would get involved. Johnson felt that the Note of 8 September indicated intent to get involved; the US could not then be caught unprepared, they agreed. The Indian leaders also approached the Soviet leaders, Leonid Brezhnev and Alexei Kosygin, less than a year into their jobs then.

The Chinese followed up with a second Note on 17 September. This was an ultimatum, and referred not to the India–Pakistan War, but to bilateral disputes, though the purpose was clear: to ease the pressure on Pakistan. It accused India of illegal constructions on the Chinese side of the border with Sikkim and demanded that these be dismantled by 20 September. There were also intrusions and firing on both the Eastern and Western sectors. Prime Minister Lal Bahadur Shastri was sufficiently concerned about this ultimatum to approach the US for consultations under the Air Defence Agreement, the only Cold War defence agreement between the two countries, signed during the Kennedy administration. The US declined, but advised that they were restraining the Chinese through the talks they were conducting between the two embassies in Warsaw.

Meanwhile, the Soviets also made appropriate démarches in Beijing, but relations between the two were already on the decline, and it is not clear what effect Soviet advice had. Nonetheless, at the end of the war, the Indian government thanked both the US and the USSR for their role in restraining the Chinese. What is important to note is that the Chinese did extend their deadline from 20 to 22 September, and that was the date on which India accepted the UN-brokered ceasefire, which then came into effect, since Pakistan did likewise. According to the then Chief of Air Staff, Air Chief Marshal Arjan Singh, he had opposed the ceasefire, and thus, it can only be speculated whether the Chinese ultimatum weighed with Shastri in disregarding Arjan Singh's advice. Perhaps it was one of the factors.

The second major episode was the 1971 War for the liberation of Bangladesh. Active hostilities began on 3 December and ended on 16 December, with the Pakistani surrender in Dhaka. The Chinese this time were much more restrained, for which there were two obvious reasons. The first was the Indo-Soviet Treaty, signed in August 1971. The archival record shows that both the US and China were greatly exercised over the fighting, and each pressed the other to do more to help Pakistan. But, the then Union of Soviet Socialist Republics (USSR) put out a TASS newspaper statement on 5 December, which effectively warned off the Chinese from any interference. In fact, the leader of the Chinese delegation to the UN General Assembly recognised the reality in the following words:

> On 5 December, TASS published a statement, which is full of the smell of gunpowder. It clamours that the tension between India and Pakistan has threatened the so-called interests of the security of the Soviet Union and that it cannot remain indifferent. This is blackmail and is a menace to China...
>
> (*Peking Review*, No 51, 17 December 1971)

> The Americans also approached the Shah of Iran, and he was even more explicit. He stated clearly that in the light of the Indo-Soviet Treaty, he was not prepared to confront the Soviet Union, and help Pakistan with arms and material. Despite this, the Chinese did try to put pressure later as the war progressed, and Pakistan and its protectors apprehended that India was preparing to attack the western half as well. Kissinger noted in his contemporary assessment of the war for President Nixon that the Chinese note warned India about encroachment and intrusion by Indian troops across the Sikkim border, and asked for this to be reversed immediately.
>
> (FRUS 1971 Vol XI, Doc 319, 16 December 1971)

The second obvious reason is that the Cultural Revolution was at its height at this time. Amid the turmoil, the armed forces were not ready for a confrontation—least of all with the USSR, which was raring to use nuclear weapons against China, if American reports are to be believed. More importantly, the designated heir to Mao and a leading figure in the armed forces, Lin Biao had also defected. He was killed in September 1971, when the aircraft he was flying in crashed in Mongolia, while he was apparently fleeing out of China, though the circumstances of this episode remain a mystery.

A similar pattern of behaviour is evident during the Kargil War of 1999, though the Chinese displayed more restraint. Again, the reason is not hard to fathom—the US had cauterised the fighting by imposing restraints on all sides, and the Chinese had worked out an understanding with the US, reflected in their joint statement issued in 1998 after the nuclear tests. But still, there was an attempt to tie down Indian forces on the line of actual control.

The important conclusion to draw from these episodes is that in the military field, the Chinese commitment to Pakistan is strong and consistent. Such restraint, as has been evident, has been the result of deterrence by the Soviets as in 1971, or persuasion by the Americans as in 1999. Today, these factors are absent or much weaker: the Soviet Union no longer exists, and Russia is the weaker of the two—as most Russians themselves acknowledge.

As for the Americans, their role in restraining China would probably continue, but the Chinese have built up their military capability to an extent where they may not heed American advice. In this context, the recent remarks of a Chinese scholar, active in the South Asia Track II circuit, are worth noting. He said that China would have to get involved, if there was any Indian attempt to destabilise Baluchistan and Pakistan-occupied Kashmir. These remarks were made following Prime Minister Modi's mention of these areas during his Independence Day speech on 15 August 2016. (*HT*, 29 August 2016)

The argument so far has been to establish that the Chinese commitment to Pakistan in the military field is serious, and Indian planners would be well-advised to take cognisance of this reality, especially in the event of a future confrontation or actual war. The factors of restraint that had operated in the past no longer apply—either Soviet pressure, or American persuasion. In fact, the growing understanding between India and the US is itself emerging as a factor promoting an adversarial attitude among the Chinese. However, the Chinese–Pakistani nexus goes beyond the military. In the economic and nuclear fields as well, and even on terrorism, there is an inexplicable and implausible alliance between them.

On the economic side, it was long argued, at least in India, that there was no real commitment to Pakistan on the part of China. This was factually true, but the answer was not because there was a lack of commitment. The answer was that as long as the US was willing to provide the funds required to keep the Pakistani economy afloat, the Chinese were comfortable standing aside. The reasons for the US to continue the funding, in the face of the destabilising role Pakistan was playing in Afghanistan were hard to fathom, and eventually even the US could not keep it going. From around 2011, US subventions have been declining and the Chinese have stepped in now with the China–Pakistan Economic Corridor (CPEC) with a pledge of USD 46 billion in energy and infrastructure projects. This is quite the biggest single-country commitment made by China. Even though many of the projects are funded by loans given by Chinese banks at commercial rates, if the past is anything to go by, much of this will end up being written off. Still, it is not a given that these projects will pay off. Many of the Chinese investments in Africa and elsewhere have failed to provide the returns, either commercial or strategic, that were expected. In the case of Pakistan, there are well-advertised differences over the substance of the projects, their geographic locations and alignments. In the case of Gilgit–Baltistan, Khyber–Pakhtunkhwa, and, above all, Baluchistan, there are demonstrations, and objections even at official and political levels. Obviously, India is concerned over the use of Gilgit–Baltistan, part of the territory of the princely state of J&K under the illegal occupation, and has made its formal démarches.

As the Chinese economy runs into its own economic difficulties, it will also find it problematic to continue such large-scale funding, even on commercial terms.

To substantiate: it is frequently pointed out that China holds the largest foreign exchange reserves in the world. But, these are being drawn down rapidly, and have fallen from USD 4 trillion in 2015 to USD 3 trillion in some eighteen months. Additionally, China also has among the highest foreign debt–USD 1.4 trillion–and servicing this will become more and more burdensome as US interest rates rise, and the dollar also rises against the RMB. All the same, what Chinese investments have done is to instil in Pakistan a sense that they can ignore American pressure, and continue their destabilising role vis-à-vis both, India and Afghanistan. The response from India has, unfortunately, been vacillating. Instead of indulging Pakistan's refusal to accord most favoured nation (MFN) treatment to Indian exports, we need to withdraw our grant of the same status to Pakistani exports to India. They are in violation of WTO rules, and this is one more example of how they are allowed to get away with flouting their international obligations.

Similarly, India should formally pull out from the Turkmenistan–Afghanistan–Pakistan–India gas pipeline. It is not enough to argue, as many do in India, that this pipeline has no real prospects. It is important for India to make it clear that it will not countenance Pakistan, sitting astride its energy lifelines. Equally, so long as India is part of the project, it remains bankable, and remains on the international agenda, with some of the multilateral lending agencies pushing it along.

With regard to terrorism, it is worth remembering that the Chinese did business with the Taliban when they were in power in Kabul from 1996 to 2001. During this period, the two sides signed several economic cooperation agreements covering civil aviation, mining and transport. And the Chinese have opened links with the Taliban once again in recent years, hosting them on two recent visits to Xinjiang, just before the four-way talks under the Quadrilateral Coordination Group (Afghanistan, Pakistan, China, USA) began. Given the growing threat from Islamists in Xinjiang, one would expect the Chinese to be wary of the Taliban. The Chinese, in fact, have laid emphasis on this in their Track I and II discussions with India, with some success. But the real logic of their approach to the Taliban may be seen through the prism of the manner in which the US used the same forces, then called the Mujahideen, and the considerations that guided them. The main aim then, in the 1980s, was to defeat the USSR. They understood the nature of the men they were using, but two considerations overruled their possible reservations. The first was that they were the only effective fighters against the Soviet forces, and defeating the Soviets was the paramount objective. The second was a conviction that Pakistan would hold these forces in check, and not allow them to threaten US interests. The Chinese, *mutatis mutandis*, are being guided by the same considerations. Their aim is to defeat the US-led forces in Afghanistan, and if that means using the same Islamist forces, they can accept the risk for a higher prize. And, of course, they are also convinced that Pakistan will ensure that these forces do not hurt their interests. How wrong this calculation is, they have had occasion to see for themselves, even if they would not learn from the bitter experience of the US. For the third time in the last two decades, the Chinese have had to close the border between Pakistan and Xinjiang because of terrorists entering from Pakistan. Still, it seems, the appeal of inflicting a humiliation on the Americans is strong enough to override all these potential troubles.

For India, there is a more troubling picture—this concerns the case of Masood Azhar and the Chinese refusal to allow him to be named as a terrorist under the UN Security Council Resolution 1267 Committee. Back in 2008, the Chinese had also blocked the naming of Jamaat-ud-Dawa and its key members, including Zaki-ur-Rehman Lakhvi, from being similarly named. This was just after the Mumbai attacks, in which 166 persons, including several foreigners, were killed. But on that occasion, the combined US and Indian pressure had persuaded China to withdraw its objection. This time, that pressure regarding Masood Azhar—if it is being applied—seems not to be working. This is further evidence that China is willing to stand up to international persuasion and pressure even in a clear-cut case of a terrorist. This is one more example of what India (and Afghanistan) can expect from the China–Pakistan nexus in the future.

The final aspect to be considered relates to nuclear and missile cooperation between the two countries. The full details of the content of this cooperation are still not known, but what is available publicly is serious enough. The Pakistanis took the decision to acquire nuclear weapons in 1972, though there had been interest in the issue ever since the Chinese nuclear test in 1964. A few years later, AQ Khan was to return to Pakistan with Zulfikar Ali Bhutto's blessings, and begin work on nuclear enrichment with the aim of developing a bomb. The story of Khan's activities in west Europe and the leniency with which he was treated is well known. However, the Chinese entered into this effort sometime in the late 1980s, as the Americans grew detached with the Afghan War winding down; they had to invoke the Pressler Amendment in 1990, and impose sanctions on Pakistan. China at this stage reportedly even tested a device for the Pakistanis in their Lop Nor test site. It may be presumed that the design for the weapon was also provided by the Chinese themselves. This emerged from the exposure of the AQ Khan papers that were discovered with the Libyans after Col M Gaddafi made his deal with the US, and handed over all the documents he had received from the Pakistanis. Many of the documents for the bomb design were in Mandarin, and the design for the bomb was similar to the early Chinese devices.

China signed the nuclear Non Proliferation Treaty (NPT) in 1992, so in a purely legal sense, it was not violating any laws by sharing this technology in the late 1980s. But, even after 1992, China has continued its cooperation to Pakistan: the Khushab reactor, which is unsafeguarded, was built in stages from the late 1990s, and is thought to be capable of producing 40 kg of weapons-grade Plutonium annually. Further, on the plea of 'grandfathering' new nuclear reactors, China continues to build Chashma 3 and 4, and Karachi 1 and 2. These are unambiguous violations of the Nuclear Suppliers Group (NSG) guidelines, but the Obama administration was reluctant to take any action on this. It remains to be seen whether the new Trump administration will take a more forthright stand.

There is a similar story of clandestine supply of missiles and missile technology from China to Pakistan through the decades. The beginning is in the early 1990s, when the US stopped all military cooperation with Pakistan after invoking the Pressler Amendment. Among the most serious issues for Pakistan was the ban on the supply of F-16 aircraft, which Pakistan had modified for nuclear delivery. Initially, China supplied entire systems, including the M-11 missile and then switched to components shipped in crates, once the M-11 supply was discovered. These were spotted by several intelligence agencies, and the US imposed sanctions on both Pakistan and China. However, the Clinton administration lifted these sanctions on both, and found a way out of the Pressler restrictions through the Brown Amendment, named after its author, Senator Hank Brown, which allowed a one-time waiver of the restrictions. Nonetheless, the missile cooperation continued. Some of it was direct and some of it was between North Korea and Pakistan. The former was seeking nuclear technology, and had developed missiles on the basis of the design of the Russian Scuds. Pakistani scientists made several trips to North Korea in order to help the nuclear programme along, and received missile components and technology in return, based on the No Dong, a medium-range missile.

China had also sought to limit India's options by amending the Comprehensive Test Ban Treaty (CTBT) draft to include the requirement that all the forty-four countries running nuclear plants had to sign the treaty for it to enter into force. This was targeting India, and was a first in the history of treaty-making to compel a third country to accede to a treaty. This was one of the major reasons that India was forced to veto the draft in Geneva in 1996, when it came before the Conference on Disarmament.

How have all these aspects manifested themselves in recent years? Probably the most important is a little-known document signed by the Chinese and the Pakistanis in 2005: their Treaty of Friendship, Cooperation and Neighbourly Relations. The text of this treaty has not been released, but there are two aspects that are worth stressing, on the basis of the summary released by the Chinese side. The first is the timing. This is the time that Pakistan was abandoning its supportive role in the US-led operations in Afghanistan and gradually reviving the Taliban. The second, one of the major clauses, states that China respects the independence, sovereignty and territorial integrity of Pakistan.

Inevitably, the Pakistanis put a spin on this to suggest that China is committed to defending Pakistan's territorial integrity. True or not, it is hard to say, but what is worth noting is that from this time onwards, Pakistan was emboldened to undermine US interests in Afghanistan. Judging by the anti-Soviet Afghan War in the 1980s, Pakistan was only willing to play the role it did if it had assurances of its security, and the Reagan administration did so, on a long-term basis. It would be safe to speculate that there is some sense of security that the treaty provides, and that enabled Pakistan to rebuild the Taliban and unleash them on the Afghan battlefield.

The existence of the treaty is important to bear in mind, for the situation in each of these countries is shaky. President Trump has reached out to, or accepted the outreach of Taiwan in a way that has unsettled China. While it is true that there is a commitment on the part of the US to 'One China' in its bilateral understandings with the People's Republic, it is equally true that the Taiwan Relations Act pulls US diplomacy in the opposite direction. But apart from Taiwan, China has been facing long-term problems in Tibet and Xinjiang. Hong Kong has also emerged as a challenge to the 'one-country-two systems' formula, with its obvious implications for Taiwan.

The Chinese economy remains unsettled, despite headline GDP figures that seek to reassure. Further, the new Trump administration threatens the economic relationship as well. All talk of interdependence cannot conceal the fact that China needs the US market for its exports, because that is where it earns over half its trade surplus. And the Chinese nervousness over monetary tightening—recently referred to by Xi Jinping at Davos—is another factor of Chinese vulnerability. On top of all this, there is a major political transition due later this year when the nineteenth Congress of the Chinese Communist Party meets.

Pakistan is similarly unsettled. The periphery is growing more turbulent, and Prime Minister Modi has become the first leader to make a public reference to the problems not only in Baluchistan, but also in Gilgit–Baltistan and Pashtunistan.

All these factors make for an emerging security environment that requires careful understanding and preparation. It is worth stressing that the Chinese have recently reorganised their armed forces, establishing joint theatre commands. Under this arrangement, new military districts in Tibet and Xinjiang form part of the Western Command, thus bringing the entire Indian border under one command, unlike the previous arrangement. Tibet is, however, under the direct control of the Beijing-based Central Military Commission, and is headed by an officer of the same rank as the theatre command. *Global Times* described the arrangement as:

> 'After the [recent] military reform, most of the provincial military commands are now under the control of the newly-established National Defence Mobilisation Department of the Central Military Commission, and their priority is to the region's militia reserves and conscription.

> The Tibet Military Command, on the other hand, is under the leadership of the Chinese ground forces, which suggests that the command may undertake some kind of military combat mission in the future,' a source close to the matter told the *Global Times*. And further: 'The Tibet Military Command bears great responsibility to prepare for possible conflicts between China and India, and currently it is difficult to secure all the military resources they need…'

There are credible reports that Chinese troops are present on the Pakistani side of the Line of Control. According to reports, they are meant to provide protection to their workers in Pakistan-occupied Kashmir, but that is not convincing, since protection is the job of the host government, and this is what Pakistan is doing along the CPEC. China has also provided Pakistan two ships for security of the maritime links to Gwadar port. Two more are to follow.

Another recent development that is a cause for concern is that Russia is being drawn into this nexus. The needless pressure that the Obama–Clinton–Kerry team was putting on Russia left it with little choice but to accommodate China into its calculation, even though it has well-recognised reservations regarding the potential risk of getting too dependent on China. But it has been compelled to do so in order to break out of the isolation the West was forcing it into. This has provided both China and Pakistan with the potential of acquiring some of the best military technology in the world. Russian jet engines fill the gap that China has not been able to fill in on its own. And it is a major provider of energy, both hydrocarbon and nuclear. It must be hoped that the Trump presidency will attenuate some of the hostility that it inherited; India is well-positioned to try and bridge the differences between the two countries, and should actively try and do so.

All this suggests that there are serious security issues as a result of the growing nexus between China and Pakistan, which India would be well-advised to track closely, and find ways of neutralising the dangers they hold. This will require a mix of economic and military means as well as active diplomacy. The Trump presidency will create sharp discontinuities, and will be even more challenging for partners and adversaries alike. India must be ready with its own strategy, and coordinate its actions with the many like-minded countries in the region. The time for passivity is at an end.

***

Prabhat Prakash Shukla is an Indian Foreign Service officer. He has served in diplomatic assignments in Brussels, London and Kathmandu and as the Indian Ambassador to Russia. He was the Diplomatic Adviser to the Prime Minister from 1996 to 2000. He is currently a Distinguished Fellow at the VIF, New Delhi.

TRACK
MS.OFFICE 2013
MS.PROJECT
WEB DEVELOPMENT
MULTI MEDIA &
GRAPHIC DESIGNING
POLICE

Evolving Dynamics in Pakistan

Tilak Devasher

Abstract

Pakistan is in a state of flux. Even though one civilian government succeeded another in 2013, democratic consolidation continues to be fragile. Despite a solid power base in Punjab, Nawaz Sharif's position has become uncertain due to the taint of the Panama Papers and the impending Supreme Court verdict. His hastiness in putting the army in its place could lead to the revival of tensions in civil–military relations. The economy continues to suffer from serious structural flaws and Pakistan could be heading for a major balance of payment crisis in the near future. Notwithstanding the ongoing military operation in North Waziristan, incidents of terrorism continue apace. Barring the one bright spot of relations with China, Pakistan's flawed security paradigms have brought it into conflict with its neighbours, and as a result, relations with India and Afghanistan continue on a downward spiral. With the US, Pakistan faces an uncertain future. Current issues apart, the degradation of the innards of Pakistan—water, education, economy and population—requires a visionary leadership to pull Pakistan back from the abyss.

PAKISTAN'S PIVOTAL MOMENT

Pakistan stands at a pivotal moment in its history. It has to take major decisions regarding its future trajectory, on issues pertaining to democratic consolidation, civil–military relations, economic development, terrorism, response to religious fundamentalism and its relations with its neighbours and beyond.

The task has, no doubt, been complicated by the winds of change that are blowing across the world. Brexit in the UK and the election of Donald Trump as the US president, point to the waning popularity of globalisation and a clamour for nationalism and protectionism. Even though Pakistan is not fully wired into the global economic system, it too will not be able to escape the impact of the flux that the world is likely to face in the coming years.

DEMOCRACY

Despite one civilian government succeeding another in 2013, democratic consolidation continues to be brittle. In its annual report titled *Assessment of the Quality of Democracy in Pakistan 2016*, The Pakistan Institute of Legislative Development and Transparency (PILDAT), a think tank focused on political and public policy research, made the following points: (i) The National Assembly continued to be sidelined as a forum for debate, discussion and resolution of national issues (Prime Minister Nawaz Sharif has attended only 13 per cent of parliament sessions and Imran Khan even less); (ii) Lack of institutionalised decision-making, since the federal cabinet that was supposed to meet at least fifty-two times in a year, only managed to meet six times during 2016 leading to poor governance (the Supreme Court had to intervene to tell the Prime Minister to get policy decisions passed by the cabinet); (iii) The internal democracy of political parties continued to be a liability for the quality of Pakistan's democracy during 2016; (iv) The civil–military imbalance tilted even further, with the military leadership taking leading roles on matters of national security and certain areas of foreign policy, while the elected government appeared to act as an auxiliary.

The report concluded that the process of consolidation of democracy continues to be not only slow but also marked by roadblocks and twists and turns. Though a formal democracy, Pakistan had serious drawbacks that have made it fragile.

POLITICAL DYNAMICS

Be that as it may, the pace of political activity is likely to quicken due to the general elections slated for 2018. Punjab, with over 50 per cent seats in the National Assembly, would remain the major battleground. During the last three years, the ruling Pakistan Muslim League–Nawaz (PML–N) has further consolidated its position in its power base of Punjab due to its performance in the local bodies polls. Using the criterion of loyalty, it has established a monopoly over the State machinery—bureaucracy, police and patronage in Punjab colloquially called *thana-kutcherry* model of governance. It has created a large pool of beneficiaries ranging from bureaucrats and government contractors to real estate businessmen and journalists. The future of these beneficiaries is now intricately linked with the PML–N and they will do their best to ensure its victory in the 2018 elections.

Despite this solid base in Punjab, Nawaz Sharif finds his position shaky primarily because of the Panama Papers case[1]. The hearing of the case has been completed and the Supreme Court, at the time of writing, had reserved its judgement that is expected any day. Though the Sharif brothers believe that they can 'fix' almost anything like they have been doing for the last three decades, Panama Papers are not going away and neither are the London flats. Nawaz faces difficulties in explaining the source of funds through which the flats were bought. Irrespective of the judicial decision in the case, these issues will remain part of the political narrative in Pakistan and would be like the proverbial albatross around Nawaz's neck.

For Imran Khan, the Panama Papers were god-sent, since they gave him a new lease of life after his election-rigging campaign received a setback following the 2015 Judicial Commission report. However, tactically, Imran was unable to capitalise on the opportunity to force Nawaz Sharif's resignation. This was primarily due to his inability to grow out of the campaign mode and to continue to depend on the power of street agitation, instead of that of the parliament. When he was unable to muster enough street power to dislodge Nawaz Sharif, he had no option but to return to parliament. The opposition remained fractious with the Pakistan Peoples Party (PPP), especially unable to countenance that it was Imran Khan, who had emerged as the main opposition leader.

The key battleground for both the PPP and the Pakistan Tehreek-e-Insaf (PTI) is Punjab, where the two would be fighting to attract the same anti-Nawaz constituency. Bilawal Bhutto has been making some efforts to reinvent the party by distancing it from the label of being a 'friendly opposition' to the PML–N. Asif Zardari, however, continues to play an ambivalent role, hedging his bets, lest the anti-corruption campaign engulfs him too. That apart, there is considerable skepticism about the party being a crowd-puller anymore. It does not have an agenda or programme like its leftist agenda in the past of *roti, kapda aur makan*. 2017-18 would show whether the PPP is politically relevant at the national level or would remain confined to Sindh.

Imran Khan has an edge over the PPP since he has had a consistent anti-corruption agenda. He dominated the political scene in 2016 and has donned the de facto mantle of the leader of the opposition. However, the moot question is whether he can convert his 17 per cent vote share in the 2013 elections into over 30 per cent in 2018 that would be required to ensure that Nawaz does not win a fourth term. For this, his corruption plank would have to fire the imagination of the people at large or make them angry enough to see the back of Nawaz. It remains to be seen whether he can create a *hawa* in the run up to the 2018 elections to defeat the well-oiled Sharif machinery, especially in Punjab.

CIVIL–MILITARY DYNAMICS

The state of civil–military relations is another cause of worry for Nawaz Sharif. With the on-schedule retirement of the popular Army Chief Gen Raheel Sharif, Nawaz was saved the blushes of another premature termination of his premiership. Having appointed his sixth Army Chief, the debatable point is, have civil–military relations become harmonious under the new Army Chief, Gen Qamar Javed Bajwa?

It is one of Nawaz Sharif's fatal flaws (the others being demanding absolute control and loyalty and considering himself above accountability) that he thinks that having appointed his own man (*apna banda*) as army chief, the army is now beholden to him. He still hasn't learnt that the army chief is no one's man and neither has the army as an institution changed because of change in command. In trying to settle scores with the army and claw back some of the space conceded to it, Nawaz is likely to land himself in trouble. A case in point has been the efforts to tarnish the reputation of former Army Chief Gen Raheel Sharif by the systematic leak of his joining the Saudi-backed Islamic Military Alliance, and later generating a controversy over the propriety of the allotment of 90 acres of land to him. This led to a sharp rejoinder from the army's mouthpiece Inter-Services Public Relations (ISPR) that the land was allotted strictly in accordance with the 'constitutional provisions' warning 'this debate with the intent of maligning the army has the potential to create misunderstanding between State institutions thus considered detrimental to existing cohesion'.

This was the second warning under Gen Bajwa's short tenure. The first was in mid-January 2017, when in response to a question about a 'dormant inquiry' into the *Dawn* leaks controversy during a visit to Kharian cantonment, he said that, 'There will be no compromise on the dignity of Pakistan Army[2].' This was not an isolated event since he was again asked about the *Dawn* leaks issue during his visit to the Lahore cantonment in February. If the PML–N thought that the leaks controversy was done and dusted with the departure of Gen Raheel Sharif, they were mistaken.

Both these statements are indicators of the potential acrimony between the civil and the military regimes early in Gen Bajwa's term, owing to Nawaz's penchant for control. Observers have noted that the ISPR went beyond the defence of Gen Raheel Sharif to warn about misunderstanding between State institutions, i.e. the civil and the military and being detrimental to existing cohesion.

Nawaz's calculations to chip away at the army are possibly based on the reality that the opposition is in disarray, his formidable power base in Punjab is intact and the fact that the new army chief will take some time to settle down. His attempts, however, could lead to a renewal of tensions in civil–military relations. An alternative strategy of providing good governance and strengthening institutions to claw back the space from the army does not seem to fit into Nawaz's style of governance.

TERRORISM AND INTERNAL SECURITY

During the last fifteen years, Pakistan has lost more than fifty thousand civilians and soldiers to terrorism. According to the State Bank of Pakistan, the total direct and indirect loss and damage to Pakistan's economy, as a result of the 'war on terror' is around USD 118.3 billion from 2002 to 2016.

It required the massacre of school children at the Army Public School in Peshawar in December 2014 to make the Pak leadership, especially the army, see the writing on the wall. A quick consensus was arrived at, which mandated that the anti-Pakistan terrorist groups, especially the Tehrik-e-Taliban Pakistan (TTP) and the sectarian groups like the Lashkar-e-Jhangvi (LeJ), had to be rooted out. The violence in Karachi was already being tackled via a sustained operation. Cumulatively, these operations have led to the security situation showing considerable improvement in 2016. While the military operation, *Zarb-e-Azb* has significantly weakened the terrorist infrastructure and networks in the North Waziristan and Khyber agencies, the killing of leaders of LeJ in Quetta, Karachi and Punjab, have lowered the threat of sectarian violence. Many of the TTP leaders have relocated to Afghanistan.

However, there have been slippages in 2016 with major attacks in Quetta, Peshawar, Mardan and several areas in FATA, and in 2017 in Lahore, Sehwan and Charsadda. These attacks show that terrorist organisations still have the capacity to wreak havoc virtually at will and cast doubts on the self-proclaimed successes of Operation *Zarb-e-Azb*. It is also indicative of the fact that rival factions of the TTP have decided to come together to form a 'united front', joining hands with other terrorist outfits. In the days ahead, tackling the regrouped, united factions would be a major challenge. Moreover, the military operation has been selective in its targeting. The anti-India terrorist groups like the Lashkar-e-Toiba (LeT) and the Jaish-e-Mohammad (JeM), and the anti-Afghan groups like the Afghan Taliban and the Haqqani network have been spared. Unless Pakistan carries out an across-the-board, holistic operation, it is unlikely to be rid of the scourge of terrorism. In addition, it would be vital to dismantle the terrorist infrastructure developed over decades that would have to include a counter-terrorism narrative so as to join the ideological debate that the Pakistani State has been losing for decades.

The focus would have to be Punjab, the hub of the terrorist infrastructure. The fight to reclaim Pakistan would have to begin here. Following the 13 February 2017 Lahore attack, despite the PML–N government being in denial about the problem, Operation *Radd-ul-Fasaad* has been launched across the country. How effective it will be, remains to be seen.

Complicating the issue is the extent of polarisation in Pakistani society. This was most apparent on the death anniversary of former Punjab Governor Salman Taseer, who was shot by his own guard Mumtaz Qadri in January 2011. A section of civil society mourned Taseer's brutal murder for trying to help a Christian woman accused of blasphemy, while another section went on a rampage to flag their support for the blasphemy law. Symbolising this polarisation is the 'shrine' that has been constructed for Mumtaz Qadri near Islamabad. The shrine is now the symbol of the blasphemy law and a foe to anyone who tries to tinker with it. This is, in a fundamental sense, the net result of politicians, starting from MA Jinnah and Liaquat Ali, using religion for opportunistic purposes and now facing the consequences of that opportunism by conceding more and more space to religious groups.

The entrenched sectarian and ideological ambiguities that continue to plague Pakistan were amply demonstrated when the Interior Minister refused, in the Senate, to equate banned sectarian organisation with banned terrorist groups even though they openly advocate *takfir* (inquisition) and violence. The reason given was that the Shia–Sunni conflict went back 1,300 years.

THE ECONOMY

The Sharif or the *Raiwind* model of economic development has major flaws. At its core are mega infrastructure projects with a focus on Punjab and massive borrowings to make the foreign exchange reserves look good. In addition, what has kept Pakistan afloat is the low price of oil. Ostensibly, the economy looks okay. The stock market is doing well, foreign reserves are healthy, the growth rate though below 5 per cent has picked up from the under 4 per cent growth of the 2000s.

However, below the surface is a different story. Workers' remittances are declining–5 per cent of the GDP in FY 2015-16, as compared to 6.9 per cent in FY 2014-15. Exports have been declining–USD 24.5 billion in 2012-13 to USD 17.9 billion in 2014-15. The trade deficit has widened to 5.9 per cent of GDP. Tax-to-GDP ratio has declined in the three years of the PML–N government and is one of the lowest in the world at 8.4 per cent of GDP in 2015-16. In the last three years, the PML–N Government has borrowed USD 25 billion in foreign loans and USD 30 billion domestically. Total level of public debt and liabilities has swollen to Rs 22,461.9 billion, which is 75.9 per cent of GDP in FY 2016 up from 72.2 per cent in FY 2015 and is likely to worsen in the next few years[3]. The Fiscal Responsibility and Debt Limitation Act of 2005 restricts public debt at 60 per cent of GDP. To get around this statutory violation, the PML–N government has pushed ahead the 2013 deadline to 2018 to reduce debt to 60 per cent of GDP[4].

The deterioration of the macroeconomic indicators reveals structural problems in the Pakistan economy that should be a major cause of worry for the leadership. This type of borrowing is unsustainable and together with declining exports and remittances from overseas workers, the Pakistani economy is headed for a severe balance of payment crisis in the near future.

FOREIGN POLICY DYNAMICS

The foreign policy challenges for Pakistan continue to be Afghanistan, the US and India. The key challenge for Pakistan in Afghanistan would be to accept the sovereignty and independence of the neighbour instead of trying to impose its own proxies in Kabul. With Pakistan trying to leverage the intra-Afghan peace process for its own gains, peace in Afghanistan would remain elusive. As a consequence, peace in Pakistan would also be elusive. This is a dynamic that Pakistan just does not seem to understand.

With the US, signs of a cooling relationship were already visible under former President Barack Obama. Under President Donald Trump, this is likely to persist if not intensify, especially if Pakistan continues fooling the Americans by using US aid to fund the Taliban. Pakistan could also suffer collateral damage due to the growing US rivalry with China. What will hurt Pakistan the most is, if as a result, the US were to deepen its strategic partnership with India.

In its relations with India, Pakistan has banked on two factors: possession of nuclear weapons and non-State actors. The challenge for Pakistan is that India's retaliatory strike after the Uri camp attack in September 2016 has rescued it from its self-imposed restraint of risking a nuclear escalation. In future, jihadi strikes from Pakistan could have far more lethal consequences.

Finally, while its friendship with China continues to be 'all weather' bolstered no doubt by the USD 46 billion (now USD 51 billion) China–Pakistan Economic Corridor (CPEC), Pakistan will have to ensure that the projects are economically, financially and environmentally viable. Lack of transparency and the fine print of the financial proposals are ringing alarm bells in several quarters in Pakistan. The alienation of the Baloch at being neglected in the planning and sharing benefits of the mega project, the water problems in Gwadar and the monopoly of projects in Punjab are equally disturbing signs for many in Pakistan.

Beyond current issues lie the major fault-lines of Pakistan. The innards of Pakistan—water, education, economy and population—have deteriorated to such an extent that the very survival of Pakistan could have been endangered[5]. Pakistan faced an emergency situation in all these four areas about a decade ago. Due to lack of action then, it should be in the disaster management mode today, but there are no signs that it is. Additionally, even seventy years after its creation, Pakistan is still not sure about its identity. Neither is it sure whether it is an 'Islamic State', or a 'democratic State'. Collectively, the resolution of these issues would require a leadership with vision, its comprehension of the multiple crises facing the country and its willingness to take resolute action to tackle each of the problems. Unfortunately, signs of such a leadership and vision are not very evident today.

***

Tilak Devasher is a former Special Secretary, the Cabinet Secretariat, Government of India. He is the author of the book titled, *Pakistan: Courting the Abyss*.

END NOTES

1 The Panama Papers are over 11 million leaked documents detailing financial information of more than 200,000 offshore entities containing personal financial information about individuals and public officials using shell companies some of which were to hide illegal wealth. The leaked documents were created by Panamanian law firm Mossack Fonseca. The children of PM Nawaz Sharif were named in the papers.

2 The Dawn Leaks refers to a news story published in the *Dawn* in October 2016 that purported to contain information leaked from a top-level security meeting held in the PM's house. The Corps Commanders declared the leaks to be a breach of national security and demanded action against those responsible. With the needle of suspicion pointing towards the media cell in the PMO headed by Nawaz Sharif's daughter, the government has been trying to scuttle any enquiry/action in the matter.

3 State Bank of Pakistan Report 2015-16. http://www.sbp.org.pk/reports/annual/arFY16/Chapter-05.pdf, p-61.

4 Ibid., FN 1 p-59.

5 Collectively called the WEEP factors. See the author's *Pakistan: Courting the Abyss*, Harper Collins, India, 2016.

Prospects and Problems of Transition and Stability in Afghanistan

Lt Gen Ravi Sawhney, PVSM, AVSM & Sushant Sareen

Abstract

There is no gainsaying that the situation in Afghanistan is very fragile. The Taliban is in the ascendant and other terrorist groups like Islamic State of Iraq & Syria (ISIS) have established their presence in the country. Security forces are stretched and have suffered heavy casualties. Only around 60 per cent of the area is under the control of the Afghan government. The economy is in a tailspin and the political situation remains fraught and factious. And yet, despite all the existential challenges confronting Afghanistan, there is a good chance that Afghanistan will be able to ride out the storm of insurgency and instability, provided its allies and partners do not abandon it. But a more onerous challenge to Afghanistan will be the new and dangerous Great Game that is being played by some of the great powers—Russia and China—and a destructive policy being followed by Pakistan in Afghanistan. Without the end of external interference, even if the Afghan State manages to reverse the gains made by the Taliban, security and stability will remain elusive in that country. A destabilised, or worse, Talibanised Afghanistan, will in turn, destabilise the entire region. This is why the Great Game is not so 'Great' for the countries playing it.

INTRODUCTION

Ever since the Taliban's resurgence around 2005-06, every new year has been billed as a critical year which would determine the future trajectory of the post-9/11 Afghan State. For the last ten years, the Afghan State has managed, even if not perfectly, to deal with the political and administrative problems and confront the security and economic challenges, and in the process belie the predictions of doom and gloom. 2017 will be yet another year which will be critical for Afghanistan's future: one, the Taliban insurgency is gaining pace and has managed to garner the tacit support of countries like China and Russia, and even Iran; two, the Pakistanis continue with their double-game and double-speak in Afghanistan and seem to have got the support of the Chinese and Russians in their misadventure; and three, the US and its allies have continued to affirm support to the Afghan government, but with a new administration taking office in Washington, there is as yet no clarity on whether the US will remain committed to Afghanistan, and if so, for how long.

Domestically, the very fragile security situation is having a very negative impact on the economy, which has been further exacerbated by the steady pulling out of many of the foreign NGOs and aid workers, along with paring down of development programmes. In addition, the drawdown of foreign troops has led to a further contraction in the economy. Meanwhile, the political situation remains fraught. Despite papering over the political cleavages that opened after the 2014 presidential election, the National Unity Government (NUG) hasn't quite been able to pull itself together very amicably, much less, get its act together.

And yet, despite all the challenges, problems and uncertainty confronting both State and society in Afghanistan, and notwithstanding the shaky confidence not just among sections of the international community but also among many Afghan citizens in the ability of the Afghan State to hold its own for any length of time, it would be a mistake to write-off the Afghan State as a lost cause. If anything, far from it being the case that supporting and sustaining the Afghan State is tantamount to reinforcing failure, any abandonment of Afghanistan would in fact be the real failure because it would make the conjecture of a collapsing Afghan State a reality.

FRAGILE AND YET, FORMIDABLE

Any assessment of the situation in Afghanistan made in purely binary terms would be prone to glossing over all the positives that outbalance the negatives, and conversely, all the negatives that undermine the positives.

Even fifteen years after the post-Bonn Conference consensus that resurrected the Afghan State, it remains a work-in-progress. Apart from the first couple of years of relative peace, Afghanistan has been wracked by a foreign-funded, and foreign supported and supplied, Islamist insurgency commanded and controlled from a foreign country—Pakistan. For a variety of reasons, the international coalition troops took their eyes off the ball and failed to address this issue when it could have been nipped in the bud.

Asides of the failure on the security front, there was also the failure on the political front. The fiddle during successive presidential elections actually created more problems than it solved. With both politics and security in a flux, the economy, which was in any case overly dependent on external aid and assistance, was never going to be able to stand on its own feet, even less so because of the colossal wastage on account of skewed development programmes, policies and priorities that undermined the nation-building project.

Unfortunately, there is so much focus on the negative news emanating from Afghanistan, that the positives are often enough lost sight of. The fact of the matter is that despite all the mistakes made, very many good things also happened over the last decade-and-a-half. The Afghanistan of 2017 is very different from the devastated and desolate Afghanistan of 2001. A lot has changed in these years, change that is not easily reversible. A new and educated middle class, which is connected to the rest of the world, has emerged in these years. Afghanistan has seen a communications revolution with a vibrant and independent media and internet-savvy young people, who express themselves fearlessly in cyberspace. A State structure exists, which even though far from being perfect, is at the same time, far from being dysfunctional. Afghanistan has a reasonably competent army, a pretty good intelligence agency, a police force, a very active parliament, and all other elements that go into the making of a State. Modern banking, airlines, roads, schools, universities, offices, hospitals, communication and electricity networks have been established. Dams have been built, irrigation canals restored and rehabilitated, trade links revived.

Probably, the most important thing going in Afghanistan's favour is the fact that despite all the ethnic tug-of-war, the Afghan identity remains very strong. There is no ethnic or sectarian movement for separatism in Afghanistan. The Afghans remain fiercely independent and are unlikely to accept being a vassal or client State under the over-lordship of a tottering and near-failed State like Pakistan, which is trying to impose itself on the Afghans. At the same time, the Afghans are pragmatic and practical enough to take assistance that they feel is in their interest. Within the security forces, there is no Bonapartism. The military remains loyal to the elected civilian leadership, something that can hardly be said for a country like Pakistan. All these positives can, of course, be overturned, if the forces of darkness represented by the Taliban and other sundry Islamist groups, including the Islamic State (IS) and Al-Qaeda were to once again either hold sway over the entire country or even over large swathes of territory. But that eventuality can be avoided by building the sinews of all the positives that exist. Despite the fatigue, even lack of interest, in the international coalition with the nation-building project, if ever there was time to double-down on nation-building in Afghanistan, it is now.

What is important is that the Western countries, which have invested so much in blood and treasure in rebuilding Afghanistan from the ashes, temper their expectations on how Afghanistan will evolve. Applying Western standards of democracy and governance to evaluate the performance of the Afghan government is utterly pointless. In fact, the West should be happy that the democracy project in Afghanistan hasn't been unsuccessful despite their botched attempts at political engineering. Even though Afghan democracy is nowhere close to the West's conception of an ideal democracy, it has not done too badly in the last fifteen years. Despite all the allegations of stolen elections and 'industrial scale' fraud in polls, it is the maturity of the Afghan politicians that they have stuck to the democratic project. So much so, that with all its imperfections, winning an election has so far been the only way to come to power. This is saying a lot because there aren't many new democracies or even quasi-democracies where an election victory, howsoever dodgy it may have been, grants legitimacy to wield power.

Clearly, like in all other democracies, Afghanistan too will have to go through a long process before democracy can be consolidated. But unlike other fledgling democracies, the prospects for democratic political consolidation are much brighter in Afghanistan, provided the political process continues to be supported by those who have a stake in Afghanistan's survival. In order to continue the support, the international community, and in particular the West, needs to adopt greater realism about the social, cultural and political peculiarities of Afghanistan. This means that apart from showing patience with Afghanistan as it tries to consolidate its democratic polity, Afghanistan's supporters must also adopt a certain amount of equanimity in judging the progress of Afghanistan's political culture. Instead of imposing alien standards and norms, Afghanistan must be allowed to evolve its own democratic system. Quite naturally, such a system, while it conforms to the basic rules of any democracy, will at the same time have characteristics that Western and more mature democracies might not consider as being up to par.

The democratic political project was always going to be a long haul. In the more immediate future, however, there is a need for an effective leadership that enjoys credibility among and confidence of all ethnic groups. Unfortunately, there is a bit of a leadership deficit on this account. President Ashraf Ghani has not quite been able to rise to the level of being seen as a pan-Afghanistan leader, whose acceptability cuts across the ethnic divide, something that his predecessor Hamid Karzai, despite his warts and all, had managed. But given that President Ghani will serve his term, and cannot and should not be ousted mid-term because that would hardly help matters, it is important for him to build mutual trust and confidence with all political players and ethnic groups. This will mean working out a credible power-sharing arrangement within the NUG, which incidentally was the main purpose of forming it and which is something it has not quite managed to do. Some aspects of this power sharing can be formal, which will require constitutional and legal sanction, but some aspects of this can be informal which in the Afghan context, can be as effective as formal arrangements. For instance, even though Afghanistan may not constitutionally be a federal State, a way has to be found to co-opt provincial leaders to give them a stake in the system by making them partners in governance.

In the security domain, the challenge is more onerous. The Afghan National Army (ANA), with all its fairly serious limitations in terms of resources, capacity and capability, has not performed very badly. Armies take a long time to rebuild, and fifteen years is just not enough time to build a conventional army, which can conduct operations on its own. In the case of the ANA, the Americans and their allies committed the blunder of building it as a conventional army but giving it the operational capability of a glorified constabulary. This was done to appease the Pakistanis who were spooked by the idea of a 300,000 odd, strong, modern Afghan army on its western front. But this turned out to be a classic Catch-22 situation: the army was not provided the wherewithal to function effectively against the foreign-sponsored insurgency in order to appease the sponsor of the insurgency, who in turn used the opportunity to bleed the newly-built army through its Taliban and other Islamist proxies.

This is a problem that needs to be fixed and some amount of work is being done to achieve this. The earlier reluctance of many of Afghanistan's friends to equip the ANA with the necessary hardware—tanks, armoured personnel carriers, helicopters, artillery, aerial platforms, for not just troop movement and casualty evacuation, but also for use in an attack role, etc—is steadily becoming a thing of the past. For example, India has started to provision some of this much-needed hardware. More importantly, the Americans too are working to provide the necessary equipment. There seems to be greater appreciation of the fact that Afghanistan does not really need state-of-the-art military equipment, only effective weapon systems which even though dated by the standards of armies of countries like India or even Pakistan, are able to meet the operational requirements of the ANA. Alongside, efforts are underway to provide training and building capacity of the ANA, to handle logistics and conduct operations on its own. A reasonably well-equipped and well-trained ANA will not only be good for the morale of the soldiery but also give Afghanistan the confidence to stand up to the bullying tactics of unfriendly countries like Pakistan.

While building the ANA's capacity and capability is necessary, it is just as important to ensure that the Afghan National Police and the intelligence service perform well. The latter has done some splendid work, but there is a lot more that can be done to make it more effective, both in collecting and analysing intelligence as well as in undertaking counterterrorism and counter-espionage operations. The National Directorate of Security (NDS) has a fairly good system of human intelligence but depends quite a lot on the Western agencies for electronic intelligence. As far as the police is concerned, it has been often facing the brunt of terrorism. Better training, equipment, resources and facilities will go a long way in improving the effectiveness of the police, which is often the first line of defence against the terrorists.

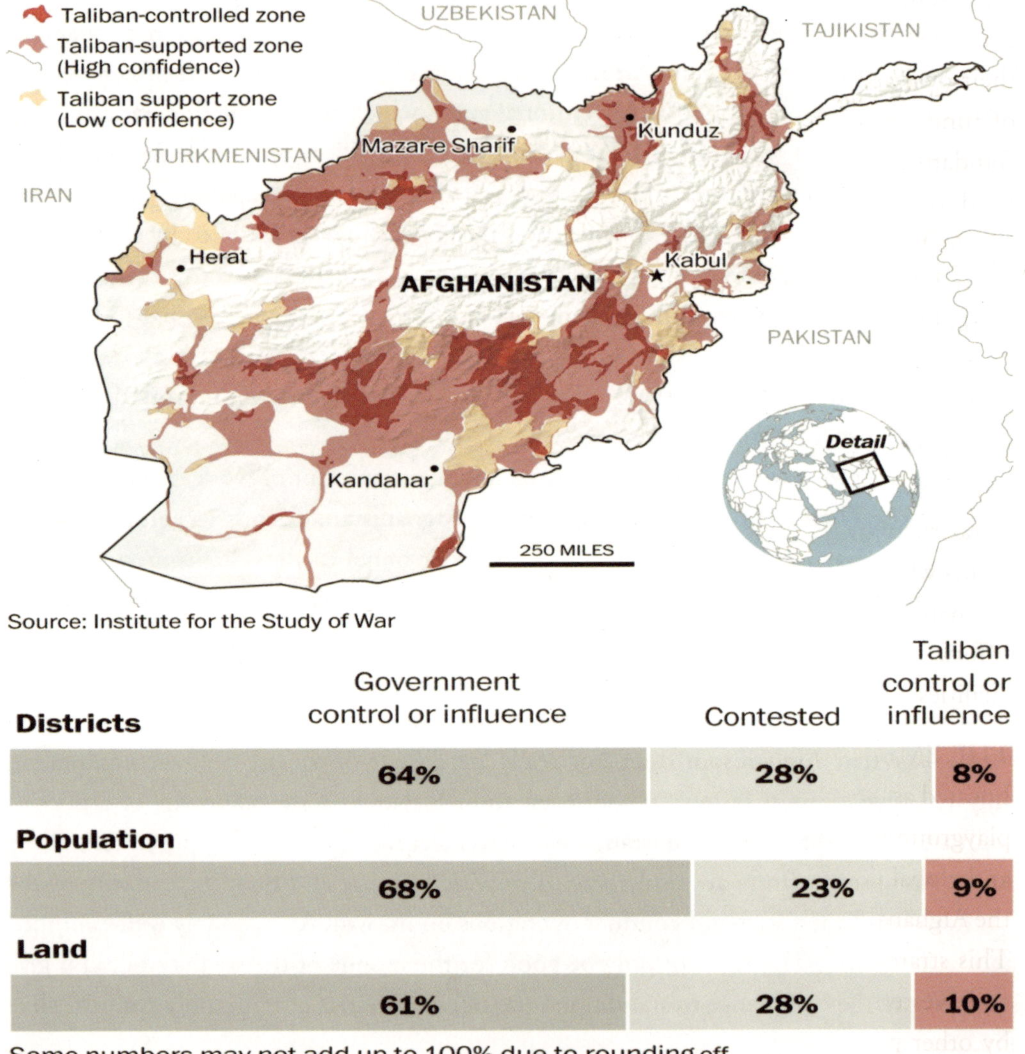

Some numbers may not add up to 100% due to rounding off.

Source: Special Inspector General for Afghanistan Reconstruction THE WASHINGTON POST

Besides rejigging politics and revitalising the security services, the third critical component of securing Afghanistan is economy. The drawdown, which has seen many of the foreigners (civilian and military) exiting the country, and coupled with the uncertain security situation, has had a very severe impact on the Afghan economy. The country is nowhere close to being self-sustaining. Afghanistan will require huge amounts of foreign assistance—budgetary, military and project implementation—over at least another decade or two, before its economy can stand on its own feet. Any premature cut-off of aid could easily see the bottom fall off the Afghan State. Although donor fatigue is entirely understandable, more so given the mounting economic difficulties in many of the donor countries, the money being given to Afghanistan needs to be seen as an investment in their own security. And while strict vigil needs to be kept to ensure there is no wastage of funds, much less any skimming of aid, there also needs to be greater realism that standards of financial probity that exist in mature democracies and efficient States will need to be relaxed somewhat while dealing with a country like Afghanistan.

As much as continued foreign assistance will be an essential condition for ensuring the stability, even survival, of the Afghan State, this assistance will have to be well directed to build Afghanistan's economic potential. Afghanistan's geographical location, at the crossroads of West, Central and South Asia, is a unique resource that can make it a regional trade and transit hub. But for this to happen, greater attention will have to be paid to infrastructure development, which not only allows connectivity through Afghanistan, but also allows Afghanistan to tap its own natural resources for its development. The infrastructure development will have to include irrigation networks and hydel power plants which will in turn ensure an agricultural revival and consequently, help in curbing the narcotics trade, which has been one of the factors behind the Islamist insurgency. Efforts will also need to be made to promote skill development and improve education facilities so that the Gen Next of Afghans can participate in the global economy.

THE EMERGING GREAT GAME

Located as it is at the crossroads of Central, South and West Asia, Afghanistan has been the playground for Great Games even before the term itself was coined. For centuries, regional and global powers have competed for influence, often at great expense to themselves and the Afghans. One Great Game's end is often enough the beginning of another Great Game. This strategic dynamic is once again playing out with the prolonged 'end-game' of US and Western presence in Afghanistan being accompanied by the unending manoeuvring by other players—Pakistan, Iran, Russia, China, and to an extent Saudi Arabia, Qatar, and Central Asian States—to secure their interests and take pole position when the next Great Game begins. The tangled web of competing and converging interests—almost as complicated as the one in Syria—and shifting alliances between various players has only added to the complexity of the task of bringing peace and stability to Afghanistan. The hapless Afghans have been reduced to mere bystanders whose fate will be decided by cynical and callous strategic calculations carried out in capital cities of both regional and global powers.

The most stunning example of this was the recent trilateral meeting in Moscow—the third one, actually, between these three countries but the first to be revealed—between Russia, China and Pakistan on the future of Afghanistan, without Afghanistan having any say in what was being deliberated or decided. In many ways, therefore, it is not so much what happens inside Afghanistan in the political, economic and security domain, but more of what happens outside Afghanistan, in the conference rooms of regional and extra-regional powers that will determine the future course of events. If anything, even the politics, economics and security of Afghanistan is being decided outside Afghanistan. This, in a sense is the real tragedy of Afghanistan and the primary reason why peace and security is so elusive.

THE TRUMP CARD

A lot will, of course, depend on the decisions taken by the incoming Trump administration in Washington. Until now, there is no clarity on what the policy of the new administration will be. While there are some indications that Trump will stay the course and not abandon Afghanistan, there is also a feeling that he might just reach the conclusion that no real good is going to come from staying on and that a totally new policy needs to be adopted. The efficacy of US decision to stay or scoot will depend in large measure on another, and perhaps more onerous decision—will the US continue to 'incentivise' Pakistan, but without any solid plan to also 'dis-incentivise' Pakistan's bad behaviour, or will the US stop mollycoddling Pakistan and start turning the screws real tight to force compellence on Pakistan? If the US continues to repeat the mistakes of the last fifteen years by only holding carrots and not wielding the sticks then it will tantamount to reinforcing failure.

In such an event, it will make little difference to the situation in Afghanistan whether US troops stay or leave. On the other hand, if the US makes a break with the decade-and-a-half-old failed policy on Pakistan, and takes the gloves off while dealing with Pakistan's double-dealing, then there is some chance of success. Most Americans know how Pakistan has been double-dealing them but refrain from taking any strong step since it could lead to a severance in relations with an unstable, Islamic, nuclear-armed country. But strangely, the US had no compunctions in taking on a great power like Russia and imposing sanctions, but has been chary of taking similar action against a tottering, middle-level power like Pakistan, which has been responsible for the death of a couple of thousand American soldiers.

Be that as it may, the real question is whether the strategic fatigue brought on by the seemingly unending 'longest war' in American history is now being replaced by strategic disinterest because of changing priorities and new hotspots that seem to be capturing the mind-space—ISIS, South China Sea and the whole China question, trade issues and so on? If so, then it will be a matter of time before the US disengages from Afghanistan. This will mean that the Western economic and military support will be reduced to a trickle. There is little doubt that such an event will sound the death knell of the Afghan State. The resulting vacuum will be filled either by the Taliban or could see Afghanistan descend into chaos, something that will once again make it a preferred destination for jihadists from around the world, who are being squeezed in the Middle East and other countries. The repercussions of such a development on regional security are extremely negative and will radiate in Central, West and South Asia, putting paid to ambitious projects like the Chinese One Belt One Road (OBOR) and Russia's Eurasian Economic Union.

Table 11. Post-Taliban U.S. Assistance to Afghanistan

(appropriations/allocations in $ millions)

Fiscal Year	2002	2003	2004	2005	2006	2007	2008	2009	2010	2011	2012	2013	2014	2015	2016	2017*
ESF	117	239	894	1280	473	1211	1400	2088	3346	2168	1837	1850	851	1225	1200	1000
DA	18.3	42.5	153	170	185	167	149	.4	.3	0	0	0				
GHCS	7.5	49.7	33.4	38	41.5	101	63	58.	92	70	0	0				
Refugee Accounts	160	61	63	47	42	54	44	77	82	65	99	13				
Food Aid	206	74	99	97	108	70	231	82	32	19	0.6	0				
IDA	197	86	11	4	0	0	17	27	30	66	61	14				
INCLE	60	0	220	709	216	252	308	484	589	400	324	6.1	225	325	250	185
NADR	44	34.7	67	38.	18.2	37	27	49	58	69	65	54		43.5	38	37.6
IMET	0.2	0.4	0.7	1.0	1.0	1.2	1.7	1.4	1.8	1.6	2	0.8	.51	1.4	1.2	0.8
FMF	57	191	414	397	0	0	0	0	0	0	0	0				
Other	33	23	36	18	0.2	0.1	21	5	5.8	7.4	8	0				
DOD—ASSF	0	0	0	995	1908	7406	2750	5607	9167	10619	9200	5124	4727	4109	3652	3448
DOD—CERP	0	0	40	136	215	209	488	551	1000	400	400	200	30	15		
Infrastructure Fund	0	0	0	0	0	0	0	0	0	299	400	325	199	0		
Business Task Force	0	0	0	0	0	0	0	14	59	239	242	179	64	5		
DOD—CN	0	0	72	225	108	291	193	230	392	376	421	372				
DOD—Other	7.5	165	285	540	0	0	0	0	0	0	0	0				
DEA Counternarc	0.6	2.9	3.7	17	23.7	20	41	19	0	0	0	0				
Total U.S. Assistance	909	970	2392	4712	3339	9818	5732	9292	14854	14800	13058	8084	6097	5725	5165	4672

Sources and Notes: Prepared by Curt Tarnoff, Specialist in Foreign Assistance. Department of State budget, SIGAR reports, and CRS calculations. Does not include USG operational expenses (over $5 billion since 2002). Food aid includes P.L.480 Title II and other programs. "Other" = Office of Transition Initiatives, Treasury Assistance, and Peacekeeping. ESF = Economic Support Funds; DA = Development Assistance; GHCS = Global Health/Child Survival; FMF = Foreign Military Financing; NADR = Nonproliferation, Anti-Terrorism, De-Mining, and Related: IMET = International Military Education and Training; INCLE = International Narcotics and Law Enforcement; ASSF = Afghan Security Forces Funding; IDA = International Disaster Assistance. Includes stipulated levels in FY2016 Consolidated Appropriation (P.L. 114-113). *Denotes Administration request.

CHINA'S CALCULUS

The Chinese have had a virtual free ride in Afghanistan so far. They have indulged in tall talk of their investments in Afghanistan but in reality have so far not invested more than a few million dollars. And yet, the Chinese have managed to manoeuvre themselves into a pivotal role in deciding the future of Afghanistan. By allowing the Pakistanis to front for them and by ensuring that they have Pakistan's back covered, the

Chinese game plan is based on making Pakistan the fulcrum of their Afghan policy. Their interest is partly stated—to stabilise the region, especially its ally Pakistan, by promoting trade, investment and connectivity, which in turn will help to rein in the rise of Islamic radicalism that is also a threat for China—and partly unstated—to ensure that the Americans do not get to establish a permanent presence in Afghanistan. To a great extent, the Chinese have allowed the Pakistanis to lead them by the nose on Afghanistan and have bought the Pakistani story on engaging with the Taliban even at the expense of earning the disapproval of the Afghan government. Clearly, the Chinese, along with the Russians, have bought into the story of IS making a base in Afghanistan, which they see as an imminent threat to their own security. The Pakistani advocacy seems to have convinced both China and Russia that only the Taliban can ensure that the IS is not able to consolidate. This is so much nonsense because not only are the so-called IS elements in Afghanistan nothing more than a breakaway faction of the Taliban, but also that there is very little to choose between the IS and Taliban when it comes to medieval barbarity and worldview.

RUSSIAN REDUX

Ostensibly, the Russians too are using the ISIS excuse to enter into a virtual alliance with the Pakistanis and Chinese on Afghanistan. Although Russia's concerns about ISIS expansion in Afghanistan are entirely understandable, these concerns are highly inflated and therefore, quite disingenuous. The Russian game plan is clearly something else. A recent interview of the Russian point man on Afghanistan, Zamir Kabulov, to Anadolu Agency suggests either muddled thinking or something else. Kabulov clearly contradicts himself when he first calls the Taliban a local force that has given up the global jihadist idea, and later admits that there are groups and elements in the Taliban which share an ideological affinity with the ISIS, cryptically adding that 'today the Taliban is predominantly a local force'. While the interview confirms that the Russians have a very benign, even positive, view of the Taliban (there were unconfirmed reports in the past of the Taliban emir Mullah Mansour having visited Russia and even meeting President Putin), the thrust of his interview was, however, on the US presence in Afghanistan and he pretty much blames the US for not just the drug mafia in Afghanistan, but also insinuates that the US might have something to do with the ISIS presence in Afghanistan. He raises questions about US objectives and expresses his reservations over the number of US bases in Afghanistan.

By all accounts, the ISIS angle is only a sideshow for the Russians in Afghanistan. The real objective seems to be to reassert its role and influence in the region and once again, become a player instead of being a bystander that it had been for over a decade. Linked to this is the new, or rather revived, compact with the Chinese, who seem to be exercising a greater influence on the Russians to forge a common policy on Afghanistan with Pakistan as a fulcrum of this emerging alliance. The Russian assertiveness is causing disquiet in the Central Asian States, who fear that Russian forays in the region are part of a plan for resource grab, including in Afghanistan. Most of all, Russians seem to have joined the strategic competition with the US and would not be averse to seeing the US bow out in ignominy—a payback, or at least poetic justice, for what the erstwhile Soviet Union had to suffer for its Afghan misadventure in the 1980s.

IRAN'S INFLECTION POINT

Iran's role is also critical in Afghanistan, more so because the old assumption of Iranian antipathy towards Taliban has been turned on its head. It is now quite apparent that the Iranians have maintained very close contact with the Taliban, something that is borne out by the fact that the now deceased Taliban chief Mansour was 'droned' in Balochistan, while he was returning from a still unexplained visit to Iran. The Iranian approach to Afghanistan and Taliban is both tactical and strategic. Given the extremely tense relations between Iran and the US, and the fact that the US was unable to make use of the opportunity offered by 9/11 and the Iranian cooperation to their war effort in Afghanistan to improve ties with Iran, it was quite natural for Iran to be seriously concerned over US presence in Afghanistan and to buy some insurance against this. This is one of the reasons why they maintained contact with the Taliban—enemy's enemy is a friend.

The emergence of ISIS also forced the Iranians to continue with their liaison with the Taliban. Quite understandably, at a time when Iran was fully occupied with trying to keep the US at bay and also defeat the ISIS (an existential threat), it made little sense to open another front against the Taliban. This was something that suited the Taliban as well. Even so, there is a fundamental problem between the Iranians and Taliban which will erupt as soon as they are free from other more pressing engagements. As a Shia State, Iran is anathema for the Sunni extremist Taliban. This sectarian divide can be bridged temporarily but not permanently. For now at least, the Iranians are dealing with the Taliban over the head of the Afghan government, something that undermines the latter and empowers the former. This equation might change if the Taliban actually manage to assume power in Afghanistan because then, unless they temper their anti-Shi'ism (a theoretical impossibility because if the Taliban could do this they would not remain Taliban), they will get into conflict with Iran.

PERNICIOUS PAKISTAN

The real villain of Afghanistan has been and remains Pakistan. Despite all the talk from the Pakistanis, such as: 'Afghanistan's enemy is Pakistan's enemy', 'It is in Pakistan's interest to have a stable, secure and peaceful Afghanistan', 'Pakistan backs an Afghan-led, Afghan-owned peace process', and other such palpably false formulations—the fact of the matter is that Pakistan has never let go of its policy of reducing Afghanistan into a virtual vassal State, control its foreign and defence policy (especially in relation to India) and exploit its geography and resources for its own benefit. These policy objectives have not changed and until that happens, Pakistan's inimical Afghan policy will continue to bleed Afghanistan. With Chinese and Russian backing, and given the steady recession of US and the West from Afghanistan, Pakistan is only becoming more insincere in its declarations and emboldened in its aggressive, terrorism-based policy inside Afghanistan to bring that country to its knees.

THE INDIAN INTENTION

The Indian policy on Afghanistan is perhaps the most Afghan friendly. Unlike most other players in Afghanistan, the prism from which India sees Afghanistan is an Afghan-centric one in which India's interests converge with the interests of Afghans. India is not seeking to steal an advantage over any other country, nor is it seeking to use Afghan resources or its location to needle any adversary or gain some strategic foothold. Instead, the Indian policy is based on a simple fact: an unstable, chaotic Afghanistan or even an Afghanistan which is run by Islamists and terror groups is neither in the interest of Afghans nor in the interest of India. Instability or Islamist ascendancy in Afghanistan will destabilise the entire region and therefore, everything possible needs to be done to secure and stabilise the Afghan government.

Until a few years ago, the Indian focus was on development assistance to build and improve Afghan capacities to handle their own affairs. But, over the last couple of years, India has also started gravitating towards supplying much-needed weapon systems that will assist the Afghan security forces to defend themselves and protect the citizenry. Obviously, there are inherent limitations—geographical, logistical and financial—to what India can do in Afghanistan. But keeping within these limitations, India is trying to do the maximum possible to bolster the Afghan government.

STILL NOT A LOST CAUSE

Afghanistan is not by any stretch of imagination a lost cause. This is not to deny that the challenge of securing and stabilising Afghanistan is going to be an uphill task. But it is eminently doable and, what is more, desirable.

Peace in Afghanistan will however be contingent on two things: the first and necessary condition is for the international community to assist Afghanistan's security forces and provide the necessary economic assistance, and for the Afghan politicians to get their act together and make the NUG work; the second and sufficient condition is to ensure that external interference, and especially external support to Islamist terror groups, is eliminated. Both these conditions are easier said than done. But these have to be done in tandem because managing the internal issues without addressing the external dimension is not going to work, just as getting the external dimension right without doing anything to fix the internal issues will also not solve the problem.

The external players need to understand that strategic myopia in Afghanistan is a recipe for disaster, as all those countries which flirted with Islamists to settle scores with the Soviet Union have found to their expense. It will be no different for Russia and China, and even Iran, if for short-term advantage, they make a deal with the devil (read Taliban and other Islamist groups) in Afghanistan. The trouble, however, is that these lessons are generally learnt only after the blowback starts. The US National Security Advisor, Zbigniew Brzezinski, who was so gung-ho about the Afghan mujahideen famously claimed: 'Which was more important in world history? The Taliban or the fall of the Soviet empire? A few over-excited Islamists or…the end of the Cold War.' Similar myopia is guiding the policy of most countries regarding Afghanistan nearly forty years later.

These countries would do well to remember that the Cold War has restarted, albeit in a different context, and the 'over-excited Islamists' are wreaking havoc and destroying societies and States, including in Europe, and pose a global challenge today. Any compromise with the Taliban and any abandonment of the Afghan State will only add to the strength of the Islamists and boomerang on the very countries that prop them up for gaining some advantage over other countries. If this realisation strikes roots, the Afghan problem can be solved without too much trouble; but if this realisation does not dawn, then Afghanistan will probably go under, but it would not go down alone.

***

Lt Gen Ravi Sawhney, PVSM, AVSM (Retd), is a former Deputy Chief of the Army Staff. A post graduate in Defence and Security Planning from the Royal College of Defence Studies, London, he was involved in conceptual development of strategies at senior levels as the Director of Military Intelligence and was subsequently responsible for the overall coordination of the deployment of Indian Army troops at various UN missions. Post retirement, he was deputed by the Government of India to monitor the situation in Afghanistan. He is presently a Dean of Defence Studies in Vivekananda International Foundation, New Delhi.

Sushant Sareen is an alumnus of the Delhi School of Economics and a former civil service officer (Railways), who resigned from service to be an observer and analyst of political situations in South Asia, specialising on Pakistan, Afghanistan and by extension, terrorism. Sareen has variously worked as editor, consultant and director in various think tanks and has authored many papers, besides authoring a book titled *The Jihad Factory—Pakistan's Islamic Revolution in the Making*. He has also been invited to deliver talks at many premier institutions. Presently he is a Senior Fellow at the Vivekananda International Foundation, New Delhi.

Daring to Dream: Restoring Connectivity in South Asia for Regional Development

TARIQ KARIM

Abstract

In this article, the author makes a strong case for restoring connectivity in the Bangladesh–Bhutan–India–Nepal (BBIN) subregion in South Asia. He draws a parallel to this newly-defined subregion having been analogous to what was historically known as the Bengal Presidency during Britain's colonial rule over the Indian subcontinent. He makes the case that the seamless matrix of connectivity that imperial Britain developed and used for its own purpose of extraction, synergising the river system of the water-dominated geo-terrain with rail and road connections, was akin to an organic circulatory system that enabled the Bengal Presidency to become the most developed and richest of its colonial domains. The author advocates that reviving the template of connectivity that imperial Britain had left behind in 1947, and which gave pre-eminence to river connectivity that was grievously disrupted in the mid-1960s, would enable the BBIN subregion in South Asia to once again become an environment-friendly yet fast growing and important driver of economic growth and development. This would enable the BBIN subregion to meaningfully address the goals of eradicating unemployment and poverty, counter marginalisation and radicalisation of peoples feeling left out, stop and then roll back environmental degradation, effectively contribute to reducing global warming and lessen its deleterious effects on climate change, and act as an effective bridge between the South Asian and Southeast and East Asian regions, for the greater prosperity of all peoples. The partitioned nation-states of the subregion can be ecologically and economically reintegrated without compromising their respective sovereign and independent status.

FROM BEING INTEGRATED TO BECOMING DISCONNECTED

The geographical landmass known historically as the Indian subcontinent was, for well over three millennia, perhaps one of the most integrated regions of the world. Ironically, a little over three centuries of colonial rule, from the advent of the Portuguese conquering Goa in 1510 until Britain quitting India as colonial power on 14 August 1947, succeeded in partitioning India into three entities and making each look on the others with hostility bordering on enmity. These post-colonial 'neo-Westphalian' nation-states, have remained largely hostage to the 'partition syndrome' since then. The newly-created borders that separated, and defined, their sovereign territorial spaces also progressively and effectively restricted free movement of people and goods across the hitherto integrated geographical space. By the mid-1960s, their ruling dispensations had physically severed road, rail and river routes that had for long served as an organically integrated circulatory system of communication for them, particularly most severely to the detriment of the eastern part that was known as the Bengal Presidency under British rule.

The Bengal Presidency that was the largest of the colonial administrative subdivisions of British India with its seat in Calcutta (now Kolkata) extended from the present-day Khyber–Pakhtunkhwa of Pakistan in the west to Burma, Singapore and Penang in the east[1]. Most of this Presidency's extended territories were gradually incorporated into other British Indian provinces or crown colonies. With partition of Bengal in 1905, Dacca (now Dhaka) became the capital and Shillong the summer capital of the truncated province, but with the reorganisation of Bengal in 1912, the reorganised Presidency embraced initially the provinces of United Bengal, Bihar, Orissa and Assam.

The *East India Gazetteer* described Bengal as 'the granary of the Indies', from where large quantities of rice were exported, along with coir, coconut oil, coconut tree produce, cowries, salt fish, turtle fish, sugar, hardware, broadcloth, cutlery, silk stuffs, coarse cottons, tobacco, etc. [2]Bernier, the seventeenth-century physician and traveller, in his historiography of his travels had also described Bengal as the granary of the east, and of its silk industry he wrote: 'There is in Bengal such a quantity of cotton and silk, that the kingdom may be called the common storehouse for these two kinds of merchandise, not of Hindoustan or the Empire of the Great Mogol only, but of all the neighbouring kingdoms, and even of Europe'.[3]

The British Bengal Presidency, including Assam, in 1874, had an area of 248,374 square miles and a population of nearly 67 million. Bengal alone accounted for one-third of the total population of British India at that time, and yielded over one-third of the aggregate revenues of the Indian Empire[4]. 'The territory teemed with every product of nature, from the fierce beasts and irrepressible vegetation of the tropics, to the stunted barley which the till-man reared, and the tiny furred animal which he hunted within sight of the unmelting snows. Tea, indigo, turmeric, lac, waving white fields of the opium—poppy, wheat and innumerable grains and pulses, pepper, ginger, betel nut, quinine and many costly spices and drugs, oil seeds of sorts, cotton, the silk mulberry, inexhaustible crops of jute and other fibres, timber, from the feathery bamboo and coronetted palm to the iron-hearted *tal* tree—in short, every vegetable product which fed and clothed a people, and enabled it to trade with foreign nations, abounded[5].'

Before the Partition and the Independence in 1947, the Bengal Presidency had the highest GDP and Shillong, the summer capital, boasted the highest per capita GDP. Following the Partition, the Indian subcontinent transformed overnight from having been the most integrated region for eons, into arguably perhaps, the least integrated region in the world[6].

TOWARDS ECONOMIC REINTEGRATION

If trade and connectivity are handmaidens to each other with the latter actively promoting exchange of ideas, goods and services, it follows axiomatically that disruption to connectivity will translate into disruption of trade and people-to-people exchanges. Land, rail and riverine connectivity continued to remain hostage to negative politics until very recently. Following a bold initiative by Bangladesh, in December 1985, leaders of seven South Asian countries came together to form the South Asian Association for Regional Cooperation (SAARC). By 1995, recognising that SAARC as originally conceived was going nowhere, Bangladesh, once more, took the initiative and in 1996 proposed to the SAARC summit the adoption of subregional approach to moving forward gradually to embrace all countries. The entire region could be conceived of as comprising three subregions: Bangladesh, Bhutan, India and Nepal (BBIN) as the eastern subregion; India, Maldives and Sri Lanka (IMS) as the southern subregion, and Afghanistan, India and Pakistan (AIP) comprising the western subregion. If one subregion was ready to move forward together on some areas and demonstrate palpably successful model of cooperation in any given priority sector, it might attract other subregions to join or emulate.

The eastern subregion had displayed inclination to move forward, following two treaties that were signed between Bangladesh and India in 1996-97. It became obvious that at least three contiguously located neighbours needed to first establish a modicum of good bilateral relations amongst themselves before those three (or four) sets of good bilateral relations could be triangulated (or quadrangulated) into a form of subregional cooperative grouping. This could expand through a process of accretion in specifically agreed areas as deemed comfortable by the partner countries.

INDIA–BANGLADESH RELATIONS ASSUME CRITICAL IMPORTANCE

In this schema, getting India–Bangladesh relations right was a sine qua non. The two countries set about determinedly attempting to do this in 2009. The Joint Communiqué at the end of the visit of Bangladesh Prime Minister to India in January 2010 set out the road map for the two countries to follow in their efforts to set right all that had been wrong earlier[7]. India and Bangladesh relations forged forward steadily and remarkably, with the two countries amicably and peacefully finalising demarcation of their land and maritime boundaries, and signing and operationalising coastal shipping and maritime shipping agreements, while the long-existing Inland Water Protocol has included additional ports of call, offering synergy with the new coastal and maritime shipping connectivity. In February 2017, the first shipping container vessel carried goods from India across the coastal waters of the Bay of Bengal and then travelled upstream to disgorge cargo at inland water port of Pangaon in Bangladesh[8].

These are phenomenal developments, considering what had existed (or rather, not existed) less than a decade ago. The number of land customs stations has expanded exponentially, with three having been upgraded into Integrated Check Posts (ICPs). Electricity grids on bilateral basis have been connected between Bhutan and India, Bangladesh and India and Nepal and India, and power trade has commenced between the three countries (with Nepal and Bangladesh being power deficit countries). Several joint ventures between Bangladesh and India to generate power for Bangladesh are currently underway. Talks are ongoing now for a tri-nation joint venture cooperation between Bhutan, India and Bangladesh for hydroelectricity generation and shared distribution of power. Bangladesh is also sharing its surplus but fallow bandwidth for augmenting information and communication technology (ICT) capacity in north-east India.

The convincing rationale behind these initiatives was the deepening realisation that economic development was imperative for growth and for fending off anti-State movements by radical and militant elements; that there was an urgent need for creating new jobs every year, given the notorious impatience of youth who needed to be offered opportunities of positively channeling their energies[9]. To be able to address these compelling challenges, leaders of the eastern subregion (BBIN) realised the need to revive and reinstate the connectivity that had existed before the British left.

ROAD CONNECTIVITY

While in most other regional groupings, whether European, South African or Southeast Asian models, motor vehicles of one member country can trundle across borders freely carrying people, goods and services, this was not so in the case of the SAARC countries. The first concrete and, for the region, revolutionary breakthrough occurred when the BBIN subregional grouping, in early 2015 decided to sign onto the BBIN–Motor Vehicles Agreement (MVA). This seminally important document symbolises the beginning of the revival of historic connectivity corridors that had existed prior to 1947. The BBIN-MVA has been ratified by Bangladesh, India and Nepal and is pending final ratification by the Upper House of Bhutan's parliament before it becomes fully operational. In the meantime, container trucks have made the trial run from Chittagong to Delhi, carrying consignment of goods for the Indian market. The visionary and farsighted leadership of Bangladesh to opening connectivity to Bhutan, India and Nepal opens new vistas of cooperative development for the subregion as well as bringing the operationalising of India's Act East policy closer to reality. Once the BBIN–MVA's full ratification process by all four countries is completed, work on the SAARC Corridor–4, stretching across Kathmandu (Nepal)–Kakarbita (Nepal)–Panitanki (India)–Phulbari (India)–Banglabandha (Bangladesh)–Mongla–Chittagong (Bangladesh); and the SAARC Corridor-8, linking Thimpu (Bhutan)–Phuentsoling (Bhutan) Jaigon (India)–Changrabandha (India)–Burimari (Bangladesh)–Mongla/Chittagong (Bangladesh) can be fast tracked and operationalised. The existing relations of bonhomie between Bangladesh and India, if extended to embrace Myanmar in trilateral cooperation, would induce the completion of much remaining work on Asian Highway-2 linking north-east India–Myanmar, and the Kaladan Multi-Modal Transit Transport Project that would reconnect Mizoram (Mobu)-Moreh (Myanmar).

RAIL CONNECTIVITY

The four BBIN countries have also commenced discussions on similar BBIN Rail Connectivity Agreement based on SAARC Regional Rail Agreement template, with the aim of reviving and activating rail routes that had existed and connected Bangladesh and India, and to some extent Nepal, until severed following the 1965 India–Pakistan War. Of eight rail links that had existed between Bangladesh and India but had been severed, three are in operation once again, while work is in progress for upgradation, unification of gauges and restoration of services on others. Once completed and fully operationalised, the distance in the Kolkata–Agartala route will be shortened from1590 kms to 499 kms.

The larger, more ambitious South Asia–Southeast Asia Rail Corridor of 4,430 kms, from Kolkata to Ho Chi Minh City, is still on the drawing board. It faces seemingly insurmountable challenges, with 2,493 kms missing links, incompatible track gauges, between regions and within each region that have to be made uniform or compatible for smooth cross passageway, since transshipment is costly[10].

RIVER CONNECTIVITY IS OF PRIMARY IMPORTANCE–VISUALISING AN ORGANIC APPROACH

The best, most efficient and most optimal way forward in restoring connectivity is to adopt an organic approach. The BBIN subregion (more or less corresponding to the pre-Partition Bengal Presidency of British India) should consider reviving the connectivity in this subregion, which conforms best to the geo-morphology of the terrain. In the largely alluvial plains of a region that is dominated by the waters of its innumerable mighty eastern Himalayan rivers, and where even the hills are essentially soft alluvial foothills of the higher Himalayan range, the countries have spent countless billions to date in trying to build and maintain highways. However, it is extremely difficult to maintain round-the-year operational highways conforming to international transportation standards, when the monsoonal climate, geo-morphology and contours of the terrain, so dominated by waters, militate against these roads being all-weather highways. The British colonial rulers had taken full cognizance of these challenges and put in place a superb organic system of communications, synergising the advantages offered by the rivers as arterial waterways, the railways that formed a network analogous to the human body's venous system, linking with junctions that became hubs at major river points; with the roads comprising the capillaries that transported goods, services and peoples to and from the farthest nooks and crannies of the land to these hubs or intersection points. The efficient use of such a synergised and organically meshed communication system is what made the Bengal Presidency perhaps the richest, not only in British India, but perhaps, among all Britain's crown possessions. Where mighty rivers were un-crossable for the railways or roads, river ferries took over seamlessly. Now, we have the capacity and capability of building bridges over these rivers.

In terms of fuel economy and carbon emission, river transportation is most efficient, reducing fuel costs by close to 60 per cent and carbon-emissions by around 65 per cent. In a visionary and far-sighted decision led from the top by Prime Minister Modi, the Indian parliament adopted The National Waterways Act, 2016 unanimously, to give a fillip to moving towards greater and wider use of inland waterways as main arterial system of connectivity. The rationale given for this decision, which would have far-reaching implications, was that developing these waterways 'will enhance the industrial growth and tourism potential of the hinterland along the waterway. This will also provide an additional, cheaper and environment-friendly mode of transportation throughout the country…inland water transport is considered as the most cost effective and economical mode of transport from the point of view of fuel efficiency…one horse power can carry

4000 kg load in water, whereas, it can carry 150 kg and 500 kg by road and rail respectively. Further, in a study as highlighted by the World Bank, 1 litre of fuel can move 105 ton-km by inland water transport, whereas the same amount of fuel can move only 85 ton-km by rail and 24 ton-km by road. Studies have shown that emission from container vessels range from 32-36 gCO_2 per ton-km, while those of road transport vehicles (heavy duty vehicles) range from 51-91gCO_2 per ton-km[11].' Water transport is 'not only environment friendly but also much cheaper as it costs Rs 1.5 per km to carry the cargo by road, while the same stands at Re 1 by rail, whereas through waterways it reduces to only 25 paisa per km…India has about 50,000 km of waterways, which on development will change the face of India, and that the government is committed to aggressively work to develop these as the environment friendly mode of transport, which is bound to decrease significantly the huge 18 per cent logistics cost in India[12].'

What is applicable for India is equally applicable to the BBIN subregion, particularly for Bangladesh, whose landmass is finitely limited, totally dominated by its myriad water bodies and crammed with a burgeoning population that makes it the most densely populated country in the world today. Bangladesh, of all the countries in this subregion, still depends the most on river connectivity serving its people. The present government in Bangladesh places great importance to reviving river navigability and restoring river health, and some major river routes of historical use and importance have been restored recently. Voices in Nepal are acknowledging the logic of the above. A former water resources minister of Nepal, advocating restoration of inland navigation stated: 'If Nepal, Bhutan, Sikkim, Arunachal, Meghalaya, Mizoram or Uttarakhand can see that containers from Europe or Japan can come to their doorsteps at Chatra or Chisapani and similar places elsewhere—and they could benefit from reduction in the cost of their goods—there would be that much more reason for them to agree to building the Kosi, Karnali, Pancheswar and other water storage facilities that would also provide flood control, electricity and other multipurpose side benefits'[13]. Bhutan too looks upon the rivers as integral to their concerns about their fragile and vulnerable ecology, and would like to see river connectivity, that once used to exist between Bhutan and India–Bangladesh, restored now as this would take pressure away from over-dependence on roads that requires cutting into and denuding their still largely pristine mountainous and hilly landscape.

Tragically, following the 1965 War between India and Pakistan, the extensive river connectivity that had inseparably linked the peoples and lands of the erstwhile Bengal Presidency and now the BBIN subregion was grievously disrupted. Plying of ships between Allahabad–Calcutta–Narayanganj and Guwahati–Narayanganj–Allahabad abruptly ceased. With these services being stopped, the regular annual dredging that used to be done to maintain and keep the navigable channels open and usable also ceased. These mighty rivers, effectively had become nationally segmented by the politics of partition, for which the peoples of the entire subregion (and arguably, even the larger region) are having to pay a burdensome cost today. The flourishing river economy that had made this part of the subcontinent so famously prosperous, wilted away, with upstream and downstream industries disappearing. The dumping of vast amounts of industrial and human-generated waste, due to lack of effective regulatory or governance mechanisms in place, and ill-considered interventions on the river, have translated into a huge and complex pollution challenge. The steady and cumulative piling-up of river beds with silt has made the channels of the rivers very shallow, rendering them un-navigable, and forced the waters to wresting their own passage from the mountains to the Bay by literally devouring land and expanding its breadth. The mighty Brahmaputra today is reportedly navigable only for three months in the entire year.

Reviving the rivers for connectivity as well as for restoring the river economy, will admittedly be a huge challenge because of the accumulative damage done to these rivers by over six decades of criminal neglect. It must necessarily involve engaging proactively with the people who inhabit the countless villages, towns and cities that dot both banks of each of these rivers, and restore to them a sense of ownership and pride in their shared commons. If we wish to restore navigability of these rivers, we would need to undertake systematic and planned dredging, perhaps initially on pilot basis along certain identified lengths of rivers, for restoring navigability; in the process, we would also be regaining considerable tracts of land, lost over the years to erosion, for human habitation, agriculture and commerce. The dredging and reclamation process could well spawn a huge, river-wide cottage industry for peoples of the river who could use geo-bags to be filled by dredged-up silt and then use these bags to reclaim and buttress redefined embankments. For shoring up the embankments of these rivers, inhabitants of riverine villages would find employment and livelihood. In the process, they would become effective guardians of the river, constantly monitoring the health of the river and the state of its embankments, and acting as early-warning system for protecting these embankments from damage by sudden floods. Fishing and ancillary fisheries-related industry would also be revived massively.

Reclamation of the rivers would also revive the ship-building industry that had existed and flourished in ancient times in Bengal. The great Moroccan scholar and traveller Ibn Batuta, wrote about his visit to Bengal in the fourteenth century where he 'saw numerous boats in the river carrying men and merchandise and testified to the existence of gigantic fleet of war-boats[14].' Caesaro Frederici (or Frederick Caesar), a Venetian who during his travels to the East, between 1536 and 1581, also visited Bengal, saw Chittagong as the centre of building ocean-going vessels. In the seventeenth century, the ship-building institutions of Chittagong were reported to have built a fleet of war-boats for the Sultan of Turkey. During the Mughal period, Bengal is said to have taken the lead in building ships and boats. The Mughal naval force had many ships built at Chittagong. The British Navy also used warships built at Chittagong, at least one of which comprised Nelson's victorious fleet in the famous Battle of Trafalgar in 1805. During the first half of the nineteenth century, the shipyards at Chittagong built ships up to 1000 DWT[15].'

Reclaiming the rivers could also see well-planned expansion of existing irrigation channels (that could also serve as overflow drainage channels during high season floods) and offset the current high dependency on tube wells extracting and grievously depleting, precious underground aquifers. In large tracts of West Bengal and Bangladesh, the underground aquifers have become contaminated with arsenic and salinity-infusion. In a comprehensive approach to water management and freshwater conservation, water conservation reservoirs and pondages could be created, where feasible, to augment freshwater access to people as well as for generation of run-of-the river hydroelectricity projects. Last, but not the least, ecotourism and cultural tourism along the rivers could be revived, reconnecting peoples with each other to rediscover their common heritage.

All these activities must involve the peoples of these rivers. This sort of collaborative activity would result in massive employment generation that would translate into a multiplier effect on the socio-economic matrix, enhancing security and stability of the peoples of the subregion. Opening the rivers to better and more optimised use for transportation, in turn will open new service sectors and industries. Dying rivers would be revived, progressive siltation of riverbeds would be reduced and the currently-endangered ecology would be resuscitated. The generation of hydroelectricity would also serve the purpose of rendering surplus hydrocarbon resources for intra-regional use, export abroad or strategic reserve. It would also dramatically reduce the current rate of deforestation for fuel as well as for illegal logging. Regeneration of forestry and increasing forest coverage would create new, and enhance existing, carbon-sequestration zones[16].

These goals are not pipe dreams. Given the growing consonance of political will prevailing, they are now well within the realm of the imaginable and doable, provided leaders stay the course that their vision has charted and their mandarins do their bidding with alacrity. Regional connectivity, now under process of resuscitation within the BBIN subregion, could well serve as the operationalising pathway to larger trans-regional connectivity, between South Asia and Southeast and East Asia. Even within the South Asian configuration, Sri Lanka and Maldives could join the current coastal shipping template inaugurated bilaterally between Bangladesh and India. This could be expanded to include Myanmar and Thailand as well, giving heft to the now-somnolent

Brazil, Russia, India, China and South Africa (BRICS) grouping, invigorating a Bay of Bengal community linked together symbiotically by the Bay that laps their shores. Instead of relying solely on one mode of connectivity, all these countries could optimise limited resources, by coordinating collaborative actions and deriving synergy, from the various modes available currently to them. We could conceivably envision a 'back to the future scenario' of this subregion and beyond to the east, once more reclaiming its great reputation of prosperity that it had enjoyed as the Bengal Presidency; this time not for any foreign power coming from distant shores to colonise and extract for its own gain, but for the shared and even greater prosperity of the peoples who are inhabitants of the region now and true inheritors of this wealth.

In conceptualising this intra and inter-regional connectivity agenda for shared prosperity and growth, a moot question would be: Can the Association of Southeast Asian Nations' (ASEAN) strength augment South Asian weakness and deficit? We must not lose sight here that what is a challenge within domestic context is often more of a challenge in regional/subregional context. Democracy, anywhere, is constantly a work-in-progress. Since we, in South Asia, are all practicing and functional democracies in different stages of perfection (or otherwise), ultimately the peoples must take charge of, and drive, this great connectivity project forward. All parties and leaderships across these regions must therefore, ensure that the full and meaningful success of this venture must, *ab initio* and necessarily, be transparent so that potential gains are perceptively large and worthwhile for all peoples concerned to wish to pursue this goal.

The compelling rationale behind the decisions of Conference of the Parties (COP)-21, moreover, dictate that in our own larger self-interest we should commence the transition to reviving riverine connectivity urgently on a priority basis. These compulsions are likely to become more demanding in future. Fortunately, there exists now a convergence of thinking that could, if seized and built upon, see this subregion once again being reunited ecologically and economically, even while retaining their respective separate sovereign status as independent nation-states.

***

Tariq Karim, in his diplomatic career with the Bangladesh governement, has served in various capacities in Tehran, Bonn, Bangkok and London. He has been the Deputy Chief of Mission in Beijing and New Delhi and has held ambassadorial assignments in Washington, Pretoria and Tehran. In recent past, he has been Bangladesh's High Commissioner to India with the status of a Minister of State. Having reverted to his academic interests, he is presently a Distinguished Fellow at the

Vivekananda International Foundation, New Delhi, besides being a Consultant to the World Bank on Regional Integration (South Asian Region).

END NOTES

1. https://en.wikipedia.org/wiki/Bengal_Presidency.
2. Hamilton, Walter. *The East India Gazetteer*: 'Containing Particular Descriptions of the Empires, Kingdoms, Principalities, Provinces…of Hindostan, and the Adjacent Countries'; John Murray, London, 1815, p 547 (Google books).
3. Bernier, Francois. *Travels in the Mogul Empire, AD 1656-1658,* trans. by Constable, A. (London, 1914), p 439 *op cit* http://www.columbia.edu/itc/mealac/pritchett/00islamlinks/ikram/part2_17.html
4. http://www.globalsecurity.org/military/world/bangladesh/history-uk.htm.
5. Ibid.
6. Karim, Tariq. *South Asia's Efforts at Regional Integration – Fantasy or Within the Realms of the Probable?*, East West Centre, Washington DC, 19 January 2017.
7. Ibid.
8. http://indiatoday.intoday.in/story/pangaon-port-india-to-bangladesh-first-cargo-vessel/1/886000.html.
9. Ibid.
10. Karim, Tariq. 'Connecting South Asia with Southeast Asia: a Reality Check', in *Emerging Trans-Regional Corridors. South and Southeast Asia;* ORF Global Policy Series, Yhome, K and Chaturvedy, Rajeev Ranjan (ed.). New Delhi, p 12.
11. Press Release, 9 December 2015, Press Information Bureau, Government of India (http://pib.nic.in/newsite/PrintRelease.aspx?relid=132900).
12. Nitin Gadkari, in interview to PTI; *Business Today*, 14 March 2016 (http://www.businesstoday.in/current/economy-politics/india-to-harness-50000-km-waterfront-raise-rs-70k-crore/story/230197.html).
13. Gyawali, Dipak. 'Will Inland Navigation Shift South Asia's Water Discourse Positively?', *New Spotlight News Magazine*, Vol 10. No. 3, 2 September 2016 Kathmandu (http://www.spotlightnepal.com/News/Article/Will-Inland-Navigation-Shift-South-Asia-Water-Disc.
14. From Banglapedia, national encyclopedia of Bangladesh; http://en.banglapedia.org/index.php?title=Shipbuilding_Industry.
15. Ibid.
16. Karim, Tariq. *Transboundary Rivers – Converting Challenges into Opportunities*, Paper under publication in newsletter of GB Pant National Institute of Himalayan Environment and Sustainable Development (an autonomous Institute of Ministry of Environment, Forest & Climate Change, Government of India).

Europe
Mediterranean Sea
Persia
China
Egypt
Arabia
India
Somalia
Indian Ocean
Java

India and the Indian Ocean—the Dynamics of Multiple Centralities

Vice Admiral Anil Chopra, PVSM, AVSM

Abstract

India and the Indian Ocean are interlinked by the word 'central' in many ways. India is geographically central in the Indian Ocean; the Indian Ocean is central to India's economy and prosperity; India is central to the security of the sea lanes of the Indian Ocean and the Indian Ocean itself is now central to global trade. As economic power shifts eastward, the Indian Ocean has indeed become the centre of gravity and the freight corridor for the world economy.

There is no gainsaying that the twenty-first century is the century of the seas, and the energies and strategies of nations, large and small, are focusing seawards. It is for India to take cognisance and advantage of the bounty of multiple centralities that providence has bestowed upon it, to emerge stronger and more prosperous. In recent times, New Delhi has indeed recognised the importance of the maritime dimension, but it still lacks the organisational wherewithal and coordination apparatus to aggressively pursue the Modi government's maritime vision.

The global quest for prosperity through trade, resources, markets and freedom of navigation is leading to many multinational and multilateral initiatives on maritime cooperation. However the same quest is also leading to competition and conflict, as can be seen in the South China Sea. There is a distinct trend towards enhancing naval force levels and maritime capacity-building all across the Indo-Pacific region, as the littoral nations aspire to strengthen maritime security which is seeing the beginning of territorialisation of the seas.

> *Global and regional development apart, for India in particular, the Indian Ocean is central and indeed critical for both its prosperity and its security. Surrounded by the ocean on three sides, and blocked off by the Himalayas in the north, India is essentially a huge island interacting with the world through the seas. More than 90 per cent of its trade is seaborne, and its energy security is completely dependent on safe sea lanes. Its influence, diplomacy and heft are also majorly linked to its visible and deployable sea power.*
>
> *In addition to strengthening the instruments and foundations of sea power such as the Navy, Coast Guard, ports, shipyards etc., India's immediate maritime thrust should be three-pronged. First, it must look west and south in addition to looking east, especially at the geopolitics and maritime developments in West Asia, the Persian Gulf, the Horn of Africa and the small island developing States of the southern Indian Ocean. Secondly, it must create significant military capability and infrastructure in the Andaman and Nicobar Islands. Last, but not the least, it must set in place an apex maritime body to coordinate and make policy in respect of the multifarious objectives in the maritime domain, which involves over two dozen government departments and agencies.*

The word 'central' has been increasingly used in various contexts and connotations in the recent geopolitical discourse on India's place and role in the Indian Ocean, as well as in the renewed geostrategic focus on the Indian Ocean itself. Clearly, India occupies geographical 'centrality' in the Indian Ocean Region (IOR), and it is fairly evident to most discerning observers that the Indian Ocean is also 'central' to India's prosperity and security. Further, it is now an accepted geo-economic reality that the Indian Ocean itself is 'central' to international trade, and increasingly to global maritime security.

All these 'centralities' are interlinked and merit holistic and continual examination, as India can truly emerge and rise only if its mostly continentally-focussed and sea-blind polity takes full cognisance of the extent to which India's vital interests, aspirations and ambitions are dependent on the Indian Ocean. The Modi government has certainly displayed a maritime vision and launched a number of initiatives—Sagarmala, Sagar and Mausam, to name but a few. Significance of the potentialities of the Ocean has broken through the confines of diplomatic, military, academic and journalistic circles, and does appear to have sunk into the polity at large. Should this now be translated into a 'whole-of-government' approach with cross-ministerial institutional commitment, the nation will surely reap the fruits of the bounty of maritime centralities that providence has bestowed upon it.

THE MARITIME DIMENSION

It is abundantly clear that the twenty-first century is witnessing nations more interconnected and interdependent than ever before in human history. The globalised economy with exponentially increased trade, the internet and instant communications, quick and reliable intercontinental transportation, space-based imagery and location, and even long-range precision guided munitions, just to mention a few factors, have served to shrink the planet to a point where one can now imagine humanity as a string of communities living on the shores—the 'Great Littoral', if you will—of the interconnected oceans—the 'Great Commons'—which cover 70 per cent of the Earth's surface, and belong, as yet, to no political entity.

These increasingly contested and vast oceanic spaces have thus naturally, and progressively, occupied strategic centre stage in recent times, and the twenty-first century has been aptly termed as the 'century of the seas'. It follows that maritime issues, such as boundary disputes, freedom of the seas, exclusive economic zone (EEZ) delineation, piracy, the right of innocent passage for military vessels, seabed mining rights, and the United Nations Convention on the Law of the Sea (UNCLOS) treaty itself, amongst many others, are now matters of significant interest and concern for all nations, and will occupy the energies of statesmen, sailors and diplomats alike.

The maritime revolution which began in the Iberian Peninsula with the nautical emergence of Portugal and then Spain in the fifteenth century, has progressed steadily over half a millennium of trade and conflict. It has, however, truly matured only over the last half-century, as the post-War technological boom, and rapid globalisation catalysed the use of sea for a host of human aspirations, whilst simultaneously enhancing the threats to peaceful maritime activity. The maritime dimension today impinges on all aspects of universal strategic concerns, including global prosperity and stability, regional and national security, reliable energy flows, the quest for resources and markets, food security, international crime, climate change and even the safety of oil pipelines, offshore structures and the ocean-bed cables of the internet.

With maritime interests of even landlocked nations growing rapidly, the maritime space has become increasingly crowded. On the other hand, the maritime battle space has become increasingly transparent and targetable, and given the vast expanse of the oceans, it is well nigh impossible for any power, even a hyper-power, to guarantee security and stability for its own assets and interests, let alone police the seas for others. Both threats and opportunities abound, and for powers-in-being, and those in the making, an effective and imaginative maritime strategy is indeed the need of the hour. For India, poised as it is geographically and economically, it is indeed an imperative.

THE INDIAN OCEAN'S GLOBAL CENTRALITY

'The Indian Ocean is the key to the seven seas.... In the twenty-first century, the destiny of the world will be decided upon its waters,' naval officers are inclined to frequently use this quote attributed to the strategist Alfred Thayer Mahan, who apparently articulated it a century-and-a-half ago. Irrespective of its authenticity, this was a remarkable piece of crystal-gazing to emanate from the nineteenth century as it does appear that the Indian Ocean is fast becoming the planet's geostrategic centre of gravity. It would thus only be fitting to first examine the centrality of the Indian Ocean in global affairs prior to looking at India's centrality within it, and the consequent centrality of the Ocean for India's own security and prosperity.

Indian Ocean, the third-largest ocean on the planet, is uniquely named after a single country, and is the only one which is completely landlocked to the north. It can thus be described as the navigable southern rim of the Eurasian landmass, commonly accepted as the 'heartland' of the world. Apart from the deep southern approaches, the ocean can be accessed by shipping only through a few choke points, all of which have gained tremendous strategic and economic significance; consequences of tension, let alone turmoil or closure in the Straits of Hormus, Malacca or Bab-el-Mandeb could severely affect the economies of scores of nations.

The IOR is home to almost three billion people, resident mostly in developing, conflict-ridden and poverty-stricken nations who are nonetheless rich in natural and human resources. As the global economic and demographic centres of gravity shift eastward after an interregnum of over five centuries, the Indian Ocean has emerged as the world's east-west expressway, its principal trade and energy corridor, but concurrently its most crisis-prone region in terms of both human conflict and natural disasters. It is therefore, hardly surprising that the Indian Ocean is attracting the strategic interest of the entire global community.

The Indian Ocean is today the principal highway which connects resource-hungry economies to their raw material reservoirs, and producers of goods to their ever-increasing and far-flung markets. It has overtaken the Atlantic as the world's busiest and most strategic trade corridor, carrying two-thirds of global oil shipments, half its container traffic and a third of bulk cargo. Apart from the Western Pacific, seaborne trade from other extra-regional and non-littoral regions such as the European Union, Russia, Central Asia, Western Africa and even Latin America is also increasingly transiting the Indian Ocean. In fact, about 80 per cent of the seaborne trade in the Indian Ocean is extra-regional. Much of this is headed to and from East Asia, including China, Japan, South Korea and the Association of Southeast Asian Nations (ASEAN) nations, and has thus led to the concept of the 'Indo–Pacific' region. The Indo–Pacific label emanates from a global realisation that the fast accelerating security and economic interdependencies between the Indian Ocean and the West Pacific have created a single overarching strategic system. This construct is essentially maritime in nature, as Asia's emerging, developing and developed nations intersect in the maritime sphere, increasingly using the sea for economic advantage and military posturing.

Around 80 per cent of China's and 90 per cent of both South Korea's and Japan's oil imports are shipped from the Middle East and/or Africa through the Indian Ocean. This is a huge strategic vulnerability for these extra-regional nations which is influencing their diplomacy and partnerships as well as naval capacity building. Beijing's One Belt One Road (OBOR) initiative and increasing forays of the People's Liberation Army (PLA) Navy into the IOR must also be seen through this prism, and not only as an economic thrust for markets and resources.

INDIA'S CENTRALITY IN THE INDIAN OCEAN

If geography is indeed a destiny for nations, then clearly a maritime future beckons India. Even a cursory glance at the map will underscore the physical centrality of the Indian peninsula jetting out into the vast southern ocean, neatly dividing its northern waters into the Arabian Sea and the Bay of Bengal. It is little wonder therefore that cartographers, both ancient and medieval, termed this essentially tropical ocean as the 'Indian Ocean'. India not only enjoys singularly fortunate location and position, but is also by far the largest country, both in terms of area and population, in the IOR, if one were to discount the Australian continent abutting the Ocean in its south-east extremities. Furthermore, India's vast coastline and extensive eastern and western sea-boards are ideal for maritime operations unconstrained by choke points, thus allowing free and multidirectional access to open waters—a significant advantage for naval forces breaking out into the maritime battle space.

Enabled by geography, size and population as it is, and with well-equipped and well-trained armed forces which are increasingly capable of rapid deployment, there is little doubt that a nuclear-capable India is by far the strongest military power in the region. With its blue-water navy, its mid-air refuelling assets and troops trained for expeditionary and out-of-area operations if so required, India already is and will continue to be the net security provider and stabilising power across the length and breadth of the IOR. As India slowly but surely strengthens its island assets into strategic military outposts, its capabilities for surveillance and interdiction will be unmatched. No other power, including extra-regional ones, can protect or disrupt on a sustained basis, the vital Sea Lanes of Communication (SLOCs) that criss-cross the Indian Ocean, as India can. Clearly India is 'central' to the security of the region.

Furthermore, India is also the region's largest and most diverse economy with a strong industrial and manufacturing base and an accomplished services sector operating in both the public and private domains. It has significant trade with almost all the nations of the IOR and is making considerable investments in many regional economies. In addition, New Delhi has increased its assistance and aid programmes to many of the smaller countries, including all the small island developing States (SIDS). Acknowledged as the brightest spot in the global economy, India is fast becoming a wealth-creating powerhouse, driving growth not only within itself, but across the wider canvas of the IOR. With its multi-faceted economic linkages from the eastern and southern shores of Africa in the west, through the West Asia, to the portals of the Pacific in the east, India is also 'central' to the prosperity of the IOR.

In addition to its indisputable salience to the IOR geographically, militarily and economically, India's paramount status is further amplified by its ancient civilisational linkages, its modern technological prowess, widespread cultural influence, the many-hued soft power, and not the least its moral leadership that it derives from its non-violent struggle for independence. It is apparent that India occupies pre-eminence in the Indian Ocean in myriad ways. This not only spells great opportunity but also demands responsibility. The IOR can witness prolonged stability and consequently great prosperity only if India matures into a significant benign regional power. There is simply no other country in the region that can play this role.

THE OCEAN'S CENTRALITY FOR INDIA

It would not be an exaggeration to state that the Indian Ocean provides India its vital core—prosperity and security. Sea is the medium through which India can strongly influence, shape and stabilise the regional environment towards the furtherance of its national and economic interests by the means of requisite maritime forces and infrastructure, maritime diplomacy, blue economy initiatives, and of course, provision of security to the smaller nations of the littoral. Instability in the Indian Ocean would significantly erode the growth of India's economy and pose an omnipresent threat to its security in many dimensions across the spectrum—from nuclear conflict to maritime terrorism.

95 per cent of India's trade by volume and 70 per cent by value are seaborne, and this oceanic trade accounts for almost 40 per cent of India's GDP. India's energy security is also inextricably linked to the maritime dimension. If one were to include offshore production, India is dependent on the sea for over 90 per cent of its total oil consumption, with 45 per cent of its imported Liquid Natural Gas (LNG) also coming by sea.

Over two million square kilometres in area, India's EEZ is almost two-thirds of its land mass and a potential economic powerhouse in terms of both living and non-living resources. India is already the sixth-largest fishing nation in the world, netting over four million tonnes of fish, providing livelihood to millions of people, and also exporting. Besides oil and gas, the seabed and the column of water above it contain many valuable minerals and metals. Future technologies also hold the promise of generating alternative renewable energy and distilled water from the oceans.

The sea-leg of the nuclear triad is unquestionably the most potent deterrent on which India's nuclear strategy of 'No First Use' is predicated, as it is the least vulnerable to an attack by any weapon of mass destruction. In combination with a strong blue-water navy, the submarine deterrent offers India, as classical sea power, the most effective military and diplomatic instrument of State policy—in peacetime, in crisis situations and in full-fledged conflict.

GEOPOLITICAL CONCERNS AND OPPORTUNITIES: VIEW FROM THE CENTRE

Given the nature of the Indo-Pacific geostrategic continuum, almost all geopolitical events and trends in this entire region, or the Indo-Asia–Pacific if you will, have the potential to affect India, with its multiple centralities, for better or for worse. There are significant tensions within and beyond the IOR, along with many opportunities. Whilst 'hot-spots', such as Yemen, the Horn of Africa, the Persian Gulf and Afghanistan–Pakistan, to name a few, are indeed of concern, India could leverage its centrality to paint the geopolitical canvas to its advantage in pursuance of its permanent long-term national interests.

Looking east to the South China Sea imbroglio, although it is not party to the territorial dispute, the emergent debate on the freedom of navigation (FON) is of utmost importance to India, as such freedom is vital to both its security and trade. FON essentially relates to the right of all vessels of all nations, including warships and military vessels, to freely navigate in the EEZs and the contiguous zones of any coastal State, without approval or permission of the coastal State. As a growing maritime power, India must unequivocally support the FON concept, and oppose the overt attempts of any nation to dilute this freedom. This would entail clear-eyed diplomacy both at the UN, whilst debating UNCLOS, and at the International Maritime Organization (IMO) and the International Hydrographic Organization (IHO). It would also entail the determination and resolve to continue to deploy maritime assets, as has been the case hitherto, in the now increasingly contested waters. Deployment need not only be exercises or patrols, but could take the form of presence through passage and transit.

By virtue of its centrality, and despite considerable economic opportunity beckoning from East of Malacca, India cannot however, be limited to looking and acting only East. It must not neglect to keep an eye on the waters both to its west and south, as there is much potential conflict as well as opportunity in the oceanic expanse towards these cardinals. India's maritime policy, diplomacy and strategy must constantly address the east coast of Africa, West Asia, and the SIDS of the IOR.

The often and increasingly articulated objective of the US to gradually pivot out of the West Asian quagmire, and the simultaneous increasing presence of the PLA Navy in the Arabian Sea, must clearly be factored whilst shaping New Delhi's overall maritime strategy. Reduction of US engagement in the Persian Gulf is a distinct possibility due to a combination of factors including the decline in its strategic interest stemming from growing energy independence, the military fatigue resulting from over fifteen years of deployment, President Trump's seemingly isolationist proclivities, the gradual resolution of the Syrian and Islamic State issues, and the present 'drawdown' in the force levels of the US Navy.

This possible US disengagement is coincident with China's arrival on the shores of the north-west Indian Ocean through the portals of Gwadar, shortly to be linked to its heartland through the China–Pakistan Economic Corridor (CPEC). This audacious 57 billion dollar venture affords Beijing strategic and military oversight over the Straits of Hormus, and needs to be fully assimilated by New Delhi in terms of the maritime threat and energy insecurity it implies. The increasing presence of the PLA Navy in the IOR, by way of both ships and submarines, is likely to become a permanent feature, although not immediately in any significant numbers given Beijing's preoccupations East of Malacca for the foreseeable future.

These developments should be of utmost concern to India given its massive interests in the region including energy security, the extensive diaspora and considerable commercial and business linkages and investment which can only be addressed through persistent maritime presence at sea and intensive diplomacy ashore. Given that not only nature but geopolitics too abhors a vacuum, any reluctance or vacillation on New Delhi's part will result in the growing Islamabad–Beijing combine jointly taking on the role of the principal maritime entity in the area spearheaded from Gwadar. This makes it imperative for India to increase its maritime footprint and general presence in the region. Any absence of credible rapid response capability in the waters to the west of India, would lead to both instability and insecurity.

The Chinese power play on the Makran Coast also needs to be viewed from the perspective of the ambitious and audacious OBOR or the Belt and Road Initiative (BRI) project. It is precisely at Gwadar that the controversial 'Belt' and 'Road' meet. It, of course, needs to be seen whether the faltering Chinese economy can fund the OBOR infrastructure, and whether its preoccupations and strategic concerns East of Malacca allow Beijing and PLA Navy the bandwidth to venture and persist in the IOR. Declining oil prices, struggling post-oil economies, and Shia–Sunni, Saudi–Iran and Arab–Israeli discord will also continue to exacerbate the general instability in the Persian Gulf, the Red Sea, the Gulf of Aden and the Straits of Bab-al-Mandab and Hormus, all of which could be detrimental to India's prosperity and interests. As both India and China will continue to be vastly dependent on unrestricted energy supplies from the region, there is bound to be competition for influence and goodwill with the littoral States of the Gulf Cooperation Council (GCC), Iran and Iraq.

India must build on its cultural and civilisational ties with Oman and Iran in particular. Muscat has adroitly established maritime infrastructure away from the Straits of Hormus in Salalah, and now in Duqm, both vital for maritime logistics. Similarly Chabahar is vital to India's interests in Afghanistan, Central Asia and beyond. Despite the signing of the Iranian accord with the P 5 + 1, renewed tension between the US and Iran, including the possibility of fresh sanctions could again alter the geopolitics in the region, and deserves close scrutiny. Further west, the Indian Navy has obtained significant experience in the waters of Gulf of Aden and the Horn of Africa, and its frequent visits to Djibouti and Salalah augur well for presence in the area. Once the immediate turbulence in Yemen has died down, the utility of engaging Sanaa, and recommencing the Indian Navy's traditional visits to Aden and Hudaydah in the Red Sea cannot be over emphasised.

One of New Delhi's marked successes over the last decade has been its engagement with the countries of the African east coast. Ships of the Indian Navy have increasingly and routinely visited ports and naval bases in Egypt, Eritrea, Kenya, Tanzania, Madagascar, Mozambique and South Africa. Besides a manifold increase in the knowledge of the operational environment along the waters of this vital continent, such engagement has established Navy-to-Navy ties, friendship and interoperability. With India's economic, energy and commercial interests thriving in both public and private sectors in Africa, the maritime connect must be kept alive, utilising every opportunity. Membership of the Indian Ocean Commission will go a long way in further cementing maritime ties in this region.

New Delhi's seaward gaze to the south-west must take in the island nations of the IOR—Mauritius, Seychelles, Maldives and Sri Lanka. Both the Indian Navy and the Indian Coast Guard have robust relationship with these countries, who are also being assiduously courted by China, Pakistan and extra-regional powers. India, however, has cultural, historical and ethnic linkages with all these nations, and provided New Delhi adopts a proactive approach and makes good on its promises without inordinate delays, there is no reason why these island nations would not be amongst India's most reliable supporters in the IOR.

The eastern part of the IOR, i.e. the Bay of Bengal fortuitously remains a relative oasis of oceanic calm, sandwiched between the Arabian Sea to the west and the China Seas to the east. It would clearly be in India's interest that the status quo prevails. Towards this end, New Delhi has sagaciously resolved its maritime boundary dispute with Bangladesh under the aegis of the Tribunal on the Law of the Sea (TLOS), and stepped up its maritime engagements with Myanmar, Thailand and Indonesia. Efforts to keep the Bay of Bengal free of multinational and extra-regional submarine operations are the key to stability and security in this water body. Indian diplomacy must therefore, aim to convince the aforementioned States of the Bay of Bengal littoral that neither a submarine arms race, nor hosting of extra-regional submarines would be in their overall interest in 'stability for prosperity'. By virtue of their location overlooking the choke point of Malacca, the Andaman and Nicobar Islands are of great strategic value. This considerable visibility over India's maritime capabilities and its potentialities in the Bay of Bengal and the IOR and with every likelihood of India's joint command, the Andaman and Nicobar Command, gaining full time maritime leadership, these islands have the inherent wherewithal to be a potent military and maritime trump card.

Whilst some benefit may accrue to India's north-eastern and eastern states through economic activity catalysed through the Bangladesh–China–India–Myanmar (BCIM) initiatives, this must be weighed against the likelihood of the dynamics of the same enterprise leading to militarisation of the Bay of Bengal on a permanent basis. A strategic review of BCIM is certainly required before New Delhi commits itself to some of its strategically questionable provisions, which may allow for ease of maritime access to non-IOR powers. The Bay of Bengal Initiative for Multi-Sectoral Technical and Economic Cooperation (BIMSTEC) construct however offers a more advantageous way ahead to harness the economic potentialities of the Bay of Bengal littoral.

CONCLUSION

The maritime domain in general, and the Indian Ocean in particular are indeed 'central' to India's security, growth and prosperity, as well as a prerequisite for its regional and global aspirations. Towards that end, initiatives such as the Indian Ocean Rim Association (IORA), Indian Ocean Nation States (IONS), International North South Transport Corridor (INSTC), BIMSTEC, Sagar and Sagarmala must receive continued and focused impetus. The Indian Navy in particular must have the means in terms of force levels as well as sustained funding to be both present and visible across the IOR, and must have the wherewithal to conduct active maritime diplomacy as also be the first responder for humanitarian and disaster relief (HADR) and non-combatant evaluation operations (NEO). Only then will it get acceptability as a credible net security provider in the vast oceanic spaces. In addition to the security aspects, commercial and economic activity is bound to increase manifold through the blue economy, oceanic research, deep-sea mining,

EEZ harvesting and infrastructure building for connectivity across the region. This would require greater policing of the coast and the maritime zones of India by constabularies such as the Coast Guard and the Maritime Police.

It would therefore be appropriate to conclude by strongly recommending the long overdue establishment of an apex maritime body to synergise the multifarious requirements, challenges and concerns of the maritime domain. Such an organisation is indeed central to the realisation of India's maritime potential in harnessing the resources and energy that are vital, and to underscore the criticality of India's maritime imperative. The opportunity must be seized if India is to emerge from the shadows and realise its tryst with destiny.

***

Vice Admiral Anil Chopra, PVSM, AVSM (Retd), is a former Director General of the Indian Coast Guard, who went on to be the Commander-in-Chief of the Western as well as Eastern Naval Command.

Emerging Contours of BIMSTEC

Rajeet Mitter

Abstract

India's imaginative and farsighted initiative to invite BIMSTEC leaders to the BRICS–BIMSTEC Outreach Summit in Goa in October 2016 refocused attention on the potential and prospects of BIMSTEC emerging as a viable vehicle for substantial subregional cooperation. As BIMSTEC approaches its twentieth anniversary, its inherent advantages are self-evident. It is home to 1.5 billion people amounting to 21 per cent of the world population with a combined GDP of USD 2.5 trillion. It is rich in natural and human resources and its unique geographical contiguity and access to the sea provide the opportunity for the establishment of an integrated economic space. Most significantly, it provides a critical bridge between South Asia and Southeast Asia and the emerging economic architecture of the wider Indo-Pacific region. Importantly, from India's point of view, BIMSTEC places the relatively underdeveloped north-eastern region of the country at the heart of India's Act East policy.

Yet, it is widely recognised that in twenty years, BIMSTEC has not lived up to its early high expectations and promise, particularly in terms of visible and beneficial outcomes. Many of its initial proposals have been pushed forward through other bilateral, subregional and regional initiatives leaving BIMSTEC without a clear vision for the future. Nevertheless various factors now point to an opportunity for BIMSTEC to reinvent itself and move ahead. The establishment of the BIMSTEC Secretariat in Dhaka and the appointment of its first Secretary General, have filled a huge void in its institutional structure. Secondly, the apparent dead end reached by SAARC, due to Pakistan's continual obstruction of its aims and programmes, has become all too evident, necessitating alternative avenues for furthering subregional cooperation. It is in this context that India's initiative in hosting the BRICS–BIMSTEC Outreach Summit in Goa in October 2016 was highly significant. It was a shot in the arm for BIMSTEC and the Outcome Document has become a comprehensive plan of action for the future.

The identification and pursuit of priority projects is the key to re-energising BIMSTEC. These may include early finalisation of the free trade agreement and adoption of trade facilitation measures. Other sectors that offer opportunities for substantial outcomes are connectivity, maritime cooperation, energy and counterterrorism, all of which have been highlighted in the Outcome Document. However, BIMSTEC must first also address the urgent need to strengthen the Secretariat with human and financial resources. As with other regional organisations, there is also the need to establish a special fund and tap international financial resources to execute major projects. Finally, BIMSTEC needs leadership and commitment and perhaps, India can play such a role in consonance with its Neighbourhood First policy.

India's imaginative and farsighted initiative to invite Bay of Bengal Initiative for Multi-Sectoral Technical and Economic Cooperation (BIMSTEC) leaders to the Brazil, Russia, India, China and South Africa (BRICS)–BIMSTEC Outreach Summit in Goa, in October 2016, refocused attention on the potential and prospects of BIMSTEC emerging as a viable vehicle for substantial subregional cooperation. The BIMSTEC Summit assumed an added significance against the backdrop of the decision of four South Asian Association for Regional Cooperation (SAARC) countries to boycott the SAARC Summit in Islamabad in November 2016 on the issue of Pakistan's failure to curb cross-border terrorism emanating from its territory. It was also self-evident that Pakistan had repeatedly obstructed various SAARC initiatives and an alternative strategy was necessary to push forward greater subregional cooperation and integration.

BIST-EC, as it was first known, was formed in Bangkok in June 1997, comprising Bangladesh, India, Sri Lanka and Thailand. Myanmar attended the inaugural meeting as an observer and joined as a full member at the special ministerial meeting in December 1997. Subsequently, Nepal and Bhutan joined as full members in 2004, and at the first summit meeting held in 2004, the name of the organisation was changed to BIMSTEC. BIMSTEC did not have a founding charter, but over time member countries agreed on fourteen priority areas for cooperation with lead countries for each[1]. These were trade and investment, transport and communication, energy, tourism, technology, fisheries, agriculture, public health, poverty alleviation, counterterrorism and transnational crimes, environment and natural disaster management, culture, people-to-people contacts and climate change. Apart from such sectoral meetings, BIMSTEC had summit-level meetings in Bangkok in 2004, New Delhi in 2008 and Myanmar in 2014. The fourth summit is in Nepal in 2017.

There are many inherent advantages in BIMSTEC as a subregional organisation. It is home to 1.5 billion people amounting to 21 per cent of the world population having a combined GDP of over USD 2.5 trillion[2]. Despite the global economic slowdown since 2008, BIMSTEC countries have been able to maintain a stable growth rate. It is rich in natural and human resources, and its unique geographical contiguity and access to the sea, provide the opportunities for establishment of an integrated economic space. Most significantly, it provides a critical bridge between South Asia and Southeast Asia, complementing India's Look East and now Act East policy as well as Thailand's Look West policy. It also provides a vital link between South Asia and the emerging economic architecture of the wider Indo-Pacific region. For the least developed countries (LDC) in BIMSTEC in particular, the prospect of wider cross-border cooperation holds out much promise. The early involvement of the Asian Development Bank (ADB) as a partner of BIMSTEC was also highly advantageous. The ADB completed in 2008 the BIMSTEC Transport Infrastructure and Logistics Study (BTILS), recommending a large number of connectivity and trade facilitation projects[3]. The ADB had earlier played a major role in the launch of the Greater Mekong Subregion (GMS), and its association with BIMSTEC was expected to address the financial and technical shortfalls. Finally, from India's point of view, BIMSTEC places the relatively underdeveloped north-eastern region of the country at the heart of India's Act East policy. The promise of an accelerated development of the north-eastern states as a part of subregional cooperation has been a long-standing aspiration of the region.

Yet, despite its many inherent advantages, it is widely recognised that in twenty years, BIMSTEC has not lived up to its early high expectations, particularly in terms of visible and beneficial outcomes. Many of its proposals have been pushed forward through other bilateral, subregional and regional initiatives, leaving BIMSTEC without leadership and a clear vision. Most glaring has been the failure to conclude a BIMSTEC Free Trade Agreement (FTA). A Framework Agreement was concluded in 2004 and a Trade Negotiating Committee (TNC) was set up, but even after twenty rounds of negotiations, consensus has been elusive. Meanwhile, the South Asia Free Trade Agreement (SAFTA) came into force in 2006 and the India–ASEAN FTA in 2010. The India–Sri Lanka FTA (2000) and the Asia–Pacific Trade Agreement (APTA) of 1976, of course, preceded the BIMSTEC negotiations. At the bilateral level, India concluded Comprehensive Economic Cooperation/Partnership Agreements with Singapore, Japan, Korea and Malaysia in the period 2005-2011. India is engaged in FTA negotiations with other countries such as Thailand, Indonesia, Australia and New Zealand, and the Regional Comprehensive Economic Partnership (RCEP) that will encompass the ASEAN Plus Six countries, including China.

Similarly, in the priority area of connectivity, the major initiative of the India–Myanmar–Thailand Trilateral Highway is being pursued outside the BIMSTEC framework. India and Myanmar are working bilaterally on the Kaladan Multi-modal Transit Transport project and the Zokhawtwar–Tiddim axis through Rhi, to establish a viable corridor between Mizoram and the Chin state of Myanmar. Similarly, India and Bangladesh have agreed to the Agartala–Akhaura rail link and the Sabroom–Ramgarh road link, which will open up vital links between Tripura and Chittagong port in Bangladesh[4]. The grant of transit and trans-shipment facilities by Bangladesh to India by means of waterways and road through the inland port of Ashuganj has substantially reduced the time and cost of transporting goods from the east coast of India to Tripura and beyond[5]. A host of other connectivity projects are being undertaken under the umbrella of the South Asia Subregional Economic Cooperation (SASEC) programme with the assistance of the ADB. Finally, new proposals which, if implemented, will have a bearing on the BIMSTEC subregion include the Bangladesh–China–India–Myanmar Economic Corridor (BCIM-EC) and the Maritime Silk Route, a part of China's One Belt One Road (OBOR) initiative.

In the area of sectoral cooperation, BIMSTEC's record is a mixed one. Two security related agreements have been finalised and are awaiting either signature or ratification. An energy-related MoU on grid connectivity has also been finalised and is awaiting signature. BIMSTEC centres for energy, weather and climate, and culture have been initiated, but are not fully operational as yet. In other areas, meetings at official, expert and even ministerial level have been held, but substantial progress and implementation has been tardy and there are very few visible outcomes. It would appear that BIMSTEC has perhaps spread itself too thin over fourteen sectoral initiatives and there is a need for focus and prioritisation.

Various factors now point to an opportunity for BIMSTEC to reinvent itself and push forward subregional cooperation. The establishment of the BIMSTEC Secretariat in Dhaka in 2014 and the appointment of its first Secretary General have filled a huge void in its institutional structure[6]. There is now the promise of administrative stability and continuity as well as close monitoring and follow-up of the BIMSTEC programmes. Of course, the need to further strengthen the Secretariat with human and financial resources remains imperative. Secondly, the apparent dead end reached by SAARC due to Pakistan's continual obstruction of its programmes has become all too evident.

The denial of most favoured nation (MFN) status to India which undermined SAFTA, the last minute blocking of the agreements on Motor Vehicles and Railways at the seventeenth SAARC Summit in Kathmandu, the strident advocacy of China's entry as a full member, and Pakistan's abysmal record in curbing cross-border terrorism, are illustrative of its lack of commitment to SAARC. There are no indications of any likely change of course in the near future, and arguably, Pakistan's focus is now concentrated on the China–Pakistan Economic Corridor (CPEC). It is in this context that India's initiative in hosting the BRICS–BIMSTEC Outreach Summit in Goa in October 2016 was hugely significant. It was a shot in the arm for BIMSTEC and the Outcome Document has become a comprehensive plan of action for the future[7]. Similarly, the official support given to the grouping of four countries, Bangladesh, Bhutan, India and Nepal (BBIN), was a response to the paralyses in SAARC, and the BBIN Motor Vehicles Agreement, now awaiting a final ratification by Bhutan, has been a solid achievement, and one, which can be easily replicated in BIMSTEC. Finally, BIMSTEC, which straddles South Asia and Southeast Asia, can be seen in the light of recent developments as an alternative narrative to OBOR. OBOR has been viewed in some quarters as a unilateral Chinese initiative whose aims and objectives have not been fully clarified. Whereas with its proximity to the Bay of Bengal and the Indian Ocean, BIMSTEC has the natural advantage in promoting subregional maritime cooperation.[8]

The identification and pursuit of priority projects is the key to the re-energisation of BIMSTEC. This should also be driven by adding value to and filling the gaps in other bilateral and regional initiatives. First and foremost would be finalisation of the BIMSTEC FTA for which, some twenty rounds of negotiations have already been held. There are reports that India is lukewarm to the modest tariff concessions that have been negotiated over a long period of time. India, being a participant in SAFTA and the ASEAN–India FTA, may not stand to benefit substantially from a BIMSTEC FTA. Nevertheless, there are compelling reasons to push it ahead. Bangladesh, Bhutan, Nepal and Sri Lanka on the one hand and Myanmar and Thailand on the other, are not linked by any FTA, and a BIMSTEC agreement could bring major trade gains for these countries. Intra-BIMSTEC trade has been growing in recent years, but still amounts to only 6-7 per cent of total trade, and as such, the scope for trade enhancement through an FTA is enormous. More importantly, it would facilitate cross-border production networks and regional value chains, which are the true measure of subregional economic integration. From India's point of view, the potential integration of the north-eastern states into these value chains would be a major gain. These states are emerging internationally competitive in a number of products such as pharmaceuticals, minerals like coal and limestone, agri-horticultural and floriculture products, stone chips, bamboo, refined petroleum products, food processing, rubber and some light engineering products[9]. The potential for the North East to export medical, educational and tourism services is also substantial.

A BIMSTEC FTA would also focus attention on various trade facilitation issues such as upgradation of border infrastructure, simplification of customs procedures, harmonisation of standards, cross-border testing facilities and non-tariff barriers. The extension of the BBIN Motor Vehicles Agreement to BIMSTEC would automatically meet a vital requirement for operationalisation of the Trilateral Highway. A trial run of a truck from Dhaka to Delhi in September 2016 under the BBIN Motor Vehicles Agreement (MVA) was strikingly successful with GPS monitoring arrangement[10]. The logical next step would be a comprehensive transit agreement to facilitate the smooth flow of goods between and through BIMSTEC member countries. Thus, even a low-ambition FTA to begin with, incorporating trade in goods, services and investment could lead to other substantial benefits.

ADB's BTILS Report has a ready-made menu of connectivity projects that can be pursued by BIMSTEC and, which have not yet been taken up under other frameworks. The completion and operationalisation of the Trilateral Highway is the obvious priority. The three countries involved have already committed to completion of most sections of the highway. Opening a link from the Trilateral Highway into Mizoram is also important so as to provide an alternative to the Moreh–Tamu border point in Manipur. India has committed to finance the upgradation of the Rhi–Tiddim section in Myanmar beyond the border point at Zokhawtwar, and the next critical section to Kalemyo is also a possible BIMSTEC project[11].

There are other long-term, high-value connectivity projects that can be considered. India has been pushing railway connectivity with the north-eastern states and the Silchar–Imphal broad gauge line should be completed within the next couple of years. If eventually the line is extended from Imphal to Moreh, then there remains a relatively short missing section to Kalay for a link-up with the Myanmar railway network. This possibility has already been discussed at the first meeting in 2013 of the India–Myanmar Joint Railway Working Group. Finally, BIMSTEC can plug into the Myanmar proposals for development of port-based SEZs. The location at Dawei in southern Myanmar is ideal for road-maritime connectivity from Thailand across the Bay of Bengal to the eastern seaboard of India and Sri Lanka. This project was considered as the Mekong–India Economic Corridor (MIEC)[12], but by involving Bangladesh and Sri Lanka, this could evolve into an important BIMSTEC initiative.

Indeed, there is a significant reference to the maritime heritage of BIMSTEC in the Leaders' Retreat 2016 Outcome Document[13]. It draws attention to the Bay of Bengal region being home to over 30 per cent of the world's fishermen, and that sustainable development of fisheries in the region has the potential to make a significant contribution towards ensuring food security and improving livelihoods of people. The document goes on to highlight the enormous potential for the development of the blue economy with cooperation in areas such as aquaculture, hydrography, seabed mineral exploration, coastal shipping, ecotourism and renewable ocean energy. These are areas of cooperation that can be pursued by BIMSTEC without large financial implications. India and Bangladesh have already concluded a coastal shipping agreement, which can easily be extended to Myanmar and Sri Lanka. There is scope for BIMSTEC countries to coordinate their port development projects so as to maximise synergies and also offer options for the landlocked countries: Bhutan and Nepal. India's Sagarmala project envisages the development of six mega ports in the coming years and Bangladesh is also looking at deep-sea ports at Payra and Matarbari. Extending cooperation in this sector to the Indian Ocean Rim Association (IORA) countries would be a logical next step for BIMSTEC to consider. In maritime matters, BIMSTEC and IORA face common challenges and opportunities. Cooperation could cover issues such as maritime choke points, safety and security of shipping lanes, building of maritime domain awareness, piracy, disaster relief and search and rescue[14].

Among other priority sectors for BIMSTEC, cooperation in the field of energy has huge potential. The India–Nepal, India–Bhutan and India–Bangladesh electricity grids are already connected and power trading arrangements are in place. Much more work needs to be done to increase cross-border energy flows so as to unlock the enormous hydroelectric potential in Nepal, Bhutan, north-eastern India and Myanmar. For instance, hydropower potential in north-east India has been estimated at 60,000 MW. This power can be most economically transmitted to Bangladesh or to Myanmar. Myanmar itself has a hydropower potential of some 100,000 MW. India and Bangladesh are already exploring a 6000 MW transmission line from Rangia in Assam to Bihar through northern Bangladesh. Sharing of this power would be a win-win outcome for both countries. The finalisation of a BIMSTEC MoU on grid connectivity is the first step in the establishment of a regional grid, with power trading and equitable outcomes for all. The MoU provides for building blocks that are both bilateral and multilateral, and the proposal for linking the grids of India and Sri Lanka has been under serious consideration for some time now. Energy sector cooperation can be extended to cover oil, gas, LNG and renewable energy. An old proposal for a Myanmar–Bangladesh–India gas pipeline never saw the light of day, and Myanmar gas is now being exported to China. However, with the recent settlement of the Bangladesh–India and Bangladesh–Myanmar maritime boundaries, exploration for hydrocarbons in the Bay of Bengal is likely to go up and future sharing of new discoveries amongst BIMSTEC countries is a prospect worthy of serious consideration. The same applies to petroleum products. Assam is surplus in refining capacity and there is a proposal to bring a product pipeline from Siliguri to Parbatipur in Bangladesh. A 41-km India–Nepal pipeline is under construction. A network of cross-border oil and gas pipelines will appreciably enhance energy security of all concerned.

Finally, the 2016 Outcome Document recognised that terrorism continues to remain the most significant threat to peace and stability in the region and called for concrete measures to step up cooperation among law enforcement, intelligence and security organisations. All BIMSTEC member countries have in various degrees faced the challenge of terrorism and in a veiled reference to Pakistan, the Outcome Document condemned in the strongest possible terms, recent barbaric terror attacks in the region. The need for cooperation instruments and mechanisms cannot be overemphasised. Such cooperation and preventive vigilance has to continue, irrespective of constraints that may arise in other sectors and may eventually be extended to coastal maritime security.

The illustrative priorities outlined above do not detract from other areas of cooperation such as tourism, culture, people-to-people contacts, climate change and disaster management. However, for BIMSTEC to become a successful vehicle for subregional cooperation, it has to seriously address the question of financial support for its programmes. As a member-driven organisation, it is largely dependent on the financial and technical support of its members. The time has come for BIMSTEC members to set up a special fund or a number of funds dedicated to specific projects to overcome the financial challenge. This is the practice followed by other regional organisations. Secondly, BIMSTEC has not adequately leveraged its unique partnership association with the ADB. It is not just a question of funding but also utilising the enormous technical resources available with the ADB. For instance, under SASEC, the ADB has spearheaded some forty projects worth USD 7.7 billion as of July 2016[15]. Most of these are in the areas of transport and connectivity, trade facilitation, energy, information and communication technology (ICT), and digital connectivity. BIMSTEC can draw on the comprehensive BTILS report and seek ADB support for identified BIMSTEC projects. Indeed, after the BRICS–BIMSTEC Outreach Summit, the BRICS New Development Bank can also be approached for funding, apart from other international financial institutions, including the China-based Asian Infrastructure Investment Bank. Finally, BIMSTEC may explore 'open regionalism', a concept first articulated at the Asia–Pacific Economic Cooperation (APEC) Summit in Bogor in 1989, but not fully defined. Essentially, this could involve bringing in outside countries and institutions on a project-specific basis without necessarily expanding BIMSTEC membership. For instance, Vietnam and Laos could be brought in to extend the reach of the Trilateral Highway or Japanese finances could be sought for the development of port-based Special Economic Zones in Myanmar.

BIMSTEC as a subregional grouping for fostering socio-economic cooperation has many inherent advantages and new life has been breathed into it in the last few years. The objective factors are favourable, but there is need for strong leadership to realise the opportunities and potential. Perhaps, India needs to play such a role in consonance with its Neighbourhood First policy.

***

Rajeet Mitter is a former Indian Foreign Service officer. His early career included postings in the Indian diplomatic missions in Iraq, UK, Yugoslavia and Singapore. He also served as Director, Department of Economic Affairs, Joint Secretary (Gulf), Ministry of External Affairs and Joint Secretary (Trade Policy), Department of Commerce. He was appointed High Commissioner to Botswana in 1998, Ambassador to the Philippines in 2006 and High Commissioner to Bangladesh in 2009.

END NOTES

1. Refer, for example, BIMSTEC Secretariat, Dhaka, available at www.bimstec.org.
2. This data refers to the year 2015, sourced from World Bank's World Development Indicators (WDI).
3. Refer, official website of Asian Development Bank (ADB), www.adb.org.
4. Refer, India–Bangladesh Joint Statement, September 2011, available at www.mea.gov.in.
5. Refer, *The Times of India*, dated 16 June 2016.
6. Refer *Dhaka Tribune*, dated 13 September 2014.
7. Refer, BIMSTEC Leaders' Retreat 2016 Outcome Document, available at www.mea.gov.in.
8. Refer, for example, De, Prabir (2017) 'Strengthening BIMSTEC-IORA Linkages' in Kumar, Yogendra (2017) *Whither Indian Ocean Maritime Order? Contributions to a Seminar on Narendra Modi's SAGAR Speech*; Knowledge World, New Delhi.
9. Refer, De, Prabir and Majumdar, Manab (2014) *Developing Cross-Border: Production Networks between North Eastern Region of India, Bangladesh and Myanmar*, Research and Information System for Developing Countries (RIS), New Delhi.
10. Refer, *The Hindu Business Line*, dated 5 September 2016.
11. Refer, Seshadri, VS (2014) *Transforming Connectivity Corridors between India and Myanmar into Development Corridor*, Research and Information System for Developing Countries (RIS), New Delhi.
12. Refer, ERIA Study on Mekong–India Economic Corridor Development, Economic Research Institute for ASEAN and East Asia (ERIA), Jakarta, March 2009.
13. Refer, BIMSTEC Outreach Summit Declaration, available at www.mea.gov.in.
14. Refer, for example, De, Prabir (2017) 'Strengthening BIMSTEC-IORA Linkages' in Kumar, Yogendra (2017) *Whither Indian Ocean Maritime Order? Contributions to a Seminar on Narendra Modi's SAGAR Speech*; Knowledge World, New Delhi.
15. Refer, Asian Development Bank (ADB) (2016) *South Asia Subregional Economic Cooperation Operational Plan 2016-2025*, Manila.

The Arab World—A Region in Transition

DINKAR SRIVASTAVA

Abstract

The Arab world spanning the Middle East and North Africa has been witnessing major changes. This is an ancient region, home to three great religions. The Arabic language provides a common link to an otherwise diverse area. Turkey, Israel and Iran are three non-Arab powers sharing the political space with varying degrees of competition and conflict. With the discovery of oil in the early twentieth century in Persia, followed by Saudi Arabia, geopolitical importance of the region increased. The twenty-first century saw three major events, which have shaped the region's history, and its impact on the rest of the world—9/11, the Arab Spring and the sectarian divide. The age of hydrocarbons is not over, but the OPEC's hold on the oil market is declining.

OVERVIEW

The Arab countries ranging from the Middle East to North Africa are witnessing a series of parallel transitions. There are political and social changes, the regional balance is changing, the role of external actors has undergone changes and the oil prices fell dramatically beginning mid-2014. A number of regional and internal conflicts have erupted in Syria, Iraq, Yemen and Libya. The rise of sectarian tensions and Islamic State of Iraq and Syria (ISIS) has had consequences beyond the region. The migrants' crisis has affected the European Union. The Middle East peace process remains stalled. What was termed as 'Arab Spring' by Western commentators, has belied its promise even to its supporters. With Russia's military intervention in Syria, and the ceasefire sponsored by Russia and Turkey after the fall of Aleppo, the great power equations have also changed. This comes at a time of transition in Washington, which may also affect the region.

For a region as varied as the Middle East and North Africa, no single cause can be attributed to the sweeping changes the different countries are undergoing. Revolution in Tunisia could be described as an internal change brought about by pent-up frustrations against the regime, which denied democratic aspirations of the people. In the case of Libya, the regime change could only be brought about by a sustained bombing campaign by the NATO. In Egypt, after a brief interlude of the Morsi government, the military regime is back in power. The Gulf countries could weather the storm better. High oil prices at the beginning of the crisis provided them with a financial cushion to offer subsidies. With the fall in oil prices, their margin has eroded. Tunisia, Egypt, Yemen and Iraq actually saw regime change. In Syria, this did not happen—only at an enormous cost in terms of civil war, refugee exodus and foreign intervention.

The rise of ISIS in Syria and Iraq is sometimes described as a breakdown of the Sykes–Picot Agreement. The ISIS proclaimed itself as a worldwide caliphate, breaking down the inter-State boundaries. But the problem goes deeper, with the ISIS challenging the Westphalian concept of nation-state. The rise of ISIS has heightened Shia–Sunni schism, though its primary aim is competition for the minds of people in Sunni heartland. This coincided with an increase of Iran–Saudi tensions. After some modest steps towards rapprochement under King Abdullah, the relations between the two regional great powers have become tenser. Saudi intervention in Yemen and formation of a thirty-four country anti-terror alliance reflects increased regional rivalries. Lifting of sanctions against Iran has created the apprehension that Iran will flex its muscles in the region. The fear is shared on both sides of the Israel–Arab divide.

The Arab countries are caught in a pincer with increased competition from Turkey and Iran for regional dominance. The Ottoman and Persian empires have been the Arab's historical enemies. This has come at a time of rise of the ISIS. Vehemently anti-Shia, paradoxically, its immediate challenge is to the Arab regimes. Its ideological appeal lies more with the Sunni population.

There was nearly 80 per cent drop in price of crude oil between 2011, when Arab Spring began, and early 2016. It has recovered since, to around USD 53 per barrel. But it is still around half the price level five years ago. There is a similar drop in price of natural gas. Underlying this steep drop is a basic shift. Shale gas revolution has ended US dependency on oil from Middle East and North Africa. Though the Organization of the Petroleum Exporting Countries (OPEC) still has a role in influencing crude prices, the salience of this factor in US policymaking has gone down. Lower oil prices and revenues have also reduced the cushion, which oil-rich countries had in coping with domestic social pressures.

Has there been any rethinking on the part of those, who advocated use of force in the Middle East and North Africa in the wake of the Arab Spring? President Obama was asked in an interview to *Fox News* in April 2016 about his 'worst mistake'. His response was: 'Probably failing to plan for the day after, what I think was the right thing to do, in intervening in Libya.'[1] He also criticised the US' European partners. He was more blunt in his May interview to *The Atlantic* magazine. Libya continues to burn. His critics hold his refusal to intervene in Syria, and quick drawdown of forces in Iraq, as failures.

Obama had been consistent in following a cautious approach. He tried to pull US troops out of Iraq. He refused to get drawn in after chemical weapons were discovered in Syria. He preferred that US should lead from behind in Libya. It was the alliance partners—UK and France, which were in the forefront, with enthusiastic support from Secretary of State, Clinton.

THE ARAB SPRING

The ferment, which swept the Arab world in 2011, had different socio-economic causes. It took place in one-party States. The Western commentators, who termed it Arab Spring, focused on the political dimension. But if the absence of democracy was the cause, it is difficult to explain why the monarchies weathered the storm better. This was true not only in oil-rich Gulf countries, but also in Morocco in North Africa, which was not so well endowed. It was driven by socio-economic causes in Tunisia and Egypt. In case of Libya, the economic situation was not a factor. The use of force to bring about regime change has discredited the phenomenon, though underlying causes remain.

The Arab Spring was seen as a Western construct by many other countries. Their discomfort was reflected in abstention by Russia, China, India and Brazil on UN Security Council Resolution 1973 of 17 March 2011 on Libya. The rise of tribal warfare and Islamic extremism has reinforced the disenchantment with the Arab Spring even amongst its erstwhile supporters, who now derisively call it the Arab Winter. Libya remains divided between different governments and rival militias. In Syria, the West found itself fighting the regime as well as those who opposed it. President Obama's interview to *The Atlantic* magazine was a candid confession of the failure of Western intervention. He blamed it on US' European allies, particularly UK and France. But the failure was not simply because the European powers did not maintain their engagement for nation building in the aftermath of regime change. Internal evolution in any country takes time. The States concerned may also lack institutions to foster democracy. Or often, the only strong institution is the Army, which provides security, but is no guarantor of democracy.

LIBYA

Libya under Gaddafi was never a democracy. Gaddafi did not hold any formal position in government, but wielded absolute control. He did, however, knit together a tribal society. He had come to power overthrowing King Idris, who was head of a religious sect from the Cyrenaica region in the east. He led a lifelong struggle against political Islam and his overthrow opened a Pandora's box.

During the colonial period, Libya was divided into three different parts—eastern Libya or Cyrenaica, western Libya or Tripolitania, and southern Libya or Fezzan. The colonial powers tried to carve out their spheres of influence, and keep Libya divided. A unified country was established in 1951 by a resolution of the United Nations. Idris, who was head of a religious group, was installed as king. These historical fault lines have persisted. The Cyrenaica region where King Idris came from, had an uneasy existence under the Gaddafi regime. Islamist influence was also strongest in this region. During the civil war, Benghazi rose in rebellion against the Gaddafi rule. Despite American help in overthrowing Gaddafi, the US diplomatic compound in Benghazi was attacked and Ambassador Chris Stevens was killed in September 2012. President Obama blamed UK and France in part for the Libya situation: 'When I go back and ask myself what went wrong, there is room for criticism, because I had more faith in the Europeans, given Libya's proximity, being invested in the follow-up[2].'

The country remains divided with Tripoli controlled by General National Congress and the eastern region controlled by the House of Representatives. Both the bodies have exhausted their mandate. The Government of National Accord (GNA) was established in Tripoli in April 2016. But it has not been able to unify the country.

Before 2011, Libya had an oil production of 1.7 million barrels per day. This included exports of 1.4 million barrels per day. Gaddafi was careful with finances. The country had no debt and foreign exchange reserves of more than USD 100 billion. Since then, its oil production has come down to 403,000 barrels per day with exports of 235,000 barrels per day.

The central part of the country, known as the Sirte region, has become a base for ISIS. Libya is barely 550 km south of Europe. The proximity has made it an ideal staging post for migrants seeking a better standard of living in Europe. The combination of terrorism and immigration crisis has torn apart EU. It has been at an enormous cost to the Libyan people.

EGYPT

The Arab Spring brought Egyptian masses into the streets. The crisis was brewing before the events of Tunisia. Egypt witnessed the Kifaya movement, wherein, people wrote the term *Kifaya* on the walls, which means 'enough' in Arabic, as a reference to Hosni Mubarak's long rule, and his attempt to bring his son to power. Socio-economic pressures too played a role. In the ensuing elections, Morsi, supported by the Muslim Brotherhood, came to power, though on a thin majority in the presidential election. In the first round, he got 24.7 per cent votes against Ahmed Shafiq, who received 23.6 per cent of votes. Ahmad Shafiq was the last prime minister under Mubarak. In the second round, he received 51.7 per cent as against 48.7 per cent votes bagged by Ahmed Shafiq. Nevertheless, election of a Muslim Brotherhood candidate in the largest Arab nation sent a signal.

Morsi's election raised two vital questions: whether political Islam can be integrated in democratic process, and whether Egypt under Morsi will maintain its international commitments, the most important being the Camp David Accord. The answer to the second was clear. Morsi not only maintained Egypt's commitment, but played a mediating role between Israel and Palestine, as well as among different Palestinian factions. Morsi however, was less successful in working with domestic institutions, including parliamentary opposition and the judiciary.

Egypt had continued to supply natural gas to Israel till 2011 when there was a terrorist attack on the pipeline. More recently, Egypt voted in favour of UN Security Council (UNSC) Resolution 2334 on Israeli settlements in the West Bank, as well as UNSC Resolution 2336 sponsored by Russia and Turkey on ceasefire in Syria.

General Abdel Fattah el-Sisi's takeover was supported by Saudi Arabia and the United Arab Emirates (UAE), who were happy to see Muslim Brotherhood ousted from power. They committed a generous financial package of USD 12 billion to bail out Egypt from its financial difficulties. They also provided crude oil. General Sisi was elected president in the election in which he won 96.91 per cent of valid votes in May 2016. Positive votes in support of the Russian–Turkish backed resolution on ceasefire in Syria may have caused some irritation in Riyadh. There may have been other contributing factors as well. Egypt sent a fleet in support of Saudi-led action in Yemen but did not commit ground troops. There have been delays in handing over two islands in the Gulf of Tirana to Saudi Arabia. Egypt has retained autonomy of its foreign policy and will continue to remain one of the most important players in the region.

MIDDLE EAST PEACE PROCESS

The adoption of UNSC Resolution 2334 on 23 December 2016 has brought the focus back on the Middle East Peace Process, which had remained dormant since the start of Arab Spring. The resolution affirmed: 'Settlements in Palestinian territory occupied since 1967, including East Jerusalem, had no legal validity, constituting a flagrant violation under international law and a major obstacle to the vision of two States living side-by-side in peace and security, within internationally recognised borders[3].' It was adopted by a vote of 14-0 with the US abstaining. The resolution, aimed at Israeli settlement activity, was adopted under Chapter VI of the UN Charter, which is not enforceable.

It reiterated the two State solution which is not new. Nevertheless, it carried a political message, particularly since it was passed by overwhelming majority.

The Israeli prime minister criticised the Obama Administration. The US PR Samantha Power, in her statement at the UN, quoted President Reagan to underline bipartisan consensus, and long-standing US policy on the subject. Then President-elect Trump said that this would not be repeated on his watch. Political process has to go on. The alternative, where Arab masses are won over by Islamic State of Iraq and Syria's (ISIS) message of hatred, posed a greater danger. There was a terrorist attack in Israel on 8 January, which Prime Minister Netanyahu blamed on ISIS.

Expansion of settlements on the West Bank also revives Israel's classical dilemma. It can choose to be Jewish and democratic, or lose both the attributes in an expanded State, where Arab majority increases. Settlements are no defence against a missile attack which Israel had to weather in the past. President Trump's comment during a meeting with Prime Minister Netanyahu's visit to Washington on 15 February 2017 suggests a rethink on US position on 'Two State Solution'. This may have major implications in future.

SYRIA, IRAQ, TURKEY AND ISIS

President Obama in his interview to *The Atlantic* magazine in March 2016 said, 'Right now, I do not think anybody can be feeling good about the situation in the Middle East. You have countries that are failing to provide prosperity and opportunity for their people. You have a violent, extremist ideology, or ideologies, that are turbo-charged through social media. You have countries that have very few civic traditions, so that as autocratic regimes start fraying, the only organising principles are sectarian[4].'

Prolonged civil war in Syria and disenfranchisement of the Sunni minority in Iraq created political space for the rise of ISIS. The speed with which it occupied Ramadi and Mosul, and the sheer brutality displayed by it attracted much international attention. ISIS is more than a terrorist organisation. It has an army, which has displayed capacity to hold territory. More importantly, it aims at dominating Muslim minds and incite attacks in Europe and America. Syrian forces, with help from Russian bombing, have recovered Aleppo. ISIS has lost Fallujah and Ramadi in Iraq, and is expected to be pushed out of Mosul. It may no longer be a winning franchise, which can easily attract recruits and funds. But if the ideology retains its pull on the minds of alienated youth, the danger of 'lone wolf' attacks will remain.

The ISIS posed a dilemma for the US and Western countries. They were fighting the Syrian regime, and its opponent, at the same time. This was bound to weaken their war effort in Syria. The sectarian killings of Shias and Kurds by ISIS raised concerns in Iraq. But precisely because of its sectarian nature, its message had no appeal for the

Shia majority. After making initial gains in Ramadi, since reversed, ISIS fell back on the Sunni majority region of Anbar.

The rise of ISIS is sometimes projected as the breakdown of the Sykes–Picot Agreement. Actually, the first challenge to the Anglo-French accord came immediately after World War I, when Abdul Aziz, then a minor chieftain from Nejd, displaced Hashemite rule over Hejaz. This forced the British to install Prince Faisal in Iraq. Abdul Aziz established his kingdom over the Arabian peninsula, and consolidated his rule by assuming the mantle of 'custodian of holy shrines'. It is this role, which is being challenged by the ISIS. The territorial status quo of the Sykes–Picot Agreement was based on the demise of the Ottoman empire, and the country focusing on internal consolidation, and secularism under Kemal Attaturk. Turkey, under Recep Tayyip Erdogan, is seeking reversal of both the internal and external dimensions of this legacy. It seeks greater Islamisation. It has also asserted Turkey's role in the Arab world. Turkey along with Russia, sponsored the ceasefire agreement in Syria.

It is interesting that Turkey, a North Atlantic Treaty Organization (NATO) member, has struck at least a tactical alliance with Russia. This directly challenges America's stated objective of replacing the Assad regime. The fact that Turkey waited till the fall of Aleppo to Russian–Assad forces backed by Shia militias, shows the extent of turnaround in Turkey's position and regional equations. Turkey was the most vociferous critic of the Assad regime. It hosts three million Syrian refugees. It has revised its priorities. It sees consolidation of a Kurdish enclave on Syrian border as a greater threat than continuation of the Assad regime, supported by Russia and Iran.

SAUDI ARABIA

The Saudi State has shown that it has the capacity to meet the territorial challenge from ISIS. However, the bigger challenge is ideological. There was an attack on Saudi outpost on its border with Iraq in January 2016. There have been terror attacks within the Saudi kingdom, which have been checked. The real danger ISIS poses is if its message of hatred is accepted by the mainstream in Muslim countries. In claiming the caliphate, and assuming Emir's title, Abu Bakr al-Baghdadi has directly challenged the Saudi monarchy, which derives its legitimacy from its role as the 'servant of the two holy mosques'.

According to a Carnegie study by Cole Bunzel, entitled *The Kingdom and the Caliphate: Duel of the Islamic State*[5], unlike Al-Qaeda for which the United States was the primary target, for Abu Baqr al-Baghdadi, the regime in Saudi Arabia is the primary target. Bunzel states: 'This revision by the leader of the Islamic State marks a significant change in the priorities of the global jihadi movement now spearheaded by the group.' The paper mentions that ISIS seeks to appropriate Wahabi ideology but considers the

Saudi ruling family as 'apostates, unbelievers, who have abandoned the religion and must be killed'. A month after ISIS had declared itself the caliphate, King Abdullah in August 2014 called on 'the scholars of the Islamic community to carry out their duty before God and confront those trying to hijack Islam and present it to the world as the religion of extremism, hate and terror.' The Saudi clergy was upbraided by late King Abdullah as 'lazy', who were not doing enough to combat the ISIS message. The study says that Abd al-Aziz al-Sheikh, the grand mufti of the kingdom and the head of the Council of Senior Religious Scholars, has characterised the ISIS, along with Al-Qaeda, as 'an extension of the Kharijites, who were the first group to leave the religion'. There are also voices outside the ranks of clergy, who have asked for reform of the Wahabi doctrine.

With the passing of King Abdullah, Saudi Arabia went through a transition. While Prince Salman became king, the appointment of Prince Mohammad Bin Nayef as crown prince, and Prince Mohammad bin Salman as deputy crown prince, the succession was passed on to the second generation. This in effect meant bypassing a number of Abdul Aziz's sons. Prince Mohammad bin Salman, the king's son and deputy crown prince, has effected changes in key portfolios. This includes the foreign ministry, where for the first time, a commoner, Adel al-Jubeir, has taken over as the Saudi foreign minister. The Oil Minister Ali al-Naimi was replaced by Khalid al-Falih.

Saudi Arabia has also followed a more muscular foreign policy. This includes military intervention in Yemen following Houthi takeover, which reflected an apprehension that it was inspired by Iran, a charge the latter denies. The kingdom also supports 'moderate opposition' in Syria. With Russian intervention in support of the Assad regime, the tide of war in that country seems turning in favour of the Syrian government.

Prince Mohammad bin Salman has also announced an ambitious plan for diversification of the Saudi economy to wean it away from dependency on oil revenues. An ambitious blueprint for the future—Vision 2025 has been released; its implementation however, will take time. The kingdom also demonstrated irritation with the US over the Obama administration's policy in Syria, as well as the nuclear accord with Iran. Since then, Joint Comprehensive Plan of Action (JCPOA), as the nuclear deal is known, has gone into effect. It is worth recalling that though there may be differences over Syria, but on the issue of nuclear deal with Iran, the US position is also supported by Russia, China and European countries. Whether there will be warming of relations with the new Republican administration remains to be seen.

Saudi Arabia announced formation of a thirty-four country alliance to counter terrorism. The group is named Islamic Military Alliance to Fight Terrorism (IMAFT) and includes Muslim countries, within and outside the region. It also conducted a military exercise 'Northern Thunder'. The announcement of appointment of General Raheel

Sharif, former Pakistan Army Chief, to head the alliance was criticised in Pakistan as potentially drawing Pakistan into the conflict between Saudi Arabia and Iran. According to an article by Syeda Mamoona Rubab, General Sharif stated that he has made his joining conditional upon the role being 'related to his training responsibilities, the advisory role and reconciliation efforts[6].' The article mentioned further that the Pakistan Peoples' Party and the Pakistan Tehreek-e-Insaf have opposed General Raheel serving the Saudi alliance.

IRAN

The nuclear deal is a multilateral agreement supported by P5+1 (US, Russia, China, UK, France and Germany) and endorsed by the UNSC. Though they opposed the deal, Gulf countries, including Saudi Arabia, have not called for its repeal since. President Obama in his interview to *The Atlantic* magazine in May 2016, advised that the kingdom should learn to share the neighbourhood in a 'cold peace' with Iran. Iran's bilateral relations with the US remain unchanged. Indeed, normalisation of Iran–US relations was not part of the nuclear deal. Iran's relations with Saudi Arabia also remain under strain after showing some promise during the last days of King Abdullah, when his son and deputy foreign minister visited Tehran. The passing away of Ayatollah Rafsanjani, who had close personal relations with Saudi leaders, may also complicate normalisation.

SHIA–SUNNI TENSIONS

Saudi–Iranian competition is a reflection of geopolitics as well as rise of sectarian tensions. The Arab–Azam tensions go back to the Arab invasion of Persia in the seventh century AD. The Iranians accepted Islam, but rejected the Arab domination. Firdaus's poetry celebrates Iran's glorious past. The rise of the Ottoman empire added another twist to this tale. The adoption of Shia theology as State religion by the Safavids was partly an ideological defence against the Ottoman empire, which had assumed the mantle of caliphate. It defined the Iranian nation as separate from the Sunni neighbours to the west.

The sectarian divide was reinforced by the geopolitical rivalry between Saudi Arabia and Iran in the contemporary period. The rise of ISIS has heightened Shia–Sunni tensions. But ISIS targets Saudi leadership, as much as Shias. The doctrinal differences would not have assumed such an edge, if the geopolitical rivalry over Syria, Lebanon and Yemen was not there.

FUTURE OF ISIS

The speed with which ISIS expanded in Iraq and Syria took most of the world by surprise, including the countries in the region. It is equally difficult to predict its future.

It has lost Aleppo, though it continues to retain its capital Reqqa and territory in eastern Syria. In Iraq, Mosul, remains its last major stronghold. Will the loss of territory destroy the movement? Or will the ideology continue to hold sway over the minds of the believers? The latter outcome is perhaps more dangerous. It will produce terrorism across the world.

ISIS arose in war-torn Iraq and Syria. If its followers gain control of a major State, the consequences would be far worse. By some estimates, the ISIS attracted more outside fighters than the Afghan jihad. Its impact on the outside world could be potentially more devastating as these fighters return to their native countries. The Afghan jihad was fought in the 1980s before the age of internet. In the second decade of the twenty-first century, the ISIS has much more powerful tools in terms of social media to propagate its creed and attract adherents. ISIS has found adherents in the Afghanistan–Pakistan (Af-Pak) region. To what extent these were ex-Talibans, who joined the winning brand, and may melt away if ISIS is successfully contained and defeated in Arabian heartland, remains to be seen.

OIL

The OPEC basket price came down from around USD 107 per barrel in 2011 to USD 22 per barrel by January/February 2016. It has recovered since then to USD 53.13 per barrel by the end of December 2016. Even this remains much below its historic level in 2011 at the beginning of the Arab Spring. The fluctuation goes beyond the traditional demand–supply cycle. There are fundamental changes at work. With the increase in shale production, the US demand for oil import has come down. In December 2015, the US administration lifted control on oil exports in place for more than four decades since the Seventies. The changed scenario has a salience on importance of Middle East in US policy calculus.

There are environmental pressures also on demand for fossil fuel. The International Energy Agency, in a 2016 report stated that in fifteen years' time, demand for crude oil will peak. This is reversal of the earlier theory of 'peak oil', when beyond a point the crude availability will enter a terminal decline. The prospect of oil running out had kept crude prices going up.

The economics of demand and supply were reinforced by politics. By the end of 2014, an interim nuclear deal with Iran had been reached. In the Vienna ministerial meeting in December 2014, OPEC ministers were to decide on production cut to sustain crude price, which had started going down since June of that year. The Iranian oil minister had personally lobbied his Saudi counterpart, and announced that an understanding had been reached to support price. This expectation was belied, when the Gulf producers led by Saudi Arabia decided to let the market determine the price, and rejected production ceiling. The crude price nosedived. The Iranian suspicion was that the decision was driven by politics, with Arab Gulf countries trying to strangle Iranian economy, just as it was coming out of sanctions. The lower production also adversely affected Russia, and hence suited America politically. There was a third rationale for the decision. Lower price was to eliminate high cost shale oil producers, and thus eliminate competition for the Gulf countries.

The Gulf countries maintained that it was purely an economic decision. Earlier production cuts by OPEC did not stabilise prices. Non-OPEC producers stepped in to increase their market share, and OPEC lost market share. Saudi Arabia did not want to be the swing producer and accept losses indefinitely. In the November 2016 OPEC meeting, this cycle was reversed. OPEC agreed on production cut to sustain crude oil prices. The OPEC agreement was coordinated with non-OPEC producers like Russia, who account for two-third of the global oil production. What was remarkable was that not only did Saudi Arabia agree to accept a cut in its production, Iran was exempted till it recovered its pre-sanction production level.

SECURITY

Saudi Arabia dominates the Gulf Cooperation Council (GCC), formed to provide collective response to internal and external security challenges faced by the Gulf monarchies. Within GCC, while Bahrain, Kuwait and UAE tend to be closely aligned with the Saudi policy, Oman plays a bridging role with Iran with whom it has maintained cordial relations. Qatar tended to be an outlier with support to Muslim Brotherhood, which is anathema to other Gulf monarchies. It has somewhat muted this role recently. GCC was founded to defend the legitimacy of monarchical system. It has so far weathered the storm.

There have been horrendous consequences of war in Syria, Iraq and Yemen in terms of refugee exodus, internal displacement and destruction of civilian life and property. According to UN High Commissioner for Refugees (UNHCR), in 2017, there are 6.3 million internally displaced persons in Syria and 4.9 million people, who have fled the country. In Iraq, there are 3.1 million displaced and 1.2 million in temporary settlement. The UNHCR estimates there are 2 million persons displaced in Yemen[7]. Unless, reconstruction and resettlement is undertaken quickly, humanitarian disaster of this scale would have far-reaching impact on the security of the region and beyond.

Saudi Arabia and Iran, two major regional powers have a convergence of interests in political and economic fields. The emergence of ISIS is a challenge to both, though for different reasons. The movement, which calls for killing of Shias, cannot be acceptable to Shia Iran. The ISIS ideology targets the Saudi regime, as they consider it 'apostate'.

The two countries have agreed to work together to boost crude oil prices, in which they have a shared interest. However, they are yet to grasp the opportunity for cooperation at the political level. If the Trump presidency brings together US and Russia, this will help control the festering conflicts in the region. The situation is more complex than the Great Game of the nineteenth century, which was played out by external actors, where local population was not a factor. In the age of social media and faith-based wars, there is multiplicity of actors.

Being the birthplace of three great religions, West Asia will retain its importance long after the age of hydrocarbons is over. But the coincidence of depressed oil prices with the rise of ISIS, has created an explosive mix. The impact of reduced oil revenues goes beyond the Gulf monarchies, with the loss of worker remittances, which buoyed up economies of many countries of the region. ISIS not only represents a challenge to the Westphalian concept of nation-state, it has aggravated theological schism within the Islamic world. Its political and military formations have to be defeated. But military defeat, and loss of territory, will not be enough until its ideological appeal is countered. This challenge has to be met from within the Islamic world. The war devastated countries of the region also need massive reconstruction effort, and inclusive State structures.

***

Dinkar Srivastava is a former Indian Foreign Service officer, who besides many diplomatic assignments, has served as India's Ambassador to Iran.

END NOTES

1. President Obama's interview to *Fox News*, April 2016.
2. 'The Obama Doctrine', *The Atlantic's* Exclusive Report on the US President's Hardest Foreign Policy Decisions, 10 March 2016.
3. www.un.org.
4. 'The Obama Doctrine', *The Atlantic's* Exclusive Report on the US President's Hardest Foreign Policy Decisions, 10 March 2016.
5. Bunzel, Cole. 'The Kingdom and the Caliphate: Duel of the Islamic States', *Carnegie Endowment for International Peace*, 18 February 2018.
6. Rubab, Syeda Mamoona, 'Dirty Work', *The Friday Times*, 27 January 2017.
7. www.unhcr.org.

JEN

Radicalisation: Developing a Counter-narrative

ALVITE NINGTHOUJAM & CD SAHAY

Abstract

The phenomenon of radicalisation has emerged to be one of the most serious security challenges before the international community today. This has been reinforced with the emergence of extremely rabid terror outfits such as the Islamic State of Iraq and Syria (ISIS) or Daesh, using Islam as a tool to promote radicalism and violence.

Beginning with the trend of radicalisation in the 1980s, under scrutiny is the current scenario of radicalisation, particularly in places where there is significant penetration of Daesh or where it is trying to establish/gain influence including India, Southeast Asia, Europe and the United States. Some of the salient features of radicalisation, use of social media as a tool, role of ideologues and institutions and vernacular publications, are also examined. A section delves into the growing trend of radicalisation in India under the influence of external groups including Daesh. The concluding sub-themes concentrate on the future threat scenario; kinetic and non-kinetic approaches to deal with the outward violent manifestation; de-radicalisation and above all, the imperatives of evolving counter-strategies including a new counter-narrative to be developed by the Islamic institutions, scholars and the relevant civilian establishments.

INTRODUCTION

Extreme violence fuelled by Islamic radicalisation has, understandably, emerged as the most serious security problem being faced by the international community today.

Impact of this global phenomenon is being felt not only in the traditionally conservative societies of West Asia, Middle East and to an extent even in the Indian subcontinent, but also in the Western countries, which have always taken immense pride in their time-tested values of democracy, secularism and multiculturalism. But these basic values have been thoroughly shaken at their roots by the emergence of deeply-radicalised terrorist outfits such as Daesh or Islamic State of Iraq and Syria (ISIS), or just Islamic State (IS) as it is now known, over the last few years. This is not to say that radicalisation is concentrated only in the Islamic societies; it also exists in areas having serious ethno-political crisis. The Muslim insurgency in southern Thailand is a suitable example[1].

Radicalisation in its current manifestation, particularly in the Islamic world and with the level of terrorism associated with organisations like Daesh and Al-Qaeda, is to be seen in a different perspective. The 'dream' of establishing the elusive 'caliphate' has caught the imagination of the followers of Islam like never before. To an extent, even Al-Qaeda in its heydays had this ambition, though it lost the focus on account of its overwhelming preoccupation with Saudi Arabia and the United States (US). Regardless of which terror organisation follows this agenda, radicalisation, as the international community perceives it, is a major threat that is not likely to fade away soon or easily.

INTERNATIONAL SPREAD OF RADICALISED TERROR MACHINE

In recent times, analysts believe that the rise of Islamic radicalisation began with the call for Afghan jihad in the 1980s, wherein large groups of Muslims from across the world were mobilised, deeply indoctrinated, trained in the art of jihadi warfare, fully armed and launched under official patronage to drive the Soviets/Russians out of Afghanistan. They did it successfully but in the process, left behind a massive body of highly indoctrinated and motivated army of mercenaries for the region and the world to contend with. Al-Qaeda and the Taliban became synonymous with this new crop of Islamic warriors, who were at war with virtually the entire established order, first in the region and then later with the world, as evidenced in the 9/11 attack in the US.

Following the punitive US bombing the Taliban regime out of Kabul and all that followed thereafter, including the US-led action in Iraq, the Al-Qaeda attacks against the US/Western establishments/interests around the world led to the emergence of a new narrative of deeply-radicalised Islam at war with rest of the world under the theme, 'Islam under threat'. The then US President, George Bush, described it as a 'Conflict of Civilisations'.

To cut a long story short, the international community is currently grappling with the impact of these developments that are being witnessed in the larger regions of Iraq, Syria and the adjoining neighbourhood, where Daesh, led by its firebrand leader,

Abu Bakr al-Baghdadi, has unleashed a reign of terror like never seen before. His call to the Muslim world to unite to establish the caliphate has found emotive resonance all around. His warriors of Islam are highly indoctrinated and deeply-radicalised. They have joined the movement from across the globe with significant numbers coming from various European countries like the United Kingdom (UK), France, Germany, etc. The presence of Daesh modules has come to notice in many other countries, including the Asian subcontinent, Afghanistan–Pakistan region, the Central Asian republics, Russia, the US, Africa, etc. Daesh recruits are, as a rule, highly radicalised, indoctrinated and intensely motivated. Where Daesh has stolen the march over other groups like Al-Qaeda and some of the African entities is the fact that they rapidly captured vast swathes of land in Iraq and Syria, built up significant financial resources and captured an enviable armoury of war weapons. They did all this in the record time of just a couple of years.

THE HORROR OF TERROR

The horror story of terror perpetrated by Daesh can be gauged by the fact that over the last three years, the group has carried out startling attacks in different parts of the world with near impunity. To establish a well-defined Islamic State to be governed by strict Sharia Law, Daesh, since the beginning of 2014, fought unrelentingly to capture as much territory as it could, and this led to the conquest of a few major Iraqi and Syrian cities, such as Tikrit, Fallujah, Mosul, Ramadi, Raqqa, Palmyra, along with other towns and villages. By the time the self-appointed caliph made his first public appearance on 4 July 2014, his outfit had taken control of territories 'stretching from al-Bab in Syria's Aleppo governorate to Suleiman Bek in Iraq's Salah-ad-Din province, over 400 miles away'[2]. The total territorial control in Iraq and Syria in the beginning of 2015 was about 78,100 square kilometres (sq km) but this dropped to 60,400 sq km in December 2016[3].

This terror war was facilitated by Abu Bakr al-Baghdadi's vast army that had even attracted thousands of foreign fighters from over 100 countries. Between 2014 and mid-2015, the number of these fighters was estimated at 30,000,[4] with majority of them coming from Tunisia, Jordan and Saudi Arabia. A study conducted by the New York-based The Soufan Group gives the following estimates region wise: 1. Western Europe–5,000; 2. Former Soviet Republics–4,700; 3. North America–280; 4. The Balkans–875; 5. The Maghreb–8,000; 6. The Middle East–8,240; and 7. Southeast Asia–900.[5] Daesh militias could carry out several brazen attacks in the region while its overseas fighters, mostly in Europe, carried out similar carnages. Since June 2014, apart from Iraq and Syria, Daesh has conducted or inspired more than 140 attacks in 29 countries, killing more than 2,000 people and injuring thousands[6]. Apart from Syria and Iraq, after 2014, some of the countries, including, Yemen (March 2015–224 deaths),

Egypt (October 2015–224-deaths), France (November 2015–130 deaths), Belgium (March 2016–32 deaths), Turkey (June 2016–45 deaths and January 2017–39 deaths) and Pakistan (February 2017–90 deaths), have faced major attacks which were claimed by ISIS and its affiliates.[7] Even now when the outfit is on retreat in Mosul, it continues to carry out suicide bombing and other acts of terror.

THE STORY OF RADICALISATION

How has Daesh achieved these within such a short span of time? The unanimous answer is: radicalisation. According to noted Indian scholar, Tufail Ahmed, 'Radicalisation is the process of directly and indirectly motivating Muslims to participate in jihadi terror, based on religious teachings and grievance nurturing by Islamic preachers, the press and other Islamic media'[8]. While religion has always been used as a tool to radicalise, current international developments around the world also play a significant role as drivers of radicalisation, which ultimately facilitates recruitment into terror outfits, especially Daesh in this context. However, it is largely agreed that radicalisation on its own does not necessarily lead to violent behaviour by every individual. There is a need to differentiate between the two. More often than not, radicalisation and terrorism have been used interchangeably. No doubt, radical beliefs are a necessary precursor for terrorism but radicalisation per se does not equate with terrorism. Global polls from organisations like Pew and Gallup suggest that there are tens of millions of Muslims worldwide, who are sympathetic to 'jihadi aspirations', and could be branded as 'radicalised'; but only a fraction of them engage in terrorism. Conversely, some terrorists, perhaps many of them, are not ideologues or deep believers in extremist doctrine; and yet have taken to terror violence.

Radicalisation takes place through different routes, such as Islamic institutions, media and literature, preachers, internet and cyberspace, etc. But there is also a growing number of self-radicalised or self-indoctrinated people, mostly belonging to the younger generation. They pose equally serious security challenges. The call given by al-Baghdadi asking sympathisers/supporters from all over the world to unite for the cause found resonance with Muslims everywhere. Focus on internal or domestic issues has been encouraged by Daesh and Al-Qaeda leaderships to augment both radicalisation and recruitment into their groups. Such messages are apparently received by impressionable lone individuals. However, as these elements lie low, it becomes difficult to track their activities. From interrogation of arrested persons in different countries it is clear that both offline and online mechanisms have been effectively used both to radicalise and recruit people. Outfits like Daesh and Al-Qaeda are known to have successfully radicalised and mobilised for action, thousands of foreign fighters into Syria and Iraq to join in the ranks of Daesh or Jabhat Fateh al-Sham (Conquest of Syria) Front, formerly known as Jabhat al-Nusra or Al-Nusra Front[9]. This has been possible due to successful radicalisation and recruitment activities in their native countries.

Role of modern communication technologies and cyberspace has been particularly 'extraordinary' in self-radicalisation the world over. Popular social media tools, such as Facebook, Twitter, Skype and encrypted messenger applications such as Surespot and Telegram, along with easy availability of publications in different local languages, have only made the task easier for the recruiters reaching out to those, who constantly surf the internet looking for any particular terror group, their ideologies, propaganda and their objectives. In this domain, Daesh has outshone all others of that ilk, both in terms of numbers and geographical outreach. Highlighting the role of the internet and social media in spreading radicalisation in the region, Singaporean Prime Minister Lee Hsien Loong said, 'By skilfully exploiting the internet and social media, ISIS has attracted malcontents and misfits, misguided souls and naïve youths from all over the world. More than 20,000 people have gone to Iraq and Syria from Europe, from the US, from Asia, from Australia, to fight—for what? But they are there, and one day, when they return home, they will bring the radical ideology, the combat experience, the terrorist networks and the technical know-how with them'[10].

In West Asia and North Africa (WANA) region, Arabic language print and online publications have played an important role in promoting radicalisation. Likewise, this tool has been effectively used in spreading radicalisation in Central Asia, Russia, the Indian subcontinent, and Southeast Asian countries where Daesh footprints are discernible, both ideologically and physically. Fighters, mostly from Central Asian countries, have set up online forums in Russian and other local languages to make the recruitment endeavours easier. Daesh quickly saw its potential and launched its Russian-language publications *Furat-Press* and *Istok* in mid-2015, published by its propaganda unit, Al-Hayat Media Centre, which also brings out English-language *Dabiq* and *Dar-al-Islam* in French. Since September 2016, the social media campaign was further reinforced with the introduction of *Rumiyah*, the latest English propaganda magazine which called upon Daesh operatives and supporters to intensify lone-wolf attacks against the infidels and the Western interests. These publications play an extremely critical role in promoting radicalisation and perpetration of some of the successful terror attacks staged in recent times. Similar approach is applied in the Asian context, too. Daesh grabbed worldwide attention with its propaganda video in which a Canadian-origin person was featured. This clip was copied into different Indian languages like Urdu, Hindi and Tamil. Similarly, in Malaysia, Indonesia and Philippines, Malay was used to establish the linkages that led to the formation, in September 2014, of a 22-member group called Katibah Nusantara Lid Daulah Islamiyya (Malay Archipelago for the Islamic States) in Al-Shadadi, Syria.

Daesh has perfected the art of exploiting linguistic affinity to attract like-minded recruits. Circulation of propaganda material in Bengali language for its audience in Bangladesh can be a concerning factor, as this language is widely spoken and understood in north-eastern Indian states and West Bengal[11]. Moreover, at this juncture, Bangladesh is undergoing a severe problem of radicalisation of youths who are increasingly going the terror way[12].

Radicalisation propagated through religious establishments, places of public gathering and educational institutions is not new. Its efficacy is astounding—mainly in Europe, a few African countries, Southeast Asia, Central Asia, etc. Mushrooming of mosques funded by the Gulf countries, particularly Saudi Arabia, even in a tiny country like Maldives, has significantly contributed to spreading radical ideologies[13]. Many young Maldivians were introduced to rigid Islamic teachings during their education in Saudi and Pakistan, which was totally different from the form of Islam followed in their own country. This has led to the indoctrination of the young citizens of this nation, and it gives a leeway to the recruiters[14]. Induction of European teenagers into Syria and Iraq mostly happened through self-indoctrination over online route followed by contact with local leaders, ideologues and mentors, often in local mosques. While the internet and the social media do play an important part at least in the initial process of self-radicalisation, the 'second person', that is the motivator and the facilitator, who takes up the task of interpreting the calls of Daesh leaderships from online materials, still plays the most crucial part in the process of final conversion of the individual into an 'asset' for the movement.

This relationship between a recruit and a mentor usually kicks off during religion-oriented seminars, community activities and casual interactions. This is quite common in the UK and in some European Union (EU) countries. The problem is more acute in France, where young Muslims feel disconnected with the mainstream French society. Family problems, societal pressures, search for identity, acceptance and purpose and peer pressure, are some of the other attributing factors for the rising rate of radicalisation amongst the youth. Local converts to Islam in Europe and the US are more susceptible to indoctrination, and they become devout and fanatical adherents to radical Islam[15]. They are more receptive to radical religious views imbibed both online and on the ground. As their numbers grow, they are identified by the recruiters and brainwashed. Over a period of time, ideologues associated with certain mosques and religious institutions are able to infuse many such soft targets with radical views. The story of Shamima Begum and her three friends, who fled to Syria after getting radicalised at a women's charity (Sisters Forum) allegedly run by a group called Islamic Forum of Europe (IFE) in an East London mosque, is an example of the involvement of religious establishments[16]. The problem of radicalisation through mosques in the UK is reportedly fanned by the presence of independent bodies such as the Mosques and Imams National Advisory Board (MINAB), the Muslim Association of Britain (MAB) and the British Council of Muslims (BCM), which are often unregulated.[17]

In Southeast Asia, Russia and Central Asian countries, many of the Kyrgyz, Kazakh and Tajiks are known to have joined Daesh through local mosques and prayer rooms. Similarly, in countries like Indonesia and Philippines, pro-Daesh radicalisation and recruitment happens in mosques and educational institutions[18]. Similar trends were noticed in some African countries where Daesh had already established some presence. A few of the recruits from countries like Ghana and Sudan happened to belong to affluent families with foreign passports of UK, US and Canada. Daniel Byman and Jeremy Shapiro from the Washington-based think tank, Brookings, have observed, '…foreign fighters who go to a war zone are young and ideologically informed, and the combatant groups convert them to their worldview as part of their mission, while training camps emphasise the teachings of "true" Islam and the duty of jihad besides weapons training. So individuals may enter the war with no intention of attacking at home, but their views change and come to encompass a broader set of goals…'[19]

In India, too, there had been instances of radicalisation of youths being carried out in educational and religious establishments. One of the earliest cases of this nature was that of a lecturer, Sufian Sheikh from Anjuman-I-Islam's Kalsekar Technical College located in Panvel (Maharashtra)[20]. In another instance, propaganda in support of Daesh was made by Jamaat-e-Islami Hind[21] and by a cleric from Darul Uloom Nadwat-ul-Ulama in Lucknow (UP) in July-August 2014[22]. While it is difficult to quantify the extent to which such activities resulted in actual radicalism, these acts could have far-reaching implications at this juncture when discontents among the Muslim youths are widespread due to sense of real or imagined socio-political and economic deprivations in the community. The role of Mumbai-based televangelist Zakir Naik, and his organisation, Islamic Research Foundation (IRF), in infusing radical thoughts to a few Muslim youths in India is worrisome[23].

This trend is going to be a worrying factor for some time to come. The growing number of highly radicalised foreign fighters returning to their native countries as Daesh continues to lose grounds in Syria and Iraq only adds to the challenges faced in dealing with the phenomenon of rapid spread of radicalisation around the world.

RADICALISATION AND DAESH THREAT IN INDIA

In recent times, India's exposure to the extreme radical brand of Islam came about with the arrival of the Taliban phenomenon in our neighbourhood in the early 1990s. However, this was, to an extent, preceded by the Jamaat-e-Islami (Pakistan) trying to export radicalised Islamic ideology to the state of Jammu & Kashmir in the early 1990s by launching deeply brainwashed Kashmiri youth, under different banners, to target traditional Sufi Islam practised for centuries in that region. They targeted moderate Islamic leaders, preachers and institutions, including the liberal educational institutions and schools in the rural areas with the aim of replacing these with Islamic madrasas that could spread radical Islamic beliefs in the Valley. The movement gained real momentum when the Taliban established firm control in Afghanistan. Almost around the same time, the Al-Qaeda too became active in this part of the world in terms of spreading radical Islamic ideology. Non-occurrence of Daesh-directed or inspired attacks should not give rise to complacency in India as radicalised individuals have the potential to perform terror attacks, as has been witnessed in other parts of the world. As a result, threats posed by radicalisation, which is being conducted in the name of religion—Islam—should not be underestimated.

As Prime Minster Narendra Modi pointed out, 'Rising tide of terrorism, especially cross-border terrorism and the rise of radicalisation are grave challenges to our security. They threaten the very fabric of our societies. It is my firm belief that those who believe in peace and humanity need to stand and act together against this menace[24].' During his meeting with the Egyptian President Abdel Fattah el-Sisi, Prime Minister Modi had said, '...growing radicalisation, increasing violence and spread of terror pose a real threat not just to our two countries, but also to nations and communities across regions[25].' Though the number of Indians travelling to the Syria/Iraq region is significantly less as compared to European or other Asian countries, the fact remains that al-Baghdadi has targeted this region for future expansion of his agenda of establishment of the caliphate. He made repeated reference to India in his Ramadan speech in 2014 signalling the possibilities of India being one of his prime targets, connecting this with the purported Muslims' dissatisfaction in Myanmar, Pakistan and Jammu & Kashmir[26].

Even as analysts, political leaders and Islamic scholars downplayed Daesh's influence in India, departure of four youths from the state of Maharashtra in June 2014 to Syria and Iraq sounded the first warning of growing radicalisation among a vulnerable section of the community. Brainwashing and radicalisation became easier as many Muslim youth felt an affinity for the outfit on theological lines[27]. Since 2015 or so, India has witnessed several instances of radicalisation taking roots in the Muslim society, particularly in some of the southern states. The charge sheet filed against eight Muslim youths from Hyderabad (India), clearly brought out the role of online radicalisation, supplemented by radical Islamic preachers, such as Anwar al-Awlaki, Abdu Sami Qasmi, Meraj Rabbani, Tausifur Rehman, Jerjees Ansari and Zakir Naik, but also their interest in *Dabiq*, the English propaganda journal of the Daesh[28]. Another example of this was seen in the case of Arif Majeed and three other boys from Kalyan (in Maharashtra, India) joining Daesh. Investigation revealed three more names, out of which two were Afghan nationals, Rehman Daulati and Ahmed Rateb Hussein Zade, and one was Govind Thapar (Indian).

This proved the existence of a large network of people, both in India and abroad, involved in radicalisation and eventual recruitment of youth for deployment in the war zone.

THE FUTURE THREAT SCENARIO

In today's reality, Daesh is obviously the most potent terror organisation, reaping maximum advantage by running an extremely effective radicalisation and recruitment machine. The impact of Islamic radicalisation is mostly noticeable in the EU countries while the US has also faced attacks which were being carried out by individuals influenced by terror outfits and Islamic preachers such as Anwar al-Awlaki. The attacks in San Bernardino in December 2015, Orlando massacre in June 2016, and bombing and knifing incidents in New Jersey, New York and Minnesota in late 2016, were all manifestations of the increasing radicalisation amongst a section of American Muslims. A study by the Virginia-based Threat Knowledge Group mentions that 'ISIS is recruiting within the US at about three times the rate of Al-Qaeda'[29]. In this, Muslim converts are the soft targets; 40 per cent of the arrestees belonged to this category. This is a significant share as 23 per cent of the Muslims in America are converts[30]. Youths as young as 15-17 years were arrested for Daesh-related activities, while the average age of its sympathisers and supporters is between 20s and late 40s.

Search for 'identity' and 'purpose' amongst young converts has motivated them towards radicalisation and ultimate recruitment. Under prolonged indoctrination, they 'emerge as some of the most dangerous and fanatical adherents to radical Islam', and their sense of disconnect from the local mosque has been attributed towards the rising rate of radicalisation in the US and in Europe[31]. For these people, extremist ideology propagated by terror groups and ideologues associated with them gives a sense of belonging as well as an alternative and a zeal to take revenge against the 'infidels'[32]. Despite the retreat of Daesh in Syria and Iraq, many of its fighters and supporters are still convinced 'of the righteousness of their cause'[33]. This is mostly applicable in the European context, which is witnessing an exponential rise of radicalisation within the natives and the migrants. A study conducted by the Sydney-based Lowy Institute categorises 'the future foreign fighter cohort in Syria and Iraq into four categories', including '...those who chose to remain in Syria and Iraq; those who leave in order to continue violent jihad in another theatre, either at home or elsewhere; those who seek to return to their country of origin; and those who go to a third country of refuge'[34].

COUNTER-STRATEGIES

Recognising the fact that radicalisation and the terrorism driven thereon will continue to pose a serious challenge to the world community and remain an international scourge with an ever-growing army of battle-hardened, intensely radicalised people, governments and their intelligence and security establishments in most countries, have started evolving workable strategies and counter-narratives to soften its impact in the short- and long-term perspectives. The counter-strategies and counter-narratives include both kinetic and non-kinetic approaches; the former in terms of detecting and neutralising radicalised terror modules through the use of force, and the latter through a combination of de-radicalisation process for those already affected, and by evolving a credible counter-narrative platform designed to neutralise the ideological drivers of radicalisation. This is important to secure the lives and properties of the citizens at large, which is the primary responsibility of the State.

The kinetic approach would essentially centre on collection of intelligence by the State within its own territories and outside, develop these into actionable intelligence and terminate the imminent threat through police action. This route has high impact, brings immediate result and above all, gives a sense of assurance to the community at large that the security establishment is willing and capable of ensuring their wellbeing. However, as pointed out by the Bangladeshi scholar, Faiz Sobhan, '...while hard power or kinetic measures have often proved successful in removing terrorists from the battlefield, it has become increasingly evident from the global fight against terror, that it is not the sole solution to counter violent extremism. In the long run, hard security measures can prove detrimental in efforts to roll back the appeal of violent extremism. While such measures may be required in situations where threats are imminent, failure to employ "soft power" measures in the long term can be counterproductive in fighting violent extremism with any degree of success...'[35]

As far as non-kinetic measures are concerned, Sobhan goes on to urge the need to formulate a comprehensive policy on counter-radicalisation and de-radicalisation, including a robust programme of rehabilitation and reintegration of violent extremists. Examining the successes and failures of various de-radicalisation programmes worldwide, he points out that even some of the best programmes have their flaws. The de-radicalisation programme of Saudi Arabia is arguably the best-known initiative worldwide, which has also helped other countries in developing similar programmes. Following the 2003 Riyadh bombings, Saudi Arabia launched its rehabilitation and reintegration programme in 2004 to counter the extremist narrative of Al-Qaeda and those terrorist detainees imprisoned at Guantanamo Bay, who had returned to Saudi Arabia. Countries like Egypt, Singapore and Indonesia follow similar de-radicalisation programmes as Saudi Arabia. Three major aspects of the programme include: (1) rehabilitation of extremists; (2) reintegration of extremists; and (3) de-radicalisation[36].

Similarly, the EU decided to focus its anti-terror/radicalisation fight with the involvement of various government, non-government, and public and private sector establishments. The efforts are mainly aimed at the initial period 'where radicalisation is nurtured and encouraged'; the next phase—planning—where 'terrorist plots are hatched'; and the final stage, during which 'attacks are undertaken'[37]. Further, the EU has outlined seven specific areas of cooperation between the member States. These are: (1) countering terrorist propaganda and hate speech online; (2) addressing radicalisation in prisons; (3) promoting inclusive education and EU common values; (4) promoting an inclusive, open and resilient society and reaching out to young people; (5) strengthening international cooperation; (6) boosting research, evidence building, monitoring and networks; and (7) focusing on the security dimension[38]. The counter-strategies have become more sophisticated against the changing operational tactics and effective use of social media tools by terror groups and their supporters operating in the region.

Alongside the policies adopted by the government and its agencies, a robust participation of the Muslim community is a must in evolving an effective counter-narrative to radicalisation. Community leaders and scholars need to show their vehement opposition to the fallacies spread by radical elements and terror outfits, which always portray Islam in a bad light. In one collective voice, Muslim or Islamic countries need to evolve counter-narratives against the prevailing narrative of 'Islam is in danger' and 'Muslims are severely oppressed and marginalised', etc. In order words, the theological underpinnings of Islamists, radical ideologues and Daesh and Al-Qaeda must be constantly challenged and lambasted in every possible forum—classroom lectures, Friday sermons, public speeches and popular media. This is a task that should be taken up by moderate theologians with support from the masses. In the absence of this, any counter-radicalisation strategy will be futile. As former US President Barack Obama stated, 'Groups like ISIL and Al-Qaeda want to make this war, a war between Islam and America, or between Islam and the West. They want to claim that they are the true leaders of over a billion Muslims around the world who reject their crazy notions. They want us to validate them by implying that they speak for those billion-plus people and that they speak for Islam. That is their propaganda. That is how they recruit. And if we fall into the trap of painting all Muslims with a broad brush, and imply that we are at war with an entire religion, then we are doing the terrorists' work for them[39].' These steps encompass a wide range of religious, economic, security and political programmes, and as a result, they can be applied in the South Asian context, particularly India and Bangladesh, which in recent times have seen a radicalisation upsurge.

Even though in India the problem is not that acute as yet, the government has planned a comprehensive strategy to counter the threat from Daesh, its recruitment and radicalisation. In July-August 2015, the Ministry of Home Affairs identified twelve Indian states including Jammu & Kashmir, Uttar Pradesh, Andhra Pradesh, Telangana, Karnataka, Maharashtra, Kerala, Assam, Punjab, West Bengal and Delhi, as vulnerable to

Daesh-related activities. It was decided to initiate counter-radicalisation steps including counselling of youth, involvement of community or religious leaders to persuade the younger generation not to succumb to any form of extremist ideology, constant monitoring of internet and social media sites, quick response to reports of young people planning to join Daesh or any terror group, counter-propaganda strategies, etc. The condemnation and abhorrence expressed by some leading Indian clerics, Islamic scholars and awareness campaigns by non-governmental organisations (NGOs) are some social approaches that need to be promoted further. These roles should not be concentrated on a specific location but be a nation-wide activity.

There is the view that more emphasis needs to be placed on developing and propagating counter-narratives against radicalisation than merely pursuing the kinetic approach. Besides, since other regional countries like Bangladesh, Pakistan and Afghanistan are also affected by this scourge, it is imperative for the governments to work out an all-encompassing cooperative mechanism to deal with the problem together, incorporating some of the best practices and models followed by other countries.

CONCLUSIONS

The twin problems of radicalisation and terror are unlikely to disappear anytime soon. Even if Daesh is physically neutralised in its present strongholds, its ideology and emotive appeal will not be completely eliminated. Another al-Baghdadi, in another part of the world, will likely reappear sooner than later and perhaps, in a more virulent incarnation. There is a humongous amount of effort that needs to be put into place to counter the rising tide of radicalisation amongst the youths in Islamic and non-Islamic societies. The long-term solution lies in fighting the ideology from within and at the grass-roots level. A multi-pronged strategy needs to be evolved. In the Indian context, it is generally agreed by all stake holders that the role of the government and its entities must necessarily remain minimal and under the radar. The lead role has to be played by the community leaders and institutions.

Meanwhile, as security and intelligence apparatuses brace themselves to deal with terror attacks not only from major terror outfits but also from self-radicalised individuals, who possess the wherewithal to cause violence, the State, society at large, religious leaders, writers and intellectuals, the vernacular media, religious and educational institutions, all have to come together to develop an effective and credible counter-narrative, projecting the benign and peaceful image of Islam. The counter-narrative must deconstruct the existing narrative of conflict and war propagated by the radicals and extremists. In other words, a new 'positive' narrative of Islam built around the true essence and beliefs that would inspire the youth and wean them away from the current narrative, needs to be evolved in right earnest. The sooner this is done, greater would be chances of success.

***

Alvite Singh Ningthoujam is Senior Research Associate at VIF. He looks after issues related to international terrorism, Middle East security dynamics, Israel's military exports and India–Israel relations.

CD Sahay is Dean, Centre for Neighbourhood Studies and Internal Security Studies at VIF. He is Former Secretary (R), Cabinet Secretariat, Government of India.

ENDNOTES

1. Bajoria, Jayshree and Zissis, Carin. 'The Muslim Insurgency in Southern Thailand', *Backgrounder*, Council on Foreign Relations, 10 September 2008.
2. Lister, Charles, 'Profiling the Islamic State', *Brookings Doha Center Analysis Paper*, No. 13, November 2014, p 4.
3. 'Islamic State and the Crisis in Iraq and Syria in Maps', *BBC*, 20 January 2017, at http://www.bbc.com/news/world-middle-east-27838034
4. 'Foreign Fighters: An Updated Assessment of the Flow of Foreign Fighters into Syria and Iraq', *The Soufan Group*, December 2015, p 5.
5. Ibid.
6. Lister, Tim and Sanchez, Ray et al, 'ISIS goes Global: 143 attacks in 29 countries have killed 2,043', *CNN*, 13 February 2017, at http://edition.cnn.com/2015/12/17/world/mapping-isis-attacks-around-the-world/
7. Yourish, Karen; Watkins, Derek and Giratikanon, Tom. 'Where ISIS Has Directed and Inspired Attacks Around the World', *The New York Times*, 22 March 2016, at https://www.nytimes.com/interactive/2015/06/17/world/middleeast/map-isis-attacks-around-the-world.html?_r=0
8. Ahmad, Tufail. 'The Radicalisation Series: Analysing the Threat to Muslim Youths in India, *First Post*, 22 August 2016.
9. Basra, Rajan; Neumann, Peter R and Brunner, Claudia. 'Criminal Pasts, Terrorists Futures: European Jihadists and the New Crime-Terror Nexus', The International Centre for the Study of Radicalisation and Political Violence, 2016, p 23.
10. 'Excerpts of Keynote Address of Singapore Prime Minister Lee Hsien Loong', at http://www.iiss.org/en/events/shangri%20la%20dialogue/archive/shangri-la-dialogue-2015-862b/opening-remarks-and-keynote-address-6729/keynote-address-a51f,
11. 'Dhaka Attack: IS Publishes Propaganda Material in Bengali, Alert Issued', *Deccan Chronicle*, 4 July 2016.
12. For further discussion, 'Karim, Tariq and Balaji, Madhumita Srivastava. Rising Trend of Religious Radicalisation in Bangladesh', Issue Brief, Vivekananda International Foundation, New Delhi.
13. Wright, Oliver. 'Islamic State: The Maldives—A Recruiting Paradise for Jihadists', *The Independent*, London, 14 September 2014. Also see Boghardt, Lori Plotkin. 'Saudi Funding of ISIS', *Policy Watch*, No. 2275, The Washington Institute for Near East Policy, 23 June 2014.

14. Ningthoujam, Alvite Singh. 'Maldives is No Longer a Paradise', *International Institute for Counter-Terrorism*, Israel, 2 April 2015.
15. Faiola. Anthony and Mekhennet, Souad. 'From Hip-Hop to Jihad, How the Islamic State Became a Magnet for Converts', *The Washington Post*, Washington DC, 6 May 2015.
16. 'Britain's Jihadi Bride Groomer: Schoolgirl Radicalised in London Mosque Recruited her Three Classmates to Join ISIS in Syria', *Daily Mail*, London, 1 August 2015. See Kassam, Raheem. 'ISIS Recruitment in London Mosque Uncovered', *Middle East Forum*, 2 August 2015.
17. 'UK Mosques Can Play a Role in Radicalisation', *The Arab Weekly*, 17 July 2015.
18. 'No ISIS Recruitment in Mindanao Schools, WMSU president says', *The Manila Times*, 12 November 2014.
19. Byman, Daniel and Shapiro, Jeremy. *Be Afraid. Be Little Afraid: The Threat of Terrorism from Western Foreign Fighters in Syria and Iraq*, Foreign Policy, No. 34, Brookings, Washington DC, November 2015, p 6.
20. 'Lecturer Quizzed for B rainwashing ISIS militant Areeb Majeed', *India Today*, 2 December 2014.
21. "Supporting the ISIS Caliphate is Binding on All Muslims, ISIS Fulfils Maulana Azad and Maududi's Aspirations for The Islamic Caliphate," says Jamaat-e-Islami Hind', *New Age Islam*, New Delhi, 26 August 2014.
22. 'Nadwa Cleric asks Saudi Government to Prepare an Army of Sunni Youth for Iraq', *The Times of India*, New Delhi, 26 July 2014.
23. For a detailed analysis, see Sahay, CD. 'Islamic Radicalisation: The Zakir Naik Way', *Articles*, Vivekananda International Foundation, New Delhi, 22 August 2016.
24. 'Excerpts of the Press Statement by PM during the visit of Prime Minister of Singapore', at http://www.pmindia.gov.in/en/news_updates/press-statement-by-prime-minister-of-india-during-the-visit-of-prime-minister-of-singapore-to-india/?comment=disable
25. 'Excerpts of the Press Statement by PM during the visit of President of Egypt to India', http://www.pmindia.gov.in/en/news_updates/press-statement-by-pm-during-the-visit-of-president-of-egypt-to-india/?comment=disable&tag_term=pmspeech
26. Swami, Praveen. 'India among jihad targets of ISIS', *The Hindu*, 2 July 2014.
27. Joseph Chinyong Liow, 'ISIS Goes to Asia', *Foreign Affairs*, 19 September 2014.
28. 'Eight Accused Charge Sheeted for Involvement in Terrorist Conspiracy in Hyderabad ISIS Module Case', *Press Release*, National Investigation Agency, New Delhi, 22 December 2016.
29. Gorka, Sebastian L and Gorka, Katharine C. 'ISIS: The Threat to the United States', *Threat Knowledge Group*, Virginia, 17 November 2015, p 1.
30. 'Converts to Islam', *Pew Research Centre*, Washington DC, 21 July 2007,
31. Faiola and Mekhennet, 'From Hip-Hop to Jihad, How the Islamic State Became a Magnet for Converts'.
32. Bergen, Peter and Sterman, David. 'Who are ISIS' American Recruits', *CNN*, Atlanta, 6 May 2015.
33. 'Ticking Time Bomb of Foreign Fighters Returning to France from Syria', *The National*, Abu Dhabi, 9 September 2016.
34. Khalil, Lydia and Shanahan, Rodger. 'Foreign Fighters in Syria and Iraq: The Day After', *Lowy Institute*, Sydney September 2016, p 7.
35. Sobhan, Faiz. 'The Urgent Need for a De-radicalisation Programme', *Dhaka Tribune*, Dhaka, 28 October 2016.
36. Ibid.
37. Behr, Ines von and Bellasio, Jacopo. 'Fighting Terrorism and Radicalisation in Europe', *The RAND Blog*, Santa Monica, 11 March 2016.
38. 'Stronger EU Action to Better Tackle Violent Radicalisation Leading to Terrorism', *Press Release*, European Commission, Brussels, 14 June 2016. For a detailed account, see Vidino, Lorenzo and Brandon, James, 'Countering Radicalisation in Europe', The International Centre for the Study of Radicalisation and Political Violence, London, 2012.
39. 'Excerpts of the Remarks by the President Barack Obama After Counter-ISIL Meeting', at https://www.whitehouse.gov/the-press-office/2016/06/14/remarks-president-after-counter-isil-meeting

ALHAYA

The New Climate Change Regime and Its Implications for India

CHANDRASHEKHAR DASGUPTA

Abstract

The Paris Agreement requires all countries to make 'nationally determined contributions' to mitigate climate change on the basis of their 'national circumstances' and 'capabilities'. It shifts the focus from historical and current emissions to future emissions. This has major implications for India since our emission levels are expected to rise progressively from very low historical and current per capita levels as we pursue inclusive development. Projections indicate that India will contribute more than any other country to the rise in global energy demand till 2040 in aggregate terms, though India's per capita emissions will still be around 20 per cent below the global average.

India should, therefore, strive to ensure that the compliance procedures of the agreement take full account of per capita energy consumption, per capita emissions and energy resource endowments as elements of 'national circumstances' and per capita income as the basic element of national 'capabilities'.

OVERVIEW

The Paris Agreement on climate change was adopted with much fanfare in November 2015. This new agreement charts a very different course of action from the Kyoto Protocol, which it will replace after 2020. A brief overview of the preceding agreements will help us understand what is new in the Paris Agreement and the changes it introduces in the climate change regime.

UN FRAMEWORK CONVENTION ON CLIMATE CHANGE AND THE KYOTO PROTOCOL

The UN Framework Convention on Climate Change (UNFCCC), adopted in 1992, laid the basis for a global response to climate change. The convention reflected the fact that the bulk of the greenhouse gas concentrations in the atmosphere had originated in the developed countries, that per capita emissions in the developing countries were still low and that they would increase in the course of economic development. It explicitly recognised that 'economic and social development and poverty eradication are the first and overriding priorities of the developing country Parties.' In accordance with the principle of 'common but differentiated responsibilities', the convention required developed countries to initially stabilise and thereafter, reduce their greenhouse gas emissions. It also required developed member countries of the Organisation for Economic Co-operation and Development (OECD) to contribute financial resources and transfer technology to developing countries with a view to enabling the latter to undertake mitigation and adaptation activities. The developing countries had no such commitments.

While it called upon developed countries to limit and reduce their emissions, UNFCCC did not lay down specific, time-bound targets. This lacuna was filled by the Kyoto Protocol (1997). Under this protocol, each developed country was allotted a specific, legally-binding emission reduction obligation for an initial commitment period up to 2008-12. This was to be followed by further reductions for subsequent periods, to be negotiated by 2012. The protocol created a 'Clean Development Mechanism', which allowed a developed country to meet part of its emission reduction commitment by financing emission limitation measures in a developing country.

The Framework Convention and the Kyoto Protocol meet the criterion of environmental justice, in the sense that they require the parties that are mainly responsible for causing climate change, to bear the burden of mitigating greenhouse gas emissions. Climate change is not caused by carbon dioxide emissions per se. Indeed, life on this planet could not have been sustained in the absence of carbon dioxide. Climate change is precipitated only when the accumulated carbon dioxide concentration in the atmosphere exceeds certain limits. If all countries had the same per capita emission profile as, say, India, our planet would not have faced the threat of climate change induced by human activities. The developed countries have exceeded their proportionate share of carbon emission and are, thus, mainly responsible for climate change. These countries are also more amply endowed with the financial and technological resources required for mitigation and adaptation actions. Thus, the Framework Convention and the Kyoto Protocol draw a sharp distinction between the respective obligations of developed and developing countries[1].

Almost immediately after the entry into force of the Kyoto Protocol, the developed countries reopened the question of mitigation commitments for developing countries. They brought pressure on developing countries to accept an attenuation of the differentiation in their respective commitments, following a salami-slice strategy to progressively pare down the principle of common but differentiated responsibilities. They also ensured the demise of the Kyoto Protocol. The United States refused to ratify the protocol, notwithstanding the leading role of the then Vice President Al Gore in ensuring its adoption. Canada withdrew from the protocol soon after its entry into force. Japan and Russia, followed by many other developed countries, refused to accept commitments beyond 2012. The European Union (EU) reluctantly agreed to accept a very modest 2020 commitment, while declaring that it would not proceed with its mitigation commitments under the Kyoto Protocol after that date. Apart from the EU, only five developed countries have agreed to a 2020 commitment under the protocol. The Kyoto Protocol has thus been sentenced to a lingering death.

THE CLIMATE REGIME AND THE CHANGING GLOBAL ECONOMIC ORDER

In 1997, the developed countries accepted the equity-based Kyoto Protocol; yet, almost as soon as it entered into force, they began to demand a radically different treaty. The explanation for the turnaround lies in the domain of economics, not ecology. In 1997, the OECD countries were still confident of retaining their leadership position in the global economy. China's rise was still in its initial stages, and India's economic reforms had been introduced very recently. The situation changed sharply within a few years. China achieved spectacular growth rates, overtaking Germany and Japan to emerge as an industrial, trading and financial power, second only to the United States. Some other large developing countries, India and Brazil in particular, also achieved impressive, if less spectacular, growth rates, emerging on the global scene as major economies. These developments resulted in a radical reordering of the distribution of global economic power[2].

This shift in the global economic balance initially gave rise to protectionist calls in OECD countries, thinly disguised as environmental measures. In the first decade of this century, new competitiveness concerns drove industrial circles in many OECD countries to demand border levies on imports of carbon-intensive goods from developing countries, on the plea that it was necessary to offset the carbon mitigation costs resulting from the commitments of developed countries under the Framework Convention and Kyoto Protocol. Fearing loss of jobs, trade unions in these countries made common cause with employers concerned about loss of competitive advantage. It was also argued that the implementation of carbon emission regulations by developed countries would only result in relocation of carbon-intensive industries to developing countries, if the latter are exempted from similar obligations.

Though superficially plausible, these arguments are not backed by convincing empirical evidence. In general, carbon mitigation costs are not the decisive consideration in investment decisions. Important factors include the condition of the physical infrastructure (ports, roads, railways, etc); quality of human resources; tax regulations; legal and dispute resolution systems, and so on. These factors generally outweigh the costs of carbon regulations required by the Kyoto Protocol. Moreover, if carbon mitigation costs had been a decisive factor, it would have led to a massive transfer of carbon-intensive industries from other developed countries to the United States, since the latter had refused to ratify the Kyoto Protocol and was, therefore, exempt from the commitments applicable to other OECD countries. Yet, the concerns voiced in OECD countries, focused on 'emerging economies', rather than the United States, reflecting their protectionist nature. The real source of these concerns was the rapid loss of competitive advantage to the 'emerging economies'.

Alongside these attempts to change the rules of the global trade regime, the developed countries also pressed for a fundamental change in the climate change regime. Their tactics were to divide the least developed countries (LDCs) and the small island developing States (SIDS) from the 'emerging economies'. They used economic aid as an instrument, holding out promises of largesse and, in some cases, threats of withholding aid. While insisting that the 'emerging economies' should bear a greater share of the burden of greenhouse gas mitigation, the OECD countries promised that the LDCs and SIDS would be exempted from these new obligations.

THE PARIS AGREEMENT

Under the Paris Agreement, all countries, developed and developing alike, are expected to declare nationally determined contributions (NDCs) of a non-binding nature. However, in the case of a developing country, the NDC need not reflect an absolute reduction in greenhouse gas emissions; it could, for instance, take the form of an emission-intensity target (i.e. the quantum of greenhouse gas emissions per unit of GDP). The aim is to achieve 'global peaking' of greenhouse gas emissions as early as possible, with a view to restricting global warming to 'well below' 2 degrees Centigrade and, if possible, to 1.5 degrees. The agreement recognises that 'peaking will take longer for developing country Parties'. Each country is expected to contribute to the global mitigation effort in accordance with its 'national circumstances'.

The parties to the agreement will undertake a periodic 'global stock-take' to assess progress towards achieving its goal. In addition, an expert committee will examine the performance of individual countries with a view to 'facilitate implementation and promote compliance' in a 'transparent, non-adversarial and non-punitive' manner, paying particular attention to 'national capabilities and circumstances'. The important question of the modalities and procedures to be followed by the expert committee is to be decided in future negotiations.

The net effect of the Paris Agreement is to weaken the differentiation between the two categories of 'developed' and 'developing' countries and to replace it with a continuum of countries at various stages of development and with differing 'national circumstances'. In blurring the line dividing the developed and developing countries, the Paris Agreement shifts the focus from accumulated historical (past) emissions present in the atmosphere to current and future emissions. It glosses over the responsibility of affluent industrialised countries to vacate the excess atmospheric space they occupy, a responsibility that requires them, under the Kyoto Protocol, to reduce their own emissions, meeting any shortfall by financing mitigation actions in developing countries. The Paris Agreement, therefore, transfers a large share of the obligations of the developed countries to the shoulders of developing countries and, in particular, to large, rapidly growing economies (such as India), whose emission trends will inevitably reflect both their rapid development and the size of their population. The focus is shifted to 'early peaking' of emissions in these countries.

Adoption of the Paris Agreement was greeted with much fanfare and it was hailed as a notably ambitious 'breakthrough'. The agreement does, indeed, set an ambitious climate stabilisation target, but it is far from clear that it provides an adequate basis for meeting the target. It may be recalled that in 1991, in the early stages of the climate change negotiations, Japan had proposed a voluntary 'Pledge and Review' accord, not dissimilar to the Paris Agreement. The Japanese proposal was rejected because it was felt that an agreement that set no legally-binding emission reduction commitments for developed countries ignoring their historical responsibility, would fail to achieve the objective of the climate change convention. The initial 'nationally determined contributions' submitted by parties, and, in particular the singularly modest contributions of the developed countries, fall far below the stabilisation target.

The prospects of the Paris Agreement are further clouded by deep uncertainty over the US policy. The newly-inaugurated President, Donald Trump, had declared during the electoral campaign his intention to withdraw from the Paris Agreement. The terms of the Paris Agreement permit a party to give notice of withdrawal only three years after the entry into force of the agreement for the concerned party and the notification takes effect after another year. However, one cannot rule out the possibility that the new administration might withdraw from the umbrella Framework Convention itself, thereby divesting itself of all international responsibility concerning climate change. At any rate, it seems certain that the US will renege on its pledges of financial support, thereby dealing a serious blow to implementation of the Paris Agreement. The agreement will survive a US withdrawal (as did the Kyoto Protocol) but its effectiveness will be greatly impaired.

IMPLICATIONS FOR INDIA

In the wake of the Paris Agreement, the International Energy Agency (IEA) brought out a study on India's energy future, highlighting the country's current low levels of energy consumption as well as the rapid increase in energy consumption and related emissions over the next few decades[3]. It observed that India's current per capita energy consumption is only one-third of the global average but also that 'India is set to contribute more than any other country to the projected rise in global energy demand, around one quarter of the total' till 2040. Because of India's dependence on its coal reserves, it is projected to account for nearly 50 per cent of net coal-based power generation capacity added worldwide. Since the Paris Agreement focuses on future emission pathways, Indian emission trends and energy options will receive very close scrutiny, notwithstanding the IEA projection that India's per capita emissions will remain some 20 per cent below the world average even in 2040.

At the same time, it will be more difficult for India to find effective coalition partners in future negotiations. Despite differences on other issues, China has so far been India's closest partner in the climate change negotiations. Right from the inception of the climate change negotiations in 1991, the two countries have cooperated closely, adopting similar positions on almost all issues. This cooperation was based on common interests: both India and China had low per capita carbon dioxide emission rates and these emissions were bound to increase as a result of their development imperatives. This situation has evolved in recent years. Because of China's spectacular growth rates, its per capita carbon dioxide emissions reached a level of 6.66 tonnes by 2014, close to that of many developed countries such as UK (6.31 tonnes) or Germany (8.93 tonnes), according to IEA estimates[4]. Moreover, with the narrowing of China's technology gap, its growth rate is registering a gradual decline. Thus, China was in a position to submit a nationally determined contribution, which envisaged peaking of its emissions by around 2030 (indeed, a number of projections indicate a much earlier peaking date). China will soon be in a position to pledge emission reductions after the anticipated peaking date, offering pledges similar to those of the developed countries. Because of India's growth trajectory, its per capita emissions will continue to rise beyond 2040. China has reached a stage of development where its interests in the climate change negotiations no longer necessarily coincide with those of India.

The procedures of the expert committee to 'facilitate' and 'promote compliance' have yet to be finalised. Though the committee is expected to work in a 'non-adversarial' and 'non-punitive' manner, there are suggestions that it should adopt a 'name and shame' approach, with a view to ratcheting up pledges of target countries. This would inevitably lead to arbitrary findings in the absence of agreed criteria for determining the entitlement of each party to a share of the global atmospheric resource. India should oppose this proposal and advance a counter-proposal for giving the expert committee a mandate to identify and publicise 'best practices' followed by countries at different levels of development and with different resource endowments. Unlike a 'name and shame' proposal, this would conform fully with provisions of Article 15 of the Paris Agreement, which requires a 'facilitative', 'non-adversarial and non-punitive' approach.

The compliance mechanism set up under Article 15 is required to pay particular attention to the 'national capabilities and circumstances' of each country. This term has not, however, been defined in the agreement. India should identify per capita GDP as the basic element of national 'capabilities'. Availability of financial resources is a critical requirement for mitigation actions. Poorer countries require financial support on non-commercial terms in order to respond effectively to climate change. India should also identify per capita energy consumption, per capita emissions and resource endowments (coal, in India's case) as the basic constituent elements of 'national circumstances'. We should aim to keep the focus on per capita, as distinct from aggregate emissions.

CONCLUSION

Unlike the UN Framework Convention on Climate Change and the Kyoto Protocol, the Paris Agreement glosses over the historical responsibility of developed countries arising from the disproportionately large share of the global atmospheric space occupied by them. It shifts the focus to future emissions and the rapidly-shrinking atmospheric space that is still available. India currently suffers from extreme energy poverty; its per capita energy demand and associated emissions will increase for some decades as it pursues inclusive development. Projections indicate that because of its development trajectory and the size of its population, India will account for a larger share of *incremental* emissions than any other country till at least 2040, even though its per capita emissions will remain much below the global average. To place these developments in proper perspective, it is essential that the compliance mechanism should give full weightage to per capita emissions and per capita GDP in estimating a country's 'national circumstances and capabilities'.

***

Chandrashekhar Dasgupta is a retired Indian Foreign Service officer. Among other posts, he served as Ambassador to the European Union and Ambassador to China. He is a Padma Bhushan awardee. Dasgupta is presently a Member of Prime Minister's Council on Climate Change, and Member of the UN Committee on Economic, Social and Cultural Rights, Geneva. He is the author of *War and Diplomacy in Kashmir, 1947-48*.

END NOTES

1. For Indian perspectives on environmental justice, see Agarwal, Anil and Narain, Sunita. *Global Warming in an Unequal World: A Case of Environmental Colonialism*, Centre for Science and Environment, New Delhi, 1993 and Ghosh, Prodipto. 'Climate change Debate: The Rationale of India's Position', in Dubash, Navroz K (ed.). *Handbook of Climate Change and India: Development, Politics and Governance*, OUP, New Delhi, 2012.
2. See Dasgupta, Chandrashekhar. 'The Future of the Global Climate Change Regime', *Indian Foreign Affairs Journal*, Vol. 7, No.3, July-September 2012.
3. International Energy Agency, *India Energy Outlook: World Energy Outlook Special Report. 2015*. Paris.
4. International Energy Agency, *CO2 Emissions from Fuel Combustion: Highlights*. 2016. Paris.

Year of Climate Departure for World Cities

Results show multi-model averages under RCP8.5 (Mora et al. 2013)

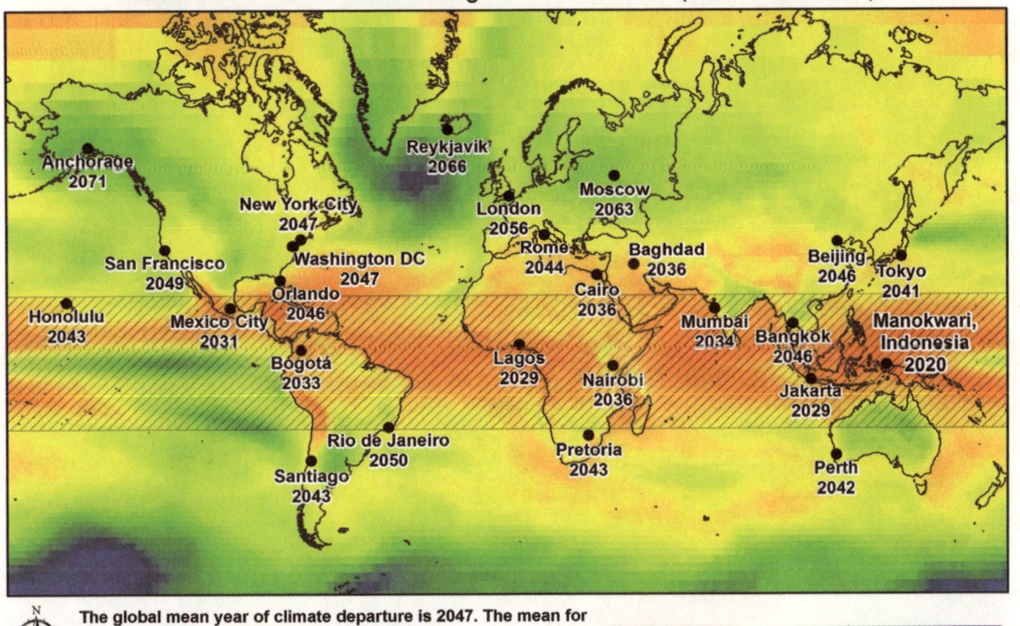

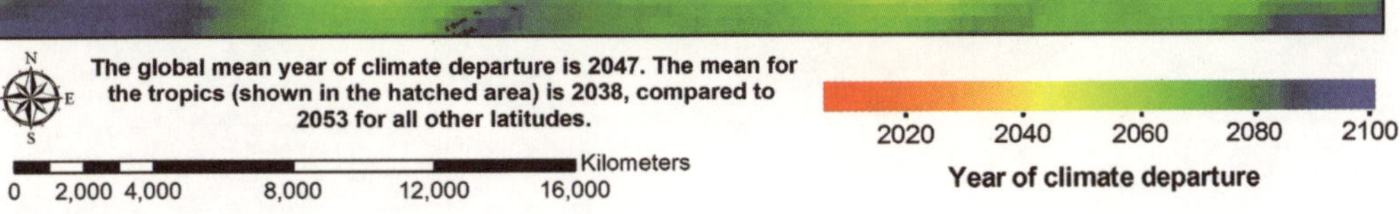

NASA

Weaponisation of Outer Space—A Major Security Challenge

LT GEN DAVINDER KUMAR, PVSM, VSM BAR, ADC

Abstract

Outer space is being used extensively for governance, development, telecommunications, weather forecasting, education, entertainment, disaster management and for a host of other commercial and military applications. Consequently, space, a very fragile and hostile environment, has become highly crowded, contested and competitive. Developed nations, due to their extensive dependence on space systems, have become very vulnerable and are involved both in the protection of their systems and developing and testing counter-space capabilities. Countries that may either have their own power ambitions or feel threatened, are also developing counter-space technologies and weapons to gain advantage through asymmetry. The situation is accentuated by the low cost and lowering of technology threshold. While space is already heavily militarised, the challenges are the debris, traffic management, development of ballistic and anti-ballistic missile systems and imminent weaponisation.

INFORMATION, SPACE AND SATELLITE SYSTEMS

In the information age, satellites have become a core element of modern societies and are largely responsible for bringing nations and individuals together[1]. While satellite-based communications and navigation systems help to improve traffic safety, disaster response and weather forecasts, they also help in education, health, earth resource management and so on. Global climate change and the concomitant increase of water conflicts and energy crises will further enhance the importance of satellites as means of information procurement, dissemination and disaster response. The advancement of the information society will also create new vulnerabilities. The more societies depend on satellites, the more important it will be to protect them as critical infrastructures.

For modern armed forces, satellites have become indispensable, especially considering the irresistible advance of network-centric warfare (NCW) and effect-based operations (EBOs), particularly since the war in Afghanistan from 2001 onwards[2]. Satellite systems are an integral part of information network, which is at the heart of decision-making process and navigation of forces. Satellites, thus, serve as force multipliers in present-day military operations.

In a space system, most of the technologies have a dual-use character and civilian satellites are increasingly being used for military purposes. This presents a dilemma to security persons as limiting them in traditional arms control measures is not possible, and, as a result, they question the very adequacy, feasibility and applicability of arms control in outer space. Dual-use technologies such as those seen in the space domain present a challenge for multilateral arms control efforts. Primarily, there are two main concerns affecting the safe and peaceful use of space: first is the increasing level of space pollution; and second, the re-emergence of arms dynamics in space.

Space-based systems and satellites will continue to increase in importance and reach[3]. There is a new sense of sensitivity and urgency emerging about the security of outer space and related techno-military superiority in space. Military blueprints by major space-faring powers now encapsulate concepts of 'space support' and 'force enhancement', which point to a central role of space assets in facilitating military operations, while notions of 'space control', 'space power', 'space situational awareness' and 'force application' suggest that not only has space been recognised as the new strategic frontier, but its weaponisation is imminent. The majority view indicates that space may soon be a theatre of military operations. Counter-space capabilities such as missile defence, anti-satellite capabilities and a new class of Directed Energy Weapons (DEWs), thus, assume critical importance for defence and security perceptions. Space-faring nations across the world are busy in developing technologies and capabilities both for defensive and offensive operations. Relevant technologies and methodologies are those for physical and electronic hardening, anti-jam systems, satellite maneuverability, redundancy at system and sub-system levels, quick launch facilities, as well as, mini, micro and nano satellites both for restoration of facilities and for use as killer satellites. The world seems to be in a state of transition from using space-based assets to support combat operations on the surface of the earth to using them for conducting combat operations in space, from space, and through space.

MILITARISATION VERSUS WEAPONISATION

A distinction must be made between 'militarisation of space' and 'weaponisation of space'. These terms are sometimes used as if they were interchangeable, but they are not. While there are no specifically deployed weapons in space yet, there are satellites that could be manoeuvred to act as weapons to disable or destroy the space assets of others. Therefore, when considering questions of space security, it must be recognised that though space has not yet been specifically weaponised, it is already heavily militarised[4]. The military operations in space have shifted gradually from scientific interest to surveillance to intelligence collection to robust combat support.

The next logical transition is the weaponisation of space. This is precisely what happened to other domains like sea and air. Space, as currently used, is a finite resource which is highly congested, contested and competitive. This competition, coupled with dependence on and the criticality of space for development and security, is likely to lead to conflicts, which will involve weaponisation of space, space control and space dominance across the full spectrum, namely orbits, space assets and ground-based facilities. In discussing the expanding role of the military in space, the term weaponisation implies an increase in the capability to conduct warfare in, from or through space. While space has not been weaponised yet, there are historical reasons for suspecting that the weaponisation of space is as inevitable as was the weaponisation of the land, sea and air domains of warfare, primarily to protect resources in those environments.

> 'People no longer can do without telecommunications, navigation and the information provided by remote sensing based on space systems.'
>
> —Russian President, Vladimir Putkov, as stated at the last UNIDIR outer space conference

Nations and societies across the world are depending increasingly on space-based systems for practically every facet and activity. The same is true for the military. As an increasing number of these critical resources and capabilities migrate to space, the need increases to protect these resources, in peace and war. Space, thus is likely to become an arena of military operations.

Having been militarised virtually since the beginning of man's experience in this medium, societies will weaponise space as they perceive threats to the ability to gather information, communicate and trade in, from or through space[5]. The question is not whether societies will do so, but when, and in response to what stimulus. Control of space is not only important to ensure access to satellites but to support military operations on the earth. Just as control of the air is a precursor to effective operations on the land or sea, control of space is a prerequisite to effective operations in all terrestrial media (land, sea and air). As reliance on space assets increases, any disruptions to military access in space would adversely affect military operations and impact national security. Space, in effect, has become the centre of gravity for national security, governance and development.

THREATS AND SECURITY CHALLENGES

Space is an extremely harsh and inhospitable environment with solar radiation, extreme temperature gradients, micro gravity and absence of external pressure, besides transfer of heat only by conduction, ultra violet radiation, space debris and meteoroids being some of the challenges, which directly impact the design, useful life and survivability of the satellites and other space assets. The net effect is that a space system is inherently very fragile and vulnerable. The irony is that ground-based space systems are equally, if not more, susceptible to interference by physical, kinetic, electronic and cyber-systems.

Since 1957, hundreds of satellites have been launched into space, many for commercial reasons[6]. However, the security of the space environment has not yet been adequately addressed. Today, we face many space security challenges, including orbital crowding, debris and imminent possibility of weaponisation of space. Orbital debris is a serious threat due to the potential for collision. Despite debris mitigation guidelines, such as those of the Committee on the Peaceful Uses of Outer Space (COPUOS), the problem remains overwhelming and a great threat to space assets. With 4256 satellites in different orbits, space is a very crowded place[7]. Out of these, only 1419 satellites are operational (June 2016). The rest are metal junk, posing a serious threat and a challenge. There is, therefore, an inescapable requirement for transparency and traffic management. The threat of weapons likely to be placed in space and weapons designed to attack space-based assets, for example, counter-space and anti-satellite weapons (ASATs), is very real. Indeed, avoidance of an arms race in outer space is the biggest challenge.

There is an urgent need to spell out strategy for the safeguarding of outer space, of the long-term viability of the use of space and of the use of space by new actors. A six-point approach, as given below, is recommended:

- First, a comprehensive and proactive strategy is needed for addressing space debris including improvements to the resolution of debris tracking systems.
- Second, traffic management should be available and applied to all in space, as a logical consequence of an increase in the number of satellites, in order to avoid collisions and to guarantee safe access.
- Third, measures to narrow the gap of technological asymmetry and ensuring equitable exploitation of space for development and disaster management should be taken.
- Fourth, a set of common and consistent rules and procedures for operating in outer space should be evolved. More integrated approach and accountability

towards space governance, including introduction of property rights envisaged in the Moon Treaty 1984, to prevent conflict are needed.

- Fifth, a way must be found to prevent conflict in space and to prohibit ASAT tests and counter-space technologies.
- Finally, space situational awareness is extremely important. Sharing of information on launch and location of space assets must be made mandatory.

DRIVE TOWARDS WEAPONISATION

In view of the criticality of outer space for national development and security, nations across the world are engaged in developing both offensive and defensive capabilities to secure and exploit space assets both in the space and those on ground. These capabilities are being built on three pillars of space power, space control and space situational awareness.

SPACE POWER

Space power can be defined as 'the total strength of a nation's capabilities to conduct and influence activities to, in, through and from space to achieve its objectives'. The definition is further expanding to being 'the aggregate of a nation's abilities to establish, access, leverage and sustain its orbital assets to further all other forms of national power'. Simply put, space is inherently a medium, as with air, land, sea and cyber, and 'space power is the ability to use or deny the use by others of that medium'.

Space power is a precondition to control the sea, land or air. It provides the ability of continuous awareness of terrestrial events and has become the concern of all organisations, regardless of their technical sophistication. It is based on the following conjectures:

- Space forces are necessary to enhance war-fighting capabilities.
- Space forces can target forces at sea, land and air.
- Adversaries must be deprived access to space to gain a decisive advantage.
- Space power is perishable and must be protected and regenerated if necessary.

SPACE CONTROL

Space control supports freedom of action in space for own forces, and when necessary, defeats adversary's efforts that interfere with or attack own space systems and negates adversary's space capabilities. It consists of:

- Offensive space control (OSC): Measures taken to prevent an adversary's hostile use of space capabilities or offensive operations to negate an adversary's space capabilities used to interfere with or attack own space systems.
- Defensive space control (DSC): DSC are operations conducted to preserve the ability to exploit space capabilities via active and passive actions, while protecting own space capabilities from attack, interference or unintentional hazards.

SPACE SITUATIONAL AWARENESS (SSA)

SSA involves characterising, as completely as necessary, the space capabilities operating within the terrestrial environment and the space domain. SSA is dependent on:

- Integrated space surveillance.
- Collecting and processing data in real time.
- Environmental monitoring.
- Status of own and cooperative satellite systems.
- Measure of own space readiness and analysis of the space domain.
- It also incorporates the use of intelligence sources to provide insight into adversary's use of space capabilities and their threats to own space capabilities, with a view to understand adversary's intent.

HISTORICAL PERSPECTIVE

Both the US and the Soviet Union developed and tested different methods of destroying or damaging satellites or causing disruption of their operations from early sixties to mid-eighties[8]. The initial Anti-Satellite weapons (ASAT) were modified Intermediate Range Ballistic Missiles (IRBMs) used as direct ascent weapons with nuclear warheads. However, the US Starfish test in space in 1962 brought the realisation that nuclear explosions in space are indiscriminate and would destroy all nearby satellites in their line of sight and damage many more in the ensuing weeks by the increased radiation in Low Earth Orbits (LEOs). Consequently, the 1963 Limited Test Ban Treaty (LTBT), signed by both the US and the Soviet Union, banned any nuclear explosion in space. The LTBT further led to the Outer Space Treaty (OST) that in 1967, banned placing of Weapons of Mass Destruction (WMDs), including nuclear weapons, in space. The OST, however, did not explicitly prohibit deliberate attacks on satellites or conduct of ASAT weapons tests. Consequently, other ASAT technologies continued to be developed and tested as space negation ability was considered integral to the larger strategic domination effort during the Cold War. Both superpowers also tested air-launched ASAT versions in the 1980s. The Chinese ASAT test in 2007 and the strategic imperative to ensuring availability of space assets changed the status quo, and many space fairing nations started work on both defensive measures and development of offensive capability.

THE CURRENT SCENARIO

The use of outer space has all along been driven by forces from two directions: one is the impetus for outer space weaponisation[9], and the other, efforts toward the prevention of an arms race in outer space (PAROS).

In the globalised world, national security imperatives have evolved beyond securing of borders to all aspects critical to the nations' political and economic well-being.

Space-based capability has become integral to military, social and commercial interests, and any disruption of these capabilities would have huge operational and economic ramifications for most countries. Today, space-based systems are at the heart of the modern revolution in military affairs (RMA) and precision targeting that is an important part of EBOs.

Proliferation of technology and its reduced cost have allowed an increasing number of States to have the ability to develop or possess more complex and devastating weapons. Similarly, there are more seekers of ballistic technology and capabilities for access to space. Hence, the threat environment confronting the existing space-faring nations is broadening and becoming increasingly complex.

THE UNITED STATES' POSITION

> 'The weaponisation of space provides the asymmetric technology the US needs to win the next war.'
>
> —Thomas D Bell, Lt Col USAF, January 1999

The US, with 576 satellites in space in different orbits, is the largest user of space with considerable dependence for national security, development and governance[10]. The US, therefore, is also most vulnerable as far as space security is concerned. Accordingly, its stand on military exploitation of space is different. It wishes to expand its military capabilities and have weapons in space and therefore, also be dominant in this fourth dimension of warfare.

In April 2005, Gen James E Cartwright, who led the United States Strategic Command, told the Senate Armed Services' nuclear forces subcommittee that the goal of developing space weaponry was to allow the nation to deliver an attack 'very quickly, with very short time lines on the planning and delivery, in any place on the face of the earth.'[11] General Lance Lord, head of the US Air Force Space Command, quoted in 'Air Force Seeks Bush's Approval for Space Weapons Programmes', *The New York Times*, 18 May 2005: 'Space superiority is not our birthright, but it is our destiny. Space superiority is our day-to-day mission. Space supremacy is our vision for the future.'

The United States considers space capabilities—including the ground and space segments and supporting links—vital to its national interests. Consistent with this policy, the stated stance of the United States is to: 'preserve its rights, capabilities and freedom of action in space; dissuade or deter others from either impeding those rights or developing capabilities intended to do so; take those actions necessary to protect its space capabilities; respond to interference; and deny, if necessary, adversaries the use of space capabilities hostile to US national interests'. The US military explicitly says it wants to 'control' space to protect its economic interests and establish superiority over the world.

'A century ago, nations built navies to protect and enhance their commercial interests by ruling the seas. Now it is time to rule space.'

—Karl Grossman, *Master of Space*, Progressive Magazine, January 2000

CHINA AND SPACE

Countries that may either have their own power ambitions or feel threatened by the US are most likely to develop counter-space technologies and weapons to gain advantage through asymmetry. In this context, China is likely to be considered a possible adversary of the US in the future, and may be one of the countries that could threaten US dominance in space, even though it has constantly opposed the use of space for military purposes. The counter-space technologies being developed by China and demonstrated at times, are of serious concern. The common belief is that China is slowly flexing its muscles and that an arms race may be underway. China's behaviour smacks of hypocrisy for wanting a global treaty to ban weapons in space on the one hand, and then developing and testing full spectrum counter-space capabilities on the other. China is of the view that to avoid taking the old path of arms control, where control comes after development, the fundamental way of preventing the weaponisation of outer space and maintaining lasting peace and security is to negotiate a legally-binding international instrument. In the meantime, it is concentrating on developing and operationalising both defensive and offensive capabilities.

INTERNATIONAL EFFORTS FOR PEACEFUL USE OF SPACE AND SPACE GOVERNANCE

Ever since the beginning of the space age, the development and spread of space technologies have been key components of globalisation, spurring international cooperation. As an ever-larger number of players enter into space activities, it has become critically important to ensure the security and integrity of outer space. One of the most effective ways of enhancing space security is to build trust and confidence among space-faring States by promoting international partnerships and cooperation.

As of date, the 1967 Outer Space Treaty remains the primary point of reference for international space law. However, the space environment has changed drastically with the end of the Cold War, the emergence of a highly profitable space services industry and a sharp decrease in the financial and technological entry barriers. Consequently, there has been a dramatic increase in the number of actors with space assets. While the importance of matters related to peaceful space operations has been for the most part undisputed, the need for arms control in outer space has been far more contentious. Proposals include both legally-binding treaties, such as the draft Treaty on the Prevention of the Placement of Weapons in Outer Space and the Threat or Use of Force Against Outer Space Objects (known as the PPWT); and politically-binding norms of behaviour, such as the proposed International Code of Conduct for Outer Space Activities.

The draft PPWT was jointly introduced in the Conference on Disarmament (CD) by Russia and China in 2008. However, the international community has failed to embrace it as an opportunity to lay down the foundation for a robust, unambiguous and universal space security treaty that unequivocally attempts to minimise the likelihood of a weaponised space domain.

The proposed code of conduct is essentially a mechanism to codify a set of transparency and confidence-building measures for outer space activities, with the aim to reduce misperceptions and miscommunications among space actors and to spell out the sort of behaviour that will contribute to a sustainable space environment such as that which limits the further creation of space debris and reduces the likelihood of unintentional harmful interference.

WHAT INDIA NEEDS TO DO?

While India advocates peaceful use of space and has strong outer space capabilities, she needs to formulate without delay her 'National Space Vision' and the associated 'National Space Security Policy'. India must take a proactive and aggressive stand and build necessary capabilities both for defensive and offensive measures in a time-bound mission mode. 'Space Command' must be raised immediately and the space programme should be given an urgent techno-military orientation in response to her national security imperatives, particularly in view of the outer space and counter-space capabilities of China. Concurrently, a strategy has to be adopted for promoting an international treaty for peaceful exploitation of outer space and protecting India's interests.

There is still time for India to develop the technology, test the same and integrate with her war-fighting capability and thereby safeguard her long-term strategic interests. The window of opportunity may close any day owing to major entry of private sector in outer space and the likelihood of a shift in the stance currently adopted by the USA. The time to act is now.

***

Lieutenant General Davinder Kumar, PVSM, VSM BAR, ADC retired as the Signal Officer-in-Chief of Indian Army after a distinguished service of forty-one years. An expert in telecommunication networks, Information Warfare and Space systems, he was the CEO and MD of Tata Advanced Systems and was on the board of directors of various public sector and private companies. He has published more than 400 papers and spoken at various fora in India and abroad.

END NOTES

1. *Space: The New Frontier of Security Policy*–CSS www.css.ethz.ch/publications/pdfs/CSSAnalyse171-EN.pdf.
2. *From Star Wars to Space Wars–The Next Strategic Frontier: Paradigms to Anchor Space Security*, Maogoto, Nyamuya and Freeland, Steven.
3. Ibid.
4. *Militarisation and Outer Space Politics*, Essay, https://www.ukessays.com/.../militarisation-and-weaponisation-of-outer-space-politics...
5. Ibid.
6. *Security in Space: The Next Generation*, Conference Report 31 March–1 April 2008, UNIDIR United Nations Institute for Disarmament Research, Geneva, Switzerland.
7. Index of Objects Launched into Outer Space maintained by United Nations Office for Outer Space Affairs (UNOOSA),
8. *Weaponisation of Space*, Puneet Bhalla, Centre for Land Warfare Studies (CLAWS).
9. *Security in Space: The Next Generation*, Conference Report, 31 March–1 April 2008, UNIDIR United Nations Institute for Disarmament Research, Geneva, Switzerland.
10. United Nations Office for Outer Space Affairs (UNOOSA).
11. *Militarisation and Weaponisation of Outer Space Politics*, Essay https://www.ukessays.com/.../militarisation-and-weaponisation-of-outer-space-politics...23 March 2015.

Index

1267 Committee of the UNSC 59, 64, 66, 80
1962 India–China War 75
1963 Limited Test Ban Treaty (LTBT) 190
1965 Indo-Pakistan War 75
1967 Outer Space Treaty 192
2015 Judicial Commission report 87

A

Abdullah, King 146, 152, 153
Abe, Shinzo 47, 52
Act East policy 115, 137
Aden 131
Afghan National Army (ANA) 99
Afghan National Police 99
Afghanistan, India and Pakistan (AIP) 113
Afghanistan/Afghan 49, 53, 54, 55, 75, 78, 79, 80, 81, 82, 89, 91, 95, 96, 97, 98, 99, 100, 101, 95, 101, 85, 101, 98, 100, 101, 102, 103, 104, 105, 106, 107, 108, 113, 129, 131, 154, 160, 161, 166, 170, 186
Afghanistan–Pakistan (Af-Pak) region 154, 161
Africa/African 48, 53, 78, 120, 124, 126, 127, 128, 129, 130, 131, 136, 145, 146, 147, 161, 163, 164, 165
Agartala 115, 138
Agartala–Akhaura rail link 138
Agreement on the Political Parameters and Guiding Principles for the Settlement of the Boundary Question (APPGP) 66, 67, 72
Ahmed, Tufail 162
Aiyar, CP Ramaswami 23
Akhaura 138
al-Awlaki, Anwar 166, 167
al-Bab 161
al-Baghdadi, Abu Bakr 151, 161, 162, 166, 170
Aleppo 145, 150, 151, 154, 161
al-Falih, Khalid 152
Al-Hayat Media Centre 163
Ali, Liaquat 90
Alibaba 68
al-Jubeir, Adel 152
Allahabad 117
Allahabad–Calcutta–Narayanganj 117
al-Naimi, Ali 152
Al-Qaeda 97, 151, 152, 160, 161, 162, 166, 167, 168, 169
Al-Shadadi 163
al-Sheikh, Abd al-Aziz 152
America First policy 63
America, United States of (USA/US) 12, 14, 15, 16, 25, 38, 39, 43, 44, 47, 48, 49, 50, 51, 52, 53, 54, 55, 56, 60, 61, 62, 63, 64, 68, 70, 72, 75, 76, 77, 78, 79, 80, 81, 82, 85, 91, 96, 99, 101, 102, 103, 104, 105, 106, 107, 130, 131, 146, 147, 148, 149, 150, 151, 152, 153, 154, 155, 156, 159, 160, 161, 163, 164, 165, 167, 169, 172, 177, 178, 179, 180, 190, 191, 192, 193
Anadolu Agency 104
Anbar 151
Andaman and Nicobar Command 132
Andaman and Nicobar Islands 132
Andhra Pradesh 169
Anjuman-I-Islam's Kalsekar Technical College 165
Ansari, Jerjees 166
Arab Winter 147
Arab/Arabic/Arabia 55, 101, 130, 145, 146, 147, 148, 149, 150, 151, 152, 153, 154, 155, 160, 161, 163, 164, 168, 172
Arabian Sea 49, 54, 127, 130, 131

Arunachal Pradesh 59, 67, 117
ASEAN Plus Six 138
ASEAN–India FTA 139
Ashuganj 138
Asia/Asian vi, 15, 30, 39, 45, 48, 49, 51, 52, 53, 54, 60, 61, 62, 65, 71, 78, 101, 103, 105, 108, 111, 112, 113, 115, 119, 120, 121, 124, 126, 127, 128, 129, 130, 131, 135, 136, 137, 138, 139, 142, 143, 156, 159, 160, 161, 163, 164, 165, 166, 169, 172
Asian Development Bank (ADB) 137, 138, 140, 142, 143
Asian Infrastructure Investment Bank (AIIB) 69, 142
Asia–Pacific 48, 53, 61, 62, 65, 129, 142
Asia–Pacific Economic Cooperation (APEC) 142
Asia–Pacific Trade Agreement (APTA) 137
Assam 112, 113, 141, 169
Assessment of the Quality of Democracy in Pakistan 2016 86
Association of Southeast Asian Nations (ASEAN) 53, 63, 120, 126, 137, 138, 139, 143
Atlantic 48, 50, 53, 126, 147, 150, 151, 153, 156
Atlantic magazine, The 147, 150, 153
Attaturk, Kemal 151
Aurobindo, Sri 22, 34
Australia/Australian 16, 44, 127, 138, 163
Azam 153
Azhar, Masood 59, 65, 80
Aziz, Abdul 151, 152
Azm-e-Nau III 6

B
Bab-el-Mandeb 126
Babur (Hatf VII) 6
Bahrain 155
Bairoch, Paul 40, 45
Bajwa, Qamar Javed 88
Balkans 161
Baltistan 78, 82
Baluchistan/Baloch 5, 78, 82, 91
Bangkok 120, 136, 137
Banglabandha 115
Bangladesh 76, 111, 113, 114, 115, 117, 119, 120, 121, 132, 114, 119, 115, 117, 119, 120, 121, 132, 136, 138, 139, 140, 141, 142, 143, 164, 169, 170, 171
Bangladesh–Bhutan–India–Nepal (BBIN) 111, 113, 114, 115, 116, 117, 119, 139, 140
Bangladesh–China–India–Myanmar (BCIM) 132, 138
Bangladesh–China–India–Myanmar Economic Corridor (BCIM-EC) 138
Basu, Sankari Prasad 22, 34
Battle of Trafalgar 119
Bay of Bengal 114, 120, 127, 131, 132, 136, 139, 140, 141
Bay of Bengal Initiative for Multi-Sectoral Technical and Economic Cooperation (BIMSTEC) 132, 135, 136, 137, 138, 139, 140, 141, 142, 143
BBIN Motor Vehicles Agreement (MVA) 115, 139, 140
BBIN Rail Connectivity Agreement 115
Begum, Shamima 164
Beijing 52, 60, 70, 76, 82, 120, 127, 130
Bek, Suleiman 161
Belt and Road Initiative (BRI) 59, 62, 64, 69, 72, 130
Belur 22, 33
Bengal 22, 34, 35, 111, 112, 113, 114, 116, 117, 118, 119, 120, 121, 127, 131, 132, 136, 139, 140, 141, 164, 169
Bengal Presidency 111, 112, 113, 116, 117, 120
Benghazi 148
Bernardino, San 167
Bhutan 111, 113, 114, 115, 117, 136, 139, 141
Bhutto, Zulfikar Ali 80
Biao, Lin 77
Bihar 112, 141
Bilawal Bhutto 87
BIMSTEC FTA 139, 140
BIMSTEC Summit 136
BIMSTEC Transport Infrastructure and Logistics Study (BTILS) 137, 140, 142
BIST-EC 136
Bogor 142
Bonn Conference 96
Border Peace and Tranquillity Agreement 67
Brahmaputra 118
Brazil, Russia, India, China and South Africa (BRICS) 48, 53, 120, 135, 136, 139, 142
Brexit 52, 60, 85
Brezhnev, Leonid 76
BRICS New Development Bank 142
BRICS–BIMSTEC Outreach Summit 135, 136, 139, 142
British Council of Muslims 165
Brookings 165, 171, 172
Brown Amendment 81
Brown, Hank 81
Brzezinski, Zbigniew 107
BTILS Report 140
Bunzel, Cole 151, 156
Burimari 115
Burma 112
Bush, George 160
Byman, Daniel 165, 172

C
Cabinet Committee on Security (CCS) 3
Camp David Accord 149
Canada/Canadian 163, 165, 177
Carnegie study 151
Cartwright, James E 191
Central Asian/Central Asia 49, 53, 54, 101, 105, 126, 131, 161, 163, 164, 165
Central Military Commission 82
Central Political and Legal Affairs Commission of the Communist Party of China 65

Chabahar 131
Changrabandha 115
Chapter VI of the UN Charter 149
Charsadda 89
Chashma 3 81
Chatra 117
Chenab 5
Chicago 21, 22, 35, 45
Chin 138
China Seas 131
China/Chinese 3, 13, 14, 15, 16, 17, 39, 40, 45, 47, 48, 49, 50, 52, 53, 54, 55, 59, 60, 61, 62, 63, 64, 65, 66, 67, 68, 69, 70, 71, 72, 75, 76, 77, 78, 79, 80, 81, 82, 83, 85, 91, 95, 96, 101, 102, 103, 104, 105, 106, 107, 120, 123, 126, 127, 129, 130, 131, 132, 136, 138, 139, 141, 142, 147, 152, 153, 177, 180, 182, 190, 192, 193
China–Pakistan Economic Corridor (CPEC) 49, 54, 64, 78, 83, 91, 130, 139
Chisapani 117
Chittagong 115, 118, 119, 138
Clinton, Bill 43, 81
Clinton, Hillary 51, 83, 147
Cold Start Doctrine 6
Cold War 48, 53, 76, 107, 190, 192
Colombo 35, 64
Committee on the Peaceful Uses of Outer Space (COPUOS) 188
Comprehensive Test Ban Treaty (CTBT) 15, 81
Conference of the Parties (COP)-21 120
Conference on Disarmament (CD) 81, 171, 193
Congress of the Chinese Communist Party 82
Council of Senior Religious Scholars 152
Council Resolution 1267 Committee 80
Cultural Revolution 77
Cyrenaica 148

D
Dabiq 163, 166
Dacca (now Dhaka) 76, 112, 135, 138, 140, 143, 171, 172
Dar-al-Islam 163
Darul Uloom Nadwat-ul-Ulama 165
Daulati, Rehman 166
Davos 82
Dawei 140
Defence White Paper of 2013 13
Deussen, Paul 29
Djibouti 63, 64, 131
Doval, Ajit 70
Duqm 131
Durkheim, Emile 38

E
East Asia/East Asian 71, 112, 119, 126, 143
East India Gazetteer 112, 121
East Jerusalem 149
East London 164
East of Malacca 129, 130
Eastern Sector 66, 72
Egypt/Egyptian 56, 131, 146, 147, 148, 149, 162, 166, 168, 172
el-Sisi, Abdel Fattah 149, 166
Erdogan, Recep Tayyip 151
Eritrea 131
Eurasian 103, 126
Eurasian Economic Union 103
Europe 25, 30, 35, 47, 49, 50, 55, 70, 80, 107, 112, 115, 117, 126, 145, 147, 148, 150, 152, 159, 161, 163, 164, 166, 167, 171, 172, 177, 182
European Union (EU) 47, 48, 49, 50, 52, 53, 55, 126, 145, 148, 164, 167, 168, 169, 172, 177, 182
Eurozone 55

F
F-16 aircraft 81
Fallujah 150, 161
FATA 89
Firdaus 153
Fiscal Responsibility and Debt Limitation Act of 2005 90
Fissile Material Cut-off Treaty (FMCT) 15
Florida 52, 60
Flynn, Michael 51
Framework Convention 176, 180, 181
France/French 17, 23, 49, 55, 56, 147, 148, 151, 153, 161, 162, 163, 164, 172
Frederici, Caesaro (or Frederick Caesar) 118
Friedman, Milton 39
Furat-Press 163

G
G-2 52
G-20 39
Gaddafi, Col M 80, 147, 148
Gallup 162
General National Congress 148
Germany 17, 49, 50, 52, 55, 153, 161, 177, 180
Ghana 165
Ghani, Ashraf 98
Gilgit–Baltistan 78, 82
Goa 112, 135, 136, 139
Gore, Al 177
Government of National Accord (GNA) 148
Greater Mekong Subregion (GMS) 137
Guantanamo Bay 168
Gulf 124, 129, 130, 131, 143, 146, 147, 149, 153, 154, 155, 156, 164
Gulf Cooperation Council (GCC) 131, 155
Gulf of Aden 131
Gulf of Tirana 149
Guwahati 117

Guwahati–Narayanganj–Allahabad 117
Gwadar 49, 54, 63, 64, 83, 91, 130

H
Haley, Nikki 49, 51, 54
Hambantota 64
Haqqani network 55, 89
Hashemite 151
Hatf 6
Hejaz 151
Ho Chi Minh City 115
Hong Kong 71, 82
Hormus 126, 130, 131
Horn of Africa 124, 129, 131
Houthi 55, 152
Hudaydah 131
Hyderabad 70, 166, 172

I
Iberian Peninsula 125
Idris, King 148
Imphal 140
India, Maldives and Sri Lanka (IMS) 113
India's Nuclear Doctrine 3
India–ASEAN FTA 137
India–Myanmar Joint Railway Working Group 140
India–Myanmar–Thailand Trilateral Highway 138
Indian Coast Guard 18, 131, 133
Indian Navy 64, 131, 132
Indian Ocean 63, 123, 124, 126, 60, 126, 127, 128, 130, 131, 132, 139, 141, 143
Indian Ocean Commission 131
Indian Ocean Nation States (IONS) 132
Indian Ocean Region (IOR) 60, 63, 64, 124, 126, 127, 128, 129, 130, 131, 132
Indian Ocean Rim Association (IORA) 132, 141, 143
Indian subcontinent 75, 111, 112, 113, 160, 163
India–Sri Lanka FTA 137
Indo-Asia–Pacific 129
Indonesia 132, 138, 163, 165, 168
Indo-Pacific 123, 126, 129, 135, 137
Indo-US Civil Nuclear Agreement 12
Indus 4, 5
Indus Valley 4
International Atomic Energy Agency (IAEA) 15
International Code of Conduct for Outer Space Activities 193
International Energy Agency (IEA) 154, 180, 182
International Hydrographic Organization (IHO) 129
International Institute for Strategic Studies (IIIS) 4
International Maritime Organization (IMO) 129
International North South Transport Corridor (INSTC) 132
Inter-Services Public Relations (ISPR) 88
Iran 18, 49, 54, 77, 96, 101, 105, 107, 130, 131, 145, 146, 151, 152, 153, 154, 155, 156
Iraq/Iraqi 95, 131, 143, 145, 146, 147, 150, 151, 153, 154, 155, 159, 160, 161, 162, 163, 164, 165, 166, 167, 171, 172
ISIL 169, 172
Islamabad 90, 130, 136
Islamic Forum of Europe (IFE) 164
Islamic Military Alliance to Fight Terrorism (IMAFT) 88, 152
Islamic Research Foundation (IRF) 165
Islamic State/ISIS/IS/Daesh 50, 51, 53, 95, 97, 103, 104, 105, 130, 145, 146, 148, 150, 151, 152, 153, 154, 155, 156, 159, 160, 161, 162, 163, 164, 165, 166, 167, 169, 170, 171, 172
Israel/Israeli 130, 145, 146, 149, 150, 171, 172
Istok 163

J
Jabhat al-Nusra/Al-Nusra Front (formerly Jabhat Fateh al-Sham) 162, 163
Jaigon 115
Jaishankar, S 70
Jaish-e-Mohammad (JeM) 89
Jamaat-e-Islami 165, 172
Jamaat-e-Islami (Pakistan) 165
Jamaat-e-Islami Hind 172
Jamaat-ud-Dawa 80
Jammu & Kashmir (J&K) 75, 76, 78, 165, 166, 169
Japan/Japanese 16, 47, 48, 50, 52, 53, 63, 117, 126, 127, 137, 142, 177, 179
Jayaswal, KP 26
Jhelum 5
Jianzhu, Meng 65
Jiechi, Yang 70
Jinnah, MA 90
Jinping, Xi 48, 52, 60, 61, 62, 63, 68, 82
Johnson, Lyndon 76
Joint Comprehensive Plan of Action (JCPOA) 152
Jordan 161

K
Kabul 79, 91, 160
Kabulov, Zamir 104
Kakarbita 115
Kaladan Multi-modal Transit Transport project 138
Kalay 140
Kalemyo 140
Kalyan 166
Karachi 63, 81, 89
Karakoram Highway 64
Kargil War 77
Karnali 117

Karnataka 169
Karzai, Hamid 98
Kathmandu 17, 71, 83, 115, 121, 139
Katibah Nusantara Lid Daulah Islamiyya 163
Kazakh 165
Kennedy, John 76
Kenya 131
Kerala 169
Kerry, John 83
Khan, AQ 80
Khan, Imran 86, 87
Kharian 88
Kharijites 152
Khushab 80
Khyber 78, 89, 112
Khyber–Pakhtunkhwa 78, 112
Kidwai, Khalid Ahmed 6
Kifaya movement 148
Ki-moon, Ban 42
Kolkata (also Calcutta) 34, 35, 112, 115, 117
Kolkata–Agartala 115
Korea 63, 81, 126, 127, 137
Kosi 117
Kosygin, Alexei 76
Krishna, Raj 40, 45
Kuwait 155
Kyoto Protocol 175, 176, 177, 178, 179, 180, 181
Kyrgyz 165

L
Lahore 76, 88, 89
Lakhvi, Zaki-ur-Rehman 80
Lama, Dalai 59
Laos 142
Lashkar-e-Jhangvi (LeJ) 89
Lashkar-e-Toiba (LeT) 89
Latin America 126
Leaders' Retreat 2016 Outcome Document 136, 139, 140, 142, 143
Libya/Libyan 145, 146, 147, 148
Look East policy 137
Loong, Lee Hsien 163, 171
Lop Nor 80
Lord, Lance 191
Lowy Institute 72, 167, 172

M
M-11 missile 81
Madagascar 131
Madison, Angus 41
Madras 23, 35
Maghreb 161
Mahan, Alfred Thayer 126
Maharashtra 165, 166, 169
Makran Coast 5, 130
Malacca 126, 129, 130, 132
Malaysia 71, 137, 163
Maldives 113, 119, 131, 164, 172
Manipur 140
Mansour 104, 105
Mansour, Mullah 104
Mao 77
Mardan 89
Maritime Silk Route 138
Marx, Karl 38, 40, 45
Matarbari 141
Mattis, James 51
Mauritius 131
Mausam 124
McMaster, Herbert 51
McNamara, Robert 76
Meghalaya 117
Mekong–India Economic Corridor (MIEC) 140
Merkel, Angela 52
Mexican 50
Middle East 103, 127, 145, 146, 147, 149, 150, 154, 160, 161, 171, 172
Middle East Peace Process 149
Migiro, Asha-Rose 40
Minnesota 167
Mizoram 115, 117, 138, 140
Mobu 115
Modi, Narendra 34, 41, 68, 69, 78, 82, 116, 123, 124, 143, 166
Mongla 115
Mongolia 77
Moon Treaty 1984 189
Moreh 115, 140
Moreh–Tamu border point 140
Morocco/Moroccan 118, 147
Morsi 146, 148, 149
Mosques and Imams National Advisory Board (MINAB) 164
Mosul 150, 154, 161, 162
Mozambique 131
Mubarak, Hosni 148
Mueller, Max 29
Mumbai 7, 80, 165
Muscat 131
Muslim Association of Britain (MAB) 165
Muslim Brotherhood 148, 149, 155
Myanmar 115, 119, 132, 136, 137, 138, 139, 140, 141, 142, 143, 166

N
Nagrota 7
Naik, Zakir 165, 166, 172
Narayanganj 117

Nasr (Hatf IX) 6
Nasr SSM 8
National Directorate of Security (NDS) 99
National Institution for Transforming India (NITI) Aayog 41, 42, 45
National Unity Government (NUG) 96, 98, 107
National Waterways Act, 2016, The 116
Nayef, Prince Mohammad Bin 152
Neighbourhood First policy 136, 143
Nejd 151
Nelson 119
Nepal 111, 113, 114, 115, 117, 136, 137, 139, 141, 142
New Delhi/Delhi 16, 17, 34, 35, 71, 72, 83, 107, 108, 115, 120, 121, 123, 128, 130, 131, 132, 137, 140, 143, 169, 171, 172, 182
New Jersey 167
New York 34, 44, 45, 56, 161, 167, 171, 191
New Zealand 138
Nivedita, Sister 22, 23, 33, 34, 35
No Dong 81
Noble, Margaret 22
Non Proliferation Treaty (NPT) 15, 80
North Africa 145, 146, 147, 163
North America 161
North American Free Trade Agreement (NAFTA) 50
North Atlantic Treaty Organisation (NATO) 48, 50, 52, 146, 151
North Korea 81
North Waziristan 85, 89
Northern Thunder 152
Nuclear Command Authority (NCA) 4, 7
Nuclear Proliferation Treaty 15
Nuclear Proliferation Treaty (NPT) 15
Nuclear Suppliers Group (NSG) 12, 15, 59, 64, 72, 81
Nunes, Devin 51

O

Obama, Barack 47, 50, 51, 52, 81, 83, 91, 147, 148, 150, 152, 153, 156, 169, 172
Oman 131, 155
One Belt One Road (OBOR) 49, 54, 103, 127, 130, 138, 139
One China policy 48, 60, 82
Operation Parakram 5, 6
Operation Radd-ul-Fasaad 89
Operation Zarb-e-Azb 89
Organisation for Economic Co-operation and Development (OECD) 45, 176, 177, 178
Organisation of the Petroleum Exporting Countries (OPEC) 145, 146, 154, 155
Orissa 112
Orlando 167
Ormara 63
Ottoman 146, 151, 153
Outer Space Treaty (OST) 190, 192

P

P 5 + 1 131
Pakhtunkhwa 78, 112
Pakistan Institute of Legislative Development and Transparency (PILDAT) 86
Pakistan Muslim League-Nawaz (PML-N) 86, 87, 88, 89, 90
Pakistan Peoples Party (PPP) 87, 153
Pakistan Tehreek-e-Insaf (PTI) 87, 121, 153
Pakistan/Pakistani 4, 5, 6, 7, 8, 9, 10, 13, 14, 16, 49, 53, 54, 55, 64, 66, 76, 77, 78, 79, 64, 3, 75, 76, 79, 80, 81, 82, 83, 85, 86, 87, 88, 89, 90, 91, 92, 95, 96, 97, 99, 101, 102, 103, 104, 105, 106, 108, 112, 113, 115, 117, 129, 130, 131, 136, 138, 139, 142, 153, 154, 161, 162, 164, 165, 166, 170
Pakistan-occupied Kashmir 78, 83
Palestine/Palestinian 149
Palmyra 161
Panama Papers 85, 87, 92
Pancheswar 117
Pangaon 114
Panitanki 115
Pannikar, KM 25
Parbatipur 142
Paris Agreement 49, 55, 175, 178, 179, 180, 181
Pashtunistan 82
Pathankot 7
Payra 141
Penang 112
Pence, Mike 51
People's Liberation Army (PLA) 63, 64, 127, 130
Peoples Liberation Army Navy (PLAN) 63, 64, 130
Perkovich, George 14
Permanent Court of Arbitration (PCA) 54
Persia/Persian 145, 146, 153
Persian Gulf 124, 129, 130, 131
Peshawar 89
Pew 162, 172
Philippines 53, 54, 143, 163, 165
Phuentsoling 115
Phulbari 115
Pledge and Review 179
Popper, Karl 38
Portugal/Portuguese 112, 125
Power, Samantha 150
Pressler Amendment 80, 81
Prithvi 10
Punjab 6, 85, 86, 87, 88, 89, 90, 91, 169

Q

Qadri, Mumtaz 90
Qasmi, Abdu Sami 166
Qatar 101, 155
Quadrilateral Coordination Group 79
Quetta 89

R
Rabbani, Meraj 166
Rafsanjani, Ayatollah 153
Rajasthan 6
Ramadi 150, 151, 161
Ramakrishna, Sri 26, 33, 35
Ramgarh 138
Rangia 141
Raqqa 161
Reagan, Ronald 82
Red Sea 131
Regional Comprehensive Economic Partnership (RCEP) 138
Rehman, Tausifur 166
Reqqa 154
Rhi 138, 140
Rhi-Tiddim section 140
Riyadh 149, 168
Rolland, Romain 23, 33, 34, 35
Rubab, Syeda Mamoona 153, 156
Rumiyah 163
Russia/Russian 16, 17, 47, 48, 49, 51, 52, 53, 54, 56, 77, 81, 83, 95, 96, 101, 102, 103, 104, 105, 106, 107, 120, 126, 136, 145, 147, 149, 151, 152, 153, 155, 156, 161, 163, 165, 177, 187, 193

S
SAARC Corridor-8 115
SAARC Regional Rail Agreement 115
SAARC Summit 136, 139
Sabroom 138
Sabroom–Ramgarh road link 138
Sagar 124, 132
Sagarmala 124, 132, 141
Salah-ad-Din 161
Salalah 131
Salman, Prince Mohammad bin 152
Sanaa 131
Saraswati, Swami Dayananda 26
Saudi/Saudi Arabia 55, 88, 101, 130, 145, 146, 149, 151, 152, 153, 154, 155, 160, 161, 164, 168, 172
Scuds 81
Sehwan 89
Senkaku Islands/Senkakus 48, 52
Seychelles 131
Shafiq, Ahmed 149
Shaheen IA, I, II, III 6
Shaksgam Valley 75
Shakti I, II, III 10
Shanghai Cooperation Organisation (SCO) 48, 53
Shapiro, Jeremy 165, 172
Sharif, Nawaz 85, 86, 87, 88, 89, 92
Sharif, Raheel 88, 152
Shastri, Lal Bahadur 76
Sheikh, Sufian 165
Shillong 112, 113
Sikkim 76, 77, 117
Silchar-Imphal BG 140
Siliguri 142
Silk Road Economic Belt 62
Sindh 5, 76, 87
Singapore/Singaporean 112, 137, 143, 163, 168, 171, 172
Singh, Arjan 76
Singh, Rajnath 65
Sirte 148
Sisters Forum 164
Sobhan, Faiz 168, 172
Social Capital 42, 44
Soufan Group, The 161, 171
South Africa/South African 48, 53, 115, 120, 131, 136
South Asia vi, 54, 60, 78, 101, 103, 108, 111, 115, 119, 120, 121, 135, 137, 138, 139, 143
South Asia Free Trade Agreement (SAFTA) 137, 139
South Asia Subregional Economic Cooperation (SASEC) 138, 142
South Asian Association for Regional Cooperation (SAARC) 113, 115, 136, 138, 139
South Asia–Southeast Asia Rail Corridor 115
South China Sea 52, 53, 54, 59, 63, 103, 123, 129
South Korea 63, 126, 127
Southeast Asia/Southeast Asian 39, 53, 115, 120, 121, 135, 137, 139, 159, 161, 163, 164, 165
Spain 125
Sri Lanka 71, 113, 119, 131, 136, 137, 139, 140, 141
State Bank of Pakistan 89, 92
Stevens, Chris 148
Straits of Bab-al-Mandab 131
Straits of Hormus 126, 130, 131
Strategic Plans Division (SPD) 6
Sudan 165
Sunderji Doctrine 5
Sydney 167, 172
Sykes–Picot Agreement 146, 151
Syria/Syrian 47, 50, 51, 52, 60, 95, 101, 130, 145, 146, 147, 149, 150, 151, 152, 153, 154, 155, 159, 160, 161, 162, 163, 164, 165, 166, 167, 171, 172

T
Taiwan Relations Act 82
Taiwan/Taiwanese 50, 82
Tajiks 165
Taliban 79, 81, 82, 91, 95, 96, 97, 99, 104, 89, 104, 103, 104, 105, 107, 160, 165, 166
Tanzania 131
Taseer, Salman 90
Tawang 66
Tehrik-e-Taliban Pakistan (TTP) 89
Telangana 169
Terminal High Altitude Area Defence (THAAD) 63
Thailand 119, 132, 136, 137, 138, 139, 140, 160, 171

Thailand's Look West policy 137
Thapar, Govind 166
Thatcher, Margaret 38
Thimpu 115
Threat Knowledge Group 167, 172
Threat or Use of Force Against Outer Space Objects (PPWT) 192
Tibet 15, 59, 82, 83
Tiddim 138, 140
Tikrit 161
Tillerson, Rex 51, 52, 60
Toby Dalton 14
Trans-Pacific Partnership (TPP) 50, 60
Treaty of Friendship, Cooperation and Neighbourly Relations 75, 81
Treaty on the Prevention of the Placement of Weapons in Outer Space 192
Tribunal on the Law of the Sea (TLOS) 132
Trilateral Highway 138, 140, 142
Tripoli 148
Tripolitania 148
Tripura 138
Truman, Harry 38
Trump, Donald 47, 48, 49, 50, 51, 52, 53, 54, 55, 60, 61, 63, 81, 82, 83, 85, 91, 102, 130, 150, 156, 179
Tunisia 146, 147, 148, 161
Turkey 56, 119, 145, 146, 149, 150, 151, 162
Turkmenistan 79
Twenty-first Century Maritime Silk Road 62, 63

U
UN Framework Convention on Climate Change (UNFCCC) 176, 181
UN General Assembly 77
UN High Commissioner for Refugees (UNHCR) 155
UN Security Council (UNSC) Resolution 2334 59, 80, 147, 149, 153
Union of Soviet Socialist Republics (USSR)/Soviet Union 39, 76, 77, 78, 79, 82, 105, 107, 160, 161, 190
United Arab Emirates (UAE) 149, 155
United Bengal 112
United Kingdom (UK) 44, 85, 111, 112, 116, 143, 147, 148, 153, 161, 164, 165, 172, 180
United Nations (UN) 37, 38, 39, 40, 42, 45, 49, 51, 54, 59, 76, 77, 80, 107, 125, 129, 147, 148, 149, 150, 155, 176, 181, 182, 194
United Nations Convention on the Law of the Sea (UNCLOS) 54, 125, 129
United States Strategic Command 191
Uri 7, 91
US Air Force Space Command 191
US Central Command (CENTCOM) 49, 54
US President's Commission on Privatisation 39
Uttar Pradesh 169
Uttarakhand 117

V
Vienna 154
Vietnam 142
Virginia 167, 172
Vivekananda, Swami 21, 22, 23, 24, 25, 26, 27, 16, 27, 28, 29, 30, 31, 32, 33, 34, 35, 56, 71, 107, 108, 121, 171, 172

W
Warsaw 76
Washington 48, 52, 53, 96, 102, 120, 121, 145, 150, 165, 172
Weber, Max 38, 40, 44, 45
West Asia and North Africa (WANA) 163
West Asia/West Asian 51, 124, 128, 130, 156, 160, 163
West Bank 149, 150
West Bengal 119, 164, 169
Western Africa 126
Western Europe 161
Western Pacific 48, 49, 53, 54, 64, 126
Work Conference on Peripheral Diplomacy 62
World Bank 39, 40, 45, 117, 121, 143
World Parliament of Religions 22
World Trade Organization (WTO) 37, 39, 49, 55, 79
World War I 151
World War II 37, 38, 42

X
Xiaoping, Deng 62, 66, 72
Xinjiang 79, 80, 82

Y
Yemen 55, 129, 131, 145, 146, 149, 152, 153, 155, 161
Yesui, Zhang 70

Z
Zade, Ahmed Rateb Hussein 166
Zardari, Asif 87
Zokhawtwar 138, 140
Zokhawtwar–Tiddim axis 138

Preface

Science and Technology have occupied almost all spheres of human life. The wonderful achievements of science and technology have glorified the modern world and transformed the modern civilization into a scientific and technological civilization. Considering the importance of science and technology, they have been incorporated in every stage of education.

This International Encyclopaedia of Science and Technology Education is developed covering a wide range of aspects related to science and technology education for the benefit of all those who are associated with science and technology education. This Encyclopaedia is consisting of eleven volumes, namely:

1. Science and Technology Education,
2. Science Education in Developing Countries,
3. Organisational Structure of Science,
4. Science Education in Asia and the Pacific,
5. Science and Technology Education for All,
6. Values, Ethics, Talent and Girls in Science and Technology Education,
7. Popularisation of Science and Technology Education,
8. Science, Power and Society
9. Information Technology,
10. Teacher Training in Science and Technology Education and
11. Science, Technology and Society—A Curriculum Framework

I convey my cordial thanks to UNESCO-PROAP, Bangkok, Thailand; UNESCO-ROSTE, Venice, Italy; UNESCO Paris, France; IIEP, Paris, France; Commonwealth Secretariat, London, UK; UNCTAD, Geneva, Switzerland, Queen's University, Kingston, Canada; and Alberta Education, Edmonton, Canada for their kind co-operation in preparing this Encyclopaedia.

DR. DIGUMARTI BHASKARA RAO
Secretary
Academy of Communication Culture Education
Science and Service
GUNTUR (A.P.)

Contents

	Preface	vii
1.	National Scientific Institutions: Western Research Council, Development of Science Policy and Organizational Changes	1
2.	An Independent Look at Organizational Structures of Science in the USA	18
3.	The System of Science and Technology in Spain	33
4.	Organizational Structure of Science in Norway: A System in Transition	66
5.	Organization and Structure of Science in the Netherlands	83
6.	European Bilateral Co-operations of the French National Centre for Scientific Research (CNRS)	96
7.	Funding of Research in Denmark	100
8.	Organization of Science and Technology in Finland: A System Facing a Challenge	115
9.	Technological R&D: Difference Between a Market Economy and a Planned Economy	124
10.	Note From the Italian Ministry of Foreign Affairs	132
11.	Bulgarian Academy of Sciences: Current Changes and Outlook	134

12. Academic Scientific Research at the Transitional Stage 142

13. Current Organizational Problems in Hungarian Scientific Research 148

14. Organization of Science and Technology in the Ex-Yugoslav Republics 155

15. Restructuring Science and Technologies in Czechoslovakia 166

16. Creation of New Organizational Structures of Science and Technology Co-ordination in the Slovak Republic 171

17. Science and Research in Czech Universities 178

18. Organization and Financing of Academic Research in Slovakia 182

19. Romanian Science between Copying and Adapting 185

20. An Evaluation of the Restructuring Processes in the Romanian R&D System 193

21. Adaptation of Romania's Research and Development System to the Mechanisms of the Market Economy 212

22. The Russian Academy of Sciences and Scientific Co-operation in Europe 228

23. Transformation of the System of Financing R&D in Poland 235

24. Science and Government—Some Notes For Discussion 240

25. The Evolution and Role of National and International Organizations in Science in Europe 248

26. Mechanisms of R&TD Policy in The Member States of the EC, with Reference to the Specific Case of the Community Itself 252

27. Science Organizations in OECD Economies: Comparative Analysis and Main Lessons 262

28. The Promotion of Science by Foundations: Their National and European Roles 274

29. Organization of European Co-operation in the Field of S&T with Central and Eastern Europe 282

30. An International and Interdisciplinary Catalyst for European Scientists 295

31. The 'Scientific Network' Concept: Benefits for the Greater Europe 304

32. Aims and Outcome of the International Seminar on Organizational Structures of Science in Europe 320

ORGANIZATIONAL STRUCTURE OF SCIENCE IN EUROPE

1

National Scientific Institutions: Western Research Council, Development of Science Policy and Organizational Changes

PAOLO BISOGNO

Director, Institute for Studies on Scientific Research and Documentation, National Research Council, Rome, Italy

"The latter cannot elude its own responsibilities *vis-a-vis* politics, and politics cannot ignore science which, on the one hand, provides it with the instruments of study, analysis and methods to achieve its aims, and on the other, through its research and innovation activity, modifies the ways of both thinking and acting and therefore of living."

Birth and Development of Science Policy

The presence of science inside society, by means of its contribution of rational action and the consequent technical progress has led to an upheaval in social patterns. The current usage and abusage of scientific and technical potential are able to extend their dominion over man's nature, with all the possible consequences that can ensue.

In other words, the natural and social reality in which man lives has now taken on a multi-scientific and multi-technical nature, the size and extent of which is adjusted to the individual and social types of reality experienced by the individual and which are always affected, wittingly or unconsciously, by the reality proposed by science.

The resulting complex relation between science and society finds its unifying expression in politics and the two spheres sometimes become complementary, owing to the reciprocal influence they have on each other.

Science cannot elude the responsibilities it has *vis-a-vis* politics and the latter cannot ignore science which provides the instruments of study, analysis, and methods to achieve its aims and through its research and innovation activity modifies the ways of thinking and acting and therefore of living. It is against this reciprocity that the phenomenon of the 'politicization of science' must be viewed and the need arises for a scientific policy in the modern sense that redeems the laboratory from subservience to the 'principle'.

Politics for science (*i.e.* the measures taken for an environment in which research activity is encouraged) and politics by means of science (exploitation of discoveries and innovations in various sectors of public interest) have an equal value, in the sense that the scientific factors influence political decisions and at the same time affect the development of various sectors (defence, economy, social conditions, etc.) which are not in themselves scientific or technical. This is why sciences policy is determined by the concept of deliberately weaving scientific and technological activities into the fabric of political, military, economic, and social policy decisions.

Prior to the industrial revolution, science made more promises than it could keep (the industrial revolution was due to more technological rather than scientific developments). It can be said that throughout that period theoretical studies preceded practical knowledge and that these studies were essentially utopian in nature.

In Bacon's *New Atlantis,* Condorcet's *Fragment sur L'Atlantide* and *Reflections on the Decline of Science,* and Renan's *L'Avenir de la Science,* the need for state support of research activities was justified by the promises made by science and by the potential exploitation of the results. Nevertheless, in relations between science and state, the doctrine of *laissez-faire* prevailed quite naturally owing to the delay between scientific research and its application. This necessarily long delay meant that state involvement in scientific matters was restricted to sectors that could guarantee comparatively quick results.

However, the state left the promotion and orientation of research in the hands of private enterprise, limiting itself to regulating the juridical and formal aspects using legislative measures, such as the first international agreement to protect patents (Paris, 1883).

Subsequently, as the scientific and technological process began to influence all aspects of a state's existence and its continuation demanded an ever increasing and prolonged outlay in terms of human and economic resources, it became inevitable that governments should intervene in a direct and widespread fashion. In practice, the era of institutionalized science policy began only when scientific authorities had a direct influence on mundane affairs, drawing state awareness to an area of responsibility that could no longer afford to be neglected.

What actually characterizes modern science, as opposed to that of the past, is its capacity for manipulation given that the mathematical formulation and experimentation permits the application of action to natural phenomena in such a way as to change them. Since science had comparatively little influence over economic, military, and technical development, the state had little or no interest in interfering in scientific matters. During the beginning of this century, national research councils were established in the more advanced industrialized countries (*e.g.* Canada and Australia in 1916, the UK in the 1920s).

Although the Great Depression of the 1930s made some people aware of science's role towards economic and social development, it was not sufficient enough for the state to intervene or orient scientific research more coherently. Only France recognized the predominance or jurisdiction of politics over science by appointing (during the era of the Popular Front) a special State Under-Secretariat, a post first held by Irene Joliot-Curine and then by Jean Perrin. The fact that two Nobel prize winners could hold a ministerial post, as well as the establishment of Centre National de la Recherche Scientifique

(CNRS), represents the first signs of recognition by the state of the role played by science in economic and social affairs and the need as expressed by political authorities that science be woven into the fabric of government decision-making.

Science Policy in the Postwar Period

In the years following the end of World War-II, governments struggling with reconstruction and economic recovery programmes became increasingly aware of the central role played by science as a productive force and the need to direct development (in accordance with more general decisions of government policy) towards an economic nature.

This reversal of tendency was partly due to consideration of the role played by scientific research during World War II and partly to the new political equilibrium set up among the major world powers when the War ended. Scientific and technological research, originally conceived for military purposes, became a source of new technological discoveries that could be applied to civilian life: atomic energy, radar, the jet engine, DDT, computers, etc.

Political authorities could no longer leave science alone with its gadgets and when the war ended, the demobilization of researchers, instead of coinciding with the demobilization of science gave rise to systematic efforts to make use of research in the context of national and international objectives, thus marking an irreversible turning point in the relations between science and state. This ultimately led to the direct intervention of governments in selecting research activities and in recruiting researchers.

Progress in the design of nuclear weapons, rockets, and computers, changed the traditional laws governing the balance of power, marking the beginning of technological escalation, with the most spectacular aspect being the competition for supremacy in space and the strategic arms system which, affecting all sectors of research, actually affects itself.

Science policy developed against this background of strategic competition as a consequence of the impossibility of achieving true peace.

In this sense, science policy evidently was only one portion of a global policy determined by rivalry and conflict which divided nations. The directions it followed has always reflected and echoed the vicissitudes linked to international tensions.

There is an obvious connection between the onset of international crises (Berlin, Korea, Cuba, Vietnam, the Middle East, Afghanistan, etc.) and increased expenditure on research and development.

For example, between 1940 and 1960, US research spending practically doubled every five years. However, the growing influence of scientific and technological matters on policy may be considered a cause and not just an effect due to the atmosphere of international uncertainty.

The *balance of fear* was measured according to progress made in technology and the proliferation of technological innovations, above all in the military sector. This meant that nations or groups of nations who disagreed over political and ideological issues lived in constant anxiety, whether real or imaginary, of being surpassed at the technological level by their enemies.

The growing role of new techniques of the industrial sectors totally based on science, the spread of rapidly increasing economic development and the profound crisis of objectives and methods of the late 1960s led to a general reappraisal of political behaviour and specifically a revision of the concept of scientific policy.

The first option was historically referred to the importance of research in maintaining and developing technological and economical potential together with science.

The plethora of debates on technological fall out and the face of innovation (that is, the incapacity of some systems to exploit the results of research based on the cost effectiveness of research and development investment in the civilian sector), represents both a cause and effect of this option. This development of two trends in the field of science policy studies were established. One at the organizational level, where a multitude of studies were carried out to improve the management of research systems (Jantsch, 1967 and 1971), and the second, at the academic level, where critical studies were written concerning the means used to attain the aims selected by the various countries (for France Gilpin, 1968; for the US Skolnikof, 1967). But while these theoretical and critical studies cast doubts on the existing priorities, science policy studies developed in the wake of a policy not so much for the objectives challenged but for its administrative procedures, its institutional means and the tensions running through the scientific community which had become one of the many 'pressure groups' (Greenberg, 1967).

The objectives indicated in the social demand (the *second option*) appeared more realistic and more universal, reflecting the widespread concern over the negative effects of technology on the environment and on society itself. In addition to the standard of living, the concepts of social security and quality of life began to emerge and science and technology helped to make them the material objectives of general action, therefore, modifying the negative fall out.

The need to respond to the new type of demand led to a revision of the actual content of science policy and to the grandiose long-term programmes abandoned in favour of more immediate action, involving concrete and universal decisions such as health, town planning, transport, safety on the job, and communications. The new concept of 'social rights in the true sense' was established.

The failure to correct the negative factors lurking in scientific activities often are the result of the shortsighted predominance of economic interests which have diminished the often irrational blind confidence in science and created a growing feeling of distrust and scepticism in the public opinion. The immediate cause of this change is to be found in a series of recent episodes which reveal the crisis that exists in man's relations with his environment and the need to radically change them.

These accusations related to the negative consequences of scientific and technological applications are accompanied by speculative formulations about the concepts of science and technology, formulating the theoretical substrata for the phenomenon of the refusal of science itself (Horkheimer, Adorno, Marcuse, Habermas, Roszak).

Despite all these obstacles, there is a general awareness that the march of science cannot be halted. There are no real alternatives to a continuation of the technological revolution; the only valid alternative being an even faster rate of progress itself. The wider the range of alternative technologies, the greater the chances of protecting nature and satisfying our needs. This stepping up of efforts should be geared to new aims, especially those of development and improvement of society, with a harmonious order of priority being established among them. This is the *third option*.

The central issue on which the general consensus seems to converge is that of control and forecasting: to control the use of scientific discoveries; to forecast the negative side-effects of technology. These two objectives can be attained only with the help of science itself where, in its various forms and expressions, it can provide rational investigation and management methods.

However, it is clear that in order to pursue aims involving the control and evaluation of scientific research, the mere good will of individuals of national agencies and institutions is not enough.

Instead, it is necessary to have international collaboration. The basis of this collaboration of the international scientific community can be identified in those national bodies, national research councils or equivalent organizations, which can and must open upto participation on a larger scale, once the barriers of suspicion and of individualism of frontiers have been lowered.

The Research Councils in Industrialized Countries

As we have seen, the establishment of research councils was a direct consequence of the new role science came to take in economic and social development. The oldest institutions are the National Council of Research of Canada (NCR) and the Commonwealth Scientific and Industrial Research Organization (CSIRO) of Australia.

Research councils were established in the UK during the 1920s after the formulation of the Haldane Doctrine (1918). The majority of the similar institutions in other countries were established during the 1930s.

Functions

Over the years, there have been changes in the tasks of many of these institutions. This has been due to both general changes in science policy trends to which the institutions themselves tended to adapt, as well as in the specific characteristics of the organization of scientific and technological research in the individual countries which the institutions themselves attempted to interpret and direct.

For example, the Canadian and Australian organizations gradually shifted their action towards basic or long period research (perhaps because of the inadequacy of the university research structures in the two countries). Also, structures such as the Max Planck Gesellschaft (which grew out of the Kaiser Wilhelm Gesellschaft founded in 1911) headed in the direction of developing new research areas that could not in any case have been adequately built up by the universities, also because of strong teaching demands placed on the latter institutions, and the disciplinary rigidity of their organizations. In addition, the French CNRS, established in 1937, satisfied the same need.

The functions of the councils seem to be related to the organization of the scientific and technological research carried out in the various countries. Some actually have a number of sectorial councils, linked together by means of a co-ordinating committee. This is so in the Nordic countries (Denmark, Sweden, Norway and Finland) but also in the Netherlands and the UK, all of which are countries characterized by a traditionally decentralized type of administration and organization.

The 'political' function is an exception (*i.e.* National Research and Development Council in Israel). The Canadian Council was specifically established for planning and co-ordinating of research activities and for providing advice to the executive board of all science—and technology—related issues affecting the country. This function had to be abandoned after the re-organization of the scientific system in Canada during the 1970s.

The consultative and sectorial planning role is quite common, as in the Danish and Dutch councils and the Finnish Tekes (the centre for technology development, established in

1983, has an essential role to play, in drawing up and planning technology policy), as well as the Advisory Board of the UK research councils which, among other things, also advises the Secretary of State of the State of science in civilian sectors, on the funding of individual sectors, and on the distribution of resources among the various research bodies.

This function of evaluating research activity entrusted to a representative committee of the scientific community is of great interest.

The role of 'treasurer' and 'manager' of their dependent institutes are without doubt of great importance for the councils but are also quite distinct. A role similar to that of a resource-allocating agency is played by the Belgian National Scientific Research Fund (FNRS), the Swiss National Research Council and by the councils of Denmark, Sweden, and Finland as well as by the (West) German Deutsche Forschungsgemeinschaft (DFG). However, the latter carries out highly structured and wide-ranging activities that are worth outlining briefly.

The DFG budget is funded jointly by the Federal Government and the Länder. The Federal share of the funding depends upon the final destination: general promotion of research (accounting for 70 per cent of DFG funds) is on a fifty-fifty basis. Top priority long-term research areas get three-quarters of their funds from the Federal government and one-quarter from the regional authorities. DFG funds also go towards the Max Planck Institute, the national research centres and other non-university research institutions that belong to what might be defined as a research network midway between university and industrial research.

The Max Planck Institute have the task of complementing university research and of establishing priorities in specific research areas, particularly in basic research of the natural, human, and social sciences.

The DFG provides financial support for research projects, promotes interdisciplinary co-operation and the training of young researchers. The DFG also handles the basic funding of the 13 national research centres (90 per cent from the central government and 10 per cent from the regional authorities) engaged in the basic research and research on advanced interdisciplinary problems.

Sectorial Research Councils

The scope of the sectorial research councils is limited from the disciplinary point of view, but their influence is considerable. Their main function is to allocate the funds earmarked by the government for research and development, not only among the institutes that depend upon them. They also finance research programmes outside of their own institutes, as well as training at universities and highter education institutes. Moreover, they are often called upon to co-ordinate scientific activities in their specific fields and to act in a pro-positive and advisory role for the government. There is usually a body, such as the British Advisory Board for the UK research councils, that is responsible for co-ordination.

The five British Councils, Science and Engineering (SERC), Medicine (MRC), Natural Environment (NERC), Agriculture and Food (AFRC) and Economic and Social Research (ESCR) are funded by the science budget and receive one-seventh of public funds spent on research and development. Each council is a highly independent body and its members are drawn from universities, professions, industries and the public service. Each council carries on research activities through its own institutes and laboratories. They are also funded through government contracts (following the principle stated by the Haldane Committee and confirmed by the Rothschild Committee as the 'client-contractor' relationship) and private contracts. Contract research is highly developed in the Agriculture and Food (AFRC) and Natural Environment (NERC) Councils.

Multidisciplinary Research Councils

The multidisciplinary councils which are not included in the category of solely financing bodies, generally have as their main task that of the direct performance of research activities through their own organizations, institutes, and laboratories. In most cases, they originally played the role of promoting basic or long-term scientific research. In recent years, following the developments in science policy, they have extended the scope of their research fields, operating skills, action, as well as their research fields, operating and funding methods and organization. Good examples of this type are the councils of Canada, Norway, Spain, and France.

The French CNRS is the body with the largest number of functions and represents the main instrument for incentivating and co-ordinating French research. Set up under its present name in 1939 (and later restricted in 1945), it was the first body specifically responsible for a country's research activities. It is administered by a Board of Directors with Director General appointed from eminent members of the scientific world, who is assisted by a Secretary General for the administrative management and by the directors of seven scientific departments. Two national institutes follow four horizontal directions (exploitation and application of research, scientific and technological information, international relations and co-operation, budgeting and financial planning). The Council which receives 11 per cent of public money spent on science and technology, spends considerable amounts of these funds outside its own structures, according to a number of different formulas: associated laboratories, groups of research teams and laboratories working on specific topics and the promotion of specific programmed thematic actions, participation in national or international scientific groups or societies for the management of large-scale apparatus. The CNRS, by means of a special body, the National Scientific Research Committee carries out continuous evaluation of the quality of work and the results of the activity of its research groups. The Committee also has the task of analyzing and evaluating the cyclical situation regarding French scientific research on behalf of the French government.

Changing Functions

As seen, the variety and multiplicity of the functions of the various councils or similar bodies and their constant evolution are the consequence of the need to adapt to the profound social and economic changes of the accelerating development of science and technology and to the growing importance of socio-economic objectives, as well as the urgency of problems of environmental degradation. In other words, the need for the research system which is integrated with the training and the industrial systems to become a direct instrument of economic and social progress, acting as a link between science and knowledge, between society, the economy, and science policy.

The process of adaptation undertaken by numerous councils is a response to changes in government objectives which tends to make a greater contribution to the efforts of innovation and technological development. The extent and depth of this adaptation emerges clearly from an analysis of the changes occurring in the methods of planning, funding, and directing research activities as well as from the utilization and evaluation of results.

During the 1950s, some councils increased their range of skills by extending their activities to fields such as agriculture, food, the environment, which were of lesser importance in the individual national context (*e.g.* the Australian CSIRO). In many cases, other research areas, such as nuclear energy and more recently space, underwent considerable development and have acquired a very important role for military prestige or industrial reasons, warranting the establishment of special bodies.

Furthermore, again in the 1950s, the public research sector extended its horizons beyond the domain of natural science and engineering and entered that of economics and social and human sciences. This tendency has been particularly noticeable in the Nordic countries where a number of different research institutions have been established in social sciences. In addition, other less apparent but equally significant types of change are recorded. In some cases, they have taken place inside a discipline, in others, there have been trends towards new sectors, different procedures, restructuring or reorganizing.

With regard to situations of the first type, it must be acknowledged that even the traditional disciplines gradually change in their content and move closer to and interact with other disciplines. The progress of research increasingly leads us towards an integrated and multidisciplinary approach which must be given direction and coherent orientation.

Other changes have occurred in science and technology, as in the economy and the society of numerous countries: some scientific and technological sectors or industrial sector have withered and died, others have been created. The new areas that have been established with regards to the economy and society as a whole, are those related to the 'information revolution', *i.e.* electronics, computer science, robotics, telematics to genetic engineering, and biotechnology to new materials, not to mention the environment, the exploration and exploitation of space and undersea resources.

Generally speaking, these new research fields have been split up and allocated to existing institutions. However, it is worth recalling that environmental research has given rise to a new research council in the UK. One of the events most strongly affecting the research councils' activities are the general reductions in funds for research and development in the public sector in the early seventies, as a result of the economic crisis of the oil shock. Ever since, government policy has been to attach greater importance to the economic fall out from research investments.

The principle of economic importance in research has gained ground, together with that of the responsibility of public research institutions for the use of public money according to governmental policy objectives. Attention has been focused upon the economic aspects of S&T policy and greater emphasis has been laid on the priority to be given to a firm's autonomous research capacity.

The first country in which this debate was translated into a government policy change in the science and technology sector was the United Kingdom. In November 1971, a government-approved document was published consisting of two reports: one on the direction and organization of the S&T research system, known as the Rothschild Report (from the name of the Director of the Central Policy Review Staff) and the other on the future of the Research Council system, known as the Dainton Report (from the name of its author, the chairman of an *ad hoc* study group). The first report claimed that, in order to raise the degree of efficiency of research management, mission-oriented and applied research should be contracted out: *"The customer states what he wants; the contractor carries this out (if he can) and the customer carries this out (if he can) and the customer pays"*. The operational scheme also envisaged the figure of a technician-intermediary with the task of helping the customer to define his research needs, and that of a technician-contractor who checked the economic feasibility of the requests. The second report stressed the need for greater integration among the research councils and with government policy and social needs.

The Resources

The variety and inequality of functions and organization of the research councils briefly outlines above must be related back to the unit to which the bodies belong in the public sector of the research system in the countries considered funding of such programmes. Moreover, closer links with the production side means a greater interest in the needs of the end users of research and development and a certain guarantee, obtained from the outset of the process of research and innovation, that the users will apply to research developed in the public sector. To this, one must add the fact that a more dynamic process is triggered in the organization of public research, thus boosting its efficiency.

Autonomy

In the case of public research organizations of the research-council type, the first problem to arise is that of the relations between this type of institution and the government to which they refer.

In practice, the problem of autonomy varies with the type of public institution, with special reference to the size of the institution considered. However, in all cases it is crucial, in view of the fundamental incompatibility between the traditional financial and administrative rules of the public sector and the typical nature of research and development activity. This incompatibility is evident, for example, in the preparation of budgets on an annual basis, in the inadequacy of the accounting system, in the rigidity of the administrative regulations in the red tape, etc.

In addition to the risk of having to pick through the inadequate administrative and financial rules typical of the public administration, research institutions also have to cope with the complex problem of what strategy to follow in order to develop. Research and development activity cannot be truly productive and commensurate with the expectations of those commissioning it, unless it is included in a sufficiently long-term strategy. A public research institution could easily find itself at the mercy of short-term political changes or burdened with more or less unrelated priority tasks, which paradoxically could stand in the way of its development, since the really important signals could be covered by the general background noise. In the case of public research institutes, the public sector could prove to be too rigid when a certain degree of flexibility is required and too changeable when a certain degree of continuity is required.

The question of autonomy thus arises very early in the history of the development of the public research sector. The UK became aware of this in 1918, when the Haldane Doctrine was announced. The Haldane Committee claimed that the autonomy of basic research should be maintained by placing it under the responsibility of the Lord presiding over the Council. This formula had the advantage of placing responsibility for research *"in the hands of a minister who was normally free from the pressure of administrative duties and exempt from the fear of being hindered by administration considerations in applying the results of the research"*. In institutional terms, the Haldane Doctrine gave rise to the Research Council of the UK, but also had a visible influence in other countries, particularly Canada, where the NRC was founded as a Crown Corporation, and in Australia, where the CSIRO was placed under the direct responsibility of a minister rather than a ministry.

Future Organization

Research councils evolve and are transformed, on the one hand, changing their scientific activity (but not the basic guidelines), and on the other hand, they proceed towards a reorganization following a path which leads them to a different distribution of funds, to a utilization of the possible synergies, and to control over the research results.

The British research councils attach considerable importance to close collaboration between basic science and industry in establishing scientific and technological priorities for the purpose of producing useful and exploitable results. The UK authorities are convinced also that a *"substantial element of strategic significance"* is inherent in basic research, that future applications exist potentially and are predictable from the outset.

Furthermore, by pursuing the objective of concentrating available resources, they are able to achieve the gradual reduction of contributions to smaller-scale research programmes in favour of longer-term projects. It should be noted that the tendency towards greater programme selectivity has led to increased central control.

Last June, the French CNRS tabled a modernization plan. The National Committee, which has the task of analyzing the scientific cycle and its prospects in the country, evaluated the objectives, development, tendencies, strengths, and weaknesses, as well as the adequacy of the research system for each separate discipline. The 1989 report has shaken off the classic breakdown of disciplines and in consultation with the various commissions and the Scientific Committee of the CNRS, has set up special groups to monitor 22 interdisciplinary themes. The themes selected reflect the synergies that exist between the departments, together with the scientific disciplines because, as pointed out, the CNRS covers all the basic research fields.

The Centre has already adopted an interdisciplinary approach to a series of programmes and activities. These consist of four interdisciplinary research programmes (PIR), environment, energy, materials, technology and labour, as well as programmes such as bio-technology, remote data acquisition, AIDS; multidisciplinary groups (large-scale scientific apparatus, large-scale scientific computing resources), multidisciplinary research units (*e.g.* in the field of communications); promotion action (*e.g.* mathematics, information science and applications); interdepartmental action.

Other interdisciplinary lines of research under discussion include new materials, the global aspects of the environment, communications and the cognitive science, information on macromolecules, and technologies stretched to the limit.

Furthermore, the Centre is implementing a number of procedures aimed at reorganizing the management of the Agency and at making it more efficient. In 1988, the Science Policy Indicator Unit was established producing a three-point plan of action. Above all, it analyzes the key factors governing CNRS research, examples of which are: resources of the disciplines and their development, balancing the budget, equipment, the research units, technical personnel, mobility, training through research, research results.

It makes indicators (each of the factors is described and measured using different indicators), two of which in particular are needed in order to describe any given research activity: indicators which measure resources and scientific production; those of a relational type which measure interaction among research groups, among disciplines, institutions and countries or the relations between research and industry or between research and society. Lastly, it operates in collaboration with other French and foreign organizations with which it carries out joint studies.

In order to evaluate its own functioning, the effectiveness of its own activity and the relevance of the way its resources are used, the CNRS has adopted a system for revising its procedures, functions, programmes, and services. Each revision operation is entrusted to a reviser who is assisted by a committee of experts most of whom are appointed from outside the Centre who have the task of guiding the study, helping the reviser, and enhancing his conclusions.

The professional competence of the reviser, the well-defined task, regular discussions with a consultative committee of revisers (composed of ten persons acknowledged as components in the particular discipline or in science management) guarantee a rigorous working method backed up by a constant flow of information on the topics treated, the persons concerned and the results obtained.

The publication of the results of the decisions taken and of the effects of revision should ensure that the sole aim of the revision itself is to enhance to Centre's capacity for doing research.

2

An Independent Look at Organizational Structures of Science in the USA

SIDNEY PASSMAN

Organization for International Science, Inc., Bethesda, Maryland, USA

Abstract

This paper describes the system of organization and allocation of national resources for scientific research in the USA. It discusses methods of prioritization and critiques the effectiveness of various institutions in providing for basic science advances as well as in attempts at improving the national capabilities for the industrial appropriability of this knowledge.

Organization of Science in the United States of America

The history of US science and technology policy since 1945

[Sidney Passman was formerly with the US National Science Foundation where he served as Special Assistant for Planning and Policy and was Executive Secretary for the National Science Board's Committee on Planning and Policy and International Science. Prior to that he was UNESCO's Director of the Division of Scientific Research and Higher Education. He served two terms on the US National Research Council and is a Fellow of the Optical Society of America and of the American Association for the Advancement of Science.]

has been divided into three periods by Harvey Brooks (1987): the growth period from the post-war years through the mid-1960s, including responses to the challenge of Sputnik; the period 1965 to 1975, which included the Vietnam War, environment, and energy crises; and the period from the mid-1970s to the present, during which the country has attempted to meet the challenge of international competitiveness by creating a science and engineering environment that stimulates technological innovation and commercial exploitation. Each period has seen substantial changes in the political autonomy of the scientific community (Brooks, 1987).

As the federal government gradually took on the role of principal supporter of scientific research following World War II, the scientific community, at first suspicious of potential bureaucratic intrusions into research prerogatives, was able to negotiate the creation of structures that somewhat insulated them from federal control yet provided ample support *via* federal contracts or grants. The establishment of the Atomic Energy Commission as a civilian agency, for example provided the vast sums necessary for the continued growth of the physics programmes in fission, fusion, and high-energy accelerators. The establishment of the National Science Foundation (NSF) under the administration of an autonomous National Science Board, gave the university community a sponsor that shared its values and understood both the importance of fundamental research, and the desirability of coupling research to education and training in the university setting.

Support to science grew rapidly in all sectors as the Cold War and the consequent arms race stimulated R&D in all sectors. Universities became the largest performer of basic research, supported first primarily by government sponsors including of the Department of Defence (DOD) and later by the various components of the Department of Energy (DOE), the National Institutes of Health (NIH), and NSF. In some instances, universities joined in consortia to operate major research facilities, beginning with the Brookhaven nuclear research facility supported by the Atomic Energy Commission (later, by DOE). NSF, explicity barred from direct operating responsibilities, has employed this university consortium approach in support of major experimental facilities serving astronomy, atmospheric sciences, oceanography, and deep-sea drilling (US Congress, 1986).

The enormous growth of American health science research came as a response to pressure from the public and especially from the Congress. NIH developed as a highly plural sponsor, with both intramural and extramural research programmes carried out under the several institutes, each ostensibly oriented around the characteristics of a different pathology and supplemented by an institute for general science. NIH now constituted the largest agency supporter of academic research in the United States.

Research in the industrial sector continues traditions established early in the 20th century (by Thomas Edison, among others), as researchers worked in applied areas related to the product lines of their parent corporations. Industrial laboratories have also been responsible for basic discoveries in physics, chemistry, and materials science that have subsequently revolutionized industrial products and processes. Several Nobel prizes have been won by scientists working at the General Electric Company and Bell Laboratories, for example, and industry is now the principal performer of applied R&D in the United States.

Of the total R&D performed in the industrial sector, the federal government sponsors one-third through contracts from various agencies. However, the requirements of government sponsored work are generally so specialized, and the efforts at technology, transfer so ineffective, that the spin-offs to civilian application have not been commensurate with the enormous R&D investments made. Nevertheless, the few examples of industries spun-off from defence R&D are among the most competitive of US industries—jet aircraft being a notable example.

In the area of basic research, industry performs less than 20 per cent of the national total. The risks and gestation periods involved in bringing such research to commercial fruition, together with the uncertain appropriability of specific research results, have convinced many industrial organizations that investments in basic research do not meet management's rigorous requirements for short-term profitability.

The challenge of Sputnik led to widespread soul-searching regarding the efficacy of various approaches to restoring US leadership. President Dwight Eisenhower was persuaded to provide the institutional setting for improved co-ordination and advice in the Executive Branch by creating the position of Science Adviser and the companion President's Science Advisory Committee (PSAC). Outstanding scientists, giving freely of their time, serve on various committees that produce studies and reports on problems and issues of national importance. This large external advisory structure, drawn from the elite of the scientific community, gives coherence and consideration to issues that had previously been handled piecemeal by rival bureaucracies.

Presidential-level science policy structures have gone through many vicissitudes over the last three decades. They were even abolished altogether in 1973 by the Nixon administration. Congress later restored the Office of Science and Technology Policy (OSTP) by explicit statute. Its director also serves as science adviser to the President and can play as significant role in national leadership and co-ordination as the President wishes and as the director's personal credentials allow. Another mechanism for co-ordination and co-operation between federal agencies, revitalized during the Bush administration, is the Federal Co-ordinating Council for Science, Engineering and Technology (FCCSET). Organized into various committees for focusing government-wide attention on particular issues, the Council has been able to formulate a number of co-ordinated, strategic plans for national action, including recent efforts concerning manufacturing techniques, education, materials research, global change research and high-performance computing (Teich and Pace, 1986; US Congress, 1986).

Basic research accounts for some 12 per cent of the total US federal R&D effort. Almost one-half of this basic research is performed within the laboratories maintained by institutions of higher education. Although there are over 3000 institutions offering higher education in the United States, the 150 major universities, with graduate departments performs the lion's share of national R&D. These universities, 35 per cent of which are privately supported, conduct the research in conjunction with graduate education. The government-supplied individual research project grant is the principal mechanism for support the basic research effort in the universities. The selection of awards is based on peer review of investigator proposals' graduate student support is provided as a part of the research effort.

Universities themselves are supported by private and state sources as well as by student fees; federal research grants partially cover research services and laboratory instrumentation through authorized institutional overhead payments. In recent years, there has been a considerable row in Congress over excessive charges and some university administrators have had to resign over bad practices. Nevertheless, the universities still consider themselves underpaid as research performers and are often at a disadvantage over industry which is reimbursed for all R&D, whereas universities must cost-share. Universities are also facing problems as they seek to raise the necessary capital to keep their physical plant and research facilities up to the rapidly changing state-of-the-art. From time to time, different government agencies have provided funds for special laboratory construction and recently the Congress has appropriated so-called 'earmarked' funds for individual institutions or departments, although generally the academic community has advocated adhering to the peer review approach to choosing research projects, acceding to the disciplinary priorities and facility requirements established by scientific community consensus.

The tradition of carrying out basic research in the university has succeeded in producing distinguished, pioneering scientific results, and in maintaining a flow of young, well-trained, new researchers. However, there has been growing concern that US industry does not use the results of this basic research effort in a sufficiently timely or innovative fashion. To correct this situation, new alliances have been encouraged which bring industry into closer relationships with universities, either through various industrial associate schemes or through direct grants from and contractual arrangements with industry (US Congress, 1988b). Academic entrepreneurs in the United States also have vitalized the information technology and biotechnology domains, greatly adding to the dynamism and competitive spirit distinguishing those sectors.

A major NSF initiative, reflecting both the industry-engineering background of its previous director, as well as a response to the pressures to have the NSF double as a National Technology Foundation, 'has been the creation of interdisciplinary engineering research centres, devoted to various promising fields of applied research. An innovative aspect of these centres is the requirement for industrial participation, both as a supporter and a participant. This industrial participation is expected to speed use of results as well as to offer access to state-of-the-art instrumentation. It is also likely that the close working relationships between faculty, students, and industrial researchers, will lead to various opportunities for potential employment or consulting, and will encourage the industrial participants to act as gatekeepers to expedite communication of nascent research results to their industrial development organizations. Examples of these centres include the Center for Ceramics Research at Rutgers, New Jersey; the Center for Integrated Systems, Stanford, California; the Manufacturing Engineering Applications Center, Worcester Polytechnic, Massachusetts; and the Robotics Research Center, University of Rhode Island (National Science Board, 1982).

The industrial associate schemes at many universities also offer industrial participants an efficient overview of university research programmes, tailored to their own corporate interests. These programmes, arranged on a payment of membership fee, are open to foreign as well as domestic industrial organizations. Proceeds of such programmes are generally returned to the research programmes of faculty participants. Other types of university-industry couplings include the establishment of 'parks' in close proximity to university sites and the establishment of 'incubator' departments on campuses to aid newly established firms to cope with the details of entrepreneurial problems. Industrial sponsorship of university research has also been growing; some firms have underwritten entire research departments or even institutions (Dimancescu and Botkin, 1986). State government plays an increasingly significant role in encouraging university-industry co-operation, partially because of their role in support of university operations, but also because they regard it as a plausible route to regional development. Industry is attracted by the intellectual and skilled work force potential of these sites.

The movement towards a greater industrial presence on US campuses has not been without problems, however. The very principle of shifting priorities towards the pragmatic goals of placing science in the marketplace, rather than maintaining the traditional university goal of knowledge for its own sake, draws heated debate. A related concern stems from the conflict between the basic university need for free and open access to knowledge in the spirit of education and scholarship, as contrasted with the needs of industry for proprietary controls to assure the appropriability of intellectual property. It has usually been possible to compromise in finding a middle way which satisfies both sides, by arranging for short delays in information dissemination until patent issues are resolved. The University-Government-Industry Round table, administered by the National Academy of Sciences, has been a useful agency for discussing these issues and the NAS has provided general guidelines for good practices (Dickson, 1988).

The federal in-house laboratories perform about 15 per cent of the basic and applied research in the United States. Recent changes in the law now permit the granting of exclusive licences for government patents stemming from in-house R&D to co-operating industrial groups. The legislation also provides generous incentives to encourages government laboratory investigators to help participate in the commercialization of their research findings. In addition, the Bush administration has appointed a Federal Laboratory Consortium to promote co-operation between industry and the federal laboratories (OECD, 1989a). And finally, the Federally Funded Research and Development Centers (FFRDCs) operated by universities or associated non-profit consortia under contract to the federal government are intended to offer a flexible and attractive research environment not always found in government structures.

In summary, basic research in the United States takes place in a wide spectrum of organizations, supported by many different sponsors. This pluralistic system encourages diversity and the system of grants and contracts, selected on merit, allows scientists relative autonomy in choosing research topics and conducting research. Much credit for the accomplishments of the US scientific community—beyond that due to the pioneering creative efforts of individuals—can be traced to this generously supported, pluralistic research environment.

Policies for Encouraging Industrial Innovation and Exploitation of Research

The United States is a democratic pluralistic society which has long enjoyed a high standard of living which it has come to attribute to its free enterprise system and world leadership position in science, technology, and industrial productivity. In recent years, facing high budget deficits and trade imbalances, the nation has been alerted to the urgency of international issues and has sought various means to redress the US position for industrial competitiveness. While taking steps to stimulate the industrial sector, which is ultimately responsible for producing the goods and services that must compete in the global marketplace, the government looks to investments in research and development as fundamental to the generation of new wealth for the future.

The issue of technological competitiveness for future economic security has come to dominate all aspects of the US R&D enterprise (Botkin, 1982; Norman, 1981; US President, 1985; Roy and Shapley, 1988; US Congress, 1988a). Institutional and organizational changes as well as priorities for allocation of resources are all being judged by their potential for improving the US competitive position. So far, the US Government has resisted both protectionism on the one hand, and an industrial policy that would subsidize certain chosen industries ('choosing winners') on the other. Instead, the Government has attempted to stimulate R&D through direct support or through changes in the tax and regulatory environment, intended to encourage industrial enterprise. Maintaining its faith in the market approach, the US Government has negotiated in bilateral and multilateral fora for reciprocity of market access and for respect for intellectual property rights to provide a favourable international environment for US trade and investment.

Direct co-operation between industrial organizations for the joint conduct of R&D is a relatively new phenomenon in the United States. Because of the strong antitrust legal restrictions with threats of large penalties to violators, industrial organizations have remained aloof from one another, thus observing both the spirit and the letter of the law. Their technical staffs have been limited in communication to participation in the neutral activities of professional scientific and engineering organizations. The National Cooperative Research Act, passed in 1984, legalized joint research consortia among industrial members. Since then, some 60 consortia have been established, including the pioneer Semiconductor Research Corporation and the Micro-electronic and Computer Technology Corporation (Petit, 1987). An incipient trend is a possible tendency for US corporations to spend an increasing portion of corporate R&D funds at facilities abroad.

Additional measures have been taken to stimulate more industrial R&D. The Economic Recovery Tax Act of 1981 contained an incentive for investors to increase corporate risk-taking by providing for a 25 per cent tax credit on *increases* in R&D expenditures. This credit was extended but reduced to 20 per cent in 1986. Qualified research is defined as research involving a process of experimentation undertaken for the purpose of discovering information that is technical in nature and intended to be useful in developing a new or improved product or improvement in manufacturing processes. This latter area is often underestimated in academic research but it is highly significant in the commercial context, both in cutting the time to get an improved product to market and in determining cost and quality. The recent co-operative effort to create Sematech, with government assistances from the US Department of Defence, was justified on the basis of achieving more advanced national semiconductor manufacturing capabilities.

In recent years, a national debate has occurred concerning the legitimate limits of a 'technology policy'. OSTP has enunciated a policy extending government support to generic technology. As concluded by a recent NAS committee to consider this issue, *"the US needs a policy that moves beyond a focus limited to support basic research and for the development of technology to meet national security needs. A new federal role should include facilitating (not directing) civil technological development in pre-commercial areas and the adoption of new technologies by US firms. Long accepted and acted on in federal policy for basic research, there is also a clear government role in suport of pre-commercial generic technology"* (National Academy of Sciences, 1992).

Research Administration and Resource Allocation

US R&D expenditures amount to 2.8 per cent of GNP. The total national expenditure for military and civilian R&D exceeds the combined totals of FRG, France, Japan, and the UK. The US government accounts for one-half of the total; the other half represents expenditures by industry. For Civilian (*i.e.* non-defence) research, the national R&D effort amounts to 1.8 per cent of GNP—placing the United States in the medium level among other industrialized countries.

Basic research amounts to 12 per cent of the total national R&D effort. Almost one-half of the total basic research effort is performed in higher education institutions; another 10 per cent in FFRDCs administered by universities or non-profit corporations. Industry performs the second highest amount of basic research, accounting for 19.4 per cent, which in turn represents only 3 per cent of the total R&D carried out in the industrial sector. The federal government's intramural laboratories perform 15 per cent of the total basic research (National Science Board, 1987, 1989). Federal support for basic research is funded principally from the budgets of five federal agencies, which account for 90 per cent of total funding: the Department of Health and Human Services (primarily, the National Institutes of Health), 37 per cent; NSF, 18 per cent; DOD, 13 per cent; DOE, 12 per cent; and NASA, 10 per cent.

The provision of research support to the universities is made primarily through grants for specific proposed research projects approved by government authorities on the advice of selection committees or individual peer reviewers. Although the peer review system has worked well and receives general approbation, there is still debate over the need for grant administrators to utilize their own professional judgment and to allow for such other evaluative factors as the investigator's 'track record' (as evidenced in previous research accomplishments and publications) or potential of innovative proposals that may involve some intellectual risk or that challenge old models but promise breakthrough possibilities.

Priorities for the allocation of resources for research naturally vary with agency mission. Change in long-standing support patterns are disruptive. The easiest path, when increasing budgets obtain, is to use, the principle of 'enlightened incrementalism', that is, to provide across-the-board, general increases, while reserving major increases for those priority areas considered particularly promising or relevant. Nevertheless, on occasion, reductions do have to be made and some drop-outs occur. Under the US pluralistic support system, sometimes another sponsor can be found when research support is reduced or discontinues. This was the case when NSF assumed funding for the university materials research laboratories, which was originally created under the auspices of the Defence Advanced Research Projects Agency (DARPA) auspices and which provided the successful general model for interdisciplinary research laboratories.

The US research system includes many different mechanisms for planning and co-ordinating this pluralistic and autonomous effort. The scientific community itself participates in the public debate on priorities through professional societies. Advisory committees to the various mission agencies play important roles in providing inputs to the priority and budget planning efforts of agencies, from the vantage point of technical community consensus. The National Science Board (NSB), the NSF's statutory policy-making board, is responsible for compiling indicators representative of outputs such as publications, patents, and so forth. The NSB and NSF frequently commission topical reports on all aspects of the scientific enterprise, including international co-operation, science and engineering education, and university-industry co-operation (NSB, 1987, 1989). In its recent report on Science Indicators (1991), the National Science Board has chosen to view the US science scene as a half-empty glass:

"In the US, the twin engines that powered the rapid growth of R&D from the mid-1970s to the late 1980s have been decelerating—

the economy has been in a recession, and the evaporation of the cold war has reduced the urgency for military R&D spending. The average annual increase in total US R&D expenditures between 1985 and 1991 (in constant dollars) was 1.2 per cent, compared with an annual growth rate of 6.9 per cent from 1980 to 1985. The most recent estimates on change from 1985 to 1991 also show declining R&D expenditures.

"Current estimates for development expenditures exhibit the sharpest down-turn—a negative trend in constant dollars since 1988. The estimated trend in applied research, too, has been negative since 1989. The federal government is estimated to have reduced its R&D expenditures significantly from 1989 to 1991; estimates for US industry R&D expenditures remained level during this period.

"Only expenditures for basic research have continued to grow, albeit at a declining rate. The most recent estimate is for a 2.7 per cent increase from 1990 to 1991. The statistics for expenditures for academic R&D also show continuing slow growth.

"Internationally, total US R&D expenditures continue to exceed those of its four closest industrial competitors combined, despite the fact that two of these countries (Germany and Japan) outpace the United States in terms of R&D expenditures as a percentage of GNP. However, as of 1989, these four countries together (the two named above plus the United Kingdom and France) spent 12 per cent more than the US on total non-defence related R&D activities."

As regards the proposed Federal Year 1993 budget, the amount proposed for R&D, including funds for facilities amounts to US $76.6 billion, representing 2 per cent of the total government budget; an increase of 3 per cent from funds appropriated in 1992. Of this total US $14.3 billion is allocated for basic research, an increase of 8 per cent over last year. Half of this amount will go towards individual investigators working on grants from NIH, NSF, and the DOE. Basic research conducted through grants from NSF will rise to US $2.6 billion. A further US $1.1 billion is targeted for basic research in co-ordination with the US Global Climate Change Research Programme. Two 'big science' projects, the Human Genome Project and the Superconducting Super Collider receive US $175 million and US $650 million, respectively. US $890 million is destined for the category of astronomy and astrophysics. One of the interagency initiatives includes the biotechnology research programme which totals over US $4 billion and involves 12 federal agencies.

The Director of the Office of Science and Technology Policy has responsibility also for long-range reports for science and technology planning, as well as for various annual reports on federal agency accomplishments.

The role of the NAS-NAE-NRC (National Academy of Sciences—National Academy of Engineering—National Research Council) complex, in both policy for scientific and engineering research and in the use of scientific and engineering knowledge in public policy-making, is valuable to government and to the public sector. The NAS, a private organization with a congressional charter, has no laboratories or research management responsibilities, but it has been able—by virtue of a prestigious membership and a solid reputation—to attract the talents of top scientists and engineers to serve purely as public-spirited volunteers on a wide variety of advisory panels. The NAS uses contracts funded by sponsoring government organizations to bring together balanced teams of experts, supported with full-time staff, to study all phases of a national issue related to science or technology. The US government has also come to depend upon disciplinary surveys undertaken by the academy to provide long-range appraisals of promising research frontiers and a consensus on needed new research facilities, in priority rank.

The Congressional Branch of Government has come to play an extremely significant role in the governance of the national science and technology effort. Each of the two congressional bodies must approve the authorization and appropriation bills for each government agency on an annual basis. The related hearing offer an 'oversight' and public accountability mechanism and the subsequent reports and recommendations can affect priorities and programme structures. The Congress has provided for a number of institutions to supply it with independent studies so as to conduct better its legislative duties. In addition to expert witnesses who testify on request at frequent hearings, and committee technical staffs, four organizations provide in-house advice to the US Congress: the Congressional Research Service of the Library of Congress; Congressional Budget Office;

General Accounting Office; and Office of Technology Assessment (OTA). OTA, in particular, focuses its work on issues relating to the impacts of S&T. Its longer-term forecasts and politically bi-partisan evaluations of sensitive issues, such as competitiveness, technology transfer, and the employment and other societal impacts of technology, are based on broad multidisciplinary analysis and wide consultation with the 'stakeholders' directly affected by and knowledgeable about each issue. This structure makes these analyses of exceptional quality and virtually unique.

REFERENCES

Bond, J., 1986. *The Science and Technology Resources of West Germnay: A Comparison with the United States*. NSF 86-310. The National Science Foundation, Washington, DC, USA.

Botkin, J., 1982. *Global Stakes: The Future of High Tech in America*. Ballinger, Cambridge, Mass., USA.

Brooks, H., 1987. What is the national agenda for science? *American Scientist*, 75, 511-517.

Brooks, H., and Cooper C. (eds)., 1987. *Science for Public Policy*. Pergamon Press, Oxford, UK.

Clogston, A.M., Smith, B.L.R. and Kidd, C.V., 1981. FRG, France and the UK. In National Research Council, *Outlook for Science and Technology*. National Academy of Sciences, Washington, DC, USA. Ch. 13.

Dickson, D., 1988. *The New Politics of Science*. Pantheon Books, New York, USA.

Dimancescu, D. and Botkin, J., 1986. *The New Alliance: America's R&D Consortia*. Ballinger, Cambridge, Mass., USA.

Irvine, J. and Martin B.R., 1984. What directions for basic research. In Gibbons *et al.*, *Science and Technology Policy in the 1980s and Beyond*. Longman, U.K.

Long, T.D. and Wright, C., (eds), 1975. *Science Policies of Industrial Nations*. Praeger, New York, USA.

National Academy of Engineering, 1984-89. *Various Reports on the Subject of National Competitiveness*.

National Academy of Engineering, 1985. *US National Competitiveness and the NAE*.

National Academy of Sciences, 1992. *The Government Role in Civilian Technology: Building a New Alliance*.

National Science Board, 1982. *University-industrial Relations: Myths, Realities and Potentials*. National Science Foundation, Washington, DC, USA.

National Science Board, 1991. *Science Indicators*.

National Science Board/National Science Foundation, 1987. *Science and Technology Indicators*. National Science Foundation, Washington, DC, USA.

National Science Board/National Science Foundation, 1989. *Science and Engineering Indicators*. National Science Foundation, Washington, DC, USA.

Norman, C., 1981. *The God that Limps: S&T in the '80s* W.W. Norton, New York, USA.

Organization for Economic Co-operation and Development, 1984. *Industry and University*. OECD, Paris, France.

Organization for Economic Co-operation and Development, 1988. *Science and Policy Outlook*, OECD, Paris, France.

Organization for Economic Co-operation and Development, 1989a. The *Changing Role of Government Research Laboratories*. OECD, Paris, France.

Organization for Economic Co-operation and Development, 1989b. *Main Science and Technology Indicators*, OECD, Paris, France.

Petit, M.J., 1987, *Industrial Research and Development Consortia*. University of Texas, Austin, USA.

Ronayne, J., 1984, *Science in Government: A Review of the Principles and Practice of Science Policy*. Arnold, Baltimore, MD, USA.

Roy, R. and Shapley, D. 1988. *Lost at the Frontier: US Science and Technology Policy Adrift*. ISI Press, Philadelphia, PA, USA.

Teich, A.H. and Pace, J.H. (eds), 1986. *Science and Technology in the USA*. Longman, Harlow, Esses, UK.

UNESCO, 1988. *Statistical Yearbook*. UNESCO, Paris.

US Congress, 1986. House Committee on Science, Space and Technology, *History of Science Policy in the United States*, 1940-1985. US Government Printing Office, Washington, DC, USA.

US Congress, 1988a. Task Force on Technology Policy. *Technology Policy and its Effect on the National Economy*. US Government Printing Office, Washington, DC, USA.

US Congress, 1988b. House Committee on Science, Space and Technology. *University/Industry Alliances*. US Government Printing Office, Washington, DC, USA.

US President, 1985. *Report of the President's Committee on Industrial Competitiveness*. US Government Printing Office, Washington, DC, USA.

3

The System of Science and Technology in Spain

GREGORIO GARCIA-HERDUGO
Advisor for Community Affairs, General Secretariat for the National Plan of Research and Development, Madrid, Spain

Historical Background and Legal Framework

The origin of the first public actions of promotion and organization of Spanish scientific policy goes back, as in the other western countries, to the first decades of this century. Nevertheless, the definitive step to reforming the Spanish System of Science and Technology for the future development of the country was the promulgation of the Law for the Promotion and General Co-ordination of Scientific and Technical Research (commonly known as the Law of Science) of 14 April, 1986, which established a new normative framework for the definition and effecting of scientific and technological policy. As well as this, a set of complementary regulations were introduced, of which mention should be made of the Patents Law 11/1986 of 20 March and that relating to intellectual property 22/1987, of 11 November, which substantiated this new framework.

Previously, a decisive moment in the development of the Spanish System was the promulgation of the Organic Law 11/1983, 25 August, dealing with university reform (Ley de Reforma Universitaria, LRU). In this Law, the importance of university research activity for the cultural, social, and economic development of the country and, consequently, for enterprises and public and private bodies, is explicitly recognized. In particular, in Articles 11 and 45 of the Law and in the subsequent acts which further develop them, the collaboration in R&D projects between enterprises and university research groups was established; that is to say, it enabled academic research to be brought closer to the productive world.

The Law of Science establishes the National Plan for Scientific Research and Technological Development as a basic instrument for the development, co-ordination and planning of scientific and technical research and creates the Interministerial Commission for Science and Technology (Comision Interministerial de Ciencia y Tecnología, CICYT) to elaborate and monitor the Plan, as well as taking the responsibility for the co-ordination of the System in the national and international spheres. In addition, it sets up two consultative bodies; the General Council for Science and Technology (Consejo General de la Ciencia y la Technología) and the Advisory Council for Science and Technology (Consejo Asesor para la Ciencia y la Tecnología).

Similarly, the aforementioned Law identifies the co-ordination of the R&D activities of the various ministries and organizations involved in research. With regard to the international programmes for scientific research and technological development that involve Spanish participation, the Law makes CICYT responsible for co-ordination and monitoring, defining the National Plan's requirements in terms of international relations and establishing forecasts for their execution.

The outcome of the development of the Law for the Promotion and General Co-ordination of Scientific and Technical Research has been a greater integration between the public and private agents which make up the System of S&T; the paths of co-ordination so created are shown as broken lines in Figure 1.

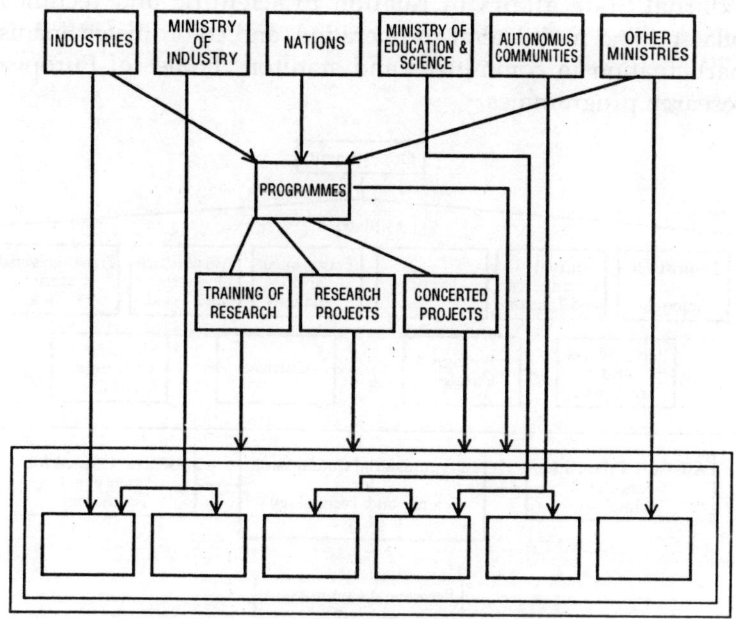

Figure 1. Spanish System of S&T.

Institutional Framework

In brief, the Law of Science and the subsequent regulations which further develop it determine the creation of new mechanisms of action: these are formed out of the various different bodies that guarantee the appropriate participation of every element forming the System. These are represented in Figure 2 on page 36.

Interministerial Commission for Science and Technology (CICYT)

This is the official body responsible for the planning, elaboration, co-ordination, evaluation and monitoring of the National Plan for R&D. It elaborates the general guidelines of scientific policy, determines the most appropriate mechanisms for their development, sets the criteria for evaluation, selection, and control of the research, allocates the economic resources of the National Fund for the Development of Scientific and

Technical Research, collaborates with the relevant bodies of external State affairs in relation to scientific and technical, bilateral and multilateral co-operation, and co-ordinates Spanish participation in committees and statutory bodies of European research programmes.

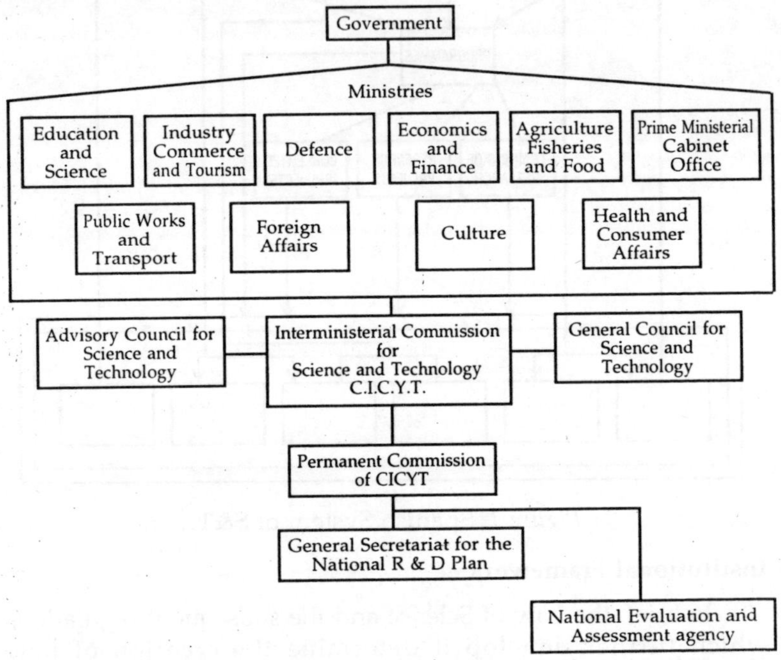

Figure 2. Bodies within the System.

CICYT is chaired by the Minister of Education and Science and comprises representatives of the ministries directly involved in research: Education and Science, Industry, Commerce and Tourism, Foreign Affairs, Defence, Economics and Finance, Agriculture, Fisheries and Food, Public Works and Transport, Culture, Health and Consumer Affairs, and the Prime Minister Cabinet. The Secretary General of the National R&D Plan acts as Secretary to the Commission.

Permanent Commission of CICYT

This is the Board of the CICYT and is chaired by the Secretary of State for Universities and Research. The General

Secretary of Industrial Promotion and Technology of the Ministry of Industry, Commerce and Tourism acts as Vice President. In addition, the General Director of Scientific and Technical Research (Ministry of Education and Science, MEC), the General Director of Technological Policy (Ministry of Industry, Commerce and Tourism), and the General Director of Planning (Ministry of Economics and Finance, MEH) belong to the Commission. The General Secretary of the National R&D Plan acts as Secretary to the Commission.

General Council for Science and Technology

This is a consultative body aimed at promoting the general co-ordination of scientific and technical research among the different Autonomous Communities and between them and the State, and evaluating the development of the National Plan in terms of overall co-ordination. It is chaired by the President of the Interministerial Commission and it is made up of representatives from the Autonomous Communities and all the members of CICYT.

Advisory Council for Science and Technology

This is the effective link between the scientific community, social agencies and those responsible for the planning of scientific activity, ensuring that the objectives of this planning meet social needs and interests. It is chaired by the Minister of Industry, Commerce and Tourism and consists of three eminent scientists, two representatives from private research associations, two representative from business associations, two trade union representatives, one representative from the General Secretariat for Industrial Promotion and Technology, one representative from the Centre for Industrial and Technology Development (CDTI), and fourteen members appointed by the President of the Advisory Council, two of whom belong to CICYT and ten of whom are from industrial management.

General Secretariat for the National R&D Plan (SGPN)

This is the support unit for the Interministerial Commission for Science and Technology and is responsible to the Permanent Commission. Among its most important functions are the co-ordination of the programmes and activities—national and international—of the National R&D Plan, technical and financial management, and administrative management. In addition, it co-ordinates and gathers together the scientific and technological information necessary for the Plan's implementation.

National Evaluation and Assessment Agency (ANEP)

This body supports and is responsible to the Permanent Commission of CICYT. Its role is to carry out the evaluation of the scientific and technical standards of projects and other proposals submitted by organizations and research groups taking part in National Plan Programmes. It also carries out studies and analyses of future prospects of scientific research and technological development as required by the Permanent Commission of CICYT. The method of evaluation commonly used—although not the only one since the proposals to be evaluated vary greatly—is that of peer review. To carry out this task, ANEP has at its disposal a bank of assessors made up of 7000 specialists, 1400 of whom are foreign experts.

Joint Congress—Senate Commission on Scientific Research and Technological Development

The remit of this Commission is to produce the annual report documenting the state of implementation of the National Plan, therefore monitoring its development and that of the Scientific and Technological Policy in general. The Commission is made up of 22 members of parliament and 16 senators.

In addition to the above-mentioned bodies, created specifically out of the promulgation of the Law of Science, there are others which have been assigned responsibility for particular functions relating to the management of certain aspects of the National R&D Plan. These include:

Centre for Technological and Industrial Development (CDT)

This is responsible to the Ministry of Industry, Commerce and Tourism. In relation to the National Plan, the Centre has been made responsible for evaluating the economic and technological interest of the projects in which enterprises participate, promoting the commercial exploitation of national technologies and collaborating with CICYT in obtaining adequate technological and industrial returns from the international R&D programme in which Spain participates. With reference to the National Plan, CICYT entrusted CDTI with the management of the Concerted Projects, the axis of the activities of the Plan, whose objectives is to promote research in enterprises and encourage the collaboration between these and public research centres (centres públicos de investigación, CPI).

General Directorate of Science and Technical Research (DGICYT)

This is a unit of the Ministry of Education and Science which, having control over its own budget, manages the Sectoral Programme for the Training of University Academic Staff and Improvement of Research Personnel, and the Sectoral Programme for the General Promotion of Knowledge (PGC) devoted to the encouragement of high quality basic research in the different areas of knowledge; both Programmes are integrated in the National Plan. CICYT entrusted this Directorate with the management of the National Programme for the Training of Research Personnel in order to co-ordinate the actions of this Programme with those of the Sectoral Programme.

National Plan for Scientific Research and Technological Development

The Law of Science established the National Plan as a basic mechanism of promotion, co-ordination and planning in the R&D area and as a fundamental instrument for the development of Spanish scientific policy. In the Plan, objectives are set, actions are given priority, and resources are mobilized toward areas of particular strategic interest for society's benefit, at the same time as supporting basic high quality research.

The national government maintains the right of approval over the National Plan and determines its activities for periods lasting several years, although it is subject to annual review. As a planning mechanism, the Plan integrates financial efforts to promote R&D, organizing research activities in a series of programmes which represent its priorities, and planning other activities aimed at achieving its objectives.

Promotion of Scientific and Technological Development

The promotion of scientific and technological development is one of the essential purposes of the National Plan. In the short-term and in agreement with the priorities established in the National Programmes, the promotional activities should lead to the expansion of the budgets available for financing research projects. In the medium- and long-term, they must ensure—through corresponding funding—the future of research potential, which will depend on the investment devoted to infrastructure and human capital.

With a view to developing the promotion of R&D activities in Spain, the National Plan is structured on the following lines of activity:

Research Projects

These are an essential part of the research activity of the public research centres and non-profit R&D bodies, whose objective is the execution of a project of work which is usually carried out over a period of three years. The funds allocated allow the research team to acquire low- and medium-cost equipment as well as consumables, to attend relevant congresses and scientific meetings, and deal with other minor expenses.

Integrated Projects

The objective of these projects is the development of products or processes which are of a considerable size and for this reason need to 'integrate' various technologies, requiring the involvement of different research groups both from public centres and enterprises.

Scientific-technical Infrastructure

This is an important line of activity with the essential aim of providing institutions and research groups with the equipment necessary to ensure the effective realization of their research projects. The infrastructure funds are mainly devoted to the acquisition of large scientific instruments and to equipping the workshop and general services areas of the public research centres and the non-profit-making research bodies.

Special Actions

These are particular actions carried out at specific times,

such as seminars, meetings of experts, etc., which are aimed at complementing and supporting the execution of research projects.

Training of Research Personnel

The National Programme for the Training of Research Personnel has mainly been focused on priority areas in the National Programmes. It has two aspects: the training of new research personnel and also of existing staff. The process extends beyond national frontiers since a proportion of this training occurs at centres of excellence abroad, and foreign scientists and technologists are involved in the work at Spanish centres. Another means of achieving this aim is the promotion of the mobility of research personnel between industries and public research centres and the training of researchers in the R&D units of enterprises.

Concerted Projects

Enterprises research projects falling within the framework of the Programmes of the National Plan are partly financed by interest-free loans. They have a two-fold objective: to foster R&D activities in enterprises and link up technological and scientific interests with economic interests, that is, to match the initiatives of the Science and Technology System with the need of industry. CICYT has entrusted the management of this line of activity to the Centre for Industrial and Technological Development (CDTI).

The budgetary instrument of co-ordination for the promotion of scientific research and technological development is the National Fund for the Development of Scientific and Technical Research (Fondo Nacional para el Desarrollo de la Investigación Cientifica y Técnica). During the period 1988-91, it rose to the amount of 80,000 million pesetas. Figure 3 shows the distribution of these funds among the main lines of activity mentioned above.

Planning of Scientific and Technological Development: The National R&D Plan Programmes

The National Plan has the responsibility of planning the public initiatives in R&D. Therefore, the budgetary funds are structured around scientific and technological programmes established in terms of the social, technological and economic interests.

The National Plan includes the National Programmes, the Sectoral Programmes, and the Programmes agreed with the Autonomous Communities.

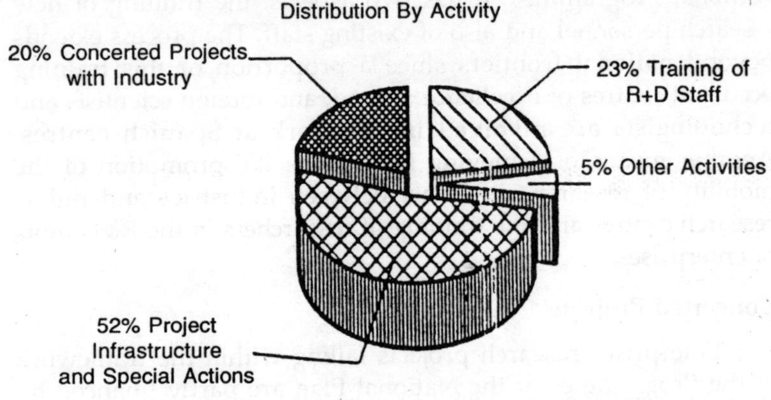

Figure 3. Distribution of the National Fund for the Development of Scientific and Technical Research (1988-91). Distribution by activity.

The *National Programmes* are approved in accordance with the defined priority lines of national interest. Their implementation has usually a multi-institutional character and they are funded from the National Fund. They include all stages of the technical and scientific process up to its culmination in the application of potential innovations to industrial development.

The *Sectoral Programmes* are orientated toward specific areas of interest to a body or ministerial department, whose scope or inter-relation with National Programmes justifies their inclusion in the National R&D Plan.

The *Autonomous Communities* can propose to CICYT inclusion in the National Plan of those R&D programmes that, because of their nature, may require co-ordination with the general national interests. The funding of these programmes is normally shared between the Autonomous Communities making the proposal and CICYT.

In Figure 4, the distribution of the total budget for scientific and technological areas for the period 1988-91 is given and in Table 1 the programmes which will be carried out during the period 1992-95 are shown.

Actions in the Area of Co-ordination

One of the historical shortcomings of the Spanish System of Science and Technology was the lack of co-ordination between initiatives originating in different institutions. The National Plan has attempted to rectify this by acting as an instrument for co-ordination, that is to say, linking the various initiatives developed by separate—public and private—agents within the System.

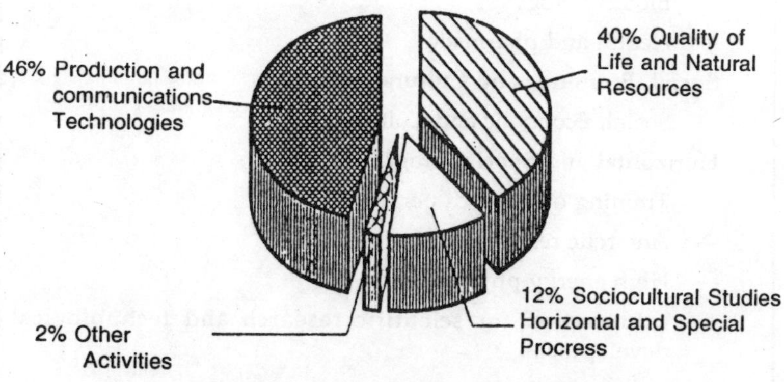

Figure 4. Distribution of the National Fund for the Development of Scientific and Technical Research (1988-91). Total 615 MECU. Scientific and technological areas.

Co-ordination occurs on three different levels: first, through the management of the different lines of activity of the National Plan, in which various administrative units, participate; secondly, with the linking up of ministerial R&D initiatives which, because of their themes, deserve general planning; finally as a result of the promotion of links between the Science and Technology System and industry, in other words, the theatre of economic activity.

Table 1. National R&D Plan Programmes (1992-95).

NATIONAL PROGRAMMES

Production and Communications Technologies

— Advanced production technologies
— Space research
— Materials
— Information and communications technologies

Quality of Life and Natural Resources

— Environment and natural resources
— Agricultural Science
— Food technology
— Biotechnology
— Health and pharmacy

Social, Economic and Cultural Studies

— Social, Economic and Cultural Studies

Horizontal and Special Programmes

— Training of research personnel
— Antarctic research
— High energy physics
— Information for scientific research and technological development.

AUTONOMOUS COMMUNITIES

— Fine chemistry (Programme of the Autonomous Community of Cataluña)

Sectoral Programmes

— General promotion of knowledge (Ministry of Education and Science)
— Training of university academic staff and improvement of research personnel (Ministry of Education and Science).

For these reasons, CICYT has entrusted CDTI with the management of the Concerted Projects so that this part of the National Plan, aimed at the enterprises, is co-ordinated with CDTI's own actions and with those of the Ministry of Industry, Commerce and Tourism, included in its Plan of Industrial and Technological Action (PATI).

This Plan was published in November 1990, and is aimed at supporting enterprises in the last stages of the process of innovation, particularly in those closest to the industrial development of the process or product.

Co-ordination with the Autonomous Communities occurs, initially, through the harmonization of the official *calls for proposals* and a specialization of actions that is only possible with an adequate exchange of information. Sometimes the co-ordination takes place through the co financing of programmes or specific actions.

The National Evaluation and Assessment Agency (ANEP) also carries out an important task of co-ordination through its evaluating activity. ANEP receives many different types of proposals coming from various bodies, and this contributes much to co-ordination, since the aggregate information so gathered helps to improve the quality of evaluation of different actions, avoiding unwanted duplication by separate sources of finance.

In short, it can help to streamline the allocation of R&D resources. In Figure 5, actions evaluated in 1990 are shown as an example.

Linking up the Science-Technology-Industry System

It has already been stated that one of the objectives of the National Plan is the promotion of R&D in enterprises and their collaboration with public research centres. This aims to promote joint action undertaken by these centres and enterprises in R&D activities and the appropriate transfer, to the productive sectors, of the results of public research that may lead to new processes or products of interest to industry. In this way, the scientific policy acts as an instrument in the various sectoral policies and the R&D activities contribute to social and economic welfare. To sum up, the aim is to replace the independent operation of the

Science-Technology System (SCT) with a linked up Science-Technology-Industry System (SCTI).

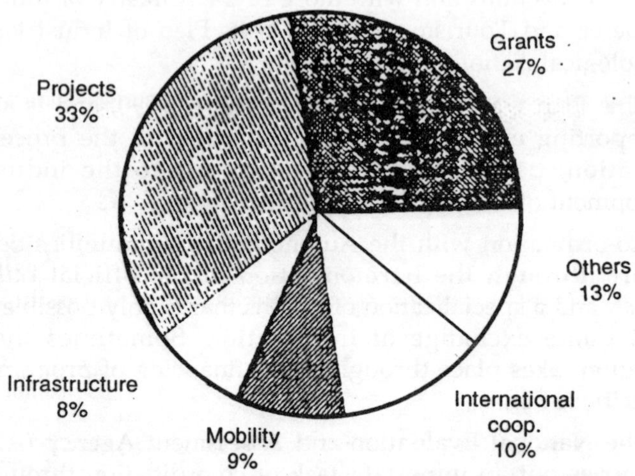

Figure 5. ANEP evaluated actions 1990. Total number of actions 15,000.

The direct relationship between R&D and technological development as well as the need for a swift transfer of knowledge with the cycle of innovation, require co-ordinated and concerted actions of all the elements making up the System. The National Plan promotes these types of actions, which facilitate fluent communication and exchanges between the elements of the Plan, and favour the creation of a network that forms the basis of SCTI.

With this aim, an interface structure has been established with the Offices for the Transfer of Research Results (OTRI) which exists in 36 universities, 11 public state and Autonomous Community research bodies, and 13 research associations. They are supported by the General Secretariat of the National Plan, through the Technology Transfer Office, which was created simultaneously.

Also, to meet the perceived need to increase the evaluation of the results of public research, the Programme for the

Stimulation of the Transfer of Research Results (PETRI) was set up. Its aim is to provide the OTRI/OTT network with a basic tool which gives them the means to offer incentives to basic and applied research groups, so that they expand part of their effort on R&D actions whose results can be transferred easily and rapidly to enterprises.

Finally, the actions of exchange of research personnel between industries and public research centres, included in the National Programme for Training of Research Personnel, referred to above, are aimed at advancing the work of R&D units in enterprises, as well as creating new units through the temporary inclusion of qualified researchers in enterprises and the temporary movement of scientists and technologists among bodies that carry out R&D.

International Activities

An explicitly stated in the Law of Science, the Interministerial Commission of Science and Technology holds responsibility for defining the activities of the National R&D Plan in the international sphere, and promoting the financial and technical follow-up of Spanish participation in the International R&D Programmes. In particular, Spain has significantly supported the R&D policy of the European Community (EC). This is understood as an instrument for the modernization of productive structures, as a means by which disparities within the Community can be overcome, and as a way of stimulating the international competitiveness of industries within the Community.

Similarly, it has been considered essential to promote and encourage the participation of Spanish public research bodies, universities, and enterprises in the Community Programmes which will produce beneficial synergies in the Science and Technology System, this itself improving the competitiveness in the Single European Market of 1993.

The European R&D Programmes in which Spain participates, and the percentage of Spanish participation is shown in Table 2. Spain also participates in the committees relating to Science and Technology within international organizations such as: OECD (Organisation for Economic operation and Development), EC (European Community), and UNESCO.

In addition, the Interministerial Commission for Science and Technology, together with the Spanish Agency for International Co-operation (Agencia Española de Co-operación Internacional, AECI), jointly finances and manages the Programme for Science and Technology for Development—Fifth Century (CYTED—D) in which Spain participates along with Portugal and 19 Latin American countries.

Table 2. European R&D Programmes with Spanish Participation (1990)

	Spanish participation (%)
EC Framework Programme	8 (1)
Other European Programmes	
AIRBUS Programme	4.2
International Co-operation in Astrophysics	20(2)
European Organization for Nuclear Research (CERN)	7.6
International Centre for Advanced Mediterranean Agriculture (CIHEAM)	21
COST Fund (Scient. and Techn. Co-op. between European Communities & third European Countries)	5.9
European Molecular Biology Laboratory	4.4
European Molecular Biology Organization	5.8
European Space Agency (ESA)	4
European Science Foundation (ESF)	5.5
European Synchrotron Radiation Facility (ESRF)	4
EUREKA Programme	6.2(3) 21(4)
Max Von Laue-Paul Langevin Institute (ILL)	1.5
Large Earth-based Solar Telescope (LEST)	14.4
Ocean Drilling Programme (ODP)	4

(1) Corresponds to Spanish contribution to the total European Community budget.

(2) Observation time.

(3) Relates to total investment in EUREKA projects.

(4) Relates to investment in projects with Spanish participation.

In agreement with the organic structure of the State Secretariat for International Co-operation and Iberian and Latin American countries (Secretaria de Estado para la Co-operación Internacional y para Iberoamérica, SECIPI), bilateral scientific and technological co-operation in R&D is basically channelled through the General Directorate for Scientific and Cultural Relations and the Spanish Agency for International Co-operation (AECI), and is developed under the corresponding scientific and technical co-operation and complementary agreements.

The modes of co-operation existing in these agreements vary greatly: the exchange of scientific and technical information, the exchange of scientists and experts, the organization of seminars, meetings and congresses of a scientific and technical character, the carrying out of research projects on themes of common interest, etc.

RESEARCH AND DEVELOPMENT INSTITUTIONS

Universities

Universities account for 50 per cent of Spanish scientists (on a full-time equivalent basis); that is, they constitute the most important potential source of research in the country. In addition to teaching, universities carry out important research and support work for the socio-economic sectors. Both of these activities have increased considerably over the last few years.

There are 37 public universities in Spain, including the Menendez Pelayo International University and the one recently created in Castellon. The map in Figure 6 shows their geographical distribution, along with percentages of students and university academic staff (except those of the Pompeu Fabra University (Barcelona) and the Jaume I University (Castellón), where courses were not held during the quoted years). Similarly, information regarding numbers of university academic staff at the public universities at La Coruña, Vigo, Carlo III (Madrid), and Navarra is omitted.

In addition to public universities, there are four private ones (Deusto University, Navarra University, Pontifical University of Comillas, and Pontifical University of Salamanca), which account for 3.21 per cent of the total number of university students in

Spain. Tables 3 and 4 show the distribution of university students by type of centre; and the total number of professors and lecturers by area of specialization. Figure 7 shows the distribution of students by study area.

Public Research Bodies (OPI)

The public research bodies develop the Sectoral Programmes within their own ministerial departments, but also participate in various National Programmes of the National R&D Plan (through the annual calls for proposals). From this point of view, the existence of the Higher Centre for Scientific Research (CSIC), responsible to the Ministry of Education and Science, a multidisciplinary body whose researchers participate in most of the Programmes, is particularly significant. Other public research bodies, sectoral in character, also participate in programmes relevant to their own area of work. Figure 8 shows the public research bodies and respective responsible ministries.

Table 3. Distribution of students by type of centre (academic year 1989-90). Source: Anuario de Estadistica Universitaria (University Statistics Yearbook), 1990

Type of Centre	*Public Centre*	*Private Centre*	*Total*
University faculties & colleges	661,024	28,134	689,158
University schools (non-technical)	213,341	2,314	215,655
University higher technical school	66,073	3,166	69,239
University technical schools	93,135	687	93,822
TOTAL	1,033,573	34,301	1,067,874

Table 4. Distribution of academic staff in public universities by area of specialization (19 June, 1990). Source as Table 3.

AREA	*Univ. profs.*	*Univ. lects.*	*Univ. school profs.*	*Univ. school lects.*	*Total*
Humanities & social sciences	1,833	5,392	580	3,080	10,885
Mathematics	1,150	4,091	190	1,035	6,466
Health sciences	720	2,403	25	313	3,461
Engineering & technology	646	1,534	261	1,218	3,659
TOTAL	4,349	13,420	1,056	5,646	24,471

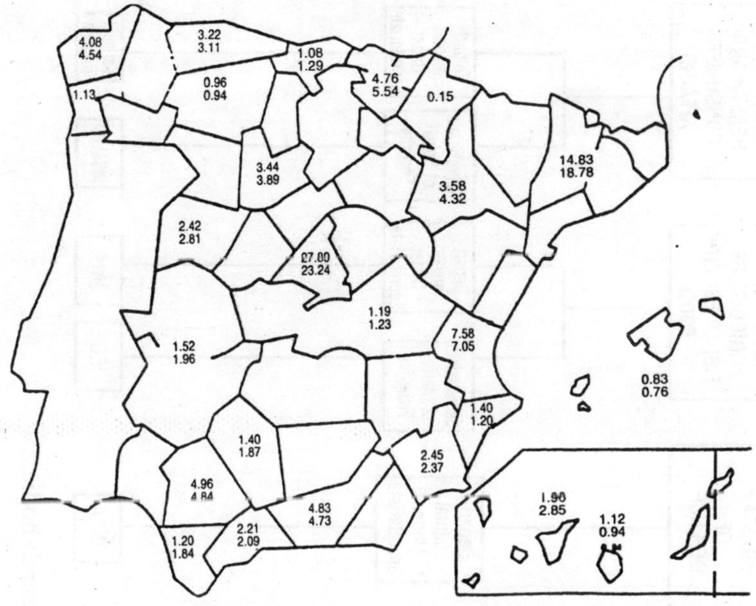

Figure 6. Geographic distribution of students (upper no.) and academic staff (lower), as per cent of total for public universities 1989-90. Academic year 1988-89: total university academic staff 50,597. Academic year 1989-90: total students 1,033,573.

Source: University Statistics Yearbook, 1989.

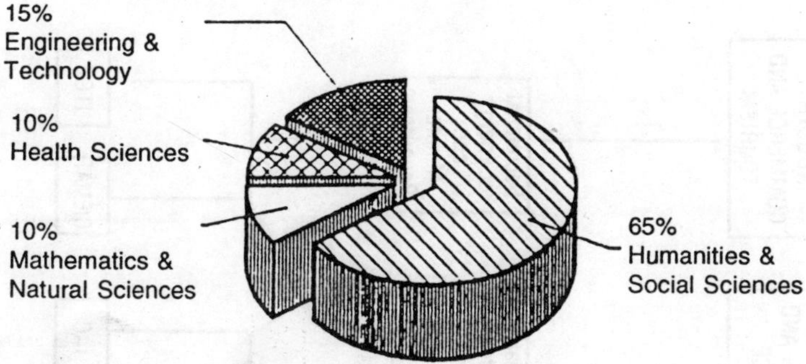

Figure 7. Percentage distribution of students by area of study. Academic year 1988-89.

Source: University Statistics Yearbook, 1990.

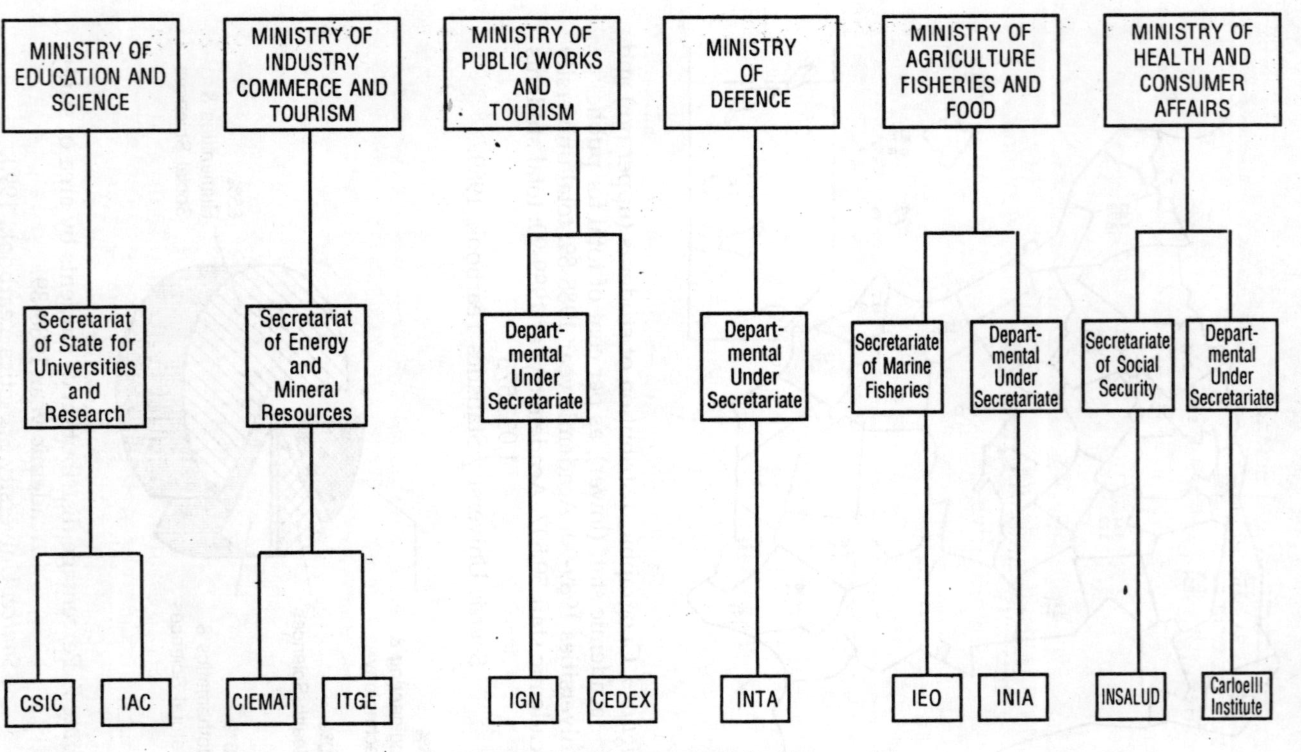

Figure 8. Public research bodies.

Ministry of Education and Sciences

Higher Centre for Scientific Research (CSIC). The CSIC is the largest public research body in Spain. Its character is multisectorial and it develops its research activity in the following scientific areas: humanities and social sciences; biology and biomedicine; agricultural sciences; space and Earth sciences; mathematics, physics, and chemistry; technology.

It also provides support centres (database, information, etc.) and central administrative centres. CSIC's total budget in 1990 amounted to 45,295 million pesetas (348.4 million ECU), out of which 33,015 million (254 million ECU) represented its ordinary budget. It has 101 centres and 6500 staff of whom approximately 2200 are researchers.

Canary Islands Institute for Astrophysics (IAC). The development of scientific research projects in the field of astrophysics and related areas is the main purpose of this Institute. Through the International Co-operating Agreements in Astrophysics, IAC's observatories of Roque de los Muchachos (La Palma) and Teide (Tenerife) have been internationalized.

Spain guarantees research activity and the protection of the observatories in accordance with the International Astronomical Union guidelines. The budget for IAC in 1990 totalled 1243 million pesetas (9.6 million ECU) and it has 178 R&D employees of whom 111 are researchers on a full-time equivalent basis.

Ministry of Public Works and Transport

National Geographic Institute (IGN). The Institute is responsible for national basic cartograpy. Among other things, it co-ordinates the R&D activities of the centres responsible to it, covering the areas of geodesy, cartographic training, astronomy and geophysics, cartographic processes, metrology, seismology, etc. Research in geophysics is carried out through the National Seismic Network and the Geomagnetic Observatories. Research in astrophysics takes place at the Astronomical Centre of Yebes and the Calar Alto Observatory among other places. The IGN budget for 1990 amounted to 5145 million pesetas (39.5 million ECU), out of which 561 million (4.3 million ECU) was allocated for research activities. This centre employs 70 research and development staff, including 24 research workers on a full-time equivalent basis.

Research and Experimental Centre for Public Works (CEDEX). This is a Centre of technological and multidisciplinary support for civil engineering and public works, devoted to highlevel development and technical assistance; from planning and work inspection to staff training. CEDEX carries out studies on materials and structures for public works, soil dynamics, harbours, coasts and oceanography, hydrology and hydraulic resources, hydraulics, general and energy mechanics, etc. The budget for 1990 totalled 4777 million pesetas (36.7 million ECU), 404 million (3.1 million ECU) of which were devoted to R&D, and some 1268 million (9.7 million ECU) to studies and technical assistance. The Centre employs 688 R&D people, 70 of whom are researchers on a full-time equivalent basis.

Ministry of Industry, Commerce and Tourism

Technological Geomining Institute of Spain (ITGE). This Institute carries out most of the R&D activities in the following areas: geology, mining, hydrogeology, geotechnics, sea-bed research, environmental geology, mining safety, and geological hazards study. In 1990, ITGE's budget for R&D activities amounted to 5529 million pesetas (42.5 million ECU). It employs 521 R&D staff, 254 of whom are researchers on a full-time equivalent basis.

Centre for Energy, Environmental and Technological Research (CIEMAT). The R&D activities carried out in this Centre are chiefly directed toward solving energy problems, paying special attention to the study of alternative energy sources which, while allowing the development of industrial activity, will protect public health and conserve the natural environment. It is divided into four departments, each dealing with a specific field: renewable energy, radiation protection and the environment nuclear technology, and basic research. In addition, it has the Technology Directorate as a support unit and the Energy Studies Institute for the training of staff. The CIEMAT total budget in 1990 was 7587 million pesetas (58.4 million ECU) and it has a staff of 1392 R&D employees including 507 researchers on a full-time equivalent basis.

Ministry of Defence

National Institute for Aerospace Technology (INTA). This research and development body specializes in the diverse fields of aerospace and aeronautic technologies. The largest projects in which it participates are EFA (European Fighting Aeroplane) in the aeronautic sphere, and the development of the Helios and Hispasat satellites, and minisatellites in the aerospace sphere. In addition, it develops other programmes and facilities such as the Official Trial Centre (OTC), the Trisonic Tunnel, and the Centre for the Treatment and Exploitation of Images of Helios (Centro para el Tratamiento y Explotación de Imágenes del Helios). Many of INTA's activities are carried out under international co-operation agreements and contracts—particularly with NASA and ESA—and by subcontracting with Spanish and foreign companies. Its budget for 1990 amounted to 9042 million pesetas (69.5 million ECU). At present it has 1153 R&D staff, 325 of whom are research workers on a full-time equivalent basis.

Ministry of Agriculture, Fisheries and Food

Spanish Institute for Oceanography (IEO). This Institute deals with the research of scientific problems in relation to oceanography and fisheries: marine biology, fishing technology and biology, marine pollution, oceanographic physics, marine geology, oceanographic chemistry, etc. Its budget in 1990 amounted to 2949 million pesetas (22.7 million ECU). It has 375 R&D employees, of whom 142 are researchers on a full-time equivalent basis.

National Institute for Agricultural and Food Technology and Research (INIA). As a result of extensive decentralization in the promotion and execution of R&D in agriculture, each of the Autonomous Communities has assumed responsibility for carrying out R&D, while the co-ordination of a national agricultural research programme, international relations, and much of the finance remains the responsibility of central government. INIA deals with agriculture, sylviculture (forestry) and livestock breeding, specifically within these categories: herbaceous cultivation, ligneous cultivation, animal husbandry, forestry development, etc. Its R&D budget in 1990 amounted to 5564 million pesetas (43 million ECU). The Institute has approximately 1200 employees, 675 of whom carry out R&D activities and 311 of whom are researchers on a full-time equivalent basis.

Ministry of Health and Consumer Affairs

National Institute of Health (INSALUD). This is the body responsible for medical and sanitary assistance policy and the promotion of health in general. It finances clinical, pharmacological, and biomedical research through the Fondo de Investigaciones Sanitarias (Health Research Fund, FIS), whose purpose is to carry out studies and activities which may contribute to the improvement of the provision of public health facilities. FIS co-ordinates its actions with the National R&D Plan through joint *calls for proposals* with the Sectoral Programme for General Promotion of Knowledge, integrated in the National Plan. The FIS budget in 1990 was 4167 million pesetas (32 million ECU).

Carlos III Institute of Health. This Institute provides scientific and technical support to the Ministry of Health and to various health services of the Autonomous Communities. The main tasks of this body are to promote and carry out research activities in the fields of health and biomedicine, as well as in those of clinical research, pharmacobiology, food safety and environmental pollution. The Institute has several National Research Centres and finances joint programmes with other public research Institutions. The R&D budget in 1990 totalled 8837 million pesetas (68 million ECU). It has 768 employees engaged in R&D activities, of whom 138 are researchers on a full-time equivalent basis.

Industrial Enterprises

The promotion of R&D activities in enterprises is one of the main objectives of the scientific and technological policy. The creation of own technology is essential in terms of increasing the competitiveness of production both in the national and the international market and it is one of the basic requirements for reducing the deficit resulting from the acquisition of foreign technology.

In conjunction with the various methods of assistance given

to achieve these objectives—mainly by the National R&D Plan and the Plan of Industrial and Technological Action (Ministry of Industry, Commerce and Tourism)—tax incentives for R&D have been made available since 1989. These allow private enterprises to reduce their corporation tax contribution by 30 per cent of capital investment and 15 per cent of other expenditures on intangible assets for the research and development of new products or industrial processes.

Spanish enterprises have increased R&D expenditure over 1982-90 by an average annual cumulative rate of 23 per cent, representing one of the largest increases in the OECD over that period. At present, the enterprise sector accounts for 58 per cent of Spanish expenditure on R&D activities.

According to various estimates, about 1000 enterprises are carrying out significant R&D activities. The most important R&D initiatives are to be found in the following sectors: chemicals (about 18 per cent), motor and transport equipment (17 per cent), electronics and electrical products (11 per cent), and computer software (7 per cent).

Around 20 per cent of the total enterprises are responsible for over 75 per cent of R&D expenditure in the business sector and utilize 70 per cent of human resources. This high concentration of R&D activities does not prevent the increasing incorporation of small- and medium-sized enterprises into these activities, as can be seen from a study of the distribution of aid given by the R&D National Plan and that given by the Ministry of Industry, Commerce and Tourism.

Public Enterprises

About 20 per cent of enterprise R&D initiatives are performed by public enterprises. Those of special note are those belonging to the National Institute of Industry (INI), a holding company subject to a policy of economic guidelines laid down by the government, as well as those belonging to the National Institute of Hydrocarbons (INH) (Ministry of Industry, Commerce and Tourism), RENFE (Spanish National Railways Network), FEVE (Narrow-gauge Railways), and the National Telephone Company (CTNE); the major shareholder is the Spanish State.

Private Enterprises

In 1990, the expenditure of R&D by private enterprises represented about 0.7 per cent of their turnover. This was very unevenly distributed, not only between different sectors but also within each sector. The most important sector carrying out significant R&D activities is the chemical industry, or more specifically the pharmaceutical sector, which devotes approximately 1000 scientists and about 6 per cent turnover to R&D; but there are other sectors that are constantly increasing the level of their R&D activity, such as electronics, computer software, and telecommunications.

In traditional industrial sectors such as footwear, wood products and furniture, textiles, toy manufacture, etc., there are enterprise research associations whose aim is to develop research projects at the competitive stage into new products or manufacturing processes, which are relevant to their sector. Over the last few years, these associations have devoted most of their efforts to the incorporation of computer and robotic technologies in their production processes, and to the development and application of new materials.

EXPENDITURE ON AND FINANCE OF R&D ACTIVITIES

General Information of Spain

Area:	504,750 square kilometres
Population:	39 million inhabitants
Currency:	peseta, 1 ECU=130 pesetas
GNP:	49.7 billion pesetas

Expenditure on R&D

In Spain financial expenditure on R&D has grown very rapidly over the decade of the 1980s, particularly since the coming into force of the Law of Science.

Figure 9 represents the growth of total expenditure on R&D in Spain over the last few years. The average annual cumulative rate of growth in expenditure on R&D (at constant prices) during the period 1983-89 was over 15 per cent, practically double the average rate of growth for equivalent expenditure in the most advanced industrial countries, which began with a total of expenditure more in line with the needs of the production system. The estimates for 1990 reflect a strong increase in expenditure in comparison with the previous year: the total expenditure amounts to a figure of 410,000 million pesetas (3154 million ECU) compared with 340,000 million (2614 million ECU) for 1989.

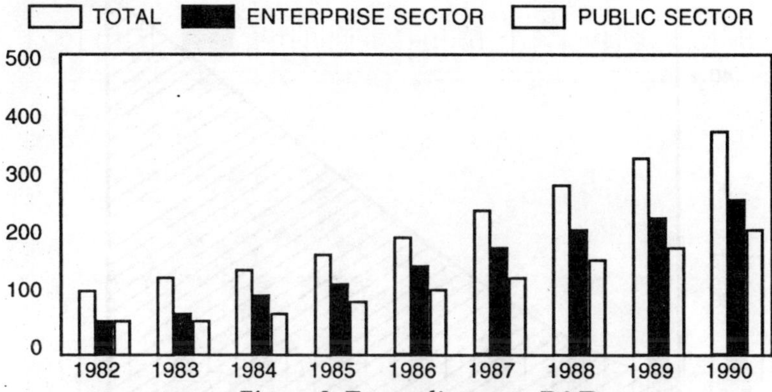

Figure 9. Expenditure on R&D.
Source: Instituto Nacional de Estadistica, *INA (National Statistics Institute)*. Note that the a information for 1988, 1989, 1990 is an estimate. *INE-SGPN.*

The relative indicator for GDP at factor cost has moved from 0.48 per cent in 1983 to 0.90 per cent in 1990 as can be seen in Figure 10. The increase is less important than that shown for expenditure in absolute terms, owing to the simultaneous increase in the GDP, as shown in Figure 11.

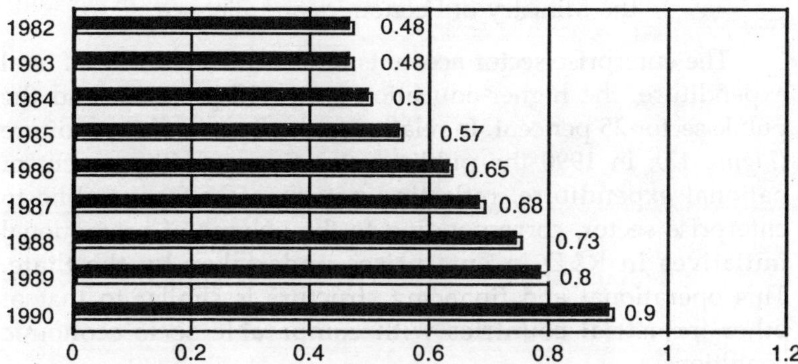

Figure 10. GDP on R&D, as per cent GDP (fc).
Source: INE. Note that the information for 1989 and 1990 is an estimate. INE-SGPN.

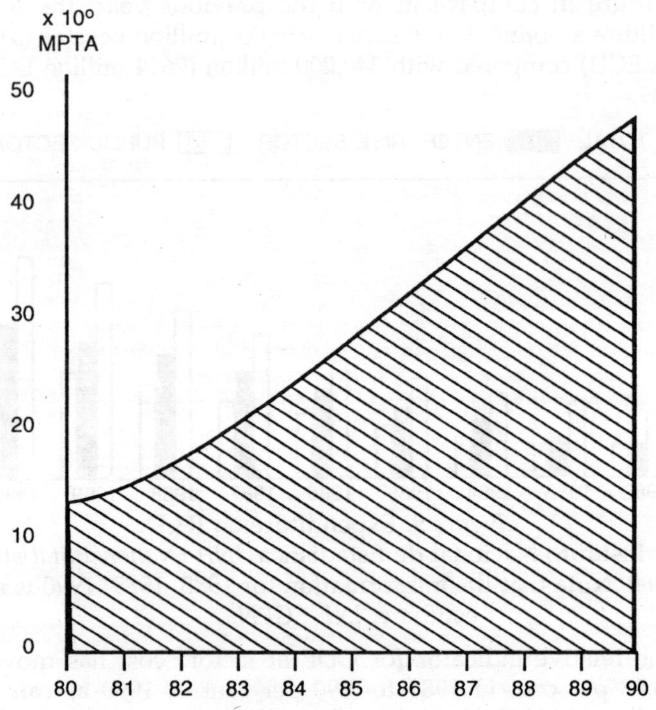

Figure 11. Growth of GDP.
Source: INE. Note that the estimate used for 1989-90 are due to the Ministry of Economics and Finance.

The enterprise sector accounts for about 58 per cent of total expenditure, the higher-education sector 17 per cent, and the public sector 25 per cent. In relation to the finance of expenditure *(Figure 12),* in 1990 the public sector financed 60 per cent of national expenditure, reflecting net transfers from public to enterprise sector, corresponding to the volume of promotional initiatives in R&D in enterprises undertaken by the State. This operational and financing structure is similar to that of other industrial countries with comparable socio-economic conditions.

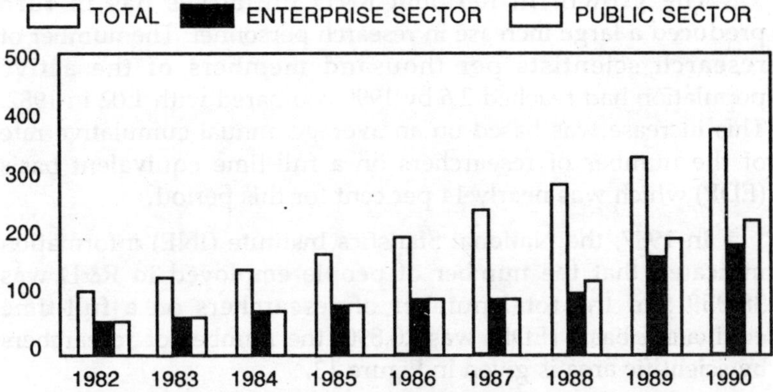

Figure 12. Finance of R&D (thousand million pesetas). *Source:* INE. 1988-89 estimates due to SGPN.

With regard to public financing of R&D, in Table 5 the sectors, by objective, and according to the information provided by NABS (Nomenclature for the Analysis and comparison of Science Programmes and Budgets) are indicated.

Table 5. Public financing of R&D by NABS objectives in millions of pesetas. Estimates for public finance (by objective, according to NABS) exclude, by definition, finance from social security. The university contribution accounts for 16 per cent of the total budget.

NABS objectives	1987	1988	1989	1990
Exploration and exploitation of the earth	12,221	11,158	15,121	13,488
Infrastructure and planning of land use	317	587	957	1,159
Control & prevention of environ. pollution	2,641	2,799	4,881	11,559
Protection & improvement of human health	13,434	13,917	15,289	18,311
Energy: prod., distrib., rational utilise.	4,110	4,199	7,143	6,701
Agricultural production & technology	9,180	10,709	13,061	13,930
Industrial production & technology	31,642	33,161	39,359	44,734
Social structures & relationships	1,317	1,281	3,061	4,077
Exploration & exploitation of space	8,148	11,718	14,643	14,950
University research	28,042	30,333	37,916	48,533
Non-oriented research	12,487	20,799	24,171	27,468
Non-classified research	4,862	5,849	8,596	12,859
Defence	12,172	24,833	49,211	49,665
Total public expenditure	140,580	171,349	233,414	267,439

R&D Personnel

The growth in national R&D initiatives has in turn produced a large increase in research personnel. The number of research scientists per thousand members of the active population had reached 2.6 by 1990 compared with 1.02 in 1982. This increase was based on an average annual cumulative rate of the number of researchers on a full-time equivalent basis (EDP) which was nearly 14 per cent for this period.

In 1987, the National Statistics Institute (INE) information indicated that the number of people employed in R&D was 38,059 and the total number of researchers on a full-time equivalent basis (EDP) was 20,890; the number of researchers by scientific area is given in Figure 13.

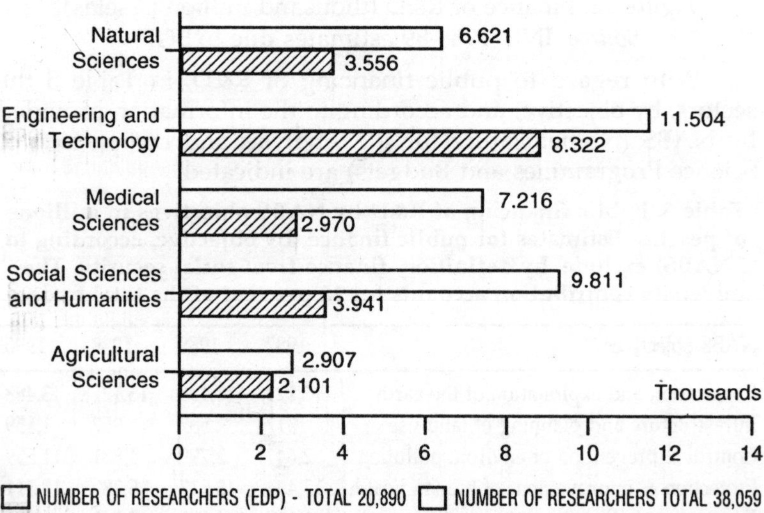

Figure 13. Number of researchers by scientific area, 1987.
Source: INE.

In Figure 14 the distribution of personnel engaged in R&D in 1990, according to the estimates of the General Secretariat or National R&D Plan, is given by sector. The substantial increase that has taken place since 1987 can be clearly seen.

On the other hand, as well as an increase in the number of researchers, there has also been a significant growth in the training of personnel, as a result of National Plan actions and other private and public initiatives.

Figure 15 shows the growth in the number of postgraduate grants, awarded to the programmes of the Plan, both in Spain and abroad, as well as those financed by the Autonomous Communities and other private and public institutions, between 1982 and 1990.

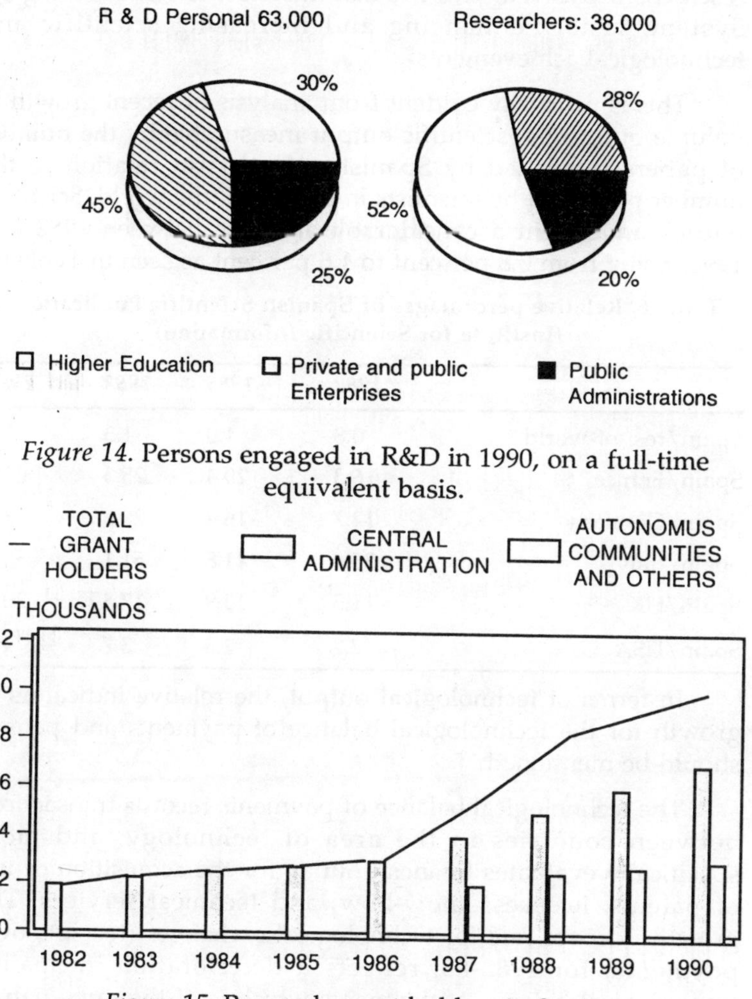

Figure 14. Persons engaged in R&D in 1990, on a full-time equivalent basis.

Figure 15. Research grant holders in Spain.

Results

From the information provided in the previous sections, it can be concluded that during the last few years the Spanish System of Science and Technology has undergone a significant expansion, not only in terms of the proportion of national resources allocated to R&D, but also in terms of the number of researchers involved. This has had the effect of consolidating the System, visibly enhancing and increasing scientific and technological achievements.

This is primarily evident from analysis of recent growth in volume of Spanish scientific output measurable by the number of papers published by Spanish scientists in relation to the number published by scientists in the rest of the world. Scientific output underwent a considerable increase between 1982 and 1990, rising from 0.8 per cent to 1.6 per cent as seen in Table 6.

Table 6. Relative percentages of Spanish Scientific Publications. (Institute for Scientific Information)

	1982	*1985*	*1988*	*1990*
Spain/rest-of-world	0.8	1.0	1.3	1.6
Spain/France	16.3	20.4	25.3	29.9
Spain/Germany	12.7	16.4	20.3	23.0
Spain/Italy	35.8	41.8	51.1	55.7
Spain/UK	11.3	13.9	17.8	20.4
Spain/USA	2.2	2.8	3.7	4.2

In terms of technological output, the relative indicators of growth for the technological balance of payments and patents should be mentioned.

The technological balance of payments records transactions between countries in the area of technology, and more specifically evaluates financial outlay for the acquisition or use of patents, licences, know-how, and technical services. The growth in cover rate for technological exchanges (receipts over payments) for 1982-88, reflects a deterioration in Spain's technological balance of payments which is of the same nature (though different in degree) as that experienced by other advanced industrial countries. However, this is a common phenomenon in countries where technological development is expanding, so requiring heavy investment for the acquisition of advanced foreign technology in certain industrial sectors.

Over the last few years, although Spain has remained with a deficit in its technological balance of payments, the growing increase in receipts from sales of technology gives rise to a tendency for hope. In 1989, in particular, there was a 66 per cent increase in the receipts for technology compared with the previous year; whereas payments increased by a mere 24 per cent, resulting in a covering rate of 18.4 per cent in comparison with that of 13.5 per cent for 1988. The movement of the covering index continues to be positive. In 1990, it had reached 19.3 per cent and the receipts increase continuously in percentage terms over those of payments.

The other chief indicator of technological output—that of patents—shows that, in the last few years, the rate of penetration of Spain by foreign patents has substantially increased. This phenomenon coincides with a sudden opening up of national markets to international competition and its corresponding interest in these markets. In any event, the movement of the indicator reflects the degree of exposure to international competition of the Spanish Technological System.

The average annual cumulative increase in the number of patents presented abroad by Spanish residents during this period is larger than that of national residents in neighbouring countries. This fact seems to reflect the greater presence of Spanish technology in the international system of science and technology.

4

Organizational Structure of Science in Norway: A System in Transition

NINA GORNITZKA

Norwegian Research Council for Science and the Humanities, Oslo, Norway

Introduction

The Norweign research organization is a rather complex structure. It has developed over the years, more as a result of a continuous series of initiatives and actions to adapt or fill voids in the existing structure, than according to a unified plan. The system operates at three levels:

(i) research policy level, with the Storting (the Norwegian Parliament), the government and the ministries as main actors

(ii) research strategy level, with the research councils as main operators

(iii) the research and development performing units: universities/higher educational institutions, research institutes, and industrial laboratories.

The research strategy level is taken as the point of departure. At this level, the most dramatic changes ever registered are taking place right now, changes that will undoubtedly lead to transformations in the science system as a whole. The Norwegian government decided on 23 March this year (1992) to replace the existing five research councils by *one single research council*.

In the following, we first give a brief overview of the structure of the new council and the process that led up to the government's decision; then some R&D statistics; and finally comments on some organizational and other aspects of Norwegian science organization in more general terms.

NORWEGIAN RESEARCH COUNCIL: A NEW STRUCTURE IN THE MAKING

General Background

The present research council organization was created after World War II and has survived so far without major changes. The five existing councils are the following:

— the Norwegian Research Council for Science and the Humanities, NAVF (sole body responsible for basic long-term research and skill building), with sub-councils for the humanities, medical and health research, natural sciences, and social sciences;

— the Norwegian Council for Fishery Research, NFFR;

— the Agricultural Research Council of Norway, NLVF;

— the Norwegian Research Council for Applied Social Science, NORAS;

— the Royal Norwegian Council for Scientific and Industrial Research, NINF.

It is worth noting that from the very beginning, the humanities and the social sciences were full members of the research council family. The councils are public institutions with considerable independence *vis-a-vis* the State and, with some variations, with close links to the academic communities. These links are particularly strong—and a characteristic of the NAVF while, on the other hand, the industrial links are what characterize the NTNF.

Over the years, the main issues of debate have been linked to questions concerning the organization of applied social science research and the sphere of competence of the industrial research council. Apparently the Norwegian system of two separate social science councils—for basic and applied research—has no parallel in Europe or in any other region.

During the 1980s, the need for changes in the research organization was the subject of several research policy papers and documents. The reasons for this were many: accelerating changes in science itself, and new research challenges arising from a changing socio-economic, political, and cultural reality necessitated a new organizational approach. Science and society were in fact becoming too complex to be handled adequately by the existing organizational research structure.

The political system, too, showed a markedly stronger interest in research in general, and, more specifically, in research as a strategic tool in the development of trade and industry. The cross-sectorial long-term priority areas established by the government from the mid-80s bear out this fact. At all levels, the present structure gave particular reason for concern as regards its disintegrative effects on science, making basic science and applied science activities appear as two distinct and different science spheres.

Finally, there was a more general need for new mechanisms to stimulate interdisciplinary research—and particularly so within the research areas of environment and development.

To cope with these new challenges and activities, a series of *ad hoc* organizational solutions were devised, resulting in new governing bodies partly within and partly cross-cutting the formal research council system. These new bodies had their own mandates and resources, and developed their own ambitions.

To sum up: rapid development and growth in science and in R&D activities continuously leading to *ad hoc* organizational solutions and, accordingly, to uncertainty as regards the lines of authority and division of labour, were the trademarks of Norwegian research organization during the 80s and the early 90s. A more cohesive, better co-ordinated and more cost-effective system had to be conceived.

Government Decision: one Norwegian Research Council (NFR)

The recent government decision to replace the five existing councils by one new one must be seen in this perspective.

The government-states that one research council will lead to better co-ordination and better use of research resources. The new one-council structure will also secure necessary links between basic and applied research.

A government appointed board will be responsible for the organization. A director general, also appointed by the government, will head the administration. Six steering committees will be in charge of the council's main activities, the activities being organized as follows:

— medicine and health

— culture and society (humanities, social sciences, public administration, public services)

— natural sciences and basic technological research

industry and energy (including oil, shipping trade and services)

— bioproduction and processing (fishery, aquaculture/ fish-farming, agriculture, veterinary medicine, forestry and food-processing industry)

— environment and development.

The NFR will be administratively linked to the Ministry of Education, Research and Church Affairs, but will co-operate actively with and receive resources from most ministries.

The existing five councils dispose of more than two billion NOK for Norwegian R&D activities. It follows that the mandate of the new council will be extensive and the resources at its disposal of considerable magnitude. The council will be operative from 1993.

The Government Committee Report on the new Research Structure: Main Features

The government's decision to change the research council system is based on a committee report proposal, an extensive hearing, and an adjusted proposal presented to the government by a group of high officials representing the most research-relevant ministries.

In the government committee's analysis of the role and position of science in society, presented as a background and intellectual basis for the proposed new structure, some of the main characteristics or dilemmas in the Norwegian science system are highlighted; the double role of science in society, that is 'science as culture' and 'science as basis for techno-economic change'; 'science as an independent academic enterprise' *versus* 'direction and use of science to attain specific social goals'; the balance between 'a co-ordinated public research policy' and 'the sectorial approach where science and research are seen as one of many modes of operation within a specific sector'. These are common dilemmas being faced by most research organizations in West Europe.

As guiding principles in the framing of a new structure, the following were established:

— integration of basic and applied research.

— strengthening the capacity for high-level political direction of research.

— modification of the principle of sector (ministry) responsibility for research, to ensure better co-ordination.

— delegation of tasks from research councils to performing units.

— well planned research direction and research administration.

Integration of basic and applied research is to be considered as the main goal of the restructuring process. Since there are no longer any sharp distinctions between basic and applied research, the Norwegian research council system, at present structured according to this very distinction, is clearly in need of some change.

The committee report, presented in August 1991, contained a set of proposals, of which the most important was the merging of all research council functions into one Norwegian research council, organized along three main axes:

— biology, environment, and health.

— technology and natural sciences.

— culture and social sciences.

A series of measures intended to strengthen the co-ordinating capacity at the ministerial level were included. The most important—and controversial—of these measures was perhaps a proposal to strengthen the appropriation of the Ministry of Research by transferring research appropriations from the other ministries.

To sum sup: the organizational changes proposed in the committee report were indeed dramatic. The mere size and complexity of the new 'baby' legitimate the question put forward by many as to whether it is at all possible to transform the concept of one council into an operative and functional unit. This is both a practical administrative challenge and a question of balancing a broad spectrum of different interests—political, sector-oriented, university-based, etc.

Also, the merging of the existing five councils into one raises the question of what is a research council. In the present Norwegian system, the research councils cover a wide range of functions, some of which lie in the 'grey zone' between research council functions and industry-related modes of operation.

When the new single-council system is made operative, a decision must be taken as to whether functions other than those normally considered strictly research council functions should be included in the system.

Nevertheless, at all levels, the reaction to the single research council concept and to the principle of integrating basic and applied research was overwhelmingly positive. This could be largely due to the report's quite sketchy description of the new structure. In the ensuing debate, sharp differences of opinion did emerge when the main protagonists started to consider what should be the flesh and blood given to the skeleton research council structure.

With the government's decision of 23 March, the main features of the new structure are in place—to be elaborated into what hopefully will be a constructive framework for Norwegian science and research in the future.

However, the final decision remains to be made by the Storting (Parliament). The government's proposal will be discussed by the Storting in June 1992. The most controversial issues will probably be the question of ensuring the research interests of the sectors (specifically, fishery and agricultural interests) in the new structure, and the question of location (joint centralized administration in Oslo versus locating parts of the administration outside the capital to accommodate regional interests).

In many countries, the idea of a single integrated research council has been considered—but it has still not been realized in any country. Even Iceland, with 250,000 inhabitants, has established separate councils for basic and for applied sector research. Will Norway succeed in her 'one-council' project?*

Financing

In Norway, total R&D expenditure in current prices has almost tripled since 1981. For 1981-89 as a whole, the average annual growth rate in real terms was 6.6 per cent initially higher then lower towards the end of the period (cf Table 1).

Table 1. Key figures from Norwegian R&D 1981-89.

	1981	1983	1985	1987	1989
Inhab. (1000s)	4,107	4,134	4,159	4,198	4,233
Employed persons (1000s)	1,932	1,957	2,012	2,126	2,049
GDP (million NOK)	328,551	402,197	500,200	561,480	622,991
R&D personnel	26,297	27,930	30,979	31,898	32,871
R&D person-years (FTE)	15,025	16,188	19,036	20,140	20,471
R&D person-years (FTE)/1000 inhab.	3.7	3.9	4.6	4.8	4.8
Total R&D expend. (million NOK)	4,267.7	5,764.6	8,202.9	10,319.4	11,662.2
R&D expenditure as %GDP	1.30	1.43	1.64	1.84	1.87
R&D expenditure/ inhabitant (NOK)	1,040	1,390	1,970	2,460	2,760

* The final decision to establish one Norwegian research council was made by the Storting on 18 June 1992.

Table 2. Total R&D Expenditure in Norway, by Performance Sector. (Million NOK.)

Performance sector	*1987*	*1989*	*Average annual growth 1987-89 (%)* *Current prices*	*Fixed prices*	*Estimate 1991*
Industry	4,549	4,590	4.6	– 4.0	5,500
Institute	3,605	4,301	9.2	4.1	4,800
Higher-education	2,166	2,771	13.1	7.9	3,100
Total	10,319	11,662	6.3	1.6	13,400
Total as %GDP	1.8	1.9			1.9

In 1989 total spending on R&D activities amounted to NOK 11.7 billion (cf Table 2), about 50 per cent of the total expenditure by public funds. The greater part of public R&D funds is channelled directly to universities and other higher learning institutions and as basic funding to research institutes. About 25 per cent of the public funds are channelled through the research council system. In addition, the councils receive a fixed share of the profits of the Norwegian Pools Organization set aside for research purposes.

Approximately 33,000 people were engaged in R&D activities in 1989. The proportion of Gross Domestic Product (GDP) spent on R&D activities increased from 1.3 per cent in 1981 to 1.9 per cent in 1989. This places Norway mid-way among the OECD countries.

Since the mid-80s, there has been an upward trend in public financing and a downward trend in industrial financing. In 1989, industry financed almost 44 per cent of the R&D activities, compared to 50 per cent in 1985 (cf Figure 1).

In 1989, 39 per cent of total R&D activities were performed in the industrial sector, 37 per cent in the institute sector, and 24 per cent in the higher education sector (cf Table 3). The institute sector's share is exceptionally high compared to OECD as a whole. During the last years, the education sector has had the highest annual real growth (8 per cent), while in industry there has been a real decline (4 per cent annually) primarily due to reduced effort from the oil companies.

The share of basic research is still low. 15 per cent of total current expenditure devoted to R&D in 1989 was used for basic research (cf Figure 2). 35 per cent was used for applied research and 50 per cent for experimental development.

Technology and natural sciences are predominant fields of science (cf Figure 3). Most resources are used to industrial purposes (28 per cent of the total current expenditure in the institute sector in 1989). In the higher education sector, the general advancement of knowledge is the main objective (cf Figure 4).

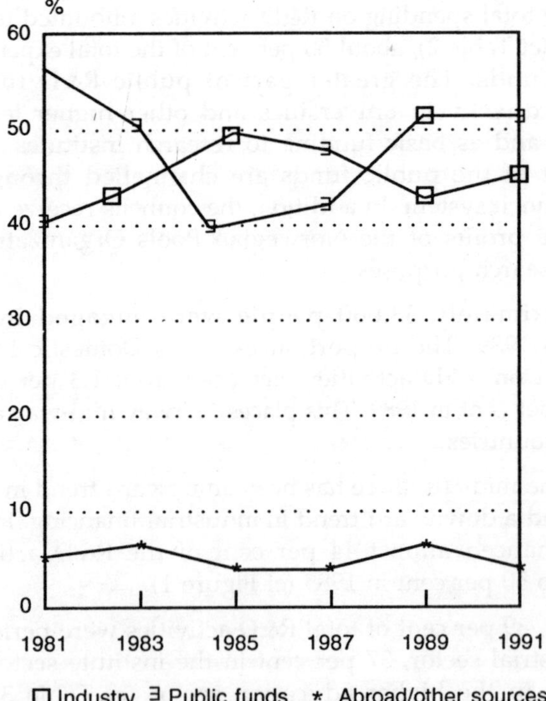

Figure 1. Total R&D expenditure in Norway 1981-89, with estimate for 1991, by source of funds. Relative amount.

Table 3. Total R&D expenditure in Norway in 1989 by sector of performance and source of funds. Estimate for 1991. Million NOK.

Performance sector	*Sources of funds*				
	Industry	*Public funds*	*Other Sources & abroad*	*Total*	*% of Total*
Industry	3,966	465	159	4,590	39
Institute	1,002	2,960	338	4,300	37
Higher-education	107	2,514	151	2,772	24
Total	5,075	5,939	648	11,662	100
% of Total	44	51	5	100	
Estimate 1991	5,900	6,800	700	13,400	

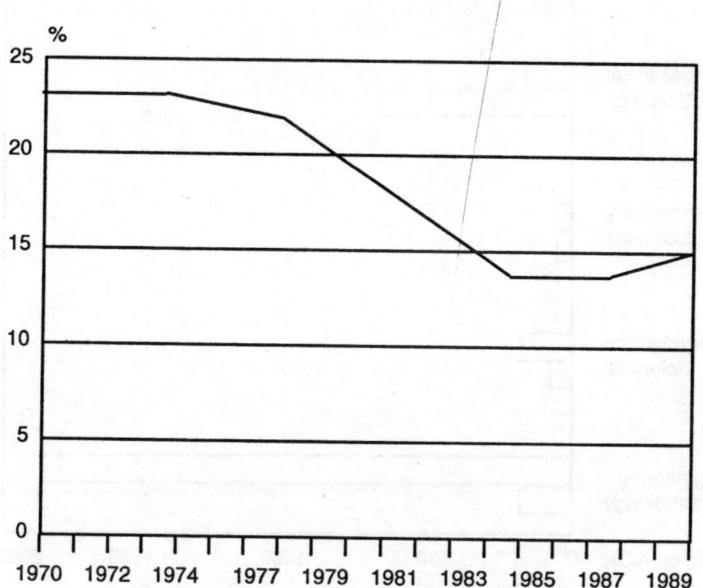

Figure 2. Share of basic research of total current R&D expenditure, 1970-89.

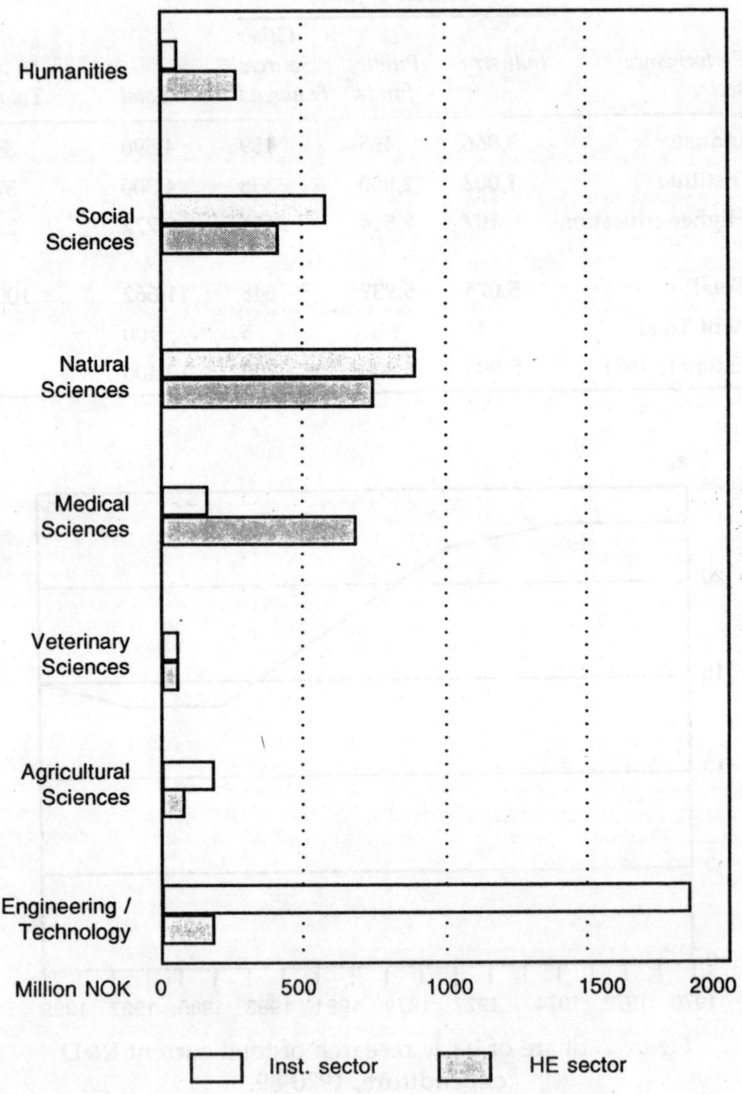

Figure 3. Current expenditure on R&D in Norway by sector performance and field of science in 1989. Million NOK.

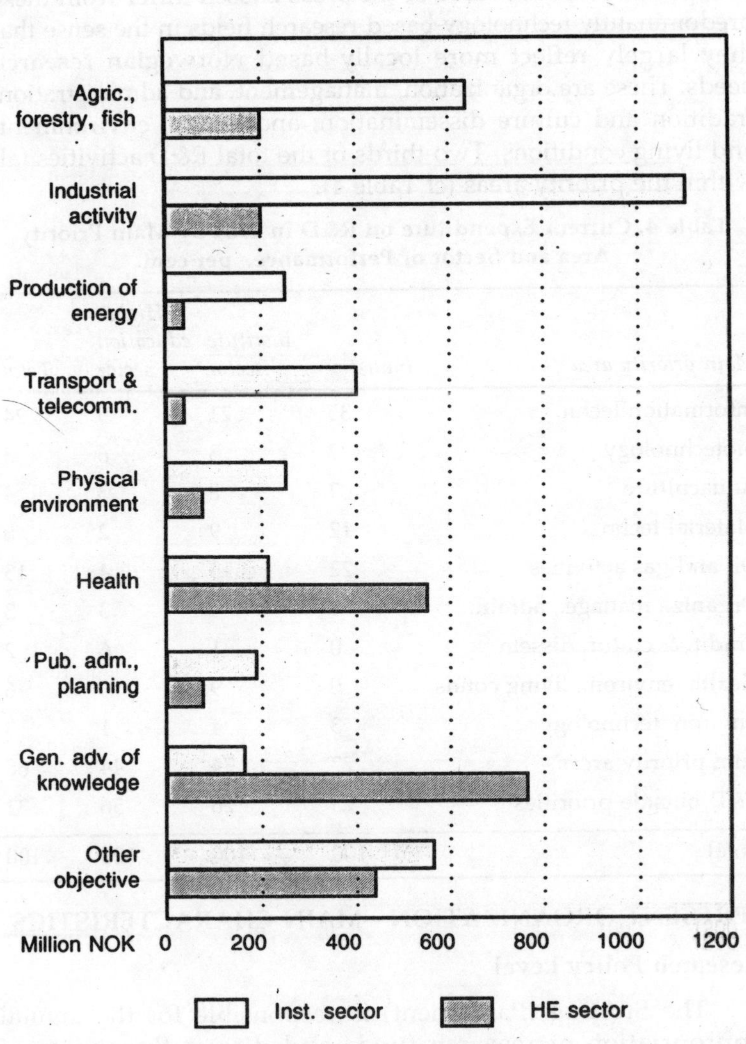

(Excluding industry).

Figure 4. Current expenditure on R&D in Norway by sector of

Eight areas have been chosen by the government as main priority areas and given preference as research fields. The majority of these coincides with the priority areas chosen in most European countries. Three of the areas chosen differ from these predominantly technology-based research fields in the sense that they largely reflect more locally-based Norwegian research needs. These are organization, management, and administration; tradition and culture dissemination; and health, environment, and living conditions. Two-thirds of the total R&D activities fall within the priority areas (cf Table 4).

Table 4. Current Expenditure on R&D in 1989 by Main Priority Area and Sector of Performance. per cent.

Main priority area	*Industry*	*Institute sector*	*Higher education sector*	*Total*
Information techn.	35	21	9	24
Biotechnology	2	3	6	3
Aquaculture	2	8	3	4
Material techn.	12	9	2	8
Oil and gas activities	22	15	4	15
Organiz., manage., admin.	1	4	3	3
Tradit. & cultur. dissem.	0	1	6	2
Health, environ., living conds.	0	9	10	6
Environ. technology	3	4	1	3
Sum priority areas	77	74	44	68
R&D outside priorities	23	26	56	32
Total	100	100	100	100

PRESENT ORGANIZATION—MAIN CHARACTERISTICS

Research Policy Level

The Storting (Parliament) is responsible for the annual appropriation of research funds and directs the course of national research activities by designating priority areas of research. Every fourth year, the government submits a report to the Storting with long-term goals for research activities. The

Cabinet Research Board is responsible for co-ordinating activities between the ministries.

Research is a high-priority area in Norway. For the years 1990-93, the government has set a 5 per cent annual growth in the R&D appropriations in real terms as its objective. The government's main priority areas are:

— more and better educated recruitment personnel (180 new recruitment positions per annum)
— basic research, trade- and industry-related research, environmental research
— international research co-operation
— better co-ordination and simplifications in the research system.

The government considers it an important science policy task to increase the proportion of women in research. This task cuts across the scientific fields and concerns both the research councils and the units performing research.

The present Norwegian research system is sector-oriented, probably more so than is the case in most other OECD countries. That means that each ministry has responsibility for science and research in its own sector. Over the years, this system has led to differences in the way the various ministries define their research responsibilities, to lack of co-ordination, and to a serious weakening in the position of long-term basic research and skill building. The proposed new research council structure has as one very important objective to strike a better balance between basic long-term research investments and appropriations set aside for applied sector research.

Research Strategy Level

The research councils are important strategic operators at this level, although they are not the only ones. Also, the universities, scientific colleges, and ministries serve important strategic functions. Unlike other OECD countries, the Norwegian government has not retained the arrangement with an advisory council on science policy questions. The Science Policy Council of Norway was disbanded in 1988.

The establishment of research councils throughout the western world must be seen as a response to what these countries felt as a growing dependence on research for social and economic development. The research councils are positioned as intermediaries between politically articulated research needs and wishes, science and its potential, and what in general terms may be called the 'users of research'. Their main characteristics are quality control and standard setting function through national competition, national co-ordination of research initiatives, strategy and evaluation. Altogether the research council model has functioned well, in Norway as other western countries. The research council system, then, does not seem to have outlived itself although, as is the case for Norway, changes in science and in society may call for changes in the system to adapt to new circumstances.

R&D Performing Units

The Norwegian research system is operating through three sectors: the university/higher-education sector, the institute sector, and the private trade and industry sector. The main characteristics of the system are:

— A complex higher education sector with four universities, six scientific colleges, and numerous, often rather small, regional colleges and research centres. The universities and scientific colleges are core institutions in the national research system.

— A relatively strong and numerous (about 225 units) institute sector, where technology and natural sciences are predominant, but where there is also quite a substantial social science component. Most institutes are established by public initiative, *i.e* by a research council (mostly the NTNF) or ministry.

— A trade and industry sector dominated by small units (41 per cent of the total of 681 with less than 50 employed) with modest research potentials.

The government has recently adopted an ambitious reform programme for Norwegian higher education. The government's goal is to create a new regional college system as part of a coherent higher-education system where universities, scientific colleges, and regional college centres develop new modalities for co-operation and labour division within the overall concept of a 'Norwegian network of higher education and research'. The ultimate aim of this reform process is a qualitatively better and more efficient system for higher education and research.

Important Issues in Norwegian Science Policy

Changes in the research council organization run parallel to processes of change in many parts of the Norwegian science system: in higher education (as indicated above), in science education, in the division of labour between the universities and the research councils, and in the role of international research co-operation in Norwegian science and research. The changes that are taking place are part of the government's long-term national science policy endeavours of creating a more unified, better co-ordinated and more efficient high quality research system.

The need for personnel with a science education is increasing, the replacement need in Norway being particularly urgent from the mid-90s. Measures to ensure a sufficient number of qualified new researchers are therefore given top priority by political authorities, the universities, and the research councils. Analyses of long-term recruitment needs, carried out by the NAVF, are used in government planning and priority setting. Analyses of long-term research system trends are a typical task for the research councils, whereas science education falls within the mandate of the universities. An important feature in Norwegian educational policy is the close relationship between higher education and research. All university education should be research-based.

The organization and content of a new science education system is at present a top-priority issue in Norway. A new model for organized science education leading up to a doctorate at a normal international Ph.D. level is being introduced at all four universities. The model has as the main prerequisite a scholarship period of four years, of which three years are earmarked for science education. There are still some bottlenecks to overcome before the structure is fully operative, above all the question of financial resources and personnel to ensure high quality in the new education programmes, and the need to develop and adequate system of co-operation and labour division between the main actors in the system.

At present, the division of labour between the universities and the research councils are changing, in the sense that some of the traditional tasks of the research councils are being transferred to the universities. This, in turn, leaves the research councils with more overall national strategic functions. This development has come about both as a consequence of the growth in the university appropriations—partly owing to a transfer of government resources from the research councils to the universities, and also as a result of organizational reforms in the university system itself. This situation will require new modes of co-operation between the research councils and the universities.

International research co-operation is emerging as a top priority in national science policy. There is no need to elaborate on this in a Norwegian context, only to state the following: the Norwegian proposal to create one research council has an ambitious goal to create a national research organization where also challenges arising from international research co-operation can be met more actively than is the case today.

5

Organization and Structure of Science in the Netherlands

HARM PINKSTER*

Netherlands Organization for Scientific Research, The Hague, The Netherlands

Introduction

For the last 300 to 400 years science and technology in the Netherlands have been publicly discussed, reflecting the requirements of society for suitable technologies to support national activities, for example an interest in geography and astronomy arose as early as the fifteenth and sixteenth centuries as a result of the activities of the Dutch merchant and naval fleets; civil engineering developed to support the battle against the sea; the interest in agriculture reflected the highly developed agrarian sector.

For the economic development of the Netherlands following World War II, priority was given to the creation and maintenance of human resources. In this way scientific and technological manpower could be secured for agriculture and

* Paper by W. Hutter, H.J. van der Molen, and H. Pinkster, partly adapted from *National policies towards the R&D system in the Netherlands* by H. J. van der Molen and W. Hutter, 1989. In P.J. Lavakare and J.G. Waardenburg (eds), *Science Policies in International Perspective*. Pinter Publishers, London.

industry based on the newest scientific and technological developments. In addition to supporting the requirements of society and industry the Netherlands has always been a meeting place (and frequently a shelter) for the different cultural and scientific schools in Europe. This has instilled a tradition of great interest in basic research, which has made it possible for a small country like the Netherlands (contributing only 1-2 per cent of scientific activities worldwide) to be reasonably informed, through active participation, in most scientifically important areas. The Dutch government spends about the same percentage of its GNP on academic research as the (former) German Federal Republic.

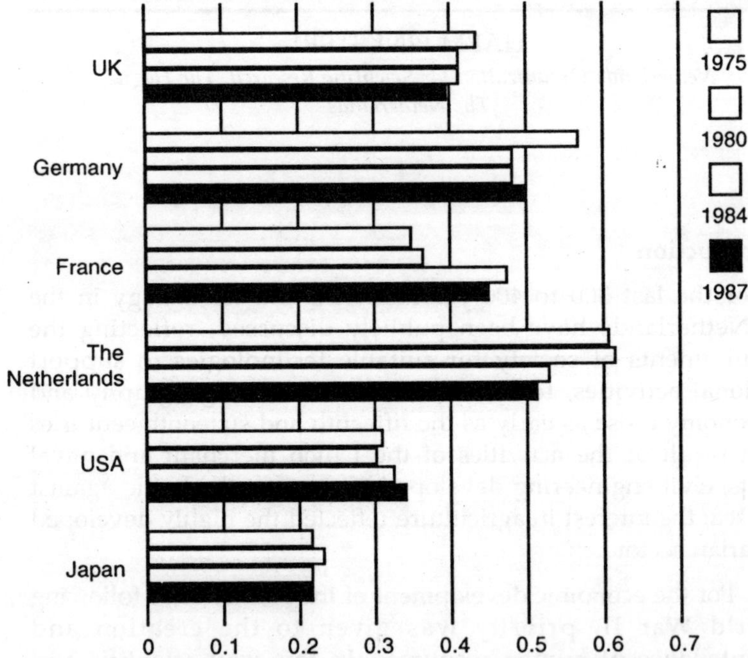

Figure 1. Government spending on academic research per centGNP 1975/1980/1984/1987.

There are many aspects of national policies towards the R&D system in the Netherlands that would justify a comparison with national policies in other countries. The present chapter aims to present some (necessarily brief and incomplete) information and thoughts about the situation in the Netherlands as background for further discussions on:

— the role of the government
— the relationship between higher education and research
— improvement of quality
— dissemination of scientific information.

Role of the Government

At present, the minister for education and science is responsible for the co-ordination of science policy. This co-ordination is carried out following a basic model in which every minister is responsible for his own policy, and related policy proposals from different departments are correlated to the main points by the co-ordinating minister. Thus the minister for economic affairs is responsible for technology policy and also for interministerial co-ordination in this field. He is particularly charged with industrially-orientated research and with energy research. The preparations for political decision-making at ministerial level on science and technology policy are structured, as in many other countries, through a committee at cabinet level that is responsible for the general co-ordination between the various ministers and has to ensure policy co-ordination. In the Netherlands, this ministerial committee is chaired by the prime minister.

Government-supported organizations and institutions of research and education which concentrate mainly on basic and strategic research include thirteen universities, of which there are three universities of technology, one agricultural university, and one open university; eight 'teaching' hospitals; the Netherlands Organization for Scientific Research (NWO); and the Royal Netherlands Academy of Arts and Sciences (KNAW).

In addition to the universities, there is a relatively modest (especially in comparison with most of the eastern countries) system of non-university research institutes. In the so-called 'para-university institutes', the emphasis is mainly on basic strategic research (many of these are funded by NWO). In other research institutes, the emphasis lies primarily on applied strategic research, particularly in the physical, agricultural and technical sciences. However, applied research, often on commission, in the social and medical sciences fields, takes place extensively in the universities as well.

Government-supported non-university research is carried out in some 180 institutes, which are characterized by their multifarious nature, a wide range of relationships and modes of financing. The government, furthermore, participates directly in international science organizations, such as CERN, ESA, NATO.

With regard to relationships between the institutes themselves, and between these institutes and the universities, there is in addition to intensive co-operation a wide-ranging diversification of research activities (*e.g.* in the field of environmental research) and even, in some cases, distinct competition.

Government expenditure on research in 1991 amounted to 4.7 billion guilders (on a total R&D expenditure—government and private sector—of 11.8 billion). This is channelled to the abovementioned (groups of) organizations in the following way:

(a)	universities	1670 billion
(b)	NWO	410
(c)	KNAW	70
(d)	applied strategic research	800
(e)	internatioinal organizations	210

Government policy for research has as important main objectives:

— promotion of quality standards, with the international context as a touchstone

— reinforcing orientation towards external questions in the medium- and long-term perspective

— increasing co-ordination, co-operation and distribution of tasks in the research system

— promoting efficient and effective operations in research institutes; attaining the best possible financial structure, investment policy, staffing policy, and management.

The Dutch government aims in particular at the promotion of processes of change which contribute towards the above objectives, including:

(a) the structure of the R&D potential, namely the organization of finance, administration, and decision-making

(b) the orientation of research efforts through stimulation policy and promotion of research programming

(c) the transfer of knowledge to users, for example by promoting the input of scientific and technical information.

In order to implement its policy and to set priorities, the government as a whole and the minister of education and science in particular rely on an elaborate network of advisory bodies and executive bodies. Among the advisory bodies we mention the Wetenschappelijke Raad voor het Regeringsbeleid (Scientific Council for Government Policy—WRR), the Adviesraad voor het Wetenschaps-en Technologiebeleid (Advisory Council for Science and Technology Policy—AWT), a newly installed National Foresight Committee, and the Royal Netherlands Academy of Arts and Sciences.

Relationship between Higher Education and Research

One of the main instruments for science policy is scientific manpower: there would be no research if there were no research workers carrying out the research in their laboratories or in their research institutes. This means two things: first, the importance of the relation between the educational system, that is the universities and the research system has to be stressed; and second, good research management in the scientific institutes—thus the need to put the right man in the right place—is very important.

Historically, the university system in the Netherlands has been the most important government-supported institutional structure for both the training of scientists and actual research. Until the 1970s, active participation of university students in research during their pre-doctoral training was the rule rather than the exception. In certain disciplines, particularly in the natural and life sciences, many graduates would continue working in the universities to obtain a doctoral degree. As a result of an increasing number of students entering universities in the 1970s and the resulting capacity problems, a restructuring of higher education has been realized which will not offer every undergraduate the possibility of participating in research.

At present, all university curricula should lead to a first university degree after four years. During this first phase—which will give the student the title of 'doctorandus'—students barely participate in original research. A limited number of graduates (in the order of 5-10 per cent, but varying for different disciplines) can obtain a research assistantship, which normally implies some form of advanced education and training. This phase—of four years—can accommodate approximately 6000 persons, which, with a four-year turnover, permits 1500 students per annum to start a research career and obtain the 'doctor' degree. This phase of combined training and research is now being organized in a system of *'onderzoekscholen'*, the Dutch equivalent of the Anglosaxon graduate schools or the Italian *dottorato dello stato.* The first of these schools will be established in the course of 1992.

Thus, the Dutch universities find themselves nowadays in an extensive process of reorientation from the traditional continental European university with intricate links or unity between education and research to a more Anglo-American system with postgraduate institutes financed for their research activities, and educating doctoral students. It was also (and frequently still is) the rule that the academic staff at universities were selected mainly on the basis of their scientific expertize and performance. This made universities the centres for basic research.

During the past forty years, however, many independent government-supported research institutions have evolved. This, in addition to the changes within the universities, has made the role of universities in the overall national research effort less dominant, even although they still pay a leading role in many scientific areas.

Also, the minister of education and science has an important policy instrument at his disposal for university research in the form of organization of finance for the universities. This policy instrument includes the following aspects:

(i) the universities are to be able to act as autonomous bodies.

(ii) the research plans for the universities are to take into account national discipline-by-discipline recommendations.

(iii) a substantial part of the research projects at universities is to be financed by the national research organization (NWO) which, unlike the universities, need not consider teaching aspects.

Consequently, research activities are funded through a system of 'multiple financing': researchers may apply to different sources with different decision-making procedures. The first souce of money is allocated directly by the minister of education and science. The universities receive these funds as a part of their total budget. Government funds are still distributed among the universities as lump sums, but a part of these sums are earmarked for research that has been positively assessed by an external review; these earmarked funds are protected from budgetary cuts by both universities and the minister of education and science.

The second source of funding is also by government grant, but allocated to the universities through the Netherlands Organization for Scientific Research (NWO) the Dutch research council; its network of councils, foundations, and study groups plays a major role in the national co-ordination of university research.

Basic stipulations in the arrangement are: (i) the funding system should be controlled by the scientists themselves, and (ii) scientific research should not be dissociated from the universities. About half of NWO's total budget (today about US$230 million) is used to finance projects in university research through this second source. A large number of these projects last for three or four years and are undertaken by Ph.D. students. Most projects are based on proposals which have been positively vetted by (expert) review, but sometimes NWO itself takes the initiative to finance a particular project.

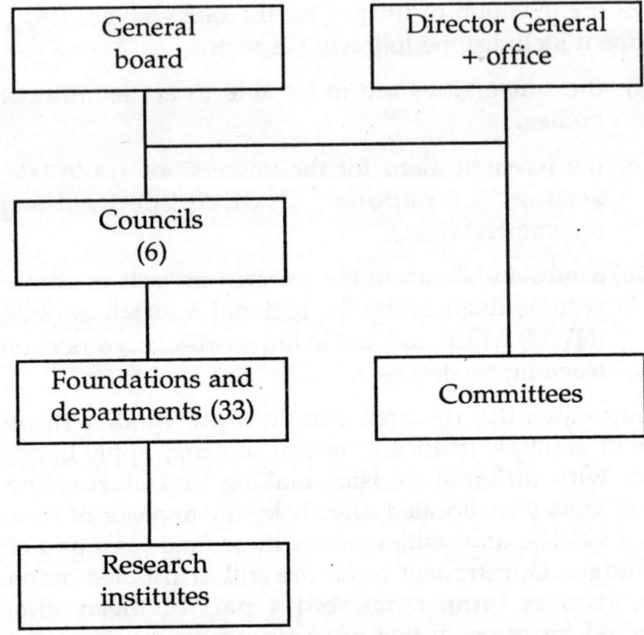

Figure 2. NWO structure.

The Royal Netherlands Academy also distributes some money to academics employed by the universities, for organizing or attending conferences, and—most importantly—for funding postdocs (50 every year). NWO's expenditure is shown in Figure 3.

The third source of funding comes from a miscellaneous collection of financial bodies: private foundations, government agencies, industry, etc. Usually the object of research projects so funded is to solve specific problems for anyone willing to pay for this service.

These are generally referred to as 'contract research' projects. By performing contract research, a university's research capacity can be expanded and the university scientist becomes better informed about problems in society.

The total research capacity of the universities comprises roughly 11,000 full-time equivalents of scientific personnel, of which 7000, 2000, and 2200 are financed by the first, second, and third sources, respectively.

Enhancement and Assessment of Quality

One of the aims of government policy in the Netherlands towards R&D has been to promote the quality of research. This aim became particularly relevant after 1975. Until then government support for research was given mainly as a lump sum (a total of 500-1000 million guilders annually) with the tacit understanding that universities and other research organizations would use the support for high-quality research. However, neither the aims and/or subjects nor the results (published papers, etc.) of the research were accounted for.

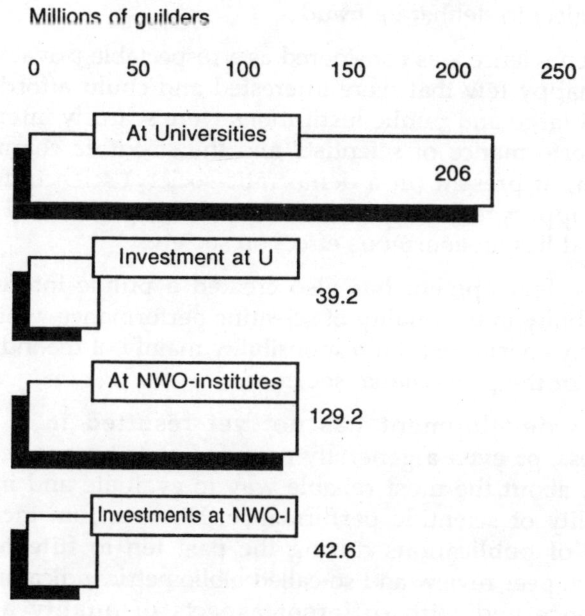

Figure 3. NWO expenditures, recurrent costs and investments total, 1991: 417 million guilders.

to such an extent that some scientists occasionally complain about the heavy administration burden in applying for and accounting for research support. However, this (often understandable) criticism about the bureaucracy involved in the administration of research plans and results should not detract from the importance of obtaining such administrative data for evaluating research quality.

It has often, though erroneously, been assumed that 'science' or 'scientific performance' is synonymous with 'quality'. History, including very recent events, has given ample evidence that scientists are liable to make errors. Not only 'reputable' errors (inherent in the process of even the most meticulously executed scientific investigation) but also disreputable errors, varying from cross neglect to deliberate fraud.

When science was considered as a respectable private hobby for the happy few that were interested and could afford it, the public at large and public institutions were scarcely interpreted in the performance of scientists and the scientific community. However, at present (in a democratic society) science depends for its support to a large extent on public opinion and public funds and has an enormous effect on society.

This development has also created a public interest and responsibility in the quality of scientific performance, which was previously considered the responsibility mainly of the individual scientist or the professional societies.

This development has not yet resulted in a public awareness, or even a generally accepted code among scientists at large, about the most reliable way to evaluate and improve the quality of scientific performance. However, an increasing number of publications during the past ten to fifteen years, mainly on peer review and so-called bibliometric indicators, have been concerned with different aspects of quality and the evaluation of quality. Also, several bodies have attempted to evaluate and compare the quality of different scientific disciplines at the national level.

In the Netherlands, for example, national survey committees have in recent years evaluated the national research activities in such areas as chemistry, biochemistry, biology, physics, health research, economics, and law.

In order to evaluate and, if possible, improve the 'quality' of scientific activities, it appears essential that 'quality' is defined in terms of 'technical norms' which guarantee the standard of rationality of the research, testing by empirical evidence (preferably through controlled experiments), reproducibility of results, proper description of methodologies used, proper presentation and interpretation of results, etc. These quality norms should be implicit in all truly scientific procedures and have been discussed in depth by several 'philosophers' of science. It also has to be accepted, however, that there is no 'absolute' or 'natural' standard of quality and that all parameters used will at best reflect a majority or consensus within the scientific discipline involved. The specification of quality in terms of 'technical norms' specifically excludes moral norms or political norms as standards for the quality of behaviour of scientists. The latter 'norms' generally offer no more than rationalizing ideologies that are merely used to justify the self-interests of scientists in comparison to those of other social institutions which also try to justify their activities through their albeit different moral norms. Such norms may be important, but should not be used in connection with quality. The guarantee for good quality research depends first and foremost on the performance of practising scientists. This will result in an overall improvement in the quality of research, however, only if the other organizational levels involved in decisions about scientific activities are equally interested in the pursuit of quality.

It is one of the main tasks of the NWO to stimulate high quality research, by giving research grants to outstanding scientists and by setting up special research programmes. Several important national research facilities in the Netherlands, such as radiotelescopes, accelerators, NMR equipment, or research vessels, are financed and operated by NWO.

Diffusion of Scientific Information, Transfer of Knowledge, and the Effects of S&T on Society

Scientific results which are not communicated will not become part of the scientific process. The diffusion of scientific information is essential for a variety of reasons, including the broadening of the publicly accessible science base, the application of scientific information for technological or social use, or the possibility of evaluating the quality and relevance of results relative to other results (as discussed above). The advantages and disadvantages of the many possibilities for communicating scientific results (private communications, congresses, scientific journals, patents, etc.) cannot be discussed in this chapter. Some considerations may be important, however, for the dissemination of scientific information which has been obtained through government-supported research as part of a national policy. At one extreme, situations will be encountered where results obtained with public money should be efficiently utilized for public needs, but which usually will not be successful when the results are only published in the international scientific literature. Particularly when results are useful for national purposes, special mechanisms for transfer of knowledge to industry or the public at large should be considered. It is an explicit government policy towards the R&D system to improve the transfer of knowledge from the research institute to possible users. In this respect, various mechanisms for transfer have been introduced such as transfer points, spinoff firms, specialized journals or meetings. Also programming committees may play a role in organizing the transfer of knowledge. In this respect, specialized journals or meetings aimed at specific national needs may be more effective. In the Netherlands the organization for applied scientific research (TNO) is by law chartered with the responsibility for the transfer of scientific knowledge through several institutes which bring together suppliers and users of scientific information in many industrial and social areas. Also, most universities and other research institutes have installed 'transfer offices' which are active in communicating information obtained within the universities to potential users and vice versa.

At the other extreme, one will encounter situations where results, for the very reason that they are important for economic purposes, should probably not be published (or otherwise communicated) before the benefits for the national economy have been secured. The latter consideration has recently stimulated an awareness of the possible need to submit patent applications in advance of publication. Because the individual scientist is not always the best informed or most alert participant in this process, it has been useful to support and co-ordinate such activities. In addition to the activities of individual universities through their transfer offices, and technological institutes (including TNO), the NWO Foundation for Technical Sciences (STW) in the Netherlands has been very active and successful in pursuing the utilization of scientific information obtained through government-supported research for technological use.

In addition to these activities of research organizations disseminating their results in specific ways, there are some government-supported organizations in the Netherlands which have as their main function the monitoring and dissemination of scientific results for the public at large, for specialized groups in society or for one of more offices in government departments. Over the last ten to fifteen years government officials have increasingly called upon research institutions to obtain scientifically based information to formulate their policies ('science for policy').

6

European Bilateral Co-operations of the French National Centre for Scientific Research (CNRS)

PIERRE RADVANYI
CNRS-MDRI, Paris, France

The CNRS (National Scientific Research Centre) is the most important French multidisciplinary research organization. Created in 1939, it covers all domains of science through seven departments: nuclear and particle physics, mathematics and physics, engineering sciences, chemistry, sciences of the Universe, life sciences, social and human sciences. In addition there are seven major interdisciplinary research programmes.

CNRS at present employs about 26,000 people—11,000 research workers (about 10 per cent of them are non-French) and 25,000 engineers, technicians and administration employees—both in its own 375 research units (laboratories) and in 991 associated research units; by convention the associatons link CNRS to universities and other institutions. There are also so-called mixed or joint laboratories, shared by CNRS with other French research organizations (Atomic Energy, INSERM, . . .).

The evaluation of research—of laboratories as well as of individual scientists—is carried out by 40 different scientific committees, each consisting of 21 members, elected or appointed for four years. In recent years, a large effort has been made to achieve a decentralized administration in twelve regions throughout France.

The international bilateral (or trilateral) co-operations of CNRS are based on the structural diversity of the various partners, on mutual information, on joint consultation and co-ordination, and on the setting-up of well reviewed joint programmes.

Of course, the laboratories maintain a large number of so-called spontaneous collaborations arising from the normal course and interchanges of scientific research. We recorded last year over 35,000 collaborations of this kind.

On the other side of the spectrum, CNRS participates in large European laboratories, like for instance the Laue-Langevin Institute in Grenoble.

For many years, we have been running bilateral agreements which each anticipate the exchange of a certain number of researcher/months. There are currently 57 bilateral agreements with partner organizations in 39 countries.

In recent years, it has been considered sensible to put more effort in joint projects are programmes and to conceive new forms of bilateral co-operation for this purpose.

One form, started in 1985, is the PICS (Programmes Internationaux de Co-opération Scientifique). These are selected programmes between scientific groups from France and one or two other countries which have already worked together (there should be already at least one common publication). The PICS have been established for three years and may be extended for one or two more.

Each side has a co-ordinator. On the French side, the selection of the projects is made by the scientific departments involved. There should be an approximate equilibrium between the partners, concerning both the scientific contribution and the human and financial resources. Our Foreign Affairs Ministry agreed to participate in the budgets of PICS.

Since 1985, 98 PICS have been launched, 39 are now completed and 59 are underway. 28 are starting in 1992. They cover a wide range of subjects: from the estuaries of major Chinese rivers to quasi-crystals with the United States; from the study of magnetic materials with Spain to the compilation of photographic archives of the Islamic world with Germany; from solar seismology with Morocco and the United States, to the study of hot nuclear matter with Poland; from the study of coral reefs with Australia to research on catalysis with Venezuela and to molecular neurobiology with Sweden.

35 per cent of current PICS concern European EFTA countries, 30 per cent Eastern Europe. The number of PICS with Eastern Europe (mostly Russia and Poland) has grown rapidly over the last two or three years: there are now 18 PICS under way, 8 of these are starting this year.

A new form of bilateral co-operation was set up in 1991 by CNRS—the creations of Associated European Laboratories (LEA). These LEAs, restricted for the moment to West Europe, are 'extra-mural laboratories' where several (in general 2 or 3) laboratories wish to combine their efforts on important jointly defined programmes. There is a partial merging of activity of the laboratories, whilst keeping to their own sites and current management methods.

The Director General of CNRS and the directors or presidents of the other organizations involved sign an agreement defining the structure adopted and the rules to be followed in order to achieve the scientific programme.

The duration of LEAs will be four years which may be extended by similar periods. A common director of the LEA is chosen and a government board is designated by the partner organizations. The human and financial contributions of each partner are defined in order to achieve an aproximate equilibrium. The first LEAs will also test the administrative and operational difficulties encountered.

The first LEA, on Astronomy, was established in December 1991 between the Institute of Astronomy of the University of Cambridge and the Leiden University Observatory. The second and third LEAs were established in January of this year (1992) between France and Spain, on materials science and process engineering between the IMP of Odeillo-Perpignan, the LPCM of Montpellier and the Material Science Institute of the CSIC in Barcelona, and on molecular plant biology between the Plant Physiology and Molecular Biology Laboratory in Perpignan and the Department of Molecular Genetics of the CSIC in Barcelona.

The establishment of other LEAs is presently being discussed in other fields of science and also with other countries.

For the co-operation with eastern European countries, a specific new form of bilateral agreements has been set up: the twinning agreements (Jumelages) Laboratories from France and from eastern European countries agree to co-operate on a joint programme, allowing extensive exchange of research workers. For instance, scientists may spend a few months each year in the same French Laboratores—this helps to maintain the scientific potential of each country.

So far, there are seven twinning agreements, in mathematics, physics, and life sciences between CNRS and Russia, Ukraine, Hungary, Poland, and Romania.

7

Funding of Research in Denmark

SINE LARSEN
Vice-Chairperson, Danish Natural Science Research Council, University of Copenhagen, Denmark

An Overview of the Danish Funding System

The expenditure on R&D performed in Denmark in 1989 amounted to just under DKK 12 billion (1 ECU = 8 DKK) or 1.53 per cent of the GDP. In 1979, the R&D expenditure amounted to 0.96 per cent of the GDP. The development of the R&D expenditures expressed in per cent GDP in the period 1979-89 is shown in Figure 1, with the equivalent development in other OECD countries.

Table 1 illustrates the distribution of the R&D in enterprises, public sources, and other sources (international sources and private funds in the same countries). The major increase in R&D has taken place in the business sector. As shown in Table 2, the business sector performed R&D to 55 per cent of the total R&D expenditure in 1989. The higher education sector performed to 25 per cent and her government sector to 20 per cent.

Business Sector R&D

About 1300 companies carried out R&D activities in 1989. Just under 21,000 employees were engaged in R&D corresponding to 14,000 R&D man-years. Manufacturing enterprises performed 78 per cent of the R&D man-years, service enterprises 14 per cent, and technological service institutes 8 per cent.

Within the manufacturing sector, the R&D activities are concentrated in five branches of industry: the pharmaceutical, electrical, measuring instruments, machinery and food industries carried out 73 per cent of the total industrial R&D. It should be noted that 20 per cent of this sector's R&D is performed at Novo Nordisk, a manufacturer of insulin and enzymes.

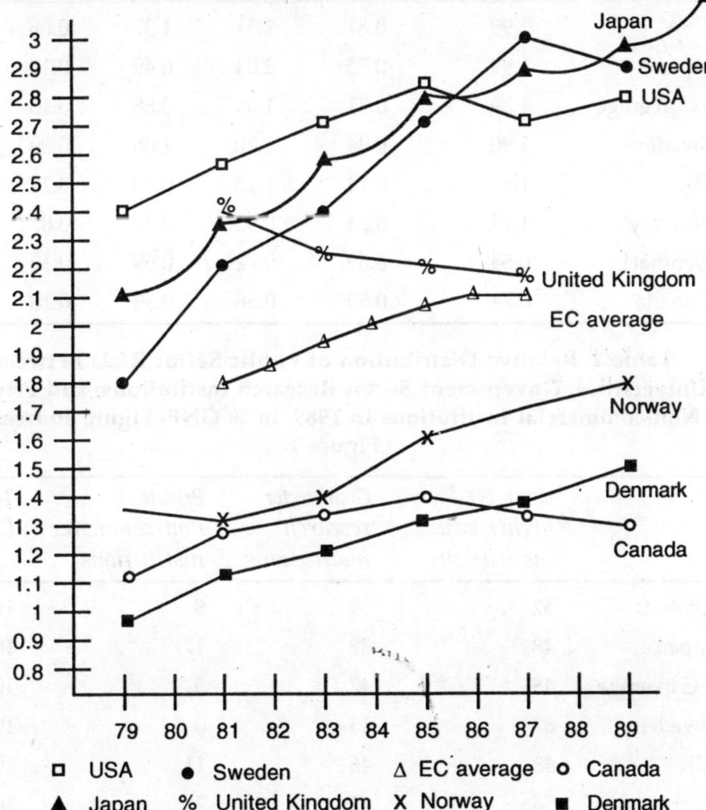

Figure 1. Developments in R&D expenditure as per cent GNP 1979-89. If the figures given are not for 1989, they are taken from the most recently available information. For a number of countries, the 1989 figures are based on prognoses.
Source: OECD, 1991.

Table 1. R&D Performed & Financed by Industry and Public Sector, 1989, per centGNP. Figure sources as Figure 1, Source: OECD, 1991.

	Research performed (%GNP)		*Financing (%GNP)*			
	Enter-prises	*Public institutions*	*Enter-prises*	*Public sources*	*Private sources & abroad*	*Total*
USA	1.99	0.81	1.37	1.37	0.06	2.80
Japan	1.99	0.73	2.04	0.49	0.19	2.72
EC average	1.39	0.71	1.09	0.88	0.13	2.10
Sweden	1.90	0.94	1.70	1.06	0.09	2.84
UK	1.46	0.74	1.13	0.80	0.27	2.20
Norway	1.17	0.74	0.92	0.92	0.07	1.91
Denmark	0.84	0.69	0.72	0.69	0.12	1.53
Canada	0.74	0.59	0.56	0.59	0.18	1.33

Table 2. Relative Distribution of Public Sector R&D between Universities, Government Sector Research Institutions, and Private, Non-commercial Institutions in 1989, in % GNP. Figure sources as Figure 1.

	Univ. & higher-edu. institutions	*Govt. sector research institutions*	*Private, non-commerce institutions*	*Total (%)*
USA	52	39	9	100
Japan	48	35	17	100
EC average	48	47	5	100
Sweden	87	13	0	100
UK	43	46	11	100
Norway	56	42	2	100
Denmark	55	42	3	100
Canada	53	44	3	100

Public Sector R&D

The public sector R&D is performed in two sectors of almost equal importance: higher educational sector and the government sector. The higher education sector comprises 17 universities and other higher education institutions. The structure of the research system within the university sector is illustrated in Figure 2.

The governmental sector consists of all other public establishments with an element of R&D, *i.e.* ministerial research institutions, hospitals, museums, etc. The 28 ministerial research institutions are funded from 11 different ministries. Table. 3 shows the distribution between ministries and the total funding for each ministry. The 28 institutions have very different levels of funding, from DKK 10 million to almost DKK 400 million which the Danish National Laboratory at Riso obtains from the Ministry of Energy.

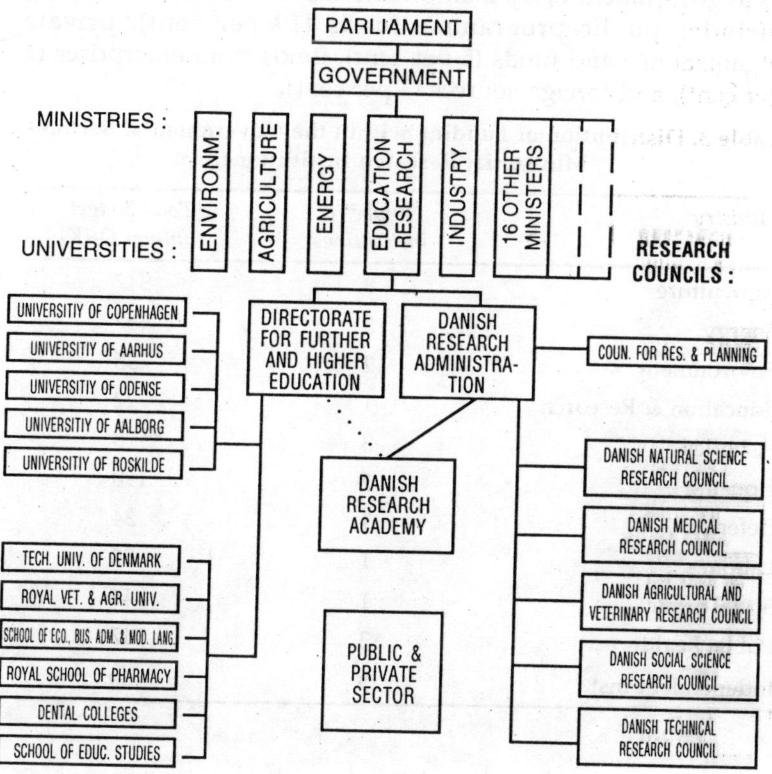

Figure 2. Research system structure within the university sector.

A total of just over 10,000 R&D man-years were performed in the two public sectors in 1989. 55 per cent of the R&D was carried out in the higher education sector. The medical and natural sciences are the two major fields of research in the public sectors, each representing about 25 per cent of the total R&D man-years. The technical sciences, agriculture and veterinary science, the humanities, and social sciences follow with 14 per cent, 13 per cent, 12 per cent and 10 per cent respectively. In Table 4, public R&D appropriations 1989-94 are listed for the different sciences.

71 per cent of the total R&D expenditure in the public sector was financed by basic budget appropriations from central or local government or by their own funds. The external financing includes public programme funds (19 per cent), private organizations and funds (5 per cent), funds from enterprises (2 per cent), and foreign sources (3 per cent).

Table 3. Distribution of Funding within the Governmental Sector—Ministerial Research Institutions.

Ministry	*Number of institutions*	*Total budget (million DKK)*
Agriculture	8	347
Energy	3	457
Environment	2	235
Education & Research	1	22
Fisheries	3	78
Housing	2	190
Defence	1	34
Labour	1	55
Social affair	1	44
Public health	3	547
Independent inst.	3	60

Table 4. Public R&D Appropriations 1989 to 1994.

Natural Science

DKK million, 1991 level Ministries	1989 Basic	 Prog.	 Total	1990 Basic	 Prog.	 Total	1991 Basic	 Prog.	 Total	1992 Total	1993 Total	1994 Total
Ministry of Education	432.9	96.1	529.0	488.8	95.3	584.1	400.9	99.5	500.5	504.7	473.0	463.0
Ministry of Culture	4.0	0.0	4.0	3.9	0.0	3.9	4.3	0.0	4.3	4.3	4.2	4.2
Ministry of the Environment	0.3	0.0	0.3	0.5	0.0	0.5	0.5	0.0	0.5	0.5	0.5	0.5
Ministry of Energy	1.0	0.0	1.0	2.6	0.0	2.6	2.6	0.0	2.6	2.6	2.6	2.6
Total	436.3	96.1	534.3	495.7	95.3	591.1	408.3	99.6	507.9	512.1	480.3	470.3

Technical Science

DKK million, 1991 level Ministries	1989 Basic	 Prog.	 Total	1990 Basic	 Prog.	 Total	1991 Basic	 Prog.	 Total	1992 Total	1993 Total	1994 Total
Ministry of Education	268.3	107.5	375.8	341.6	91.6	433.3	351.3	90.7	442.0	454.0	436.4	424.1
Ministry of Energy	1.0	0.0	1.0	0.0	0.0	0.0	0.0	0.0	0.0	0.0	0.0	0.0
Total	269.3	107.5	376.8	341.6	91.6	433.3	351.3	90.7	442.0	454.0	436.4	424.1

Medical Science

DKK million, 1991 level Ministries	1989 Basic	 Prog.	 Total	1990 Basic	 Prog.	 Total	1991 Basic	 Prog.	 Total	1992 Total	1993 Total	1994 Total
Ministry of Health	123.4	12.5	135.9	123.1	10.9	133.9	123.3	10.9	134.2	134.2	134.2	134.2
Ministry of Education	308.6	62.5	371.1	291.4	66.0	357.5	251.0	66.9	317.9	323.3	304.5	291.3
Ministry of Culture	4.0	0.0	4.0	3.9	0.0	3.9	4.2	0.0	4.2	4.3	4.1	4.1
Total	436.0	75.0	511.0	418.4	76.9	495.3	378.5	77.8	456.3	461.8	442.8	429.6

Agricultural and Veterinary Science

DKK million, 1991 level Ministries	1989 Basic	 Prog.	 Total	1990 Basic	 Prog.	 Total	1991 Basic	 Prog.	 Total	1992 Total	1993 Total	1994 Total
Ministry of Foreign Affairs	0.0	1.0	1.0	0.0	0.0	0.0	0.0	0.0	0.0	0.0	0.0	0.0
Ministry of Education	95.3	50.7	146.0	123.2	46.1	169.3	118.9	50.8	160.7	171.3	156.1	153.7
Ministry of Agriculture	4.4	0.3	4.7	0.0	0.0	0.0	0.0	0.0	0.0	0.0	0.0	0.0
Total	99.7	52.0	151.8	123.2	46.1	169.3	118.9	50.8	169.7	171.3	156.1	153.7

Social Science

DKK million, 1991 level Ministries	1989 Basic	1989 Prog.	1989 Total	1990 Basic	1990 Prog.	1990 Total	1991 Basic	1991 Prog.	1991 Total	1992 Total	1993 Total	1994 Total
Ministry of Foreign Affairs	8.3	0.0	8.3	9.2	0.0	9.2	12.6	0.0	12.6	14.5	14.9	15.4
Ministry of Education	208.3	36.6	244.9	262.2	37.6	299.8	280.0	38.1	318.1	320.2	311.9	307.3
Ministry of Culture	27.3	0.0	27.3	26.6	0.0	26.6	27.2	0.0	27.2	27.2	27.0	27.0
Total	244.0	36.6	280.6	298.1	37.6	335.7	319.8	38.1	357.9	361.9	353.8	349.7

Humanities

DKK million, 1991 level Ministries	1989 Basic	1989 Prog.	1989 Total	1990 Basic	1990 Prog.	1990 Total	1991 Basic	1991 Prog.	1991 Total	1992 Total	1993 Total	1994 Total
Ministry of Education	282.4	51.2	333.7	326.2	64.3	390.6	318.9	53.8	372.7	368.9	353.1	347.5
Ministry of Culture	56.4	0.0	56.4	57.0	0.0	57.0	62.8	0.0	62.8	62.5	63.4	62.3
Total	338.9	51.2	390.1	383.3	64.3	447.6	381.7	53.8	435.5	431.4	416.6	409.8

Trends in Danish Research Policy

The Danish research policy is laid down in a co-operation between the ministries which have R&D activities under their responsibility.

The Minister of Education and Research has the overall co-ordinating responsibility for the total research policy of the government. Of the total state R&D appropriations, approximately 55 per cent are administered via the Minister of Research budget.

With the purpose of assisting the Minister of Education and Research in his function as the research policy co-ordinator, the government has set us a research committee consisting of the ministers who administer the largest R&D appropriations. The Minister of Education and Research chairs this committee.

Principal Research Policy Lines

The government has set out the principal lines of the research policy which are to contribute to a continued strengthening of Danish research. The Danish research policy of the 1990s has the following aims:

1. To ensure the country's reserve of knowledge through education and research by laying the foundation for a business sector based on research and high technology.
2. To create a number of research institutions which are leading in Europe within their special subject-areas.
3. To strive to have research institutions of only international standard.
4. To ensure that there are qualified researchers for both private and public sectors.

The means to reach this target are:

— specialization and concentration, thus creating effective units which on the one hand reflect the importance of the research in question for the national development and on the other hand are capable of performing research which is competitive at international level.

— control and competition by introducing market-like conditions in the research system in order to optimize the national economic effort on the one hand and on the other hand to create competitive institutions.

— to strengthen the education of research scientists by intensifying both its extent and quality.

New Means in the Danish Research System

During the past ten years, the Danish research system was innovated by the establishment of new institutions and by the creation of special programmes for strategic research.

The Danish Research Academy

The Danish Research Academy (Forskerakademiet) was established in 1987 as a part of the government's action plan to further Danish research and development. This plan aims at a doubling of R&D in proportion to the GDP before the year 2000.

The Danish Research Academy was meant to be an untraditional and efficient organization responsible for the co-ordination of the graduate programmes offered by Danish universities and academic colleges.

The immediate objectives were to increase the training of researchers in Denmark in terms of both quantity and quality. The university sector was to provide society with a dramatically increased number of 'trained brains' at an internationally competitive doctoral level.

The Academy actively responds to the future research needs of society, and collaborates with universities and other bodies to ensure the production of adequate numbers of research workers in relevant fields of research, in arts as well as in sciences. All activities are related to formalized Ph.D. studies. The main objectives are to double the amount of Ph.D. students and internationalize the Ph.D. programmes. Through its Stimulation Programme, the Academy supports studies abroad for Danish Ph.D. students.

In less than two years, the Academy has funded studies outside Denmark for more than 450 Danish Ph.D. students. They have visited foreign universities and institutions for extensive periods as part of their formalized Ph.D. programmes. More than 50 per cent of Ph.D. students now wish to include a study period in USA as part of their doctoral study. But many other countries are also given preference (see Figure 3). In general, grants are not given for periods of less than six months. Support to visiting professors and guest students from other countries are also allocated through the Stimulation Programme

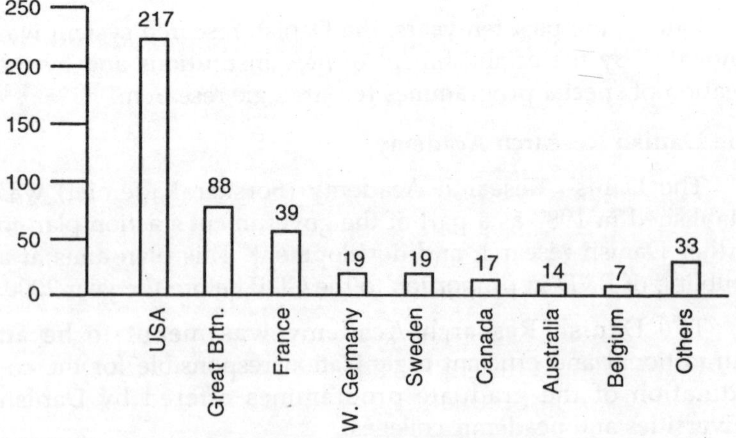

Figure 3. Ph.D. students, abroad, June 1987 to June 1989.

Another innovation was the creation of special programmes. A programme for biotechnology was the first. Its aim was to intensify the effort in biotechnology research, education, and development needed to ensure success in the modernization process and to enable Danish companies to compete on an international scale.

A biotechnology R&D programme for the period 1987-90 was proposed by the government in May 1986 and approved by Parliament on 25 May 1987. The programme has three elements: biotechnology research centres, education, and information and technology assessment. Part of the funding was allocated to the education of master's degree level scientists with relevant training, as well as to modernizing and increasing the biological content of many educational curricula.

The core of the Biotechnology Programme is the establishment of a number of research centres. A centre is not a new institution but rather a formalized association of research teams in existing institutes and private companies. These laboratories without walls are a new concept in Denmark. This construction is meant to encourage collaboration between university institutes, other public research institutes, technological service institutes, and research division in private companies. Funding was provided to 14 research centres and a single independent project. Table 5 illustrates the Programme's level of funding for the years 1987-90.

Table 5. Total Funding in Million DKK, 1987-90.

Biotechnology Programme	1987	1988	1989	1990	Total
Research centres	25	100	130	130	385
Education	20	20	15	15	70
Information & technology assessment	5	5	5	5	20
	50	125	150	150	475

The experience from the first programme was so positive that a second Biotechnology Programme for the period 1990-95 was initiated after the termination of the first programme.

The educational aspects are not included in the second Programme which finances 11 'centres without walls'.

A similar programme in materials technology development was initiated in 1988. It will receive a total grant of 495 million DKK for the period 1988-92.

One of the objectives of the Materials Technology Development Programme is to expedite the utilization, within industrial development, of opportunities presented by advanced materials research and technology. Another is to create and provide a foundation for the increased innovative content and improved quality of graduate studies and vocational education and training. These objectives are to be attained by increasing research and technological development in selected areas of materials technology, and by intensifying and expanding the transfer of this technology and related information to a wider range of Danish industrial projects. Participation in this process has been seen from various university institutes, institutes of higher education, sector research institutions, and development-oriented industrial companies.

The programme is co-ordinated under the auspices of the Council of Technology, the Danish Technical Research Council, and the Danish Natural Science Research Council. These three councils co-ordinate their respective contributions to this programme through a joint co-ordination committee. This joint committee is also responsible for the ongoing evaluation of the programme.

The programme includes the following main activities:

- implementation of applied basic, technical and scientific research at international level, with a view to future industrial utilization of the results of the research.
- technological development concerning new and existing materials/processes, and application thereof.
- transfer and demonstration of technology and know-how to a wider range of Danish companies.

In order to achieve an effective co-ordination of programme activities, a substantial part of them is to be carried out through the formation of centres (about 50 per cent), and in the form of framework programmes (about 30 per cent), whereas individual projects play a lesser role.

A programme in information technology was launched in 1991 with a similar organizational structure as presented previously for the other programmes. This programme is for the period 1990-95 with a total budget of 210 million DKK.

In 1990, an R&D programme was initiated in the area of food technology with the aim of consolidating and boosting the position of the Danish food industry on the international market. The total financing of DKK 525 million came from the Ministries of Industry, Agriculture, and Education and Research.

International Research Co-operation

Internationalization and participation in international research programmes have a very high priority in the Danish research policy, and there is the continuous aim of co-ordinating Danish research programmes with development at international level.

In 1989, 3.1 per cent of all public and private R&D activities were financed through the international co-operation in which Denmark participates, corresponding to approximately 370 million DKK.

This research is carried out mainly at public research institutions (universitites, other higher education institutions and sector research institutions) and in industry.

The heavyweights in the international co-operation are the research programmes of the EC and those of a number of international organizations. The responsibility for Denmark's participation in the organizations and in the research co-operation of the EC lies in the Ministry of Education and Research.

Furthermore, the six national research councils participate in large-scale international operational co-operation, in Nordic research co-operation, as well as in the work of the ESF.

SYSTEMS OF RESEARCH POLICY COUNSELLING

Research Councils

Six independent research councils have been set up to watch over the national co-ordination responsibility in Denmark:

— Natural Science Research Council

— Medical Research Council

— Agricultural and Veterinary Research Council

— Social Science Research Council

— Research Council for the Humanities

— Technical Research Council.

It is the task of the councils to assist the government and the parliament in research matters, and the six research councils assist the above-mentioned Council for Research Policy with subject-related advice within their respective research areas.

It is an important task for the councils to contribute to the subject-related development of the Danish research institutions and to contribute to a co-ordination of research environments across institutional and geographical boundaries.

The councils for instance see it as an important taks to advice about the subject-related long-term plans of the research institutions. It is furthermore an important task to give advice about the best possible education of research scientists.

The councils lay great emphasis on an active internationalization of Danish research.

The councils also give advice about Danish participation in major European organizations and in the research co-operation of the EC.

In research matters of a transverse nature, the advice is co-ordinated by the Conference of Research Council Chairman.

The councils can advice private research institutions, if there is a mutual wish to this effect.

Each council consists of 15 members who are appointed by the minister in their personal function. It is emphasized that the majority of the members are active researchers and that each council is ensured a broad and qualified coverage of the subject-areas which belong under the council in question.

The members sit on the council for three years and may be re-appointed for a further three-year period.

FINANCING OF RESEARCH

The six national research councils administer a number of government appropriations allocated of Danish research. The councils administer a total of approximately DKK 640 million per year (1991 figures).

Funding

The councils allocate support both to purely national projects and to projects which form part of an international co-operation.

Every four years, the councils make a long-term subject related planning. This planning identifies research areas which are to be given a particularly high priority in the period of the plan in consideration of the scientific development and/or the meeting of important society needs. The planning of the councils is co-ordinated through the Conference of Research Council Chairmen.

The areas which have been given priority are published with an invitation to the research community to submit applications. The support of the councils is allocated according to a subject-related evaluation of the submitted applications. In several cases, the councils use international experts in their subject-related evaluation. The support for the special high priority areas is generally allocated as relatively large multi-annual grants.

If a council finds the need to do so, it may itself take the initiative—and administer the implementation of a research assignment. This will naturally only be the case within areas which have been given special priority.

In their planning, the councils have earmarked a considerable part of the funds for support to research areas which have not been given a special priority. It is the policy of the councils that all particularly qualified projects should be eligible for support, irrespective of the priority given to the subject-area in question.

Programme Appropriations

On the mentioned 640 million DKK, 230 million DKK are spent on programme appropriations discussed earlier. The programmes are typically implemented in a co-operation among several research councils. The appropriations are allocated—most often after an international evaluation of the applications—as multi-annual appropriations for co-operating researcher groups. A typical appropriation is in the area of 10 million DKK per year for five years.

Conclusion

Spending on Danish R&D rose sharply during the 1980s, in the public and not least the private sectors. In composition and financing Danish research does not differ greatly from that in the other smaller OECD countries. In relation to GDP, public-sector R&D was close to the EC average while, in an international context, and despite strong growth over the past ten years, R&D in the business enterprise sector remains modest. Danish industry is predominantly one with a low research intensity and its structure is characterized by many small- and medium-sized, and only a few large enterprises.

REFERENCES

Ministry of Education and Research, 1991. *The Research and Development Programme of the Danish Government*. ISBN 87-503-9264-6.

OECD, 1991. *Main Science and Technology Indicators 1991:1*. Paris.

8

Organization of Science and Technology in Finland: A System Facing a Challenge

ULLA EKBERG

Assistant Director, Science Policy and International Affairs, The Academy of Finland, Helsinki, Finland

THE ORGANIZATION OF FINNISH RESEARCH

The organization of science and technology in Finland is based as in other market economy countries both on the public sector and on the private sector. These two sectors are in close co-operation and also interdependent.

A total of 11.6 million FIM (2.11 billion ECU) is estimated to be allocated to research and development in Finland in 1992, of which the share of the private sector is 60 per cent and that of the public sector 40 per cent.

The structure of public research in Finland is presented in Figure 1. The highest body for science and technology is the Science and Technology Policy Council chaired by the Prime Minister. The Council has been assigned the task of assisting the Council of State in questions relating to science and technology and to co-ordinate Finland's objectives set for S&T policy. In the Finnish Parliament, questions relating to S&T are discussed at the Cultural Committee, at the Industrial Policy Committee and at the Science and Cultural Section of the Finance Committee, which is the most important specialized body in Parliament dealing with S&T questions. The Council of State submitted two reports to Parliament, in 1973 and 1985, on its objectives to promote S&T.

The two important ministries are the Ministry of Trade and Industry and the Ministry of Education. These two ministries together answer for 77 per cent of the state research funding.

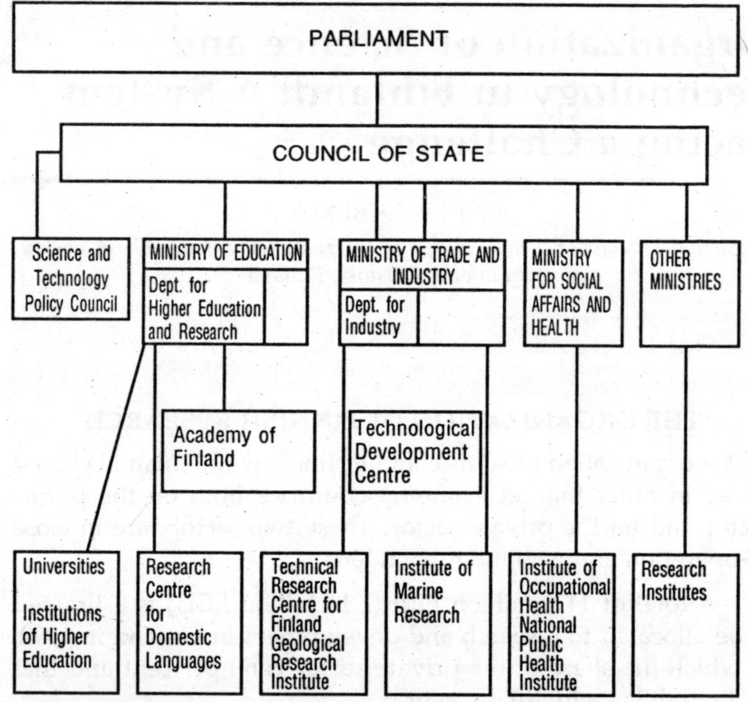

Figure 1. Decision-makers, financiers, and performers of research in the public sector.

The Technology Development Centre subordinate to the Ministry of Trade and Industry has a central position in the planning and financing of industrial R&D. Subordinate to the Ministry of Trade and Industry is also the Technical Research Centre of Finland, which is the biggest research institute in the Nordic countries and executes also a significant part of commissioned research in Finland's private sector.

Subordinate to the Ministry of Education is the Academy of Finland, which is composed of seven research councils and the central board of research councils. The organization of the Academy of Finland is presented in Figure 2. The Academy of Finland is the central financing agency of basic research carried out primarily at universities but also in research institutes. All the universities are also subordinate to the Ministry of Education.

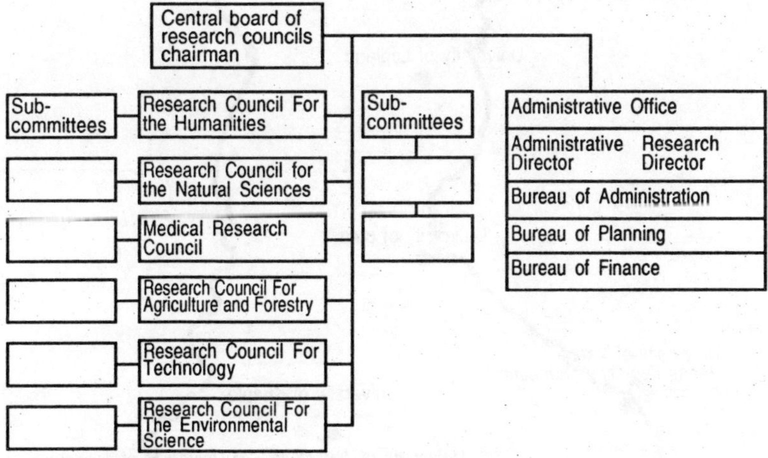

Figure 2. The Academy of Finland—organization.

The regional distribution of the universities in Finland is presented in Figure 3.

The system of higher education institutions covers the whole country, consisting of 17 science universities and 3 art academies, all having the same rights and obligations to carry out scientific research and to give doctoral education in their own field. A system of higher vocational colleges (Fachhochschule) is currently being launched as an experiment.

In addition to the Technical Research Centre of Finland there are about 20 state research institutes. Among the largest are the Agricultural Research Centre and the Forest Research Institute, both subordinate to the Ministry of Agriculture and Forestry. The research institutes operate under the ministry relating to their own areas. Research funded by public resources

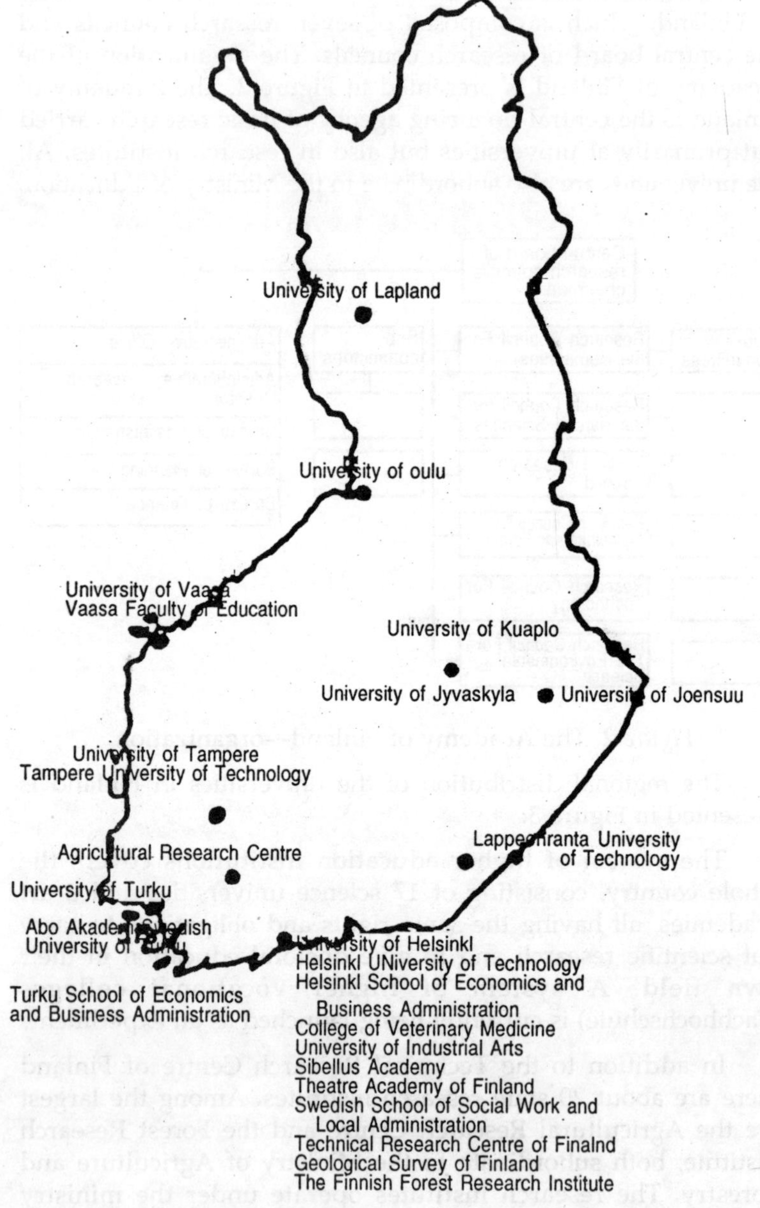

Figure 3. Universities and main research institutes in Finland.

is also carried out at the research departments of the ministries and in the expert organs under the ministries. Part of the research funding of the ministries is used for commissioned research carried out at state research institutes and universities.

The industrial sector performs research in its laboratories, and had also one important research institute of its own, the Central Laboratory within the wood-processing industry. State research institutes and universities also carry out commissioned research for industry.

Some Research Trends

Finland's research input grew very rapidly in the latter part of the 1980s. The share of GDP grew from 1.34 per cent in 1983 and the estimate is 2.1 per cent for 1992. This favourable development was primarily caused by the rapidly grown input by the private sector but also the public sector increased its share. Priority was given to the development of technology. The Technology Development Centre launched its activities in 1983 and soon became a successful funder of industrial research. The Development Centre uses two forms of funding: it allocates target research appropriations on application or grants conditional loans for industrial R&D. The budget of the Technology Development Centre amounts to 955.9 million FIM (173.8 million ECU) in 1992.

Unlike in other European countries, higher education has been supported very strongly in Finland in the latter part of the 1980s. The Higher Education Development Act was issued in 1986, in accordance with which the resources should be kept on least at the real level until the year 1995. In this connection the Council of State also made a decision-of-principle on an annual increase of 15 per cent in the resources of universities, excluding resources for building activities and permanent salaries. This decision increased the appropriations of universities considerably. The decision also included a recommendation for universities to develop their administration efficiently, to increase the number of graduates, and to reduce the number of drop-outs. During this period, the annual number of new Ph.Ds. has increased considerably: from the yearly output of less than 400 to 527 in 1991.

The restructuring of the system of the research councils of the Academy of Finland was discussed in 1990 and 1991 (the Academy's organization in Figure 2). In addition to six research councils, the Research Council for the Environmental Sciences was established at the Academy of Finland in 1983. The sphere of the Research Council covers environmental research very widely. In 1989, the then President of the Academy of Finland, E. Allardt, started discussions on the number of research councils. According to E. Allardt, the boundaries between disciplines have blurred and scientifically interesting findings are made at the intersections of various disciplines. By concentrating the decision-making on fewer research councils, the activities of the Academy of Finland would be enhanced, and scientifically trained people could be recruited for preparatory work despite the scarce growth perspectives of resouces, if the number of councils were less than at present.

The Basic Research Working Group agreed with E. Allardt's proposal and suggested that the number of research councils be reduced to three, *i.e.* the research council for big science, for biosciences, and for the humanities and social sciences. Another working group later examined the matter further and proposed that a fourth research council be established for health sciences. The proposal for restructuring gave rise to lively discussions. The advantages of the reform were seen by many but the fate of their own discipline worried many. The most typical statement submitted on the report supported reform elsewhere but not in matters concerning one's own research council. The reform has been tabled as the Ministry of Education decided that the activities of the Academy of Finland be evaluated by foreign evaluators. The evaluation is expected to be completed by the end of 1992.

The Challenge of Today

The Finnish research system is facing great challenges today. In this connection I would like to take up three challenges which are inter-linked, namely the adaptation of the economy to smaller volume, the change of the management system within the public sector, and the strongly expanded participation in the international research co-operation.

Finland is in the midst of the deepest recession of her independence. The collapse of trade with the ex Soviet Union affects negatively the long-term planning of economy; also export to western countries is decreased. Unemployment is higher than ever, of the country's five million people over 300,000 are unemployed. The tax revenues have fallen and because of unemployment and the recession, new needs have emerged for the use of tax revenues.

The public sector must implement large cuts in costs. Special attention has been paid to the staff costs within the public sector. The government has planned to reduce the number of government employees by 5 per cent during this electoral period (four years), which could mean for example a loss of some 1000 jobs at Finnish universities. The Higher Education Development Act is in danger.

Simultaneously, all governmental institutes are changing over to a new management system called result-oriented management. Earlier the resources were allocated to government institutes by detailed decisions given in the state budget on the basis of the plans submitted by the institutes. The aim of the result-oriented management system is to reduce detailed control and to delegate decision-making to the administrative units themselves. The aim is also that the ministries and the institutes and other bodies subordinate to the ministries agree upon the results to be achieved by the given resources, and monitor their activities and report on the results. The defining of the achieved results, the follow-up and commitment to result targets means a new kind of thinking at least within the Finnish public administration and causes great pressures for those involved. Anxiety is widely felt because of the decreased resources.

In the government's programme, priority is given both to R&D and higher education. In the 1992 State Budget, the resources of the Technological Development Centre of Finland grew significantly whereas the resources of the Academy of Finland fell by 3 per cent and the resources of universities by 2.8 per cent. The reductions were mainly due to cuts in the personnel costs.

The necessary cuts have been made evenly so far, *i.e.* something has been taken away from almost everything. When needs for more cuts grow and extend for several years, this method can no longer be used. New criteria for more cuts must be found, *e.g.* the closing of larger units should be discussed. My English colleagues are familiar with this problem.

There are four units of dentistry at Finnish universities. The closing of one of the units is being discussed at present. It has been proposed that the oldest of the units, the Faculty of Dentistry at the University of Helsinki, be closed. The proposal was made in the working group composed of representatives of *inter alia* the directors of administration of universities. At the follow-up discussions, the importance of each unit was considered in terms of both its scientific merits and by stressing the significance of the units for the dental care of the local population. The Minister of Education has proposed the closing of the Faculty of Dentistry of the University of Kuopio in eastern Finland, whereas the Minister of Culture has expressed her dissenting opinion, both working in the same ministry.

In this speech in March on the future of higher education, E. Allardt proposed that the closing of a whole university should also be discussed. Such decisions are, however, very difficult to make.

Decreases in the research volume and cuts in the staff especially affect young graduates at the beginning of their research careers, as posts such as temporary lectureships, assistantships, etc. have often provided smooth access to research careers. A whole generation of researchers could be lost and a career in research could be seen as less attractive. The negative impacts could be felt for a long time. I believe that we, in Finland, must soon discuss measures to be taken to maintain the natural turnover of researchers. No real shortage of, for example, competent applicants for vacant professorships, should be expected, but applicants' age structure will be unfavourable.

For a long while, Finland was a marginal participant in international research co-operation. This was primarily due to the scarce research input and to Finland's aim to participate only in co-operation activities that were open to all nations. The direction was changed in the mid-seventies when Finland joined or otherwise arranged her contacts with several West European research organizations. This development was especially rapid in the late 1980s, when Finland became a full member of CERN, an associate member of ESA, and also concluded a co-operation agreement with the European Communities on participation in the EC framework programme of research.

Finland will be a full member of the EC framework programme of research after the EFTA countries have concluded the agreement on EEA with the EC. The annual costs arising from this membership will total up to 200 million FIM in the coming years. This co-operation can be best exploited only if Finnish researchers compete for funding in co-operation with European researchers. Within many programmes the competition for funds is very keen.

The Academy of Finland has carried out several evaluations on various research areas by using foreign experts. The inadequate international contacts of Finnish researchers have been criticized in most evaluations carried out. Special attention has been paid to the fact that Finnish researchers publish much too little in international scientific publications. Research carried out by Finnish scientists and scholars is therefore not well-known internationally. Finnish researchers also have stronger contacts with the US than to Europe. Finnish research administrators, *e.g.* the Academy of Finland, have therefore strongly encouraged Finnish researchers to create new international contacts especially with European research institutes, so that Finnish international commitments could be fully exploited. As I said earlier, there is a risk that research resources will also be cut, and Finnish researchers must therefore learn to find research funding through international competition.

The target level of 2.7 per cent of GDP by 1995 has been set by the Science and Technology Policy Council for Finnish research input. This goal should be reached by balanced development of all areas within the research system. The estimate of the research input in 1992 is 2.1 per cent of GDP. This development is due to a decrease in GDP rather than an increase in research input this year. The share of research funding directly benefiting technology and competitiveness seems to develop more favourable than others. There may be considerable problems in the future for these fields to find competent researchers if the university system is reduced. Other goals set by the Science and Technology Policy Council include the intensifying and increasing of researcher training, the estimated yearly need for new Ph.Ds. by 1995 is 600, and the internationalization of research, which is currently being realized.

9

Technological R&D: Difference Between a Market Economy and a Planned Economy

PAOLO BISOGNO

Full Professor, University 'La Sapienza', Rome, Italy

Introduction

Technological change is a decisive dynamic factor in modern economic systems. The close relationship between economic development and change, on the one hand, and technological process, on the other, is now a generally accepted fact. Innovation is one of the most important factors accounting for the different growth rates and different trade balances among the OECD countries. The problem with economic research is how to identify on a theoretical basis a possible random relationship, the degree of freedom technological change may have *vis-a-vis* endogenous market mechanisms, the role played by institutional factors, and the factors determining the incidence and direction of innovative activity.

CHARACTERISTIC FACTORS IN THE INNOVATIVE PROCESS IN CENTRALLY PLANNED ECONOMIES

The analyses and surveys carried out on the economies of East European countries have confirmed the following characteristics:

— comparatively weak increase in the general productivity coefficient,

— high investment in training and scientific research,

— high development and consequent closing of the gap with the more advanced countries, in the 'strategic' technologies: defence, aerospace, nuclear energy,

— scanty development with consequent increase in the technological gap in 'basic' civilian technologies: precision engineering, computer science-electronics-robotics, fine chemistry,

— strongly passive, comparatively small, overall technological balance of payments.

RESOURCES FOR SCIENTIFIC AND TECHNOLOGICAL INNOVATION R&D

R&D

In market economies, industry finances research to an extent which varies from 50 to 80 per cent of the total, depending on the country. A comparable percentage of the research is carried out in the company's own laboratories.

Table 1. Expenditure on R&D in some OECD Countries in 1985 (US$ million).

	Total R&D expenses	*Civil R&D expenses*	*Military expenses (% of total)*
USA	109,730.00	75,291	31.4
Japan	40,064.40	37,017	7.6
Germany	19,774.00	18,868	4.6
France	14,571.10	11,905	18.3
Italy	7,014.50	6,654	5.1
UK	14,358.70	11,335	21.1
Canada	5,352.50	5,187	3.1
Sweden	2,946.50	2,667	9.5
Total OECD	2,309.01	182,781	20.9
EEC	638.49	54,911	14.0

In centrally planned economics, all research is funded by the state and most of it carried out in the laboratories of scientific institutions which are completely distinct from the production units, as regards background, aims, philosophy of action, and organizational practice. Companies are therefore exposed to a mainly abstract type of scientific and technological information, which is hard to relate to specific problems and to specific industrial topics, with only a limited capacity for training and stimulating, and lacking any material advantages of use for the purposes of inter-company competition, which is in any case institutionally very low. The difference between the two systems of funding and performing research consists in the fact that in countries with a market economy, scientific and technical information with a technological bias is generated largely inside the firm and therefore the process of assimilating it and transforming it into a stimulus for innovation is greatly facilitated. Furthermore, information generated inside the firm is naturally market-oriented and thus easier to transfer to and be used by productive units inside or outside the individual firms. For some years now, western companies have developed in-house capacity to clean scientific and technical information from the technical literature, from participation in international bidding from the analyses and comparison with machinery with incorporated technology, etc.

Moreover, in some sectors, in particular in that of capital goods, one factor that acts as an innovation multiplier is missing, namely the knock-on effect due to having a large number of small specialized firms designing and producing capital goods for the large firms. The result is a constant flow of experience and knowledge under the stimulus of the needs and requirements expressed by the large firms. This constant flow calls for a high degree of mobility of specialists and experts and is translated into a highly differentiated series of technological applications based on a number of basic technologies. The comprehensive and wide-ranging differentiation of the technological applications on the one hand prevents complete acquisition by the large firms, and on the other, allow a large number of specialist suppliers, in the form of small, flexible and competitive firms to flourish.

Postgraduate Training and Basic Research

The clear distinction drawn in the eastern European countries between the two functions linked to two different institutions, namely Academy and University, has produced a negative effect and has generally speaking stood in the way of the necessary exchanges of experience and knowledge. What are in fact needed are close relationships between the two components in order to ensure that basic research really does have an effect on economic and social conditions. It should be stressed that basic research affects technology above all through the transfer of researchers with a large stock of knowledge, experience, and problem-solving capacity, and via the network of professional contacts at national and international level.

Priority in Technological Activities

The general limitations imposed on both financial and human resources and the increased number of opportunities for innovation occurring in the recent years have rendered the problem of which decisions to make more critical in the more industrialized countries of the West.

The growing complexity of the new technological systems and the increasing effect they have on society's problems are reflected in the size of the required financial resources and the consequent need for the public authorities to shoulder part of the risks involved.

Two trends have arisen simultaneously in the western countries. On the one hand, there is the tendency towards increased public funding in the case of those technological developments lying closest to the investment and research ceiling of individual industrial sectors and involving unsustainable risks. Public funding may be used in individual advanced sectors (*e.g.* aerospace in the USA, France, and the UK, the defence and nuclear energy industries in almost all countries, etc.) or in the case of separate projects covering certain particular aspects in several sectors (*e.g.* in Italy) or else to develop technologies in key sectors (*e.g.* in computer and information science in the UK and in Japan).

On the other hand, in a number of countries having the advantage of a more mature financial structure there is a strong tendency for a financial firm to invest in the acquisition of technological developments lying outside the reach of small or medium enterprises or which originate inside the Universities (*e.g.* the conglomerates and venture capital in the USA and incentives in Sweden, etc.).

Research and Development in the Defence Industries and Civilian Technologies

Arms and weapons research absorbs a considerable amount of resources in all the industrialized countries in both West and East.

Considerable discussion has been centred on the topic of the fall out from military research in the civilian field. With the exception of aerospace research and other limited sectors, investment in military research has not produced any significant fall out in the civilian field. This is even more apparent in countries with a centrally planned economy because of the rigid distinction made between the two activities and because of the huge technological gap between the two sectors which is much wider than in the West.

The conversion of a military economy, no easy matter even in countries with a market economy, is an extremely complex undertaking in the East and the first steps that have been taken in this direction are aimed essentially at the sale of technology or the setting up of joint ventures to exploit such technology (see for instance the review of Soviet military technology held at Bologna, Italy in June, 1991 and similar market exhibitions held in several other European countries).

On the other hand, much fewer resources, in both absolute and relative terms, have been dedicated to research and development in the civilian sector in countries with a planned economy than in the West. This is due both to the different priority assigned to military research and to the 'schizophrenic' (*i.e.* completely distinct and sometimes divergent) organization as we have already seen in research and experimental activities on the one hand, and productive activities on the other.

One final consideration: in a planned economy, productive innovations are induced by the central planners by means of the instrument of price increases granted to innovators. Producers thus tend to 'produce innovations' quite independently of the latter's actual utility to firms linked to the market's needs or to factors of productivity, quality, cost, etc. They are not filtered through competition and the evaluation of the results of the use of products and processes.

Incentives for Innovation

In the East European countries, unlike the western countries, financial incentives for innovation are comparatively rare and are allocated on the basis of an *a priori* (and of course inaccurate) evaluation of their knock-on effects. The consequent innovations are offered to firms operating under monopoly conditions and thus having little incentive towards development and exploitation.

The introduction of a market system will improve this situation, although a way will have to be found to protect intellectual property, particularly in a number of industrial sectors (*e.g.* chemistry, mechanical engineering, etc.).

A second negative aspect lies in the intrinsic weakness of the other, non-financial incentives for innovation.

In the West, competition and therefore the insecurity of one's performance, which must therefore adapt to or even be in advance of a rapidly changing market, acts as a powerful incentive to innovation as a factor for survival and not just of development. The introduction of market economy elements into the eastern European countries means that a considerable in-house training effort must be made in order to create a technological learning capacity achieved through imitation and the adaptation of productive technologies.

Factors of Change in the Transition

Three factors of change are involved in the transition towards a market economy:

1. decentralization
2. diversification

3. pluralism.

1. *Decentralization* entails the creation of a network of capabilities for handling information and making decisions which will complete and stimulate the various units of which the system is composed. Decentralization down to firm level means great sensitivity to change, enhanced flexibility and capacity for adaptation, more effective capacity for decisions concerning products, processes, suppliers, clients, prices.
2. *Horizontal product-based diversification* is a characteristic of firms operating in the electrical-electronic and chemical sectors; *vertical process-based diversification* is a characteristic of mass production, continuous process firms that make use of small innovative firms; *qualitative diversification* is a characteristic of service firms that manage complex information systems and interact with small specialist firms that supply the software; *external diversification* is a characteristic of firms that make use of innovations produced outside their own sector (*e.g.* agricultural and textile firms).
3. Technological pluralism, typical of the market economy and almost totally absent in the planned economy, is without doubt an effective way of exploring and evaluating still unknown alternatives and thus represents a powerful innovation tool.

Market Independence

The greater degree of economic openness and interdependence distinguishes the market economies from planned markets, as does the degree of linkage between the scientific-technological system within the world system. The flow of collaboration and information enhances in-house technological activities and guarantees a high qualitative level in the training of scientists and engineers by providing access to information, to the best international sources of patents, know-how and codified knowledge.

Preliminary Conclusions

It is conceivable that the centrally planned economies will

go through a period of transition which will elicit incentives and stimulate the need for renewal of the industrial system. In particular, there will be a tendency towards:

— the decentralization of decision-making down to firm level,

— the introduction of competition and the possibility of the consumer making a choice,

— the establishment of closer links with the world economy.

At the scientific and technological level, the tendency will be towards:

— the development of an in-house innovation policy, either by acquiring the innovation directly or indirectly, or by funding and implementing one's own research and development activity,

— the establishment of close links between basic research, postgraduate training and the international scientific system,

— the conversion of military R&D into civilian oriented activities.

The following auxiliary R&D tools will be required:

— protection of intellectual property,

— setting up of standards,

— research and services for agriculture,

— regulation of negative external factors (health, safety, pollution).

10

Note From the Italian Ministry of Foreign Affairs

STEFANO ZIRILLI
Scientific Advisor, Ministry of Foreign Affairs, Rome, Italy

The Italian Ministry of Foreign Affairs is deeply involved in the acquisition of information on organizational structures of science in Europe, this forming the basis for a better co-ordination of research and development policies, and permitting a fuller embedding of Italian institutions in the international frame.

The acquisition referred to is seen as fundamentally important today in view of the closer prospective integration that will result from the changing structure of a major segment of Europe.

The dissemination of knowledge resulting from a seminar of this type is an essential contribution to improving the approach to both bilateral and multilateral agreements. These agreements represent the main instrument by which the Ministry of Foreign Affairs and the Ministry of University and Scientific and Technological Research plan their policy of international co-operation.

Initiatives such as this of ROSTE are clearly invaluable in allowing useful comparisons of, and monitoring of, the evolution of the organizational structures of science in Europe, and the

Ministry of Foreign Affairs supports any further meetings of this type.

The Ministry would like to express its gratitude to all participants, the organizers, the hosting institute, the city of Venice, and in particular UNESCO-ROSTE and the Italian National Commission for UNESCO.

11

Bulgarian Academy of Sciences: Current Changes and Outlook

BLAGOVEST SENDOV
Academician, Vice-President, International Council of Scientific Unions, Sofia, Bulgaria

The current political and economic situation in central and eastern Europe is well known. By decision of the Great Powers, after the Second World War, the countries of the region were included in the sphere of influence of one of the victors—the Soviet Union. They formed the socialist bloc: indeed, a real bloc, based on total alignment, in the form of co-operation and mutual assistance in economy, politics, science, defence, and so on.

The marriage, imposed from outside, lasted about half a century. It produced many children, who do not deserve to be just thrown out into the street. One of the spoilt but nevertheless gifted offspring is today's academies of sciences in the former socialist states. They were founded and consequently took shape after the model of the Soviet Academy of Sciences, now the Russian Academy of Sciences. These academies not only developed along the same pattern, but also closely collaborated with each other.

In spite of all the turbulence and vicissitudes of life, it would be just to assume that during the past socialist period, Bulgarian science made serious progress. This progress, in turn, was to a great extent the result of its co-operation with the Soviet Academy of Sciences and other academic establishments of the former socialist states.

SHORT HISTORY OF THE BULGARIAN ACADEMY OF SCIENCES

The BAS was established in 1869, nine years before the liberation of Bulgaria from the Turkish yoke. Until 1945, it functioned as a West-European type academy. Laws were passed in 1947 and 1949, which led to its restructuring according to the Soviet model. Many institutes were rapidly set up under its aegis, and its full-time staff reached its peak number of 15,000 in 1987 (see Figure 1). The BAS became the leading research centre in Bulgaria not only in terms of scope, but also regarding quality of research personnel. This can be proved by a statistical fact. In 1988, about 12 per cent of Bulgarian scholars and researchers were employed by the BAS, while 52 per cent of the scientific publications in foreign academic journals were authority by its associates.

The international scientific exchanges and Bulgarian participation in the international scientific organizations were carried out mainly through the channels of the Bulgarian Academy of Sciences.

The number of academicians (otherwise ordinary members) during the last 50 years varied between 40 and 60, while that of the corresponding members did not exceed 100.

In pursuance of the laws of 1947 and 1949, the supreme governing body of the Academy is the General Assembly. It consists of the academicians and the corresponding members. This General Assembly elects the Praesidium of the Academy, and the executive leadership—President, Vice-President, Secretariat, etc. But like other structures in the socialist period, the Academy was under the direct supervision and control of the Central Committee of the Bulgarian Communist Party.

One of the serious shortcomings of the former socialist 'Academy' model was its *de facto* isolation from the universities and the training of young scientists. This shortcoming is not a crucial one while there is large quantitative growth. The big influx of cadres to the newly founded institutes and laboratories compensates for this structural drawback. But when this growth decreases, or for some reason ceases, the isolation from the educational process begins to tell.

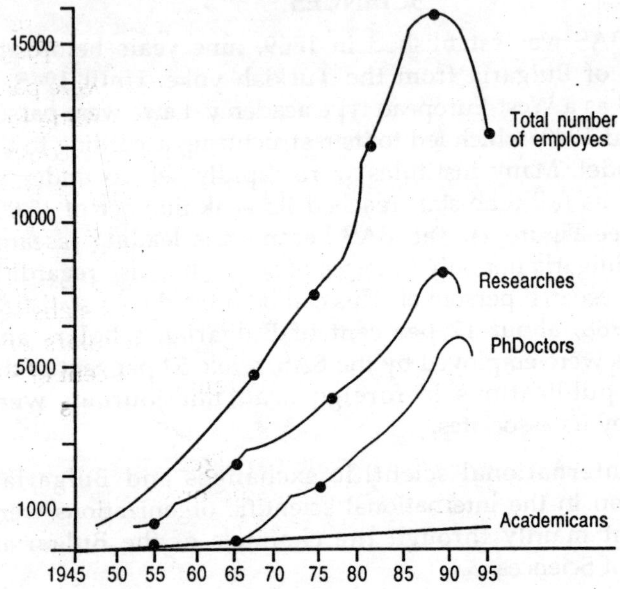

Figure 1. Number of staff of the Bulgarian Academy of Sciences over the years since 1945.

To overcome this defect, an experiment was launched in Bulgaria, unique for all former socialist countries. It was aimed at integrating the BAS and the University of Sofia, and initiated as early as 1972.

In my opinion, it was an ambitious, purposeful, and promising endeavour, containing many practical ideas. Unfortunately, it did not meet with an enthusiastic response: its ideas challenged some basic tenets of society of that time.

Let me cite an example. During the socialist period, universities were regarded not merely as an important institution of professional and scholarly training, but also as an instrument for ideological education, for communist indoctrination of the future specialist. Cases were seen where talented scholars happened to disobey party instructions, and were promptly transferred to the Academy, just to cut off their contact with students. The separation of the Academy from the university was deemed necessary for this mechanism to function.

The integration between the Academy and the University failed, since it defied some political and organizational postulates of socialism. In the final account, it was paralyzed, and what was left of it dismantled. More than ten years of strenuous efforts were wasted on a doomed cause.

This and other mishaps of the BAS in the socialist era were the product of some specific features of the system. Suffice it to mention the priority of political criteria and the life appointment system. This practice benefited bureaucracy and severely hindered innovation, competition and genuine scholarly quests.

Beginning of Changes

There was increasing talk about restructuring of the BAS as early as 1987, when its growth was brought to a halt. There were rumours about a decision by the highest party authorities to close the Academy down. This was not at all unbelievable, since such a fate had just befallen the Romanian Academy of Sciences.

In 1988, a complete package of proposals on the structure, functions, and management of the BAS was prepared. It was submitted for initial approval to the party leadership as the existing procedure required. These documents were held up for more than one year and did not live to be given the go-ahead.

The General Assembly of the BAS approved instead provisional rules at the end of 1988, which were co-ordinated with the top party officials. According to these rules, the institute directors had to be elected by general assemblies of the scientists working at those institutes. That procedure, although imperfect, was a first step towards democratization.

After 10 November 1989, when the democratic transformation in Bulgaria began, the BAS took an active part in it. In the first freely elected Parliament, more than 10 per cent of the deputies were collaborators of the BAS. The Parliament, which discussed and adopted the new Bulgarian Constitution, at the beginning of October 1991 passed the new Law of the BAS. This Law contains some very important text, which I shall take the liberty of quoting:

Article 5:

(1) The General Assembly of the BAS is the supreme body that performs its governance and management. Eligible to membership are senior research scientists and scholars, holders of doctoral degrees, corresponding members and academicians.

(2) The General Assembly of the BAS adopts and amends its Statutes.

(3) The General Assembly elects the President, the Vice-Presidents, the Scientific Secretary-General and the members of the Board of the BAS. Eligibility to presidency is restricted to academicians and corresponding members of the Academy.

Article 10:

(1) The property of the BAS and its independent units comprises property rights and other real rights, claims, securities, patents, donations, shareholding in economic organizations and associations, as well as other rights and liabilities.

(2) The Parliament (National Assembly) commits into possession of the BAS state-owned land, real estate, machinery, equipment, appliances, library collections, funds and other movable property. Disposal of this property is only possible in conformity with a decision taken by the Academy's General Assembly and in the Academy's interest.

(3) The real estate of the Academy may be expropriated only by force of a decision taken by the National Assembly.

Article 12:

(1) The BAS and its independent research units are exempted from taxation on their income in Bulgarian and foreign currency.

(2) On the recommendation of the Board of the BAS, the Government may exempt from taxation, firms associated with the Academy or its institutes that commercialize research results, and may relieve from taxation research and production enterprises, firms, and other business units attached to the Academy that perform their activities in accordance with the Law of Commerce.

(3) The entire property and funds of the BAS as well as property bequeathed or donated are exempted from taxation, duties, and other fiscal duties.

(4) Printed matter, scientific equipment, appliances, materials, etc., imported or exported by the Academy with a view to providing for its research activities, are exempted from taxation and duties.

(5) Funds of business organizations within the country and abroad intended to support the Academy's research activities are deducted from their profit prior to taxation.

From the Transitory and Final Provisions:

Paragraph 2:

The General Assembly of BAS should be constituted no later than two months from the date of entering into force of the Law. It should adopt the Statutes at its first session. The General Assembly to adopt the Statutes shall consist of 200 members.

The provisions that I have just cited testify to two basic assumptions, namely that:

(i) The Bulgarian Academy of Sciences is authorized to work out its own destinies as far as structures and management are concerned,

(ii) The Bulgarian Academy of Science is the owner of a huge and expensive property which can be utilized for income and self-support.

The new General Assembly of the Academy was constituted after overcoming certain difficulties, and set to work in early December 1991.

Unfortunately, the General Assembly of the BAS became strongly politicized and started working as a Parliament, using decrees on all major and minor problems of the Academy.

At the same time its first and most outstanding task—to consider and adopt a new Statue of the Academy—remained unfulfilled.

What kind of statute will be adopted, and when, is still far from clear. A political party, which is ruling now and dominates the General Assembly of the Bulgarian Academy of Sciences, wishes to revise the new Law of the Academy, especially its provisions on membership. This could further delay the adoption of the Statute.

Basic Problems

The most acute and painful problems for BAS is financing.

Lay-offs and closure are unavoidable. Regrettably, such fateful decisions are not preceded by serious consideration and professional evaluation of institutions and specialists. Political motivations rule supreme.

My personal opinion is that the BAS should cease to dismiss qualified researchers, and concentrate on commercial activity instead, optimizing all possibilities that the new Law provides. But this is still a highly controversial issue and views on it diverge sharply.

A point of principle is the role and status of the members of the Academy, the academicians and the corresponding members. The mere fact that 80 per cent of the membership were members of the former Communist party, is good reason for its distrust. This has been the main motivation behind the proposal that membership of the General Assembly under the new Law is not confined to Academy members only, but may also include other outstanding scientists.

21 members of the Academy (7 academicians and 14 corresponding members) were elected in the acting General Assembly. Two solutions seem feasible:

(i) the institutes of the BAS are separated in different structures and the members of the Academy form once again a typical West-European type academy,

(ii) BAS retains the present relationship between the institutes and the members of the Academy, but the latter do not have exclusive prerogatives in this structure.

I share the view that after a time, may be in 10-15 years, variant (i) will finally materialize. But at present there is no alternative to variant. (ii) The position may be substantiated with the following arguments:

— the immediate separation will give rise to property disagreements which would be extremely difficult to solve under the present economic hardships,

— the separation will deprive institutes of valuable communication with western scientific centres, since this communication has been implemented through BAS channels, or through personal contacts of Academy members,

— the separation will destroy the existing organizational infrastructure,

— if institutes are inevitably to be separated from the members of the Academy, this act should be preceded by a clear-cut decision abut the future of these institutes.

The crucial problem of today's academic restructuring is the preservation of the scientific and intellectual potential of the country. Bulgaria will badly need these people for its economic, cultural and spiritual progress. Today, the large number of scientists is considered a liability, since there is no understanding of how to use them. Under normal conditions, the availability of educated people is an asset. Our efforts should not be directed at reducing this potential, but rather at its optimization in the best interests of society.

12

Academic Scientific Research at the Transitional Stage

GEORGI ANGELOV

Director of Centre for Science and Education, Ministry of Science and Education, Sofia, Bulgaria

Let me first define more precisely the title of my report. When I am talking about academic research I do not mean basic research, but a set of scientific institutions within the R&D system in Bulgaria and the problems they face in the period of deep political, economical, and cultural changes in our society. When I refer to science I mean not only the natural sciences, but also the social sciences and humanities.

Like all ex-communist countries, the national R&D system in Bulgaria was fully budget-supported and from the organizational point of view is divided into three main sectors: academic scientific institutes, research centres in universities, and applied research institutes which serve the large state-owned industries or firms. The research carried out in the first two sectors—universities and academies—I call academic research. These are the scientific institutions that lie in the sphere of activity of the Ministry of Education and Science. Almost all basic research in Bulgaria is performed in these institutions, but this is only a part of their scientific activity.

I will consider the problems that Bulgarian academic research is suffering with respect to its: (i) role in society; (ii) organization; (iii) resources; (iv) system of science policy. Some problems are inherited from the communist regime, others are results of the abovementioned changes that our society is now undergoing.

The Social Role of the Academic Research

If we assume that science has two roles in society—as culture and as economy, or else as a source of moral correctives (cultural function) and of technological innovations (economical function)—then academic research in Bulgaria was and is not able to play them well. Very often the science was accused of lack of innovativeness. But the social functions of a national R&D system depend on the receptiveness of society for innovations.

Now it is obvious that the highly centralized socialist system was incapable of innovating successfully. The economical and political reasons for that are beyond the scope of this paper. In simple words, the ruling Party based its decisions on scientific arguments, but in fact science was isolated from the social life. And this was not a happy 'ivory tower' isolation, but a pressure that undermined the social role of science.

Soon after seizing power, the communist regime made deep reforms in the Bulgarian Academy of Sciences and in the University of Sofia, which was the biggest and most prestigious educational and research institution in Bulgaria at that time. Under the pretext of following the most advanced soviet examples, the University and the Academy were deprived of autonomy and reorganized. Nearly all prominent, independent, and reputed scientists were dismissed from educational and research activity. The formal and informal relations of Bulgarian science with European ones and with the other areas of social activity were broken. In this way, Bulgarian academic research was placed under state and party control and was surrounded by the typical for every totalitarian state 'iron curtain'. The most drastic and enduring results are:

— The relations of the academic research with the international scientific community and with society were built and supported on the base of centralized planning, organization, and control. To a great extent, these relations were artificial, and hence unproductive. Paradoxically, but in fact they were meant to isolate academic research, to reduce its social role.

For example in the 70s, the Politburo decided that no-one should be permitted to accept a personal invitation for specialization or teaching. It was up to administrative and party authorities to decide who was 'worthy' of an invitation.

The sets of relations with all cultural and economical spheres of activity in society were based on state-supported and state-controlled formal organizational mechanisms. So academic research was deprived of its basic role to make independent critical analyses of social processes and openly to try to influence public opinion and social values.

— Most of the sound scientific schools and traditions were destroyed. Instead, a profusion of purely ideological quasi-scientific disciplines emerged. Traditional research areas (in the first place in social sciences and humanities) were placed under strong ideological control.

— The academic research was fully budget-supported. Those 'greenhouse' conditions were envied by some western colleagues, but in fact they contributed to the strengthening of the 'iron curtain'.

As a result the influence of academic research upon society was very limited.

To these inherited problems, the current period of transition has added some new ones. These result from the very fast destruction of the 'iron curtain' and the transition of our society to market economical mechanisms.

In general the situation of academic research now could be defined as a 'situation of weightlessness', or as a deepening of crisis of relations, or as a process of further isolation. In the conditions of sharp economic crisis and international obligations, the state reduced drastically its financial support to science. On the other hand, private capital hardly exists and cannot compensate for this reduction. The state supported and controlled set of relations is dissolving. So the old ties are broken, but no new ones have been set up. Now academic research is ideologically free, but it is not only still incapable of playing its main roles in society—the problem is how to survive.

The Organization of Academic Research

I might say that the communist regime organized the academic research in accordance with the old Roman rule: 'divide et impera'.

As a first step, scientific research was separated from higher education. All research was concentrated in the Academy, which was transformed from a purely representative institution to an ever-expanding set of national scientific institutes. The Academy also took the responsibility for the third grade, Ph.D. qualification.

For a long time, the University and the Academy were strictly divided into sectors according to traditional disciplines. At the same time, the Academy was determined as a centre only for basic research and in this way it was isolated from applied and interdisciplinary research. Much later a number of academic institutes with a more applied and interdisciplinary orientation were set up.

As a result of all this, academic scientific community was torn apart. The discriminatory and ever-changing attitude of the state towards different subcommunities gave rise to still persisting conflicts and animosity among them.

Later, a number of attempts were made to establish organizational links between various parts of the very divided science. But all these attempts resulted abortive. One of the most ambitious projects was to integrate the University and the Academy, but it too was fruitless.

The reason was that all organizational connections were introduced by force, simply imitating integration, but were not in accordance with the real interests of scientists. The last parliament dominated by communists passed in the last days of its existence laws for full autonomy of the University and the

Academy. In this way, even the last loose connections between different parts of academic research vanished.

Now the financial restrictions required at least 20-25 per cent of the scientific personnel of the Academy to be dismissed. In these conditions, the Academy is acting in accordance with a strategy which I call 'the strategy of the lizard'. This animal when in a dangerous situation sometimes tears off its tail which later regenerates. The ruling bodies of the Academy, where as a result of traditional criteria for scientific careers the representatives of 'pure' science have predominance, began to liquidate or to dismiss institutes which were oriented to more applied and/or interdisciplinary research. The hope is that in more favourable conditions academic science will regenerate. But I think that its wholeness has been put into danger.

The research which remains in the Academy has very loose connections with the problems of the economical recovery of the country. This research is rather oriented towards the international scientific community. The Academy also reduces its capability to take part in international projects with more applied orientation and thus to gain additional financial support. I will not talk about the moral problems which arise from this drastic change of evaluation criteria for scientific work.

The Resources of Academic Research

One of the most difficult problems which academic scientific organizations face is how to preserve their resources. I will point out two aspects of this problem.

First, the most advanced scientific instrumentation is concentrated in institutes with more applied orientation. The dismissal of these institutes seriously reduces the technical resources of academic research.

Secondly, owing to financial restrictions a massive emigration of scientific personnel began. By the end of 1991, more than 7000 scientists left the country. This is more than on quarter of all Bulgarian scientists. With this classical 'brain-drain' a parallel process is observed which I call 'hand-drain'. A number of highly qualified engineers, technicians and other supporting scientific research personnel are leaving the country.

The National System of Science Policy

During the communist regime this system was closely connected with the ruling party which took all strategical decisions in the field of R&D. As a result of the political change the system which formatted and implemented the national science policy was destroyed. That is why one of the most important tasks of the Ministry of Education and Science is to set up a new system for science policy. In this connection:

(i) the Ministry is preparing a 'White Book' which will contain the strategy of the government in the fields of science and education,

(ii) a new law for science and education is prepared,

(iii) A National Council for Scientific Research and Technology, an Accreditation Committee, and various funds for scientific research will be established soon.

(iv) the Ministry had created a new research centre for science and education.

13

Current Organizational Problems in Hungarian Scientific Research

JOZSEF HERMAN

Member of the Hungarian Academy of Sciences, Former Director of the Research Institute for Linguistics, Budapest, Hungary

In Hungary, the organizational framework of scientific research—essentially a clear-cut binary system, with research being carried out partly in the universities and partly in research institutes without teaching functions of their own*—was essentially set up during the decades since World War II. It remained unchanged despite the deep political and social changes of 1989-90, and, although a clearly visible and sometimes energetic streamlining activity is under way, it will probably retain its fundamental pattern in the following years and perhaps even for some decades. This apparent immobility seems surprising in the given circumstances, when almost all other institutions of the country are undergoing an inevitable and profound remodelling. It has to be said, however, that this essential continuity is the result of a long, sometimes very

* In this paper, I concentrate on research *stricto sensu* and not on the whole R&D sector. Consequently, when speaking about research institutes, I refer to the institutes and centres of the Academy, and not to industrial research units; besides, the problems concerning the latter are very much outside my personal competence.

passionate, discussion within the research community, as well as between the universities, the Academy of Sciences, and representatives of the Government, and seems to correspond to a majority opinion inside all groups concerned. We should add that the formal continuity of the institutional pattern does not exclude essential modifications in the life and internal structures of the institutions, re-examination of the relations between the Academy and the universities, a large-scale transformation of the funding system, and so forth. Given all this, a closer look at the Hungarian case might be of interest to our colleagues from other European countries.

Let us begin with a very rough outline of the present organizational situation.

The research network of the Hungarian Academy of Sciences is composed of 36 research institutes (without taking into account at this point a number of small research units attached to university departments, but financed by the Academy). The research institutes (21 in the field of natural sciences and 15 in social sciences and the humanities) cover all the essential fields of 'pure' knowledge (physics, chemistry, mathematics, biology, geography, etc. as well as sociology, linguistics, economics, ethnology, etc.) but also some fields of applied research (*e.g.* computer science, technological chemistry); in the majority of so-called applied disciplines, however (e.g. clinical medicine, engineering), the bulk of research activities are confined to the framework of universities and other higher education institutions. On the other hand, in some branches of the humanities (foreign languages and literatures, classical philology, most fields of oriental studies), with some personal rather than institutional exceptions, all research work is pursued in the universities.

It has to be underlined—given the fact that, on the basis of superficial analogies with other countries, different views are sometimes expressed, especially abroad—that except for some highly unfortunate trends or rather slogans in the early fifties, research was never banned from Hungarian Universities, and since the late fifties and early sixties, it was unimaginable for a lecturer or professor in an established academic field of knowledge to be accepted by a faculty and appointed by the government without the credit and concrete proof of substantial personal research activity; this is equally true as far as the fields partly or totally covered by research institutes are concerned.

Turning to some indications on the size and structures of the two main institutional sectors: at the end of 1990, the research institutes of the Academy had a staff of about 7000 persons, with about 2700 qualified research workers inside these groups. If the number of research personnel is calculated on the estimated working time actually spent on research, universities present about double this number. It has to be taken into consideration, however, that research personnel in universities work in relatively very small research units, mostly departments or autonomous chairs, and, consequently the number of research workers and of research projects per unit is 8 or even 10 times higher in the research centres of the Academy than in the universities. This means that conditions for team work, for complex projects necessitating elaborate organization as well as concentration of funding, of laboratory resources and so on, are much more favourable in the research institutes than the universities. Current expenditure actually spent on research in the two sectors being roughly comparable, the concentration per capita of financial means is significantly more favourable in the institutes of the Academy, and the concentration per unit even more so.

It is difficult to compare the outputs of the two sectors. As is natural in the case of fragmented, largely individual, research work, global publication numbers as well as their per capita incidence in the university sector are high, somewhat higher in most fields than the levels presented by the research institutes.

On the other hand, some strongly quality-sensitive indicators seem to point to a clear advantage of the latter: the per capita incidence of the number of papers written and published in foreign languages, of articles published abroad by leading international periodicals, of patents granted abroad, of international travel, congress participations and the like is two or even three times higher in the research institutes than in the universities.

It should be added that even in those remote years when no body really questioned the separate existence of these two subsystems of research, real separation of the two—as is natural and unavoidable in a small country like Hungary—was much less profound than it might seem: a majority of leading researchers of the academy network—were—and still are—teaching in universities or other higher education institutions as part-time professors, invited scholars, and so on, whereas a number of university professors act as advisers or even part-time heads of research groups in academy institutions. For years now, there have been jointly founded and supervised units, and their number is increasing.

The system as described was never considered to be without its problems. Attempts at its re-evaluation, reform or even radical restructuring—by integrating in some way the research institutes into the universities—had been planned since the early eighties, well before the deep political changes of 1989-90. It is only natural that in the last two years, everyone—those against as well as those in favour of the actual research organization—considered that the time had come to reach some decision on the issue. It seems that, after years of discussion, a sort of solution, a sort of state of equilibrium, is now at hand, so that we can resume here the main arguments of the debate and its results.

I should first mention with the intention of passing over it quickly rather than dwelling on it, a rather superficial political argument, never endorsed by any responsible political force or body, but publicized more than once in the media and some public meetings: the system of the research network subordinated to the Academy of Sciences was created—so it was said—essentially around 1950. It is the copy of a 'Stalinist' model and has to be abolished as such. This reasoning met with a very dispassionate answer: it is true that in creating a partly new research network the authorities of the period followed broadly the nearest model to hand which was the Soviet one; but, as similar models exist even in countries which never belonged to the so-called 'socialist' world and as the necessity, in itself, of full time research institutions is not really questioned, the organizational pattern has to be evaluated on its own merits. However, if political considerations were decisive, it would be possible to cite some which are rather favourable to this kind of binary system. Since their foundation and as early as the late fifties, the research institutes of the Academy became, at least in their majority, the refuge for dozens or even hundreds of people whose presence, given their hostility or open scepticism towards the regime, was not tolerated in the politically closely controlled higher education institutions. Moreover, under the umbrella of the Academy, always reluctant to accept any 'ideological' approach to science, the institutes enjoyed a notable intellectual freedom and were able to become centres of innovative thinking and of introduction of 'western' trends not only for Hungary, but in some cases for the whole Soviet-dominated part of the world.

Formulated as the problem of rational and economical governance, however, the problem appeared much more serious and substantial. These institutes represent a considerable human research potential, offer relatively well developed facilities, laboratories, libraries, and a wide variety of international links. They are also involved, some with widely recognized results, in complex and important research projects. Consequently, they can be considered as sizable parts of the nation's cultural and even material wealth, their simple liquidation, for responsible politicians and other decision-makers, was never a possibility to be considered. As regards their simple integration into the universities, it soon appeared on the whole, and except for the minor research groups, as unrealistic: no Hungarian university—least of all the most concerned, the University of Budapest, with its own tremendous problems and ongoing internal reforms—is organizationally, economically, or even psychologically prepared to take over the immense burden and responsibility of such an institutional network.

The solution of creating a new administrative umbrella—probably under the form of a Ministry of Higher Education and Research, or even a Ministry of Research—was proposed by some and has still influential supporters. It seems, however, that this solution, although adopted in some European countries, cannot be considered in the Hungarian setting as bringing about administrative and bureaucratic simplification, cost-reduction and an increase of professional competence: some fear that with all the inevitable drawbacks of large-scale reorganizations, such a step could easily be counterproductive in all these fields.

It seems that for the time being, at least in the medium term, the solution to keep the research institutes under the umbrella of the Academy does not have convincing alternatives. The Academy, as a scientific body, can be held responsible for a continuous, professional evaluation of the work carried out in its institutes; with its light administrative secretariat, it can uphold the necessary minimum financial and legal control whilst granting a maximal, non-bureaucratic self-governance to the institutes themselves; finally being a non-political organization, without governmental subordination and responsibilities, it can grant to the research centres complete intellectual and scientific freedom. There are, naturally, problems implied in this solution; let us examine some of them.

— The problem of duplication: advocates of a unitary structure, an exclusively university-based research system, often underline the essentially economical dangers of parallel and allegedly superfluous work carried out on similar problems in similar disciplines—a danger that could and should be avoided through the installation of a monolithic, 'pyramidal' system where research tasks in a given discipline are concentrated in unique institutions.

This seems to most of us an essentially outsider's view. In reality, concentration of facilities or heavy laboratory equipment is a reasonable way to facilitate some specific, large-scale and expensive research, and concentration should be encouraged only where such an effort is needed. But, in scientific competition in most fields, mainly theoretical, emulation of different schools of thought seems to be the best way to create or maintain a dynamic and creative scientific life. In our experience, the current binary system permits such a healthy competitiveness within the research community, whilst still leaving open the door to any type of co-operation between different, even competing, institutions, whatever their institutional affiliation.

— The problem of co-operation between the subsystems. I mention it simply because I have already raised the issue. This seems to be the prerequisite for economical, cost-effective work: if the existence of different schools and competition between different research units are a necessary part of a healthy scientific life, this should not imply a lack of co-operation in the sharing of costly equipment, library facilities, training, international contacts, etc. Any means of expediting the end of the already interminable, lengthy discussion on research structure will, in the near future, certainly facilitate the development of effective and new co-operative links between Academy-based institutions and universities. Besides, the ongoing gradual but relatively rapid transition—which I can but mention in this context—from an essentially 'annual institutional budget' type research funding system towards one mainly based on project-funding through task-oriented grants, should sooner or later eliminate pre-established advantages and disadvantages among institutions of different types and organizational affiliations, thus creating the necessary conditions and an atmosphere favourable to normal inter-institutional co-operation.

At present, the Hungarian Academy of Sciences, with the help of a considerable number of specialists coming from other organizational environments, is working on a detailed, critical, thorough evaluation of the achievements and the situation of its research institutes. This process, to be pursued through much of the year, will certainly bring to light a large number of hidden results and hidden deficiencies, and will necessitate the reshaping of some institutes, perhaps the re-shaping of the institutional network itself inside the Academy.

It can be hoped, however, that this evaluation, whose results will be made available not only to the scientific community but also to government agencies and public opinion, will essentially strengthen, through the units attached to the Academy, the whole of the research system in Hungary.

14

Organization of Science and Technology in the Ex-Yugoslav Republics*

MIRA LENARDIC

Senior Research Fellow, Institute of Economics, University of Zagreb, Croatia

Introduction

The question of what one nation can learn from another especially when it seeks to change, radically change, its whole system, has suddenly become very important as East European countries seek to create new economic, legal, and political orders. We can put the same question to the Ex-Yogoslav republics, which in the rush to democracy and the market economy are now in the midst of historic transformation.

Having replaced authoritarian one-party regime with pluralistic democracy, the ex-Yugoslav republics are intent on moving rapidly to develop major elements for market economy (reprivatization, restructuring of economy, re-establishing a labour market, financial market, etc.). In this sense, there is also the need for major changes in the area of science and technology.

* The former Yugoslavia was a federation of six independent republics and two autonomous provinces. In this article, only the more developed republics will be analyzed: Croatia, Slovenia, and Serbia.

Organization for Science and Technology

To speak about the organizational structure of S&T in the ex-Yugoslav republics means, first of all, to point out the specific relationships of republics to each other and to the ex-Federal authorities (see Figure 1). Namely, according to the Ex–Yugoslav constitution, scientific and technological development was the responsibility of the individual republics, so that the organization of S&T was decentralized.

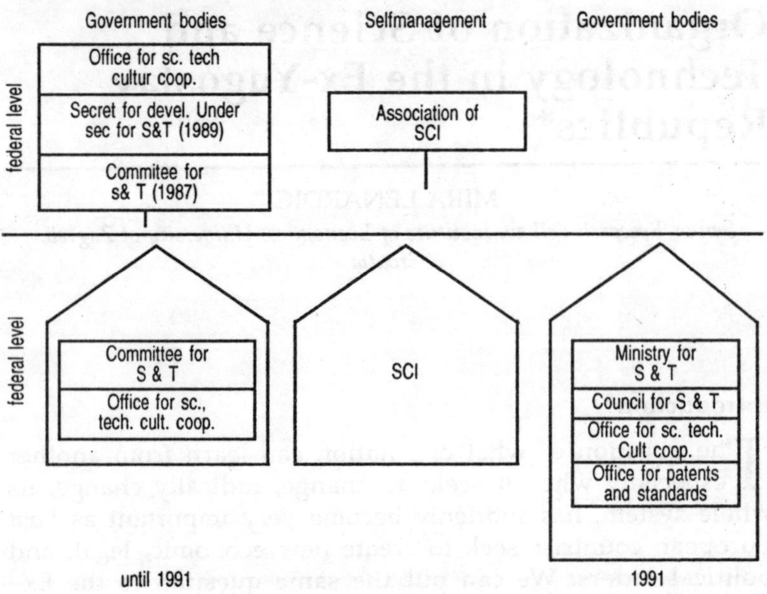

Figure 1. Relationship between republics and federal authorities in S&T (Ex–Yugoslavia).

In this sense, a unique feature of the ex-Yugoslav system was the Self-management Communities of Interest for science (SCI) as the basic and major institutional form responsible for the realization of local, regional, and republic S&T policy (from 1975). Throughout the country as a whole, there were eight SCIs—in each republic/province. These were responsible for determining the objectives and priorities in research and development, formulating the methodology of directing, selecting and evaluating projects (*ex–ante, ex–post*), resource allocation, and co-ordination of research carried out by various research organizations (independent institutes, universities, research and development in industry). The republics' organization system of SCIs, especially their financing system, created a very closed structure, so that no inter-republic exchange or researcher mobility existed at all. Among these eight SCI, communication was only possible through the federal Association of Self-management Communities of Interest for science.

At the same time, on the federal level there was no federal government institution responsible for science and technology, or federal research institutions, nor any financial support for R&D. The major role of the Ex-Yugoslav federal government in science and technology was to control international co-operation. As late as 1987, the federal government adopted its first official policy on science and technology and established a federal committee for science and technology and a federal fund for the promotion of technological development.* Meanwhile one of its functions was to link the republican committees for science and technology.

It is evident that one peculiarity of the Ex-Yugoslav organization system in S&T was the existence on the republic level of parallel organizational forms that also dealt with S&T—republic committees for S&T. As republic government bodies, they had broad authority to influence republic science and technology policy, but no responsibility for the consequences of their decision.

The federal committee structure was abolished in 1989 and replaced by an Undersecretariat for science and technology, so from that period as a result the federal system for science and technology consisted of three major organizations:

(i) the Undersecretariat for science and technology which had operational programme responsibilities for the federal science and technology fund,

(ii) the federal Association of Self-management Communities of Interest for science which linked the republics' SCIs,

---

* The federal fund for the promotion of technological development had an annual budget of approximately US$ 100 million (1990).

(iii) the office for scientific, technological, and cultural co-operation, as an independent office that dealt with international co-operation and also linked offices at republic level.

It is obvious that until 1990 the science and technology system in each republic, while independent, followed nearly the same pattern. With the break-up of the Federation and the onset of transition to a market economy, each republic was changing its S&T organization system. This process of change varies from republic to republic, but the main direction of adjustment was towards present trends influencing the development of the scientific and technological system in the world (Europe). For example, after 15 years, the self-management system in Croatia has been replaced by the Ministry for Science and Technology as the responsible governmental body for S&T policy. This Ministry and its Council are the supreme representative and legislative organ which, through the law passed in October 1990, plans the scientific and technological development in the Republic of Croatia. At the same time, this is augmented with the newly established (presently only two people) Science and Technology Council in the office of the president. Almost the same changes are in progress in all Ex-Yugoslav republics (Serbia, Slovenia, Bosnia-Hercegovina).

The ministries for science and technology in each republic are responsible for policy formulation and implementation, and advised from a council of science and technology. Some of them, under the new ministerial system, support research and development through two major sources: (i) scientific research fund, (ii) fund for the stimulation of technological development (Croatia, Serbia until 1992), which were autonomous funds as, for example, in Serbia, or as a budget item in Croatia.

In an effort to create a new system of S&T, the republics' ministries of S&T have:

— changed the previous support system (institutional grant with a system of project grants based on peer review—Croatia, Serbia, Slovenia),

— together with the ministry for education re-created a high education system (Croatia),

— established a closer relationship between universities and research institutes (Slovenia, Serbia),

— created a well-trained new generation of scientists (Croatia, 1600 young researchers),

— reduced the isolation of researchers from industry (Slovenia, 2000 young researchers),

— established bureaux of standards and metrology, patent offices (Slovenia, Croatia), etc.

Unfortunately, many of these transformations have been halted or delayed by the war, and the whole community is making efforts for survival in temporary but very difficult economic and political conditions.

Some Issues of National S&T System in Transition

Ex-Yugoslav Republics are still unable to become part of the global economy. Only 20-25 per cent of Yugoslav export value to European markets is of a satisfactory performance which is the basic prerequisite for partnership in the global economy (Federal Secretariat of Development, 1990, p. 2).

Over the last decade, the Ex-Yugoslav republics have bought increasingly less technical know-how from other countries, not a sign of their technological independence, but rather of their isolation from technological trends and world economy. Some authors estimate the development lag between first discovery of medical experiments and their application in Croatia to be 10.2 years on average (For more details, see Buneta *et al.*, 1991). The ratio domestic reported to registered patents (2:1) illustrates a poor quality of domestic patent production. The bulk of manufacturers base their market position on the price-competition with standard product quality. Most have no explicit export strategy as a result of inadequately developed activities, such as market research, product design, financial and technical services. These are only a few characteristic parameters that illustrate the weaknesses of the ex-Yugoslav economy and its S&T.

As regards the national S&T system, we can say that it is structurally unco-ordinated and non-integrated. Nevertheless the accomplishments in the R&D system in ex–Yugoslav republics

Table 1. The National R&D Effort, Selected Data, 1989 (Percentages).

	CRO	*SL*	*SR**
GERD as %GNP**	1.02	1.75	0.88
Ann. GERD growth Rate ('81-89)	6.0	5.3	0.6
S/E engaged in R&D (YU=100)	27.9	16.6	39.1
S/E per 10,000 population	20.3	29.0	13.5
Ann. S/E growth rate ('81-89)	5.2	3.1	4.0
R&D Organizations (YU = 100)	19.0	21.6	36.7
Research Organizations	49.1	30.9	49.4
R&D Units	12.3	53.1	10.3
University	38.6	16.0	40.3
GERD by source			
— industry	56.7	50.5	50.9
— public***	30.4	39.6	27.4
— other****	12.9	9.6	21.7
GERD by performer			
— industry	na	na	na
— government	na	na	na
— university	23.7	18.0	15.0
— non-profit organizations	na	na	na
GERD by scientific field			
— natural sc., mathematics	9.3	18.1	7.6
— technical science	60.7	59.7	64.1
— medical science	14.3	6.4	8.8
— biotechnology	7.5	4.9	13.5
— social science	6.5	8.5	4.5
— humanities	1.8	2.4	1.5

* Included provincial (Vojvodina, Kosovo)

** Only civil R&D

*** Included SCI of science, SCI of education, and other SCI

**** Included sources: Social services, Foreign, Patents and Licences, and other.

Source: Republics Statistical Bulletin. Scientific-Technological and Development Organizations (Croatia, Slovenia, Serbia).

are significant, especially for a small country with a lower GNP per capita. Selected data on the national R&D efforts in Croatia, Slovenia, and Serbia (see Table 1) reveal the present R&D development situation in these ex-Yugoslav republics. A large part of these R&D accomplishments remain isolated, non-integrated with the economy.

The beginning of the transition to the market economy (1990), more spontaneous than co-ordinated, produced many changes during the adjustment throughout the whole economy (bankruptcy, unemployment, social problems, etc.), with dramatic erosions of R&D capacities in general, and, in particular in industry. The research community was divided by economy: on the one side universities and independent institutes, and industrial R&D and industry on the other. Much industrial R&D is faced with imminent collapse (bankruptcy, brain-drain) or must aim to develop a new management strategy.* The universities and independent institutes as the bulk of the Yugoslav R&D system are mostly oriented towards basic research rather than applied R&D which relies on useful results. Such orientation is enhanced by the official science-push (big science) policy which, according to the current budgeting system, operates to ensure the survival of all researchers engaged in R&D ('salary budget'). In this situation, there is no need to seek contact with industry. Even the few relationships which existed before between industry and research community have now been broken off. At the same time, non-market and non-competition-oriented industry as well as a poor micro-climate for technological development expressed little demand for R&D services. So, relations between industry and research community are frail and there is apathy on both sides. Consequently, an overextended basic research establishment has developed, achieving world-class research quality, but lacking the means to

* For example, the industrial R&D institutes placed in large companies such as 'Rade Koncar' in Zagreb, once employed over 650 scientists and engineers, but because of the new market-oriented transformation today employ only 85 scientists/engineers. The independent institute 'Mihajlo Pupin' in Belgrade faced with losing the Yugoslav army as the largest support source, also made drastic large staff cuts.

provide a relatively sophisticated product design or engineering service.

The level of investment in R&D is relatively low (about 1 per cent GNP) and at the same time ineffective and expensive.* Owing to the relatively low level of appreciation of S&T, public financial support is generally low too (25-26 per cent of total R&D expenditure), and even that investment, *e.g.* in Croatia, is 5 per cent of the total government budget (1991). One principal problem is poorly defined procedure for managing research, and lack of strong research priorities. This problem, whose roots lie in the earlier system, brings out the fact that research funding is conducted essentially on the basis of personal contacts and without real project selection. In that sense, the evaluation (*ex–ante, ex–post*) is very poor, without international impact or high quality criteria.

The next crucial issues of Ex-Yugoslav S&T development in transition are clearly human resources and the education system. Ex-Yugoslav universities provide excellent undergraduate training in science and engineering, but lean towards teaching with little research and requisite equipment. They also have inflexible structures; narrowly defined departments; overlong study courses; and rigid curricula. Post-graduate education (masters/doctorates) is organized as part of the traditional academic career (scientific apprenticeship), without research training or formal courses for graduates to broaden or extend their knowledge.

The quantitative dimension of scientists and engineers engaged in R&D is almost satisfactory,** but their qualitative supply is structurally inadequate. In that sense, the most important component is the shortage of specific research skills

* Yogsolavia has invested US$ 423,500 per researcher to produce one scientific paper in SCI. For Austria, Hungary, Portugal, and Turkey this figure is US$ 184,016-358,850. Only Czechoslovakia and Bulgaria show higher levels (over US$ 500,000). Estimated R&D figures per researcher for OECD countries are US$ 112,000 (1983). (Buneta *et al.*, 1991 and OCED, 1989.)

** Annual average S/E growth rate in Ex–Yogsolav R&D was 4.4 per cent (1981-89), fairly high compared to some OECD countries.

(*e.g.* software specialists; materials scientists; electronics and mechanical engineers; management technology specialists; business management specialists; etc.) as well as knowledge and experience adequate for competitive economy. In the long-term, the age structure of scientists and engineers will also represent the second qualitative limitation factor.* Researchers' mobility is very low. Where it exists, it is one way: from industry to university or independent institute.

The political crises together with the war have caused a strengthening of the role of the republic governments. Many efforts made at the beginning of transition to the market-economy have now ceased. The governments are trying to create some basic conditions for survival, and at the same time they are creating new individual development strategies, *e.g.* general economic development plan (Slovenia, Croatia) or programme of technological development (Serbia).

Some Recommendations for the Future

At the moment it is impossible to forget the war in Croatia and Bosnia-Hercegovina, with its negative long-term effects (ruined R&D institutions and equipment, interrupted ongoing research activities, accelerate brain-drain, etc.) which has put some new priorities in currently reviewing R&D system in Ex-Yugoslav republics (especially in Croatia and Bosnia-Hercegovina) as well as in the achievement of desired objectives. Nevertheless, it is obvious that the level of structural integration and quality of the national S&T system will have a major influence on the long-term success of the Ex-Yugoslav republics as effective participants in the international market.

In that sense, the priorities are:

(i) To adopt present trends influencing the development of scientific and technological system in the world as a general strategic approach in the domestic S&T

* For Example, the age structure of scientists and engineers engaged in R&D in Croatia (1990) was as follows:

age				
.. – 29	7.7%		40 – 49	30.9%
30 – 34	11.5%		50 – 49	21.1%
35 – 39	13.5%		60 – ..	15.3%

policy, and to exploit this transformed domestic S&T policy as a key element in national long-term development strategies of each republic.

(ii) To ensure co-ordination and integration of the system and institutions. This requires a strengthening of the governmental role to be able to survive the difficult period ahead and control the transition period.

(iii) To strengthen two-way links between industry and university giving a more effective interaction (contacts and co-ordination with industry in the form of science and technology parks, industrial representation on university board and *vice versa*, consulting, jointly financed research institutes and laboratories, etc.). Such co-operation should be government-supported.

(iv) To set research priorities for academic research and to create a mechanism for support of scientific and technological development into programmes covering the areas of: strategic priorities; promotion of the diffusion of selected technologies; promotion of intermediate institutions in technological development; etc.

(v) To upgrade qualified manpower and training of S&T personnel through programmes that respond more directly to the specific needs of industry, and encourage the mobility of researchers (horizontal and vertical) as an important factor in the career development of researchers (*e.g.* special financed support for 'mobility programmes' and 'young researchers').

(vi) To reinforce the relationship between teaching and research by bringing the independent institutes and faculties together, so that the 'best brains' are involved in both. At the same time, to promote organization of National Research Council or Councils as central bodies in the organization of national research.

(vii) To define the procedure for funding and managing research, as well as establish strong evaluation mechanisms: develop an ability to evaluate critically the results of national investments in industry and at university, with less bureaucracy (involvement of international experts and international education criteria).

(viii) Reigonal development as a source of growth and its structural adjustment, especially in small countries, plays an important role in the transition processes. In this restructuring, foreign experience and technical assistance are needed.

(ix) To develop, on the basis of international standards and definition, an extensive S&T data base, providing international comparison and compatibility.

(x) Intensifying international co-operation (bilateral, multilateral).

REFERENCES

Buneta, Z., Lackovic, Z. and Cecuk, L.J., 1991. Pokazatelji tehnologijskog razvitka primijenjeni na medicinu. In Z. Lackovic, L.J. Cecuk and Z. Buneta (eds), *Rezultati Empirijskih Istrazivanja Biomedicinskih Znanosti u Hrvatskoj i Jugoslaviji*. Medicinska Naklada, Zagreb.

Federal Secretariat of Development, Belgrade, 1990 (December). *Basic Principles of the Scientific and Technological Policy of Yugoslavia*, Proposal.

Lenardic, M., 1991. Reform of the science management system of Yugoslavia: a case study of the Republic of Croatia. Presented at Workshop *Eastern and Western Lessons for S&T*. Int. Conf. *Hungary in the World*, Budapest.

Lenardic, M., 1992. *Scientific Activity in the Republic of Croatia from 1991*. Ekonomski Pregled, Zagreb. To be published.

OECD, 1989. *Science and Technology Indicators*, Report No. 3, OECD, Paris.

OECD, 1991. *Higher Education and Employment: The Changing Relationship—Recent Developments in Continuing Professional Education*, Country *Report, OECD, Paris.*

Radosevic, S., 1992. Scientific-technological system in transition and strategic alternatives for technological development in the Republic of Croatia, Zagreb. Private communication.

Yugoslav Survey, 1991. *Scientific Technological Policy* 1980-90, Survey No. 3, Belgrade.

YU-TEP, 1991. *Lessons of the findings of the Technology-Economy Programme for the Scientific and Technological Policies in Yugoslavia*. Summary report, YU-TEP Seminar, Brioni.

15

Restructuring Science and Technologies in Czechoslovakia

VLADISLAV HANCIL

Vice-President, Czechoslovak Academy of Sciences, Prague, Czechoslovakia

This timely meeting aims to foster positive changes in the support structures for science and technology in East European countries, in our case Czechoslovakia. Its outcome can influence the finalizing discussions on our new science and technology law in the Czech Republic. At the same time, the Federal Parliament is developing a new law on the learned societies.

The new Czech Academy of Sciences which replaces the old Czechoslovak Academy of Sciences has a similar structure to the German Max Planck Gesellschaft. It also adopts the principle of subsidizing the Czechoslovak universities.

The inherited structure of science and technologies in Czechoslovaki differs significantly from systems in working democracies. The main criticism is therefore directed at the principal differences:

— existence of the Academies, the learned societies, which also control the research institutes system,

— absence of industry-controlled high-quality market-oriented research,

— lack of co-operation between the universities and other research institutions,

— lack of high-quality research in many of the universities,

— absence of targeted financing in research,

— lack of mission-oriented programmes,

— absence of any peer-review assessment,

— lack of efficient support to technology transfer.

Many of these problems arise from the basic aims of the former totalitarian system. The 'old structure' had kept its power. It hence also followed that very often autonomous scientists, free human beings, could influence young people at the universities. And this meant a total separation of science from the universities.

The communist party kept every part of the people's lives under close observation, and consequently it created huge central offices for detailed control of science and the development of technologies: the State Commission for Science and Technologies, the State Planning Commission. Their old bureaucracy still acts as a block to successful negotiation owing to the fact that after the collapse of their former institutions they spread out into a vast array of new offices and are often more (in!)efficient than before.

We have all absorbed many negative aspects from this system and we still differ from people in western democracies in many respects. George Orwell describes one dangerous and common feature—generalized nationalism—through three concepts, compulsion, instability, and ignoring of the facts. We have suffered from all three by enduring purges, and it does not appear easy to accept a new system now.

It seems that we could apply measures to enable the existing system of science and technologies to find proper controls and balances by creating suitable driving forces. In the process, we should take into account current influation. In the field of science and technology we should not spend too much energy of mediocre scientists. The pressure from the Ministry of Finance almost guarantees that we will only have the same

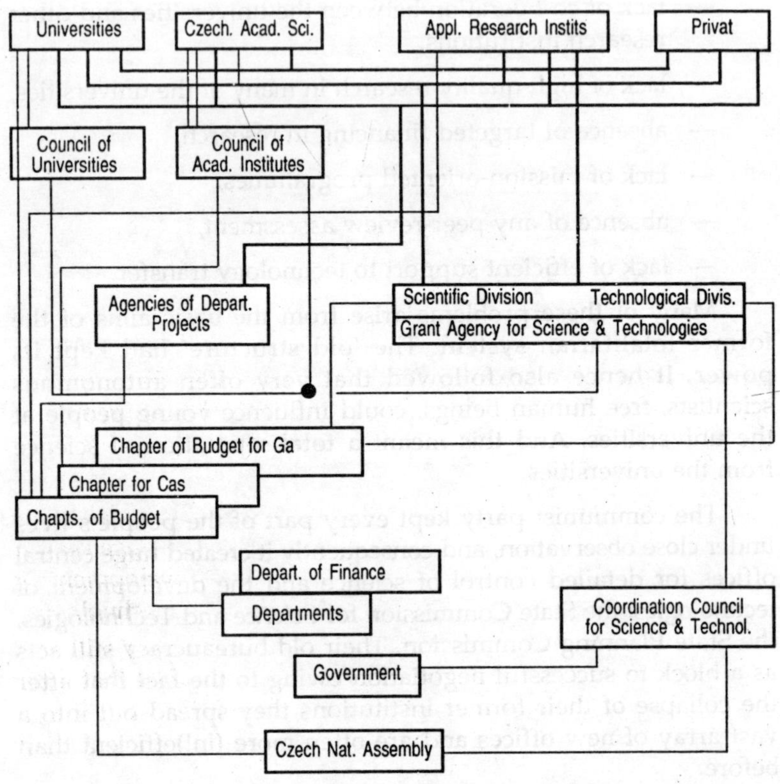

Figure 1. Financial support for science and technologies, proposed law by the Czech National Assembly on Science and Technologies.

Legend:

——— information flow, administration link;

▬▬▬ application of project, financing of grants—this financing is initialized by the application for grants;

═══ financing of projects in mission-oriented programmes of GA—this financing is initialized by GA, which calls for projects;

. . . . . institutional financing ensures the basic operations of the scientific institution, and is affected by success in grant competition in recent years;

▬▭▬ financing of projects in mission-oriented programmes.

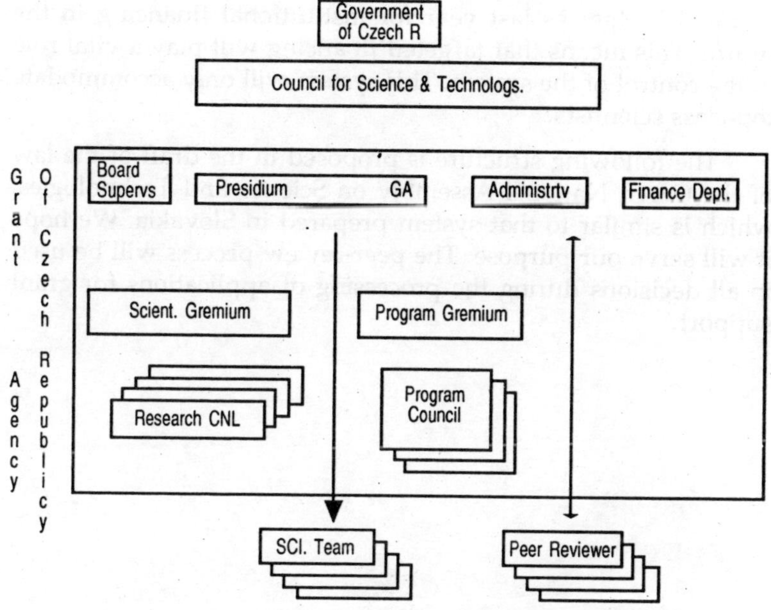

Figure 2. Scheme of the supposed grant agency of the Government of the Czech Republic.

Legend: Presidium GA According to the law, this has one president and four vice-president. The vice-presidents are responsible for: scientific section; priority programme section; international relations; finance. The presidium determines the individual research council portion of the budget to be distributed with high priority to joint programmes. These programmes will initiate co-operation of existing institutions and help to overcome old activation barriers.

Administrative information centre of GA and of the Council for S&T.

Finance Department, Science Gremium like NSF Strategic PRG Gremium co-ordinates activity of individual programme councils.

Research Councils expected 10 research councils; mathematics and physics; technical sciences and informatics; Earth and Universe sciences; chemical sciences; biology; medicine; environment and ecology; agriculture; social sciences and economical sciences; humanies, historical and philogical sciences.

Strategic Programme Council 7 proposed councils: informatics and telecommunications; production technologies and material sciences; agricultural and food technologies; environment and energetics; health protection; social problems education.

nominal budget as last year for institutional financing in the future. This means that targeted financing will play a vital role in the control of the system. This system will only accommodate top-class scientists.

The following structure is proposed in the draft of the law of the Czech National Assembly on Science and Technologies, which is similar to that system prepared in Slovakia. We hope it will serve our purpose. The peer-review process will be used in all decisions during the processing of applications for grant support.

16

Creation of New Organizational Structures of Science and Technology Co-ordination in the Slovak Republic

STEFAN BEDERKA

Director of Science and Technology Development Co-ordination, Ministry of Education, Youth and Sports of the Slovak Republic, Bratislava, Czechoslovakia

Introduction

The Slovak Republic is a component of the Czech and Slovak Federal Republic. It has about 5.3 million inhabitants (one-third of the total number of inhabitants of the CSFR), its own national government and its own legislative body, the Slovak National Council. The control of education, science, and technology is vested in the capacity of the individual republics, *i.e.* the individual Czech and Slovak Republics.

The majority of the higher educational institutions and research and development institutes of the Slovak Republic were established during the last 50 years. This development under conditions of a planned economy and a totalitarian political system was characterized by the following features:

— extensive development,

— direct intervention of the state political power in the research content, structure, and staffing of institutions,

— subordination to the ruling ideology of research, mainly humanitarian, often by a rough prescription of research results in this area.

Under these conditions, the following structure of research and development organization in the Slovak Republic was created (the situation in the year 1991):

The Slovak Academy of Sciences: an independent institution, authorized by an Act of 1963 to co-ordinate basic research. Basic research is performed predominantly at institutes of the Slovak Academy of Sciences with nearly 5000 workers and accounting for 31 per cent of the state budget allocations of the Slovak Republic for science and technology.

The Higher Education Institutions: the major part of their research activity is basic research. The 40 faculties of 13 universities employ 7500 teachers participating formally with 25 per cent of their activity on research programmes and 2500 research workers. These institutions draw 14 per cent of the state budget allocation of the Slovak Republic for science and technology. Applied research at higher education institutions is pursued on the basis of financial contracts. At present applied research at higher education institutions is stagnating because of enterprise insolvency.

The Research and Development Base in the Public and Economic Sector: pursues basic research, applied research, and develpment in the direct link-up with economy, industry, agriculture, health service, forestry, and other branches. The public and economic sector draw 35 per cent and 20 per cent, respectively of the state budget allocation of the Slovak Republic for science and technology. Nearly 40,000 workers are employed in 85 institutes in these sectors.

Each of these above components of research and development was financed from the state resources under its own budget-heading for science and technology. In this way, obstacles to co-operation of these subjects in the area of science and technology arose and still persist. This isolationism, accompanied by the financially disadvantaged university research, caused the fall in level of basic research at the universities.

Conditions for removal of these obstacles were created only when one central body of the state executive, for the time being the Ministry of Education, Youth and Sports, was authorized to co-ordinate research development activity.

In the area of basic research, where mainly the higher education institutions and the Slovak Academy of Sciences participate, the process of objectivization and evaluation of its content and results began during the last year by establishment and activities of the grant agencies for science and technology, covering the whole Slovak Republic. On their basis, a grant agency for science with 14 commissions with inter-scope capacity was established at the end of last year (1991). Its commissions evaluate the level, orientation, and results of science projects. Analogously, the grant agency for technology with 20 commissions was established to evaluate science and technology projects and their results. For the time being, both agencies are working as if with the approved situation, which will have legal status only after approval of the Fund for Science and Technology. This Fund can be created after the passing of the Act on Organization and Support of Science and Technology. (The organizing scheme of the State Fund for Science and Technology, as well as the organizing schemes of both grant agencies, are presented at the end of this paper.)

This is considered to be the first step towards a closer link-up of these two areas, where a considerable science and technology potential is now building up.

Legislative

The following acts should be basic regulations of relations in the area of science and technology bases:

— the Act on Organization and Support of Science and Technology: this is currently being debated by the Slovak National Council,

— amendment of the Higher Education Act,

— amendment of the Labour Code,

— Act on Taxation.

The central idea of the Act on Organization and Support of Science and Technology is the establishment of one central body of state executive with capacities in the area of science and technology. With the participation of elected representatives of the science and technology community, this body will observe, analyse and evaluate the state and level of science and technology. In this way, conditions for development of science and technology, in line and proportion with the tasks and goals of societal, economical and general development, will be created. This solution allows the nurturing of conditions for closer linking of higher education institutions with the institutes of the Slovak Academy of Sciences and with other research and development institutions by the launching of projects, student education, and postgraduate/doctoral studies. It remains the task of the future government to decide which body will be authorized for capacities in this area. However, it is suggested that the Ministry of Higher Education, Science and Technology of the Slovak Republic be established.

A new organizational structure of science and technology in the Slovak Republic is being established on the basis of information on successfully operating mechanisms in this field. We highly appreciate your interest and helpful co-operation in our endeavour to transform our organizational structure of science, technology, education, and economy, in order to come in line with other developed European countries.

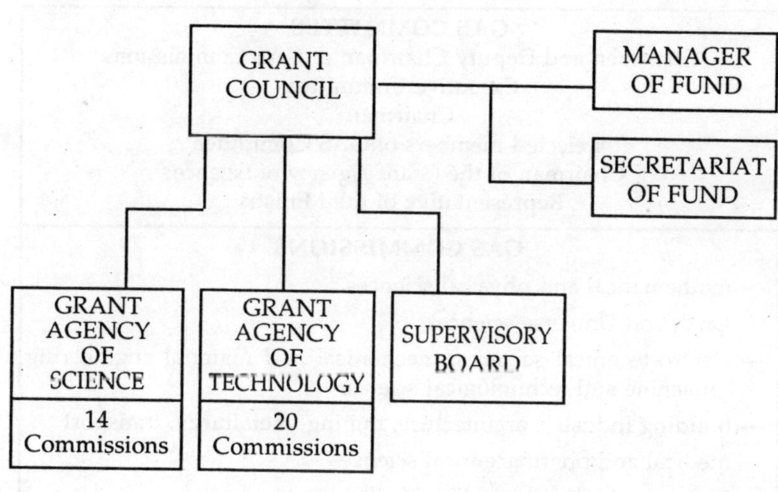

Figure 1. State Fund for Science and Technology (organizing scheme).

Table 1. Ministry of Education, Youth and Sports of the Slovak Republic, Science and Technology Division: Grant Agency of Science (GAS).

GAS COMMITTEE
Chairmen and Deputy Chairman of GAS Commissions Executive Committee: Chairman 4 elected members of GAS Committee Chairman of the Grant Agency of Science Representative of the Ministry
GAS COMMISSIONS
— mathematical and physical sciences — Earth and Universe sciences — electro-technical sciences, mechanical and material engineering, machine and technological science — building industry, architecture, mining, metallurgy, transport — medical and pharmaceutical sciences — molecular biology, genetics, biochemistry — biological and ecological sciences — agriculture, forestry and veterinary sciences — chemical and chemical-technological sciences — social sciences — human sciences — historical sciences — fine-art history, aesthetics, linguistics — economics, law

Table 2. Ministry of Education, Youth and Sports of the Slovak Republic, Science and Technology Division : Grant Agency of Technology (GAT).

GAT COMMITTEE Chairman of GAT Commissions Executive Committee: Chairman 4 elected members of GAT Committee Chairman of the Grant Agency of Technology Representative of the Ministry
GAT COMMISSIONS
— low-tonnage chemistry and chemistry of new materials
— petrochemistry, organic/inorganic chemistry
— health service
— pharmaceutical production
— agricultural production
— food production
— forestry and complex wood processing
— management of water supplied
— light and consumer industries
— mechanical engineering, new technologies
— metallury and material engineering
— electrical engineering, electronics
— transport
— energetics
— building industry, architecture
— information science
— geology
— commerce, travel, services
— security of work
— environmental protection

17

Science and Research in Czech Universities

JAROSLAV DROBNIK

Professor, University Council of the Czeh Republic, Prague, Czechoslovakia

The universities in the Czech Republic are now going through a period of rebuilding, following damage resulting from the forced implementation of Soviet organization of science and education in the fifties. The Soviet-style Czechoslovak Academy was founded for scientific work and the universities were ordered to look after education alone. The 'pedagogic norms' determined how many hours full, associated and assistant professors should spend in classes, student laboratories, and tutoring students. These 'norms' left no time for research, nor allowed a scientist any time to follow up his field.

The financial support for science was directed towards the Academy, and the universities received funds for education only. University research was considered as some sort of private 'hobby' of the teachers. Better salaries and reasonable support of research, together with the official presentation of the Academy as 'The Representative Body of Czechoslovak Science' caused an exodus of the best scientists from universities into the Academy where the title of 'Academician' brought a considerable amount of material and political benefits, never to be available to the university professor.

In this way, university science and research dwindled and the best scientists were drained off. Even if they did not leave, the 'norms' burden caused their slow but deep scientific degeneration. The teachers who left were replaced by political prominent people. Devotion to the communist ideology and practice was more important than their professional qualities in science. The ultimate step of education—study for the Ph.D.—was step-by-step transferred to the Academy, transforming the universities to the level of colleges.

This situation lasted 36 years—almost two generations. It was also reflected in the international position of the universities. The official presentation of the Academy by the communist regime as a 'representative' of Czechoslovakian science was recognized by many international bodies that in this way supported the communist party leadership in our science (the President of the Academy was usually a member of Central Committee).

Fortunately, this situation was not equally bad in all fields. In medical sciences, engineering, and the arts, science and research was not dominated by the Academy.

I have given this historical introduction in order to clarify the understanding of our present situation. In may fields, scientific research is much stronger in the Academy than in the universities. Also, better specialists are very often found in the institutes of the Academy. For the sake of survival of our academic community, it is necessary to engage the best scientists in education and to bring back scientific research to the universities. Many steps in this direction have already been taken, but several obstacles still have to be overcome.

At the universities, for the reasons presented above, many teachers were demoted from their scientific position. They fell into a routine, comfortable, life-style, obeying directions 'from above' protected from any decision-making. Their scientific record is poor. They were isolated from the development of world science and were unable to compete. These scientists command our respect, having sacrificed their scientific careers for the sake of the education of the younger generations who are now working in science at the institutes of the Academy.

Without these teachers, our scientific community would not have survived the period of totality. Nevertheless, these members of the university staff are the roots of the resistance felt by scientists at the Academy who want to join the university system. This is understandable, but an untenable situation.

At most universities, the lack of teaching staff is very serious. It has several causes. First, positions occupied by prominent communists were removed. Second, schools are using all opportunities to send teachers abroad to refill the great lack of international contacts. In the frame of the TEMPUS programme alone, 659 Czech and Slovak teachers travelled abroad in 1991/2. Third, the number of universities was increased by establishing new regional schools. Fourth, more students are enrolled at all universities. Again, the situation is there—the university teacher has no time or energy to work in scientific research as he should. This time, not because of the 'norms', but as a result of the situation which arose after the revolution.

In the Academy, there is no motivation to go and teach at universities. The scientist level is appraised according to the number of papers published, patents issued, and membership of international scientific bodies. Teaching at undergraduate and graduate level would steal time from this activity which is subject to evaluation. Having several 'aspirants' is another story: they help to fulfil research tasks and produce papers co-signed by their supervisors. Considering the low level of equipment and usually poorer scientific milieu, those who decide to leave the Academy for the university system are definitely to be admired.

What should be done about the situation?

If education—starting from freshman level—is made widespread throughout the entire academic community of our country, then there will be no local overload in particular areas. On the other hand, university teachers should participate in scientific research in the Academy's institutes. Good results are being registered in the former direction: several joint units (laboratories) between universities and the Academy have been established, educational boards composed of members of both institutions were assembled. University graduate students are working in Academy laboratories and programmes for Ph.D. study have in many cases been worked out by joint bodies.

In the latter direction—teachers working in the Academy laboratories—the record is very poor, mostly because of the above-mentioned lack of teachers, and also because of the lack of science funding.

We therefore consider the direction of combining the functions split up under the communist regime, between the Academy and universities, back into a single body as the correct cure for the totalitarian disease our scientific community is suffering. Because of human nature, all steps in this direction should be taken very carefully, taking into account the situation in both institutions. Nevertheless, the separation of education and science cannot survive in our country. Models such as the CNRS or the Max-Planck Institutes may be considered in the future when our national product per capita reaches the level of Germany or France. But for at least two decades we do not have the economic power to support two parallel bases of good science.

18

Organization and Financing of Academic Research in Slovakia

ANTON HAJDUK

Scientific Secretary, Slovak Academy of Sciences, Bratislava, Czechoslovakia

The research institutes of the Slovak Academy of Sciences are putting considerable effort into sustaining advances across a broad front in the understanding of natural and social phenomena. More than 5000 individuals, including 3000 scientists, working in almost 70 research units, constitute a significant part of the scientific activity in Slovakia.

As rapid changes occur in eastern Europe, the Slovak Academy of Sciences has eagerly accepted its role as a major builder of future growth in Slovakia, a weighty responsibility not being taken lightly. The Academy is now working aggressively to diversify its research and define its academic quality in a truly global view.

I would like to specify, briefly, the main changes in the organization and in the financing of the research in our Academy.

These organizational changes since January 1990 are:

— A completely new scientific body, the Council of Scientists, has been created (January 1990) through the election of the entire number of scientists at all institutes, which replaced the role of the body academicians (learned society) from the old regime.

Very few academicians have been elected to the Council of Scientists.

— The old body of academicians has been moved out by a new law accepted by the Slovak Parliament. The extra sums paid to academicians (2 million CSK) were transferred to the Fund supporting young scientists.

— A new Presidium of the Academy was elected by the Council of Scientists and then (February 1990) nominated by the Government.

— In about two-thirds of the institutes, new directors have been nominated by the Presidium via competitive selection processes.

— Some institutes which had lost their sense of activity have been disbanded (*e.g.* the Institute of Scientific Atheism or institutes manufacturing old generations of computers), many institutes were restructured, and new disciplines opened up (such as theoretical informatics or politology).

— The institutes of social sciences have changed their research activity orientation (Institutes of Philosophy, Sociology, History, etc.) but this is still the weakest point of our Academy.

— The number employed in administration was reduced in 1990 by 20 per cent and this process is continuing as a consequence of the new system of financing.

— A system of research grants was implemented in January 1991.

The main changes in the financing of research are:

— Since January 1991, the system of financing was changed from the old system based on some traditions where the best paid institutes were those to which members of the Presidium belonged, to financing proportional to the scientific production of the institute and via research grants to groups of scientists. In this way, parts of 25+37.5 per cent of the total budget of Academy were distributed, the rest devoted to supply energies and other necessities for the survival, since owing to inflation and government budget restriction, the real budget represented in 1991 about two-thirds of the budget from previous years. The consequence of this financing system was a decrease of 18 per cent of the Academy staff (over 1000 people). It was interesting to observe that the scientific production, primarily publications in current journals, but also in other journals (weighted less) or symposia proceedings, etc. in 1991 was even higher than in previous years. This mean without any doubt that the system works properly.

— This system of financing was applied very strongly (in about 80 per cent of the total budget) for the year 1992, since, moreover, financing of buildings and energies was also limited according to the same criteria. Upper and lower limits were set up to 15 per cent of the previous budget of a particular institute. The Presidium decided not to control the number of people in institutes (as previously), but the ratio of the scientific product and the volume of the budget of the particular institute. This way, productive individuals are not eliminated, and the best can be supported, hence also considerably stemming the brain-drain process. About 90 per cent of international co-operation is paid by the institutes (previously it was fully paid and controlled centrally by the Presidium). Also the financing of scientific journals is no longer central, the budget being distributed to the institutes seeking the most effective way of apportioning them.

— A Science Park was created mostly for people leaving institutes as a result of the selection system. They may use Academy buildings and equipment free of charge but they have to exist on their work for industry by contract. This represents not only social support for people leaving the institutes, but also support in the transitional stage of industry which is not yet sufficiently productive. This is also a possible attractive means for effective international co-operation.

The results of increasing scientific production, despite the considerable decrease in manpower in our research, give us grounds to believe that within a very few years we will be able to transform our academic research to a high standard.

19

Romanian Science between Copying and Adapting

RADU GRIGOROVICI
Academician, Vice-President, Romanian Academy, Bucharest, Romania

About one month ago, at a Workshop on the Methodologies for Evaluating the Future Potential of Research Institutes, held in Prague, Benno Parthier from the Leopoldina Academy in Halle placed Romania among the small countries in Europe. In fact, only 8 out of some 33 European countries have a higher population than Romania. So why should Romania lie so low on the scientific scale? And how can Romania organize its scientific research so as to occupy as soon as possible an honourable place on this scale?

This is not the place or the time to insist on the causes of this situation. But a short account of our historical past may offer the best answer to the first of the above questions.

After having stood for many centuries in the way of the migration of Asian peoples and after arousing and partly satisfying many imperial appetites, modern Romanians saw their political ideal embodies in a Western type national state that would include most of our nationals. No wonder then, that very soon after the merging of two Romanian principalities, Moldova and Muntenia, into a single state, Romania, the first all-Romanian learned society, the Romanian Academy came into being in 1866. The two Romanian universities in Jassy and Bucharest were founded earlier in 1860 and 1864.

The characteristics of the structure and evolution of the Romanian Academy are worth mentioning. First, its members were recruited not only from the territory of Romania proper, but also from regions forming part of Austria, Hungary, Russia, and the Balkan peninsula, where Romanians live in tight and numerous groups. As a consequence, the Romanina Academy became and remained a symbol of our political unity.

Secondly, as a Learned Society, its activity started by first studying the Romanina language, the basis of our right to form one single nation. The study of our nation's history, its Latin origin and character, was its second goal: while the sciences and arts were included about a decade later. In all these fields, the concept of clearly oriented and organized study groups was defined from the very beginning in the statutes of our Academy, thus marking its double role of an autonomous forum of both consecration and creation.

Between the two world wars, both hard and soft scientific investigation was performed in united Romania mainly in the country's universities and polytechnics, but also in a series of research institutes that had sprung up through the personal endeavour of Romanian scientists of international status, many but not all of them having studies abroad. These institutes were connected with the Academy, the universities and a series of ministries. None of them was linked to modern industry which lay mostly in the hands of foreign capital. They covered a variety of fields like linguistics, history, archaeology, sociology, agriculture, medicine, etc.

After the Second World War, a communist regime was imposed by the three Great Powers in Romania. The consequences for scientific research were profound, because implanting the communist ideology in all aspects of life in a country where the number of party members was about seven hundred was no easy task. Therefore, for some ten years, scientific research was forbidden in high education institutions. Professors had to teach and nothing else. Humanistic sciences had to be 'purified'; 'bourgeois' ideologies had to be eliminated;

of all philosophies only Marxism-Leninism was allowed; the Latin origin of our language had to be denied; sociology was treated with caution; history had to be distorted conveniently; and so on. Politicization of the humanistic faculties not only eliminated the old professors, but the new ones were selected mainly on partisan criteria. Chunks were cut off the universities and new totally politicized education and research units were set up in the social, economic, and history fields.

In the field of hard sciences the attitude was different, at least in part. Specialists were still needed. The whole Soviet system, including Romania, was enveloped in a semipermeable membrane: the inward flow of information, even scientific, was throttled to a minimum: the outward flow was pure propaganda. Under these conditions, science became autarchic, ie efficient scientific research became a first degree priority, if the industrial and military technology had to be competitive with that of the arch-enemy, the USA. Therefore both fundamental and applied research had to be hurried along or, where needed, started.

Initially research was completely separated from teaching and ideological barriers erected against some 'bourgeois' sciences like genetics, cybernetics, relativity, quantum mechanics, quantum chemistry, the application of quantitative methods to social science, etc. The disastrous results of these restrictions soon became obvious and after Stalin's death research became a refuge for many independently thinking are creative people all over the Soviet system. It was a relatively happy time when hard science research flourished for some ten years in Romania.

In the early seventies, things started changing again for the worse, this time only in Romania: a State Committee for Science and Technology, headed by Elena Ceausescu, systematically destroyed the whole system of research institutes built up over the years by the communist regime, by eliminating fundamental research altogether, introducing research contracts that contained clauses so absurd that only by a tacit consensus between researchers and managers could the inefficiency of the system be covered up by cheating and lying to their masters. Obviously, without any journals and books from the West for the five to nine years prior to 1989, with visitors denied access to the laboratories, and only a few people from our country being allowed to travel and to work abroad, research of every kind could only wither away. If it was not completely destroyed, then any papers by Romanian scientists still appearing in foreign journals, albeit at a much reduced rate, were due entirely to their strong dedication to their profession and to their intellectual quality.

The best illustration of this contradictory evolution was the fate of the Romanian Academy. It lost its autonomy in 1948, being transformed into a State institution. Its history section was nearly completely destroyed; more than half the members of the literary section were thrown out and replaced by communists or obedient people. However many of the hard scientists and technologies not only survived the reorganization but their number doubled. A network of about 50 research institutes was set up. Some 35 of them worked in hard fundamental and applied sciences. So did many technological research institutes too, subordinated to different ministries or affiliated directly to big factories. From 1960 onwards, Romanian scientists published increasingly in foreign journals, and studied and worked abroad. The libraries were well supplied with foreign books and journals. Research schools sprang up everywhere. Political barriers were lowered. In 1970, however, by pure wantonness Elena Ceausescu took away all research institutes from the Academy and some of the best were split up or dismantled and, after forcing her election to the Academy against strong opposition in 1974, she let it die out 'biologically' by forbidding any new election to its body. In 1989, the average age of its members had reached 76, thus exceeding by far the national life expectancy.

Only two weeks after the triumph of our revolution, the Romanian Academy was resurrected under its old name and form as an autonomous institution. It recuperated most of its former research institutes, if they so wanted, whose main focus now is fundamental and advanced research. It is funded mainly through the state budget. All other technically-oriented research institutes are subordinated to the Science Department of the Ministry for Education and Science, being funded partly by the State, partly by a global tax contributed by industry, and partly by contracts with the ministry or with industry.

This is the present organization and funding scheme of scientific research in Romania after some two years of undecided wrangling over a law that is supposed to pass through our Parliament. I have thus reached the moment to give an answer to the second question: how to restore Romanian scientific research at least to the level it had between the two wars in humanistic sciences and in the sixties in the hard sciences.

The first problem is funding. Napoleon said that for waging war he needed three things: firstly money, secondly money, and thirdly money again. The same goes for research. In the dire state of our economy, I can only completely agree with our Secretary of State for Science who said publicly that for the time being there is no question in Romania of developing research: the only thing we can fight for is its survival. However, whilst waiting for the happy moment to arrive when our Government and our industry are able to offer us more than just our salaries—but no equipment, no materials, no journals and books, no travelling funds—we cannot stay with our arms folded.

We now have to decide whether we can solve the complex problems involved in the revival of scientific research in our country ourselves or if we need foreign guidance and help.

Soon after 1989 we were subjected to a considerable amount of offensive and threatening advice—as though we had lived until then in the wilderness, but not the slightest offer of help. The common denominator was that we had to adopt western organizations forms immediately and forego our supposedly entirely Soviet-type past. We were and still are told sometimes that, consequently, we must shift all research activities to the universities and liquidate all existing research institutes, especially those recently recovered by the Academy, neglecting all the traditions we have. Others have even told us to reinstate the recently abolished National Committee for Science and Technology, because its title sounded so similar to one of their own institutions. They had however, never experienced the NCST's destructive role in our country and are not aware that the whole bureaucratic staff of the fomer NCST makes up even today the nucleus of our Science Department of the Ministry of Education and Science, continuing to exert its malefic influence on the science policy of our Government. What we discovered after gathering authentic information about the so-called western organization of scientific research was that it varied strongly from country to country, being equally successful despite this diversity. The only element common to all is that these countries can easily afford to spend a lot of money on research but are nevertheless acting as economically as possible and, secondly, they very carefully avoid letting the main decisions be taken by politicians and bureaucrats.

The following wave of contacts with our western colleagues resulted in what we needed most: efficient help and consistent information about the real organization of research in different countries. Almost without exception, our attempts to resume the broken links with international organizations and other learned societies were accepted benevolently, and we were exempted from paying our outstanding debts which had accumulated during recent years to significant sums. Our scientists who had their papers accepted at international conferences usually had their conference fee waived and very often all their expenses were paid by the organizers. Short- and long-term study grants for young and not so young people came in increasingly: exchange schemes with other learned societies or offered by international foundations are in full swing: scientific co-operation agreements were concluded: those offering documentation and donations or access to modern equipment, with no strings attached, are most acceptable to us and are increasing in number as the quality of the researchers we are selecting becomes obvious. We do not like at all the pretentions of some organizations who only grant stipendia to people nominated by themselves, not on the basis of nominal proposals coming from Romania and accepted by them. This smacks too much of a means of obtaining cheap, qualified labour instead of offering help where it is most needed.

We know we have to evaluate in due course our research potential. In the Academy we have started this process, but we are also aware that under the present circumstances the results can be heavily flawed. Individual researchers of equal value react differently to the lack of adequate means and due appreciation: some continue to work against all odds: some give in and stop working.

We also know that in experimental sciences one needs about a decade to turn an undergraduate into a fully grown, independent researcher capable of guiding the next generation on a similar course; that two or three years are needed to become really familiar with a subject under investigation in order to achieve an original breakthrough in this matter; but that only a few months are needed to make new equipment work properly. Therefore, the first thing we have to do is to send young talented people to work abroad for as long as possible, to learn what true research work means, even at the risk that some of them will never come back.

We must also exert ourselves to initiate international scientific co-operation in fields where there is some tradition at home, with foreign research groups that will make modern equipment available to our groups, and enough information to enable them to add a significant contribution to that of the entire team.

In the meantime, the mature generation has to overcome their rivalries and find an organizational scheme which, in my personal opinion, has to fulfil the following conditions:

— It should clearly separate fundamental from applied research. Planning fundamental research and not guiding applied research is equally wrong. Not a single important fundamental discovery has been foreseen: only *a posteriori* can one plan research in order to verify or to falsify a new theory or to explain the result of an unusual experiment.

  Now, the scope of a fundamental research programme can be defined, but still the result cannot be predicted. Applied research has from the very beginning a rather well defined goal. If its results are promising, planning and achieving their transfer to industry, biotechnology or whatever form of technology constitutes the real problem.

— Research councils composed of highly qualified professionals should guide the Government and other central organizations in defining their science policy, and find the best arguments in favour of an adequate funding system. Bureaucrats should be allowed only limited access to decision-taking. The influence of politics should be reduced to a minimum, the real danger consisting of the amateur-like approach of ministers towards science and technology.

— Teaching and research should form part of a single system, differing only in the weight given to the two activities in different institutions.
— Funding should not come from one single source. Diversity of funding sources is essential if unconventional ideas are to have a chance of being accepted and supported.
— Evaluation of research groups and institutes should be based mainly on peer review and on direct contacts between reviewers and researchers, with recourse to scientometrics and other criteria only as a secondary measure.

This list is certainly incomplete but surely contains some of the essential points. As regards the advice we are hearing from various quarters, I can assume you that we are very attentive, but also quite critical listeners. We also believe that we can adapt ourselves to a system based on those successful models which agree as far as possible with our traditions, thus avoiding dramatic changes that always generate conflict and turbulence.

20

An Evaluation of the Restructuring Processes in the Romanian R&D System

ILEANA IONESCU-SISESTI
Commission for Science Policy Studies, The Romanian Academy, Bucharest, Romania

The R&D system in Romania is undergoing a major reorganization, but it is difficult to see clearly the final stage of this process. The reorganization of the R&D system under way at present is part of the general restructuring process of the country, this undergoing full debate and evaluation. The patterns and experiences of other countries cannot be reproduced to the letter, their validity depending on the particular socio-political and historical context. Moreover, solutions now adopted in the developed countries were arrived at by trial and error, evolving with time.

The problems being faced by East European countries are quite new. Time restricts natural evolution. Major restrictions are provoked by a lack of resources (mainly financial), needed for organization on a national scale, and by the limited individual and social learning capability. Man's way of thinking and behaviour cannot be changed overnight.

Countries in East Europe encounter problems similar to those of the developing countries, but also enjoy certain achievements comparable with those obtained by the developed countries. Their economies are passive and inefficient, each one to a different extent: most countries undergoing transition already have R&D systems with high scientific and technological potential but their inadequate structures impede their efficacy.

This is indeed the case for Romania. Top-level visitors from other countries acknowledge the potential here. Indirect evidence is seen in the lack of commitment of foreign systems to invest effort in Romania, a move which could elevate the country to the position of competitor on the international market.

The conclusion is that each country's case has to be considered individually though with the wisdom of accrued international experience.

Moreover, for identifying the problems and solutions, generally speaking—for accelerating the restructuring processes—the development of a function of evaluation, critical analysis, 'watch' and forecasting, is also necessary. At present, the role of science policy studies is to supply the decision factors in the R&D field, and other relevant factors, with elements on which to base future decisions and actions.

The usefulness of such an evaluation function is also connected to the fact that the new structures are growing with time. Since the starting functional, institutional, and managerial skills in the country are underdeveloped, this time could indeed be long. The key is to avoid going in the wrong direction in the future.

With this in mind, I have initiated an evaluation of the results of the restructuring processes that have taken place recently in the R&D system in Romania. The difficulty of this approach was to identify the evaluation parameters: which R&D system should be used for comparison when the problems are new and the solutions cannot be other than highly specific?

A valid source of establishing such parameters could be the analysis of the overall experience of developed countries in the field of R&D. The aim is to show the logic underlying their R&D systems and identify certain fundamental functioning features. Some of these in brief are:

— running using mechanisms
— setting priorities
— the action of market mechanisms, quasi-real or symbolic, in R&D activity
— the systemic character
— the specific character
— the evolutive character.

The general conclusion yielded by the evaluation of the restructuring of the R&D system in Romania, as seen from the above-mentioned point of view, was the following: the changes are considerable, are being brought about at several levels of the system, and involve various directions. However, the restructuring processes are incomplete and often designed or led with a degree of amateurism.

Several justifications could be given: new situations, a special dynamism of the events and the need to operate on the fly, sometimes even in desperate situations. However, these explain but cannot excuse certain continuing mistakes.

In the following, we submit briefly results of an evaluation based on the parameters considered above. Given the lack of space, we confine ourselves to the problems linked to the first three parameters.

Running of the R&D System is Ensured by Specific Mechanisms, not by Administrative Measures

Mechanisms channel and articulate the interests of various factors involved in the R&D activity. A fundamental role is played by the financial level, *i.e.* by direct stimulation—namely by financing the R&D activities, and by indirect stimulation, *e.g.* by tax reduction for the economic agents which contribute to the achievement of certain research activities, as well as granting other facilities.

In Romania, during the totalitarian period, the system was to a great extent obstructed, acting through administrative measures and based upon ideological criteria.

The funds ear-marked for research (as a portion of the state budget and the New Technique Fund—set up as a percentage applied to the production costs of an enterprise), were far from being sufficient. Moreover, embezzlement of funds from research to investment was practised for realizing certain pilot plants. This happened because the investment approval-reception mechanism was far too clumsy, hence introducing subjective criteria in granting the existing funds.

Also, the scientific research/technological engineering-production cycle did not dispose of a mechanism to set it going, being left in the state of a slogan without its necessary economical and social levers. That is why research had become an intellectual exercise that could not in any way a propelling force of progress. For instance, results obtained in the laboratories of the Institute of Physics in Magurele were at a world level (lasers, opto-electronic disc) but not one Romanian industrial product incorporate such results (Tibuleac, 1992).

After December 1989, owing to a misunderstanding of these problems, the funds necessary to finance research were lowered still further, seriously compromising the R&D system.

Within the overall R&D activities, fundamental and advanced research carried out in the institutes of the Romanian Academy (returned to the Academy or newly founded) were in a somewhat better situation, being subsidized at a minimum level that was at least budgeted for.

The majority of research activities are taking place in the institutes of applied and technological research, representing 90 per cent of the Romanian research potential. Their situation presents the most problems.

The New Technique Fund was abolished following decentralization, and direct research contracts with financing agents have been much reduced given their difficult economic situation, reflecting that of the whole economy. The state budget continued to provide a low amount of money, as had previously been the case, but at that time the New Technique Fund was still in existence.

After firm steps taken by the National Union of R&D Units, in co-operation with the trade unions, the research units, as well as with representatives of the then newly founded Department of Science within the Ministry for Education and Science, the government decided at the end of 1990 to constitute a provisional Special Fund for research, by applying a 1 per cent levy on the gross output of state enterprises (Government Decision (GD) 1284/December 1990), in 'Romanian Hotarire Guvernamentala' (HG). However, this fund was not supplied according to the provisions (*i.e.* in due time and completely), and being a levy and not a tax, its delivery by the economic units cannot be made compulsory.

Moreover, the provisional character (decision concerning its existence has to be renewed every year) creates a psychological climate of incertitude, little favourable to the research activities (Colegiul Consultative pentru Cercetare Aplicativa si Dezvoltare, 1992a).

In percentage of GNP, the expenses for R&D in Romania rise to little over 1 per cent.

The new regulations have conditioned the restructuring process both positively and negatively. The Finance Law provides a tax reduction for the financing agents that finance research activity. But the reduction is so small that it cannot be considered an important factor of encouragement.

A much talked about regulation was the optional transformation of R&D units into commercial or autonomously managed societies, the main object of their activity being to generate profit (GD 1284/December 1990). The trouble is that although by law the transformation was optional, many institutes were obliged to adopt the new statute under pressure and by administrative measures. No criteria were established to indicate the research fields in which, aiming to make profit at all costs, even pursuing minor themes, scientific advance would be damaged.

Generally speaking, the role of the state was misunderstood. Decentralization of the R&D system, combined with one-sided *laissez-faire* (the state disappears as a main investor in R&D activities, before the financing agents could consolidate themselves enough to take over and replace the financial obligations the state had earlier assumed), brought about a financing vacuum at R&D Unit level as well as a flight from responsibility at state level.

The responsibility is understood here from the standpoint of the intervening liberalism practised by most western states nowadays. This responsibility is even more vital at present in Romania where there is in fact a state economy trying to broaden the market sector, the state still maintaining important economic prerogatives (Comisia de Scienticā, 1991).

At the present time there is in Romania a lack of the deeper understanding of the role of S&T in the development of society. The strategy of economic restructuring should see, in supporting research, a basic factor of change. Research is able to contribute to re-technologization of the economy, and furthermore advances in S&T can lead to creation of competitional advantages on the international market.

Setting Priorities in the R&D System is a Balancing Act between Financing Requirements and Available Resources

The financing requirements in R&D systems have always and everywhere exceeded the available resources at any moment, and always will. Moreover, a great number of factors act upon the requirements, bringing about their increase, while the resources have a slower and a more contradictory evolution, recording decreases too. Consequently one major problem emerging at the upper political layer of every national R&D system is to establish certain priorities and to allocate available funds according to these priorities.

In particular for small countries with limited resources, the problem of objectively establishing the role of different fields of research raised the questions: In which fields could the concerned country be a leader at international level? In which fields should its role be that of a follower, the assigned funds being a necessary condition to maintain these positions? In the other fields, how should a strategy be developed of keeping in touch with achievements at international level, still satisfying internal needs with minimal expense?

In *'socialist'* Romania, the obsession with 'multilateral development' has manifest in research programmes according to which the R&D potential could and had to cover completely all R&D fields, even if there was no clear evidence of having the necessary resources to finalize the research (Colegiul

Consultative pentru Cercetare Applicativa si Dezvoltare, 1992b).

The policy provisions of S&T were recorded in party documents. These displayed in fact non-differentiated lists of fields and subfields of scientific research and technological development, compiled under the co-ordination of the former National Council for Science and Technology, the central body in this field.

That has led, naturally, to a dispersion of the R&D potential, to an impossibility of reaching the 'critical mass' below which scientific progress cannot take place and financial investment means waste of funds.

However, certain priorities were imposed by circumstantial emergencies, by economic and administrative pressure, or by personal ambitions, to solve certain acute economical problems. Consequently, most long-term needs were neglected or ignored, and particular developments in areas of major importance were absent (Sandi and Ionescu-Sisesti, 1990). The absence of a priorities-setting mechanism was replaced improperly by a centralized planning routine.

At the level of the R&D Units, the dispersion of research potential led in many situations to the impossibility of carrying out projects of high scientific value. As a consequence of this and also of the drastic limitation of imports of any kind, the research subjects were too directed towards assimilating products and technologies necessary to make the investments profitable. Most were based on foreign licences or were mere imitation. Therefore, the number of original products and technologies elaborated by Romanian research was small (Colegiul Consultative pentru Cercetare Aplicativa si Dezvoltare, 1992c).

At present, the situation of establishing certain national priorities in the R&D field has not improved significantly.

The Romanian Academy has established an overall strategy up to the year 2000 for the fundamental and advanced research it subsidizes. Certainly, this strategy can only have an indicative and orienting role, since the degree of unpredictability of the results and even of the approached topics in the field of fundamental and advanced research is high (Constantinescu, 1992).

By taking counsel with financing departments, the Department of Science of the Ministry of Education and Science drafted in 1991 the following National Research Programmes (each also having a number of sub-programmes):

1. Ecology
2. Energy and raw materials
3. Technological development
4. Information technology
5. Biotechnology and agriculture
6. Seismological research
7. Socio-humanist science.

Their launching was accompanied by the explicit statement that the Romanian government considers them aș priority, implying that the Department of Science should guide and financially support the execution and implementation of research contracts within this framework (Ministerul Invatamintului si Stiintei, 1991). However, the time schedule and the total funds earmarked for their finalization were not specified.

In fact, the actual way of distribution of the Special Fund in 1991 was brought about by the specific requirements of the ministries and economic departments, was not based on national programmes, and was aimed at the survival of R&D fields existing at that date.

In 1992, a certain shift towards the initial, modern concept of priority programmes occurred. The above list of seven programmes, taken as the preliminary framework, could in some way be found again in the structure of the current national research programmes agreed with or to be agreed with, by the Advisory Council for Applied R&D.

The present distribution of the Special Fund was justified as follows:

— The difficulty of suddenly giving up the previous divisionary structure of organization and financing the

R&D activities in Romania, in order to turn to priority programme,

— the absence of a macro-economic strategy at national level that should clarify the problems of re-organization and re-launching the Romanian economy.

In conclusion, we have to admit therefore that some steps were taken in Romania towards establishing priorities in the R&D field, without however having attained this goal entirely.

In short, some present faults are:

— the sharing of research funds is still without 'relief', as the specialists call it. The major objective nowadays is the survival of certain R&D fields and institutes,

— the present approach of selecting as priorities objectives of secondary importance derived from economical needs, in contradiction with the declared purpose of using the Special Fund, namely to solve problems of general national interest,

— the lack of overall co-ordination in R&D in Romania practically renders national priority research programmes unattainable.

The R&D System Provides the Framework for the Adjustment Mechanism Specific to Science Markets

The concept of market, as a social institution where a systematic exchange of 'commodities' is made for money (or other value elements), between 'vendors' and 'customers', has a special relevance in describing the dynamics of science and technology.

In science the competitive behaviour is a major dimension, being present in most situations encountered. Ziman (1991) identifies in the case of Great Britain the following system of markets, through whose interaction the dynamics of academic research is adjusted (the first four types are very close to the real market (quasi-real), the last three types belong to the symbolic category): the national institutional market, the research projects market, the internal institutional market, the academic job market, the research results validation market, the scientific reputational market, and the intellectual property market.

Using the concept of a system of quasi-real and symbolic markets in science allows a deeper understanding of the way of structuring the R&D system in some developed countries. This system is generally organized on three qualitatively different layers, with specific objectives and processes (Ionescu-Sisesti, 1991):

1. The operational layer, of carrying out the research activities in autonomous institutes or centres, groups within the higher education institutes, within private firms, or by independent research workers. The actors' behaviour at this level is (or should be) adjusted by mechanisms specific to the 'system of markets in science', quasi-real and symbolic.
2. The layer of issuing the science policy. Reasons connected to the national policy in the field of economy, social development, natural environment conservation, etc. or to the national contribution to the advancement of world science, are translated into a series of political decisions concerning the extent of the financial support granted to science from the budget, as well as concerning the major directions of S&T development during a specified period of time. The behaviour of central bodies with advisory or decision role of co-ordination and directing the S&T development illustrates the command model in science through which the political options, particular to this level, are imposed.
3. The layer of adjustment mechanisms proper to the system of quasi-real and symbolic markets in science and of mediating between the various objectives and means of action of the organizations at the extreme layers 1 and 2.

An adjustment role (validation of results, confirmation of values) has always been played through the invisible colleges by the scientific community. In view of accelerating and normalizing its role, as well as in view of adjusting the interactions between the scientific objectives and the socio-economic and political ones on the two extreme layers of the

R&D system (mediatory role, through decodification and connection), specialized bodies have been created, generically termed 'research councils'. Through their mediatory function, they bring about a protection of the R&D activity against the impulses originating from other subsystems: economic, political etc.

At present, the adjustment functions specific to these bodies are:

- Selection through peer review in view of funding the project proposals submitted by research workers, research items, units, or bidding at auction themes required for specific reasons. The criteria used are those 'internal' to the science dynamics: competitiveness, scientific efficiency, vitality, etc. (Ziman, 1991).
- Correlation of priorities and own objectives, with those set up on the political level, and consequently orienting the research programmes in the same directions.

The main means of action is to finance the selected programmes from funds coming from different sources, the governmental ones having an important share. This type of body usually has high autonomy in using the financial resources at its disposal. The research councils are delegated with the responsibility of managing the research funds.

Before December 1989, Romania excelled in hypercentralization. Present decisions were pushed to the peak of the totalitarian pyramid. The R&D system did not constitute an exception from this organization pattern either. Consequently the intermediary adjustment level was missing and the command pattern ruled everywhere.

Very soon after the change of regime in December 1989, the centralized system in S&T was abolished. But the hurry and the radicalism of the transformation had as a consequence the suppression of also certain positive existing elements. This was again connected to the political criteria as in the past period. This breaking new ground action, exceeding by far what was happening in other parts of the economy, had a negative influence on the R&D system, throwing it into confusion.

A series of structuring and restructuring processes started gradually. At the beginning they had a remedial character due to the fact that science had been sent to the periphery in Romania during the previous period: re-organization of the Romanian Academy and of its network of institutes (Decree Law No. 4 of 5 January 1990), promotion of R&D personnel, reactivation of international relations, etc. A series of principles for the restructuring processes: decentralization, self-government of R&D units, co-operation, self-government of R&D units, co-operation, free promotion of values (GD 458/28 April, 1990 and 17 May, 1990) were formulated and applied in practice.

Subsequently, the increasing needs to avoid decentralization evolving 'at random', led to the re-organization or creation of certain bodies having functions of co-ordination, orientation, correlation, elaboration of science policy, proper to a society making its way towards democracy and to an economy in transition to market structures.

The Romanian Academy is the highest forum of scientific consecration in Romania. Having a history of 126 years of high scientific tradition, the Romanian Academy is one of the institutions of this type well-known worldwide. As a type of institution, it was conceived according the French pattern.

In the first part of the period of communist ruling, the Romanian Academy was granted a certain social and economic authority, a network of fundamental research institutes being created under its co-ordination.

Their profile belonged to a broad spectrum of science fields, engineering included. During that first period, the developing pattern of the whole R&D system, including that of the Academy of Sciences, was the Soviet one, with all its deficiencies.

In spite of all drawbacks and misfunctions, the consequence of all these efforts was the creation in Romania of a system of scientific research of national relevance. Under its auspices the Academy institutes were playing an important role.

During the last twenty years, the Academy's authority was diminished little by little, its institutes taken away or dismantled. In the last years before 1989, the Academy was more an aging assembly in a decaying building with a famous library than a functioning institution.

After the change of regime in 1989, the Romanian Academy went through a re-organization process during which its prestige and its condition as a forum of consecration were recognized and reconfirmed.

The Academy revived its previous pattern, reconstituting its network of research institutes. At present, the Romanian Academy subsidizes and co-ordinates about 60 institutes of fundamental and advanced research in various fields of the exact, natural, and socio-humanist sciences. The engineering sciences are no longer dealt with in the institutes of the Romanian Academy, and medicine and agriculture are co-ordinated by two field academies.

Within the layer structure of the R&D system and with the terminology used above, the functions of the Romanian Academy tally with the mediatory level, having an adjustment role. By its function of consecration it concentrates into a single institution the role generally performed by the scientific community, namely, by activating the mechanisms proper to the symbolic market in science, *i.e.* validation of results, strengthening scientific reputation.

The Romanian Academy also belongs to the intermediary layer of the R&D system by having assumed the role of a 'promoter of fundamental and advanced research'. From this point of view, the *Romanian Academy* is generally acting as a 'research council'.

The effect of its efforts would be greater if the adjustment functions incumbent to the assumed role were better defined. In this context we can note the following aspects:

- At present, financing the research themes or programmes proposed by research workers or by institutes does not involve a competitive selection based upon peer-review evaluation.
- For resources the Academy makes available for solving problems it initiates itself, for specializations or co-operation periods abroad, an action-type procedure

would be welcome (selection by competition between the attending bidders, based on strict criteria).

— The Academy utilizes budgetary funds, granted by the government for research funding. This situation makes it difficult to accomplish a complete autonomy, the financial channel offering the government the possibility to impose certain priorities and major directions. The autonomy necessary to subsidize efficiently fundamental and advanced research, and to protect it against the action of the disturbing stimuli from the economic, social, political life implies at present an attitude often perceived as 'aggressive'. This creates a tense situation in the scientific community and, in inter-institutional relations within the R&D system. The solution could be either actual financial self-governing of the Academy based on the recovery of its profitable properties, or the acceptance of certain limits to its autonomy against the decisions and actions proper to the political layer, referring to the field of S&T.

— The mixture of roles of both a forum of consecration and of a promoter of research in its own institutes reciprocally alters the performance of each role.

The Department of Science of the Ministry of Education and Science was set up in two stages: firstly, as a General Board of Scientific Research and Technological Development (GD 223/27 February, 1990), subsequently under the present form (GD 940/ August 1990). Its most important tasks aim at promoting and co-ordinating the research: elaboration of studies and analyses for the substantiation of the proposals and strategies of science development and technological progress; elaboration of intersectorial and multidisciplinary type R&D programmes; ensuring interdepartmental co-operation in the R&D field; management of the funds granted from the budget for intersectorial, multidisciplinary R&D programmes (financing, conclusion and operation of research contracts); supervision of the execution of programmes (Ministerul Invatamintului si Stiintei, 1991, pp. 7-8).

Besides the administration of the budgetary fund for R&D, it is the task of the Department of Science also to administrate the Special Fund, based upon the recommendations of the Advisory Council for Applied Research and Development.

The assigned action area of the Department of Science is limited to the research activity in higher education institutions (at present in Romania with a low share of the overall research potential), the research in its own institutions and the multidisciplinary and intersectorial research programmes subsidized from the budget and the Special Fund, carried out in the branch R&D institutes.

The Advisory Council for Applied Research and Development was founded under a provisional title until the Research Law Act passed through parliament. Its main tasks are: elaboration of proposals and recommendations concerning the national policy within the field of R&D; distribution of the Special Fund and of the budgetary funds for R&D; the periodical evalution of the results obtained after using up the allocated funds (GD 1284/8 December, 1990 and 66/23 January, 1991). It is an advisory body of the government, non-parmanent, made up of 45 experts, reputed specialists representing the Romanian Academy, the Department of Science, the field academies (agricultural, medical), branch R&D institutions, ministries, and economic department. It works in plenum and in commissions; within the framework of the latter numerous specialists, non-members of the Council, are co-opted.

Let us further analyse the contribution of the Department of Science and of the Advisory Council to the fulfilment of the adjustment functions in the R&D system, from the point of view of the layered description given above:

— The responsibility of elaborating the S&T is diffuse. The Advisory Council makes proposals to the government, which deals with the problems of S&T in plenary meetings, every now and then, although these would require a permanent concern, a particular understanding, and a specialized approach. On the other hand, the Advisory Council has not yet succeeded in elaborating an adequate set of priorities, requesting the government to put forward the strategy of long-term economic development, in order to establish the priorities that will result from the strategy, while the present distribution of funds has considered mainly the survival of the present structure of fields. For the time being, the Department of Science has not gone beyond the role of an operative secretariat of this mechanism.

— The responsibility of managing the funds for applied research and development is fragmented. The government agrees in plenum to the Advisory Council's proposals of distributing the Special Fund. But without a specialized subgroup for the R&D problems within the government, this approval has only a formal administrative character. Neither does the Council take upon itself this responsibility, because it bears the label 'advisory'. It operates as a debating and negotiating forum—in fact a modern and very positive feature, but not enough in this case.

  In its condition as an operative secretariat, the Department of Science assured the actual running of the contracts concluded for the projects included in the research programmes by the Advisory Council. A great deal of bureaucratic obstacles render the tasks of the Department of Science more complicated.

  The problem is in fact that of one or several missing bodies, of the type of a 'research council', that should perform in an independent and exhaustive way the specific adjustment functions: (i) assignment of the funds it disposes of, under competitive circumstances; (ii) correlating their own priorities with the national ones.

To sum up, within the R&D system in Romania, there are two sources performing adjustment functions, both doing it incompletely:

1. the Romanian Academy—for fundamental and advanced research.
2. the ensemble consisting of the Advisory Council for Applied Research and Development, the government, and the Department of Science—for applied and technological research.

There is an area of the system which is completely unexposed to the action of any adjustment mechanism. According to the GD 66/23 January, 1991, the budgetary funds assigned to the Department of Science should be distributed through the Advisory Council through the same procedure as the Special Fund. That does not actually happen, the Department assigning the funds directly. It follows that the new board, the Superior Council for Science, very recently set up at the Department of Science, should take over this function henceforth.

— The terminology used does not mirror the reality quite satisfactorily. The attribute 'advisory' is unsuitable, the Council's role being more extensive than the advisory one. On the other hand, the Superior Council for Science of the Department of Science does not call itself advisory, though its prerogatives correspond exclusively to this role.

— Within the framework of the Advisory Council, a very important role is played by the field commissions. In fact, it is at that level that the field programmes are assembled, that the financing of projects is negotiated, and the intrafield priorities created. The orchestrators of these processes are the commissions' co-ordinators, a very great responsibility within the framework of the Council resting upon them. Nevertheless, these responsibilities are in no way standardized, adjusted by normative documents, the decisional behaviour of the head of each commission depending very much on his character and his managerial skills.

To contrast with the past, when the flight from responsibility was driving the decision up on the hierarchical scale of the hypercentralized system, we are witnessing at present an opposite tendency: another style of avoiding responsibility by driving it, in a disguised way, down, where things seem to be settled somehow by themselves. Nevertheless, this does not mean that the responsibility has disappeared.

NOTE

A complete discussion would have taken into account the other three reference parameters:

Systemic features—the natural relation between the research types (basic, oriented, applied, technological) and the specific meaning within the system of the main types of research units: public institutions, units/groups within the higher education institutes, research units within the framework of the private firms; the fragmented character of the R&D system in Romania; multi- and interdisciplinarity; conflict of interests of the involved and affected parties (scientists, scientific community, financing organizations, public opinion, etc.) related to a theme or a research programme; the problem of rendering the results profitable and the connected research/using of the results.

Specificity features—the R&D system cannot be known without the presence of the scientists themselves; the problem of risk in research; the taking over of methods of evaluation, planning, management, etc. from other fields has to be done very carefully and with the necessary adjustments, otherwise the results could be a disaster; the specific behaviour of research workers and of the scientific community.

Evolutive features—the system is in permanent evolution; the structures and mechanisms have a historical character, they are shaped in time and change in time. There is the danger of skipping certain stages without the fundamental processes coming to maturity.

REFERENCES

Colegiul Consultative pentru Cercetare Aplicativa si Dezvoltra (Advisory Council for Applied Research and Development). 1992a. Discutii Consemnate (Recorded Discussions).

Colegiul Consultative pentru Cercetare Aplicativa si Dezvoltare (Advisory Council for Applied Research and Development). 1992b. Program national de cercetare-dezvoltare pentru constructia de masini, 1992-2005 (National R&D Programme for Machine Building, 1992-2005).

Colegiul Consultative pentru Cercetare Aplicativa si Dezvoltare (Advisory Council for Applied Research and Development). 1992c. Schita pentru o strategie a evolutiei industriei chimica—baza pentru fundamentarea program. de cercetare (Outline of a strategy for the chemical industry as a framework for research programmes).

Comisia de Scientica (Commission for Science Policy Studies), 1991. Rolul si interventia statului in dezvoltarea stiintei si technologiei. Sinteza a dezbaterii din 17 mai (The state role and intervention within the science and technology development. Synthesis of debates of 17 May).

Constantinescu, N.N., 1992. Report privind strategia si programul cercetarilor fundamentale si avansate ale Academiei Romane in urmatorii ani prezentat Adunasii Generale a Academie Romane (Report of the strategy and programme of basic and advanced research in the coming years addressed to the General Assembly of the Romanian Academy). *Academica*, 3(15)—4(16).

Ionescu-Sisesti, I, 1991. Studiul tendintelor si orientarilor pe plan mondial in stiinta si technologie—Dezvoltarea si stemelor S&T. Contract de cercetare pentru Departmentul Stiintei (Trends in S&T systems development. Research contract for the Department of Science).

Ministerul Invatamintului si Stiintei, Departmentul Stiintei, 1991. *Bulletin de Informare (Information Bulletin)*, No. 1.

Sandi, A.M. and Ionescu-Sisesti, I, 1990. R&D organization and management in Romania during the transition period. Paper at UN Economic Commission for Europe, Senior Advisers to EEC Governments on Science and Technology, Ninth Session, 25-27 September, 1990.

Tibuleac, D., 1992. The complexity of the decentralization problems in science. NRC for *UNESCO Journal*. In press.

Ziman, J., 1991. Academic science as a system of markets. *Higher Education Quarterly*, 45 (1).

21

Adaptation of Romania's Research and Development System to the Mechanisms of the Market Economy

NICOLAE NAUM

Deputy Director General, Ministry of Education and Science, Bucharest, Romania

Scientific creation is a human activity that is very sensitive to changes in its surroundings and, at the same time, highly dynamic, in relation to economic and social progress. For this reason, the State should protect and promote it through an appropriate regulatory, organization and financing system.

The organization of Romania's scientific research has experienced two dramatic periods marked by the moment of transition from the communist dictatorship to democracy and the market economy. We are still in a transitional period, and so it is most expedient to make a critical presentation of the previous period.

The Evolution of Scientific Research in Romania's Present Economic, Social and Political Environment

The last years of the communist regime in Romania were characterized by a significant decrease in industrial and agricultural production, as well as the R&D level which were denied by the political leadership through widespread propaganda, using false statistics.

The huge investment projects in industry, agriculture, and public building accompanied by severe restrictive measures for paying foreign debts and the general mismanagement of the economy resulted in rapid reduction of the economic and technical-scientific base and in living standard, and caused severe discontentment among the population.

Centralization and economic planning produced negative effects on the R&D sector. Activity in this sector was concentrated in some huge institutes, in some cases one alone for an individual field (central institutes, such as those in chemistry, mechanical engineering, and electrical engineering). A degree of communication between the political and public structures succeeded in producing unanimous decisions.

The former National Council for Science and Technology, to which all the research units were subordinate, concentrated strategical decision in research under the direct command of higher political leadership.

At the time, Romania's Academy of Sciences had no operational responsibilities, since the Academy had lost its subordinated institutes in 1977.

Research in the higher-educational institutes, whose activity had a mainly didactic role, was performed in their specific departments.

Research was generally financed from a centralized fund consisting of the dues collected from the state enterprises, and allotted by the National Council for Science and Technology and the State Planning Council to the research users on the basis of a previously determined destination.

The entire research activity was the object of agreements concluded by the research institutes with the holders of the fund.

The research worker was then paid a fixed salary, just like any public officer, regardless of his/her results or labour value. Patents were state-owned while inventors received a nominal reward of encouragement.

The organization of scientific research provided a certain stability and a rigorous control by the State of scientific creativity, but it was inflexible and, in the long-run, it had a paralyzing effect on the research system and industry, and social and cultural life.

However, a strict contractual system provided a perfect legal framework for scientific research, which, at present, is a favourable premise for transition to a market economy.

Another specific feature of the R&D system which existed in Romania until the revolution was the indifference shown to university research in general, and to fundamental research in particular. Officially, emphasis was laid on applied and industrial research in such a manner that, in order to solve the problems despite prevailing conditions, some sectors of the research institutes were converted into units for manufacturing small-series products.

However, it is worth mentioning that in Romania, after World War II, the pressure of a forced economic growth produced many valuable technological projects, and important basic, advanced, as well as applied research work was carried out which compensated for the technological and information deficiencies of the socialist system. On the other hand, the qualification of the personnel has always been competitive, a fact demonstrated by the favourable way in which the scientific world accepted the studies and participation of Romanian scientists into the international scientific circuit.

After the fall of the dictatorship, the revolutionaries took the first measures for dissolving all the power structures of the former regime, for democratizing the economic, social, and political life, for introducing the multi-party system, and for a market economy-oriented strategy.

The first government constituted after the general elections in May 1990 put forward a radical reform programme, for whose implementation more than 200 laws have been passed by Parliament.

The economy-decentralization process was carried out by transferring the economic decisions from the central administration directly to the economic units, by setting up businesses based on public capital, a strategy also used for the applied research, development, and design institutes.

After 1989, the governmental body for science and technology was dissolved and the activity for R&D co-ordination was taken over by the Department of Science, newly established within the Ministry of Education and Science.

Through this Department, the Government sought to solve the above-mentioned problems specific to the Romanian research activity, but limited funding allowed only partial solution.

New problems were added to the existing and unsolved problems, as a result of the fundamental changes taking place in the Romanian economy, reflected in the research activity.

A number of institutes, especially those for research, engineering, and design, have become commercial undertakings or public autonomous corporations, adapting their activity to market-economy demands, based on the new legislation. The brain-drain phenomenon—both external and internal—has swollen, as many scientists have been tempted to work abroad or to change their jobs because of the advantages offered by businesses or private industry.

The State is therefore still compelled to supervise the formation of a central fund for research financing and its distribution.

The organization of the research institutes as autonomous businesses represents a step forward on the route towards authoritative decentralization. It nevertheless implies the risk that these new companies could change their concern towards a small-series production or trade as alternatives for increasing revenue, whereas scientific activity could be a secondary preoccupation.

Another risk which research must cope with at present is the change of interest of highly-skilled personnel towards more profitable activities.

The attraction exerted by private affairs, following after a long period of total interdiction of free initiative is legitimate and in many ways useful to research. The result will be a source of private managers for R&D.

Only a short time has elapsed since the fall of the communist regime. The old conceptions and organizational structures are still vivid, and the reorganization of industry, trade, research, and development has generated unemployment and an economic downturn. Under these conditions, the responsibility assumed by the State to protect scientific creation and provide an adequate environment for its implementation is extremely onerous.

To make a start, several organizational solutions have been found which combine stability with dynamism, autonomy with economic discipline, shortage of material and financial supplies, with people's ingenuity.

However, in the next phase, the organization of science, allotment of funds for scientific and technical creativity, as well as the protection of the research results beyond the borders of the country, must be a priority.

The process of creating new organizational structures in the economic, social, trade union, and technical-scientific activities is rapidly developing, while the risks inherent to this rhythm must not be overlooked. The lack of managers trained under normal conditions makes this activity very difficult and full of risks for all involved.

Romania's Present Conception on R&D-Activity Organization during the Market-Economy Transition

For the moment, it is not possible to talk of a research activity intended to bring profit to private companies: these are just being established and do not have the necessary capital to fund important research investments.

We thus evaluate here public research profitable for all economy sectors, for science in general, as well as for social programmes.

The goals suggested by Romania in relation to this evaluation are as follows:

— Definition and guiding the national policy in the area of research and technology—a duty fulfilled by the Higher Council for Science and Consulting Council for Technological Research, as representative bodies.

— A co-ordinated implementation of the sectorial policies in science and provision of the necessary funds, a task assumed by:

Romania's Academy for Basic Research,

Department of Science for the Inter- and Multi-Disciplinary Programmes, for the Research carried out in higher education institutes and its subordinate institutes.

Competent ministries for the implementation of the programmes of research, development and assimilation of new technologies.

These are the higher organizational bodies of the research and development system.

A particular role in this structure is played by the Department of Science, whose organization chart is presented in Figure 1.

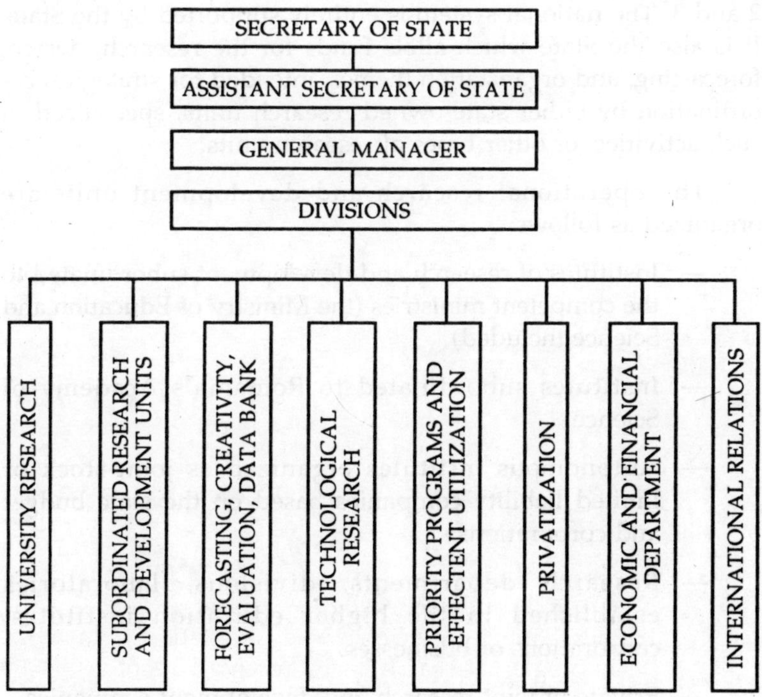

Figure 1. Organization of the Department of Science.

The Department of Science is the body entitled to prepare the policy in science, based on the studies made in all fields of activity, to submit draft acts to the Government's approval in order to initiate regulatory initiatives. This Department has the task of substantiating the necessary funds for the extra-budget-financed research: after the Government's approval they become holder of the fund. They allot a part of the capital to the ministries for specialized research, and they are direct managers of the fund and an active party of the research contract.

A major responsibility devolving upon the Department of Science concerns a programme for reorganizing the activity and the privatization of the research units, for which a specialized division has recently been established. Its organization chart, activity and specific tasks are presented in Table 1 and Figures 2 and 3. The national system is entirely supported by the State. It is also the State which allots funds for the research, design, forecasting, and organization themes, intended for strategical co-ordination by either state-owned research units, specialized in such activities, or other types of research units.

The operational research and development units are organized as follows:

— Institutes of research and development subordinated to the competent ministries (the Ministry of Education and Science included)

— Institutes subordinated to Romania's Academy of Science.

— Autonomous institutes organized as joint-stock or limited liability companies based on the state budget and corporations.

— Research departments, divisions, laboratories established in the higher education institutes, corporations or businesses.

— Private or joint research and development companies.

Table 1. Duties of the Division for the Privatization of Research, Development, and Design Units.

In order to fulfil the duties reverting to the Department of Science concerning the reorganization and privatization of scientific research and design units, the Division for Privatization, established by Order No. 3174/17.01.1992 is entitled to:

— devise the conception and strategy of privatization in the area of research, development, and design.

— devise the privatization criteria in the categories of research, development, and design units and fields of activity.

— co-ordinate the preparation of a methodology to evaluate the assets of research, development, and design units (land, premises, equipment, capital, intellectual potential, and assets).

— provide the data bank and necessary information concerning privatization.

— provide connection to the National Agency for Privatization and other ministries and departments, and make proposals for initiation of new regulations in the area of privatization.

— approve the applications for privatization of the research, development, and design units.

— advise and provide expertize in the area of privatization taking into account the needs of the respective period.

— study and consign the list of research units willing to become private to the National Agency for Privatization.

— support private research, development, and design units by appropriate actions.

These decentralized research units can be funded from the state budget and by agreements concluded with the holders of the funds earmarked for research purposes (see Figure 4).

In the long run, decentralization results in an increased extra-budgetary funding to the prejudice of budgetary financing. However, taking into account the financial difficulties of the transition period, the state is compelled to maintain a fair balance of the state subsidies for research.

The involvement of the State in the centralized distribution of funds for research purposes should be adjusted by changing the allotment system:

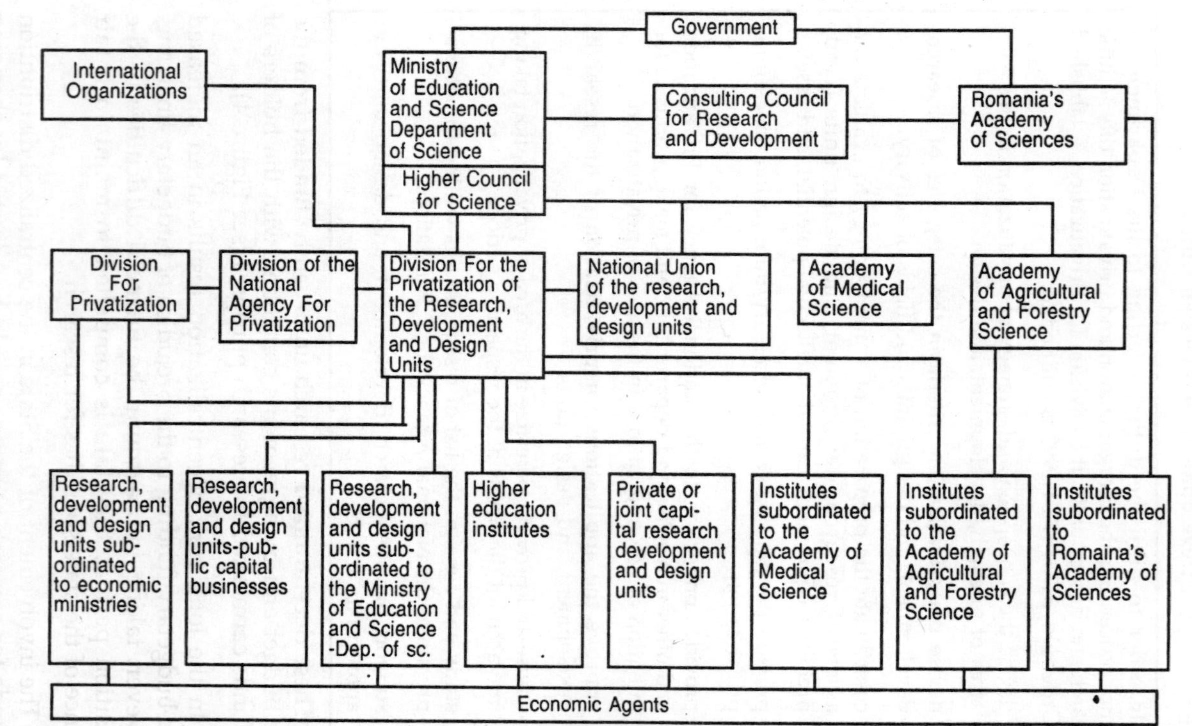

Figure 2. Organization Chart of the Division for Privatization of Research, Development and Design Units.

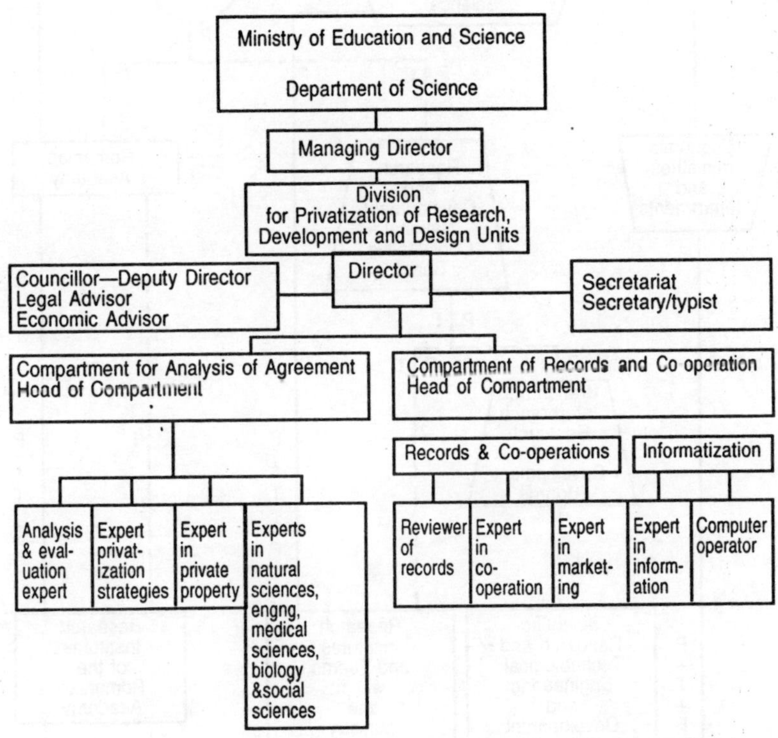

Figure 3. Diagram showing connections within the Division for Privatization of Research, Development, and Design Units.

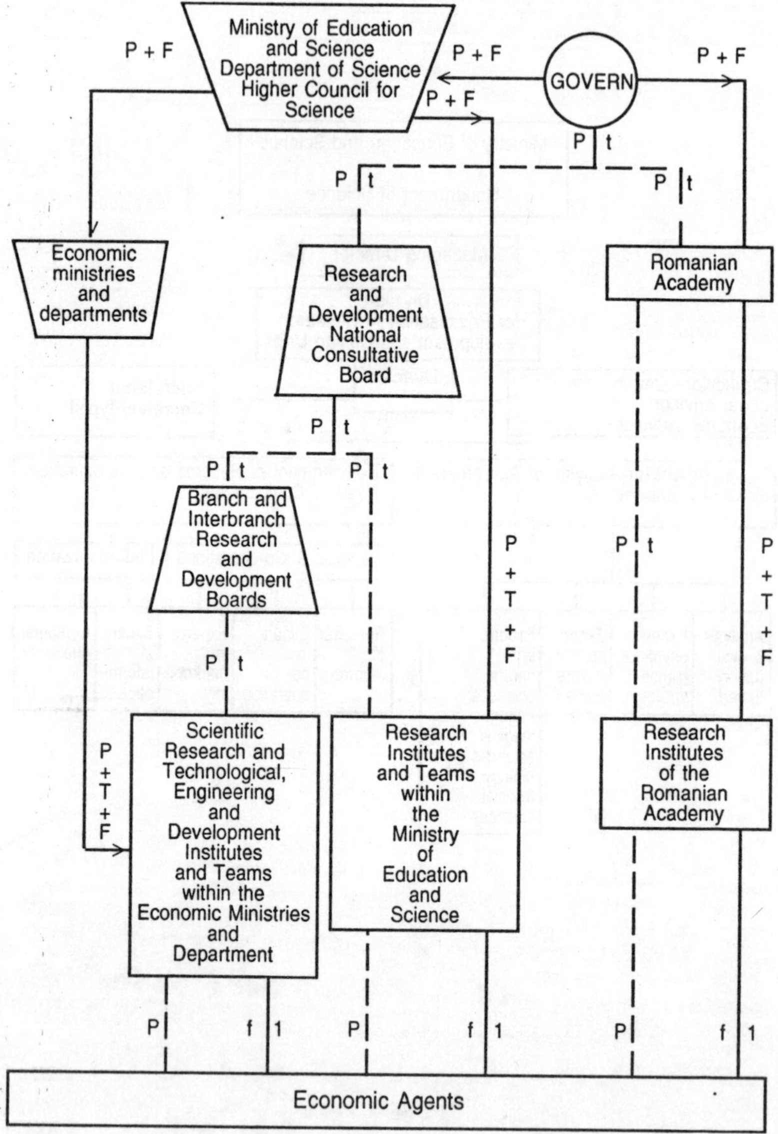

Figure 4. Diagram of activities regarding the scientific research programme in Romania.

Key to Figure 4.

P.	scientific research programmes of national interest, multi-branch, multi-disciplinary, and departmental programmes	
F	budget research funds	
T	approved research projects	
C	proposed research projects	
P	research problems of the economic agents	
f	research funds of the economic agents	
l	advanced, applied, and basic research projects.	
@	formed of	-researchers -research managers -representatives of economic agents -ministry and department specialists
&	formed of	-academicians -scientists -researchers and highly qualified specialists -professors and academic personnel
#	duties	-analyse -evaluate -approve -distribute funds
$	duties	-analyse -evaluate -approve -co-operate
- - - - - - -		proposals
————		approvals

Note: the diagram presents the activities (prepare, justify, approve, subsidize) and bodies concerned in the scientific research programmes in Romania, August 1991.

Instead of allotting funds to institutions, the state should impose funding as a function of the research themes and initiate a system of actions, so that the funds could be efficiently managed.

If a selective allotment system is adopted, it would already be possible to speak about an integration of the research activity into the market economy. Competition will stimulate quality and the immediate interest of scientists.

Moreover, this will facilitate a modular reorganization of the research institutes, as a function of the market demands and exigencies, and direct involvement of private managers, which entails a change of the rigid structures into dynamic and flexible ones.

Capital or assets in private property will be an additional stimulus for triggering the creative forces. The research manager and business owner will be interested in obtaining the necessary funds, in the competitively of the personnel, and in stimulating positive results. The same is true if the working team wishes to contribute by shares to the capital.

We consider ungrounded the objection according to which scientists must be left alone in their 'ivory tower', protected against the risks of the free market in order to devote themselves to science. In fact, the managing staff in charge of the control of the funds and the business are always appointed and paid in the knowledge that they carry on their shoulders the burden of the private company, the owners being only the immediate users of the profit and the only ones in a position to decide upon the necessary investments.

An interesting solution to the research organization in the transition period from the public to the private property is the holding company, whose evaluation is in progress and which is interesting for making comparisons with the scientific experience of other countries.

Several Alternatives for Privatization, Applicable to the R&D Sector

The Act of Business Privatization operational in Romania mentioned the following alternatives:

— capital sale, under the form of shares or state-owned social shared

— sales of the state-owned assets

— leasing or rent for state-owned possessions.

In this way, businesses based on public capital can be reorganized under the form of co-opting private firms onto the business, or under a modular form, some of the modules or even all of them liable to be sold to private firms.

Another alternative is to associate businesses based on public capital with a private firm, the immediate effect being an increase of the capital.

At present, this last alternative is most often applied owing to its smaller risk concerning the protection of public capital.

The above-mentioned alternatives are equally applicable to research and development businesses and under certain conditions (for the capital resulting from extrabudgetary funds) to the research and development institutes which are not businesses proper yet.

Several Characteristics

— In a transition periods it is more cautions to create small research and development units which can count on a well-defined segment of the market for technologies, ideas and experimental products. The most appropriate form of organization for them is the limited liability company. Such a company is also advantageous in that any capital transfer is limited to a small group. The risk to purchasing shares by capital holders who are not warned against the problems of research is smaller than in the case of joint-stock companies.

— In all circumstances of privatization, an evaluation of the public patrimony is compulsory. The evaluation of the industrial and intellectual property is difficult and, at the same time, essential for the penetration of the research results on the market (either directly or by industrial users).

— The accumulations of the socialist epoch, which as already mentioned are significant, resulted in a unitary network of technical and material supplies in any field of activity. The alienation of any such outfit, before an assimilation of new research technology is certain, represents a major risk for the very existence of research in Romania. Privatization by selling or leasing assets is therefore conditioned by the acquaintance with and the evaluation of the purchaser as a good manager or specialist, capable of maintaining the object of activity and fulfilling the responsibilities assumed by the former research units before the financiers. A research and development company is not just any business affair, but a creation by the state for a well-defined purpose. Privatization can serve immediate economic interests, but cannot neglect the purpose.

— A clever and extremely fruitful solution for privatization of the research and development activity is the Business Innovation Centre.

  Subordinated to higher education institutes, research institutes or industrial parks, Business Innovation Centres facilitate the acquaintance with the possible buyers or owners of the outfit, their assistance in business affairs and marketing, in the control of prices and application of technologies and finally in the legal transfer of ownership.

— An Act concerning the free initiative ratified soon after December 1989 has enabled the sporadic formation of small private research teams based on their own funds. They perform research activities on the users' outfit, provide technical consultation, perform analyses, measurements, studies.

— Due to the small overhead expenses and the reasonable cost of labour, private authorized groups or persons are preferred by some of the private businesses all the more as the specialists involved are very often remarkable personalities recently retired or retiring. Their market is limited, for the time being, to the public companies which show confidence in them. In future, they can participate in auctions for research themes of national interest and, in their capacity as good organizers and persons already experienced on the market, they can organize larger, more complex and competitive private groups.

— It is expected that the germs of privatization could result in the high and expensive directing bodies, bequeathed by the former regime, becoming insolvent.

— However, considering the general environment of the market economy, the transition period with its financial and technical difficulties, such activities as research and development, scientific creation, and innovation cannot be left at the mercy of the harsh rules of competition and profit. They are just like the land, the soil and subsoil resources and nature, the real wealth of a nation. Therefore, the state is compelled to protect them for their survival and, moreover, for their economic strengthening.

We consider worthwhile the allotment of funds for research and development or the warranty of credits from both Romania's public banks and foreign financial sources.

It seems natural that the joint negotiations and the actions initiated by international bodies should include distinct divisions for the support of science development, for international co-operation in this area, for granting unredeemable credits to the research teams concerned with general technical and social problems.

Science is not only a natural matter, and scientific research is a value *per se* whose legal and financial conditions should be well defined, with the agreement of the international community, at least in the way that man's rights or armaments control are.

It is worthwhile relying, at least partially, on the solutions of implementation adopted by private businesses.

The experience gained by the East European countries, obliged to save their own research activity under the conditions of fierce competition on the international market and an economic, social, and political crises, inherent to the transition period, can serve as a subject of meditation.

22

The Russian Academy of Sciences and Scientific Co-operation in Europe

IGOR MAKAROV

Academician, Chief Scientific Secretary, Russian Academy of Sciences, Moscow, Russia

Preamble

Today it is difficult to tell the absolute and relative figures or the percentage from the state budget which are allocated to fundamental studies in Russia. I remember very well what these figures were in the USSR but now this belongs to the past and is no longer interesting. So, I am going to build up my report about the Russian Academy of Sciences, which I represent.

Only two structures have so far survived in Russia—they are: the Russian Academy of Sciences and the Russian Orthodox Church.

I will try to construct a model of the survival of Russian Fundamental Science which has its own specifics, and the development of which might successfully contribute to world science. Generally speaking, I am not for universal models and I cannot assume responsibility for building them up.

I suppose we should rather pay more attention not to models but to the principles providing favourable conditions for the development of fundamental science. In this respect I would like to show the role of Russian Academy of Sciences.

The Russian Academy of Sciences and Scientific Co-operation in Europe

Distinguished colleagues! Ladies and Gentlemen!

In December 1991, a new page was added to the history of Russian science. The General Meeting of the Academy of Sciences adopted the decision to revive the Russian Academy of Sciences—the supreme scientific-technical establishment in Russia.

The Russian Academy of Sciences is the historical successor to the Academy of Sciences of the USSR. The history of the Academy of Sciences goes back 268 years. Created in 1724 in St. Petersburg under the direction of Peter the Great, the Academy made a great contribution to Russian prosperity, studying and mastering its wealth, the rise of intellectual and spiritual potential of many generations of Russians.

Nowadays the Academy unites 365 scientific establishments with more than 160 thousand people involved, including 66 thousand scientific workers. A set of unique installations are successfully functioning in the Academy. In the first place, there are the two giant astronomical instruments, the telescope-reflector BTA with main mirror diameter of 6 metres, and the radio-telescope 'RATAN-600'. They are widely used for conducting scientific research by astronomers from many different countries. In addition, the deep-water inhabitable apparatus 'MIR', provided with a system of modern-measuring equipment allows complex expedition research of the ocean world to be conducted down to a depth of 6000 metres. Finally, the 1 MeV high-voltage electron microscope enables the most complicated tasks to be solved.

We see that investigations over the widest spectrum of modern science are conducted in the Academy of Sciences. Of great significance is its contribution to the solution of the nuclear problem, to the elaboration and fulfilment of the space programme, to the minerals-prospecting activity. A set of results of the research is at the highest level now and has worldwide recognition. The scientific schools of the theory of figures and theory of probability, in the sphere of nuclear physics and quantum physics, in the theory of combustion, in low-temperature physics and other fields, have gained high international regard. The scientific establishments of the Academy participate in the carrying out of the all-national programmes involving the study and use of outer space.

The Academy issues more than 200 scientific journals, more than half translated abroad regularly. It is closely integrated into the world scientific association. It includes 130 foreign members. The Academy has more than 70 agreements on scientific co-operation with foreign countries, takes an active part in the activity of 236 scientific international governmental organizations in the most up-to-date directions of the natural and humanitarian sciences. Our scientists take active part in the international scientific programmes on space, climate, world ocean, Arctic and Antarctic studies, geological correlations, in international projects and research on current problems of physics, mathematics, chemistry, microbiology, biotechnology and other major directions of research work.

Now a few words about financing and organization of scientific research. The system of financing investigations does not correspond to Western ones. We finance scientific institutes that have defined the scope of their investigations by themselves. Experience shows that such systems of 'basic' financing works effectively enough. At the same time, without giving it up we are gradually starting to use the grant system and target financing of scientific projects or programmes.

The Russian Academy of Sciences in its organizing structures combines scientific-industrial and territorial principles. It consists of 18 specialized units on mathematics, physics, chemistry, biology, earth sciences, humanitarian, and public disciplines; three regional departments in Siberia, the Urals, the Far West, and 11 scientific centres.

The problem of a co-ordination of fundamental investigations in Russia is now taking on the highest significance as in all scientific associations. Historically it happened that scientific research in Russia is carried out in the establishments of three sectors—Academic; higher educational; and establishmental and industrial. All are co-ordinated by the Academy. The co-ordinating work is conducted through the specialized departments of the Academy and through its scientific councils on the most important problems. The staff of the councils is formed from the leading scientists of those three sectors of science. The Russian Academy takes an active part in the work of the governmental scientific-technical programmes of Russia, aimed at the socially significant goals. It also gives the Academy a chance to strengthen links with the scientific collectives, participating in the development of those programmes. The future for organization of the interaction of science, education, and manufacturing in the country lies in technological parks—associations created on the basis of the leading scientific centres and universities. In the Russian Federation, 13 technological parks have already been registered: these are engaged in practical work and seven more are in the course of creation.

Here I will allow myself to finish off with the official representation of the Russian Academy of Sciences. Please note that the superficial resemblance of my view with the works of Chagall is mere coincidence.

The Russian Academy has pursued a policy of scientific-technical co-operation in science and technology. European co-operation in scientific and technical research, the European Community programme, operates to encourage the further development of existing contacts in the framework of the European Council, heuric and international scientific organizations on European and international level.

The many years' experience of such co-operation testifies to the necessity of shifting the priority to targeted scientific-research programmes and projects with concrete forecastable results. Direct connections between the scientific collectives and separate scientists should form the basic for fulfilment of any programme. These connections may be carried out in various forms: from the holding of regular working seminars and working specific tasks in laboratories to the organization of joint scientific centres.

Despite some serious difficulties, which the Russian Academy of Sciences is currently experiencing, we are entering the all-European scientific market not with empty hands. Even now we are ready to suggest a wide programme on joint scientific research. Our scientists are well acquainted with their colleagues from the various countries of Europe. We can forward such suggestions in the near future.

The spectrum of suggestions with sufficient scientific reserve is very wide; mathematics and computing techniques, plasma physics, non-traditional energetics and energy-saving, high temperature fuel elements, possible future systems of energy-saving 'Space-Earth' on the ground of new-generation solar transformers, high-efficiency chemical works, development of a new progressive technology in engineering industry, development of new effective forms of mineral prospecting, and others.

With the backing of all-European co-operation, we hope to complete the construction of several unique objects on the territory of Russia with the purposes of creation on their base of international scientific centres. Here we can include the high-pressure research nuclear reactor PIK which is being build in St. Petersburg. This will make it possible to get a flux of thermal neutrons higher than 10^{15} neutrons per square centimetre. The presence of the large number of experimental installations, including sources of cold and ultra-cold neutrons and neutron systems more than 300-m in length, opens up vast possibilities for organizing an international centre for neutron research on the basic of that reactor. The participation of European countries in the creation of such a centre would allow us to overcome a long-term deficit in the sources of intensive neutron beams for fundamental research workers, above all in the field of condensed-matter physics, including high-temperature super-semiconductors.

Another interesting proposal could consist in the creation of the first ever deep-water wide-scaled Cherenkov detector of elementary particles in the Baykal lake. This would allow us to investigate the flux of the cosmic neutrino in the range of energies 10^{11}—10^{14} electron-volts. It would be possible to study the active stages of the evolution of the universe as a whole and its separate objects, the search for new elementary particles and rare process, at levels of sensitivity inaccessible by other methods of investigation.

It might be possible to consider the proposal of the creation in Moscow of an international scientific-technical centre for the physics of extreme conditions and investigation of the security of the nuclear-energetic, chemical, and energetic technologies, with the aim of conducting fundamental investigations in high-pressure and high-temperature physics and chemistry. As a basis for this centre, there could be the world's largest explosive cell, with a weight of 800 tonnes and an 11-m diameter. It would be possible to carry out explosions where the explosive's weight is 2000 kg, as well as creating in Russia the cavity laser and high-current electronic and ionic installation.

Ten and sometimes hundreds of millions of roubles are invested in these projects, and their level of readiness is over 70 per cent. For this reason, a comparatively small capital investment is needed to make unique complexes like these available to the world scientific community. I am sure that the support for putting up such objects, as well as Russian science, which is a link to the world science, on the whole, will open up good opportunities for European scientific co-operation, with subsequent integration of science in Europe.

Thus the variety of forms of organization of Euroscience testify to the fact that the integration of science in this region will not be an easy process and will need a long period of time. Nevertheless, I find it useful to pursue co-operation in the mutual scientific field with the aim of turning it into an immense scientific complex later on, and there an important role must be played to UNESCO-ROSTE.

Every possible opportunity should be used to support ROSTE, to strengthen its links with the national academies and centres and international organizations, and primarily with ICSU, which has already founded a Special Committee in Science in Central and Eastern Europe.

I believe it is possible to identify the main problems on which ROSTE must focus its attention, as follows:

(i) Working out all European scientific policy, determining priorities, and in particular problems which could not be solved by one European country alone.

(ii) Working out the fundamental science support programme in Eastern Europe. Giving possible support to young scientists with the aim of stemming the brain-drain from these countries.

(iii) Solving the problems of prevention of scientific duplication, avoidance of waste of scientific effort, reduction of financial expenses, with the aim of accelerating the solving of global scientific problems.

(iv) Creating the all-European idea and technology market.

(v) Working out forms and methods of scientific study.

(vi) Standardization.

(vii) Organizing an exchange of scientific and technical achievements with the ultimate aim of creating a uniform system of European scientific information on the basis of the already developing computer network.

One cannot enter the same stream twice. For too long a period of time we have been thrashing about in the 'West-East' waters. At the present moment we are cautiously coming into another stream called inter-European co-operation. I hope sailing in it will be more successful—all the necessary grounds for it are there.

In conclusion, I wish to express deep gratitude to UNESCO, George Sorosa Fund, and the various organizations in France, USA, Austria, and other countries, for their support of fundamental research in Russia.

Thank you for your attention.

23

Transformation of the System of Financing R&D in Poland*

BOGDAN ROKOSZ

Senior Officer, State Committee for Scientific Research, Warsaw, Poland

The organization of science in Poland after World War II was based on the Soviet model, in which all scientific institutions were divided into three groups:

Polish Academy of Sciences (PAS).

Universities and other higher schools of university rank.

Research and development institutes administered by ministries (*e.g.* industry, forestry, agriculture).

The main feature of this model was the dominance of the PAS institutes in the area of basic research, while a large network of sectorial R&D institutes was charged with undertaking most of the applied R&D work.

From 1985 to 1990 policy and funding were determined centrally by the Committee for Development of Science and Technology at the Council of Ministers, a governmental body composed of nominated members and chaired by a Deputy Prime Minister. The Committee was responsible for drawing up

* Prepared on the basis of papers by Karczewski W., Frackowiak J. K., and Ziabicki A., in Kuklinski A. (ed.) *Transformation of Science in Poland*, Warsaw, 1991.

forecasts of needs and opportunities for research, formulating central research and development programmes and supervising their implementation. R&D works were financed through Central Fund for Development of Science and Technology made up of economic establishments' payments (a turnover tax of 1.5 per cent on the value of an enterprise's production). The Committee decided upon distribution of resources to ministries and PAS which, in turn, distributed allocated funds to subordinated universities, institutes and laboratories.

An important role in the administrative decisions was played by ideological, personal and bureaucratic factors, while the quality of research was often ignored. People employed in scientific units had little or no influence on the management and financing of research, and in certain disciplines (especially in social and economical sciences) their research activities were restricted.

A thorough reform of the organization and financing of S&T was demanded by various groups of scientists already in 1980. However, martial law introduced in December 1981 forced the reformers to stop their work or to continue it underground. When the former political system collapsed after parliamentary elections in June 1989, the discussions on necessary changes in the S&T sector were resumed.

Following long public debate on the new administrative structure for managing and financing research, the Polish Parliament passed the Act on Establishment of the State Committee for Scientific Research, which came into force on 12 January, 1991. The Committee is composed of 19 members, 12 of whom are elected representatives of the scientific community (all academic and research staff with Ph.Ds. have a right of vote); the remaining 7 are: Chairman elected by parliament, Secretary, and 5 ministers appointed by the Prime Minister. The same applies to the Committee's Commissions—one for basic and the other for applied research—divided into specialist teams and responsible for proper assessment and financing of scientific institutions in Poland.

The committee has been given a wide range of responsibilities:

— to produce draft guidelines on government S&T policy for debate by the Council of Ministers

— to identify areas of research that are likely to yield particularly fruitful scientific, social, and economic benefits

— to prepare and submit annually to the Ministry of Finance a draft plan for budgetary spending on R&D.

— to determine criteria and procedures for allocating resources to R&D.

— to allocate founds for R&D.

— to monitor and evaluate the R&D activities financed by the State budget.

The fundamental change as compared with the former system of financing consists in that now R&D are founded entirely by the State budget whole resources are channelled by the Committee in charge of full or partial financing of:

— statutory activities of R&D institutes as well as research carried out by higher schools of university rank.

— research projects submitted and approved in open competition.

— research projects stemming from strategic government programmes.

— R&D works of social and economic importance, implemented upon order by enterprises, state administrative bodies or local governments.

— international scientific and technological co-operation resulting from intergovernmental agreements.

— general technical and research supporting activities (*e.g.* publishing activities, information services, libraries, learned societies).

One of the most important features of the present system is introduction of competition for the financing of research projects (grants). The grant mechanism is based on western, especially America, patterns which had to be adapted to incomparable, very specific circumstances. It is aimed, among other things, at overcoming some fossilized personal ties and giving a chance to young researchers who often have had to wait for many years for the possibility of proving their talent.

During the first funding round in February 1991, 9600 project proposals are submitted, 2420 of which were granted. The low experience of the staff, and lack of necessary information technology equipment in some of the early weeks protracted the peer-review process, though the competition for grants nevertheless proved to be a useful tool for preliminary identification of the abilities and activeness of Polish scientists.

The grant mechanism is sometimes criticized for initiating a brutal struggle for funds. But experience gained in other countries has shown that grants lead to more efficient utilization of resources, the feature particularly important in Poland where the wastage of public money is all too common. It is therefore hoped that the system of grants will be accepted in scientific circles and will help towards raising the standard and competitiveness of Polish research in the coming years.

In 1991 it was planned to assign about 20 per cent of the research budget to grants: it is assumed their share will be gradually increased to 50 per cent.

It should be stressed here that the Committee started its activities in the very difficult period of transition from a centrally planned to market economy. Owing to the servere economic crisis, significant increase in the science budget will obviously be impossible during the next few years. In this situation, the Committee has been forced to decide whether it should provide almost every scientific institution with a very limited, inadequate amount of money, or else whether the same financial resources should only be offered to the best people. The latter strategy seems to be painful but the only reasonable solution. Therefore, the Committee is opting for a smaller number of properly equipped institutes and laboratories, manned by the best scientists and working in these fields of S&T which both represent the highest level in terms of scientific achievements and are most significant for the economic and civilizational development of the country.

It is expected that the transformation of financing system will be followed by the systemic changes that are crucial for the future of Polish science. The role of basic sciences as a necessary component of the nation's civilizational development is now better understood. That is why institutions performing research in basic sciences should be financed by the State budget. The situation of applied sciences is different. State-owned industrial enterprises lost interest in innovation through the economic crisis, and the private sector is still too weak to substantially support R&D institutions. The Committee decided therefore to support temporarily these institutions, which should normally be financed by the industrial sector. However, they will not be financed in the future when they are supposed to start earning money.

The solutions described above are, of course, far from perfect. For this reason they are often criticized, especially by those scientists who argue that the system is overcentralized. There is no doubt that it will be changed in the future. The first step in this direction could be a revision of the Parliamentary Act on Establishment of the State Committee for Scientific Research. Discussions concerning a possible revision have already begun.

24

Science and Government—Some Notes For Discussion

ANTONI KUKLINSKI

Undersecretary of State, State Committee for Scientific Research, Poland

Introduction

The history of the state is, at one and the same time, that of the relationship of science and government. It is necessary to recognize that science and government have different logics of development and it is dangerous and harmful if the government tries to impose its logic on science and *vice versa*.

In different historical conditions, different pragmatic solutions in this field have been designed and implemented. The decade of the nineties will be crucial years in Europe, and will see deep structural changes in the nature of the state and in the nature of science. It is, therefore, advisable to have a hard look at our experiences in this field.

Let me suggest ten topics for comparative studies, conferences, and publications:

1. science and government—three models
2. strategic choices in the development of science
3. science and technology—science policy and industrial policy
4. thematic choices in the development of science

5. regional approaches in the development of science
6. science and market economy
7. the autonomy of the scientific community—potentialities and limitations
8. the role of the state in the development of science—the efficiency of governmental agencies
9. the role of international organizations in the development of science
10. the changing nature of science and the changing nature of government at the turn of this century.

Science and Government—Three Models

There are three models of the relation science-government:

(i) The model of the unlimited autonomy of science

(ii) the model of the unlimited domination of the government

(iii) the equilibrium model.

(a) in the first model science enjoys an unlimited autonomy and is guided only by its own internal logic of development. It is extremely difficult to find implementation of the pure version of this model in any historical experience;

(b) in the second model science is just a servant of the government. But some independent scholars have survived even in hard totalitarian regimes;

(c) in the third model, now dominating in the most important countries, there is an equilibrium between the internal autonomy of the scientific community and the long-term interests of society, economy and state.

Strategic Choices in the Development of Science*

Each society is obliged to make three strategic choices related to the role of science:

---

* Cf Kuklinski, 1991, p. 356.

1. How important is the role of science in the development of national culture and identity?
2. How important is the role of science—in the development of the spiritual and material foundation of competitive society?
3. How important is the role of science in the development of a competitive globally-oriented national economy?

So the crucial choice of the given society is to answer the fundamental question—is science important for the development of the society and economy or is it not? This strategic choice of society and government is expressed in the share of science in the GNP of the given country.

There are three groups of countries here—the most advanced allocating above 2 per cent GNP, the advanced allocating 1-2 per cent, the third allocating less than 1 per cent. The geographical and historical change of this index is a good measure of the role of sciences in different countries.

S&T—Science Policy and Industrial Policy*

The relation of science and technology creating the R&D system is the foundation of each national economy—which is trying to win the competitive struggle on the global scene.

There are two approaches to the R&D system:

1. a *laissez-faire* approach based on the assumption that market forces will spontaneously shape this system.
2. a guided-change approach based on the assumption that the promotion of this system is impossible without a strong science and industrial policy.

Let us quote an important statement of the *International Business Week*** on industrial policy, printed on the front page.

---

* Cf *OECD*, Paris, 1991.

** *International Business Week*, 6 April 1992. Cover Story—Industrial Policy—Call It What You Will, The Nation Needs A Plan to Nurture Growth. "*Government can become a key player in the knowledge economy. It should boost research spending across a wide range of technologies and offer hefty financial support to the next generation of scientists and enginneers.*"

Industrial Policy! The very phrase rattles the teeth. It implies bureaucracy. It suggests government will pick winners and losers. Done badly, it would certainly hurt America. But with the cold war over and a global economy taking shape, America needs to shore up its competitiveness. How? Certainly, by investing in education and infrastructure. But that's not enough. We much recharge the 'knowledge base'—the basic science and technology that are the foundation of an advanced industrial society. Perhaps we should call it a growth policy.

This growth policy is a crucial problem in global scale but especially in Central and Eastern Europe.

Thematic Choices in the Development of Science*

The thematic choices are most exposed in the judgement of the scientific community and society at large. In the model of organic growth of science, a balance should be kept among preferences allocated to:

— technical sciences
— natural sciences
— economic and managerial sciences
— human sciences/humanities.

This balance is necessary if science is seen as an element of national, cultural and national identity. In this approach there is a strong place for social sciences and humanities.

In a model of unbalanced growth, especially in short-term considerations, strong preferences are allocated to technical, natural, economic, and managerial sciences—directly contributing to development of technology, economy, and also armament industries.

It would be extremely interesting if UNESCO or OECD could sponsor a study examining the thematic priorities in different countries, let us say, over the last two decades.

Regional Approaches in Science Development**

In the recent OECD publication cited, we find the following statement:

* Cf Kuklinski, 1991, p. 358.

** OECD, 1991, p. 57.

"Science and technology policy is no longer planned, drawn up and implemented only by national strategic and policy institutions.

In a very large majority of OECD countries, the development of the regional dimension of science and technology policies has been one of the most important trends over the last decade. This dimension, in fact, consists of two factors in combination which need to be distinguished even if they are in part inter-related:

— The first is the growing awareness of the central role of science and technology in economic growth and social development shown by political and economic decision-makers in what we shall designate in this report as 'regions', whatever their exact designation—state, province, land, country, etc.;

— The second is the realization by national governments that some of their science and technology policy objectives, particularly those relating to the technological development of industrial enterprises, are best achieved by locally based activities, *i.e.* activities designed and, above all, implemented in close connection with regional and local conditions."

Science and Market Economy

In the present discussion on market economy there are two approaches in this field:

1. the first approach sees the market economy as a spontaneous phenomenon more or less in the perspective of the 19th century traditions,
2. the second approach sees the market economy as a guided institutionalized phenomenon incorporating the whole transformation of the global economy of the 20th century (Wade, 1991).

We need serious studies and discussions to answer the question—to what extent in the most advanced capitalistic countries (science, knowledge, and know-how) are conventional market commodities exposed to the normal supply and demand rules of price?

I think that science, knowledge and know-how are special commodities very often not exposed to the normal market rules. Let us mention only two extreme examples: one, the fundamental sciences, and two, the military R&D system.

But this is the question that should be answered in serious empirical studies.

The Autonomy of the Scientific Community—Potentialities and Limitations

The autonomy of scientific communities can be seen as a final or instrumental value. If it is accepted as a final value then it will be promoted even in situations where other solutions are more efficient as regards the development of science.

One should promote a comprehensive set of comparative studies on the development of scientific communities (Marks, 1991) in different countries, and the role of endogenous and exogamous factors in this field; and answer the question *inter alia* of whether the present science-globalization phenomenon is expanding or restricting the autonomy of scientific communities.

Role of the State in the Development of Science—Efficiency of the Governmental Agencies*

There is universal agreement that the state performs an important role in the development of science. However, in the opening part of this paper, I have stressed that the equilibrium model is *grosso modo* accepted as the model outlining the relation science-government.

In the analysis of the governmental agencies acting in this field, there are three approaches:

1. An approach of individual description presenting the case in the climate of uniqueness.
2. An approach of comparative analysis, seeking similarities and differences in relation to the solutions developed in other countries.
3. An approach of pragmatic analysis, that attempts to answer the question of how efficient are the solutions developed in country A in comparison with the solutions developed in country B.

   For example, it would be interesting and useful to compare from this point of view the Polish State

---

* Cf Karczewski, 1991.

Committee for Scientific Research and the French Ministére de la Recherche et de la Technologie.

Unfortunately, the efficiency of governmental agencies is in practice beyond the scope of comparative analysis.

International organizations are accepting a tracit assumption that value judgements of this type are outside the limits of their competence.

Role of International Organizations in the Development of Science*

The development of science is incorporated in a global network of relations, inducements, co-operative and competitive behavioural patterns. International organizations are an important and creative element of this global network. International organizations have developed a comprehensive system linking not only activities at intergovernmental level but also the activities of individual scholars, institutes, universities, academies, academic societies, and R&D institutions.

In relation to the classical agencies of the government, the system of international organizations should be seen in both co-operative and competitive perspective.

One should try to prepare a comprehensive cost-benefit analysis of the activities of international organizations in terms of the development of science and technology.

This study should also answer the question of the relative efficiency of different international organizations in the field of development of science and technology.

The Changing Nature of Science and of Government at the Turn of the Century

We observe very deep changes in the nature and structure of science. The globalization of scientific and technological activities is creating a new reality and a new environment for the individual and social behaviour of academic communities (Science and Technology Agency, Japanese Government, 1991).

---

* Cf Kuklinski, 1991, pp. 89-167.

However, we have to remember that the global scene is largely determined by the strongest and most advanced countries, transnational corporations, and international organizations. The co-operation, competition, and conflict among those strong actors is the main driving force of the global scene.

It is a formidable task to outline the real sphere of manoeuvre of the smaller actors. Are they able to design and implement creative science and technology policies or are these policies only those of adaptation to the global relatity?

This is the fundamental question for the governmental agencies involved in S&T policy at the turn of this century, especially in Central and East Europe.

Conclusions

Critical comments on this note would be very highly appreciated. Especially important is the question to what extent the ideas presented in this note should be an inducement to design and implement an International Research, Conference, and Publication Programme: *'Science and Government at the Turn of This Century'* (Kacprzynski, 1991).

REFERENCES

Kacprzynski, E., 1991. The transformation process of science and technology in Poland. In A. Kuklinski (ed), *Transformation of Science in Poland*. Warsaw.

Karczewski, W., 1991. Some remarks on S&T in Poland. In A. Kuklinski (ed), *Transformation of Science in Poland*. Warsaw.

Kuklinski, A (ed), 1991. *Transformation of Science in Poland*, Warsaw.

Marks, J., 1991. Science at the turn of the 20th century. In A. Kuklinski (ed), *Transformation of Science of Poland*. Warsaw.

OECD, 1991. *Choosing Priorities in Science and Technology*. OECD, Paris.

Science and Technology Agency—Japanese Government., 1991. White Paper on Science and Technology.

Wade, R., 1991. *Governing the Market—Economic Theory and the Role of Government in EAT Asian Countries*. Princeton University Press.

25

The Evolution and Role of National and International Organizations in Science in Europe

AUGUSTO FORTI

Secretary General, European Institute for East-West Co-operation, Venice, Italy

First of all, I would like to acknowledge the long established but irreplaceable role played in the transformation of science structures in Europe by UNESCO, WHO, the International Atomic Energy Agency, UNIDO, and the other organizations belonging to the UN system in the years since the fifties.

As regards UNESCO, I believe it is fair to remember that this organization has been for decades that only open channel of communication between scientists from East and West.

We should also recall its contribution to the progress of science through programmes which were developed in Europe, such as the international geological correlation programme, the various activities related to man and the biosphere, and the proliferation of advanced postgraduate training programmes run jointly by scientists from East and West.

UNESCO through its science policy division is also instrumental in the support and assistance to European member states in the working out and reconstruction of national science policy and of national infrastructures in science and research.

UNESCO also provided a fundamental key in maintaining the European scientific community in the region, thus avoiding the brain-drain problem of outstanding physicists in particular, through the creation of CERN in Geneva, EMBO, and other regional scientific organizations. Most notably, at the end of the 80s, with the decentralization of the European Office for Science and Technology, attention is being given to the needs of Europe and its evolving situation.

Today, many other inter-governmental organizations like the European Community (EEC), the OECD, and the Council of Europe, have major programmes which are also involving Eastern European countries. I believe that everyone here is aware of the programmes which ROSTE has developed on specific topics such as energy, new materials, AIDS, and also the role of ROSTE in crucial issues like the brain-drain and the need for better management of research. V. Kouzminov will provide any literature you might request.

If one were to inquire deeply into a study of the evolution of science in Europe, I know that a great deal of interesting material would be found in the Science Policy Unit of UNESCO, as well as at OECD and other governmental organizations. Of course, we should not overlook the growing role of non-governmental organizations like ICSU, the European Science Foundation, the European Institute for East-West Co-operation, and many others.

But today, the question we are posing to ourselves is the following: are the structures that we set up in the fifties and sixties (CNR and the Academies) still valid? And are those structures responding to the needs which have been generated by the deep changes of our society? Structures that were created after the Second World War, linked to the industrial reconstruction and typically connected with the industrial society, have experienced over the years a very arduous process of adaptation to the new European post-industrial society. Today, living in a very rapidly changing age, we have to recognize that the CNR and the Academies are suffering from the same malaise as the other paleo-industrial structures.

Just to quote some of the problems which are afflicting these organizations:

- bureaucratization
- elephantiasis: unwieldy structures with wastage of funds, duplication of effort, and lack of flexibility, rendering them incapable of responding to the recurrent crises of our society.
- poor management and unadroit evaluation of the relevance of the programmes and of any type of cost-benefit analysis.
- lack of managerial skills of the laboratory directors. Furthermore, these structures cannot cope with the increasingly significant research-innovation-market chain. The laboratories of the academies and national research councils are bursting with important research findings that will never reach the marketplace, resulting in significant economic loss to the nation as a consequence.

Should we then envisage a shutting down of the academies and national research councils? This is certainly too formidable a step: should we instead try to reorganize and give better focus to their vast mission? I believe this is a question taking shape in the minds of many in Europe. Certainly the restructuring of these bodies could be one of the future tasks of many European countries. Here I believe there is a rich opportunity for innovation for those European countries that are reshaping their science and research structures.

As A. Kuklinski and many others have mentioned, Europe for its deep-rooted strong cultural tradition presents a wide variety of cultural approaches to science. Again, I consider this an extremely positive element for Europe because cultural diversity also means creativity and wider opportunity for fertile innovation which will reinforce Europe in its competition with giants like Japan or the USA. Member states and international organizations have therefore to engage in designing new structures for science and research. I believe that the first task will be to make better use of universities, academic laboratories, and professional organizations. A large percentage of investments in research and development should continue to be funded mainly by national resources to universities and academic institutions.

Without a reservoir and continuous supply of results from fundamental research, there is the risk that the chain that runs from basic research to technological products could be blocked by a lack of research resources, whenever an unpredictable technological demand or a socio-economic crisis appears.

There are types of research I would describe as having strategic relevance—electronics, new materials, the environment, etc.—which are demanding a major national effort in order to give a country the capacity to compete on the international market. This research should clearly involve also private and public industries. Then there are research programmes that require, for reasons of their dimensions, the involvement and co-operation of several European countries (here we see the importance of international organizations). This is the case of CERN, space research, and other crucial areas.

In the effort of revolution of European structures, some basic ideas could be borne in mind. With reference to what I have said above, I think that first of all:

- we have to assure that the reservoir of basic scientific research is always full in order to face the frequent and unpredicatable crises.
- creativity and innovation should be encouraged in order to face the challenge of international competition.
- we should also try to avoid excessive intervention of the state, particularly in the field of applied and industrial research, where it may be limited to a grant-giving role which should include the private sector.

The international organizations as we have already described should cover costly co-operative projects ('big science') of strategic importance for the region or of planetary importance. Interntional organizations should also assist national science bodies in setting up peer review or overall analysis of the soundness of a research programme or policy without imposing any ready-made scheme. They have a very important catalyzing role to play.

Finally, there is an increased role of the international non-governmental organizations which are closer to the scientists' problems and interests.

26

Mechanisms of R&TD Policy in The Member States of the EC, with Reference to the Specific Case of the Community Itself

MICHEL PAILLON

Head of Divison, Directorate General for Science, Research and Development, Commission of the European Communities, Brussels, Belgium

It was in the 1930s in the aftermath of World War I that certain western governments, mindful of the role of science in their defence policies, initiated scientific research policies and approved the budgetary resources necessary to maintain them. However, it was not until the 1950s, following World War II, that the importance of the links between science, technology, and the economy were recognized and genuine policies for scientific research and technological development began to take shape in most of the industrialized countries. The various national governments established different structures and procedures according to their particular traditions and needs. Some, like France, opted for a centralized approach. Others, like the UK, developed a decentralized model, each ministerial department implementing its own research and technological development (R&TD) policy. Whichever approach was chosen, they are all contingent on the release of budgetary appropriations enabling certain objectives to be pursued as part of a more or less detailed strategy. The differences between them lie in the manner in which these policies are implemented rather than in their principles.

There are three underlying principles:

- subsidiarity
- continuity
- inter-relationship.

The purpose of the principle of subsidiarity is to define the respective roles of the players involved in R&TD, that is to say public authorities, undertakings, and research organizations, According to this principle, action should be taken at a particular level only if it cannot be taken at a lower level. For example, in some countries, the State will take action only in cases where private sector undertakings are not in a position to do so. In any event, it will be up to the State to lay down the ground rules and to determine the strategic sectors in the light of choices made at national level. These strategic sectors will naturally be eligible for preferential national support.

The purpose of the second principle is to guarantee the continuity of R&TD by proposing a medium or long-term R&TD programme. This is the only way of ensuring that the appropriate resources are made available in good time. By resources we mean not only financial resources but also the human resources necessary for accomplishing R&TD. Because research and technological development is a continuous process, no-one can guarantee the eventual result, particularly in the area of fundamental research, and it may turn out that further resources have to be committed or the duration of certain programmes has to be extended.

The purpose of the principle of inter-relationship is to match the objectives of R&TD policy to those of other policies. Leaving aside support for pure fundamental research, it is impossible to imagine how the public authorities can take action in the field of R&TD without a clear idea of how this policy ties in with, say, economic, industrial, energy or defence policy. Moreover, in our market economics it is essentially these policies that will determine the objectives of R&TD policy. Interestingly enough, where R&TD initiatives have been taken without being closely co-ordinated with the aims of economic, industrial, energy or military policy, they have, for the most part, ended in failure.

This being so, the way in which R&TD policies are put into practice in most western countries is still strongly influenced, as we said earlier, by history and tradition. In some countries, a Ministry for Research and Technology policy has been set up, while in others responsibility for science and technology policy has been entrusted to the Ministry for Education; elsewhere the task has been given to the Ministry for Industry or the Ministry for Economic Affairs. It is interesting to note that in the English-speaking countries, R&TD policy has tended to fall within the remit of technical government ministries, whereas in the Latin countries it tends to be associated with the universities.

There are others, such as France and, to an extent, Belgium, that are still under the centralizing influence of the Napoleonic system and consequently adopt a Cartesian approach, bringing all scientific policy programming together under one umbrella. These different approaches to the implementation of R&TD policy lead in turn to different attitudes to funding, and this sometimes makes it difficult to compare various national R&TD budgets and to evaluate the precise role played by the public authorities in the area concerned.

While in most member countries of the OECD the proportion of gross domestic spending on R&TD financed by national governments is between 45 and 50 per cent, it can be as high as 70 per cent, especially in those countries which are least developed in terms of S&T, or as low as 20 per cent in the most developed countries, like Japan.

Another interesting finding is that the proportion of R&TD actually carried not by the State, which is between 20 and 25 per cent of gross domestic expenditure of R&TD in the majority of OECD countries, can be as high as 50 per cent in the least developed countries and under 10 per cent in the most developed countries (8 per cent in Japan). This shows that the higher the level of scientific and technological development, the smaller is the role of the State and the less direct the influence of national R&TD policy.

The Decentralized Approach: Example of the UK

As we have seen, a decentralized approach can have certain advantages, particularly if market forces are allowed a free rein. The application of the costume-contractor principle in the UK has prompted the government to allow each ministerial department to conduct its own R&TD policy. The main political responsibility for civil R&TD lies with the Department of Education and Science (DES) and the Department of Trade and Industry (DTI). The DES (responsible for funding the Research Councils and R&TD in universities) alone accounts for 66 per cent of the public sector finance allocated to civil R&TD, the DTI being responsible for 9 per cent. The rest is shared mainly between MAFF (Ministry for Agriculture, Fisheries and Food) 4 per cent; Demp (Employment Department) 2 per cent; DoE (Department of the Environment) 3 per cent; DEn (Deapartment of Energy) 4 per cent; DH (Department of Health) 3 per cent; Scottish Office 2 per cent).*

There is no-ordination of sectoral R&TD policies as such between the various ministerial departments, but the UK government is advised by its Chief Scientist on the main policy guidelines to be followed consistent with the national interest, for example in matters of defence and international co-operation. The Cabinet Office also assists the Chief Scientist, particularly, with regard to the role and interest of the UK government in the implementation of Community R&TD policy.

It is quite clear that the primary responsibility for R&TD under this type of approach will lie with private sector. We have seen that in the United Kingdom, the private sector finances nearly 51 per cent of total R&TD and is actually responsible for carrying out 66 per cent. This means, however, that the private sector receives considerable support from the public authorities. A cursory analysis of the breakdown of R&TD funding by sector indicates that this support for undertakings is largely in the form of government defence contracts. Indeed, the figures show that government funding allocated to this sector accounts for some 45 per cent of total budgetary appropriations for R&TD.** This

* All data are based on estimated R&TD civil expenditure for the fiscal year 1991-92.

** On the basis of expenditure for 1989.

only serves to highlight the importance of military research and its impact on the civil sector.

What are the merits and demerits of this decentralized model?

On the minus side, over-dependence on the market makes it difficult to take a medium- and long-term view and thus interfered with the continuity of R&TD activity. Research institutions and councils have long regretted the lack of any guarantee of continued support for R&TD activity, a situation which tends to have a demotivating effect on the research scientists concerned. Moreover, in the United Kingdom, R&TD potential appears to be stagnating somewhat judging by the expenditure and manpower levels committed to R&TD over the last ten years or so. The private sector, more preoccupied with producing the short-term results dictated by its proximity to the market, does not seem to have shouldered the responsibility of developing R&TD in the UK to match the level achieved in the most developed western countries.

On the other hand, this decentralized approach has certain advantages, the chief among them flexibility and pragmatism. It avoids effort being devoted to R&TD activities that are too remote from the objectives of economic development which are part of the process of globalization of technology and which most western countries are currently pursuing. But, on the other hand, there is a major risk of fundamental research being affected, as British scientists have repeatedly emphasized.

The Centralized Approach: Example of France

Though not always consistent, France's R&TD policy, unlike that of the UK, is subject to the centripetal forces which are a feature of French political life. Particularly since the 1950s, France has concentrated most of the government funding for R&TD within a specific budget heading which is for the most part managed by a ministry or ministerial department whose responsibilities include R&TD. For example, the Ministry for Research and Technology currently administered until 2 April, 55 per cent of government civil R&TD appropriations, with the balance being allocated mainly to the Ministry for Industry and the Ministry for Space and Transport. From 2 April, this Ministry is now in charge not only of Research and Technology but also of Space. In addition, the Ministry for Research, Technology and Space is responsible for co-ordinating overall public sector R&TD activity and ensures that this dovetails with the international co-operation effort in which France is involved, for example within the Community framework.

It is obvious that under this centralizing approach the French Government has a major say in the running of national R&TD policy and as a result has sometimes put forward large-scale national programmes which unfortunately have not always lived up to expectations. On the other hand, it meant that France was able in the 1970s and 1980s to build enough nuclear power stations to guarantee it a measure of self-sufficiency in energy, with 75 per cent of France's electricity now being generated by nuclear energy. However, the French government does not implement R&TD policy alone; private undertakings also play a very important role. The private sector finances 44.3 per cent of total R&TD expenditure and actually carries out 62 per cent of the work. But in France, as in the United Kingdom, government defence contracts make up a considerable proportion of the work (with 39.5 per cent of total budget appropriations for R&TD being allocated to defence) and so, in the last analysis, the private sector's role in the development of R&TD is a limited one.

What are the merits and demerits of this approach?

As in the case of the UK, the picture is mixed. A major benefit of this approach is the way in which it allows greater synergy between R&TD activities and activities in other areas of government policy. Of particular note is the fact that over the last ten years, R&TD policy, in common with education policy, has enjoyed priority in the allocation of national funding. As a result of this approach, France has been able to pull itself up to the level of the most developed western countries in the field of S&T. It has also been able to maintain its level of activity in the area of fundamental research, which is an insurance policy for the future of France's technological development. On the other hand, the private sector has probably not fulfilled its obligations in the area of R&TD, namely the transferring of R&TD results to the marketplace. The end result is similar in this respect to that observed in the case of the UK, albeit for different reasons. In particular, the State has left it to major national research bodies to develop applied research. This is an aspect of French policy which is arguably responsible for the excessive red tape in research and deprives it of the pragmatism which characterizes R&TD in the UK. However, there is no doubt that scientists benefit from this approach and, as we have seen, the increase in manpower can be regarded as an insurance policy for the future of French R&TD.

But can every State continue to lay claim to an independent R&TD policy when frontiers are disappearing and when the economies of our countries are run according to the dictates of international competitiveness? The answer, clearly, is no—which brings us to the example of the European Community.

The Community Approach

Devised in the 1960s with the aim of making the Community self-sufficient in energy through the promotion of nuclear power, Community R&TD policy has gradually developed in the direction of socio-economic objectives and, more recently, the objectives of economic competitiveness and economic and social cohesion in the Community. Originally based largely on the French model, it is now moving towards an intermediate model which has some features in common with the UK approach. Pragmatism is now tending to predominate, with the market and cyclical economic forces being left to determine the objectives of this policy. The Maastricht agreements are explicit on this point: the objective is to strengthen the scientific and technological bases of Community industry, encourage it to become more competitive at international level and promote the research activities deemed necessary by virtue of other Community policies. To these ends, the Community intends to mobilize all the players involved in the R&TD process in joint research and technological development activities of high quality and support their efforts to co-operate with one another. These are the conditions set out in Article 130F of the new Treaty for implementing this Community policy, which from now on will focus on the following activities:

- implementation of research, technological development, and demonstration projects based on two main themes, namely S&T for industrial innovation and S&T for society and Europe,
- promotion of co-operation with third countries and international organizations, with particular emphasis on 'big science',
- dissemination & optimization of R&TD results,
- stimulation of the training and mobility of researchers in the Community.

The successful implementation of this policy will depend very largely on achieving the conditions that are conducive to enhancing the Community's competitiveness. With this in mind, Community action is essentially directed towards bringing together the partners involved in R&TD, *i.e.* public authorities, undertakings, research organizations, universities, under the aegis of shared-cost contracts, the Community generally paying 50 per cent of the costs. These multi-partner contracts are also multinational, thus helping to promote co-operation within the Community. Another important aspect of the R&TD work part-funded by the Community is its interdisciplinary nature, which encourages the networking of research scientists from every discipline.

In addition to these shared-cost projects, the Community is also developing its own R&TD activities under the auspices of its Joint Research Centre, since the implementation of some sectoral Community policies calls for certain specific research activities to support them. Examples include prenormative work in the field of environmental protection, safety research, and statistical surveys related to the agricultural policy (for example, the use of remote sensing to compile an inventory of resources). The Community also helps with the training of researchers through arrangements allowing researchers easier access to major European scientific facilities. All of these activities are covered by a multi-annual framework programme.

Naturally, Community R&TD policy is governed by the principle of subsidiarity. Indeed, the Maastricht Agreements specifically state that the Community will only be required to exercise its responsibilities in those cases where the Member States are unable to assume theirs. In terms of R&TD, this means that Community policy will be confined to activities of common interest which could not have been carried out more effectively at national level. This also means that *"the Community and the Member States shall co-ordinate their research and technological development activities so as to ensure that national policies and Community policy are mutually consistent"* (Article 130H). These provisions give the Member States strict control over Community R&TD policy in terms of both programming and the implementation of R&TD activities. This has also prompted the Community to develop innovative procedures for evaluating the results of its activities.

As far as the principle of continuity is concerned, Community R&TD policy is the epitome of this principle in action. It is one of the few examples of an R&TD policy implemented through the medium of a multi-annual programme, coupled with a commitment by the public authorities to provide the necessary funding for the activities covered by the programme. This has definite advantages, particularly in the field of basic research, as the example of controlled thermonuclear fusion shows. But at the same time it also guarantees contractors engaged in applied Community research, including undertakings and more especially small businesses, the medium-term financial support without which they would be reluctant to launch out into precompetitive R&TD activities. It must be emphasized that the rules of the market and, in particular, Community competition policy limit the support public authorities can give in this area and that undertakings, even though they are the driving force behind innovation, do not always have the necessary capability to engage in research and technological development which is a long way upstream of the market.

The other principle to which the Maastricht Agreements drew attention is the principle of inter-relationship, *i.e.* close interdependence between the objectives of Community R&TD policy and those of the Community's other sectoral policies. It means that the Community must seek not only to maximize the combined effect of all its policies but also to ensure that the objectives of those policies are both mutually consistent and complementary.

The effort directed towards achieving economic and social cohesion in the Community, for instance, enhance the R&TD capability of its Member States, particularly in regions that are less developed or in industrial decline. This not only allows them access to Community R&TD programmes on an equal footing, but also means they can play a full part in the process of technological development in the Community.

This is perhaps an idyllic picture but there is, as always, another side to the coin. The checks and balances introduced in the Community decision-making process are now resulting in time-scales for R&TD that are incompatible with the desire for efficiency inherent in the abovementioned principles. Another criticism often levelled at Community R&TD policy is that it is excessively bureaucratic. But is this problem not inevitable when public authorities try to implement a structural policy?

On final word on the results of this policy. Over the last ten years, Community funding of R&TD has tripled, to the point where it is now equivalent to nearly 6 per cent of R&TD civil funding by the national governments. In accordance with the Community's aims, the bulk of this funding is allocated to technological objectives (compared with almost 10 per cent of government funding in the Member States), while Community funding for human and social objectives is 8 per cent of the amount allocated by the Member States. Paradoxically, despite the size of the common agricultural policy, the share allocated to agricultural research is only 2 per cent.

As R&TD has now been recognized as a Community priority within the Maastricht Agreements, the Commission has proposed a doubling of the budget set aside for R&TD funding by 1997. If the Council agrees to this proposal, this will enable the Community to act increasingly as a catalyst in the European arena, especially since the agreement on the European Economic Area is intended to lead to the eventual association of most EFTA member countries in the framework programme for Community R&TD activities.

27

Science Organizations in OECD Economies: Comparative Analysis and Main Lessons

JEAN-ERIC AUBERT*

Principal Administrator, Organisation for Economic Co-operation and Development, Paris, France

The Organisation for Economic Co-operation and Development (OECD) was established in 1960 as a result of the expansion and transformation of the Organization for European Economic Co-operation (OEEC), set up after the Second World War to manage the Marshall Plan. In addition to the Western European countries and the United States, OECD membership includes Canada, Japan, Australia, and New Zealand. Thus OECD has been formed by grouping together the so-called 'market economies'.

OECD is an intergovernmental organization devoted to analytical work, statistical monitoring, policy dialogue, and formulation of guidelines in selected areas. OECD does not provide any form of financial support, nor assume any form of executive power.

In the addition to economic policy analysis, which has constituted the core of its activities, OECD has been involved

* The views expressed in this paper do not engage the OECD in any fashion.

in all 'peripheral' areas sustaining economic and social development such as trade, industry, education, environment, science, . . . The studies of science policies date back to the foundation of OECD. Specific tools have been developed for this purpose, including, in particular, country reviews and later on a 'policy outlook'.*

This paper is divided into three sections. In the first, we discuss common features and policy trends of science systems in OECD countries. In the second, we provide elements of comparative analysis between countries, emphasizing the socio-cultural dimension. In the last section, we represent some remarks on the problems being encountered by the economies in transition, of Eastern and Central Europe.

Common Features and Policy Trends

Science policies were shaped, broadly speaking, over two major periods. The 1950s and 1960s were a sort of golden age of science policy, when science featured at the top of the agenda. Governments spared no expense, and research structures proliferated. The subsequent two decades experienced economic disruption, with keener competition between countries, and governments asking research and innovation to serve primarily the interests of economic and industrial development. Increasing weight was given to the technology side of policy. It seems possible that, with the early 1990s, we are entering a new era. The objective is to reposition science and technology policy more effectively with regard to developments in our societies, also in the international community. Governments need to redefine their action both to cope with increasingly important environmental

---

* The country reviews began in the early sixties; they have gradually been expanded beyond science policy to include technology policy and even policy aspects related to broader 'innovation systems' such as industry and education; most OECD countries have gone through this examination process (undertaken on their request), several times for some of them. The policy outlook, launched some ten years ago, reviews trends and issues in the OECD area. It has been considerably expanded in its latest version completed in 1991, including an annex with profiles of recent policy initiatives and S&T indicators for all OECD countries.

problems challenging the course of economic development itself, and to adapt to a new 'global' deal following the crumbling of the Communist system.

Science organization and science policy present some common basic features in all market economies. The most important probably, compared to the formerly centrally planned economies, has been the relatively low importance given to the research made in the government sector. In most OECD countries, and in particular in those that are more advanced, government-based research represents less than 30 per cent of the whole R&D effort, while it was previously over 70 per cent in centrally planned economics. In market economies, the bulk of the R&D activity used to be performed either by industry in relation to production concerns, or by the universities in relation to education concerns. This distinct feature has resulted in a much better integration of science into the economic and social fabric than has been the case in the centrally planned economics, and is consequently more efficient for the whole economic development process.

Policy making and the management of the science system have seen continuous improvement over the years. Several points derived from this common experience are worth mentioning here. They concern the whole policy management mechanisms, funding aspects, and the instruments for linking science with the market place.

As regards policy management, there has been a distinct trend to link science and technology, in line with the above comments on the different ages of science policies. Policy making has generally resulted from the combined responsibility of S&T councils and *ad hoc* agencies or ministries, the former having generally the tasks of advice and supervision, the second being in charge of administering policy measures and supporting instruments. Another important trend has been the search for increasing interaction with other key policy areas such as education, trade, industry, . . . with appropriate interministerial co-ordination. There is no doubt that fairly good progress has been made in these areas, but on the other hand the integration with economic and finance policies—which are at the centre of government action and concern—remains rather weak.

The funding of science systems can be broadly divided in two main streams: institutional or 'base' funding, and support or 'free' funding. The latter represents generally around one quarter of the total R&D effort. Experience gradually acumulated in OECD countries has led policy makers to use distinctly different criteria for administering this funding, notably the 'free' money. When it comes to support of basic research, the criteria to be used are primarily international excellence based on peer reviews. When it comes to support of strategic research, the criteria to be used are those related to national relevance, taking into consideration those scientific areas where the country shows particular skills and experience, industrial structures with outstanding competitiveness, etc. Then when it comes to support of industrial research, it is the quality of the individual projects a firm presents that matters primarily.

Increased effort and continuous invention of new mechanisms have aimed at better linking of science with the market place. This process demands the systematic involvement of industry in financing significant parts of project costs (notably in strategic programmes) and the setting up of *ad hoc* centres (*e.g.* for engineering science, basic technological research, technology transfer, etc.) jointly funded by industry and government. More broadly, there has been a general trend throughout the OECD area towards increasing involvement of the private sector in the financing of the whole R&D effort.

Two other 'mega-trends' deserve mentioning in this brief survey. The first relates to the regionalization of R&D policies with the increasing involvement of regional and local authorities, especially as regards technology transfer and diffusion aspects and a *fortiori* the development of new technology-based industries, which tends to take place in well defined sites appropriately endowed with intellectual and other infrastructures.

The second main trend is the internationalization of science systems due to a series of concurrent factors. The profusion of big science projects (which require cost-sharing among nations) stimulates the interpenetration of science communities, while in all disciplines more generally international research projects are being developed at an increasing rate. In addition, the proliferation of strategic alliances between firms, going hand-in-hand with the 'globalization' process, leads to a strong internationalization of the technological development process. Finally, the processes of economic and political integration drive those of science and technology: this is a major factor of integration for the countries concerned.

Thus the nation-state is gradually challenged by supra- and infra-national developments, and this is particularly apparent in the field of science and technology. However, the socio-cultural legacy that characterizes each nation is still having a strong influence on the form and impact of its science effort.

Inter-Country Comparisons of Science Efforts and Impacts

Inter-country comparisons of science effort can be conducted at different levels. At macro-level, R&D financing structures (public/private ratio) and performing structures (government/industry/university), for example, can be compared. At meso-level, one can compare organizational patterns such as the status and structures of government-based research, the mechanisms for funding research and agencies. At micro-level, one can compare individual behaviours as expressed for instance through specialization in scientific fields, international mobility of researchers, and so on.

It is not the place here to enter into a detailed analysis of OECD countries on such different and fine parameters.* We can just emphasize that were this analysis executed, one would discover a strong coherence between the features used to characterize the research system of an individual country, and that countries could be grouped, to a certain extent, in relation to their socio-cultural background.

This also appears striking when using a series of broad data on research effort and industrial performance, allowing a consolidated overview of science effort and impact for twelve OECD countries over a period of 15 years from the mid-seventies to the end of the eighties (see Table 1).

---

* The contribution made by M. Paillon (EC) provides insight into the French and British systems for the macro- and meso-levels.

Four types of data are recorded in the table: for the 'input' side of the innovation process, the level of the R&D effort at the end of the period, the intensity of the effort (as measured by the average annual growth rate over the period); and for the 'output' side, the trend of the self-sufficiency ratio in high technology industries and the trend of the manufacturing balance.* The OECD countries included in the table are the seven major economies and the five others most involved in the industrial goods trade.

Notwithstanding the size of the country as well as the level of its R&D effort, five basic profiles can be roughly identified out of the stylized facts presented in the table:

- an Anglo-Saxon profile characterized by an R&D effort less intense than average and by a marked weakening of the competitive position.
- a Latin profile with a fairly good research effort but with a certain difficulty in maintaining a competitive position.
- a Germanic profile with little change for the whole set of variables, with a slight improvement of the competitive position.
- a Nordic profile characterized by a strong research effort and a sensible improvement of the competitive position.
- a Japanese profile characterized by remarkable results on all variables.

Adding to these data others describing the overall economic performance (*e.g.* growth rate, unemployment, . . .) would

---

* The use of trade indicators to appraise a country's competitiveness is criticable to the extent that we are living in an increasingly open world in which enterprise's competitiveness may appear increasingly significant compared with a country's competitiveness. Moreover, this form of indicator is somewhat penalizing for those countries that are by their very nature largely open to the outside world through imports or foreign direct investment and that tend to delocalize abroad their production units. However, this indicator retains a certain validity in measuring an overall performance, and at least it characterizes a certain type of economic behaviour.

strengthen the above-proposed typology; further data on scientific and industrial specializations would make it more detailed.

To explain differences between countries' performances, one would have to examine in detail the organization and functioning of 'national innovation systems' that combine sub-systems such as the research, industry, finance and education, which are in fact the basis of long-term economic development. In brief, the most successful countries (over the last two decades) have in common the following:

- research structures in which the private sector holds a large place and where defence-related expenditures are modest,
- industrial structures characterized by strong competitive resources, but also by a certain degree of co-operation between firms,
- financial structures well organized for the financing of industrial and long-term investments,
- educational structures providing the vast majority of the population, and not only an elite part, with appropriate qualifications.

Pursuing our investigations further, and in view of the apparently important role played by the socio-cultural background in a country's economic development, it is worthwhile looking also at those features that the most successful countries have in common. Among those features, let us briefly sketch out here:*

- as regards the knowledge and skills valued and widespread in society, technical know-how and concerete knowledge receive a status at least equal to scientific and abstract knowledge.

---

* The features listed in this paragraph have been identified by the author through his experience and reading; a detailed justification and documentation of the different points selected would require major analytical and bibliographical work.

Table 1. Trends in Research Efforts and Industrial Performance for twelve OECD Countries over the Period 1975-87.

	Level of R&D expenditure at the end of the period (1)	Annual average growth of the R&D effort (2)	Trends in self-sufficiency ratio in high-technology	Trends in the manufacturing balance
US	High	Weak	Deteriorating	Deteriorating
Japan	High	Strong	Improving	Improving
Germany	High	Moderate	Stable	Improving
France	High	Moderate	Stable	Deteriorating
UK	Medium	Weak	Deteriorating	Deteriorating
Italy	Low	Moderate	Deteriorating	Improving
Canada	Low	Weak	Deteriorating	Stable
Sweden	High	Strong	Stable	Improving
Netherlands	Medium	Weak	Deteriorating	Stable
Switzerland	High	Moderate	Stable	Stable
Denmark	Low	Strong	Improving	Stable
Finland	Medium	Strong	Improving	Improving

(1) RD/GDP High: over 2.5% medium: 1.5—2.5% low: below 1.5%

(2) Growth rate Strong: over 3% medium: 1.5—3% low: below 1.5%

High technology industries include: aerospace, electronics, electrical machinery, pharmaceuticals, and scientific instruments.

Source: data from *Science and Technology Policy: Review and Outlook 1991*. OECD, 1992.

- as regards the economic ethos, there is a marked domination of the community-oriented ones over the individualistic ones as seen in management of enterprises, relations between the public and the private sectors, etc.
- a state well integrated into society which does not fall into the extreme practices of pure *laissez-faire* or of centralized dirigism.
- a low tolerance to social exclusion—and unemployment in particular—of which the low level is both a cause and a consequence of good economic/industrial performance.
- relationship with foreigners combining both a large receptiveness to outside inputs in science and technology and a selective openness to industrial, financial and commercial entries.
- an identity full based on economic success due to the historical circumstances.

These different elements also form somewhat coherent sets which appear as kinds of socio-anthropological systems underpinning the innovation systems mentioned above.

Science Organization in Economies in Transition

Bearing in mind the picture given above on market economics, it might be worthwhile to say a few words on the economies of Eastern and Central Europe which are experiencing currently a dramatic transformation.

Their science systems are suffering serious drawbacks.

The R&D effort, as measured by the total expenditure, tended to be oversized, reaching in a number of countries about 2 per cent of the domestic product (or equivalent). This seemed considerably higher than OECD countries used to accomplish with apparently similar levels of development, *e.g.* as measured by revenue per capita. Recent economic recession has had a strong impact on research investment as other variables. R&D expenditure has strongly declined and a serious brain-drain process has been developing.

In general terms, the scientific workforce in Eastern and Central Europe countries is considered to be fairly well educated and industrious, despite having worked with poor, outdated equipment, and in general in fairly inadequate economic and technological conditions, vastly different from those prevailing in OECD countries.

In contrast to science systems in market economies, as already mentioned, the planned economies were strongly weighed down by government-based R&D organizations. Following the Soviet pattern, the institutes of the academies of sciences dominated the basic and applied science activities with university research being considerably limited. Industrial research tended to be developed in sectorial institutes and R&D capabilities in enterprises were rather poor. Today with the economic recession and industry's crash, industrial research tends to be reduced to nil.

The general context for science policy is chaotic. Old frameworks have disappeared, and there is a dramatic lack of government direction. Simplistic adoption of free-market ideology and institutional fights make it extremely difficult to establish priorities and preparation of sound reforms. Moreover, the 'climate' is still poisoned by a scientism which used to be particularly virulent (by scientism we mean the belief that every progress in technology and economy only derives from scientific achievement).

OECD is currently embarking on country reviews of some Eastern European countries and possibly Russia. The first review has just been completed for Hungary. The main recommendations concern the need to:

- define an overall strategy based on a country-wide technology audit to be performed without delay.
- adapt the S&T institutional framework in redistributing responsibilities, increasing transparency in the decision-making process and the allocation of resource processes.
- restructure the R&D system in rationalizing existing R&D institutes, developing university research, providing strong incentives for industrial research, and

establishing a legal framework for non-profit organizations.

- improve management of funds supporting research and innovation in aligning them to OECD practices.
- prepare immediately a White Paper to set the grounds for an overall reform and legislative action.

Eastern and Central European countries expect a good deal from international co-operation to contribute to the support and transformation of their research and innovation systems. In fact, there has been an impressive proliferation of initiatives of both bilateral and multilateral nature. However, these approaches are suffering from certain drawbacks that reduce the expected impacts. Most of these initiatives remain sectorial, while higher efficiency would obtain by combining efforts in science, industry, education, finance, . . . following the general patterns of the innovation/development systems outlined above.

These initiatives are also quite uncoordinated among the different international organizations concerned, which are at times embarked on inadequate competition-inducing waste of resources.

No-one should neglect forms of mutual misunderstanding between Eastern and Western partners, the latter tending to impose models that have proved to work in market economies, the former being highly sensitive to any form of solution proposed from outside, which seems to appear as a new kind of imperialism.

In fact, the transformation of the countries of Central/ Eastern Europe and of the former Soviet Union raises considerable challenges and formidable uncertainties. There is a non-negligible risk that a number of those countries fall into a sort of 'permanent-transitory' state, developing a large underground economy, and unable to introduce the rules and pressures of a true market economy. Some countries, victim of a deep 'deficit of hope,'* would then be in great danger of social and political trouble.

---

* As stated by A. Kuklinski in a presentation to the Promethée Conf., Budapest, 29 January 1992.

Along with the so-called 'developing economies', we are also in a state of ignorance as to those truly deep mechanisms of a socio-cultural nature that make for economic success. There is on this side a 'deficit of knowledge'. To a certain extent, the radical medicines inspired by the structural adjustment philosophy are an expression of this ignorance, resembling those medical cures such as bleedings, administered by doctors to their patients whatever the sickness, as was the practice some three hundred years ago, sometimes with dire results.

There is a definite need for establishing and enforcing basic rules of market economy and associated pluralistic democracy. But at the same time new approaches to development should be sought rather than imposing ready-made models. In this perspective it might be appropriate to implement well thought out actions on focused projects of reforms and programmes in involving scientists, industrialists and politicians from both East and West. A process of self analysis has to take place, helped by inter-country comparisons to be developed through regular meetings with a view to taking stock of progress achieved and obstacles encountered. One may call it a form of 'ethno-analysis' by anology with psycho-analysis which applies to individuals, while this would apply to peoples.

Is there any organization better fitted than UNESCO to pioneer such a venture?

In conclusion it will not surprise anyone if we underling the need to introduce truly new approaches based in cultural anthropology in order to make significant progress in helping the economic developing of countries—in particular when based on technology. This would apply equally as well to developed OECD countries.

28

The Promotion of Science by Foundations: Their National and European Roles

JOAO CARACA
Director, Science Department of the Calouste Gulbenkian Foundation, Lisbon, Portugal

Foundations: What They Are

In his interesting report on *The Law on Foundations* prepared for the Foundación Santillana, Hondius (1989) traces the origins of the institución of foundations back to religiously motivated causes, such as the provision of shelter for pilgrims and of care for the sick and needy. He asserts that foundations reflect the social and interdependent nature of man, as they correspond to the setting of immovable properties outside the jurisdiction of secular rulers with a view of extending the care and transmitting the ideals of their founders to future generations.

The founding of universities in the Middle Ages was accompanied by the creation and endowment of self-governing colleges and scholarship funds. Later, during the renaissance and the reformation, secular foundations devoted to community purposes were also created by towns and wealthy citizens. More recently, with the advent of private enterprises, a new wave of philanthropic foundations was produced.

Foundations and associations share the principle that both incorporate the dedication of resources that have (or assume) the private nature of furthering the public good. However, associations draw their resources from the activity of individual persons, whereas foundations have their source in capital or other types of property. Both also share the principle of 'non-profit' or no financial gain in their actions, the level of 'self-interest' (of members) introducing a demarcation between classes of associations.

Foundations, then, follow in the liberal tradition of Europe (as opposed to the monarchic tradition) which conveys the conception that public good is not bestowed exclusively by the State. They are private entities serving public purposes. Foundations are neither entirely within private law, nor entirely within public law.

We will not proceed along with Hondius here in discussing possible legal harmonization issues, but we would like nevertheless to support strongly his view that the proliferation of 'beggar foundations' (*i.e.* of foundations that despite their name have no capital fund of their own and rely on the public or on other foundations) is highly undesirable and creates cunfusion in the public opinion.

Modern foundations operate basically in two different ways or in a 'composite' way, depending on their primary purposes:

1. as 'operational' foundations, when they plan, finance and execute their own programmes, or
2. as 'grant-giving' foundations, when their function is to support financially the activities of others.

According to the Hague Club (The Hague Club, 1988), the three foundations with a more voluminous annual expenditure in Europe are: the Volkswagenwerk Foundation in Germany, instituted in 1961 by an agreement between the governments of the Federal Republic of Germany and of the State of Lower Saxony; the Wellcome Trust in the United Kingdom, created in 1936 by the will of Sir Henry Solomon Wellcome; and the Calouste Gulbenkian Foundation in Portugal, established in 1956 by the will of Calouste Sarkis Gulbenkian. The Volkswagenwerk

Foundation and the Wellcome Trust are grant-giving foundations, whereas the Gulbenkian Foundation functions both as a grant-giving and as an operational foundation in specific areas.

All these three major foundations have the promotion of science as their purpose: in fact, all S&T including humanities, by sponsoring research and university teaching, in the case of the Volkswagenwerk Foundation; and the support of research in human and animal medicine and the history of medicine, by the Wellcome Trust.

Of the large foundations, only the Gulbenkian seems to encompass much wider purposes: the promotion of charitable, artistic, and educational as well as scientific goals—these representing some 12 per cent of the total activity.

The Science of our Global World

National languages emerged in Europe after the 15th century, with the advent of printing and the needs and characteristics of publishing activities. National economies and markets (and the nation-states) arose in the late 18th and 19th centuries following the industrial revolution and the needs, values, and procedures that it created and promoted. The 20th century, which has witnessed fantastic changes and the growing weight of immaterial factors in our societies, is striving towards inventing new and adequate political and institutional mechanisms from world governance.

In fact, as Cleveland (1992) so nicely puts it, how can cultural diversity be reconciled both with economic opportunities at global level and with the expression of individual human rights (the 'trilemma')?

Knowledge-based activities occurred even before the first human societies acquired the capacity to use fire. But the command of fire brought cartainly the attitude of dominance over nature which has been with us ever since. The needs to survive (and thus to make relevant collective choices in a frequently hostile environment) and to strengthen the cohesion of their own groups motivated the early humans to develop their systems of communication into languages and to improve their technical and other cognitive skills and capacities. In fact, as Braudel (1979) so deftly asserted, the whole thickness of the history of mankind is the result of technique.

What are the relations between knowledge and power?

The deployment of power always involves the institution of a body of knowledge, which emerges as the source of its own legitimization and cultural identity (Foucault, 1989); concurrently, the rules that govern the operation of this body of knowledge induce a set of power relations in the group of its practitioners.

Therefore, we can say that knowledge and power function as mirrors of each other in human societies, to the extent that the conditions for their respective enactment spring from mutual co-existence. In all epochs and communities, both knowledge and power set their indelible mark, one upon the other.

The overwhelming impact of the transformations brought about by the industrial revolution showed that a considerable body of scientific and technological (S&T) knowledge plays a central role in the performance of modern economies. The conduction of S&T research activities is now seen to be crucial to the generation of technological innovations, and also to the construction of meanings, values, and representations that enable the diffusion of innovations in society.

The growing level of interdependence and integration of the economy at world level—and the subsequent globalization of the markets—inevitably motivated the globalization of S&T knowledge associated with the production, marketing, and strategic management of the enterprises that protagonized those processes. Market globalization is thus intertwined with intensive knowledge incorporation.

Globalization is changing the world: enemies turn into partners, former competitors co-operate, but, really, are foes becoming friends?

We are experiencing deep changes: whereas in the past national cohesion was mainly maintained by physical strength, a role primarily fulfilled by the armed forces, we are living in times where cohesion is being obtained—with increasing frequency—by immaterial factors, by corporate culture, and national identity.

The emergence of a new source of wealth brings inevitably a redistribution of power. Space (and location) is being re-evaluated—this must not seem extraordinary in our times, when the new immaterial dimension is establishing its empire: the same occurred when the energy (and material) dimension pervaded economic life following the invention of agriculture. But space (or energy) will not cease to have a value—obviously—therefore countries and states will not cease to exist.

They may evolve into new political configurations, though, more suited to new organizational frameworks. But what will be the shape of the world of tomorrow? No one knows, surely, as we are dealing with an ever-evolving object with meanings that are relevant only in the context of each social culture.

Evolutionary processes are complex, with time-frames that are not easily made compatible. Furthermore, they answer to conflicting goals. But nothing has more devastating consequences than avoiding the issues.

The concept of economy we must nowadays use, based on the theory of 'dissipative structures' of Prigogine (1955), shows us that any society, in its drive for organization and order, needs to 'export disorder' to its environment. Absorbing this entropy is the main function of the 'predation space' of any successful economy.

However, when an economy attains a planetary dimension—like the global economy—physical predation space gets exhausted at the surface of the Earth. The 'export of disorder' can only proceed through the intensification of available and existing schemes. This is how we must envisage environmental pollution: the dimension of the container is becoming comparable to the size of the associated machine that it supports.

Social deprivation can also be seen as a direct result of discorder which cannot easily be exported to a far distance from the 'centre'. Human societies have, over the course of millenia (with greater or lesser success) handled this question through different mechanisms: slavery, women's inferiority, racial segregation, class discrimination . . . .

Radical social changes and upheavals occur when the existing institutions can no longer absorb (*i.e.*. be economically efficient in) a framework of mounting demographic pressures.

So, this is the world we live in nowadays—a world whose finiteness we are slowly beginning to understand. But something is also emerging very strongly from this analysis: that there is no egotistic easy way out—our collective future binds us together as long as we populate this planet.

The Promotion of Science: Roles of the National Authorities and Foundations

In the 1960s, a universal model for S&T was accepted, that corresponded to an instrumental concept of S&T in relation to social and economic development. Nowadays, however, we know that it is not possible to isolate research activities from the social content in which they are conducted; this is reflected by the growing 'scientification' of the cultures of contemporary societies as well as by the increasing social involvement of S&T, of individual scientists and researchers, and of their organizations. A new need has been created: the need to make sure that public funds spent on S&T and R&D are used in a benefical way for society—evaluation performing primarily the role of mediator in this process.

This is the reason why science policies at national level have been changing from a mission-oriented nature (from the launching of strategic sectors to the emphasis on the generation of technological innovations and the support of national 'champions') to a more diffusion-oriented one, enhancing the mechanisms of technology transfer and valorization of research results. The role of the state in a modern economy is incompatible with the conduction of operations too close to the market (*i.e.* a 'precompetitive' character of state intervention has to be preserved).

What is left then to action by the state is the building-up of infrastructure (including the development of human resources—the notion of human capital); the support of networking activities (hence the notion of human mobility); the financing of research programmes (with an increasing precompetitive tendency) in basic 'pervasive' technologies; and provision of S&T services at national level.

What about the action by foundations?

In the past, the role of foundations in the promotion of science was easier to play in two aspects:

1. they were concerned, at most, with the national level.
2. the national S&T systems were in a clear development phase.

Nowadays this situation has changed drastically.

This also poses the problem of the specific character of the need of intervention by foundations or other private institutions dedicated to purposes of public good. Will there be areas where public good can be seen as being endangered?

Foundations, non-profit organizations, grant-giving bodies, entities established for the public benefit, all are living institutions proliferating in our society.

The economy, as well as technology, is becoming global. Technological innovation and commercialization of new products and services are the result of increased co-operation networks between firms across sectors and countries, and between enterprises, universities, and public agencies. Global science, technology, and economy will expand rapidly in the next decade.

What roles can foundations thus fulfil in a world where networks are means for being competitive and new organizational concepts are bursting?

The natural domain of action in science by foundations has always been vested in the time variable, *i.e.* in promoting or demonstrating excellence and top quality in the most fundamental and basic disciplines, or through projects of a highly innovative or pioneering nature.

Foundations have nowadays to resist the illusion of being able to compete with institutions emanating from national authorities and with economically-driven organizations that have been eager to adopt and reap prestige and benefits from foundation-type operations. Foundations will not succeed in this competition as the volume of their endowments will always be necessarily connected to their time of creation and will not expand at the rate of economic growth and complexity of modern nations.

The action by foundations will thus have to be strictly circumscribed to the time variable: to be ahead and look ahead; they must function as centres of reflection and rationality without any borders, promoting the understanding of issues of present societies and in their development; promoting and enforcing prospective attitudes and values; promoting systematically excellent science projects, thus contributing to the creation of a favourable climate to science, knowledge, and culture; and, finally enhancing the (sometimes unsuspected) capacity we all have, as human beings, to work together.

REFERENCES

Braudel, F., 1979. Les structures du quotidien. *Civilization Matérielle, Economie et Capitalisme XV-XVIII Siècle.* Armed Colin, Paris.

Cleveland, H., 1992 (March). Trilemma on three continents. World Academy of Art and Science News.

Foucault, M., 1989. Resumés de Cours. Quoted by M.M. Carrilho, in *Itinerários da Racionalidade.* Dom Quixote, Lisbon.

Hondius, F., 1989. *The Law on Foundations.* Report for the Fundación Santillana, Strasbourg.

Prigogine, I., 1955. *Introduction to the Thermo dynamics of Irreversible Processes.* Wiley, New York.

The Hague Club, 1988. *Foundation Profiles,* The Hague.

29

Organization of European Co-operation in the Field of S&T with Central and Eastern Europe

MANFREDO MACIOTI
Chief Adviser, DG XII, Commission of the European Communities, Brussels, Belgium

Introduction

The European Community (EC) is one of the political success stories of the second half of the 20th century.

- The European adventure began in 1951 when six war-shattered nations decided to pool their basic industrial resources of coal and steel so that war between them would be unthinkable (ECSC).
- Forty years later, the EC has grown into a 12 nation Community (Belgium, France, Germany, Italy, Luxembourg, Neatherland, Denmark, Ireland, UK, Greece, Portugal, Spain); the EC is a major economic power, with a clear political dimension.
- Together with North America and Japan, the EC represents one of the three pillars on which the global system of pluralist democracy and market economy is based. It is hoped that the new democracies of Central and Eastern Europe, and the CIS, will develop into alternative pillars of the world system.

The year 1992 means for the EC:

- The final year for completing the Single (integrated) European Market.
- The first post-Maastricht year. The Maastricht European Council (December 1991) confirmed and charted the road towards a European Economic and Monetary Union (EMU) and, ultimately, a European (Political) Union.

As European integration advances, the EC is bound to have a growing international role in a world whose political map is being redrawn.

In co-operation with its partners, the EC can provide a strong and stable framework, promoting democratic values, the virtues of the market economy and giving a helping hand to the less-privileged nations of the world.

The EC in the World

One principle lies behind the EC policies towards the world: enlightened self-interest. The EC's own well-being depends on a liberal, multilateral world economic order (GATT), as well as on the welfare of its partners, including the Third World (North-South dialogue). The example of the Airbus proves it: Europe has over 50 orders from India; over 40 from Thailand; and 30 from Korea.

After the unprecedented expansion of world trade initiated in the 1950s, the world has witnessed, since the 1970s, a growing internationalization of financial markets; it is currently experiencing a third wave of globalization, dominated by investment and technology (the agent is the transnational corporation; the means are the revolutions in information and telecommunications, and major advances in transportation).

The world is becoming a smaller place, not only because of trade, investment, communications, and information technology, but also because of man's growing exploitation of the world's natural resources and the release of by-products of human activities into the environment.

The EC Economy

The EC represents a small fraction of humanity (345 million people: 6.5 per cent of the world population . . . within 30 years it will be 4 per cent). Its land is barely 1.8 per cent of the land area of the world, less than that of Argentina, and a quarter of that of the US or Canada.

In contrast with some of its partners, the EC is not self-sufficient in any of the critical areas and metals (Al, Cu, Co, Fe, Mn, Cr, Pt) or energy source materials (Coal, oil, gas, hydro, nuclear).

Europe has to create new resources through skills, science, and technology; and has an interest in being perceived as a reliable international partner (trade, investment, acquisitions, joint R&D ventures, technology exchanges).

The EC is one of the world's great actors in investment (183 billion ECU* of cumulated 1951-89 investment by the EC in the US and 126 billion ECU by the US in the EC); it is by far the largest exporter and importer of services in the world; it is one of the great trading powers on Earth (in 1990, the EC accounted for 19 per cent of world merchandise trade, excluding intra-EC trade; the US accounted for 15 per cent).

EC Science and Technology

A look at two indicators of science (publishing authors, Nobel Laureates) underlines the pre-eminece of the United States (US: 36.5 per cent of the wrold's total scientific output over the years 1981-85 versus 26.5 per cent for the EC); but notice the EC strength in chemistry (41,500 publications versus 35,000 for the US). The US had 40 Nobel Laureates in the natural and economic sciences over the past 10 years versus 22 for the EC).

In technology, we may look at two indicators: trade in high-tech and patents (though we should remember that these reveal not only degrees of technical strength but also degrees of global interpenetration).

The EC comes out on top in trade (out of eight high-tech branches, the EC dominates five, the United States two) while

* 1 ECU is currently worth about US$ 1.25.

Japan is a very remarkable Number One in patents (330,000 patent applications filed by residents in 1990 versus 95,000 for the EC and 91,000 for the United States).

Europe '92

The main problem with the EC is its fragmentation. The Community is busy dismantling all internal barriers among the Twelve in order to allow the free circulation of people, capital, goods, and services (and ideas).

We are convinced in Brussels that in a large, integrated, open market there will be scope for achieving a more rational productive and distributive structure, improving productivity, reducing costs and prices, and facilitating amortization of investment (including research).

The market will be transparent and accessible to our partners; there will be vigorous competition and a healthy climate for innovation in the market; subsidies, monopolies, and distorting practices will be progressively phased out; European technical standards, common regulations and tests, and harmonized certification practices will be introduced.

The Single Market of the Twelve is being enlarged to encompass the Seven countries of the European Free Trade Area (Austria, Finland, Iceland, Liechtenstein, Norway, Sweden, Switzerland), thus achieving the largest consumer market in the world (almost 380 million people).

EC External Relations: Multilateralism

There are at least two dimensions to the EC policy *vis-a-vis* the world: multilateral and bilateral.

The EC is a member of several international organizations such as GATT (the EC is a *de facto* contracting party and the negotiator for the Twelve in the Uruguay Round) and the OECD (where it endeavours to speak with one voice).

The EC is an observer at the UN and its various agencies and specialized institutions, and is a party to a host of international UN agreements (such as the Montreal Protocol on the protection of the ozone layer). The EC has an important role in the preparation of UNCED to be held in Rio de Janeiro in June 1992.

The EC has special agreements for commercial and economic co-operation (including science and technology) with other regional organizations in the world, such as the Central American Common Market (MCCA), the Andean Pact (in South America), the ASEAN (in South Asia) and the Gulf Co-operation Council (in the Middle East).

The EC has long been involved in a major multilateral North-South partnership with 69 countries in Africa, the Caribbean, and the Pecific, the so-called ACP Group (the current 'Lomé-IV' Convention runs for 10 years—1990 to 2000—and provides for 12 billion ECU of European aid in the form of grants and soft loans over the first five-year period).

Since 1989, the EC co-ordinates the G-24 economic assistance to the countries of Central and East Europe to restructure their economies towards the market-oriented system, and is a major contributor under its PHARE* action plan.

The commitment by the Twelve (including the EC) represents about three-quarters of the G-24 total of approximately 30 billion ECU earmarked for the economic restructuring of Central and East Europe (international financial institutions contribute another 11.5 billion ECU bringing the total to 42 billion ECU). The Twelve have a majority share in the EBRD (EC+EIB+EUR—12 = 53.5 per cent of the 10 billion ECU capital).

As new democracies were emerging in the East, the EC promptly concluded agreements with them for trade and economic co-operation. At present, the EC is negotiating with them comprehensive 'association agreements', the so-called 'European agreements'. Those with Poland, Hungary, and Czechoslovakia were signed in December 1991, and negotiations are under way or planned with Bulgaria, Romania, Albania and the Baltic States.

---

* Bulgaria, Czechoslovakia, Hungary, Poland, Romania and Yugoslavia (although the position of 'Yugoslavia' is under review). Albania and the three Baltic States have been members since the beginning of 1992.

The Europe agreements are mixed agreements, covering areas of both Community and Member State competence. They will have a common framework adapted to the specific situation of each partner-country, and will provide for, in addition to trade, commercial, and economic activity, almost all aspects of economic activity, for political dialogue and for cultural co-operation. The agreements will be concluded for unlimited periods with transition periods of ten years and aim at the possible integration of the Central European countries into the Community.

A major agreement linking collectively the EFTA and the EC countries into a European Economic Area should be in place by the beginning of 1993 to coincide with the birth of the Single European Market.

For twenty years, COST (European Co-operation in Scientific and Technical Research) has provided a framework for research co-operation among some 20 European countries (among them, three Central European countries which joined a few months ago). To date, 160 projects are co-ordinated through COST in areas ranging from transport to industrial safety.

Eureka is a framework for co-operative research launched by 19 European countries and the EC in 1985; it currently covers about 500 projects involving some 2800 companies and institutes, with an overall financial volume of around 8 billion ECU.

EUREKA has established fruitful links with several countries from Central and East Europe (active National Information Points are established in Hungary, Poland, Czechoslovakia, and Russia).

The EC also co-operates in certain projects of CERN*, EMBL, and the ESF.

EC External Relations: Bilateralism

Bilaterally, the EC has a diversified set of relations with its industrialized partners, as well as with the major countries of the developing world. The first priority is, of course, in Europe,

* Poland has been a member since March 1991, Czechoslovakia since December 1991.

where a number of countries have applied for membership (Turkey, Austria, Cyprus, Malta, Sweden . . . Finland).

As to the Commonwealth of Independent States of the former Soviet Union, the European commitment (estimated at some 60 billion ECU so far) is by far the largest in the world—representing approximately 75 per cent of the total commitment (the most important provider is Germany with about 55 per cent of the world effort). The EC *strictu senso* has contributed over 3 billion ECU in grants and credit guarantees, of which 400 million ECU was earmarked in 1991 for technical assistance to improve financial services, transportation, distribution of agricultural products, energy production systems, and training in the public and private sectors. This figure has been increased to 450 million ECU for 1992.

The EC has also recently (19 March 1992) signed a Technical Assistance (TA) programme for Russia to the value of between 110 and 130 million ECU in order to help with the most acute economic and social priority needs of Russia. This is the second TA programme for Russia following the 1991 programme with the USSR which will be continued on a bilateral basis with the eleven republics of the CIS and Georgia. The 1992 Technical Assistance programme will concentrate on four main areas: food production and distribution, human resources, networks, and enterprise support services. In many respects, the implementation of the programme will be a race, since the EC is conscious of the urgency of the needs. The process will be aided by the foundation of national co-ordinating offices in each of the countries.

Another region with close links to Europe is the Mediterranean; the countries bordering on it share a common history and a variety of social, economic, financial, and trading interests. The EC has a network of 12 separate agreements, linking it with almost all the Mediterranean countries (including Israel).

Bilateral agreements (covering *inter alia* industry, energy, science and technology, and the environment) link the EC with the major countries of Latin America (Mexico, Argentina, Brazil) and Asia (China, India, Pakistan).

Over 150 countries now have diplomatic missions accredited to the EC. For its part, the EC has set up a network of external delegations and offices abroad, currently numbering over ten. The most recent major EC diplomatic representation opened a year ago (February 1991) in Moscow.

Research and Development

The EC effort at creating a true Single Market is accompanied by a number of flanking policies such as competition, environment, training, etc. Among these is the policy for (precompetitive) scientific research and technological development. The aim is to strengthen the scientific and technological bases of European industry and encourage it to become more competitive. Since the Maastricht Summit last December, the EC R&D strategy will also develop those research activities which are deemed necessary to underpin the other policies of the Community. Thus *inter alia,* the EC research programmes will contribute towards the development of trans-European network (*e.g.* in the areas of transport, telecommunications, and energy infrastructure); ensuring a high level of human health protection (including the fight against drug dependence); the development of a European dimension in education, training, and youth exchanges; and the restoration and conservation of European cultural heritage.

In order to reach all these ambitious objectives, the financial means for implementing the EC R&D action will have to be increased (the current 'Framework Programme' provides for a yearly science budget of slightly over 2 billion ECU).

The successful achievement of the goals of the EC research policy entails co-operation with Europe's international partners (and international organizations).

The international tradition of science and the globalization of technology can be harnessed to stimulate the creativity of the European research community, allowing it to share the costs and the risks involved in advancing the frontiers of research.

While international co-operation in science and technology may involve the public sector (including the EC's own JRC) and the university/academic area, ultimately it will be up to the private sector to take the lead (the EC role being mainly to act as a catalyst).

The prime objective of industrial co-operation internationally is, of course, profit (market share, securing finance, understanding strategies and managerial practices, acquiring technology, developing new products, keeping an early watching brief abroad, etc.).

The EC is ready to support these objectives, while being interested in the normative aspects (technical standards. certifications, testing, etc.), in the possible synergies and the sharing of expenses and risks (ITER, Human Genome), in planetary issues (*e.g.* Global Change) and a few other 'public' sectors.

The environment provides an example of these different levels of co-operation. As European industries discover the opportunities provided by a 'green market' and the stimulus to competitiveness offered by the challenge of 'clean and lean technologies', they are entering into a growing network of co-operative arrangements with overseas partners.

For its part, the EC has developed a diversified programme in environmental research with a budget of some 250 million ECU (1991-94), and executes it with industrial and other partners through shared-cost contracts. The programme is open to all persons and organizations established in the EC (industrial firms—including multinationals—universities, research organizations, etc.). The programme is open to organizations established in other European States who have specific agreements with the EC (*e.g.* from EFTA countries). Other European organizations (*e.g.* from Central and East Europe) may participate on a project-by-project basis. In the 'global change' area of the EC programme, the participation on a project-by-project basis is extended to non-European countries.

Let us now have a look in more depth at co-operation in S&T with Central and East Europe:

Central and Eastern Europe and the Commonwealth of Independent States of the former USSR

The EC has opened its Third Framework Programme for Research and Technological Development (1991-94) to participants from Central and East Europe and the CIS. As a first step, five specific European programmes are seeking scientific partners in the East: Environment, Biomedical and Health Research, Renewable Energies, Nuclear Fission Safety, and Human Capital and Mobility.

The EC Environment Programme has four parts: Global Change (including the greenhouse effect, ozone layer, etc.); technologies for the protection and rehabilitation of the environment (ranging from hazardous wastes to the protection and restoration of historic buildings and monuments); economic and social aspects of environmental issues (including cultural, ethical, and historical aspects of the environment); and technology and natural risks (seismic, meterological, forest fires, desertification, etc.).

The Biomedical and Health Research Programme focuses on four areas: harmonization of methodologies and protocols in epidemiology, biology and clinical research (including test networks for new medicinal products, diagnostic methods, biomaterials, etc.); diseases of major socio-economic impact (such as AIDS, cancer, mental illness, age-related disease and health problems, etc.); human genome analysis (within the framework of HUGO); and biomedical ethics.

The Non-nuclear Engeries Programme covers new energy sources that are economically viable and environmentally sound, as well as energy conservation. The Programme covers four chapters: analyses and modelling; improved use of fossil fuels; renewable energy sources; and rational use of energy and energy conservation.

The Nuclear Fission Safety Programme covers two areas: radiation protection and reactor safety.

The Programme on Human Capital and Mobility includes fellowship, networks, access to large installations, and euro-conferences.

Eventually, it is intended that most, if not all, of the 15 specific programmes under the Framework Programme be accessible to participants from selected East European countries (*e.g.* Czechoslovakia, Hungary, Poland).

Overall, the 1992 EC budget provides for over 1 billion ECU for PHARE assistance to the economic restructuring of Central and East Europe. This is up from 500 million ECU in 1990, 785 million in 1991 (including about 30 million commited to R&D and 70 million to higher education). PHARE allocations (1990 and 1991) have been oriented toward agriculture (17.5 per cent), environment (16 per cent), humanitarian aid (13 per cent), industry (13 per cent), etc. Among recent initiatives under PHARE, the regional project in telecommunications supporting the connection of universities and research centres of the region to the COSINE (Co-operation for Open Systems International Networking in Europe) network (EC contribution 2.5 million ECU).

In 1991-92, 885 million ECU are available in the EC budget for technical assistance to the CIS which is over 60 per cent of the internationally committed funds for technical assistance to the former Soviet Union (if we add the EC Member States' own contributions, the EUR-12 share of technical assistance climbs to some 83 per cent of the world's pledges). In addition, the 1992 EC budget includes 55 million ECU for S&T co-operation with Central and East Europe (40 million ECU to support joint R&D projects; 10 million ECU to support the participation of organizations from Central and East Europe in the EC Framework Programme on a project-by-project basis; 5 million ECU to further their participation in COST). Four countries from the eastern part of Europe (Czechoslovakia, Hungary, Poland, Yugoslavia), together with the EC member states and the EFTA countries, are members of the COST forum for research and development in the natural and social sciences.

Another EC scheme intended to promote the development of the higher education systems in the countries of East and Central Europe is TEMPUS. This programme is targeted to meet the specific needs of 11 European countries (Albania, Bulgaria, Croatia, Czechoslovakia, Estonia, Hungary, Latvia, Lithuania, Poland, Romania, Slovenia). Its main goals are to promote the quality and support the development of higher education in the eligible countries and to encourage their growing integration with partners in the EC. TEMPUS should have a 1992 budget of some 120 million ECU. TEMPUS is implemented through joint

European projects, mobility grants for staff and students, and complementary activities (associations of teachers or students, youth exchanges, etc.). TEMPUS is complemented by a specific programme in the field of management and economics, ACE (a large part of the programme being related to economic research projects and networks).

The weakness and shortcomings of the soviet scientific system are well knonw: the rigidity of its organizaiton, the separation of theoretical work from applications, the under-equipping of laboratories, the difficulties of access to international scientific literature, etc. Moreover, a large section of the scientific potential was devoted to defence needs.

However, these weaknesses have had some advantages: leading to a much larger sense of originality, and because of a lack of worry about the immediacy of results, a theoretical deepening of the subject. Arising from this and the political reforms, the republics of the former Soviet Union must confront a series of inter-linked problems. The first problem is organizational—how is the mainly centralized, mainly Russian, scientific network going to be transformed in order to embrace all the new independent republics? Other problems are the transformation to a market economy (who pays for the research work?), the need to convert a vast number of researchers from mainly military research to civil activities, and the growing 'brain-drain' of researchers from the former Soviet Union who, faced with numerous threats to the scientific system, uncertainties over the future, and a deterioration of their work conditions and salaries, are migrating to other parts of the world.

In order to prevent the exodus from Russia of a large number of scientists and engineers with specialist knowledge in a number of sensitive areas, the EC, in conjunction with the US, Japan, and Russia, is to contribute financially (20 million ECU) to, and participate in, the establishment of an International Science and Technology Centre (ISTC) in Moscow. The ISTC will provide incentives and support to enable scientists and engineers to engage in long-term scientific activities involving the peaceful applications of their expertize. It will also be instrumental in the conversion of defence-related industries to peaceful activities and will encourage the adoption of standards and practices conducive to environmental protection.

The EC will, *inter alia,* be ready to employ scientists and engineers recruited through the ISTC for nuclear safety projects supported by PHARE and TA programmes.

A parallel initiative directed at stemming the brain-drain in the civilian R&D sector (Mitterand/Rubbia initiative) is being discussed in OECD.

The Future

In a world of transition, the EC represents a pole of stability and progress, and exerts a strong attraction on its neighbours (not only from EFTA, but also from Central and East Europe and the Mediterranean area). The EC must use this attraction to co-operate with its neighbours, especially those of Central and East Europe, by bilateral and multilateral co-operation in the fields of economic restructuring, science, and technology, towards their own stability both in terms of a sustainable economy and innovative ability.

With the implementation of the Single Market, the construction of a European Economic Area, the moves toward a European Economic and Monetary Union and, ultimately, the goal of a European Union, the EC is bound to be an exciting place in the years and decades ahead. This dynamism will be an important factor in the progress of the whole of Europe.

30

An International and Interdisciplinary Catalyst for European Scientists

DAVID WAINWRIGHT

Publications Consultant, European Science Foundation, Strasbourg, France

Introduction

The European Science Foundation is the voice of European scientists. It is an association of its 59 member research councils, academies, and institutions devoted to basic scientific research in 21 countries. The ESF brings European scientists together to work on topics of common concern, to co-ordinate the use of expensive facilities, and to discover and define new endeavours that will benefit from a co-operative approach. The scientific work sponsored by ESF includes basic research in the natural sciences, the medical and bio sciences, the humanities and the social sciences.

The ESF links scholarship and research supported by its members and adds value by co-operation across national frontiers. Through its function as a co-ordinator and also by holding workshops and conferences and by enabling researchers to visit and study in laboratories throughout Europe, the ESF works for the advancement of European science.

It must be understood that the ESF operates by the goodwill and enthusiasm of its Member Organizations. More than a third of those present at this Seminar are representatives of Member Organizations of the ESF, from ten countries. It is significant that two of those countries are Hungary and Poland: the Hungarian Academy of Sciences was welcomed to membership of ESF in 1990 and the Polish Academy of Science last November.

Despite its name, the European Science Foundation is not an organization comparable to the National Science Foundation of America. NSF is endowed with responsibilities as a grant-giving body that are similar to those exercised by the Research Councils that are Member Organizations of ESF. The ESF works through the co-operation of its Member Organizations, whose delegates formally approve, at the ESF General Assembly held in Strasbourg each November, the direction of ESF activities.

These activities include Research Programmes in widely differing disciplines. There are now 23 such Programmes, fully active or in an advanced stage of preparation, involving about a thousand scientists. They are Programmes that have been proposed and assessed by the four Standing Committees of ESF: the European Science Research Councils (ESRC), concerned with the natural and technical sciences, the European Medical Research Councils (EMRC) concerned with the medical and life sciences, the Humanities Committee (SCH) and the Social Sciences Committee (SCSS).

In addition, the Foundation currently co-ordinates 20 Scientific Networks, linking teams and individual scientists (some 500 to 600 in all) from the countries represented among the Member Organizations and beyond. For example, on the Committees organizing some of these Programmes and Networks, there are already five scientists from Russia, one from the Ukraine, and one from Belarus: more are from the independent states of the former East Europe.

The difference between ESF Scientific Programmes and ESF Scientific Networks is broadly that Programmes are established to conduct substantive research over a period of years, while Networks provide a forum at which scientists may meet (usually with the participation of young researchers) to exchange views and experience in a particular field of science, usually over a period of two or three years, after which contacts will be maintained informally. It is becoming clear that Networks may lead to the establishment of Scientific Programmes in the field.

Programmes have been a feature of ESF activity almost from its foundation in 1974. Networks are a later development, introduced in 1985 at the request of the Conference of European Ministers responsible for research. The underlying concept was based on the belief that scientists in any field saw as their immediate community those working in the field in their own country, and had relatively little contact with colleagues in other European countries. Networks have now become a welcome feature of ESF operations.

The Funding of ESF

The ESF does not have a cumbersome bureaucracy—its total headquarters staff consists of only 28 people, based in Strasbourg. Its basic budget for 1991 including the Network Account, amounted to less than 23 million French Francs. This does not include the *à la carte* funding of specific Scientific Programmes by Member Organizations; if these are added to the basic budgets, the total annual cash flow is about 45 million French Francs.

The ESF basic budget is provided by annual contributions from the Member Organizations, the amount assessed in each case from published figures of GNP. The *à la carte* funding to support specific research programmes is provided by those member organizations expressing an interest in the programme. This provides Member Organizations with an additional means of monitoring the direction of ESF activities, since if adequate funding cannot be gathered together by ESF staff during the preparatory stages of a scientific programme, then it cannot run, and cannot proceed to the stage of approval by the ESF Assembly.

Relations with the Community

The ESF works in association with the Commission of the European Communities in several of its activities. There are currently two joint committees—on environmental change, and on ocean and polar sciences, reporting and making recommendations to both CEC and ESF. Under Line 6 of the

Community's Framework Programme, Human Capital and Mobility, considerable resources are to be dedicated to research training fellowships. ESF hopes to participate in this action through our Networks and Programmes, most of which deliberately and positively include the active participation of young researchers with leading scholars.

The Foundation has already acquired expertize in this field, organizing a series of European Research Conferences (Euroconferences), 19 of which were financed and co-sponsored by the Commission, six in 1990 and 13 in 1991. The programme of about 20 conferences taking place in Spring and Summer this year is being funded by CEC on the same *ad hoc* basis as last year. ESF hopes that a more stable and organic link can be established between the Community's Framework Programme and the ESF programme of Research Conferences in the future. Research Conferences reinforce and expand Networks and provide opportunities for the exchange of ideas giving young researchers, with priority for those from centres in less favoured regions, access to the latest developments in their fields.

In West Europe, the Member Organizations of ESF continue to be the main promoters of basic science. European industry also plays its part in funding research while the Commission of the European Communities is assuming an increasing role. These are all big spenders compared to ESF which is relatively very poor. A key issue is the extent to which in Europe it remains optimal to finance nationally most of basic science. There is an increasing tendency for research funders to look for wider areas of co-operation or concentration.

This has long been the case where projects are very expensive and costs have to be shared, as with CERN for example. But ESF has acted as an enabling body in such matters, and was instrumental in bringing countries together for the study which defined the European Synchrotron Radiation Facility (ESRF), which machine is now nearing completion. In addition, ESF provides fora of individual scientists through its Space Science Committee to comment on the totality of space science research in Europe, through the Nuclear Physics European Collaboration Committee (NuPECC) to comment on facilities for nuclear physics, and through the ESF Committee on Radio Astronomy Frequencies (CRAF) to be part of the international processes of frequency allocation.

European Science

The ESF has also responded to ministerial requests for advice on priorities in European Astronomy and about Human Genome research. Advice has also been given to the Ministerial Meeting of the European Space Agency (ESA). The CEC recently commissioned a report from ESF on social science research in Europe.

Naturally not all excellent science needs to be done on a European scale. Many Member Organizations of ESF have bilateral agreements with similar bodies in other European countries, working creatively without ESF intervention. But there are many examples of programmes that benefit from the international relationships that ESF can offer.

For example, the European Committee on Ocean and Polar Science (ECOPS), which ESF runs jointly with the European Commission, has been considering an initiative in the Antarctic analogous to the highly successful Greenland Ice Core Project (GRIP). This new activity—the European Programme on Ice-Coring in Antarctica (EPICA)—would be carried out via an ESF Scientific Programme providing the necessary interconnections, meetings and workshops, co-ordinating the work and analyzing the results.

Another example relates to interdisciplinary activity, especially in areas where the social sciences contribute to work in the natural technical and medical sciences. A specific instance of this is within the Environment Science and Society Programme which studies complex environmental systems, concentrating on selected economic and institutional aspects. This programme seeks to enhance environmental economics as an established area of scientific enquiry at the international level. Last November the ESF was co-sponsor (with the International Council of Scientific Unions, ICSU) of the international conference on an Agenda of Science for Environment and Development into the 21st Century (ASCEND 21), held in Vienna, in preparation for the UN Conference in Rio de Janeiro this June (1992). The ESF Programme on Environment, Science and Society, and such conferences, contribute to the analysis of the social dynamics associated with global change and demographic change.

In the medical sciences, ESF has been helping forward what was originally a French initiative in clinical networks to bring together doctors and laboratory researchers. These are now termed Clinical Collaborations: a top-down practical application of basic research to a clinical contingency, with no common fund and no international co-ordinating committee. They may act as germs of future ESF Networks and Programmes. Open to extended European participation in the medical area, and growing out of an earlier Network, is one of ESF's most ambitious current programmes, that on Molecular Neurobiology of Mental Illness, in which the ESF has become closely associated with the US National Institute of Mental Health.

The concept of networking goes beyond the natural sciences to the humanities. The ESF Programme on the Non-Governmental Ethnic Groups, which ceased to be funded last year, has nearly completed the publication of eight volumes. The Programme on the Origins of the Modern State is soon to begin publication. Dealing with pressing issues in the new context of Europe, the volumes from these two Programmes are not separate monographs but result from a process of consensus-building among researchers: that is, from networking in the fullest sense.

Relations with the Wider Europe

Finally, ESF has for a considerable time been concerned with the changes affecting the scientific communities in East Europe and the former USSR. As long ago as September 1990, the previous President of the ESF, E. Seibold, called an informal meeting at the Strasbourg headquarters to which scientists from Eastern Europe were invited to discuss the possibility of future institutional links. The occasion led to an open and constructive exchange of views between visiting scientists from Eastern Europe and the ESF Board.

Throughout the Winter, the changes affecting science in the former Soviet Union were discussed widely within the ESF and its member organizaitons. In December a member of the ESF Executive Council (A. Epstein, formerly Foreign Secretary of the

Royal Society) attended, on behalf of the ESF President, the meeting in Moscow which marked the end of the Soviet Academy of Sciences and the beginning of the new Russian Academy.

In January 1992 the ESF Board (the ESF President, U. Colombo, with the three Vice-Presidents and the Secretary General) met the Board of the Academia Europaea, the association of individual scholars throughout the wider Europe. Following that meeting, a joint statement was issued by the ESF and the Academia Europaea on problems in the scientific community of the former Soviet Union. This statement was generally welcomed.

Subsequently other meetings have been held, several in Brussels under the aegis of CEC, one arranged and chaired by the Secretary General of the Max Planck Gesellschaft. The ESF, through its Secretary General M. Posner, presented to that meeting a paper on *The Crisis Facing Research in Europe, East of the Oder*.

This paper included the following points.

"Some might argue that basic research, even in the institutions where it is well conducted and of top quality, is a luxury the former communist countries will be unable to afford for years to come. But what these countries certainly need is a continuing investment in well trained graduates of Universities and Hochschule with minds open and alert to scientific and technological changes. In Eastern Europe, as in the West, campus-based research institutions must play a key role in keeping both teachers and students close to the moving frontiers of knowledge. And links between basic research and industry are, as is well known, also essential if inward technology transfer (from Western to Eastern Europe and also within Eastern European countries) is to be successfully accomplished on a wide front.

"It is this inter-related system to which, in the view of the ESF, the scientific institutions of Western Europe should provide urgent support. That support will necessarily be limited, and cannot be committed for a long period. But it should be a co-ordinated operation, so that we help the maximum amount of science for each ECU we spend.

"Decisions on the practical implementation of such support would of necessity have to be based on a numerate analysis of the magnitude of the problem and an evaluation . . . of which sectors of science could use most effectively and rapidly the help which could be given.

"The ESF, being an organizaiton whose main interest is in fundamental science, could contribute to this process by organizing a detailed but rapid examination of the scientific priorities for the protection and development of chosen sectors. The Foundation could play a useful role in the subsequent discussions and decision-making by mobilizing the judgement and knowledge of all its Member Organizations in identifying the scientific groups and individuals on which support could be concentrated, and in proposing detailed support measures best justified on scientific grounds.

"The following support measures for basic science might need in particular to be addressed:

— mobilization (not just conservation) of the best scientists and equipment, so as to enhance their capacity to work creatively at the relevant frontiers of knowledge.

— creation of an evidently national system of distributing scarce funds, so as to build confidence and an element of stability in a system in which scientists can work effectively: this may require some help in setting up the relevant procedures.

— links with cognate work in the West—the ESF system of Programmes and Networks provides a good starting point, and our contacts with member organizations can help to widen the range of opportunities.

"In parallel, measures should be taken in the areas of higher education, industrially-related research and technology transfer—the science system as a whole. The ESF would not want to assume responsibility for these areas.

"The selection of targets and the choice of mechanisms play a central role."

The ESF made three proposals for action:

1. First, the setting up of thematic scientific panels to assess in each sector the human capital available and

the mode of support most appropriate: and to prepare an action plan including the numbers of scientists/ groups to be supported and the resources required.

2. The provision of support mechanisms, including the training of science managers, a scheme for the award of fellowships to selected scientists for short reciprocal visits, and direct support to research groups and individuals. The ESF believes that it is well placed through its existing structure of ESF activities and Standing Committees, to identify suitable panel members and to initiate activities quickly. ESF member organizations are already active in sustaining science in various countries of Central and East Europe and are thereby attuned and sensitized to the problem.
3. Thirdly, participation in existing ESF activities: European Research Conferences, Networks, Programmes and thematic 'Schools'.

In his address to the ESF General Assembly in November 1991, President U. Colombo said that *"we should not leave the scientific communities of Central and Eastern Europe to fend for themselves at such a critical time . . . The Foundation can build effective bridges, provided member organizations are prepared to take a measure of responsibility"*.

The European Science Foundation depends upon its member organizations and upon the Commission of the European Communities for its funding, year after year. Many of ESF's member organizations find their budgets under extreme pressure domestically, at a time when they face growing appeals to support science internationally. The ESF has virtually no reserves of funds that can be directed towards urgent action, however, desirable. By its constitution, the ESF must argue the need for action case by case, raising funds as it goes along year by year to support science.

In President Colombo's words, *"ESF and its member organizations seek to apply their skills and knowledge to the support of science in Europe as does the European Community. Our slogan might be: Helping forward excellent science on a European scale"*.

31

The 'Scientific Network' Concept: Benefits for the Greater Europe

JEAN-PIERRE MASSUÉ

Executive Secretary, Open Partial Agreement on Major Disasters, Council of Europe, Strasbourg, France

The aim of this presentation is to demonstrate through two examples the important role the 'Scientific Network' can play in responding to the needs of the Greater Europe. In the first step, we will describe the 'Scientific Network' concept given by the European Ministers on the occasion of their meeting in Paris in September 1984. In the second step, we will present two examples where the Network played a key role: one in the field of material sciences and a second in the field of major hazards.

The 'Scientific Network' Concept

The first Conference of European Ministers of Research was held in Paris on 17 September 1984. It followed a proposal made by the President of the French Republic, Francois Mitterand, to the Parliamentary Assembly of the Council of Europe on 30 September 1982, in which he said that: "it would perhaps be wise to keep Europe's brains in Europe and, hence, to offer them sufficient scope for their powers of research and expression".

The Ministers unanimously expressed their wish to:

— promote the establishment of a 'European scientific and technical area', open to all States taking part in the

Conference of European Ministers of Research organized by the Council of Europe; and thus,

— intensify European concerted action and co-operation in the field of research and, accordingly, foster contact and exchange among scientists, laboratories, universities and other higher education and research institutions in Europe.

The Ministers decided to:

— encourage the continued and reinforced development of existing networks and, if need be, to promote the preparation of new networks of scientific and technical co-operation in Europe

— propose arrangements whereby mobility conditions in Europe would be improved.

During this Ministerial Conference, organized in close co-operation with the European Science Foundation and the Commission of the European Communities, the European Ministers defined the European networks of scientific and technical co-operation as follows:

"A network should, within a field designated by the scientists themselves, bring together ideas and efforts, human resources, and equipment, training possibilities and expertize.

"A network should be self-administered; in other words, the scientists should themselves ensure their network's organization and scientific supervision. The scientific community should seek appropriate support structures and financial means from national, community, or international sources.

"A network should enjoy many forms of communication and co-operation: liaison, contact, information, exchange, joint research and high-level training projects."

The European networks are composed of researchers from public and private laboratories and are valuable tools for furthering co-operation and concerted action in:

— training

— research

— technological development.

The list describing the European Network created is given in Table 1.

Table 1. European Network of Scientific and Technological Co-operation

EUROPEAN NETWORK
CULTURAL FIELD
PACT network (sciences and technologies applied to the cultural heritage)
Network on scientific culture and development of astronomy in Europe.
FIELD OF LAW
CERP network (European centre for research into political practices)
EUROREGIONS network (decentralization and local autonomy in Europe)
Network on Medicine and Human Rights.
FIELD OF HEALTH
CEC network (European College of Surgeons)
Network European Academy of Anaesthesiology
ETRO network (European Thrombosis Research Organization)
EICOR network (European Interdisciplinary Centre for Oral Research)
FIELD OF NATURAL SCIENCES
E-MRS network (European Materials Research Society)
AESTM network (European Association of Marine Sciences and Technologies)
EARSeL network (European Association of Remote Sensing Laboratories
Exobiology network (life in the universe)
CERCO network (European Committee of Heads of Official Mapping Agencies)
EUROCIT network (European network for research, development, dissemination, and training in computer-aided manufacturing for the textile and clothing industry)
Environmental Counselling
FIELD OF SOCIAL SCIENCES
European network on Women's studies.
European Secretariat for Scientific Publications.

IMPACT OF EUROPEAN NETWORKS OF SCIENTIFIC AND TECHNOLOGICAL CO-OPERATION: A FEW CONCRETE EXAMPLES

The Role of the Networks in Promoting a Concerted Effort Among Scientists to Respond to Opportunities in Europe

Throughout the network system, established links between European scientists have favoured concerted reactions to opportunities in research, technological development, and training that exist within the framework of major European programmes. The network plays a vital role in bringing together a great number of researchers and laboratories from different countries so that they may share their expertize and, together, achieve the best results.

Implementation of European Platforms for Meetings, Training Schemes and Information

For example:

- in the field of geodynamics: the 'Journées Luxembourgeoises de Géodynamique' which take place in Walferdange (Luxembourg) constitute a regular meeting forum for European Researchers.
- in the field of sciences and technologies applied to cultural heritage: the European University Centre for Cultural Heritage, located in Ravello, Italy, where postgraduate courses are organized regularly.
- in the field of decentralization: European university summer courses organized by the University of Fribourg, Switzerland.
- preparation of the project 'images and science': European research images, obtained through research, for research; further impetus given to dialogue, creativity, and knowledge.

Creation of Scientific Press and a Series of European Publications

For example:

- in the field of material science: 32 books published (the result of five years of network activity: 1984-89)

— in the field of sciences and technologies applied to cultural heritage: 29 books already published or about to be published.

— in the field of human rights: the research carried out by the European network that deals with medicine and human rights resulted in the publication of one reference book on this subject. The paperback edition, which should very shortly be available in French, English, Greek, Spanish, Italian, Polish, and Russian, will serve as an educational tool for the teaching of medical ethics in medical schools and faculties in eastern and western Europe.

Printing of newsletters:

— in the field of remote-sensing (EARSeL)

— in the field of cartography (CERCO)

— in the field of oceanography (AESTM).

With the tremendous changes that have taken place in eastern Europe, its scientists, encouraged by a rebirth of democratic principles and an increasing number of co-operation projects, have expressed their desire to participate in the activities of the European networks: PACT, E-MRS, EARSeL, Medicine and Human Rights networks, etc.

Special attention should be paid to the area of advanced materials.

We are entering an age in which materials and related technologies form a single entity. New materials are no longer familiar substances reshaped to built objects. They are created in the minds of scientists, designed with computers and fabricated by robotics. Clearly, modern materials and technology for a competitive economy are becoming synonymous.

In order to appreciate their importance, new materials must be recognized as more than just substances with special performance properties. These materials are the actual media by which new technologies diffuse throughout industrial economies. Advances in materials science also are prerequisites for success today in sophisticated technologies. For example, recent progress in telecom and computerization would have been impossible without the development of optical fibres and silicon chips.

By the year 2000, advanced materials are expected to constitute by far the largest market of 12 emerging technologies identified. Advanced materials are expected to command a world market of ECU 300 billion for which Europe will have a share of about one-third.

The expected market share includes: superconductors (ECU 5 billion), advanced superconductor devices (ECU 75 billion), digital imaging technology (ECU 4 billion), high-density data storage (ECU 15 billion), high-performance computing (ECU 50 billion), opto-electronics (ECU 4 billion), artificial intelligence (ECU 5 billion), flexible computer integrated manufacturing (ECU 20 billion), sensor technology (ECU 5 billion), biotechnology (ECU 15 billion), medical devices and diagnostics (ECU 58 billion).

Besides the development of these specific new functional materials, there are also a variety of structural materials, including metals, alloys, intermetallic compounds, metal-matrix composites (7.5 billion ECUs), ceramics (45 billion ECUs) and polymers.

It is in this context that, following the Conference of European Ministers of Research (September 1984 in Paris), the European Materials Research Association (E-MRS) was founded with active backing from the Council of Europe and the European Communities.

To achieve its objectives, E-MRS, together with the EEC and the Council of Europe, took the following initiatives:

— to organize high-level scientific and technical conferences to discuss the latest developments in the field of advanced materials. At each Spring and Autumn session, these conferences bring together specialists in the field. In 1990, approximately 2000 researchers and engineers took part.

— to set up European networks that bring together representatives of Europe's most renowned laboratories (both public and private) to discuss various problems in details as well as to work co-operatively beyond national boundaries.

— to organize high-level and intensive training courses with some of the finest experts in the field of advanced materials.

Indicative of a European revival in the field of scientific publications and in response to the need for excellent dissemination of information, a survey of all the work so far undertaken has been published in a series of books (over 40 to date).

We are now facing the NEW CHALLENGE IN A WINDER EUROPE.

Examples of the Network's Success

Let us now look at two examples where the Network has played an important role:

Materials Science in Europe

MatTech'90—'The First European East-West Symposium on Materials and Processes' with about 850 participants from 40 different countries was organized by the Institute of Materials Science and Technology of the Helsinki University of Technology with an active participation of the Fransevitch Institute for Problems of Materials Science, Kiev, Ukraine, and held in June 1990 in Espoo, near Helsinki, Finland. The wide spectrum of participating nationalities and specially the impressive participation of Soviet R&D through 200 experts and decision-makers from 70 institutes and research centres of the Soviet space and defence industries manifested the urgent need for this kind of forum for dialogue for the scientists as well as for technology transfer between East and West.

The second MatTech, *i. e.* MatTech '91, was again organized in Espoo, Finland at the end of May 1991. Strong moral support for the MatTech-concept itself was given through the personal greetings of M. S. Gorbachev, President of the USSR and J. Delors, President of the Commission of the European Communities. MatTech has thus strengthened its position as an internationally acknowledged event contributing in an important way to the general aim of improving co-operation in the new wider Europe. Therefore, the E-MRS, in common with the activities of the EEC and of the Council of Europe, has decided to invite eastern scientists to participate in the activities. An agreement has been reached between the *MatTech East-West Conference* organization in Helsinki (Professor Lilius) to join efforts with the E-MRS for a joint venture starting 1992 by organizing a common European East-West Conference in Strasbourg (3-6 November, 1992) on advanced materials processes.

In addition, an exhibition of the most recent developments in this field will also be held.

The reaction of scientists from both public and private sectors of all eastern European countries wishing to join the E-MRS activities has been considerable, and we are expecting a broad participation of our eastern European partners in the Strasbourg meeting in November.

This example illustrates the value of the 'Scientific Network' concept in facilitating the participation of eastern European scientists in the existing platform of co-operation.

The Second Example is Related to the Field of Major Hazards

The PACT and Geodynamics Networks played a decisive role in the creation and implementation of the Council of Europe's Open Partial Agreement on Major Disasters.

The Open Partial Agreement on major disasters was established following the adoption of resolution (87) 2 on 20 March, 1987, by the Committee of Ministers. The principal objective of the Agreement is to further the co-operation between member states from a multidisciplinary point of view, in order to assure the best prevention, protection, and organization of relief in the case of major catastrophes.

This agreement is designated Open Partial Agreement: it is partial in the sense that only interested members of the Council of Europe may take part in it. The agreement is also open to any non-member state that asks to join.

At present, this agreement is adhered to by 14 member states: Algeria, Belgium, France, Greece, Italy, Luxembourg,

Malta, Monaco, San Marino, Portugal, Spain, Turkey, the Russian Federation, and Israel. The Commission of the European Communities participates in its activities, as do WHO, UNESCO and UNDRO.

At the operational level, the Agreement's decision-making body is the meeting of the ministers of the Open Partial Agreement, which meets every two years and is prepared by Permanent Correspondents who meet at least annually. The last Permanent Correspondents' meeting was held in Moscow on 3-5 April, 1991 and the last Ministerial meeting was held on 9-10 July 1991 in Ankara, Turkey.

The following activities, falling within the Agreement framework, are pursued at 3 levels:

— research and training activities implemented by the 12 specialized European centres situated in the different countries taking part in the agreement.

— relief activities and subsequent co-operation in the event of a disaster, notably with regard to a European warning system.

— specific programmes: research on earthquake prediction, a project for a system of epidemiological information and assistance in medical decisions following the Chernobyl accident, the conservation project of the coral eco-systems in the Gulf.

RESEARCH AND TRAINING ACTIVITIES

European Centre for Disaster Medicine (CEMEC), San Marino: In the area of provision of medicine and aid in the event of an emergency, CEMEC promotes European training programmes and international and inter-regional exchange programmes. Its courses cover areas that include, for example, emergencies, severe burns, and epidemiology. The research activities of the Centre are concerned with risk factors, prevention, control, and therapeutic approaches. The CEMEC acts as a clearing house for information on existing disaster medicine programmes.

European University Centre for Cultural Heritage, Ravello, Italy: This Centre conducts research and training activities at postgraduate level on the utilization of science and technology for the benefit of the cultural heritage. Its contribution to the activities of the Open Partial Agreement relates to questions of the protection of cultural heritage from major risks.

One of the objectives of the Centre is the development of appropriate techniques for the protection, preservation, and restoration of ancient buildings in seismic areas. In this area, a particular effort is underway to consider the behaviour of communities in regions affected. One can cite the research undertaken in Calitri, San Lorenzello, and Paestum in Italy, in the South-East French Alps, Piedmont in Italy, and Leucade in Greece. An atlas of seismic 'cultures' in risk areas of member states, principally in the Mediterranean region, will be established. This will make it possible to determine the value of local anti-seismic techniques.

A research programme will be undertaken to improve the methodology of reinforcing existing buildings (notably concrete structures and small masonry buildings) and the construction of new buildings of the same type.

European Training Centre for Natural Disasters (AFEM), Ankara, Turkey: The activities of AFEM are principally centred on the training of responsible technical and administrative personnel in preparation for a disaster, as well as of teachers in order to provide a better co-ordination of the efforts of relief services involved. One can point to the examples of courses held regularly in 1990 and 1991 on the prevention and management of catastrophes and on rescue operations for handicapped persons and children.

In addition, research is also being carried out on the public impact of televized films on the subject of earthquakes. Research is now taking place using techniques especially formulated for use in rural areas.

European Centre for Geodynamic and Morphodynamic Hazards (ECGDH/EMSC), Strasbourg, France work at the European Centre for geodynamic and morphodynamic hazards has passed from experimental to operational level with regard to rapid dissemination of information. The ECGDH remains the European focal point for collection and diffusion of technical and scientific information in the event of a major earthquake. With the help of permanent correspondents in various nations, the Centre has seen its responsibility grow with regard to the potential users of this information: civil authorities, scientists, relief agencies, mass media, etc. The ECGD constitutes an important data base of international seismic information. The Centre is now also developing geomorphological activities.

European Centre of Geodynamics and Seismology, Luxembourg: The objective of the Centre is to promote research programmes and education in geo-dynamics applicable to studies on tectonic deformations as related to earthquakes, while placing special emphasis on space techniques. The colloquia and regular symposia cover all aspects of the physics and dynamics of solid earth studies, and of natural and artificial satellites and the specific interactions between ocean and atmosphere. There is also a commitment to subjects of great importance and relevance to specific topics which involve intercomparison of measurements of gravity including those derived from superconductivity.

European Centre on the Prevention and Forecasting of Earthquakes, Athens, Greece: This Centre concentrates its efforts on earthquake prediction, minimization of casualties and civilian training. It is in the process of preparing a new European code for para-seismic building standards.

The Centre also supplies educational material on the protection of the general public in the event of an earthquake. The International Conference on Earthquake Prediction: State of the Art, held in Strasbourg, 15-18 October, 1991, was organized by this Centre.

In addition, the Centre also made a call for propositions in order to launch a European research programme on earthquake prediction.

European Mediterranean Centre on Marine Contamination Hazards, La Valletta, Malta: The Centre collects, treats, and disseminates information on cases of major marine pollution and on research in this area. The activities of the Centre are concentrated on:

— microbiological methods for the measurement of accidental marine contamination in the Mediterranean (1989–1990–1991)

— the evaluation of risks in cases of major maritime accidents (22–26 October, 1990).

On the research level, the major themes concentrate on marine pollution in the mediterranean area, primarily with regard to:

— the epidemiological evaluation of risks to swimmers

— the use of spatial means for surveillance of the ocean environment, and teledetection in particular (March-December, 1990).

European Centre for Information to the Public in the Event of Disaster Situations, Madrid, Spain: The objective of this centre is to provide all parties of the Agreement with new techniques of informing the public in emergency situations. To this end, psycho-sociological research is performed on several real-life cases and sites. In 1989, research was carried out on the behaviour of the population after the ship 'CASON' leaked toxic products along the north-west coast of Spain, as well as during floods in the Levante province. An analysis of the behaviour of the populations after the breakdown at the nuclear power plant in Vandellos, Spain and after the floods in Malaga in 1989 was produced in 1990.

In 1991, the European Centre of Madrid began its contribution to the SIEAD/APO/CHERNOBYL programme, epidemiological information system and assistance for medical decisions, with regard to information and training processes.

European Oceanology Observatory: Prediction of Major Risks and Environment Regeneration, Monaco, Principality of Monaco: The Centre's purpose is to receive research teams from different countries, with the aim of developing these projects:

— to develop selective perception (indicator species) and synoptic perception teledetection/remote sensing) in order to detect ecological disturbances and monitor their progress,

— to develop simulation techniques using theoretical and/ or experimental models (mesocosms = scale models of ecosystems) in order to acquire a better understanding of how ecosystems function, how ecological disturbances come about, how they are likely to develop, and how to evaluate the risks,

— to organize the production of species selected for their importance of potential usefulness in:

conserving threatened species,

restocking impaired habitats (species having a key role),

easing the pressure on natural stocks of overexploited species (aquarium species, collector's items, objects of curiosity, etc.),

particular attention is paid to corals because they are susceptible to reactions to ecological stress.

— to prepare a European programme on the conservation of coral eco-systems in the Persian Gulf.

European Centre for Non-Linear Dynamics and Theory of Seismic Risk, Moscow, USSR. The Centre's principal goal is to improve the theoretical and computational base of seismic risk reduction. This base includes:

— modern non-linear dynamics, with its concepts of chaos and self-organization, which started to merge with earthquake studies just a few years ago,

— modern exploratory data analysis and mathematical statistics, adapted for the analysis of a wide variety of data relevant to seismic risk.

This Centre will contribute to the preparation of a common research programme on earthquake prediction.

Since the ministerial meeting in Ankara on 9-10 July, 1991, two other European centres have been established:

— The European Centre on the Legislative Aspects of Disasters, Florival, Belgium

— The European Centre on Major Industrial Disasters, Aveiro, Portugal.

The European Warning System

In the event of seismic activity or potentially destructive tsunamis, the European Mediterranean Seismic Centre (EMSC) is in charge of gathering the necessary data, calculating the preliminary parameters of the seismic activity, and distributing the collected information.

In the event of a major seismic incident (magnitude equal to or greater than 6 on the Richter scale), the EMSC informs the Council of Europe 'in times of potential emergency', the latter immediately informing the Permanent Correspondents of the Open Partial Agreement in order, by means of a teleconference, to make a concerted response to the immediate demands of the affected state or states.

For example, the alert was activated in the event of the earthquake in Georgia which registered 6.9 on the Richter scale, followed by a teleconference to co-ordinate aid, from the member states of the Open Partial Agreement on major disasters of the Council of Europe, to the affected regions of Georgia.

Research on Earthquake Prediction

It was decided to propose the participation of the Agreement in problematic earthquake prediction as a European contribution to the United Nations International Decade for Natural Disaster Reduction.

This programme has focused on three elements:

1. Organizaiton of an international conference in Strasbourg, 15-18 October, 1991 on 'Earthquake Prediction : State of the Art':
   - seismology and theory
   - geochemistry and undergrouwa water
   - geophysics
   - deformation of the earth's crust
   - integrated projects
   - evaluation and strategies
   - social and economic impacts.

2. Drafting of European code of social ethics for scientists concerning the information on earthquake prediction made available to the public.

The project would develop an ethical code with the objective of identifying a certain number of principles regarding the role and proper behaviour of scientists working in the area of earthquake prediction. The challenge of this project is in meeting the rights and duties of the scientific community in relation to its own research structure, and in relation to the media, the public, public authorities, etc.

The creation of a European scientific evaluation committee would guarantee respect for the ethical principles defined by this code in Europe.

It should be noted that at the September 1990 session of the European Seismological Commission in Barcelona, the scientists adopted a proposal suspending all public information regarding earthquake prediction until the October 1991 Conference in Strasbourg had been held.

3. Preparation of a joint research programme on earthquake prediction.

The Programme: SIEAD/OPA/CHERNOBYL PROJECT

— system of epidemiological information and assistance for medical decisions

Project Objective: To set up a System

— with computerized epidemiological monitoring, allowing the population in irradiated zones to be followed, making clear the repercussions that the Chernobyl accident has had on the health of the population

— assisting medical decisions in the health treatment of the populations concerned.

Organization of the Project:

Geographical level:

— Ukraine, Byelorussia, Russian Federation

— Black Sea Region (Trabzon) and the Centre (Nigde) in Turkey.

Time-table level:

The project will be carried out in 2 phases:

— a pilot phase of 24 months followed by an evaluation

— a generalization phase.

Conclusion

In conclusion, I would like to take this opportunity here in Venice to launch one idea. In the 'Scientific Network' concept, we have to consider two levels of activities:

— level 1 deals with the management of the network itself: board meetings, liaison between the members, exchange of information, newsletters, etc.

— level 2 deals with scientific activities: co-operative programme for research, training or development will be defined in 'time' and 'space'.

The budgetary allocations for network activities of the second level can be found in answering the call of opportunity launched in the framework of the international and European programmes.

For level 1 activities, the budgetary needs are more difficult to obtain; however, the existence of the network as a 'potential of resources' is a prerequisite for the setting up of activities of level 2.

Under these assumptions, I would like to propose to the major intergovernmental organizations working at the level of the Greater Europe like UNESCO, EEC, Council of Europe, that they consider the possibility of a joint activity to facilitate the running and management of the Network (level 1 activities).

32

Aims and Outcome of the International Seminar on Organizational Structures of Science in Europe

Introduction

The transitional period through which Europe is passing affects not only countries in central and eastern areas, but in fact the whole of the region. Scientific communities in many countries in Central and East Europe are now involved in the adaptation of the R&D process to completely new socio-economic and political conditions. These countries need new frameworks in which their science is to operate, a new structure to accommodate moment towards a free market economy, to allow their industries to flourish, their research in science and technology to take off, to take advantage of the prosperity of market economies. A restructuring of these dimensions can be accelerated by East-West and indeed North-South interactions.

Objectives

The seminar on 'Organizational Structures of Science in Europe', held in Venice on 27-29 April, 1992, was organized by the UNESCO Regional Office for Science and Technology for Europe (UNESCO-ROSTE) to bring together top-level scientists, experts, and policy-makers from the countries of Central, East and West Europe, including representatives of national research councils from West European countries, and of the academies and ministers for science from Central and East European countries, international organizations, the Italian Ministry for Foreign Affairs, and other prominent institutions. The aim was to air various problems, identify and develop recommendations for an improved organization of science in Europe, to create new frameworks for science and technology, through the discussion, analysis, and exchange of ideas between countries, regarding the organizational structures of science in these countries, bearing in mind the transit of Central and East European countries towards a free market economy. Discussions between nations were also exchanged, of great potential given their vast differences in experience.

The seminar was deemed to be of vital assistance to the scientific community of the countries in Central and East Europe which need to reshape their research in science and technology in the context of new socio-economic conditions. It was also considered of great value for the western research institutions, not least for the new working contacts that can be forged with colleagues from central and eastern countries. Indeed, science could be the major area of co-operative effort towards unifying the countries of Europe.

Opening of the Seminar

The meeting, convened by UNESCO-ROSTE, had the honour of being hosted at the Istituto Veneto di Scienze, Lettere ed Arti, on the invitation of its President, F. Benvenuti. Welcome addresses and opening remarks were made by the Institute's President himself, and also by A. Badran, Assistant Director-General for Natural Sciences, UNESCO; the Deputy Mayor of Venice, F. Livieri; V. Kouzminov, Chief of UNESCO-ROSTE; and Senator T. Carettoni, President of the Italian National Commission for UNESCO.

Working Sessions

The programme of the seminar was composed of three major working sessions:

- First working session. Organizational Structures of Science: Western Case

- Second working session. Organizational Structures of Science: Eastern Case
- Third working session. International Organizations and Science in Europe.

The participants' presentations during working sessions were followed by intense discussions: summaries of the debates were presented by Rapporteurs at the closing session.

The demanding contributions made by the Chairpersons and Rapporteurs are strongly acknowledged: first working session Chairpersons P. Bisogno and A. Kuklinski, Rapporteur S. Passman; second working session Chairpersons U. Ekberg and V. Hancil, Rapporteur N. Lenardic; and third working session Chairpersons A. Forti and J. Caraca, Rapporteur V. Kouzminov.

Some 50 people attended, of whom 30 made formal presentations. Annex I contains a list of participants, whilst their presentations can be founding in Annex II.

Discussion

The discussion pursued during the meeting took two overlapping forms—questions and comments arising directly from the presentations, and more protracted exploration during dedicated sessions. In the following, the main points have been assembled under various categories to aid the reader, beinging out the main points raised.

Exchanges revolved around certain fixed stars: the real role of science and technology in Europe; the value of the experience of West, Centre, and East; the extent to which the experience of the West can or should be carried over to the Centre and East; the perils of popularism; the state-of-affairs prevailing in a particular country; the need to work with reality; the essential need to recognize each country's individuality, and in turn its need to act responsibly within its new environment; the need of the Centre and East to avoid dismantling valuable elements inherited from the past; the need to support the centre and East while they catch up; the role of the universities and of the academies; the public/private balance of investments in science; assessment and peer review; the need for flexibility; minimization of intellectual losses and the brain-drain; the enormous scientific potential in the Centre and East; the need to identify criteria; the value of not only talking but also listening; the role of the international organizations.

General Funding and Support

In West Europe, science and technology (S&T) receives considerable support, nevertheless considered inadequate. In contrast, S&T in countries in Central and East Europe are suffering from severe underfunding, and industries, largely in the public sector, are struggling.

State-of-Affairs

Finding. It was apparent that all western countries are devoting considerable fractions of their public and private sector funds to supporting science and technology, in a shared faith that research and development offer a path to economic and social progress. At the same time, the concern was expressed that the material and moral support given to science in western countries does not match the latter's role in society.

Finding. In Central and East European countries, there is at present in almost chronic lack of money for S&T. Funds have been extremely restricted because (i) the conditions of economic crisis have meant that governments have cut their budgets; and (ii) the newly emerging industrial sector, unable to express its interest and demand for R&D services, cannot make up for the shortage of funding. It is expected that during the course of privatization in these countries, the private sector will play a more supportive role in the R&D process.

Finding. It was recognized that where the private sector existed, it should be encouraged to increase its efforts to finance and carry out the relevant R&D, but that the public sector must continue to support fundamental science, education and training, and also encourage its application to industry. In this connection, concern was expressed that the results of fundamental science could not be foreseen or forced, but that excellence and creativity must be encouraged.

Philosophy and Approach

Intense discussions revolved around the philosophy and approach to the problems set before the meeting, some participants expressing innovative views. Provision of support and assistance through peer review, research and innovation management, and creation of scientific markets, were also considered.

Reconstruction of Society in Europe

Finding. According to one opinion, the world, Europe in particular, is undergoing a period of post-virtual-war reconstruction, rather akin to the time that followed World War I. Unlike the visionary planning that followed World War II, leading to an era of successful rebuilding, a mismanaged reconstruction period is currently under way. In vain one can talk about transition with no specific date of departure or of arrival. The exercise needs a fictitious address.

Finding. It was also stated that the most important characteristic is flexibility. Overreaction to sudden change would destroy all that has been built up in the past over the centuries. In fact, one of the skills to be learnt is to manage change itself.

Criteria For Choices

It was stated that criteria are needed so that objective decisions can be made when distributing budget, for example in a body like an academy. Although some participants spoke of absolute criteria, there are some which are a function of initial conditions. This brings us to the notion that each country has its own signature.

Finding. the Centre and East have problems of a political nature. All countries are in a learning process where models cannot necessarily be exploited because these nations are lying heavily on tradition. This puts each nation into a different position. In this situation, the market cannot solve anything alone. It was generally agreed that certain rules of good practice on which to operate—some efficiency criteria based on a process of mutual understanding—were needed. Efficiency must not be sacrificed on the alter of popularism.

Finding. In general, common to practically all countries, there is a dilemma between the principle of excellency and global competition; between social equality and popularism.

Finding. The meeting was invited to identify modalities of government interaction with science and technology that are considered good practice, with nations who wish to move into a market economy, *i.e.* to uncover certain basic principles such as means of interaction, discussions with international organizations, what are pre-competitive activities, international mechanisms, and so on. Of course, these can impose constraints.

Individuality of a Nation

The opinion was expressed that it is irresponsible to maintain that each nation can do what it chooses regardless. Certainly, each country's background, culture, history, need to be respected. However, there are some basic trial and error processes that emerge from the international situation. It is senseless to repeat errors.

Finding. It was recognized that each country has its own historical and cultural traditions reflected in the individual organizational structures of science. Practical solutions for restructuring the S&T system in Central and East European countries should respect national socio-political, cultural, and historical context, at the same time adopting where relevant input gained from international experience. Indeed, the West is in a position to offer suggestions or recommendations to Central and East Europe with regard to the transformation of science in Europe, as a result of its experience. For example, OECD has a good 30 years of experience. However, some participants from central and eastern Europe warned that their countries are weary of being issued with orders, and that there is the danger that these would be opposed by their very nature. They commented that the West wanted to give out only, and not receive or listen. It was also emphasized that there may be general themes in common, but there cannot be one single set of rules for all countries—experience shows that the situation is not that simple.

Finding. It was very evident that there are vast variations from country to country in organizational structures. Whilst science may be truly international, the scientific structure should not be expected to follow a single model or constrained to a single mould.

Recommendation. It was recommended that ROSTE bring to the attention of UNESCO the idea of studying the individualism of nations. This is the basis of the case for 'anthropological psychoanalysis' of individual nations in the area of R&D.

The Brain-Drain

The current massive intellectual migration from and within Europe witnessed recently was pointed out by a number of participants as a negative indicator of the position of science in the region, emphasizing its inadequacy. Two years ago, UNESCO-ROSTE brought to the attention of the international scientific community the increasing alarming trends in the brain-drain in Europe. However, it is important to recognize that the migration of scientists from country to country it not a real brain-drain—it is a human right. It was noted that not only is there a brain-drain from countries in Europe, there is a brain-drain from science itself. This is a new concept—that of intersectorial drain, where people are leaving science for completely new areas, representing a deplorable loss for European science and European culture. Science must be made attractive to young people, though avoiding the trap of popularism already referred to. Interestingly, the risks of the 'hand-drain', where technicians and other support personnel are also leaving their countries and professions, were also mentioned.

Recommendation. Urgent and well co-ordinated efforts should be undertaken at governmental and non-governmental levels to eliminate or at least diminish the negative impact of massive intellectual migration both direct and intersectorial which could lead to serious intellectual losses in the region, especially in Central and East Europe.

Recommendation. It is suggested that the international organizations and UNESCO in particular continue their studies and monitoring of this phenomenon in order to work out recommendations addressed to governments and national and international funding organizations on this issue.

Scientific Support

Finding. Independent analysis, assessment, and evaluation were considered to be important. Better evaluation systems, project grant systems, ministries for science, technology, and education, research councils, various intermediate institutions, etc. are new organizational forms and mechanisms that characterize the adjustment processed in progress in Central and East Europe.

Recommendation. The initiative of UNESCO, through UNESCO-ROSTE, to organize wide European discussions of critical issues of science in the region, such as brain-drain, peer review, research and innovation management, should be welcomed and continued in close co-operation with major organizations and foundations in the region.

Peer Review

Participants noted that on the issued of grants and peer review, for example, it would be judicious to identify certain criteria which could be strictly adhered to. International excellence needs peer review, and here the western countries have accrued solid experience that could be shared with colleagues from central and eastern countries of Europe.

Finding. Deciding upon national priorities for research consistent with centres of excellence and industrial opportunities and natural resources is vitally important. Objectivity and excellence in the choice of research efforts should be achieved through per review, etc. It was emphasized the criterion used must be one of excellence.

Recommendation. Peer review should be an essential element of the R&D process at all stages of the latter's implementation, in all countries, and particularly in central and eastern parts of the region.

Recommendation. International organizations and western research institutions could provide assistance to central and east European countries in carrying out peer review.

Management Training

It was maintained that more training in management is needed, a situation that is recognized to prevail in Third World Countries. Managers can all too easily lose contact with events in their own laboratories.

Finding. Technological and structural shifting towards a market economy in central and eastern Europe demands acquisition of new and changing skills, requiring a new strategy for the management of human resources, especially scientists and engineers, as well as the research process itself.

Recommendation. A better understanding of the links between scientist and management was identified as essential for better integration of scientific planning.

Recommendation. Intense training in research and innovation management in central and eastern countries of Europe during the transition to market economy should be promoted by international organizations and western management schools.

Central/East—Specific Observations and Mechanisms

The discussion dwelt on the care that must be exercised in accommodating individual characteristics of a nation in the restructuring plans. The public/private sector, industry, and academies/universities were considered, and the vast potential to be tapped in the Centre and East.

> Finding. *All countries emphasized the dramatic changes issuing from the transformation process, and the consequent need to protect the scientific community, especially the presents fundamental research capacities and human resources, in which the investment costs are substantial and long-lasting.*

Finding. All central and eastern countries show a strong desire to adjust their organizational structures of S&T to new market economy conditions. The adjustment is a long-term process, and as a result, operation must take place on there levels: macro (R&D financing and performing structures), meso (organization *e.g.* government-based), and micro (individuals).

Finding. The changes in progress in the Centre and East in organizational structures of S&T should be ensured by specific mechanisms, and not by administrative measures. These changes need assistance from the governments, which must play a very important role.

It was noted that the 'scientism'—meaning the belief that all progress in technology and economy derives from scientific achievement alone—of Central and East European research institutions should be overcome in order to adapt as soon as possible national science to new socio-economic conditions and to render science closer to human needs. A role can be played by international organizations, qv.

Scientific Potential of Central and East Europe

More study is needed. OECD-country figures are known, but there are none for Central and East Europen countries. The links between scientists and other involved in the scientific circuit need to be understood better, in order to improve the integration of science.

Some participants, addressing the delegates from Central and East European countries, commented that there are very strong and imaginative schools there, in Russia for example. The best mechanism to promote the survival of these institutions for the young generation, in terms of philosophy and methods, was discussed. The meeting agreed that the school survival was vital, and a very real problem being confronted. The economic situation in Russia is critical, but can be overcome during the transition to market economies, provided that a high level of education is maintatined.

Recommendation. The enormous scientific potential artificially dammed up in the Centre and East, as emphasized repeatedly by the participants, must be released and put at the disposal of all European nations in their entirety, and humanity in general.

Recommendation. It was suggested that attention be given to co-operative set-ups, to preserve top-level scientific centres of excellence. For example, in Russia, international mathematical and theoretical physics institutes have already been agreed.

Recommendation. An invitation was extended to European nations and major interantional and regional organizations to provide assistance for the survival of the schools, given the basis in Russia of good staff, etc.

University Teaching and Research

It was asserted that there is no link with reality in Central and East European countries, owing to their past. The universities and research institutes must be distinguished. The universities' main role is to teach, but teaching *for what* must be made clear. A new look at reality was recommended. New links between the universities and the research institutes are needed. Universities can teach *for* research. Institutes can teach *by* research. But throughout, the universities and institutes have to adhere to the reality of the market.

Finding. Weak relationships between teaching and research characterize the R&D system in all central and eastern countries.

Recommendation. Teaching and research need to be reinforced so that the best brains are involved in both.

With respect to the problem of universities being involved in full-time teaching, leaving little time for research, it was underlined that flexible mechanisms such as consortia, open to innovation, are needed to be competitive. The idea of taking study leave for university staf is relevant now that the Centre and East are moving into a market economy.

Industry—Catching up with the West

In general, it was recognized that, as in the West, the private sector in the Centre and East should be encouraged to increase financing and execution of the relevant R&D, but that the public sector must continue to support fundamental science and education, and also give backing to its application to industry.

Hungarian experience, for example, shows that the economy and the industrial part have not been functioning properly for a number of years. Normally that economy and industry give impulses to science. In Hungary, there are now fresh stimuli in technology, but these are imported. Science in nations like Hungary must survive 5-10 years without the active input from industry, or else find a way to pass it on to industry. It is an unhealthy indicator that at present it is cheaper to import.

In Czechoslovakia, scientists in industry are working in a stable, forward direction. However, there is not the feedback that exists in the West—feedback in everday life, moving off to the universities. Industry is moving towards privatization, and the universities do not show strong interest in research. So the feedback is missing. A nation like Czechoslovakia must thus look to the West for a system most similar to that prevailing in its own country, on which to model. In the same vein, in these countries, for example Hungary, there is a lack of competition, which means that there are no demands for research results of the institutes. Thus the institutes have been adjusted to the economy.

Finding. All central and eastern countries show very strong university and academy level in R&D activities, which have weak linkage with industrial R&D.

Recommendation. All countries should aim at creating appropriate mechanisms for integrating academic science and higher educational systems, and to establish new relationships with industry to create a new intellectual environment appropriate to free market conditions.

Recommendation. Industry should take into deeper consideration factors like quality, validity, competence of its companies and managers; provision of some marketing assistance should be made.

It was suggested that the new task to solve is to bring industry up to date rather than wait for it to catch up, by creating advantageous conditions through adequate budgeting and financing.

Public-Private

Figures indicate that in the late 80s, in Central and East European countries, 70-80 per cent of research was being carried out in government-supported institutions. In OECD countries the figure is about a half of this. How can the situation of the Centre and East be changed? In order to reduce government-supported research, reduction must be *planned*. Some regulations have to be eliminated, such as those which restrict people's mobility. Salaries need to be equalized. It would take 10 years to gain ground here. The problem is that for a human being 10 years is a long time.

According to some opinions expressed, basic science must be mainly government-supported—the objectives of industry are too short-term. For example, Hungary expressed the need for legislation for government support to preserve basic research.

It was also maintained that the public-private proportions should not be fixed, and the principle of flexibility should be keep in mind in all budgetary issues.

INTERNATIONAL ORGANIZATIONS AND SCIENCE IN EUROPE

The session focused on the role of international organizations and major grant-giving bodies in promoting bilateral and multilateral mechanisms for the transformation of science in Europe.

Co-operation

Finding. All present stressed the importance of international and regional co-operation in science as a necessary and desirable aspect of the present environment. Many organizations and foundations in Europe are currently undertaking tremendous efforts to aid scientific communities in Central and East Europe by providing direct financial support, organizing large-scale research projects, promoting staff mobility. There is a lack of co-ordination, however.

Recommendation. The need for a permanent body for co-ordinating all the initiatives such as the setting up of consortia, joint projects and programmes, areas supported by the Commission of the European Communities, Council of Europe, etc., that are functioning in Europe, was underlined in the session as priority action. There is a risk of losing out through delay.

Recommendation. Multilateral and bilateral co-operation should be intensified through working together, mobility, exchanges, etc., as well as networking with existing European networks. This should reinforce that national R&D efforts in central and eastern countries, and bring them into contact with the 'outside world'.

Recommendation. It was requested that UNESCO through ROSTE continue to find potential research partners for the countries of Central and East Europe. In the same vein, the importance of networks to support nations without critical mass was underlined.

Recommendation. The need for a Centre for Strategic Studies for Europe was emphasized. The creation of this type of institution could be undertaken by the major international organizations in R&D in Europe.

International Government Organizations and Foundations

The meeting emphasized that the role of international organizations including UNESCO is one of catalyst, executing a promotional role, operating as indeed it has for this meeting as a means of providing an open forum. Each national scientific community should select what is most appropriate for the elements of science managerial systems according to their historical and cultural traditions and legacies. At the same time, returning to the point about 'scientism' mentioned earlier, the international organizations can provide various types of assistance to scientific communities in Central and East Europe in the creation of innovation infrastructures in which science is an integral part.

Some participants gave their interpretation of the role of UNESCO and its Regional Office for Science and Technology for Europe in the region, that it can be used to pursue co-operation in Europe in the mutual scientific field, eventually to develop one giant scientific complex. UNESCO-ROSTE's links with the national academies and centres and international organizations, primarily with ICSU, is of major importance. Moreover, ICSU can assist in the peer-review process, having access to a reservoir of experts. ROSTE could focus on working out European scientific policy, the science support programme in Central and East Europe, clarify means of avoiding waste, duplication, etc., promoting the all-European idea, standardization, evaluating forms of study, organizaing exchanges. Of course, all these activities should be closely co-ordinated with other international and regional organizations.

It was also stated that foundations and similar organizational structures are taking on a more important role than government bodies, and it is desirable to see them grow. A view was expressed that foundations can serve as a critique to governments, and as examples the Rockefeller Foundation which furnished grants in the pre-war period, the Carnegie Foundation, or the McArthy Foundation which provided funds to the Centre and East, were quoted.

On the subject of the European Community's strategy, it was noted that some tasks are the duty of the Community. It cannot be said that in the future there will be no national policy—each country in the region has its own specificity. Nevertheless, there are areas where the Community can play a co-ordinating role, for instance in large-scale research projects which are of mutual interest to the majority of European nations.

The importance of the networking approach in developing regional co-operation under the umbrella of international organizations was underlined by the participants.

Finding. Whilst most countries in the region are seeking to achieve efficiency in their scientific support and governance organizations (national research councils, academies, foundations and funds, ministries, etc.), there were constraints due to inertias in the systems and political and social influences. These constraints could be overcome with the help of international organizations and foundations especially under new, very favourable conditions for exchange of experience in Europe.

Recommendation. International organizations and foundations could contribute substantially to the evaluation of existing organizational structures of science in different countries and advise national scientific communities on existing opportunities within concrete organizational structures.

Recommendation. UNESCO-ROSTE convened this seminar as a result of prior meetings. The role of UNESCO may be viewed as one of catalyst. The essential role of UNESCO was underlined, and it was noted with dismay that S&T funding had been cut in recent years. It was hoped that this seminar would reinforce international projects, crucially important for this transitional period of Central and East Europe. Follow-up meetings to this seminar are desirable in different areas, to help scientific communities not only survive, but flourish. The desire that initiatives such as this of ROSTE be repeated for establishing useful comparisons and monitoring in the evolution of the organizational structures of science and of other basically important issues in Europe was a common sentiment.